Mastering Sheet Metal & Weldments with SOLIDWORKS 2026

Lani Tran, CSWE

SDC
PUBLICATIONS

SDC Publications
P.O. Box 1334
Mission, KS 66222
913-262-2664
www.SDCpublications.com
Publisher: Stephen Schroff

Download all needed model files from the SDC Publication website (www.SDCpublications.com/downloads/978-1-63057-795-7).

ISBN-13: 978-1-63057-795-7

ISBN-10: 1-63057-795-2

Printed and bound in the United States of America.

Acknowledgments

Thanks as always to my dad, Paul Tran, a semi-retired design engineer, for always being there and providing support and honest feedback on all the lessons in the textbook.

I would like to give a special thanks to the team at SDC Publications for their editing and corrections. Thanks also for putting together such a beautiful cover design.

Finally, I would like to thank you, our readers, for your continued support. It is with your consistent feedback that we were able to create the lessons in this book with more detailed and useful information.

Preface

My SOLIDWORKS journey began in my youth, while observing my dad operate his engineering company. As I developed my career, I became more involved in different facets of the software, from design work to project management. After more than two decades of exposure to SOLIDWORKS, I found myself working through distinctive projects, where hundreds of components are considered small assemblies.

Throughout this time I've had the opportunity to focus on reoccurring challenges and develop unique solutions. One such challenge I faced on a daily basis was the need to quickly create efficient models to print or prototype for testing. In a deadline driven work environment, it is crucial to create accurate and manufacturable designs.

The lessons in this manual reflect much of what I do at my work place. I wanted to share the techniques I've developed to create various models using different techniques and approaches. I hope you will find this manual useful and that you can apply these lessons to grow your own skills.

Class Files

To download the files that are required for this book, type the following in the address bar of your web browser:

SDCpublications.com/downloads/978-1-63057-795-7

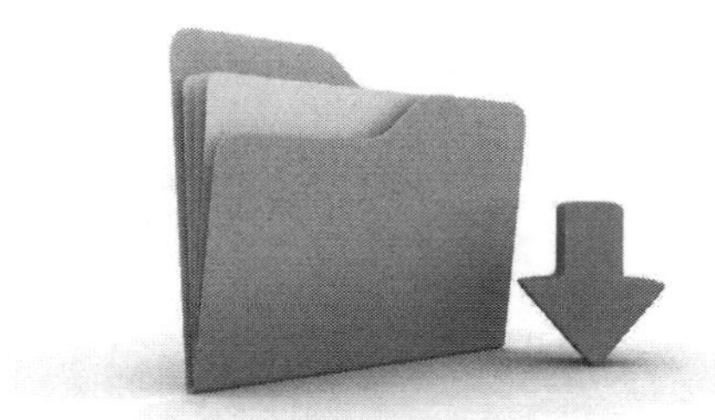

TABLE OF CONTENTS

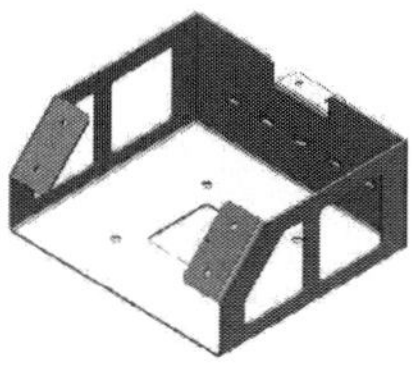
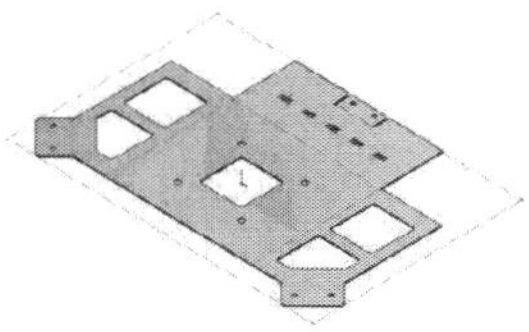

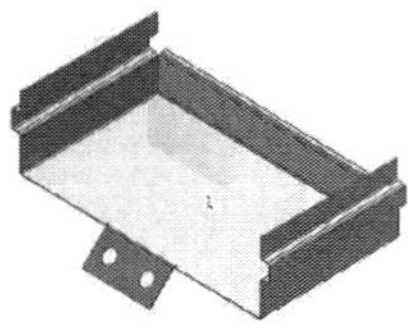
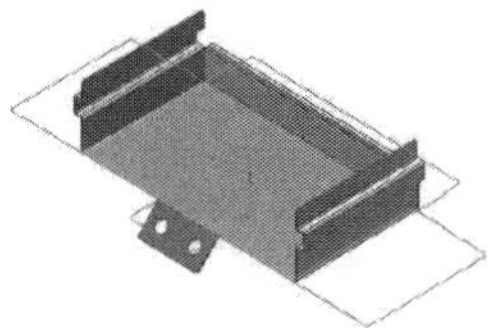

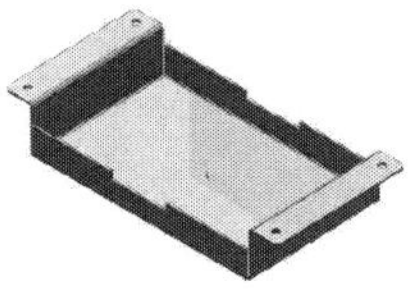

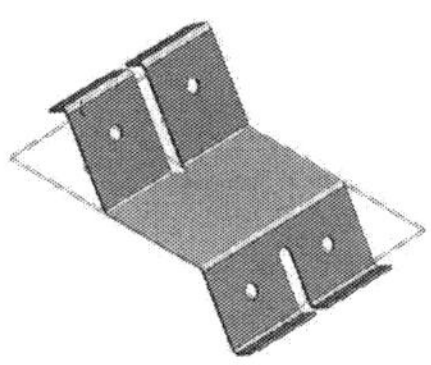

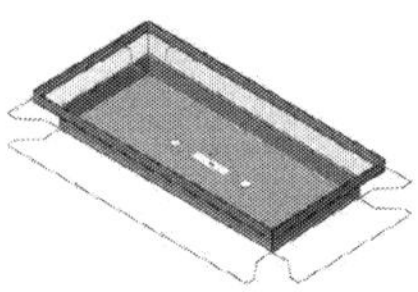

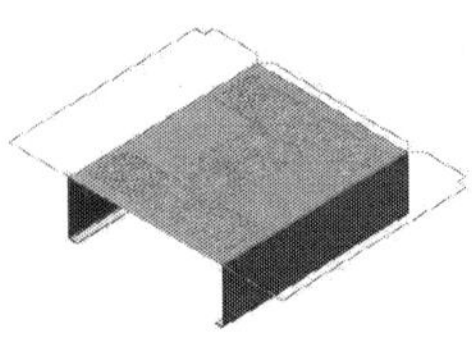

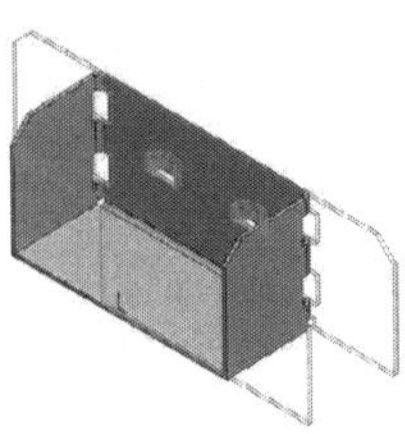

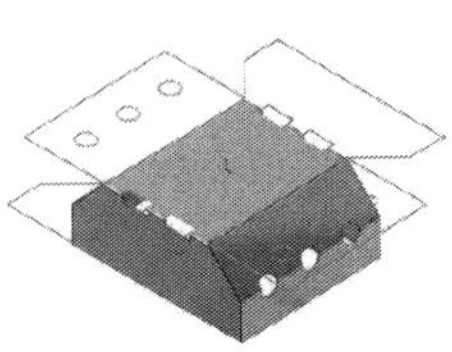

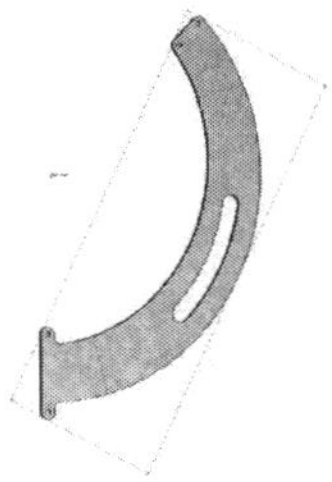

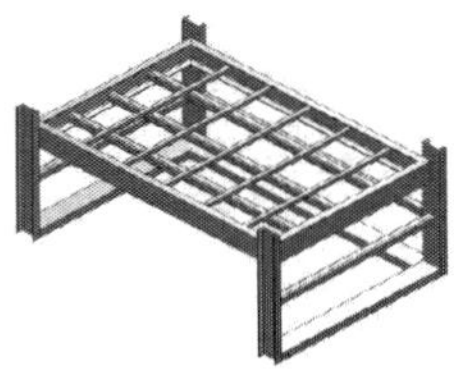

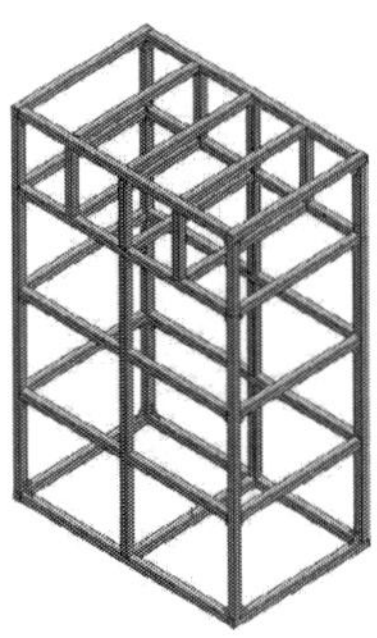

ITEM NO.	QTY.	DESCRIPTION	LENGTH
1	8	TS4x4x0.1875	116
2	4	TS4x4x0.1875	76
3	13	TS4x4x0.1875	68
4	4	TS4x4x0.1875	56
5	4	TS4x4x0.1875	142
6	1	TS4x4x0.1875	140
7	4	TS4x4x0.1875	34
8	3	TS4x4x0.1875	44
9	6	TS4x4x0.1875	32
10	8	End Caps	3.8125x3.8125x.25
11	40	Gussets	3.0x3.0x.5

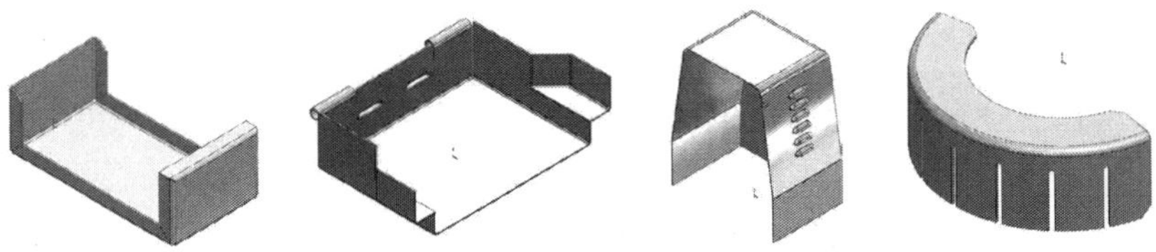

Measure your SolidWorks Skills. Take one or all of the exams below and become **SOLIDWORKS CERTIFIED.**
For more information, go to: www.solidworks.com/certification

Lesson 1: Introduction to Sheet Metal Parts

Sheet metal components are metal parts formed from flat sheets by cutting, bending, and shaping. They are widely used in various industries due to their versatility and ease of fabrication. These components can be made from various materials like steel, aluminum, stainless steel, copper, and brass, and can range in thickness from thin foils to thicker plates.

Depending on the complexity of the design and production volume, various methods can be used from laser cutting and welding to CNC punching and stamping. After the metal sheets are cut and formed into the required shapes, they are assembled and welded to create the final products.

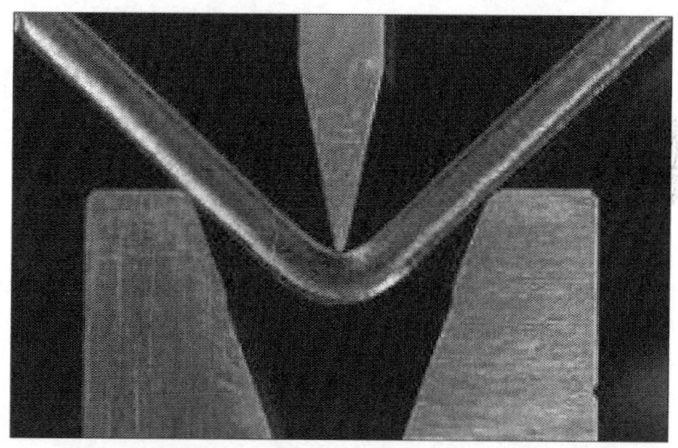

The cheapest type of sheet metal is usually low-carbon or mild steel due to its affordability and widespread availability. It is a cost-effective choice for general-purpose applications.

Sheet metal finishes are applied surface treatments that enhance the appearance, durability, and functionality of metal parts. These finishes can range from simple coatings like powder coating and galvanizing to more complex processes like electropolishing and electroless plating. The choice of finish depends on the specific needs of the application, such as corrosion resistance, aesthetics, and cost.

1. Opening a part document:

Browse to the Training Folder and open a part document named: **Sheet Metal_Part1**.

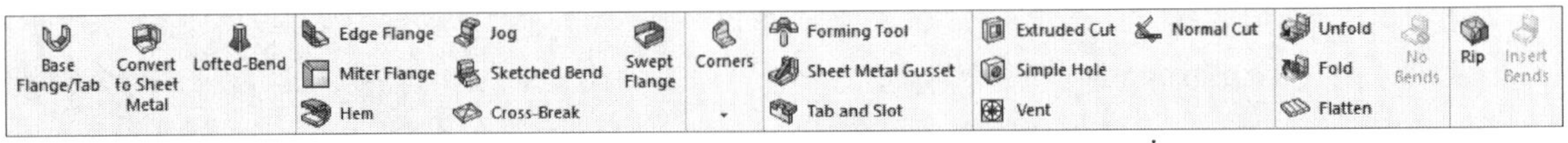

2. Creating a Base Flange:

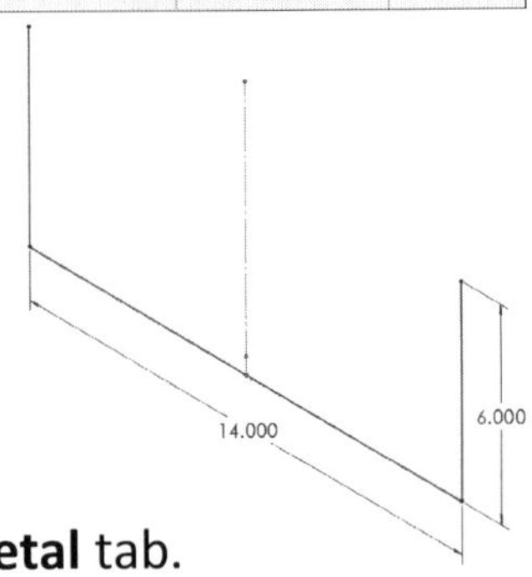

The 1st feature in a sheet metal part is the parent feature; it usually gets created with the **Base Flange** command.

Select **Sketch1** and click **Base Flange** on the **Sheet Metal** tab.

For Direction 1, select **Mid Plane** and enter: **12.00in** for depth.

Enable the **Use Gauge Table** checkbox and select:

* Sample Table - **Aluminum**
* Gauge **10** (.11811024 in.)
* Bend Radius: **.157in.**
* K-Factor: **0.5**
* Auto Relief: **Rectangular**
* Ratio: **1**

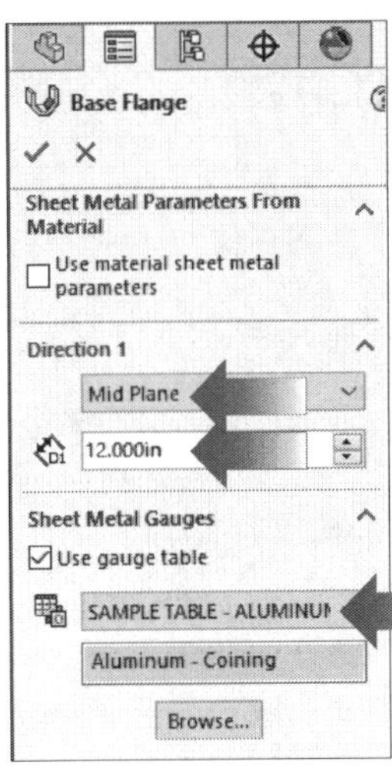

Click **OK**.

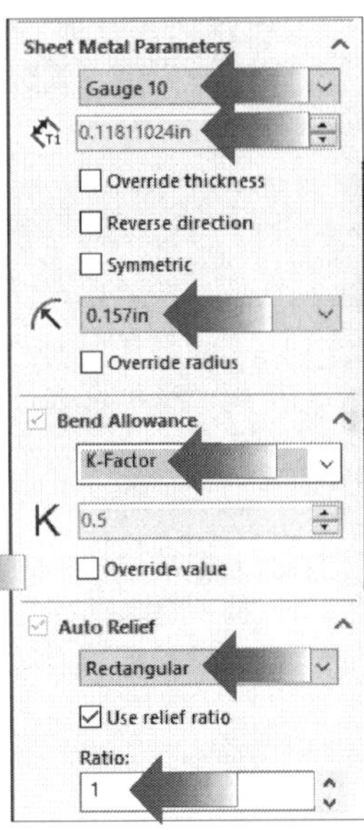

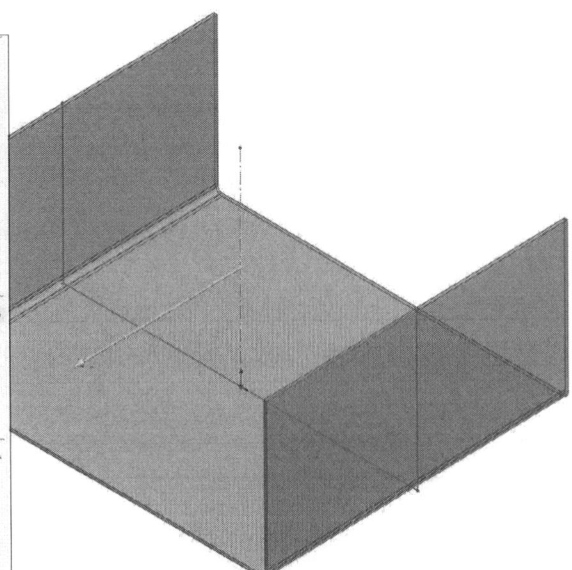

3. Making an Edge Flange:

The **Edge Flange** tool combines a bend and sheet metal tab in a single operation. Switch to the **Sheet Metal** tab and click **Edge Flange**.

For Flange Parameters, select the **upper edge** on the right side of the model.

For Flange Length, select the **upper vertex** as noted.

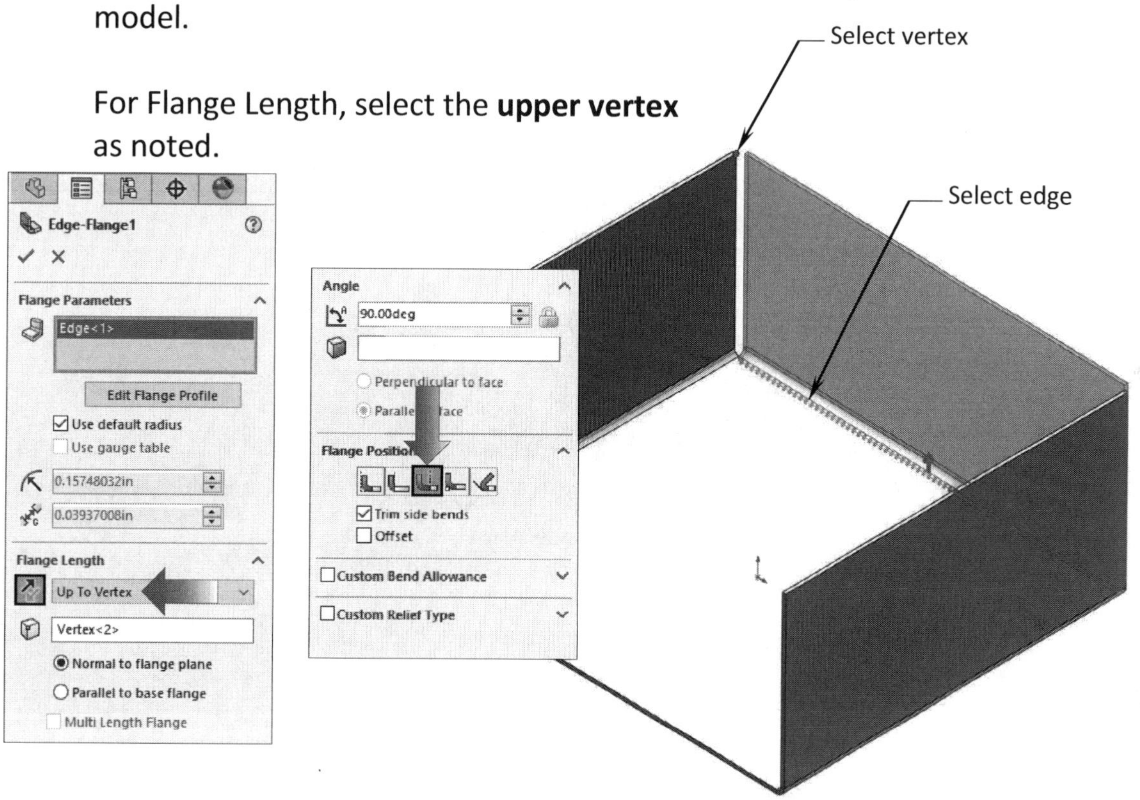

Enable the **Use Default Radius** checkbox.

Keep the Bend Angle at **90deg**.

For Flange Position, select:
Bend Outside.

Click **OK**.

The gap between the flanges will be extended and closed-off in the next step.

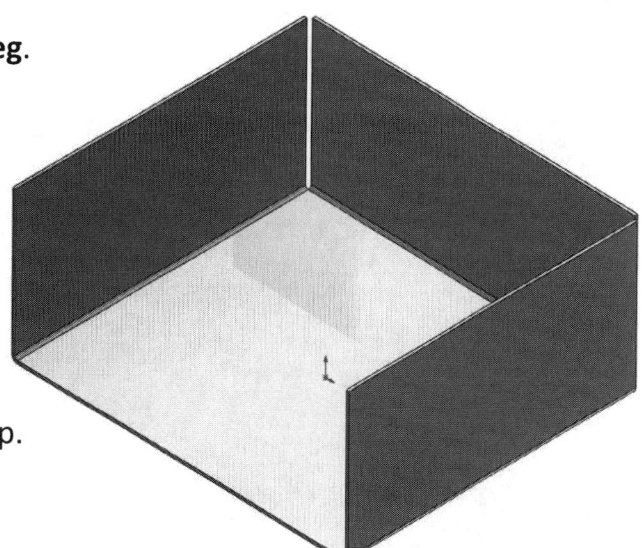

4. Closing the corners:

The **Closed Corner** options are used to close the gaps between flange corners and control if and how they overlap.

Select: **Corners, Closed Corners** on the **Sheet Metal** tab.

For Faces to Extend, select the the **thin faces** on the left and right sides of the new edge flange.

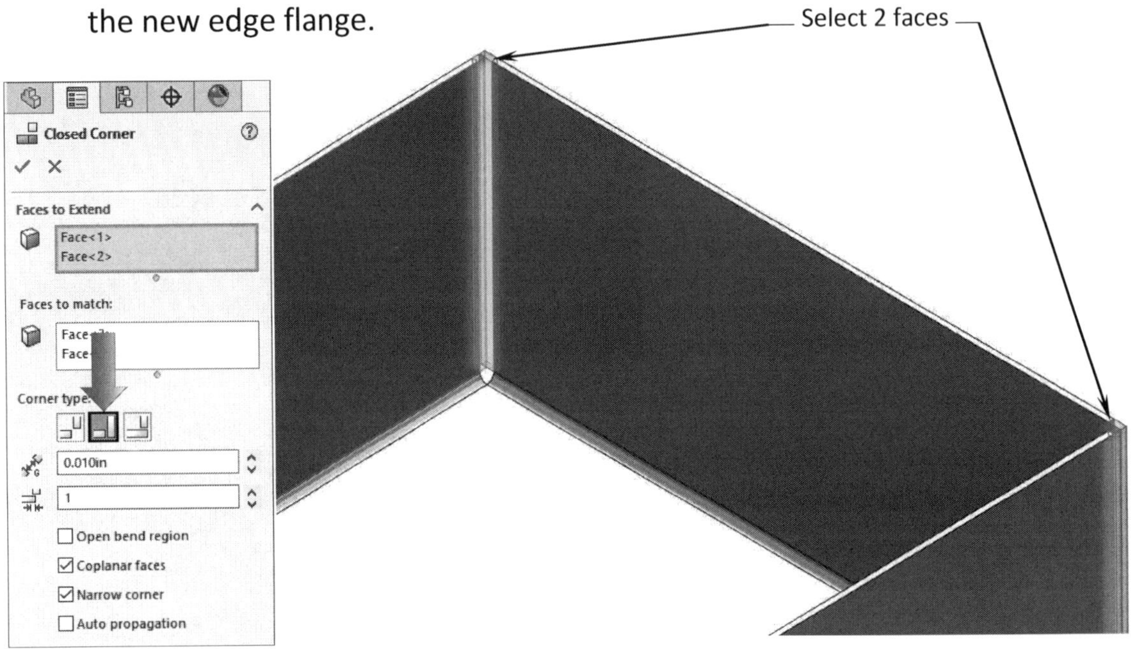

The Faces to Match are selected automatically.

For Corner Type, select: **Overlap**. Keep the gap at the default **.010in**.

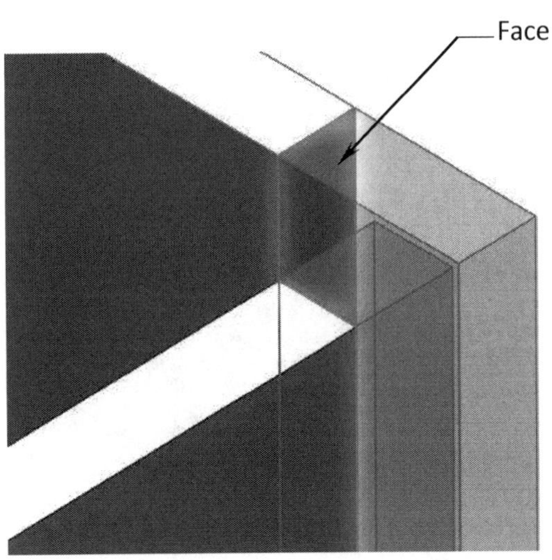

Click **OK**.

5. Making a cut:

Select the Right plane and open a **new sketch**.

Sketch a **line** and add the dimensions shown in the image to fully define the sketch.

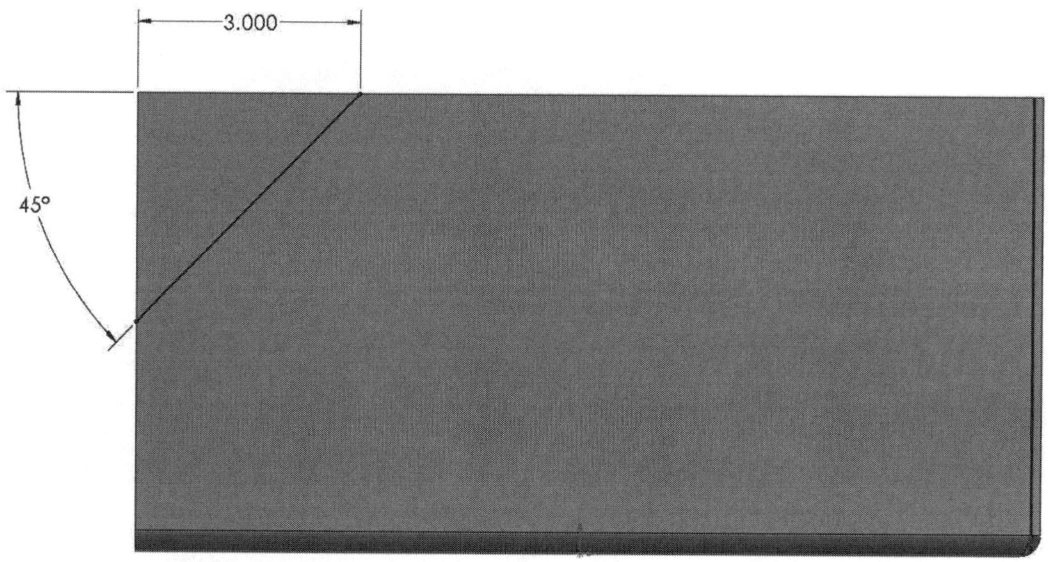

Switch to the **Sheet Metal** tab and click **Extruded Cut**.

Select **Through All Both** and enable the **Flip Side to Cut** checkbox.

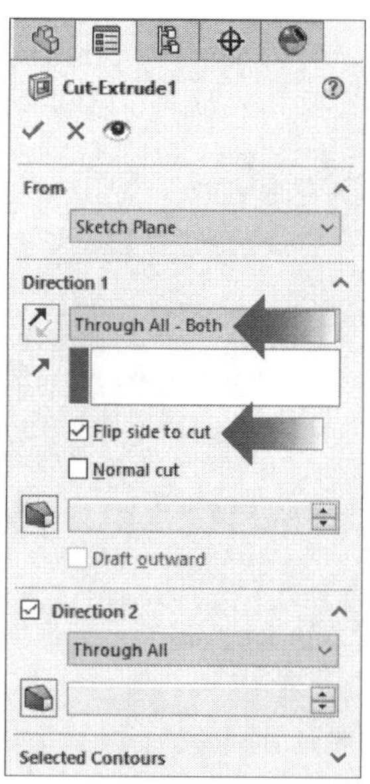

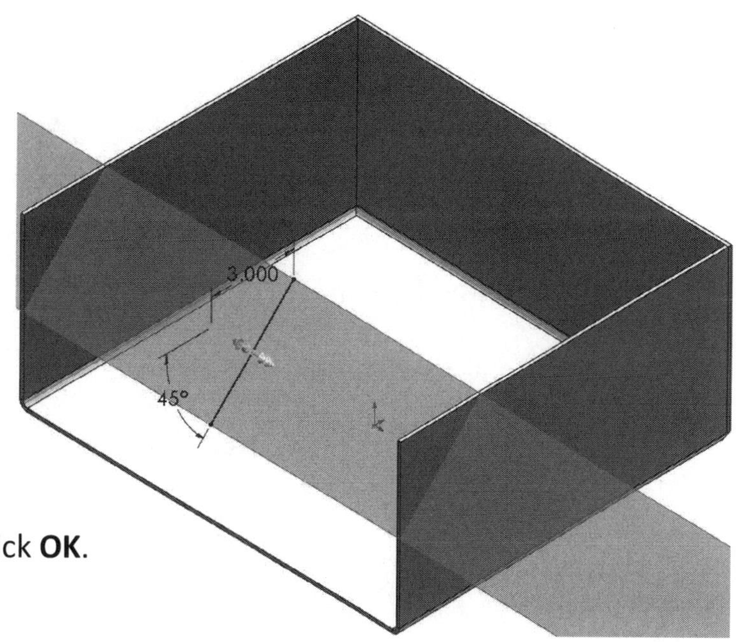

Click **OK**.

6. Adding the angled flanges:

Click **Edge Flange** on the **Sheet Metal** tab.

For Flange Parameters, select the edge as indicated below, move inward and click the mouse to lock the direction.

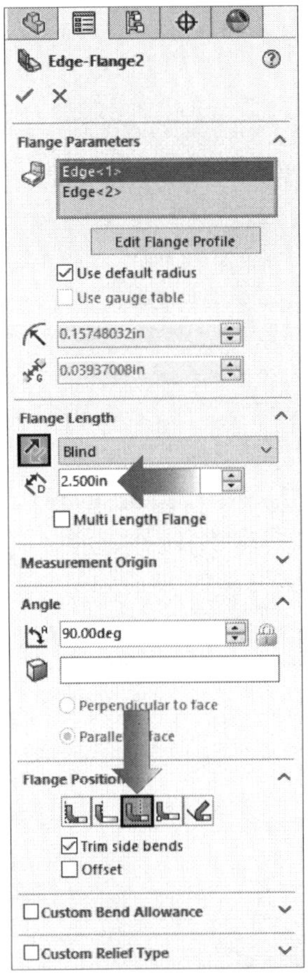

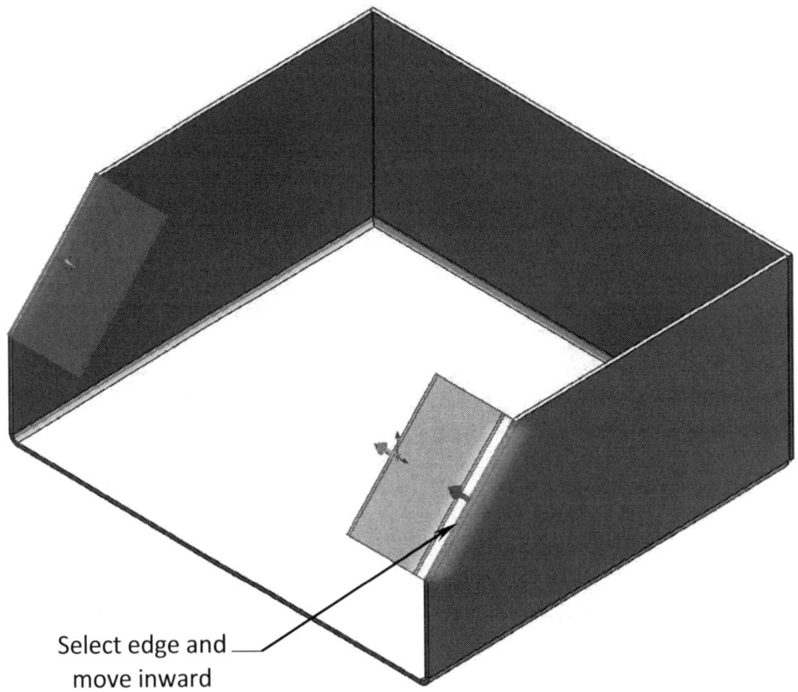

Next, select the edge on the opposite side.

For Depth, enter **2.500in**.

Keep the Angle at **90deg**.

For Flange Position, select: **Bend Outside**.

Click **OK**.

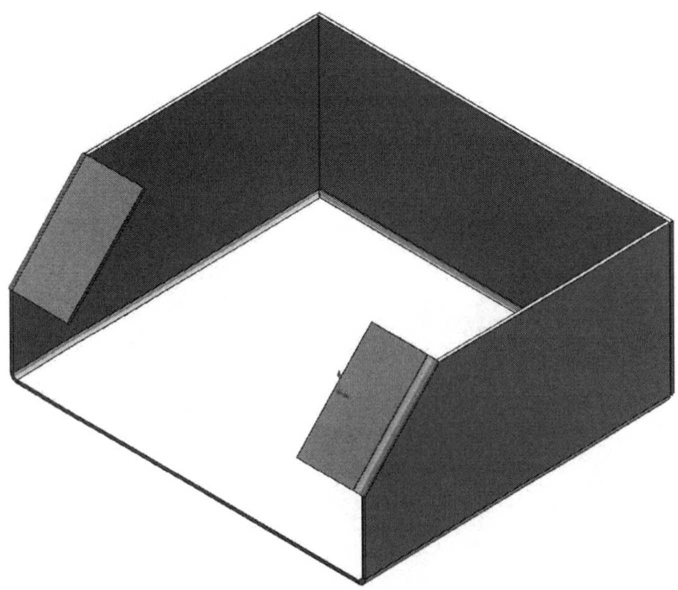

7. Making a manual relief cut:

Relief cuts are generally used to prevent splitting, binding, or cracking when bending sheet metal parts.

Select the <u>face</u> in the back of the model and open a **new sketch**.

Sketch the profile and add the dimensions and relations to fully define the sketch.

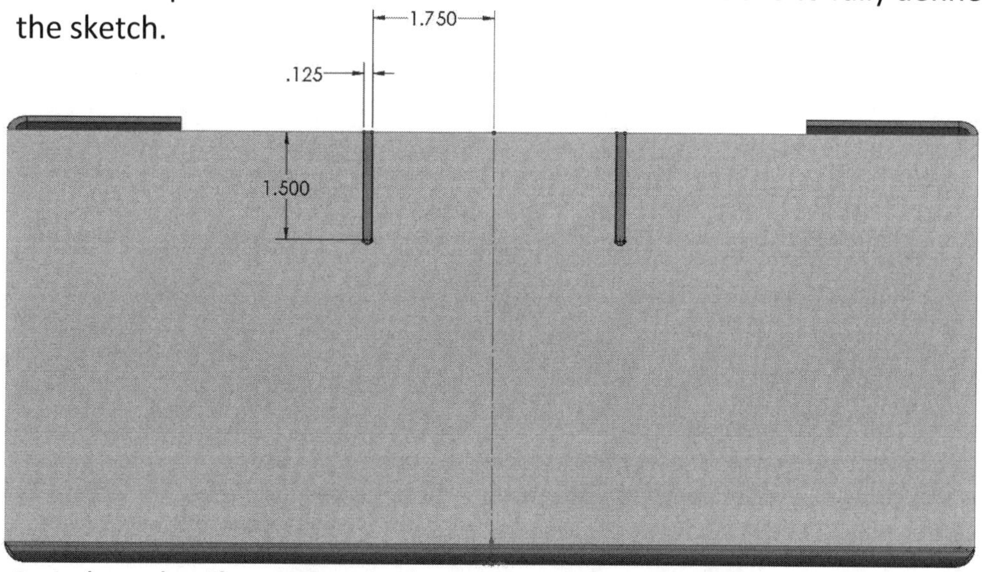

Switch to the **Sheet Metal** tab and click **Extruded Cut**.

For Direction 1, use the default **Blind** option.

Enable the **Link To Thickness** checkbox.

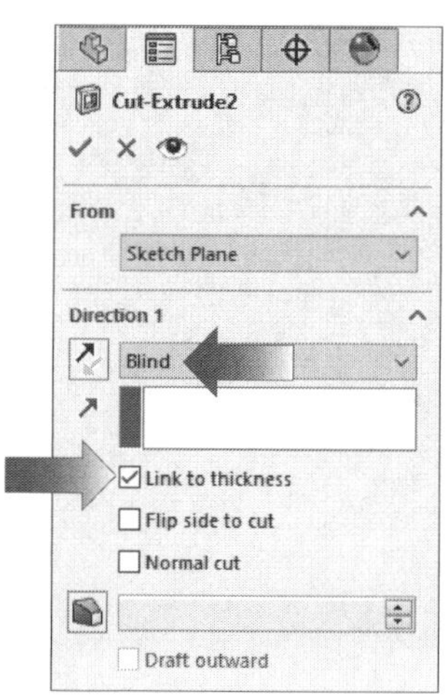

Click **OK**.

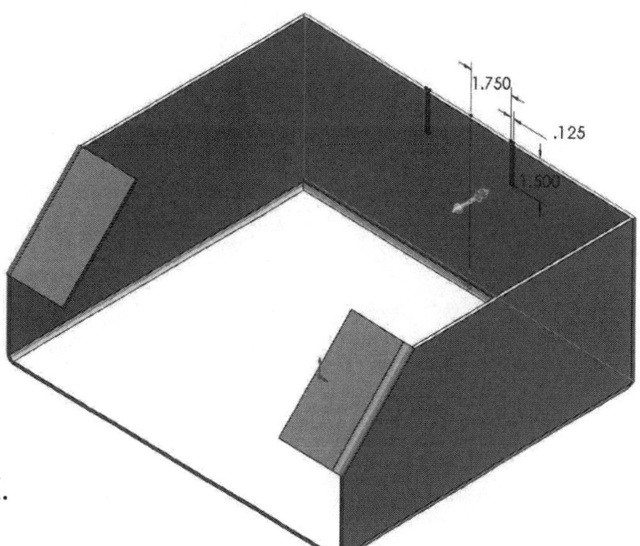

8. Creating a Sketched Bend feature:

The **Sketched Bend** tool uses sketch lines to bend sheet metal parts. Only lines are allowed in the sketch.

Select the face in the back of the model and open a **new sketch**.

Sketch a **line** and add the dimension shown below.

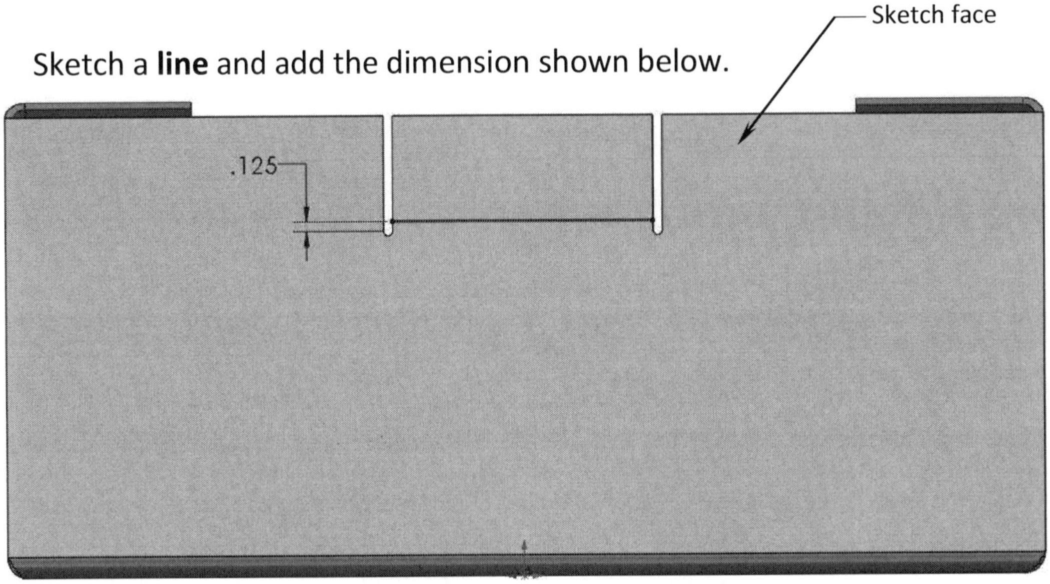

Switch to the **Sheet Metal** tab and click **Sketched Bend**.
For Fixed Face, select the area below the line.
For Bend Position, use the default **Bend Centerline**.

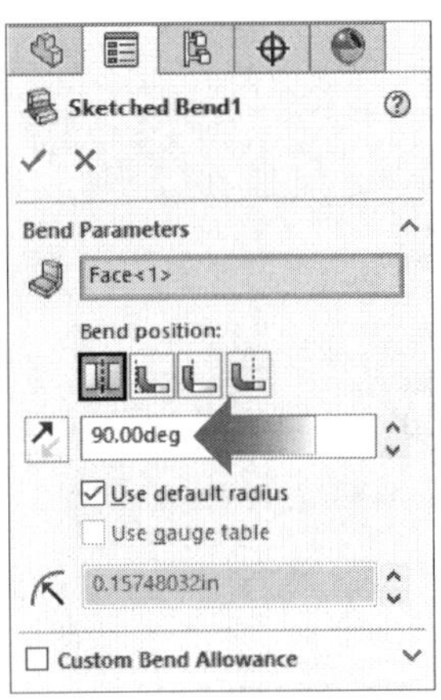

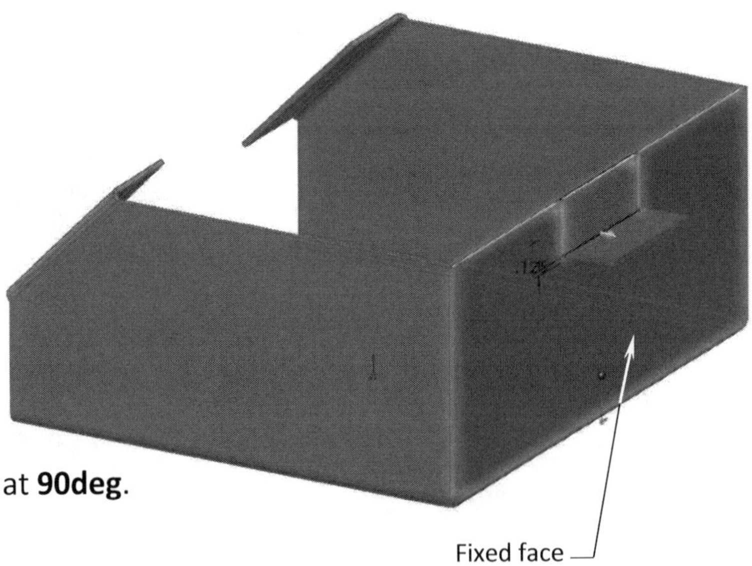

Keep the Bend Angle at **90deg**.

Click **OK**.

9. Adding the bottom cuts:

Select the face as noted and open a **new sketch**.

Sketch the profile shown in the image on the right.

Use the Mirror tool to speed up the process and to keep sketch entities symmetrical to each other.

Add the dimensions shown to fully definethe sketch.

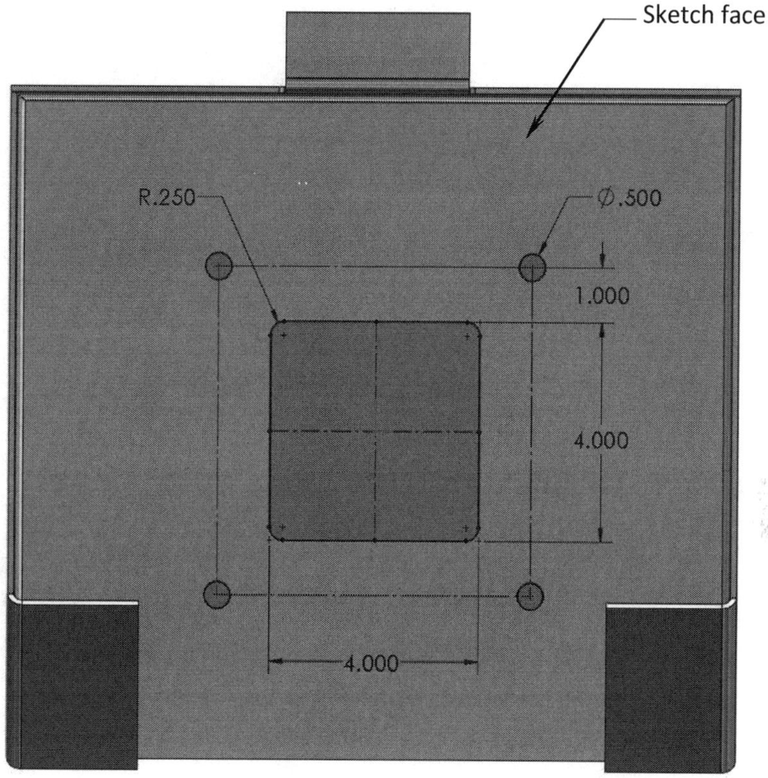

Switch to the **Sheet Metal** tab amd click **Extruded Cut**.

Use the default **Blind** type and enable the **Link To Thickness** checkbox.

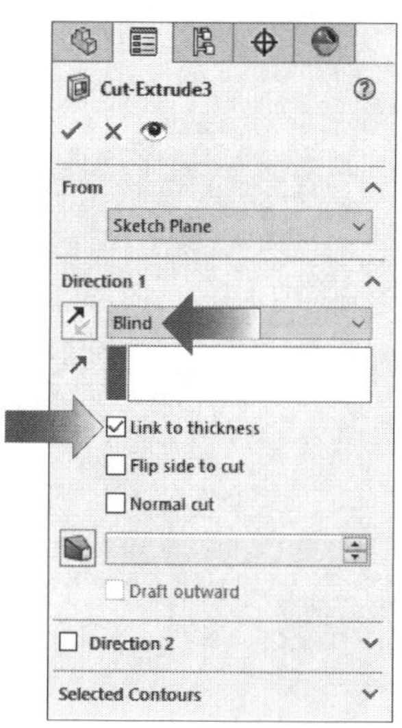

Click **OK**.

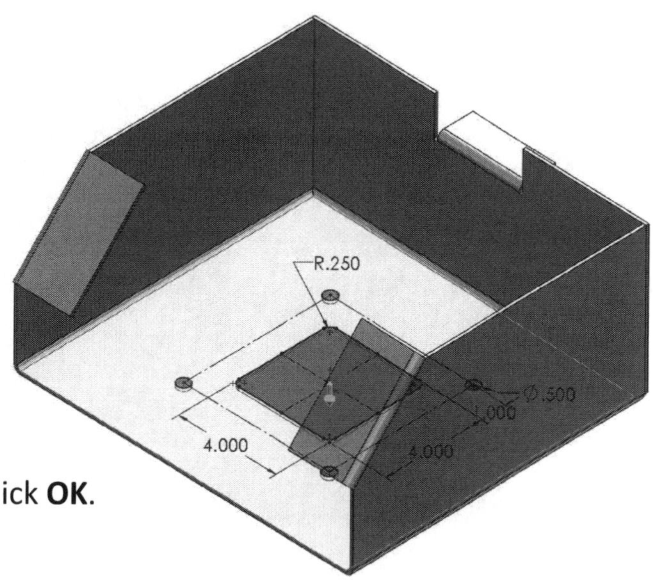

10. Adding the side cuts:

Open a **new sketch** on the side face.

Sketch the profiles and add the dimensions and relations shown.

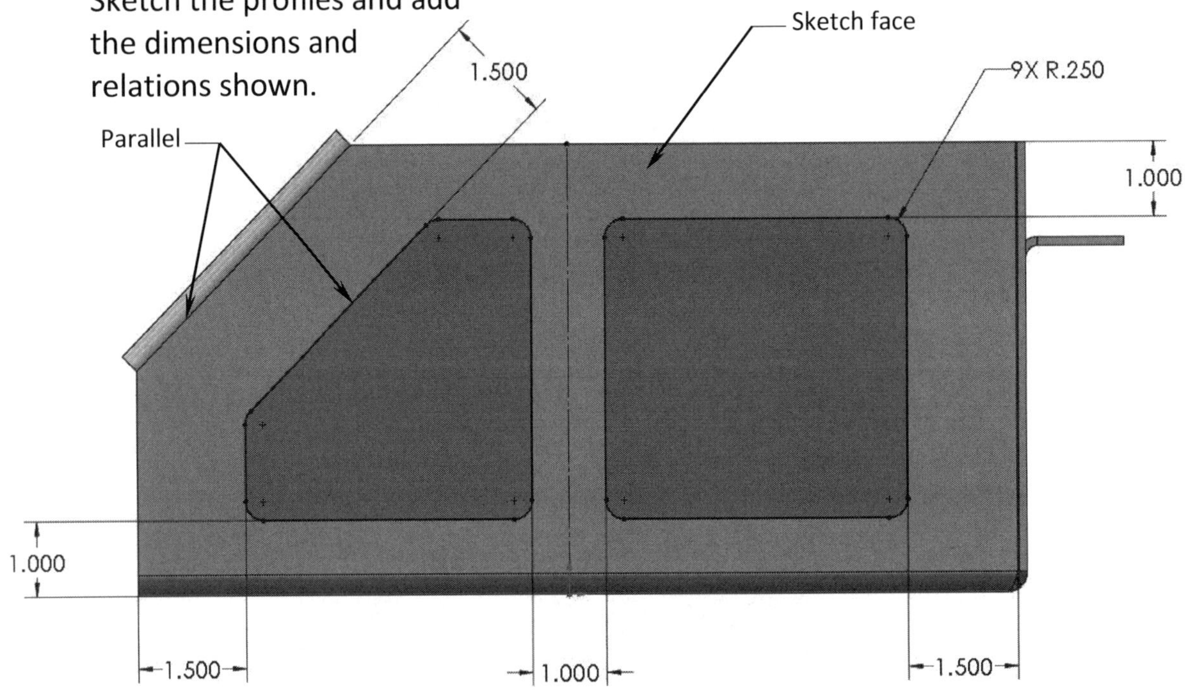

Switch back to the **Sheet Metal** tab and click **Extruded Cut**.

For Direction 1, select **Through All - Both**.

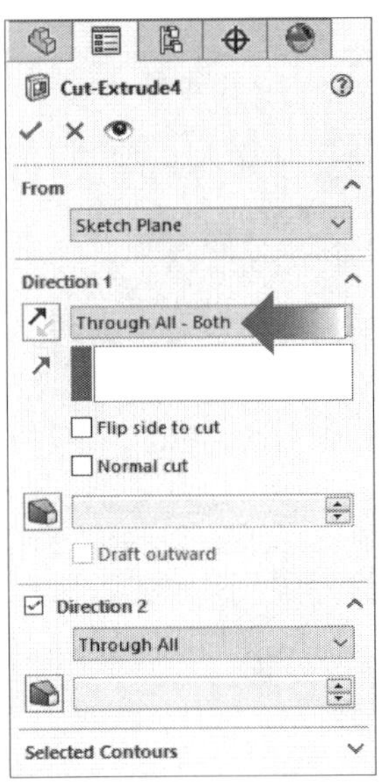

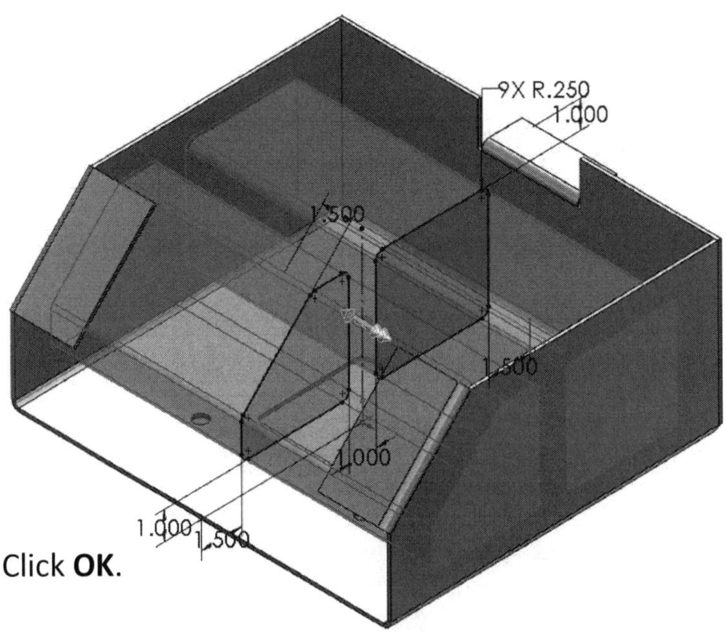

Click **OK**.

11. Adding the 3/8″ holes:

Switch to the **Features** tab and click **Hole Wizard**.

For Hole Type, select **Simple Hole**.

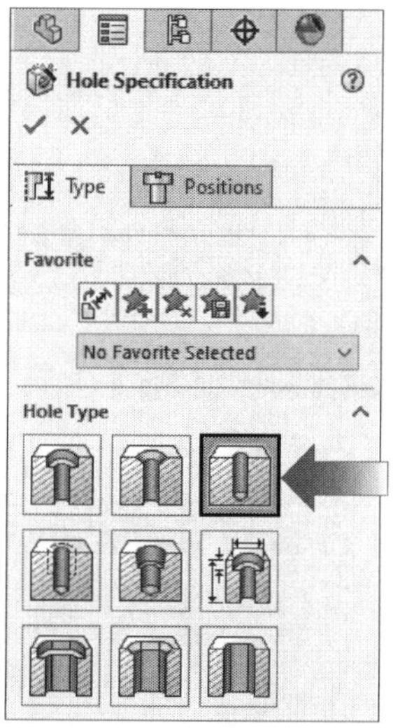

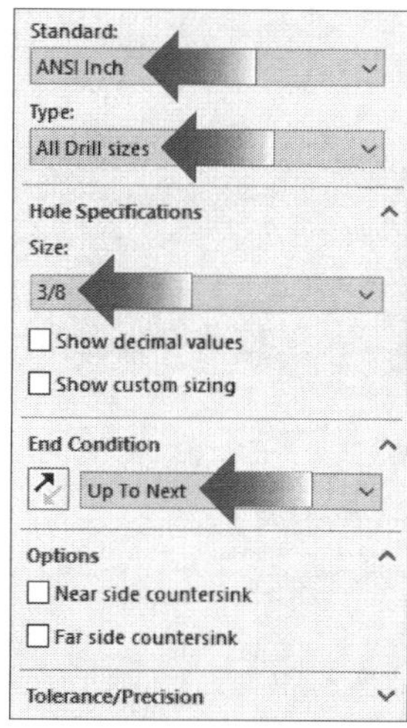

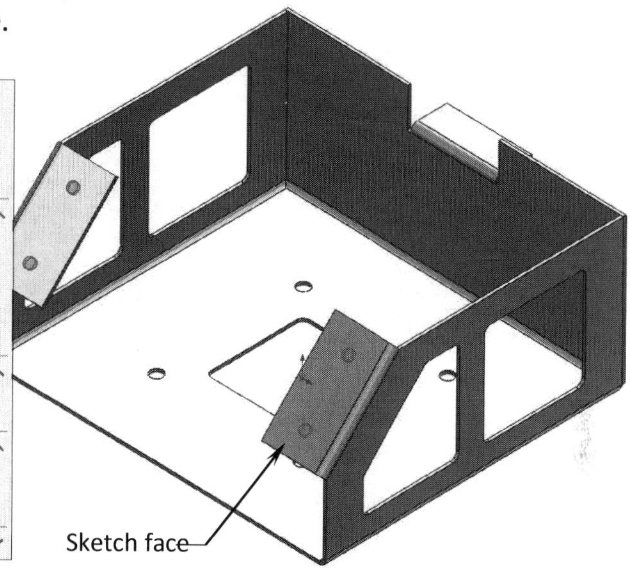

Standard: **ANSI Inch**
Size: **3/8**

Type: **All Drill Sizes**
End Condition: **Up To Next**

Click the **Position** tab and select the **Sketch Face** to rotate the view normal to you.

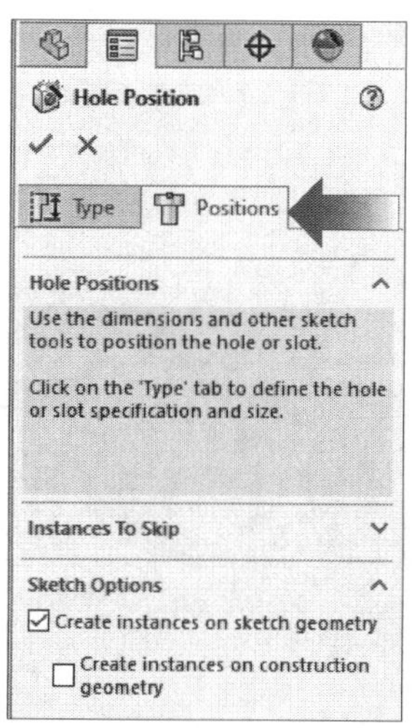

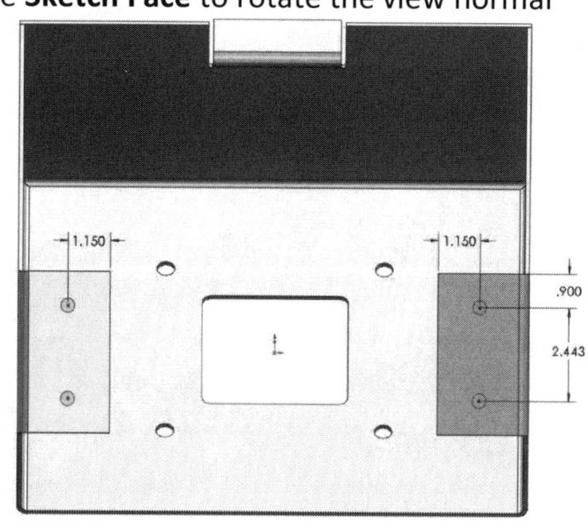

SOLIDWORKS enables the **Point** command automatically.

Place **two points** on each tab, and add the vertical, horizontal relations between the points, then add dimensions.

Click **OK**.

12. Adding the additional holes:

Change to the **Top** orientation (Control + 5).

Click **Hole Wizard**.

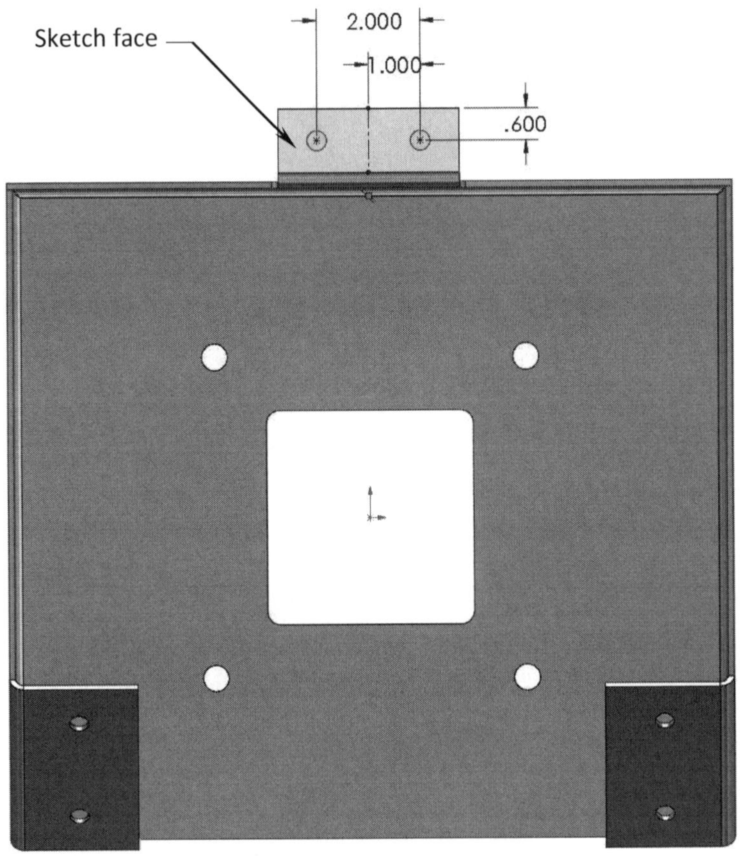

Use the same hole settings as in the previous step and **add two additional holes** on the face of the tab, as shown in the image on the right.

Click **OK**.

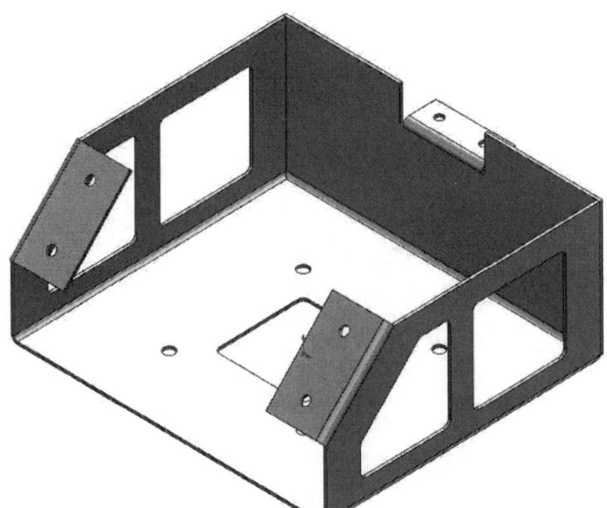

<u>Note:</u> When using the Hole Wizard, the 3D Sketch option allows the holes to be added to multiple surfaces, on multiple elevations or different planes.

13. Inserting a form tool:

Forming tools are solid parts that act as dies that bend, stretch, or otherwise form sheet metal to create form features such as louvers, lances, flanges, and ribs.

Click the **Design Library** tab and <u>expand</u> the **Forming Tools** and the **Lances** folders.

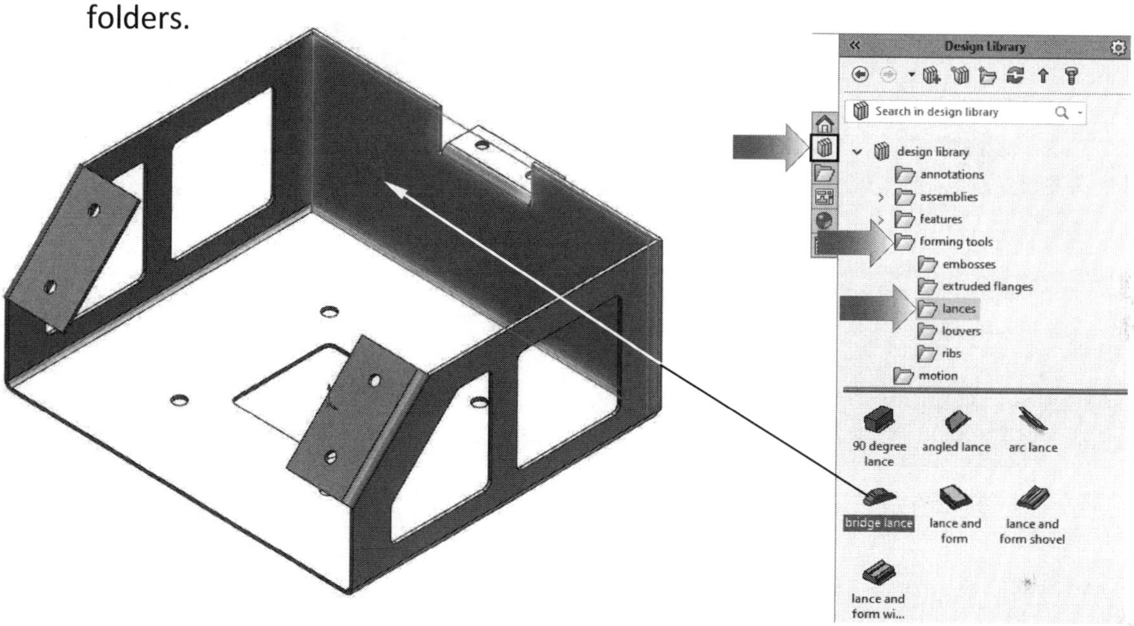

Locate the **Bridge Lance** form tool and drag/drop it to the <u>inside face</u> of the model.

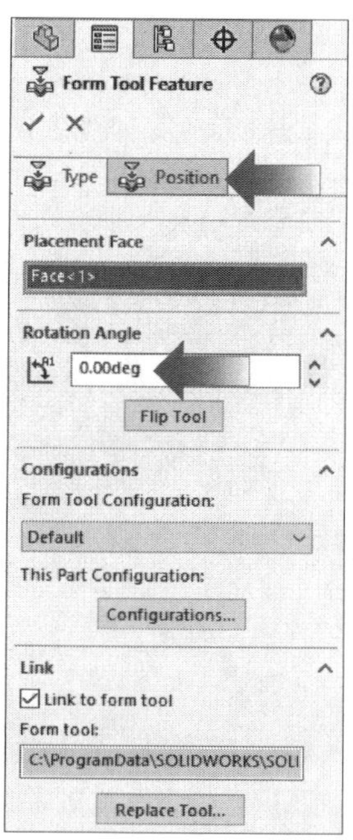

The form tool should protrude outwards and orients horizontally. Change the **Angle** or click **Flip Tool** if needed.

Click the **Position** tab and add the location dimensions.

Click **OK**.

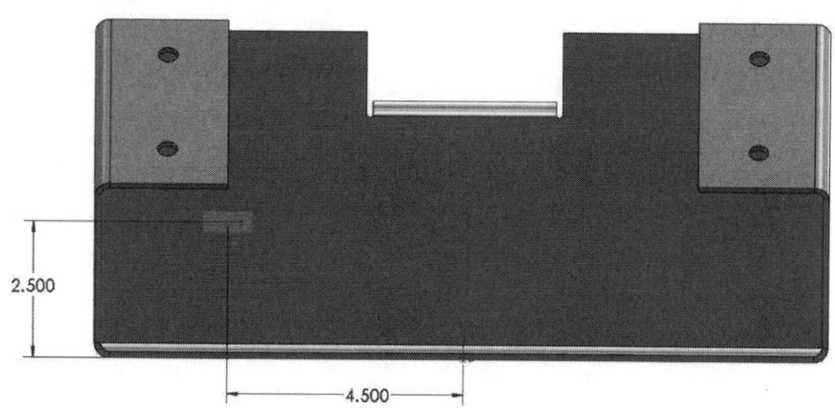

14. Patterning the Bridge Lance:

Switch to the **Features** tab and click **Linear Pattern**.

For Direction 1, select the horizontal edge as indicated in the image below.

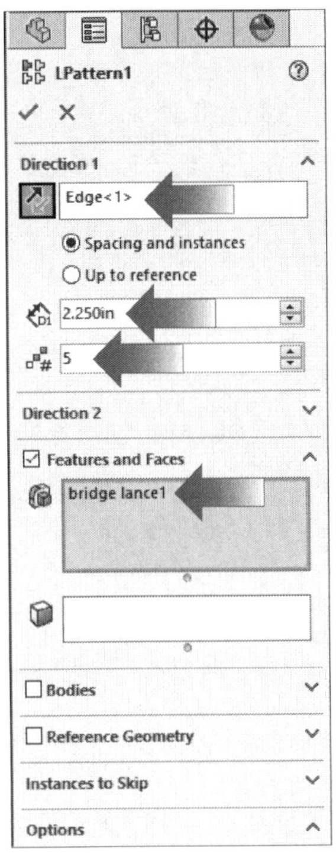

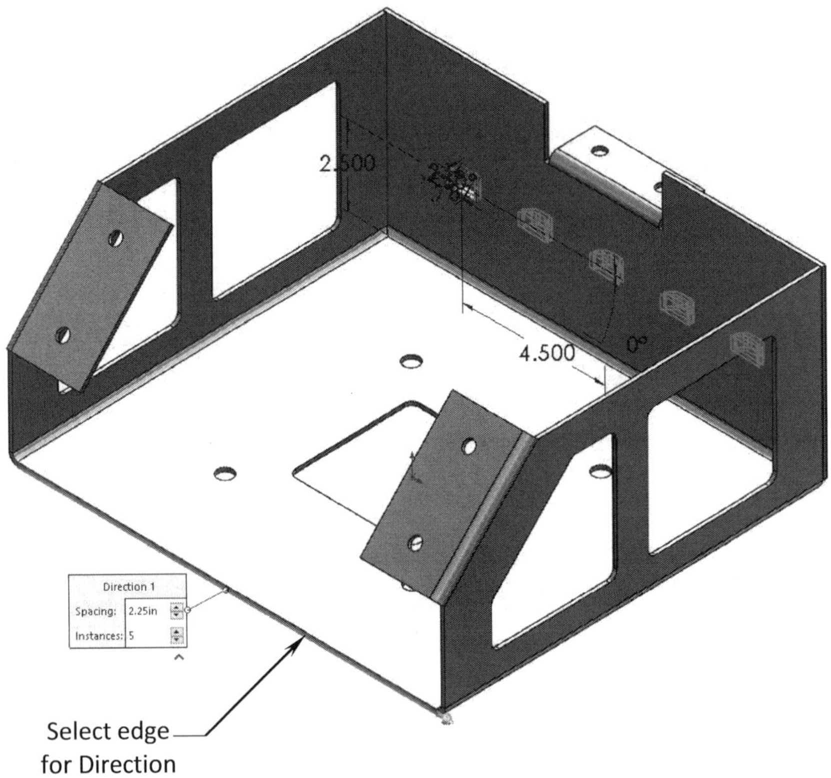

Click Spacing and Instances and enter **2.250in**.

For Number of Instances, enter: **5**.

For Features to Pattern, select the 1st **Bridge-Lance** and the **Pattern1**, either from the graphics area or from the Feature tree.

Click **OK**.

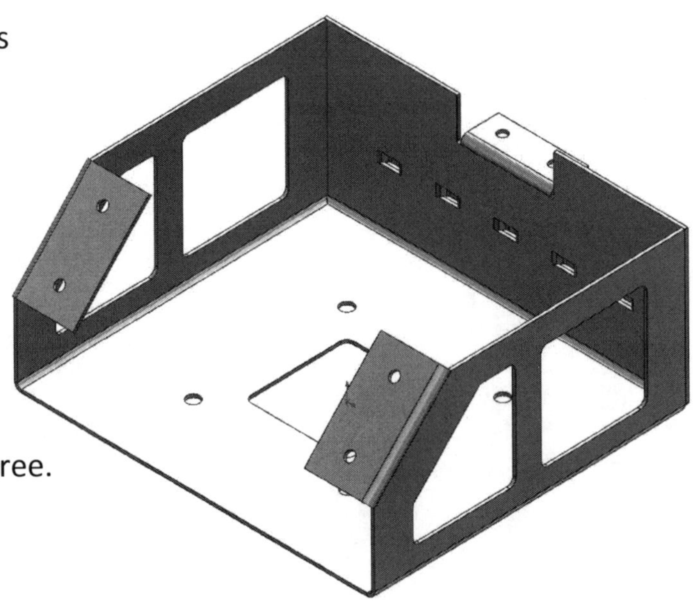

15. Adding chamfers:

Expand the **Corners** drop-down list and select: **Break-Corners/Corner-Trim**.

Click the **Chamfer** button and enter **.250in** for Distance.

Select **8 edges** as shown in the image on the right.

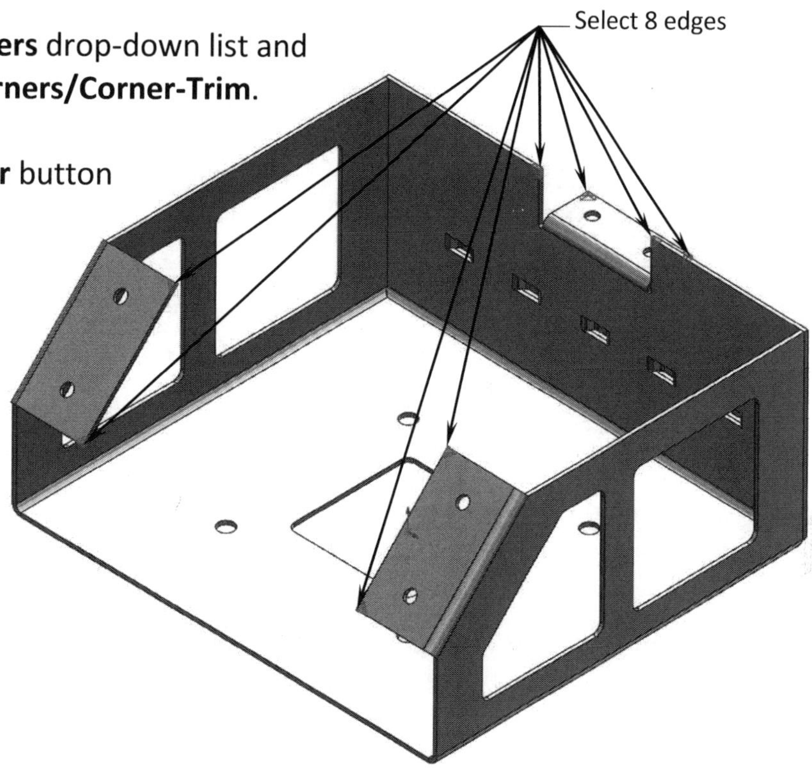

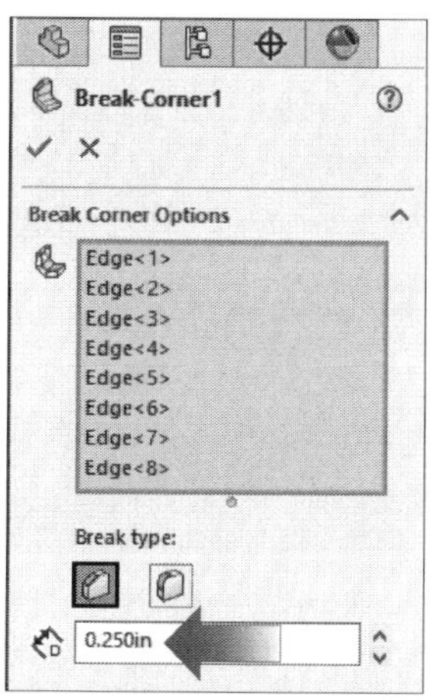

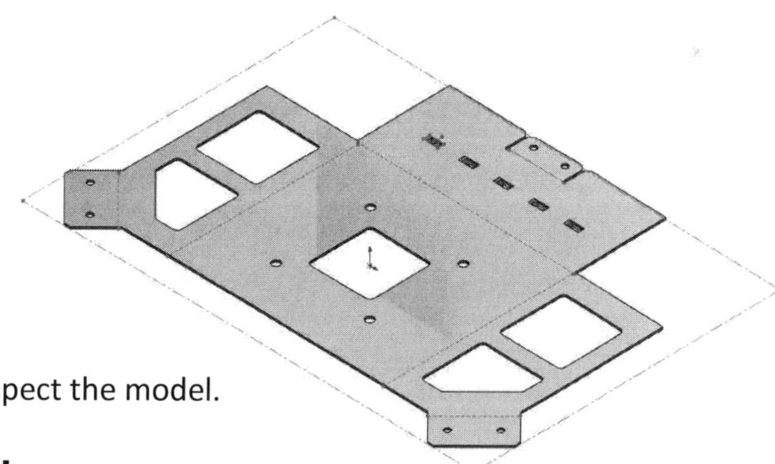

Click **OK**.

Click **Flatten** to inspect the model.

16. Saving your work:

Select **File, Save As**.

Enter: **Sheet Metal_Exe1_Completed** for the file name.

Click **Save**.

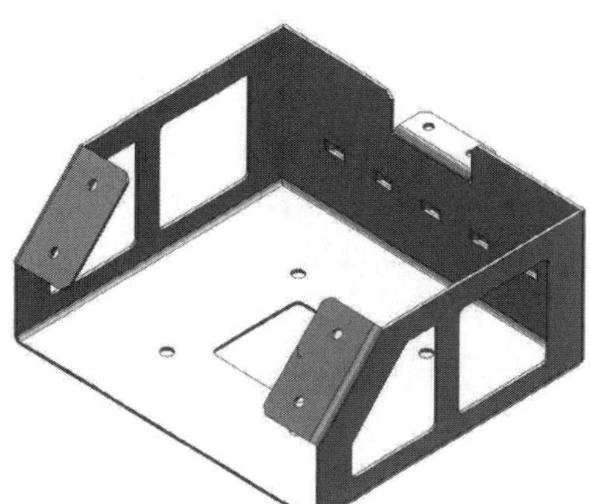

Exercise: Basic Sheet Metal Parts

1. Making the Base Sketch:

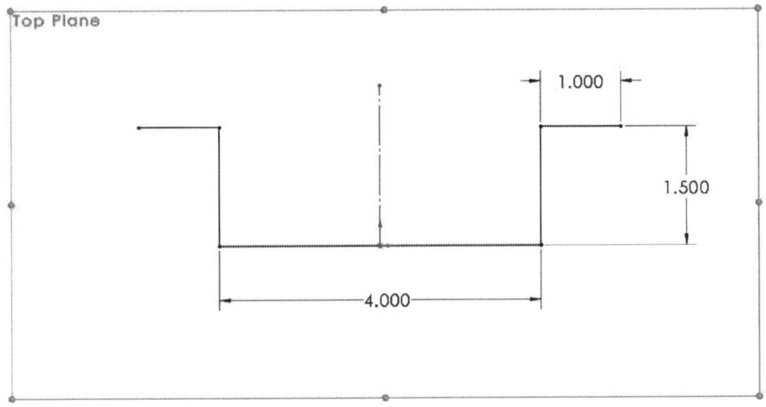

Select the TOP plane and open a **new sketch**.

Sketch the profile shown on the right. Use the **Mirror** option to keep the entities symmetrical to one another.

Add dimensions to fully define the sketch.

2. Creating a Base Flange:

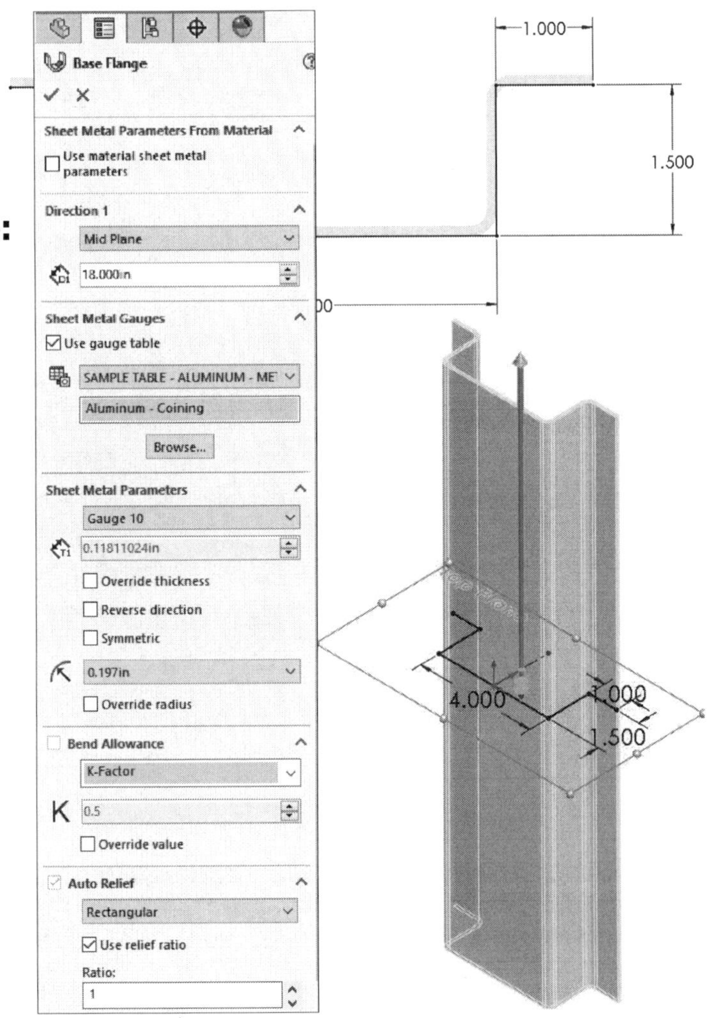

Click **Base Flange**.

For Direction 1, use **Mid Plane** and **18.00in**.

Enable the **Use Gauge Table** checkbox and select:

Sample Table – **Alum.**
Gauge **10**
Bend Radius **.197in**

K-Factor: **0.5**

Auto Relief **Enabled**
Rectangular Ratio **1**
Click **OK**.

3. Adding the Hole Wizard holes:

Switch to the **Features** tab and click **Hole Wizard**.

For Hole Type, select **Hole**.

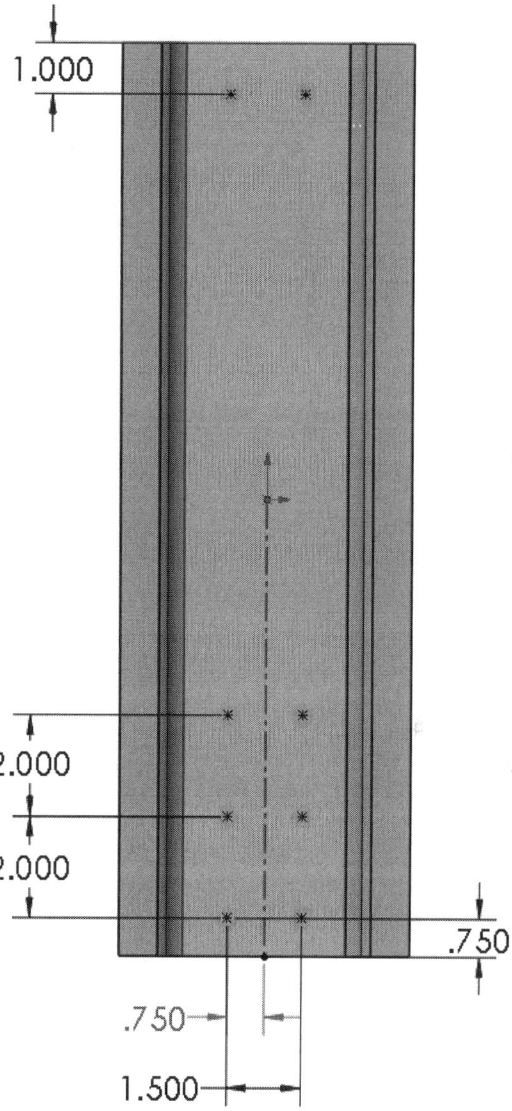

Standard: **ANSI Inch**.

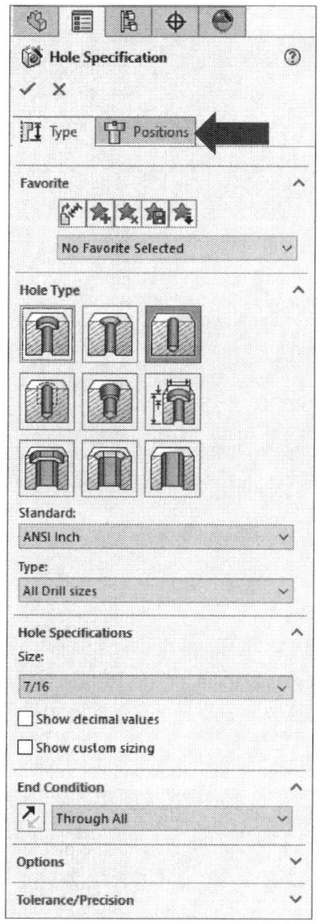

Type: **All Drill Sizes**.

Size: **7/16**.

End Condition: **Through All**.

Click the **Position** tab (arrow).

Select the center-face to rotate the view normal to you.

Place 4 dots on one side and sketch a **Centerline** to mirror the dots. (Each dot represents the center of a hole.)

Add the dimensions shown in the image to fully define the sketch.

Click **OK**.

4. Adding the Slotted-Holes (Clearance Holes):

Click **Hole Wizard** once again.

For Hole Type, select **Slot**.

Standard: **ANSI Inch**.

Type: **All Drill Sizes**.

Size: **7/16**.

Slot Length: **.500in**.

Dimension Scheme: **Arc Tangent**.

End Condition: **Through All**.

Click the **Position** tab (arrow).

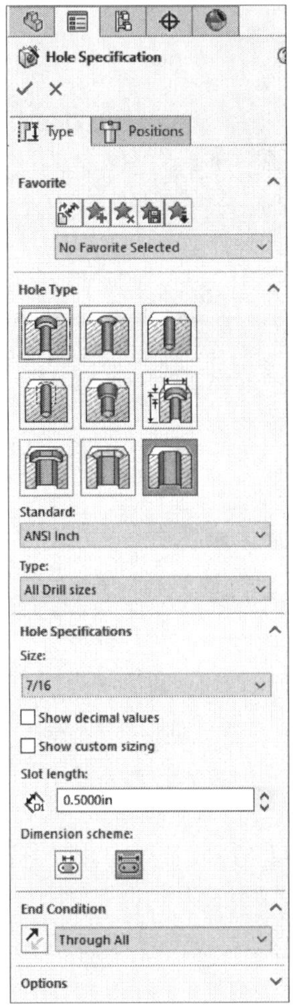

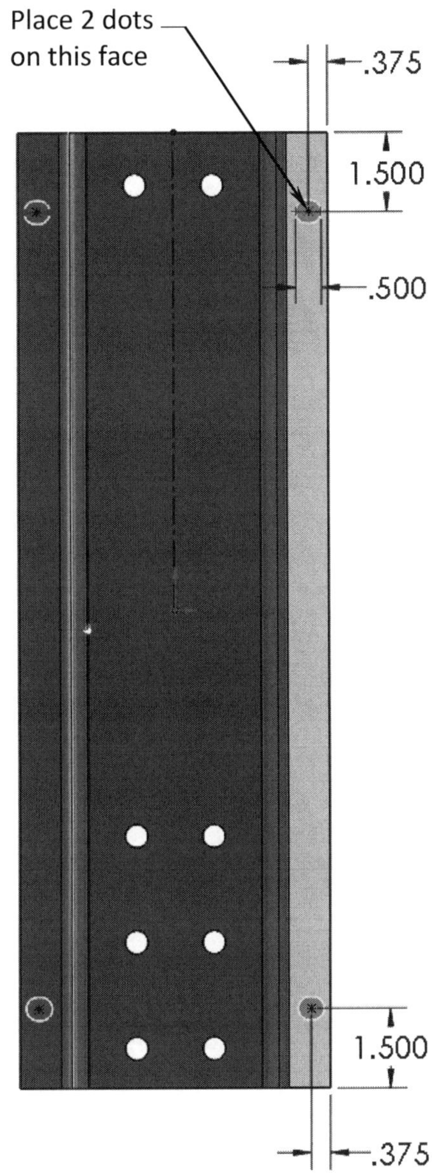

Click the side-face to rotate the view normal to you.

Place **2 slotted holes** on one side and sketch a **Centerline** to mirror the slotted holes.

Click **OK**.

5. Adding the corner fillets:

Switch to the **Features** tab and **Fillet**.

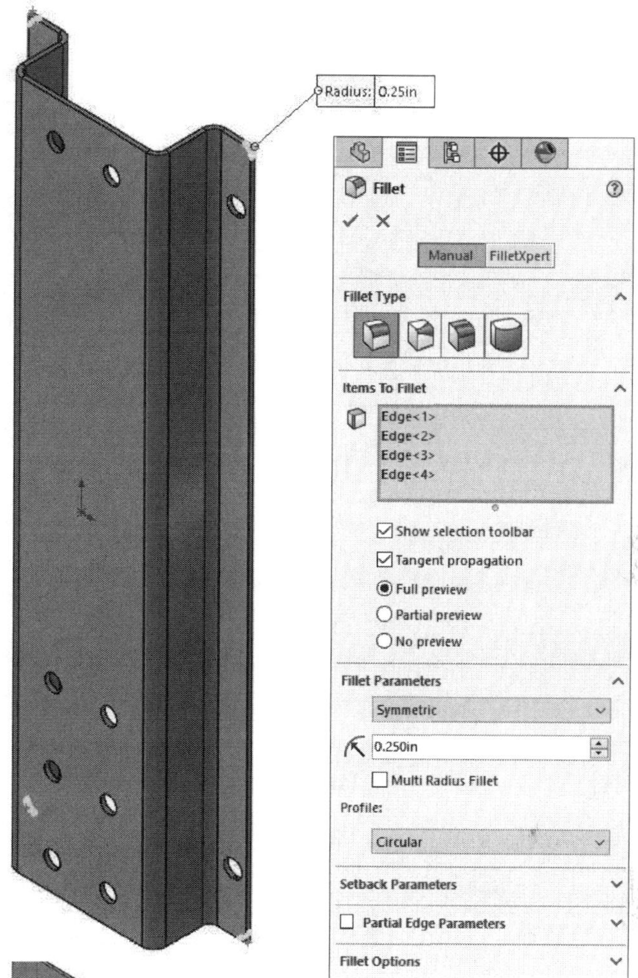

For Fillet Type, use the default **Constant Size** option.

For Radius, enter **.250in**.

For Items to Fillet, select the <u>4 edges</u> at the 4 corners of the part.

Click **OK**.

Switch to the **Sheet Metal** tab and click: **Flatten**.

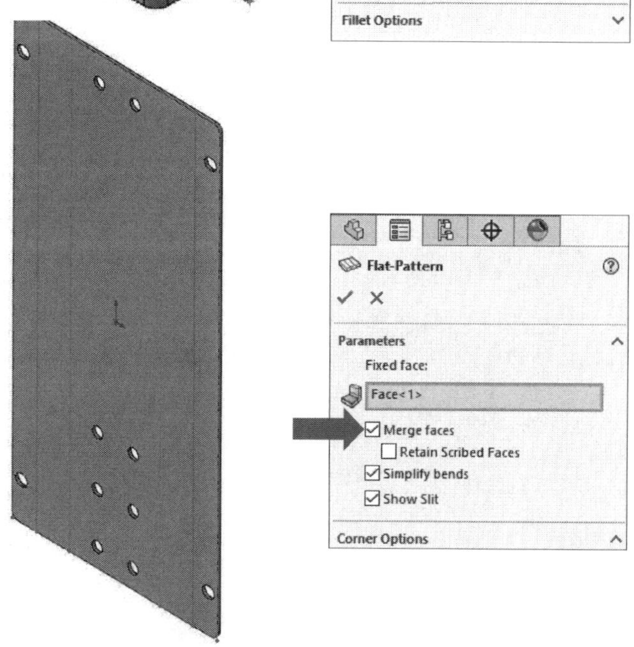

The part should show the flat pattern without any errors on the FeatureManager tree.

The Bend-Lines can be toggled on/off by editing the **Flat-Pattern1** and enabling the **Merge-Faces** checkbox.

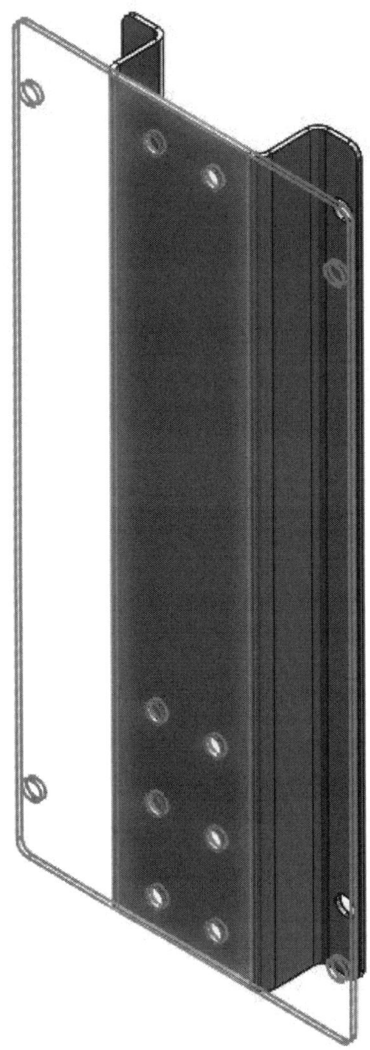

Right-click anywhere on the part and select: **Toggle Flat Pattern**.

The Flat Pattern is projected onto the Fold Pattern. This is one of the quicker ways to view the flat pattern of a sheet metal part.

6. Saving your work:

Select: **File, Save As**.

Enter: **Basic Sheet Metal Parts.sldprt** for the file name.

Click **Save**.

Lesson 2: Sheet Metal Flanges

When designing a sheet metal part using SOLIDWORKS, one of the most common features are the flanges. They can be made using the Base Flange tool, the Edge Flange tool, the Miter Flange tool, and other sheet metal tools.

In this lesson, we will explore the use of different sheet metal tools to create flanges.

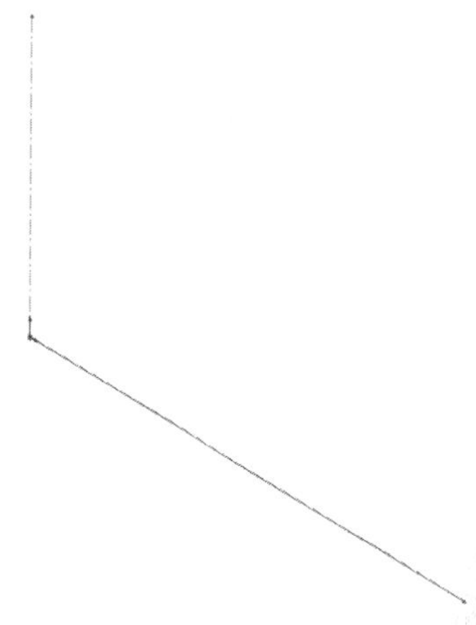

1. Opening a part document:

Browse to the Training Folder and open a part document named: **Sheet Metal Flanges**.

There is only 1 sketch in this model; we will use it to create the Base Flange, or the parent feature of this part.

2. Creating a Base Flange:

Select **Sketch1** from the FeatureManager tree and click **Base Flange**.

For Direction 1, select **Mid Plane – 8.00in**.

Sample Table **Aluminum**

Gauge 14 – Radius **.079in**.

K-Factor: **0.5**

Rectangular – Ratio: **1**

Click **OK**.

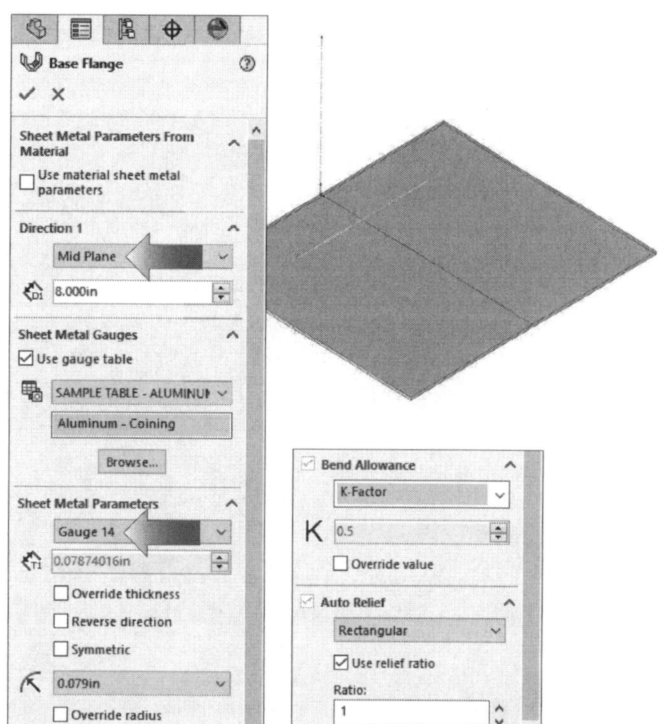

3. Making the 1st edge flange:

The part has symmetrical features. We will create all features on one side and then mirror them to the opposite side, towards the end of the design.

An edge flange is created from an existing edge of the part. It will have the matching thickness as the sheet metal part, and the thickness can be toggled in or out. The built-in sketch can also be altered to change the shape or the size of the flange.

Select the edge as noted and click **Edge Flange** on the **Sheet Metal** tab.

Move the mouse cursor upwards and click to lock the direction.

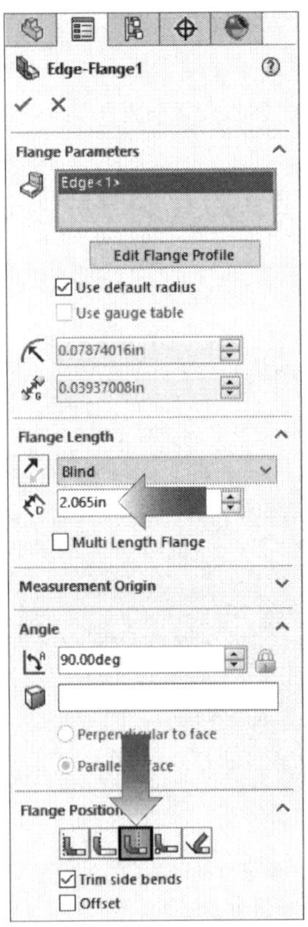

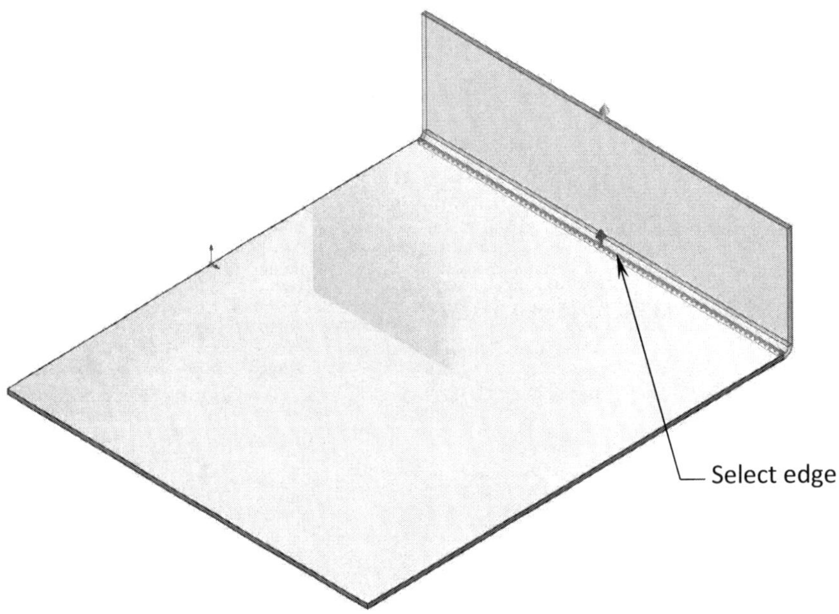

For Flange Length,
select **Blind** and enter: **2.065in**.

Leave the Bend Angle at **90.00deg**.

For Flange Position, click **Bend Outside** to move the flange and the bend radius outward. Also enable the **Trim Side Bend** checkbox.

Click **OK**.

4. Making the 2nd edge flange:

Click **Edge Flange** on the **Sheet Metal** tab.

Select the edge indicated below and move the cursor downwards to lock the direction.

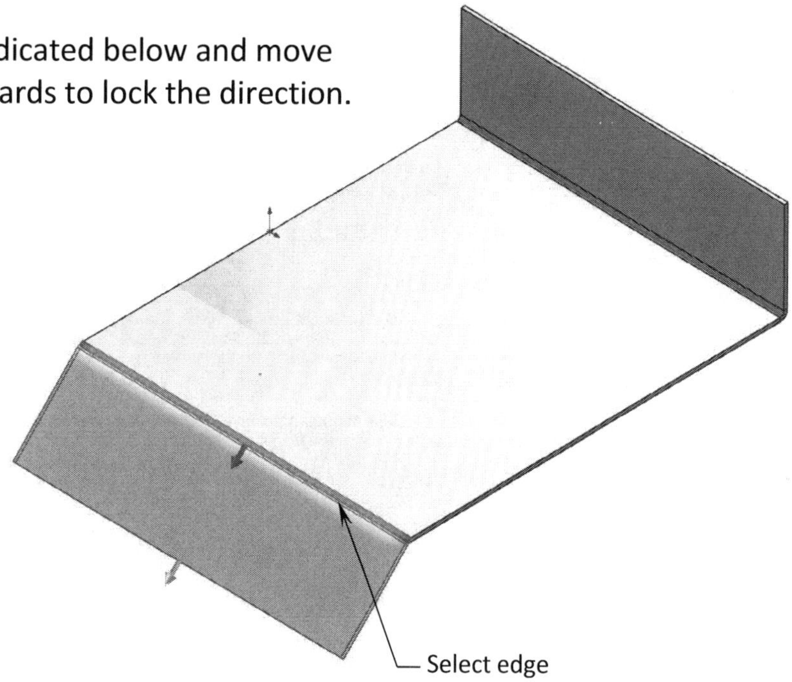

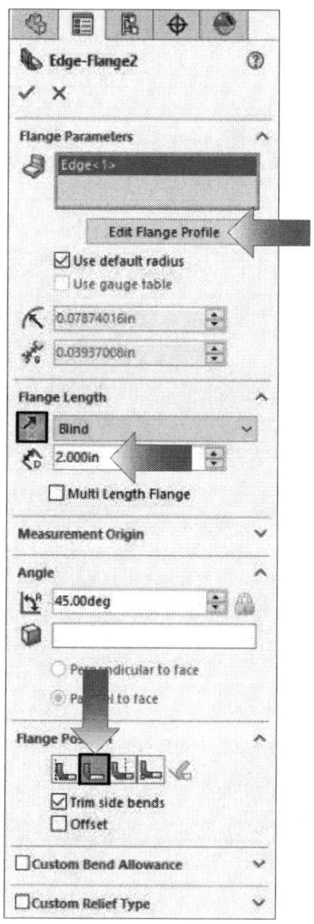

For Flange Length,
select **Blind** and enter **2.00in**. Click **Reverse** direction.

Bend Angle: **45deg**.

Position: **Material Inside**.

Click: **Edit Flange Profile**.

Drag the line inward as shown in the image.

Add the **2.00in**. dimension

Click **Finish**.

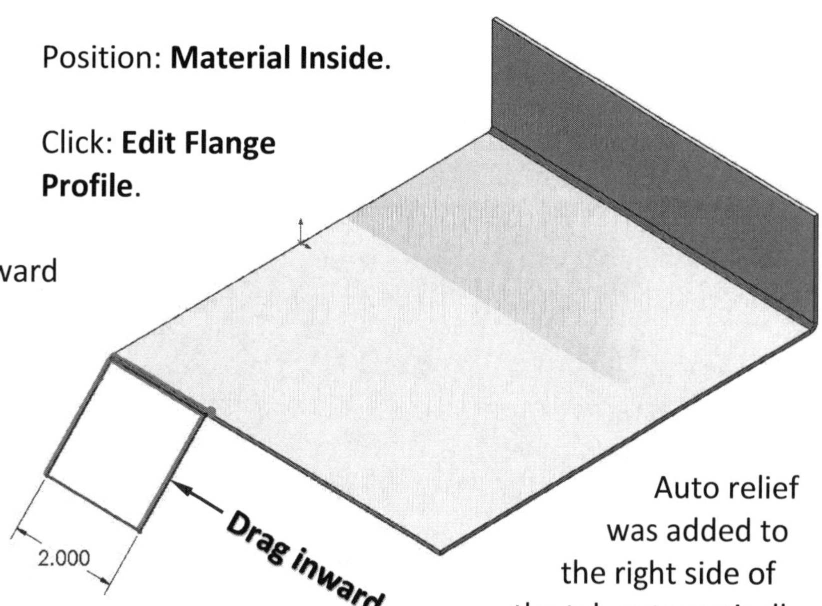

Auto relief was added to the right side of the tab automatically.

5. Making the 3rd edge flange:

Click **Edge Flange** again.

Select the edge on the right side of the part, move upwards and click the mouse to lock the direction.

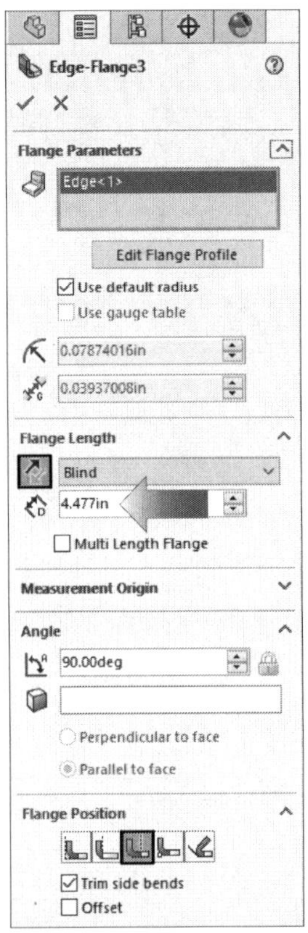

For Flange Length, select: **Blind** and enter **4.477in**.

Click **Reverse**.

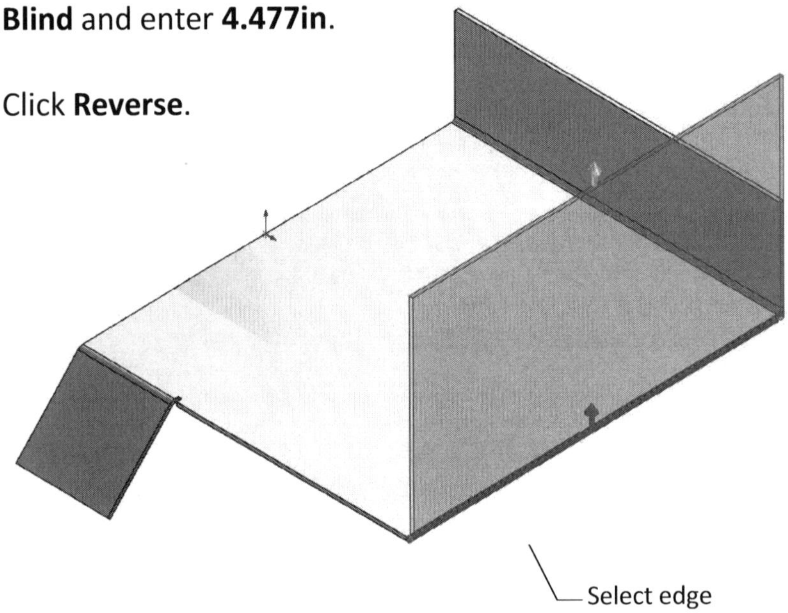

Keep Bend Angle at **90.00deg**.

For Flange Position, select **Bend Outside**.

Click **OK**.

3 Edge Flanges are created. They shared the same thickness and bend radius as the Base Flange.

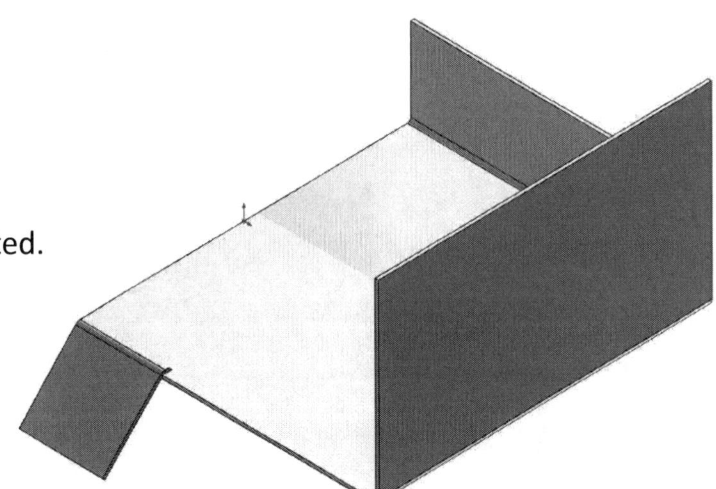

6. Creating a jog feature:

The Jog tool adds material to a sheet metal part by creating two bends from a sketched line.

Select the <u>face</u> on the right side and open a **new sketch**.

Sketch a **Line** and add the **2.00in**. dimension.

Switch to the **Sheet Metal** tab and select the **Jog** tool.

For Fixed Face, click anywhere <u>below the line</u>.

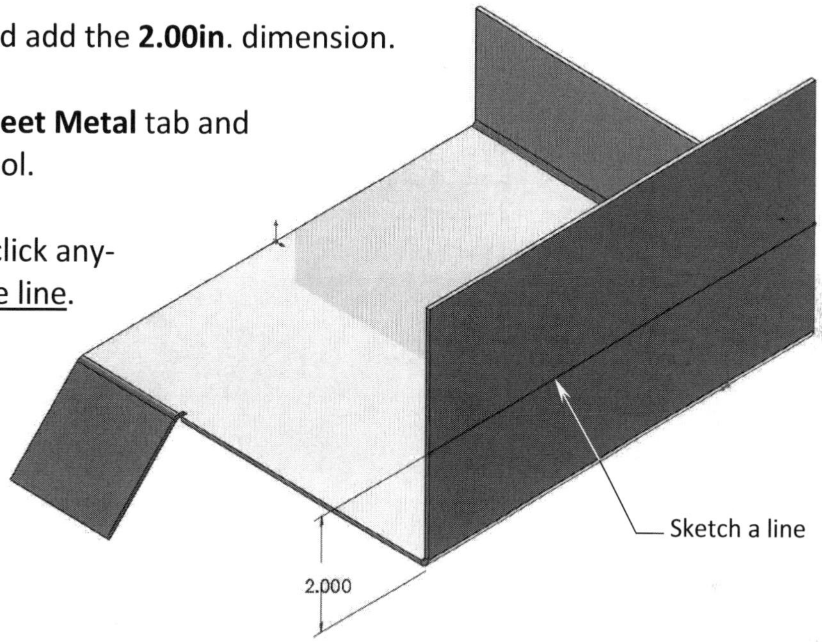

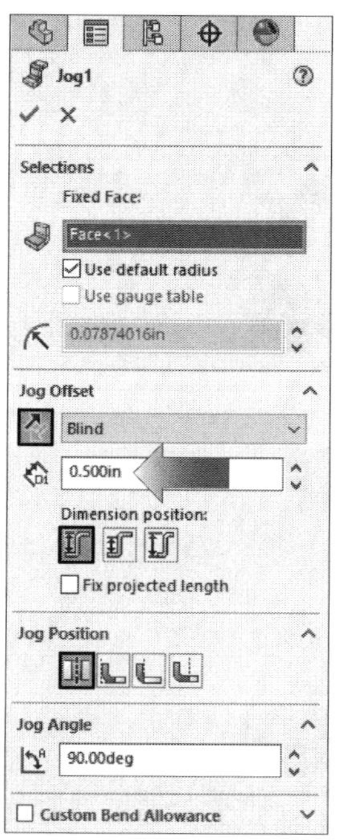

For Jog Offset, select **Blind** and enter: **.500in**.

For Dimension Position, select: **Outside Offset**.

For Jog Position, click **Bend-Centerline**.

Keep the Bend Angle at **90deg**.

Click **OK**.

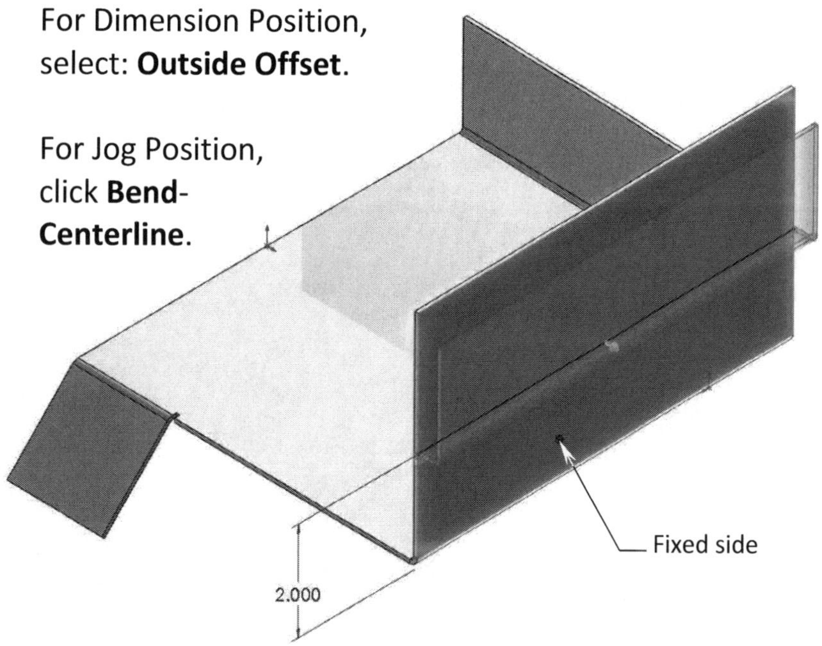

7. Adding another jog:

Select the face on the right side and open a **new sketch**.

Sketch a **Line** and add the **1.00in**. dimension.

Switch to the **Sheet Metal** tab and click **Jog**.

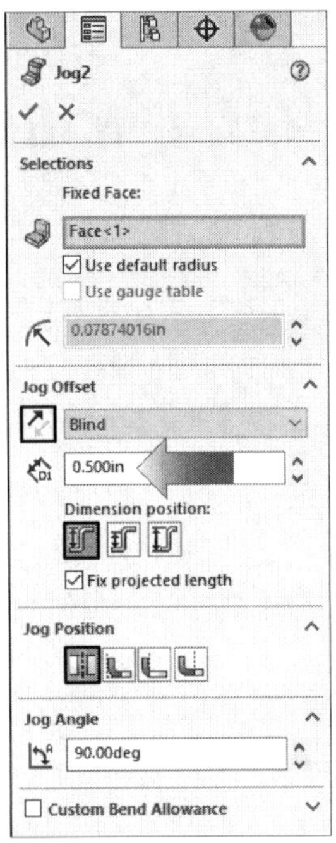

For Fixed Face, click anywhere below the line.

For Jog Offset, select **Blind** and enter: **.500in**.

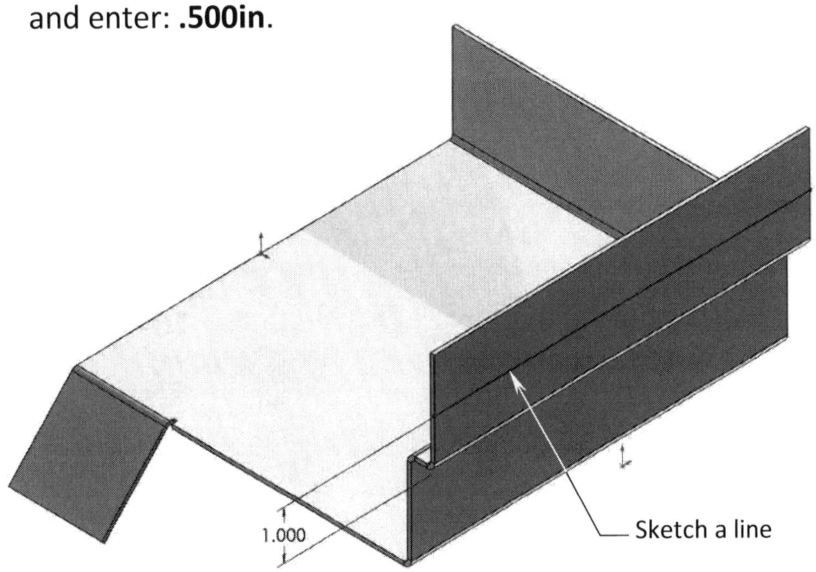

For Dimension Position, select: **Outside Offset**.

For Jog Position, click **Bend Centerline**.

Keep the Bend Angle at **90.00deg**.

Click **OK**.

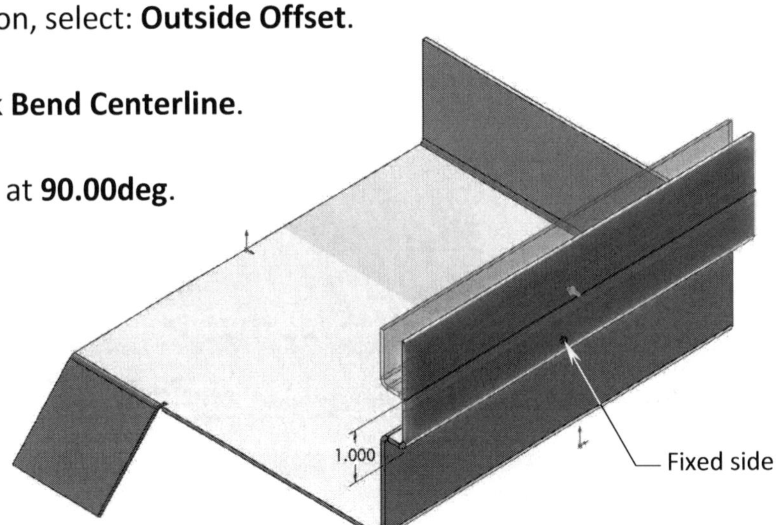

Note: Only 1 line can be used each time to to create a jog feature.

8. Creating a Miter Flange:

A miter flange tool adds a series of flanges to one or more edges of a sheet metal part. Only lines and arcs can be used to create miter flanges.

Press **Control + 4** to change to the **Right** view orientation.

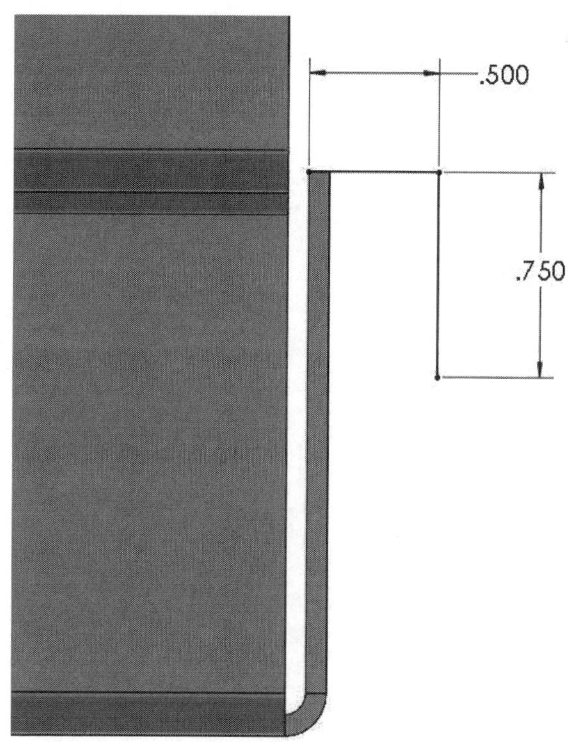

Select the small, vertical face of the Miter Flange and open a **new sketch**.

Sketch **2 lines** starting at the upper left corner of the flange.

Add the dimensions shown in the image to fully define the sketch.

Switch to the **Sheet Metal** tab.

Rotate the model to see the back side, where the flange is being made.

Select the **Miter Flange** tool.

For Miter Parameter, select the edge as indicated.

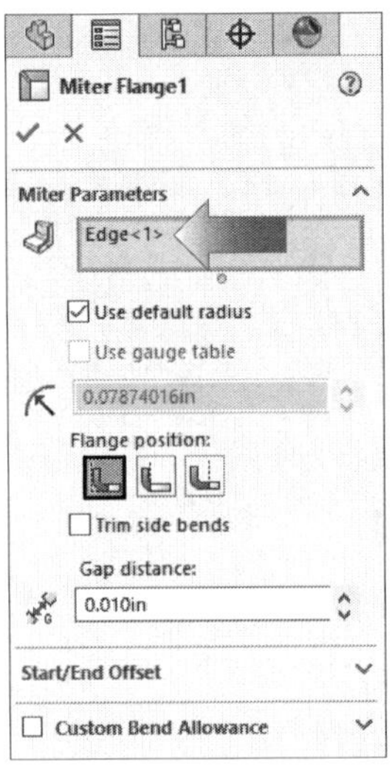

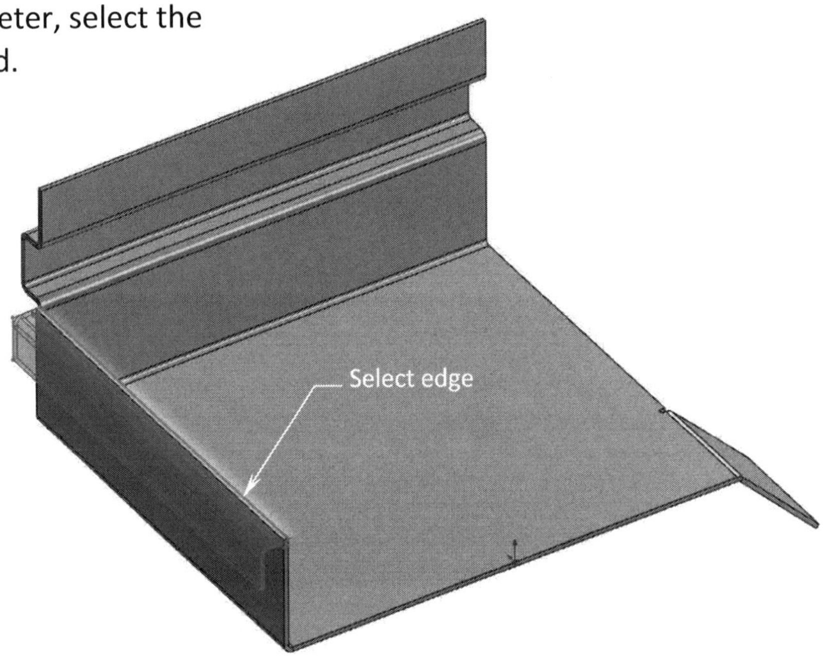

For Flange Position, select: **Material Inside**.

Clear the **Trim Side Bend** checkbox.

Keep the Gap at **.010in**.

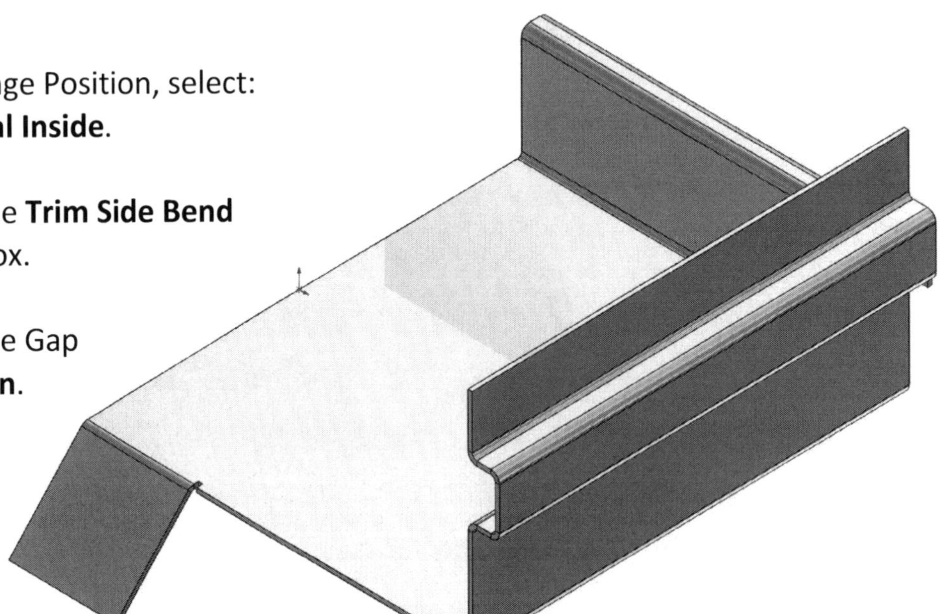

Click **OK**.

9. Mirroring a solid body:

All flanges have been created. We can mirror the body at this time.

Switch to the **Features** tab.

Click **Mirror**.

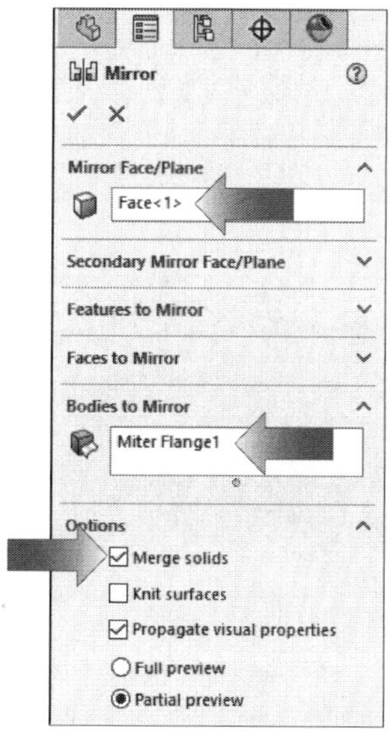

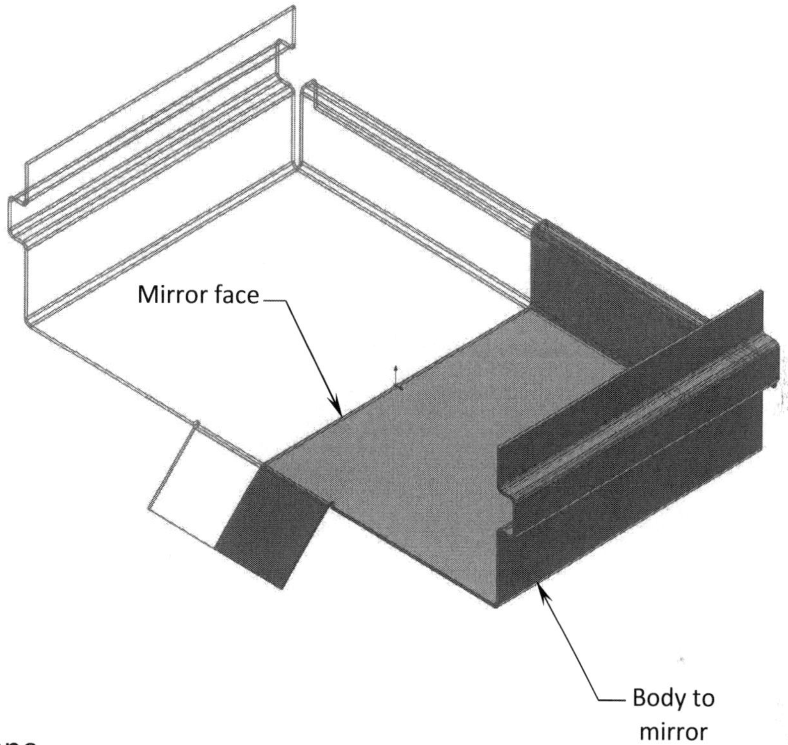

For Mirror Face/Plane, select the face on the left side of the part.

Expand the Bodies to Mirror section and select the part from the graphics area.

Enable the **Merge-Solids** checkbox.

Click **OK**.

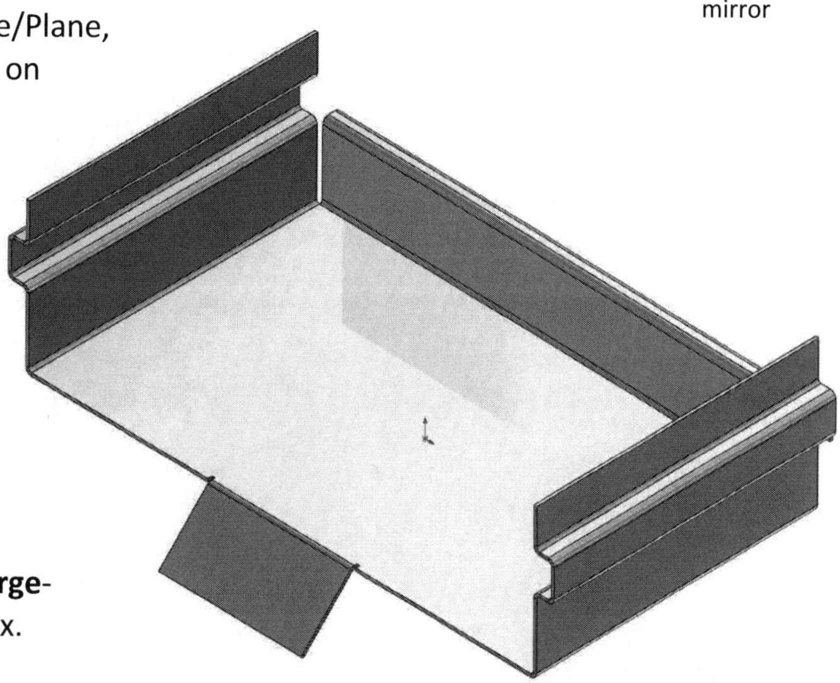

10. Closing the corners:

Switch back to the **Sheet Metal** tab.

Select: **Corners, Close Corner**.

For Faces to Extend, select the **2 end-faces** as noted below.

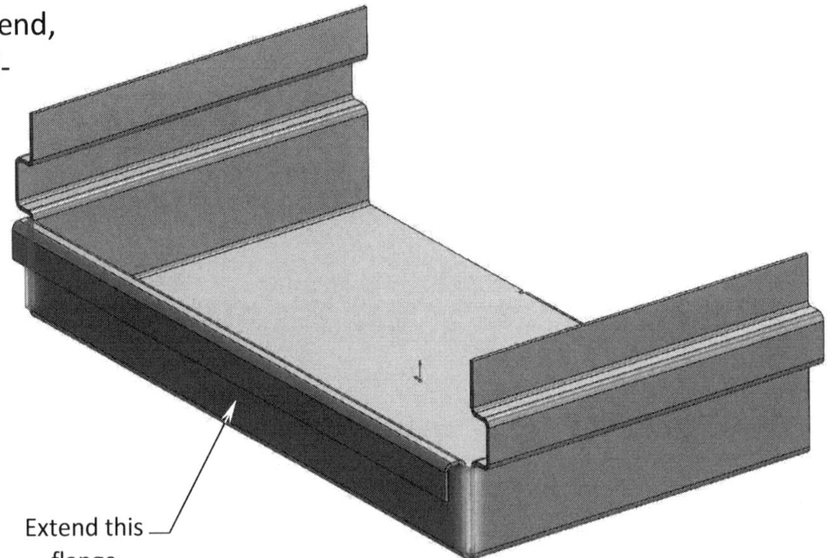

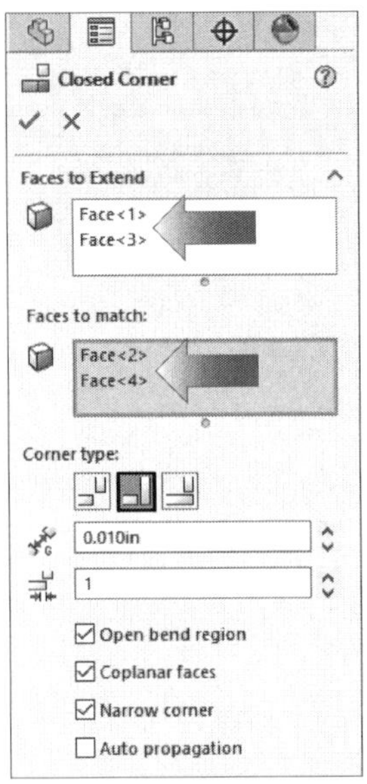

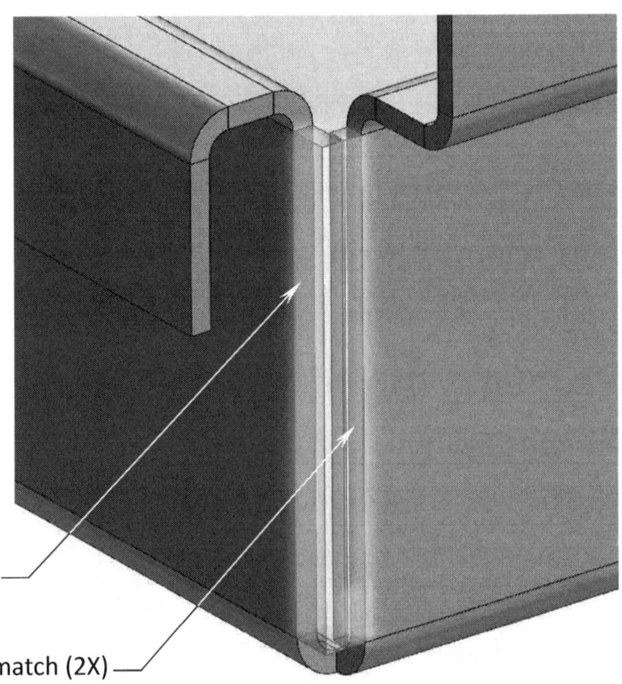

For Faces to Match, select the **2 end-faces** of the other flanges, as indicated in the image.

For Corner Type, click **Overlap**.

Keep the Gap at **.010in**.

Click **OK**.

11. Adding holes:

Select the face of the 45deg. flange and open a **new sketch**.

Sketch a **Centerline** and **2 Circles**.

Add a **Symmetry** relation between the 2 circles.

Add the dimensions shown to fully define the sketch.

Switch to the **Sheet Metal** tab.

Click **Extruded-Cut**.

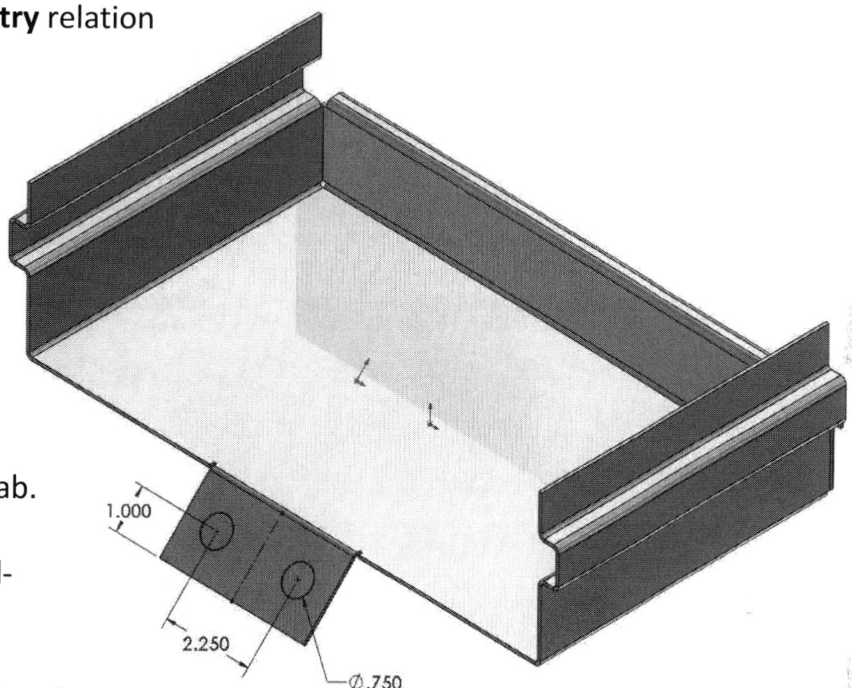

For Direction 1, select **Blind** and enable the checkbox: **Link-To-Thickness**.

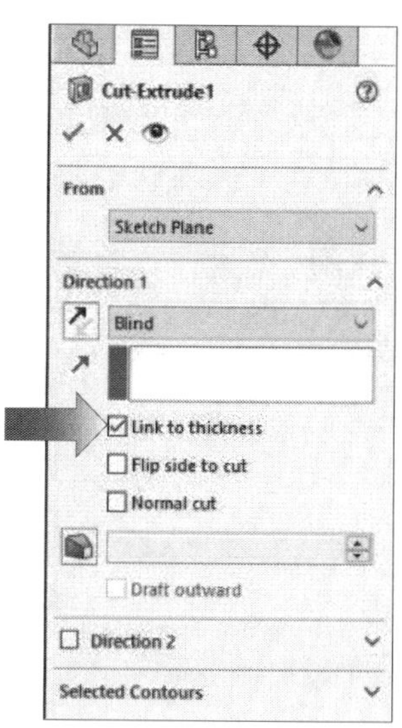

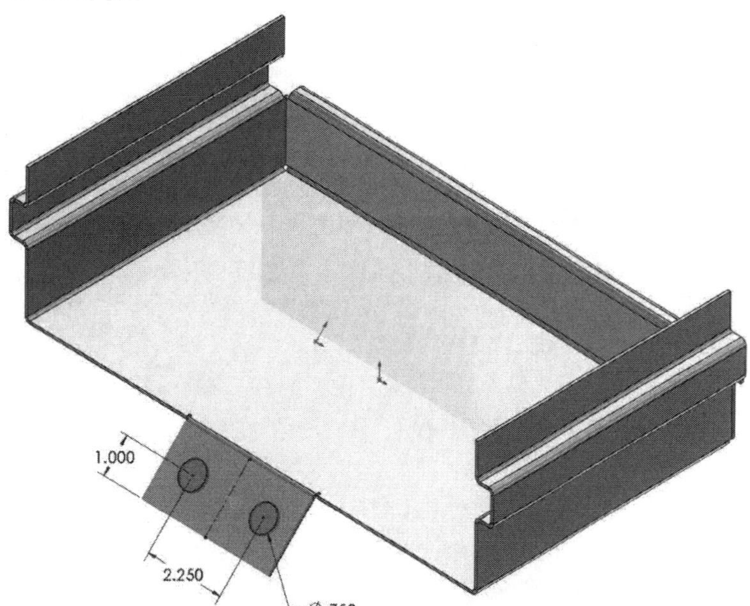

Click **OK**.

12. Adding chamfers:

Select **Corners, Break Corner**.

For Corners to Break, select **8 edges** as indicated.

For Break Type, click **Chamfer**.

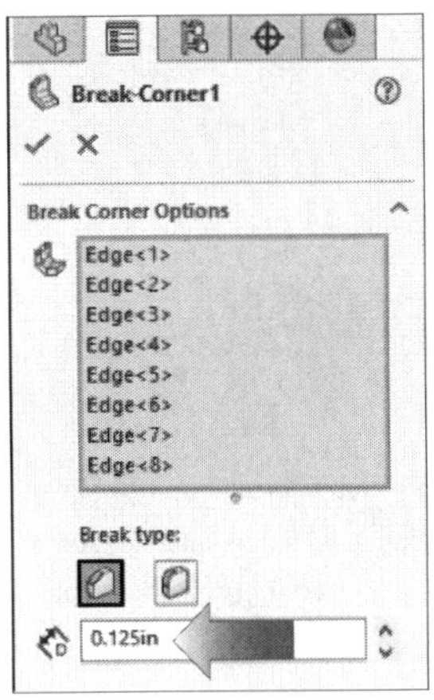

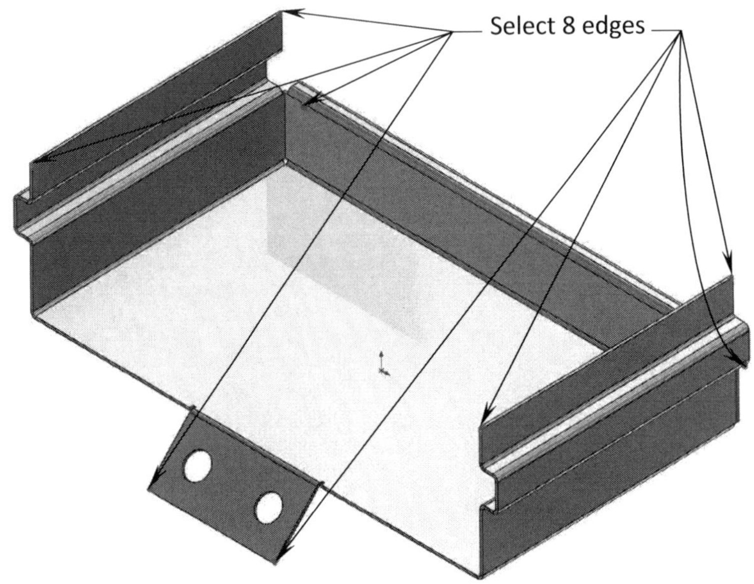

For Distance, enter **.125in**.

Click **OK**.

Right-click on the part and select: **Toggle Flat Pattern**.

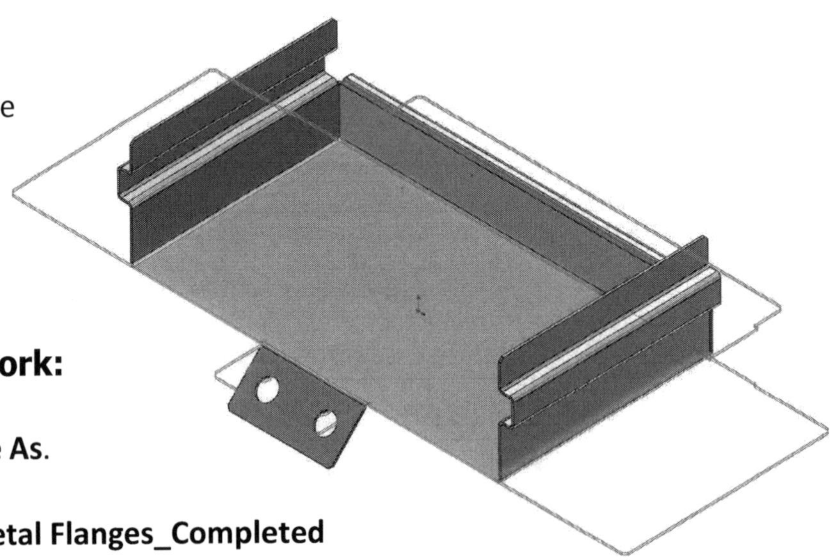

13. Saving your work:

Select **File, Save As**.

Enter: **Sheet Metal Flanges_Completed** for the file name.

Click **Save**.

Lesson 3: Sheet Metal Sketched Bends

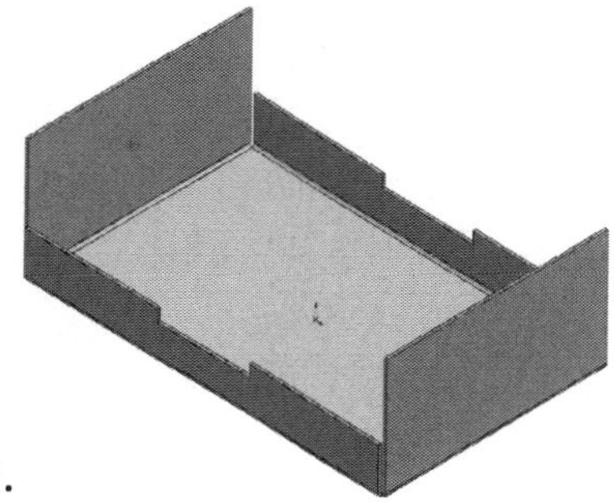

Bend lines can be added to any flat face of a sheet metal part with a sketched bend feature.
We can dimension the bend lines to other geometry.
There are a few rules to keep in mind when using Sketched Bend:

* Only lines are allowed in the sketch, but multiple lines can be used on the same face, for each sketch.
* The bend line does not have to be the exact length of the faces you are bending.
* Use sketched bends with flat faces that are not in the flattened state.

1. Opening a part document:

Browse to the Training Folder and open a part document named:
Sketched Bends1.slddrw

2. Creating the 1st sketched bend:

Select the right side face of the part and open a **new sketch**.

Sketch a horizontal **Line** and add the **1.00in**. dimension.

Switch to the **Sheet Metal** tab and click **Sketched Bend**.

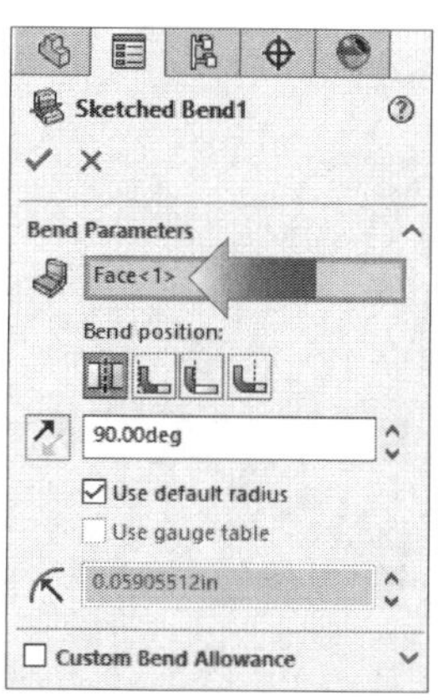

For Fixed Face, select the area below the horizontal line.

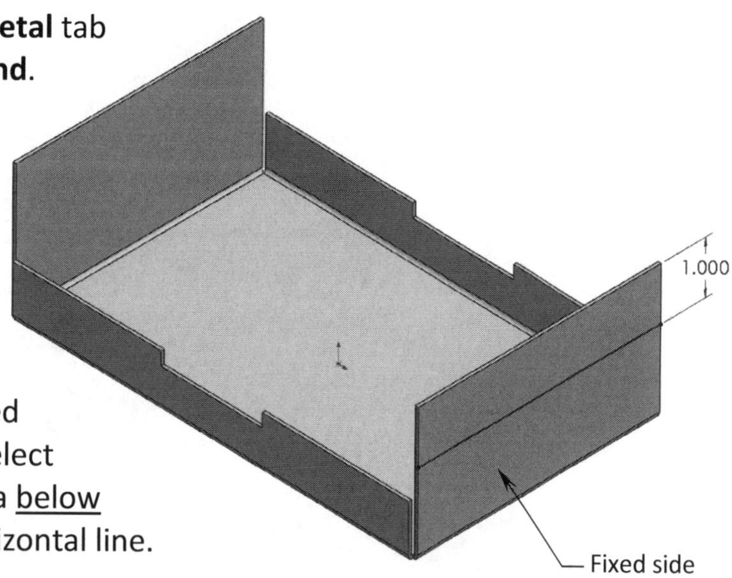

For Bend Position, use the default **Bend Centerline** option.

For Bend Angle, enter: **90.0deg**.

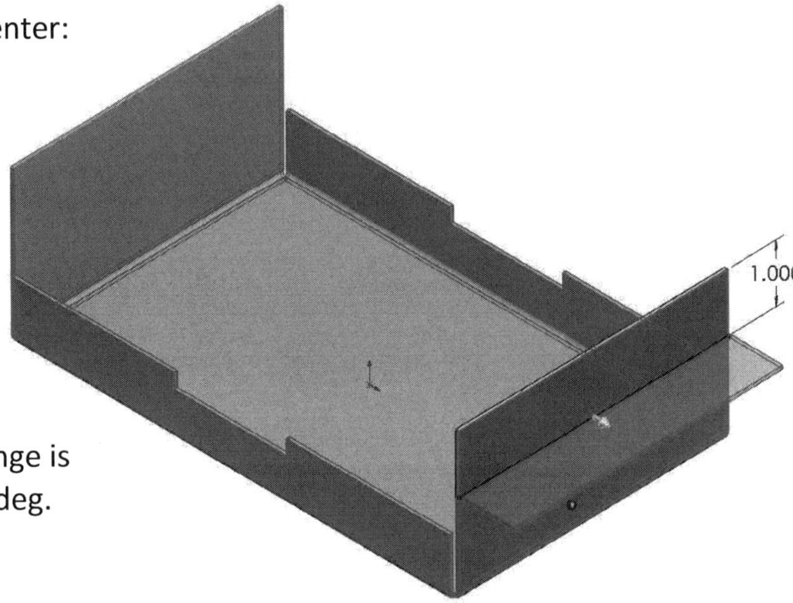

Enable the checkbox: **Use Default Radius**.

Click **OK**.

The right side flange is bent outward 90deg.

3. Creating the 2nd sketched bend:

Select the left side face of the part and open a **new sketch**.

Sketch another horizontal **Line** and add the **1.00in**. dimension.

Switch to the **Sheet Metal** tab and click **Sketched Bend**.

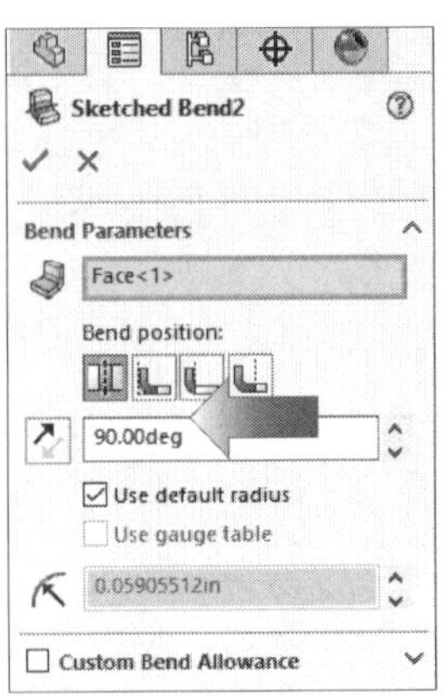

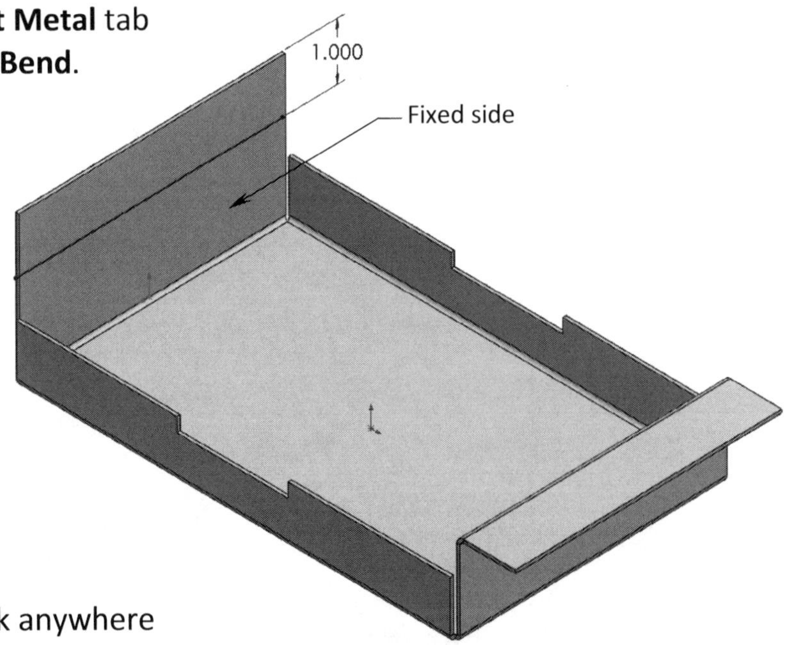

For Fixed Face, click anywhere below the horizontal line.

For Bend Position, use the default **Bend Centerline** option.

For Bend Angle, enter: **90.0deg**.

Enable the checkbox: **Use Default Radius**.

Click **OK**.

The left side flange is bent outward 90deg.

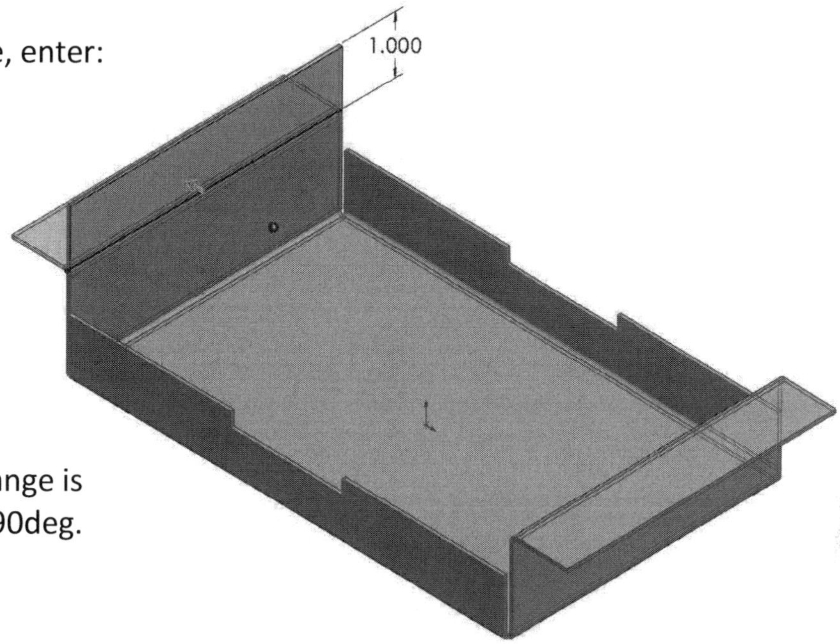

4. Adding holes:

Select the upper face of the flange and open a **new sketch**.

Sketch **2 Circles** and **2 Centerlines**, then mirror the circles.

Add the dimension shown below to fully define the sketch.

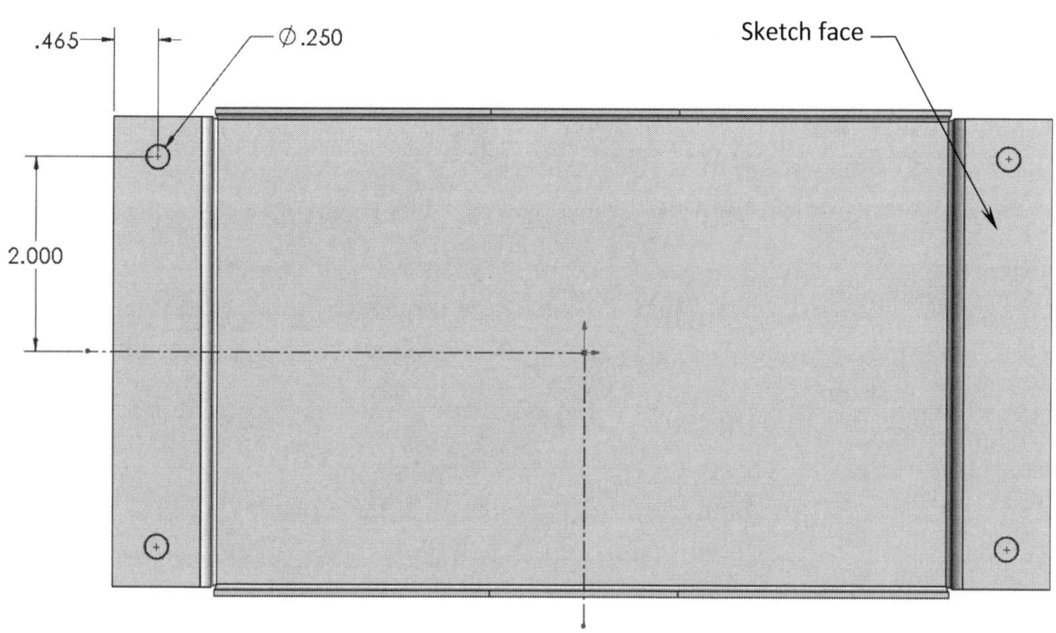

Switch to the **Sheet Metal** tab and click **Extruded Cut**.

For Direction 1, use the default **Blind** Type.

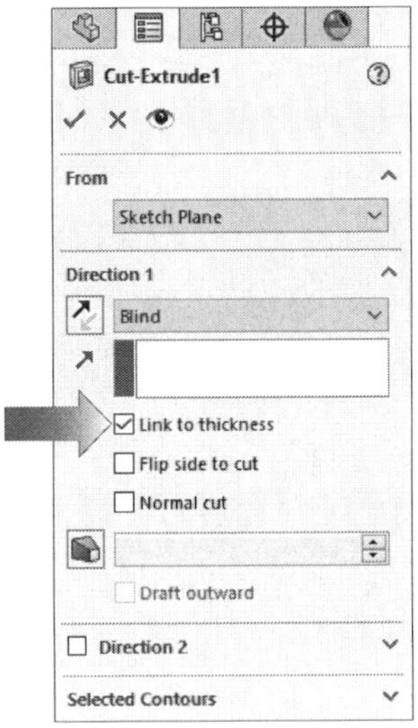

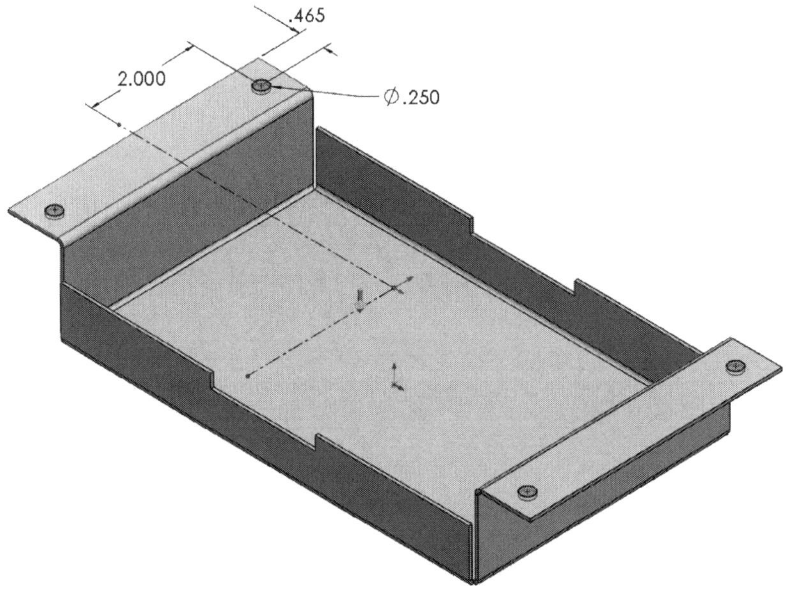

Enable the checkbox: **Link To Thickness**.

Click **OK.**

5. Adding chamfers:

Click **Corners, Break Corner**.

Select **Chamfer** and enter **.125in**.

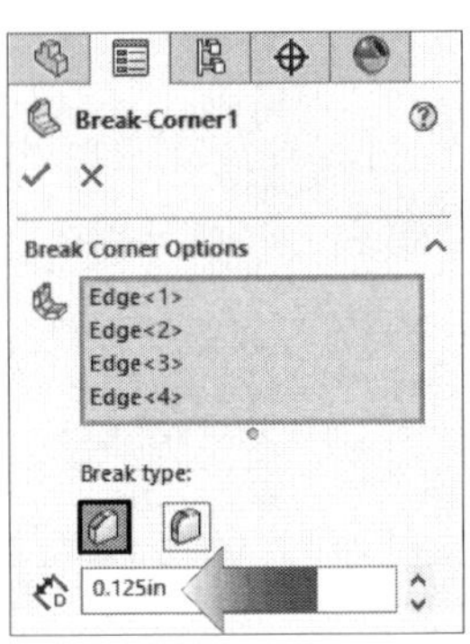

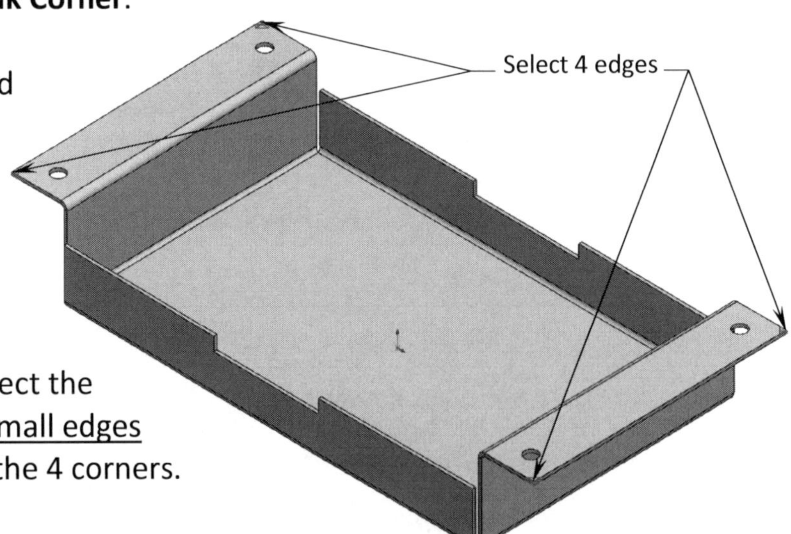

Select the <u>4 small edges</u> at the 4 corners.

Click **OK**.

6. Saving your work:

Select **File, Save As**.

Enter **Sketched Bends_Completed** for the file name.

Click **Save**.

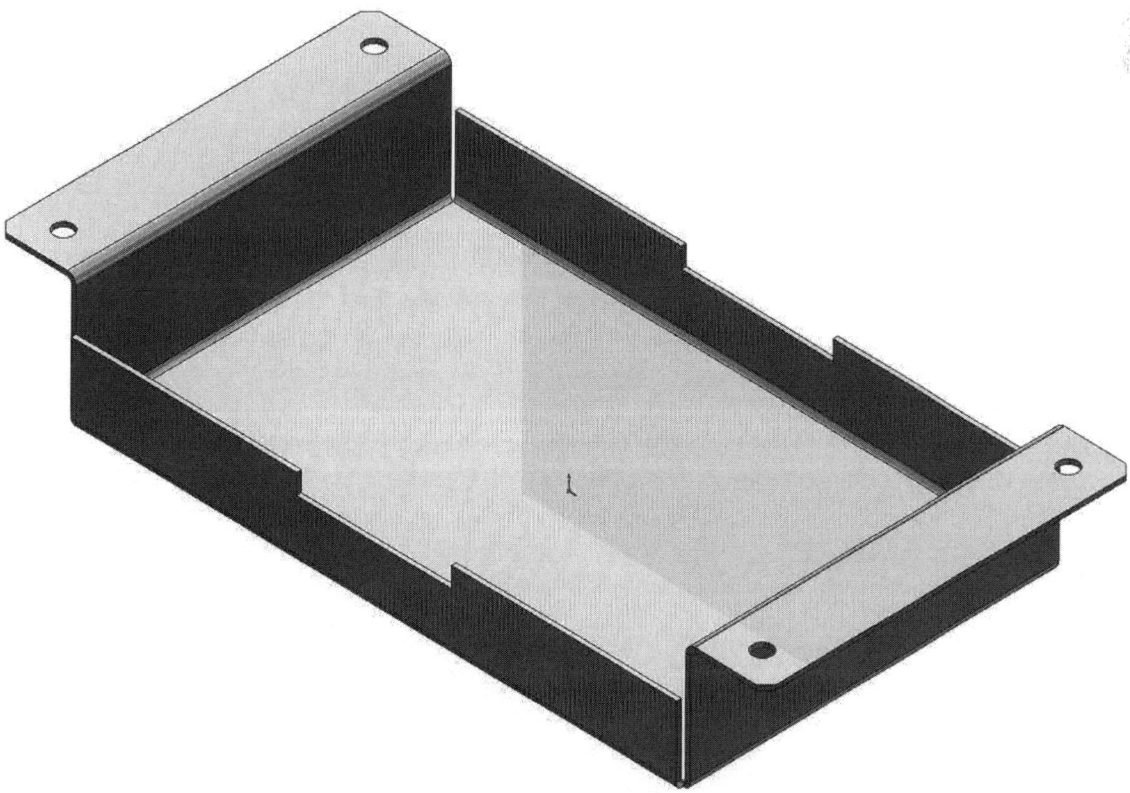

Exercise: Using Sketched Bends

The exercises in this text book are intended to give you an opportunity to explore and apply what you have learned from the previous chapters, at your own pace.

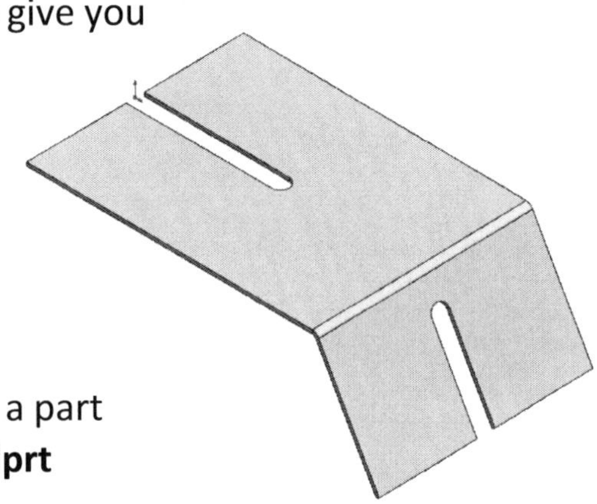

1. Opening a part document:

Browse to the Training Folder and open a part document named: **Sketched Bends2.sldprt**

The sheet metal parameters such as Material, Thickness, Bend Radius, K-Factor, etc., have already been assigned to this part.

2. Creating the 1st Sketched Bends:

Select the upper face of the model and open a **new sketch**.

Sketch a **vertical Line** across the slot as shown.

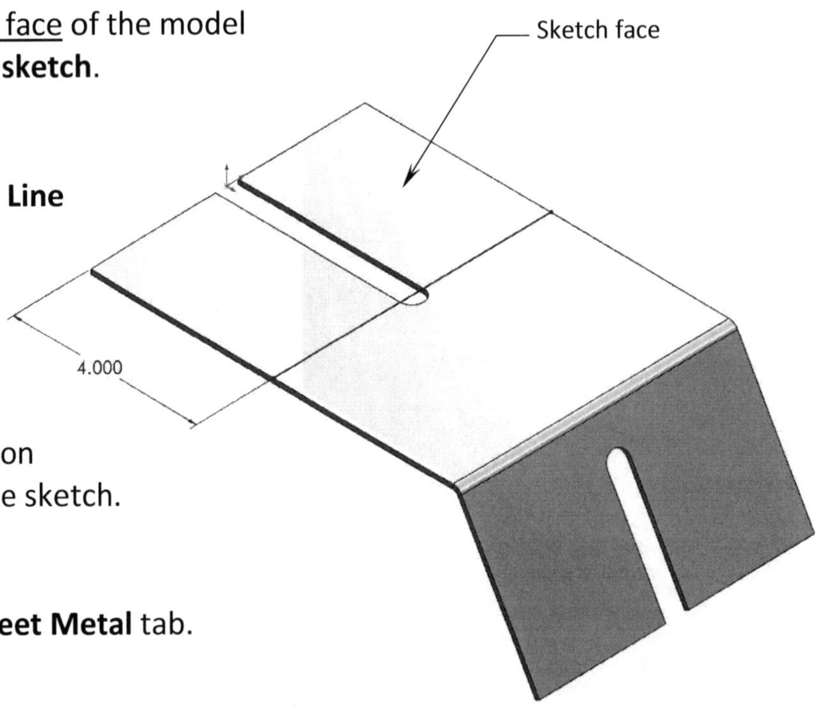

Add the **4.00in.** location dimension to fully define the sketch.

Switch to the **Sheet Metal** tab.

Click **Sketched Bend** on the **Sheet Metal** tab.

For Fixed Face, click anywhere on the <u>right side</u> of the line.

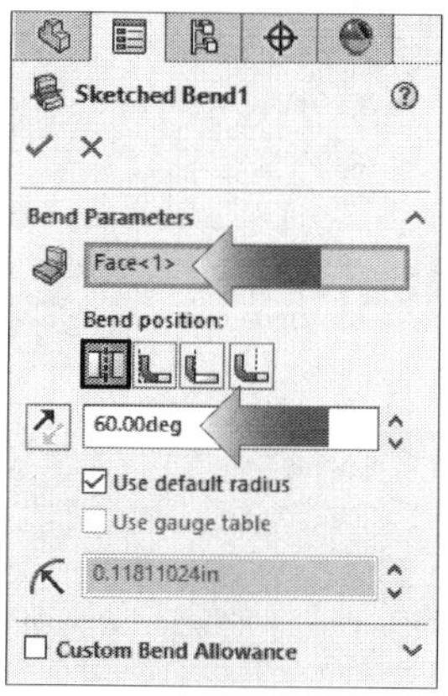

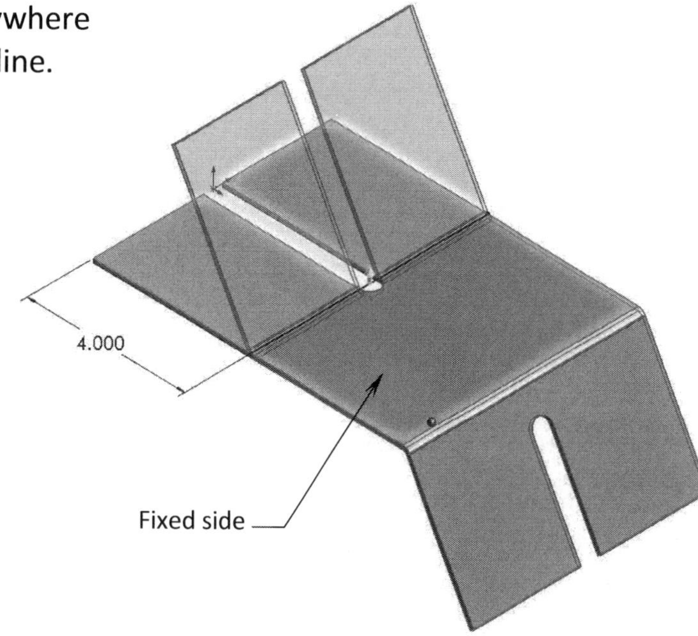

For Bend Position, select **Bend Centerline**.

For Bend Angle, enter: **60.00deg**.

Enable the checkbox:
Use Default Bend Radius.

Click **OK**.

A bent feature is created using a single line to bend.

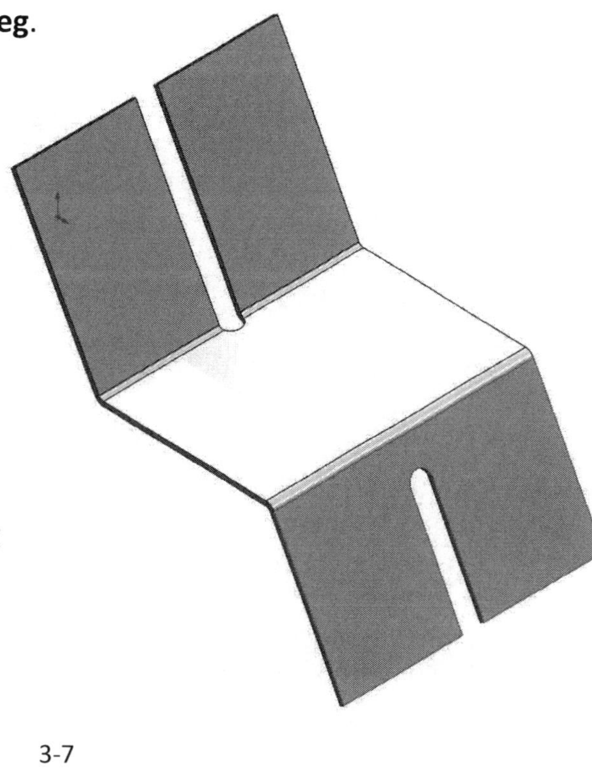

3. Creating the 2nd Sketched Bends:

Select the face indicated in the image and open a **new sketch**.

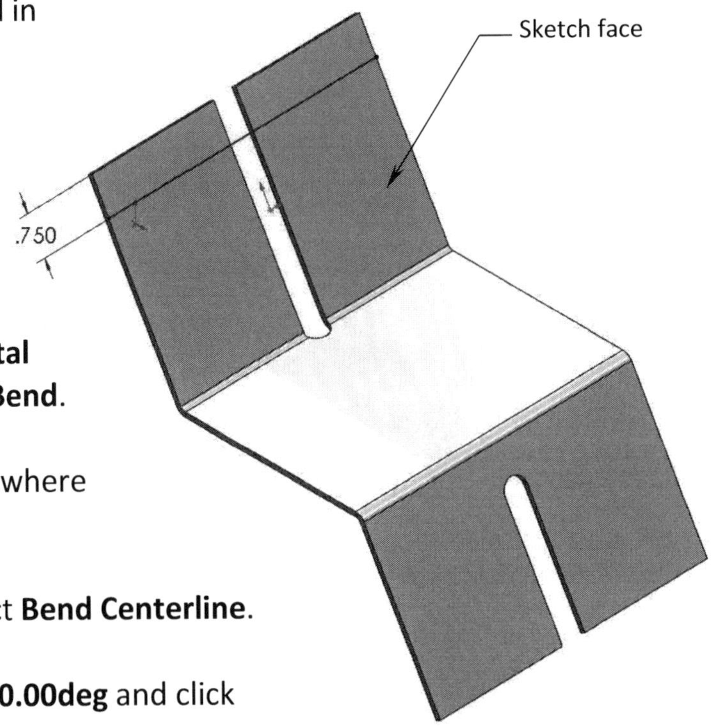

Sketch a **Line** and add the **.750in.** location dimension.

Switch to the **Sheet Metal** tab and click **Sketched Bend**.

For Fixed Face, click anywhere below the line.

For Bend Position, Select **Bend Centerline**.

For Bend Angle, enter **90.00deg** and click **Reverse**.

Enable the checkbox: **Use Default Radius**.

Click **OK**.

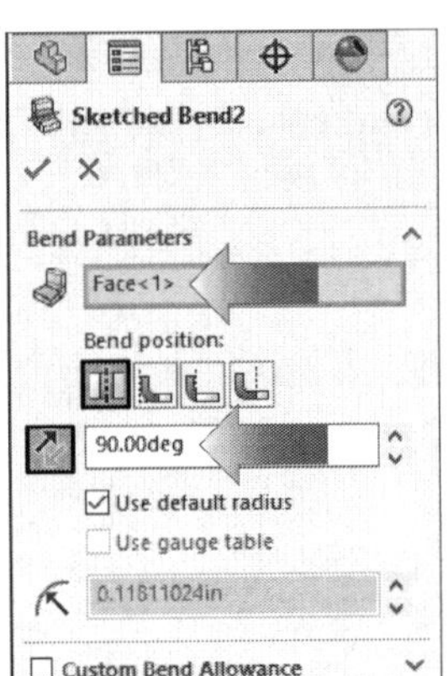

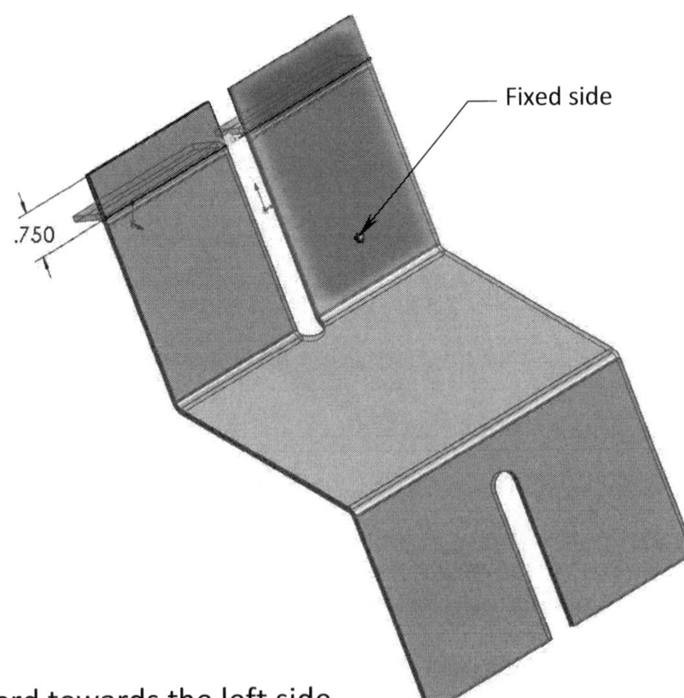

The 2 tabs are bent outward towards the left side.

4. Creating the 3rd Sketched Bends:

Select the <u>face</u> as noted in the image and open a **new sketch**.

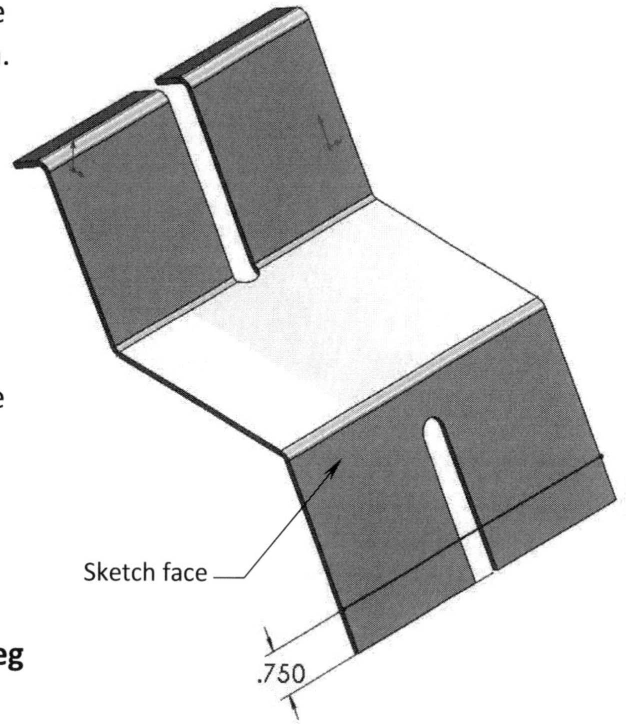

Sketch a **Line** and add the **.750in**. location dimension.

Switch to the **Sheet Metal** tab and click **Sketched Bend**.

For Fixed Face, click anywhere <u>below</u> the line.

For Bend Position, Select **Bend Centerline**.

For Bend Angle, enter **90.00deg** and click **Reverse**.

Enable the checkbox: **Use Default Radius**.

Click **OK**.

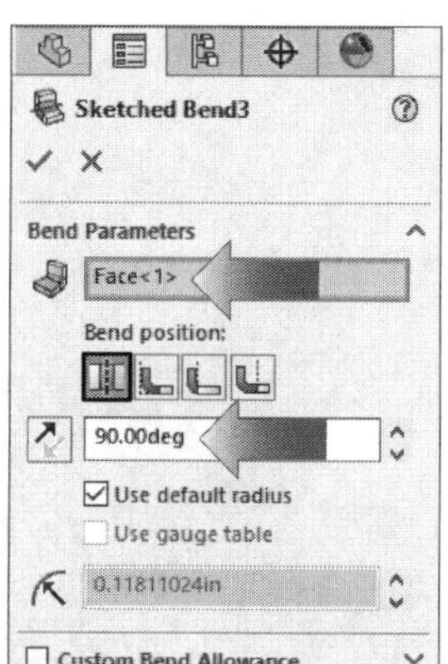

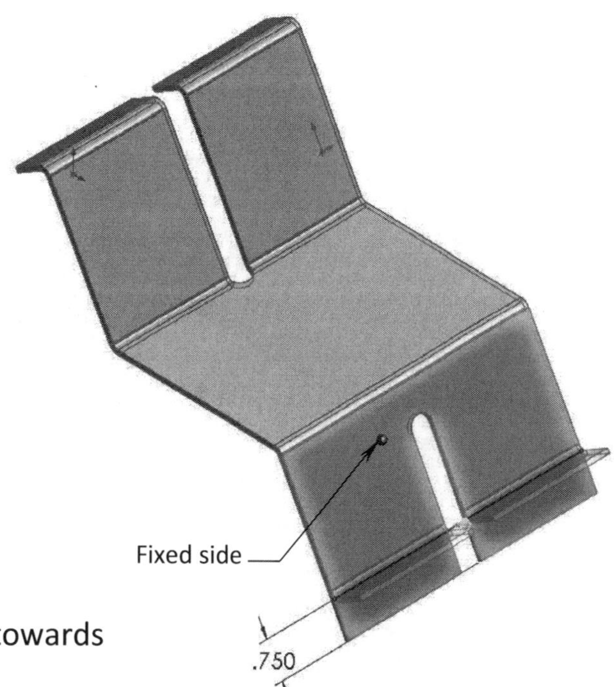

The 2 tabs are bent outward towards the right side.

5. Adding holes:

Select the face indicated and open a **new sketch**.

Sketch a **Circle** and a **Centerline**.

Mirror the Circle about the centerline.

Add dimensions to fully define the sketch.

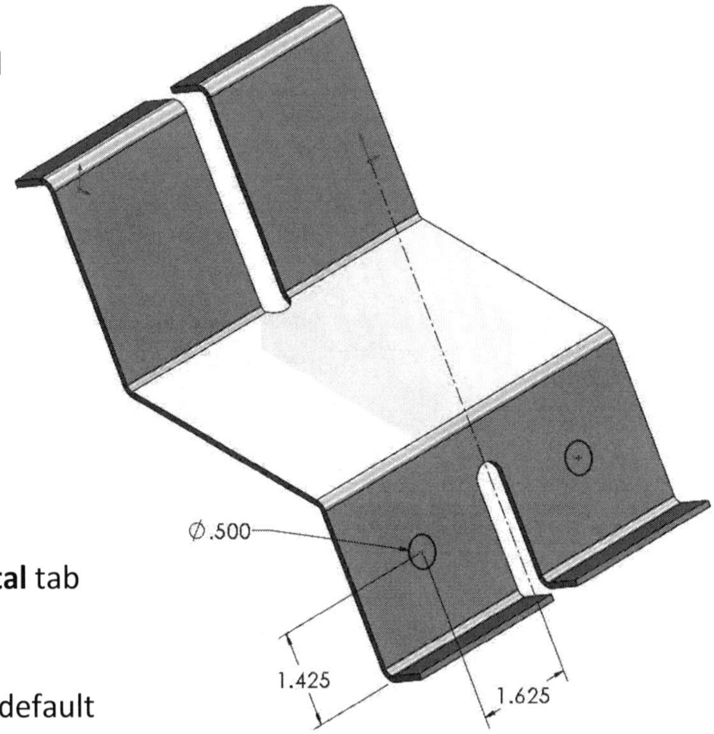

Switch to the **Sheet Metal** tab and click **Extruded Cut**.

For Direction 1, use the default **Blind** type.

Enable the checkbox: **Link To Thickness**.

Click **OK**.

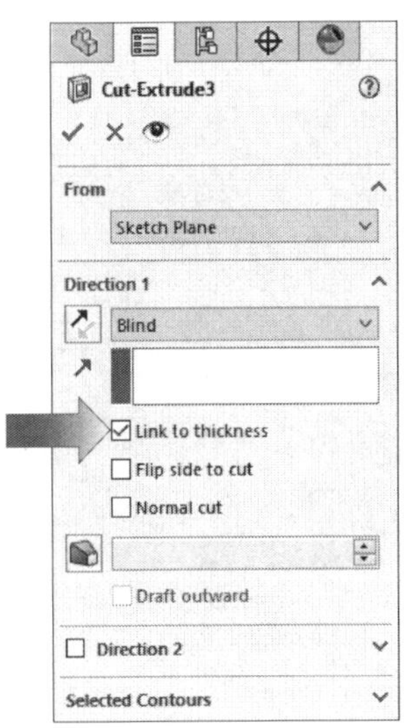

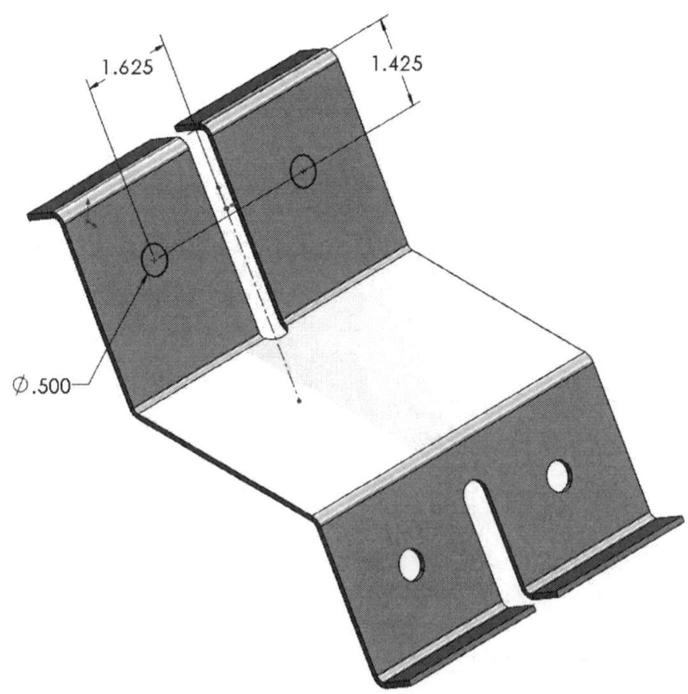

Add the same holes on the upper flange as shown.

6. Viewing the Flat Pattern:

Right-click on a face of the part and select: **Toggle Flat Display**.

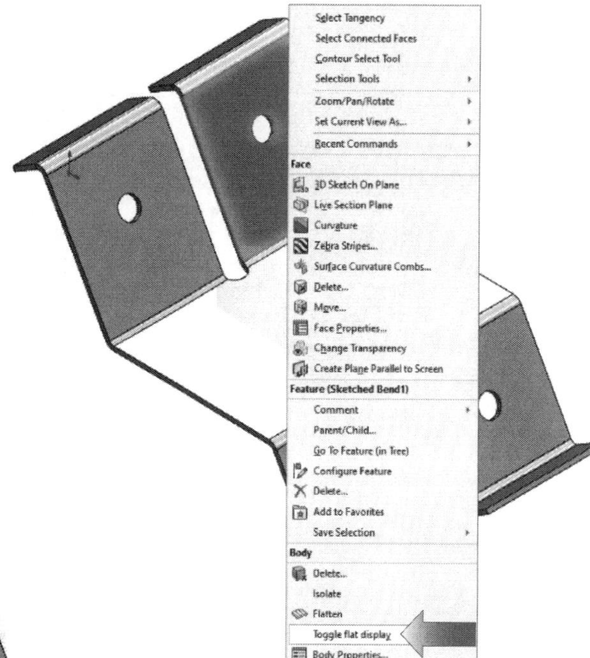

The Flat Pattern is super-imposed onto the Fold pattern.

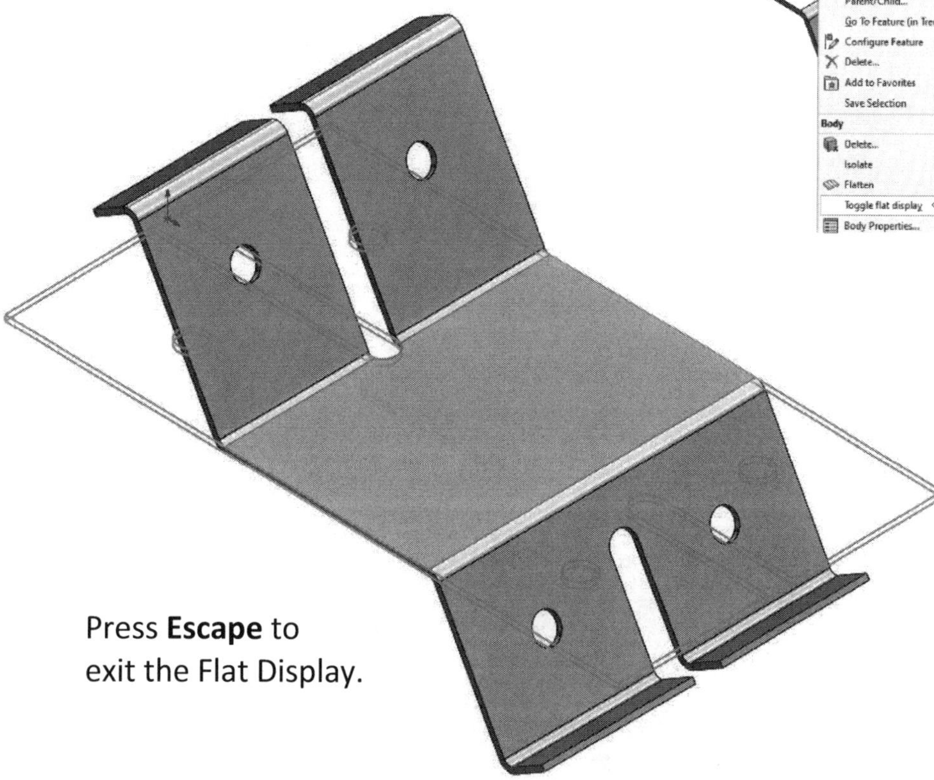

Press **Escape** to exit the Flat Display.

7. Saving your work:

Select **File, Save As**.

Enter **Sketched Bends2_Completed** for the file name.

Click **Save**.

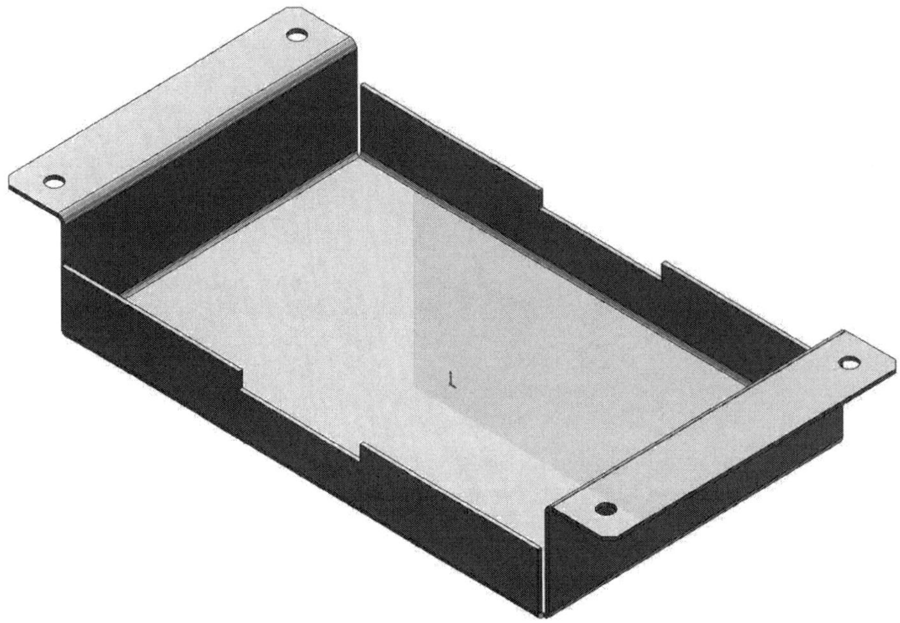

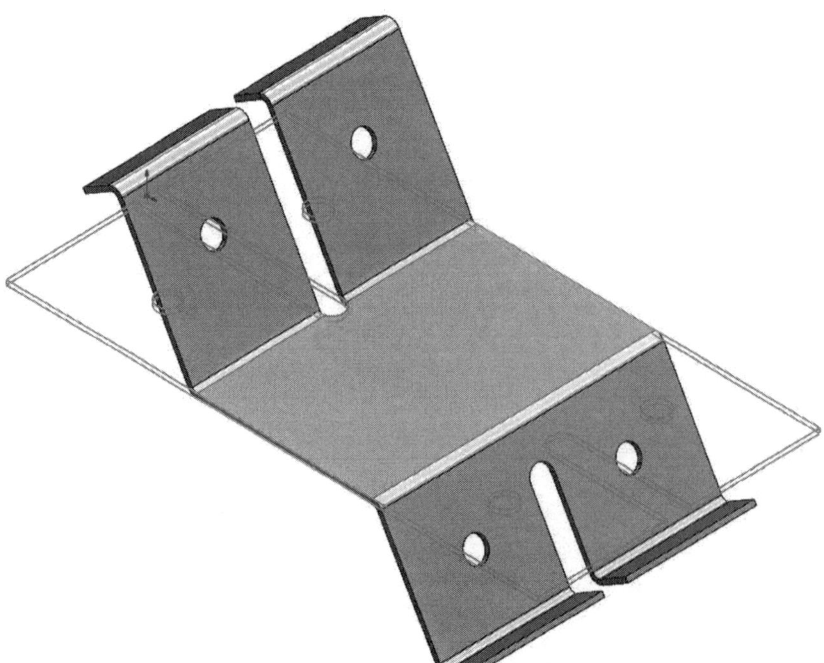

Lesson 4: Sheet Metal Miter Flange & Fill Pattern

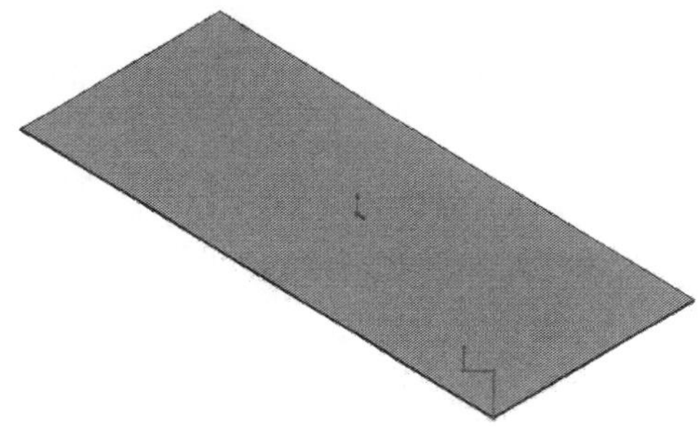

A miter flange tool adds a series of flanges to one or more edges of a sheet metal part.
Keep in mind the following rules when making the sketch for a miter flange:

* The sketch can contain lines or arcs.
* The miter flange profile can contain more than one continuous line.
* The sketch plane must be normal to the first edge where the miter flange is created.
* The thickness is automatically linked to the thickness of the sheet metal part.

1. Opening a part document:

Browse to the Training Folder and open a part document named:
Sheet Metal Miter Flange.sldprt

2. Creating the Miter Flanges:

Select **Sketch2** from the FeatureManager tree.

Switch to the **Sheet Metal** tab and click **Miter Flange** 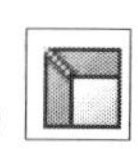.

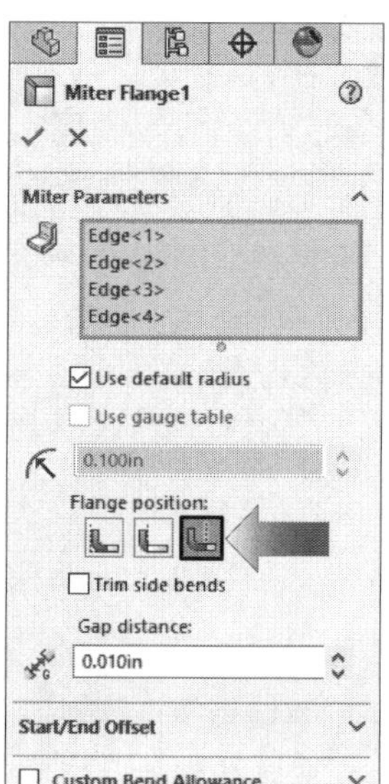

For Miter Flange Parameters, select **4 edges** as noted.

For Flange Position, click **Bend-Outside**.

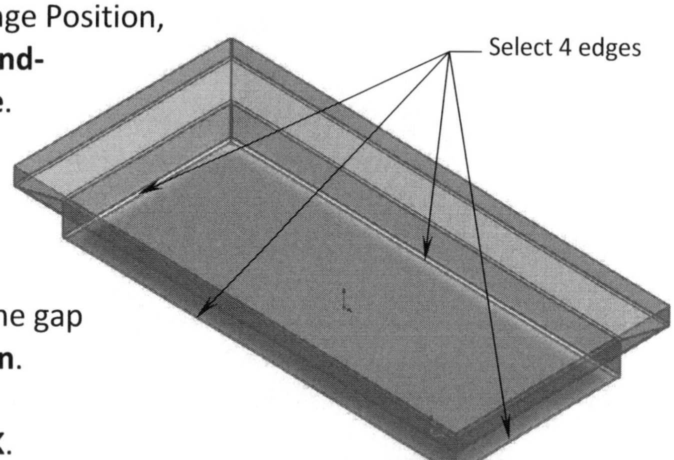

Leave the gap at **.010in**.

Click **OK**.

The sketch of the Miter Flange sweeps along the 4 selected edges.

The corners were trimmed to 45° and a gap of .010in was added to all 4 corners.

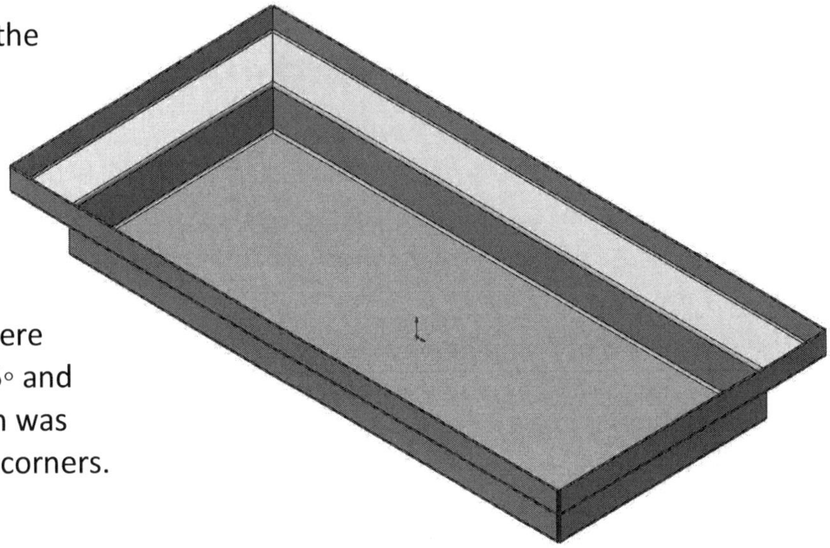

3. Adding the cuts:

Select the face as indicated in the image and open a **new sketch**.

Sketch a **Rectangle** and **2 Circles**.

Use the Mirror function to keep the sketch entities symmetric to each other.

Add dimensions and relations to fully define the sketch.

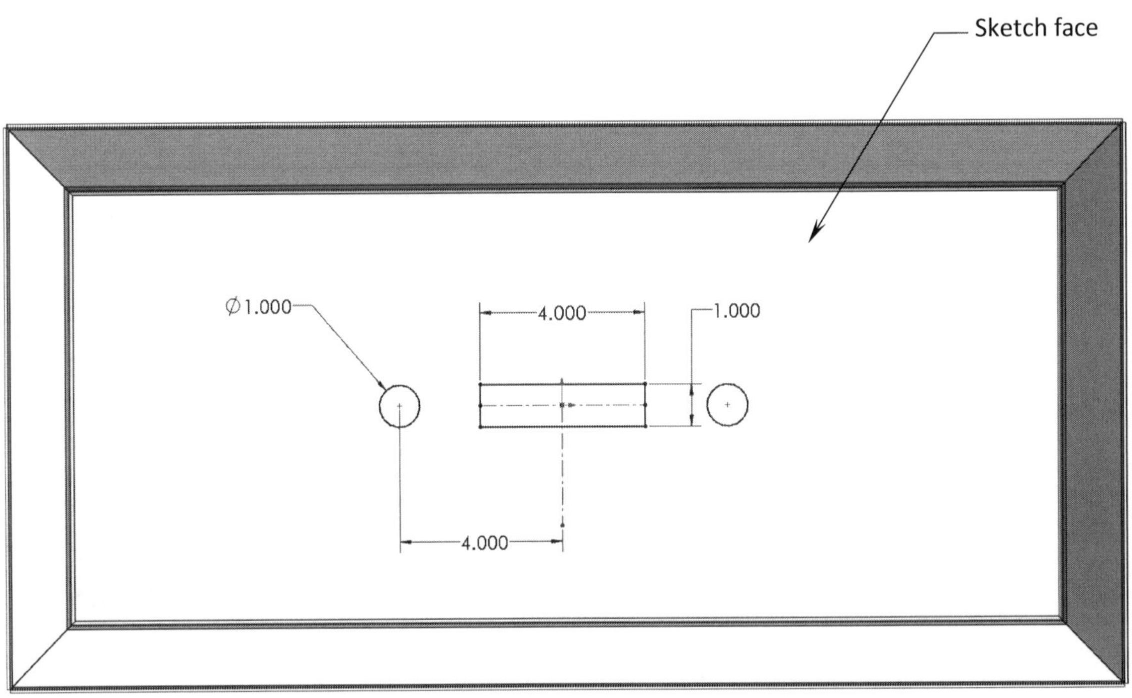

Switch back to the **Sheet Metal** tab.

Click **Extruded Cut**.

For Direction 1, select **Blind** and enable the checkbox: **Link To Thickness**.

Click **OK**.

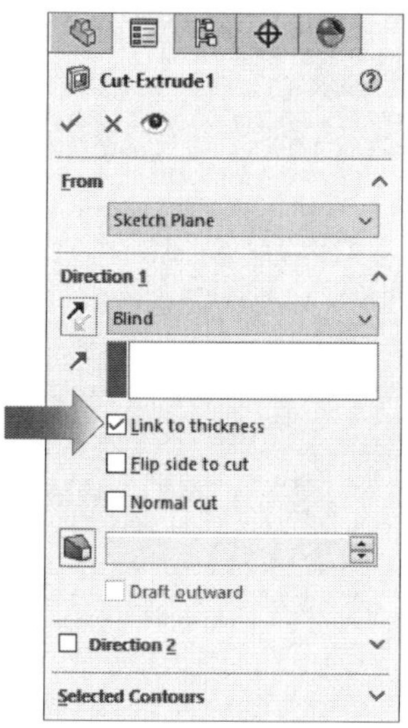

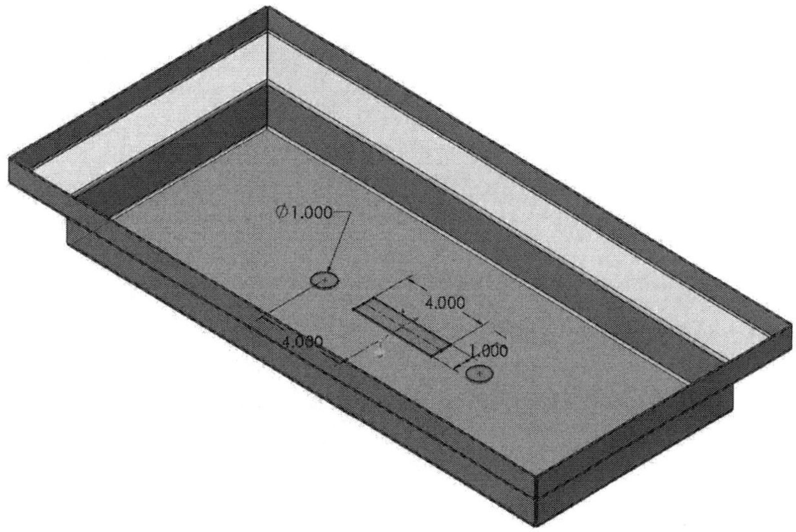

Right-click the part and select: **Toggle Flat Pattern**.

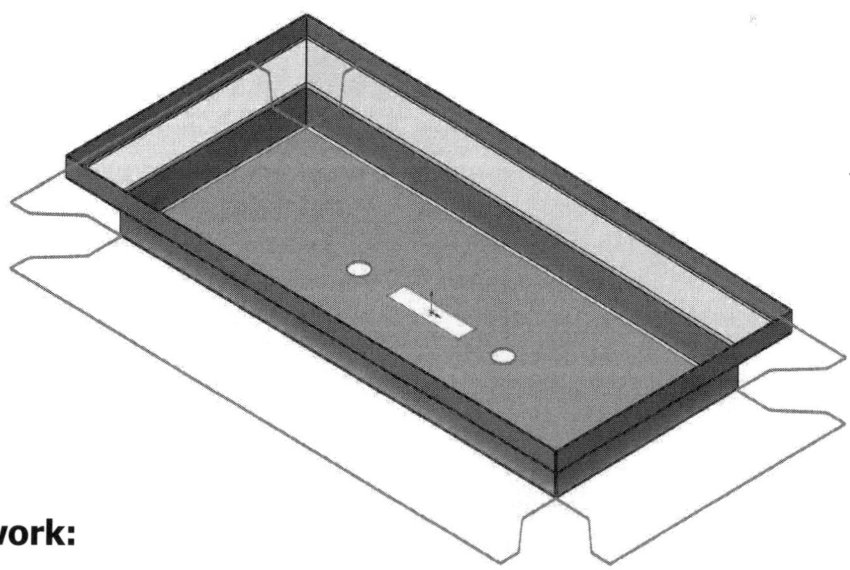

4. Saving your work:

Select **File, Save As**.

Enter: **Sheet Metal Miter Flange_Completed** for the file name.

Click **Save**.

Sheet Metal Fill Pattern

The Fill Pattern feature lets you select an area defined by co-planar faces or a sketch that lies on co-planar faces. The command fills the defined region with a pattern of features or a predefined cut shape.

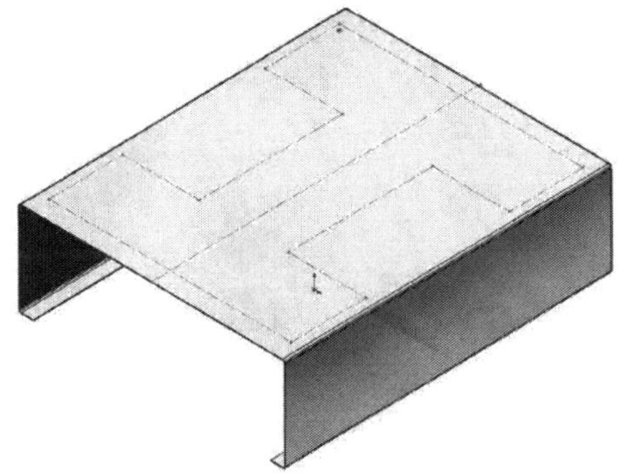

1. Opening a part document:

Browse to the Training Folder and open a part document named:
Sheet Metal Fill Pattern.sldprt

2. Sketching the pattern boundary:

Select the <u>top face</u> of the part and open a **new sketch**.

<u>Expand</u> the **Cut-Extrude1** feature.

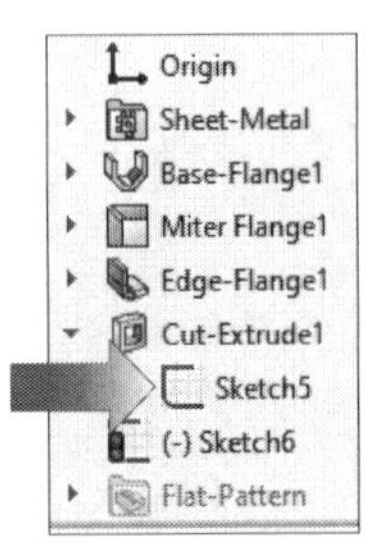

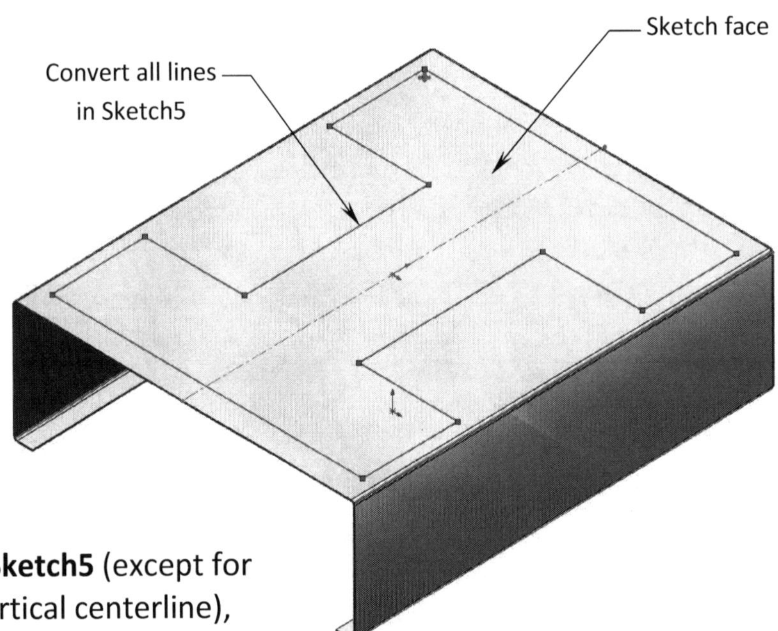

Select all lines in **Sketch5** (except for the square and vertical centerline), and click: **Convert Entities**.

All lines in Sketch5 are converted into a fully defined sketch. This new sketch will be used as the pre-defined boundary, to use in the Fill-Pattern.

<u>Exit</u> the sketch.

3. Creating a Fill-Pattern:

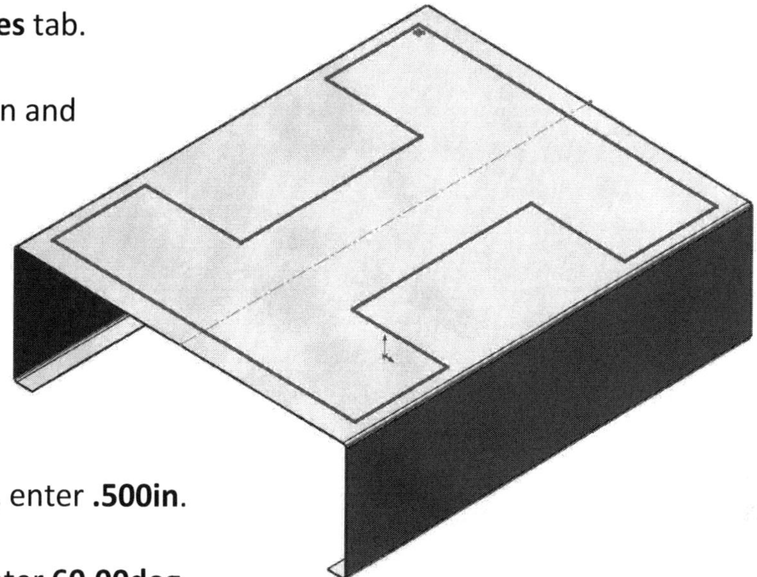

Switch to the **Features** tab.

Expand Linear Pattern and select **Fill Pattern**.

For Fill Boundary, select **Sketch6**.

For Pattern Layout, select **Perforation**.

For Instance Spacing, enter **.500in**.

For Stagger Angle, enter **60.00deg**.

For Margin, enter **0.00in**.

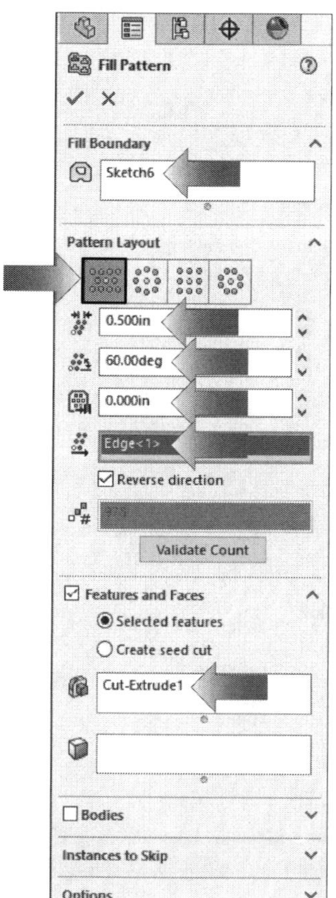

For Pattern Direction, select the **edge** shown in the image below.

For Features to Pattern, select **Cut-Extrude1** from the Feature-Manager tree.

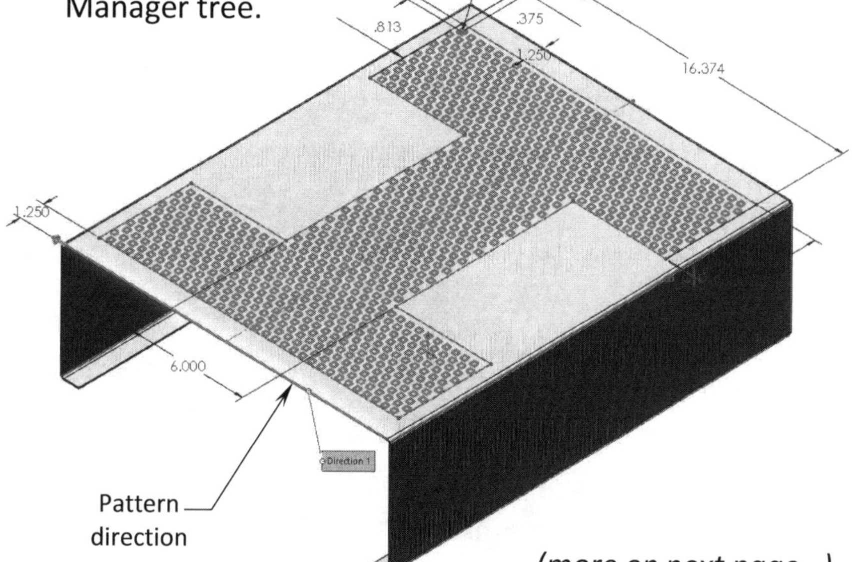

(more on next page...)

Change to the **Top** view orientation (Control+5).

Change the Stagger Angle to **0.00deg**.

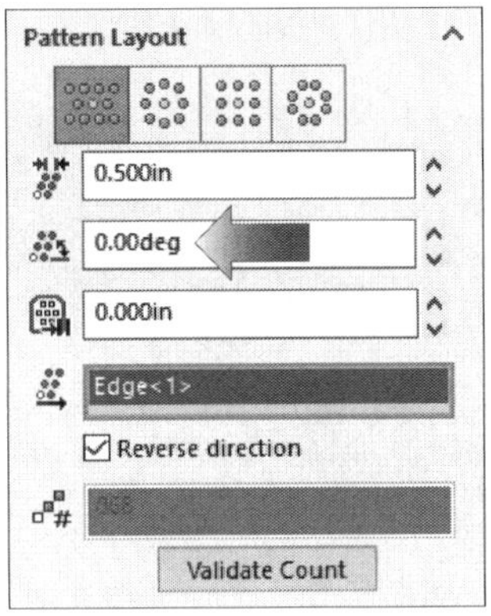

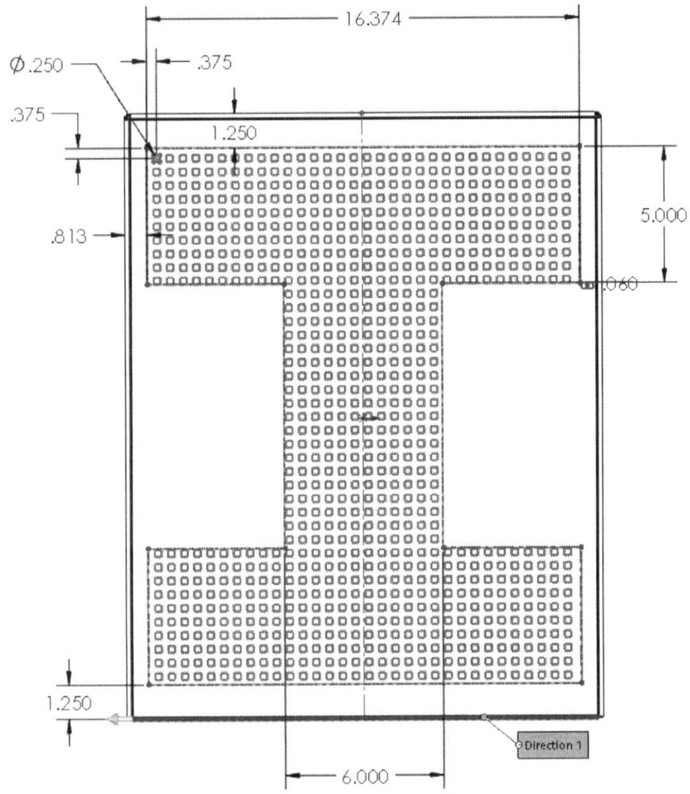

All instances are aligned with one another, both vertically and horizontally.

Change the Stagger Angle to **45.00deg**.

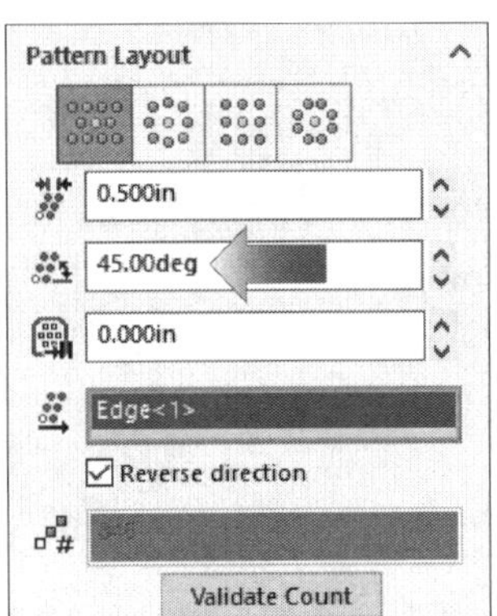

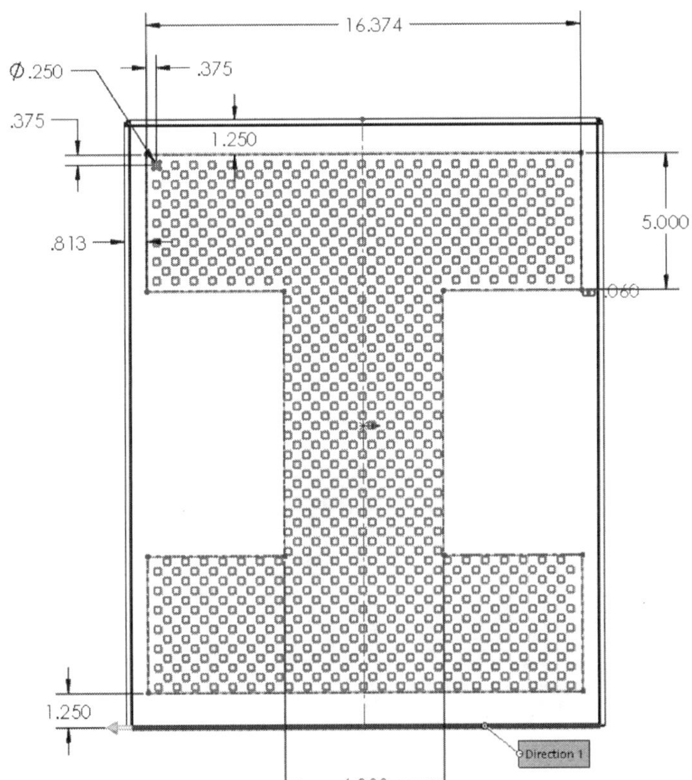

All instances are shifted 45deg from each other.

Change the Stagger Angle back to **60.0deg**.

Click **OK**.

Unlike Linear Pattern, the Fill Pattern command uses a defined-boundary to replicate the feature(s).

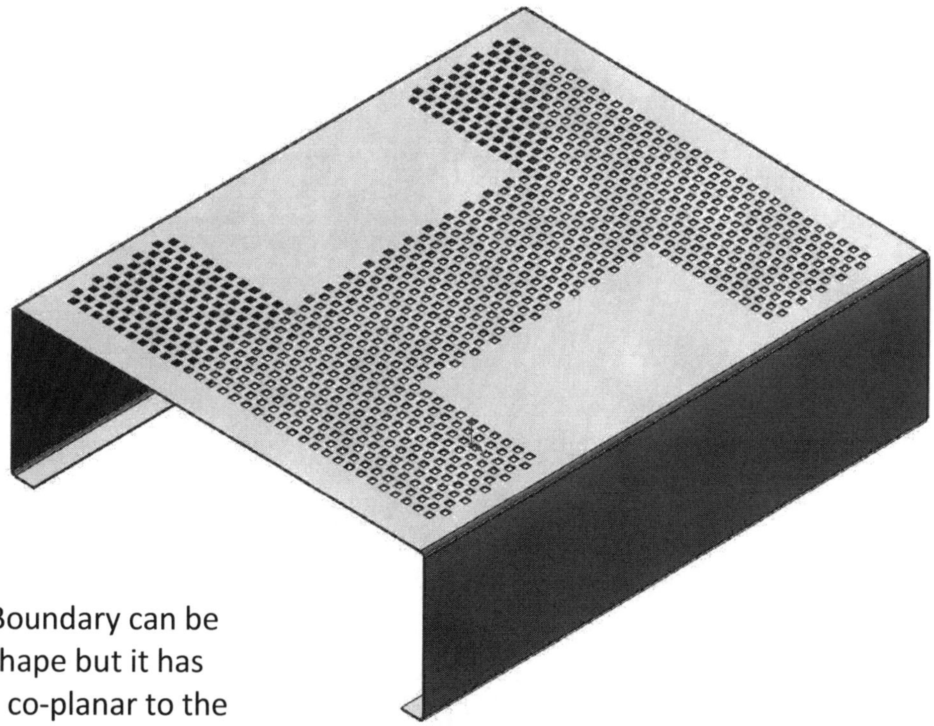

The Boundary can be any shape but it has to be co-planar to the feature(s) that is being patterned.

4. Saving your work:

Select **File, Save As**.

Enter: **Sheet Metal Fill Pattern_Completed** for the file name.

Click **Save**.

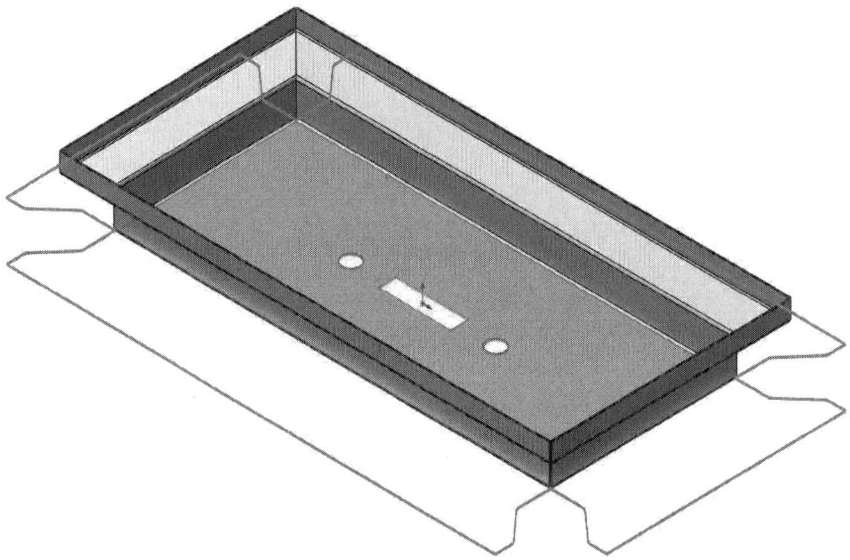

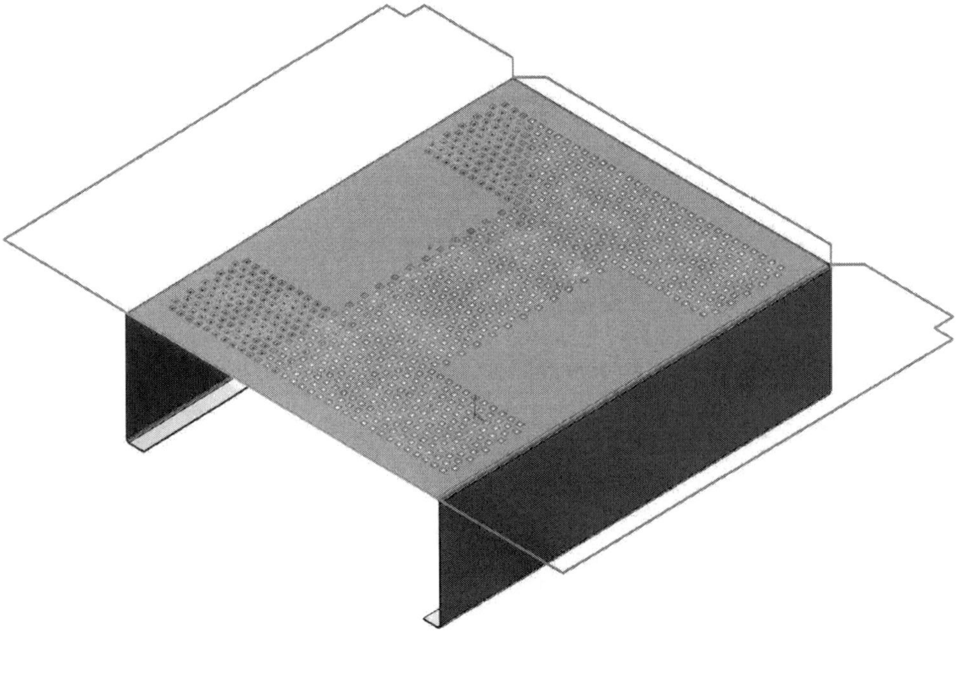

Lesson 5: Sheet Metal Fold & Unfold

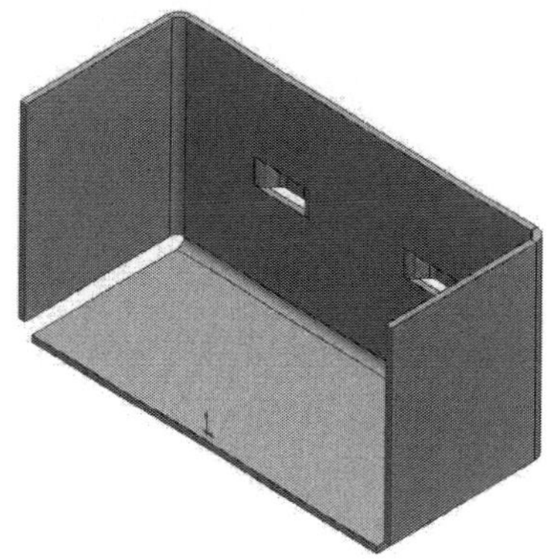

Using the Unfold and Fold tools, we can flatten and bend one, more than one, or all of the bends in a sheet metal part. This combination is useful when adding a cut across a bend. First, add an Unfold feature to flatten the bend, then add the cut feature, and lastly, add a Fold feature to return the bend to its folded state.

1. Opening a part document:

Browse to the Training Folder and open a part document named:
Fold & Unfold.sldprt

2. Closing the corners:

Select **Corners, Closed Corner**.

For Face to Extend, select the 2 bottom-faces of the 2 vertical flanges.

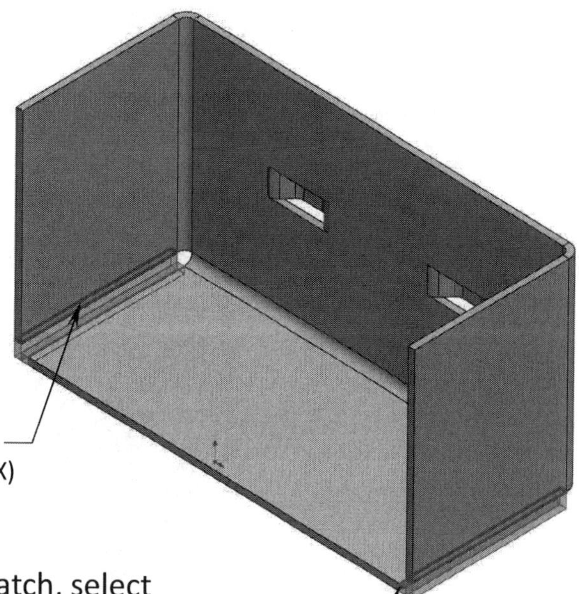

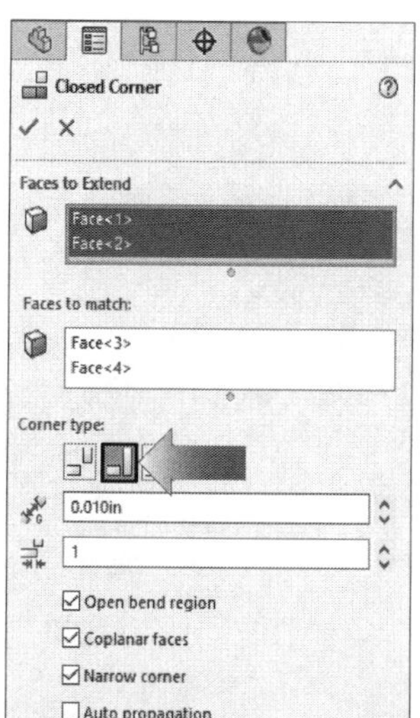

For Faces to Match, select the 2 side-faces of the bottom flange.

For Corner Type click **Overlap**.

Click **OK**.

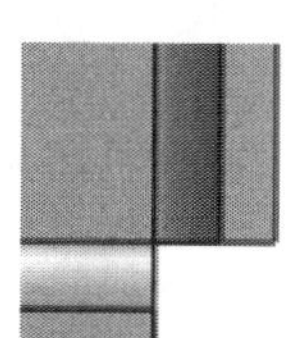

Without Closed Corners

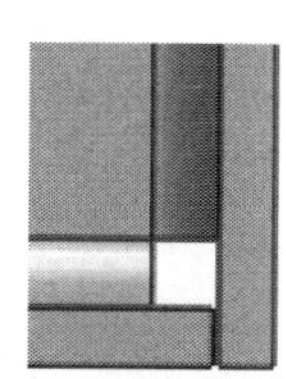

With Closed Corners

3. Unfolding the bends:

The cut features are usually created before the bends. One way to achieve that is to unfold the bends, add the cuts, then return the bends to their folded state.

Click **Unfold**  on the **Sheet Metal** tab.

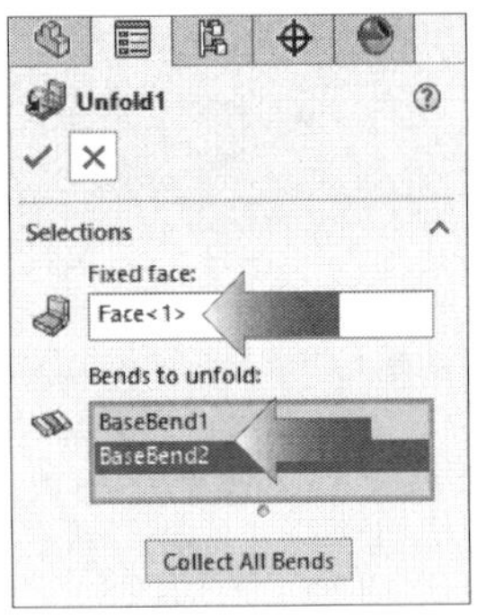

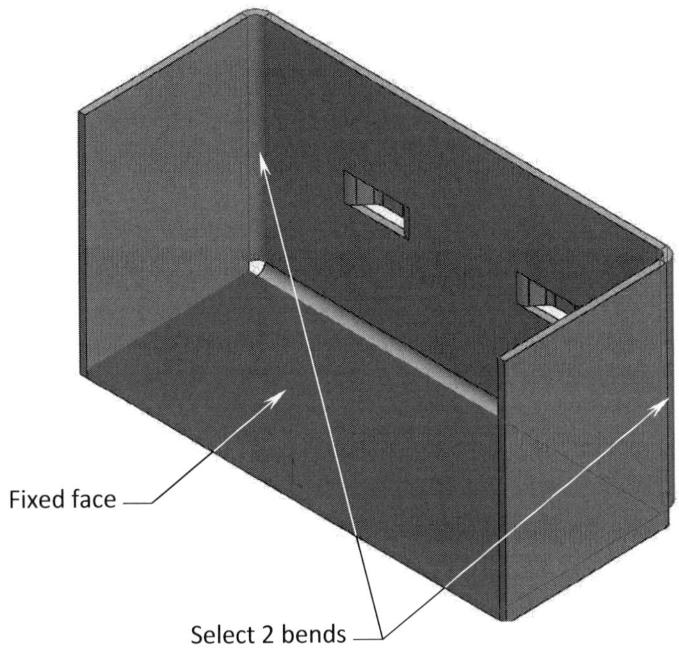

For Fixed Face, select the face of the bottom flange as indicated.

For Bends to Unfold, select the **2 bends** as shown.

Click **OK**.

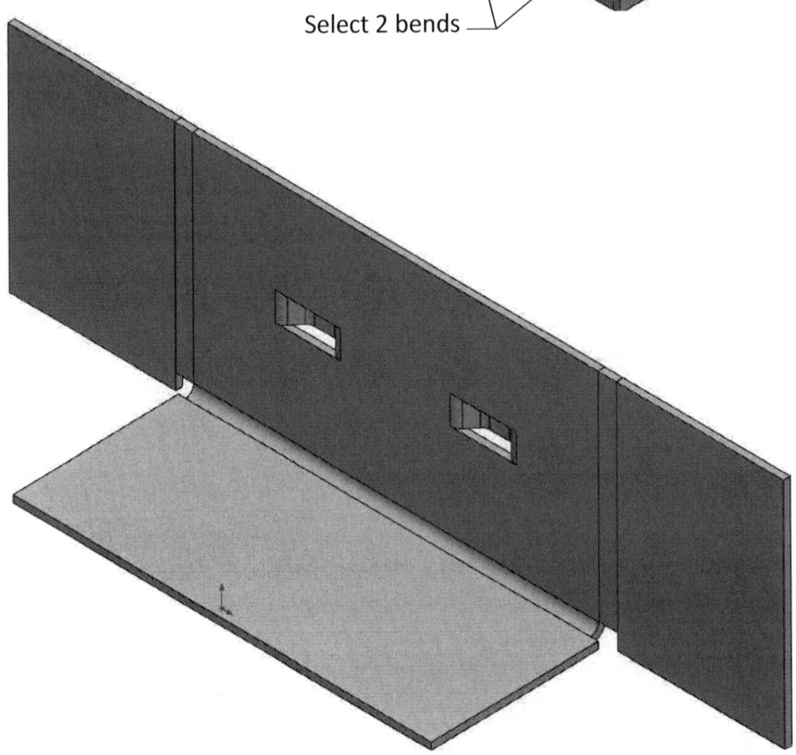

The 2 selected bends are unfolded while the bottom face remains fixed.

4. Adding cuts across the bends:

Adding the cut features are much easier at this point.

Select the face as noted and open a **new sketch**.

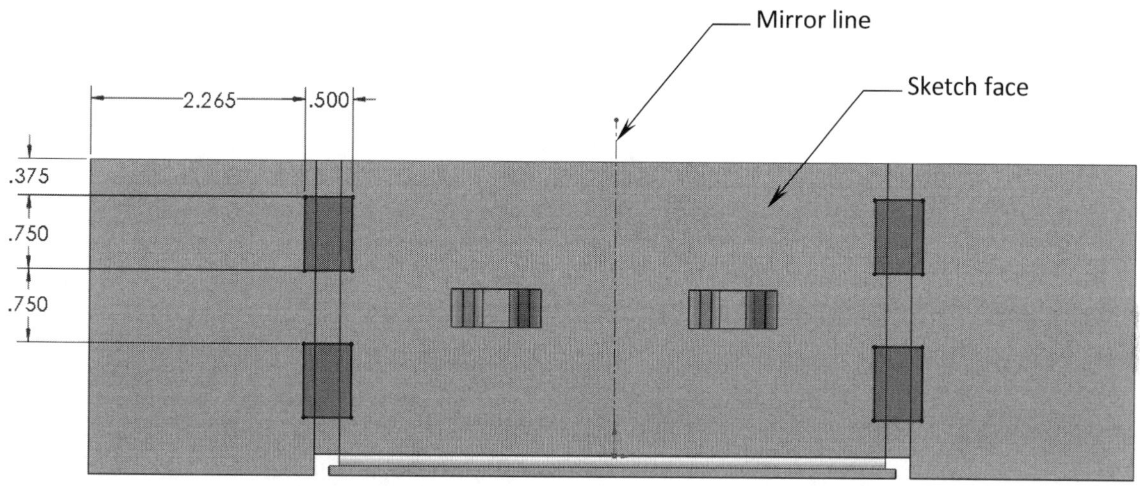

Sketch **2 Corner Rectangles** and mirror them as shown in the image above.

Add the size and location dimensions to fully define the sketch.

Switch to the **Sheet Metal** tab and click **Extruded Cut**.

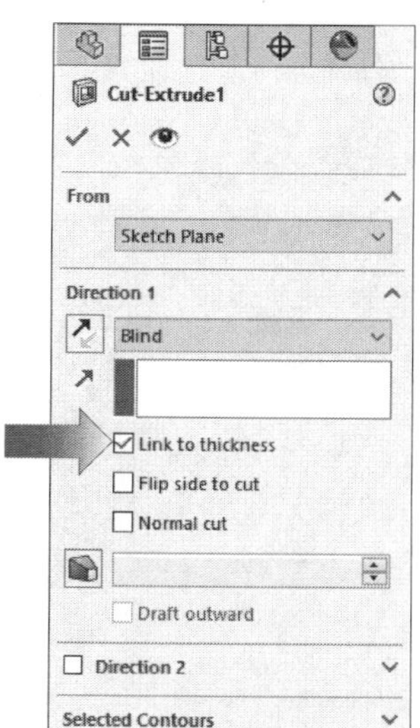

Enable **Link-To Thickness** checkbox.

Click **OK**.

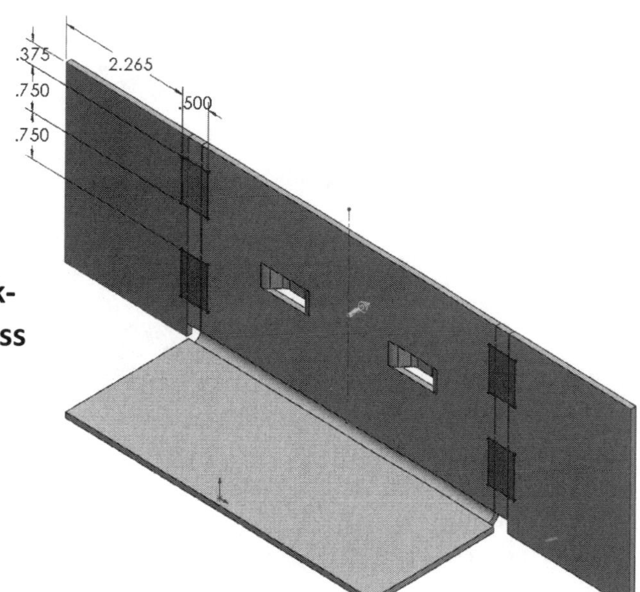

5. Folding the bends:

Click **Fold**  on the **Sheet Metal** tab.

The same **Fixed Face** should be selected automatically.

For Bends to Fold,
click **Collect All Bends**.

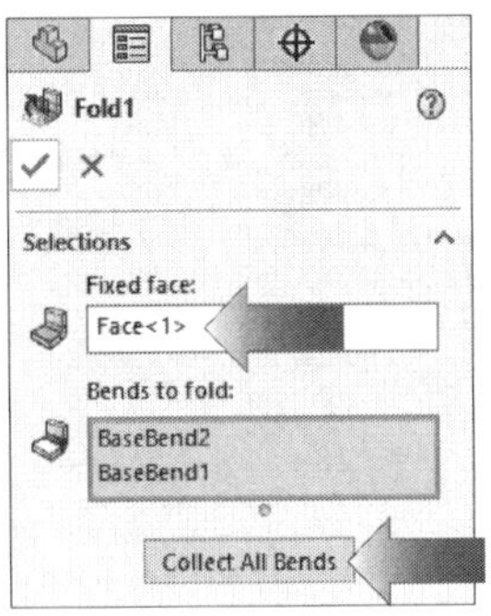

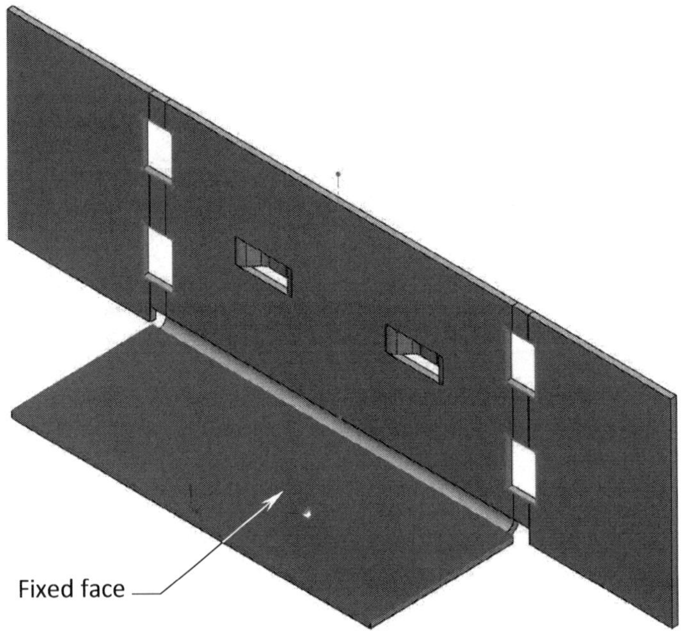

Click **OK**.

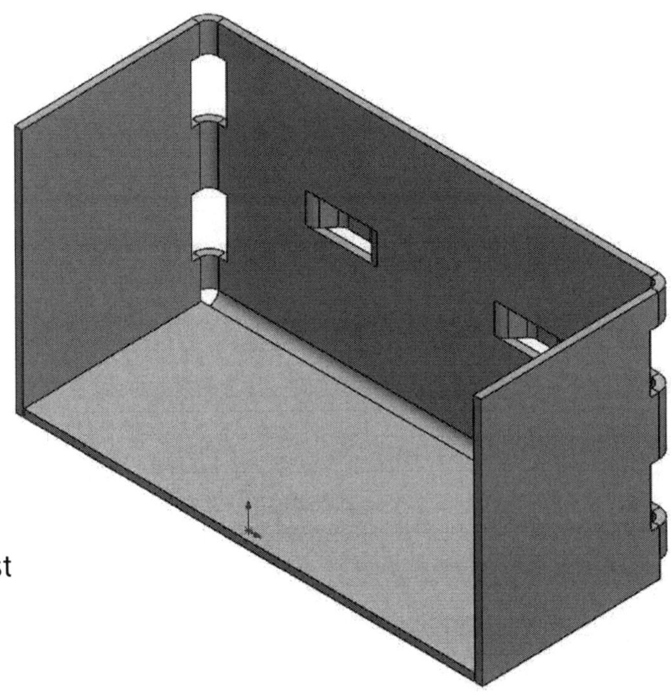

The bends are returned to their folded state, and the cut features are also folded.

Inspect your model against the image shown here.

6. Breaking the corners:

Select **Corners, Break Corner**.

For Break Corner Options, select the 2 small edges as noted below

For Break Type, select **Chamfer**.

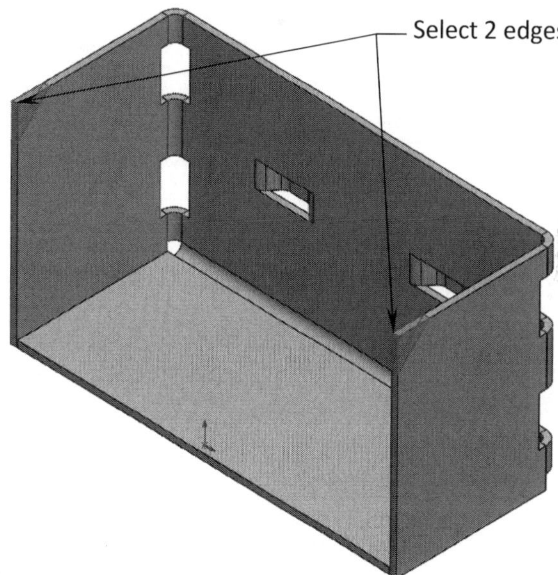

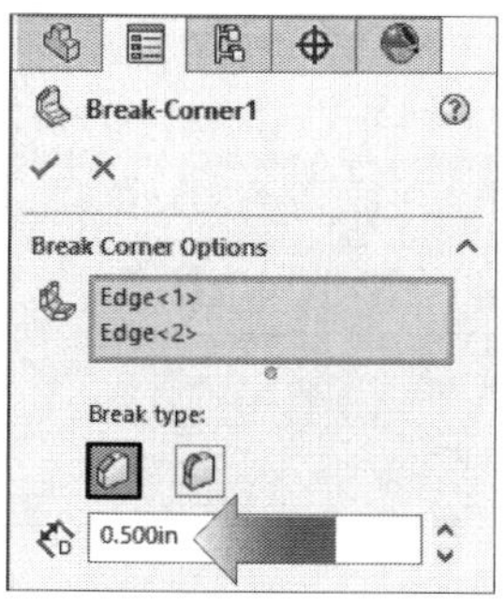

For Chamfer Distance, enter **.500in**.

Click **OK**.

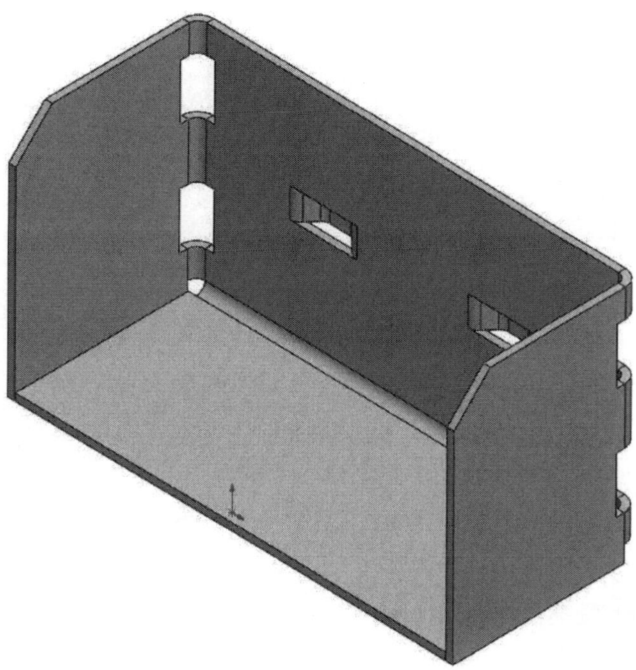

7. Flattening the part:

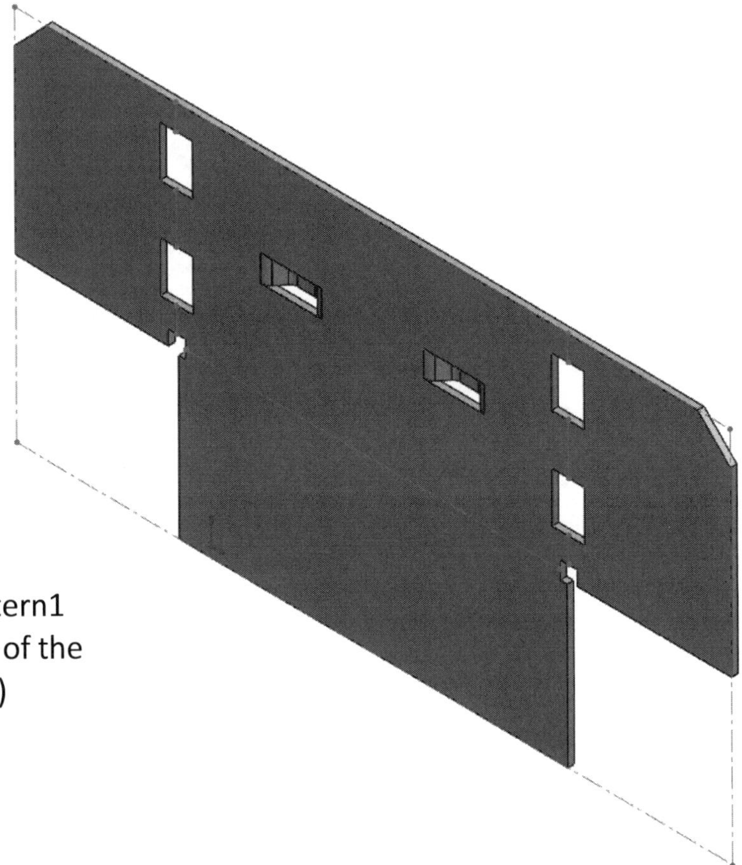

Click **Flatten** on the **Sheet Metal** tab.

The Bounding Box and the Bend Lines are visible in the flat pattern by default.

(This option can be toggled on or off by accessing the Flat-Pattern1 feature at the bottom of the FeatureManager tree.)

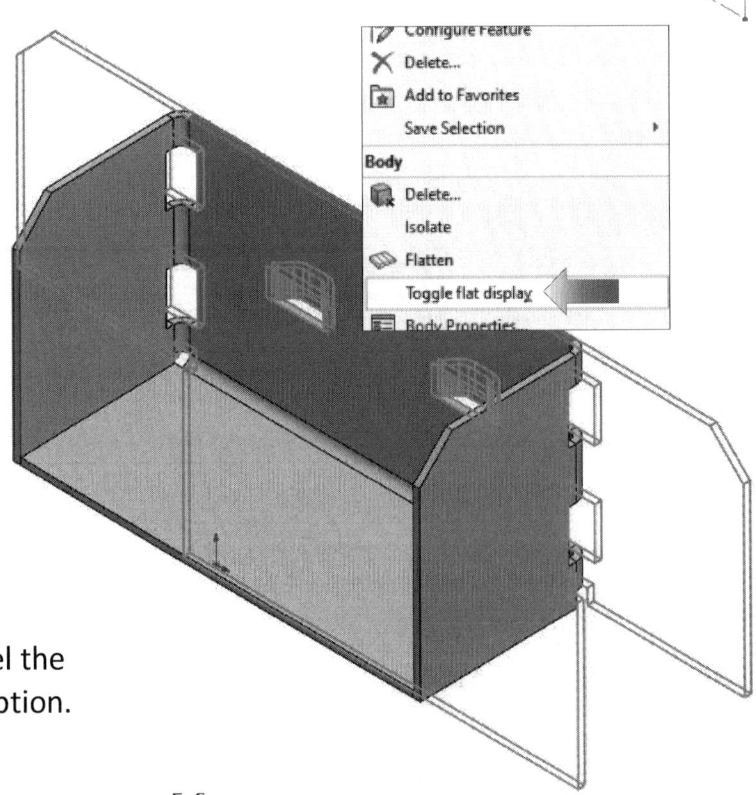

To show the Flat-Pattern on top of the fold, right-click the sheet metal part and select: **Toggle Flat Display**. The Flat-Pattern is superimposed over the fold pattern.

Push **Escape** to cancel the Toggle Flat Display option.

8. Saving your work:

Select **Files, Save As**.

Enter **Fold & Unfold_Completed** for the file name.

Click **Save**.

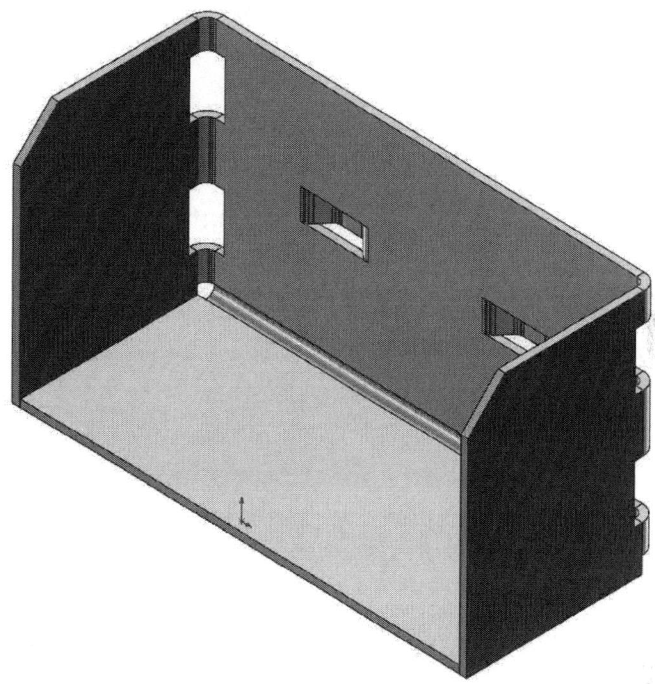

Exercise: Sheet Metal Fold & Unfold

The exercises in this textbook are intended to give you an opportunity to explore and to apply what you have learned from the previous chapters, at your own pace.

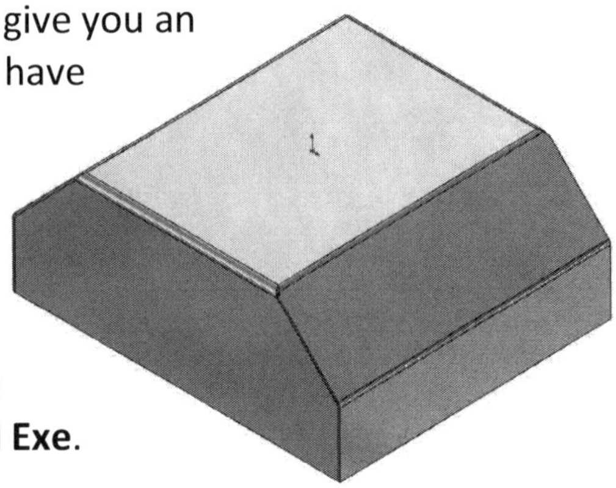

1. Opening a part document:

Browse to the Training Folder and open a part document named: **Fold & Unfold Exe**.

2. Unfolding the bends:

Switch to the **Sheet Metal** tab and click **Unfold** .

For Fixed Face, select the top face of the part.

For Bends to Unfold, select the upper 2 bends as indicated below.

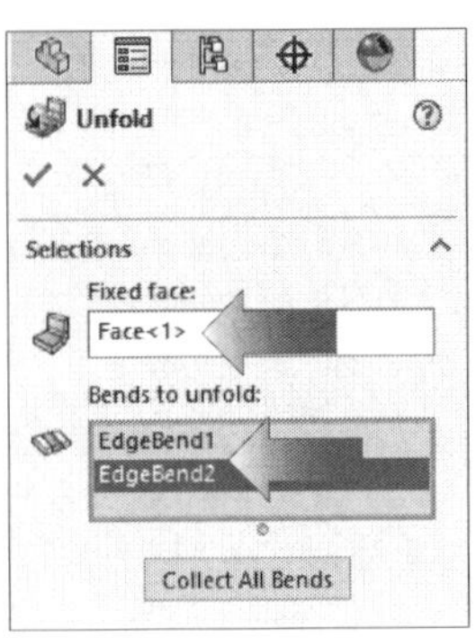

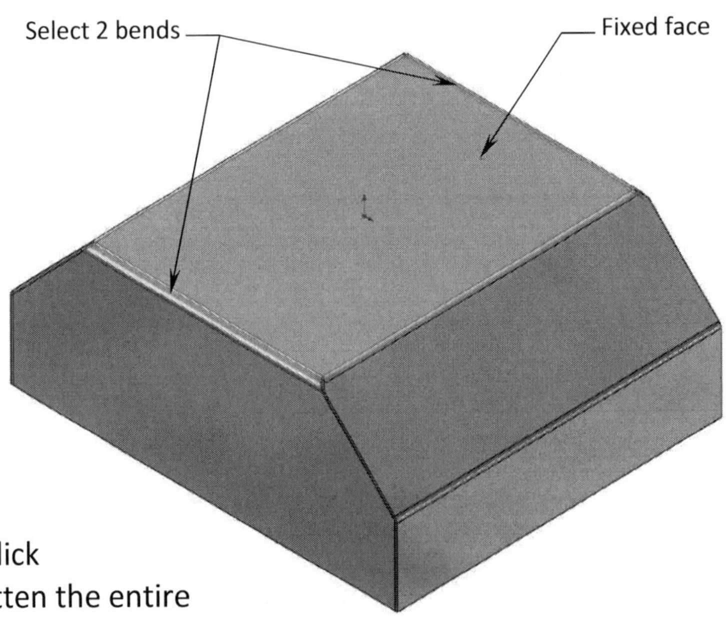

Click **OK**.

Alternatively, we can click Collect All Bends to flatten the entire part, but unfolding only the bends that we need would make it easier to understand how the tool works.

3. Making the 1st cut:

Select the face as noted and open a **new sketch**.

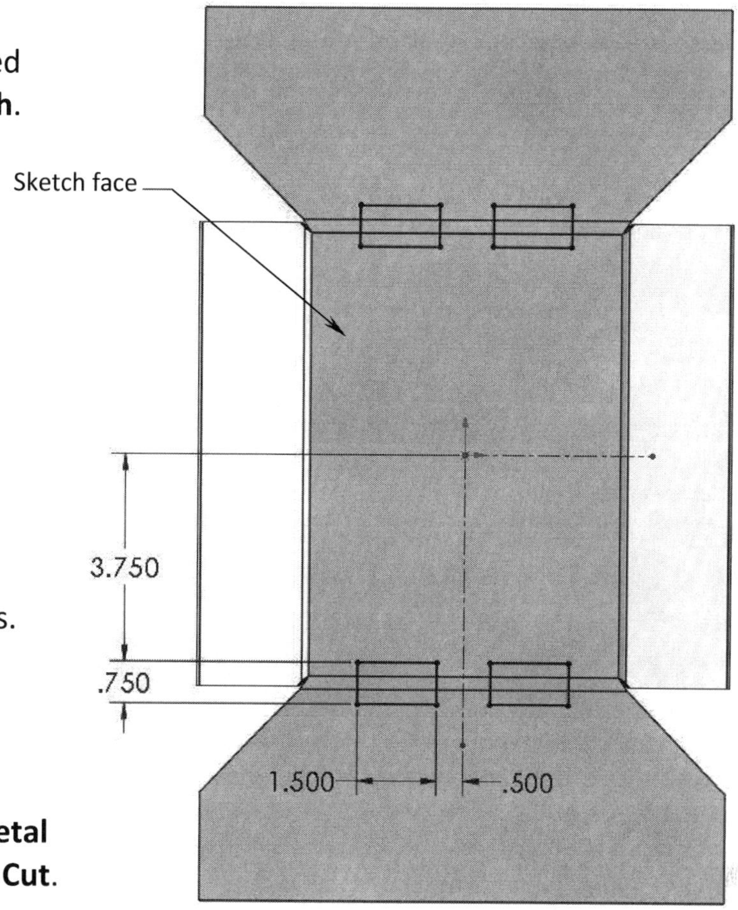

Sketch 2 **Corner-Rectangles** and **2 Centerlines**.

Add the dimensions shown in the image to fully define the sketch.

Mirror the rectangles about the 2 centerlines.

Switch to the **Sheet Metal** tab and click **Extruded Cut**.

For Direction 1, select **Blind** and enable the checkbox: **Link To Thickness**.

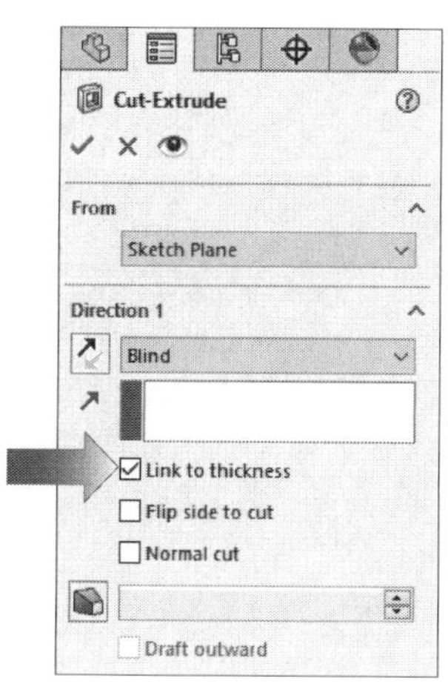

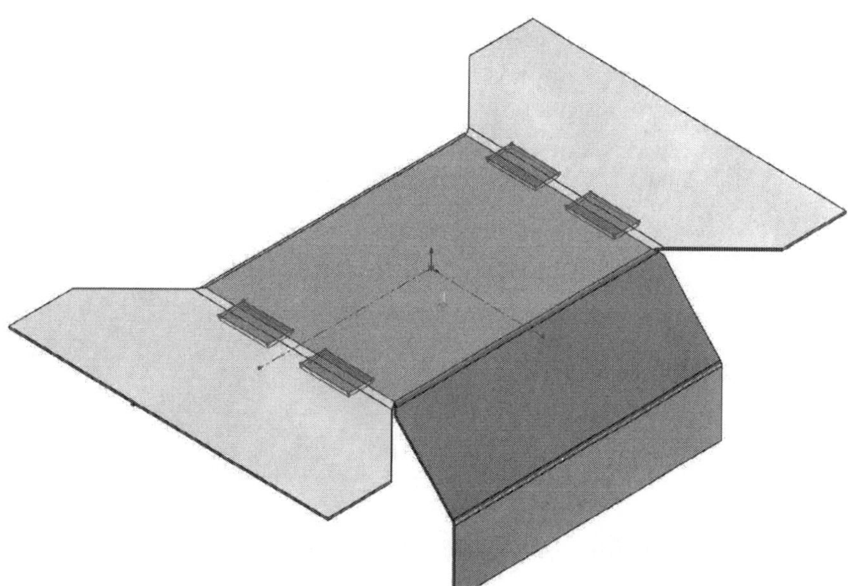

Click **OK**.

4. Folding the bends:

Click **Fold**  on the **Sheet Metal** tab.

The Fixed Face is selected automatically.

Click **Collect All Bends**.

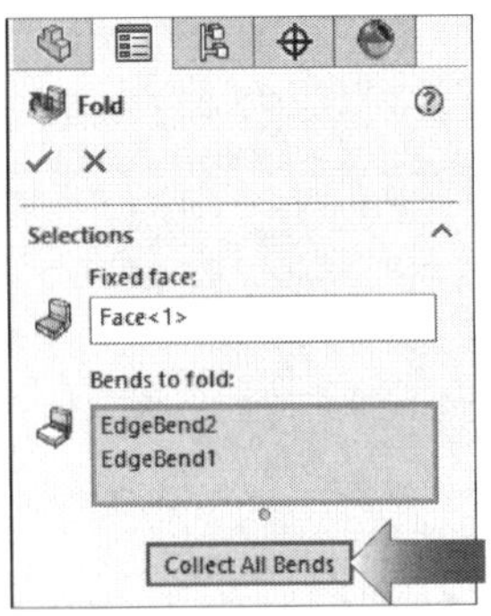

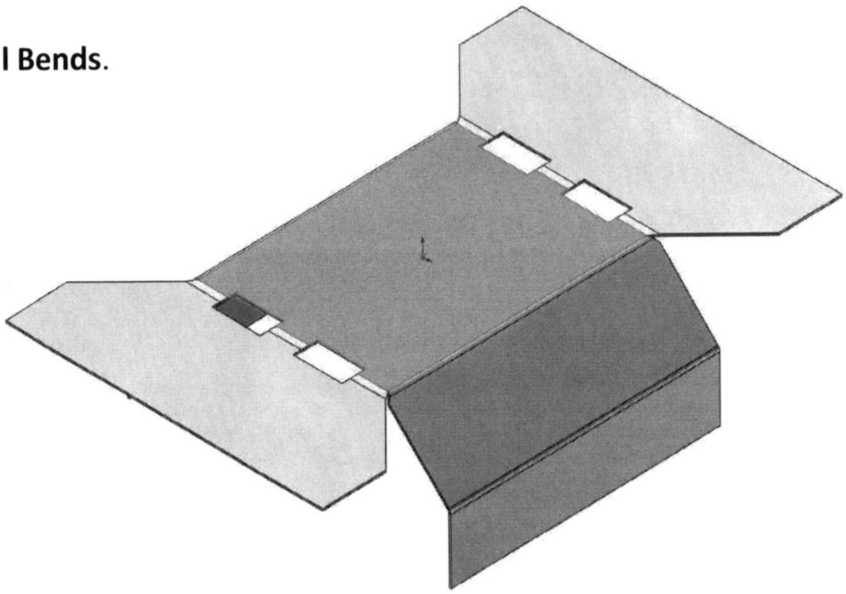

Click **OK**.

The 2 bends are folded back to their original state, along with the cuts features.

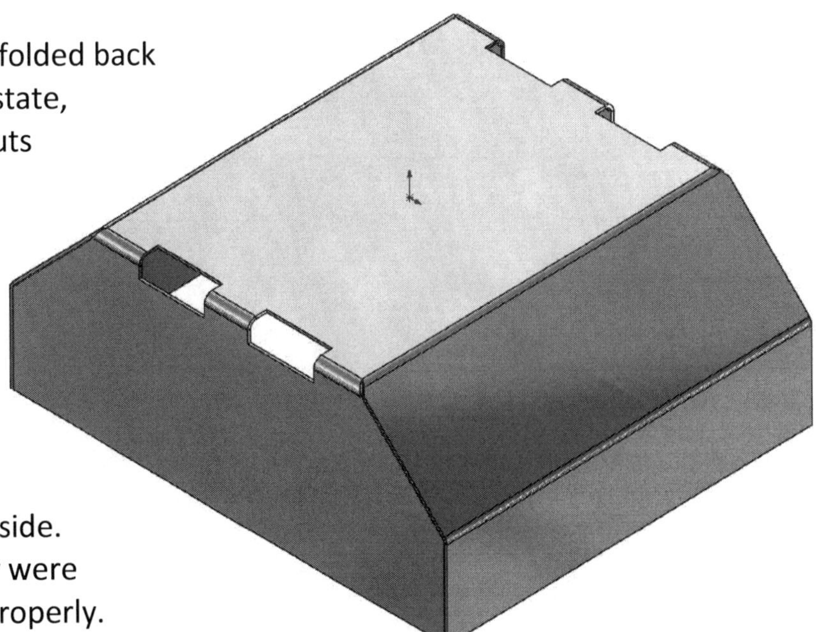

Rotate the model and inspect the cuts on the opposite side. Ensure that they were cut and folded properly.

5. Unfolding the bends:

We will need to unfold the part again to make another cut.

Click **Unfold** on the **Sheet Metal** tab.

For Fixed Face, select the top face of the part.

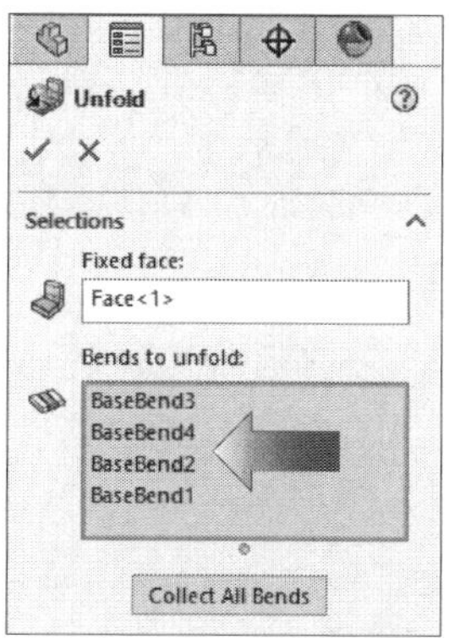

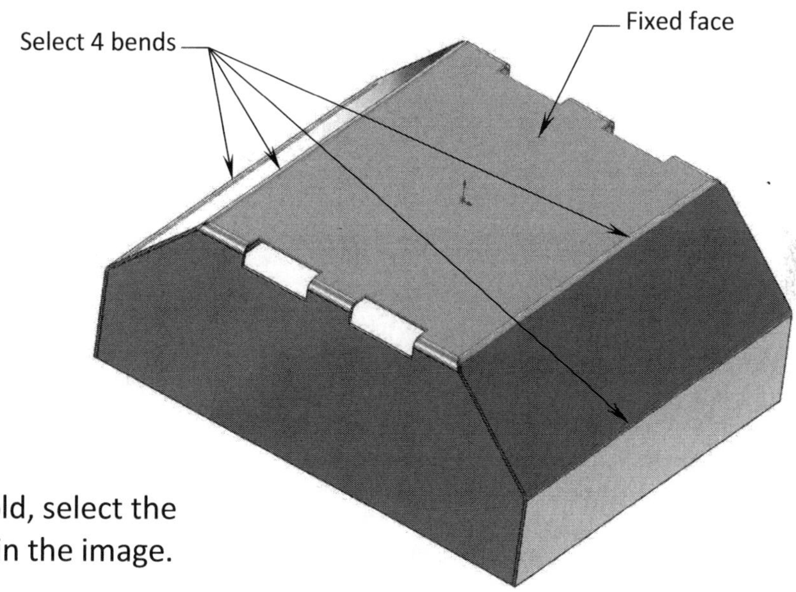

For Bends to Unfold, select the 4 bends as noted in the image.

Click **OK**.

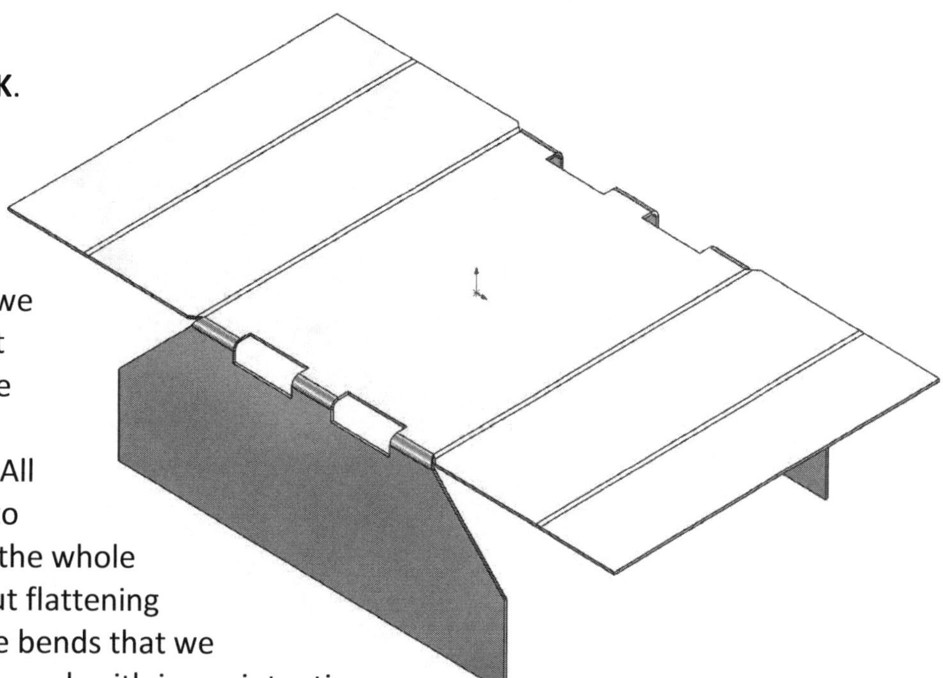

Again, we can just click the button: Collect All Bends to flatten the whole part, but flattening only the bends that we need to work with is our intention.

6. Making the 2nd cut:

Select the top face of the part and open a **new sketch**.

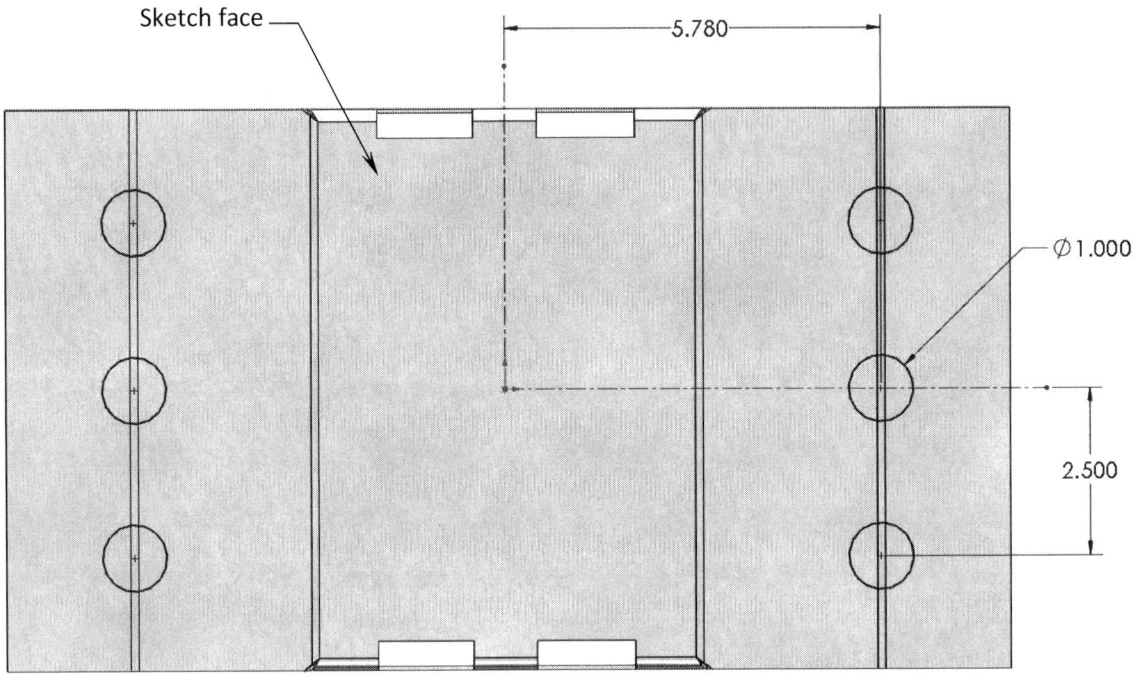

Sketch **3 Circles** and **2 Centerlines**. Add the dimensions shown in the image.

Mirror the circles about the vertical centerline.

Create a **Blind** cut, enable **Link To Thickness**.

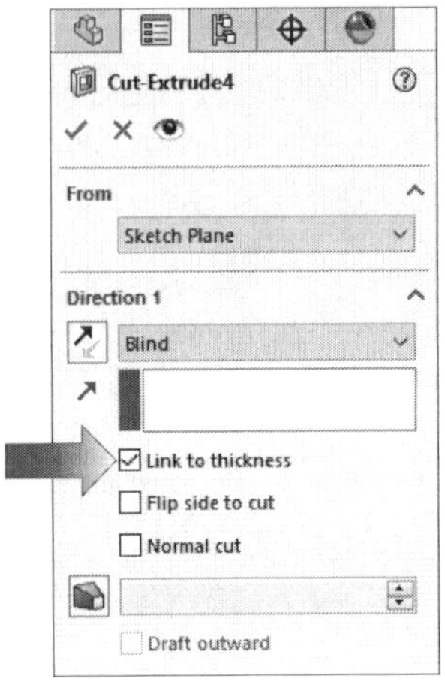

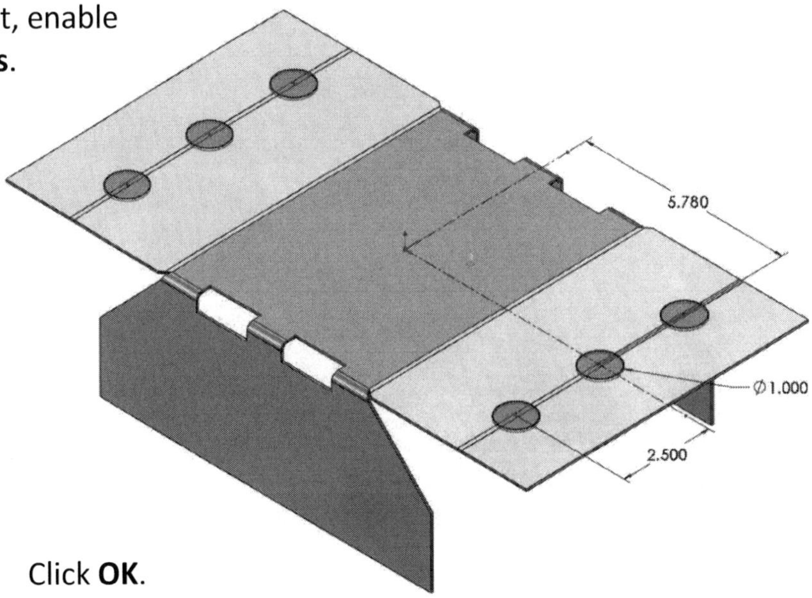

Click **OK**.

7. Folding the bends:

Click **Fold** on the **Sheet Metal** tab.

The Fixed Face is selected automatically.

Click **Collect All Bends**.

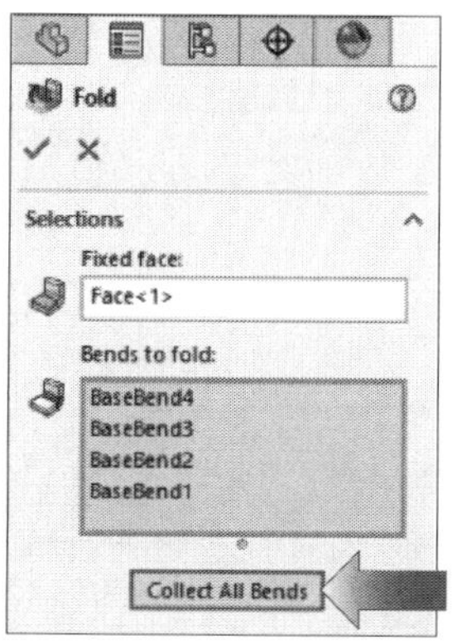

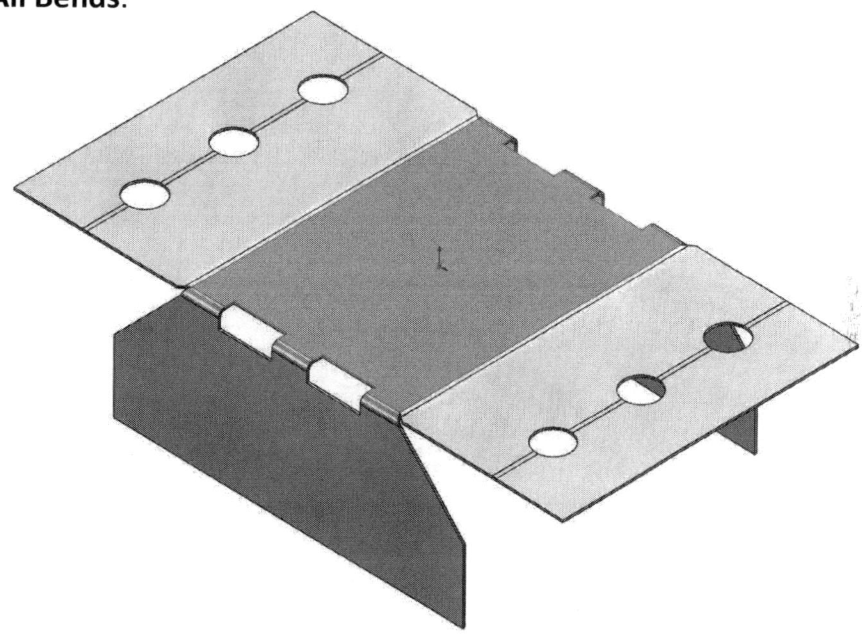

Click **OK**.

All bends are returned to their folded state. The cuts that were created in the unfold state are also folded.

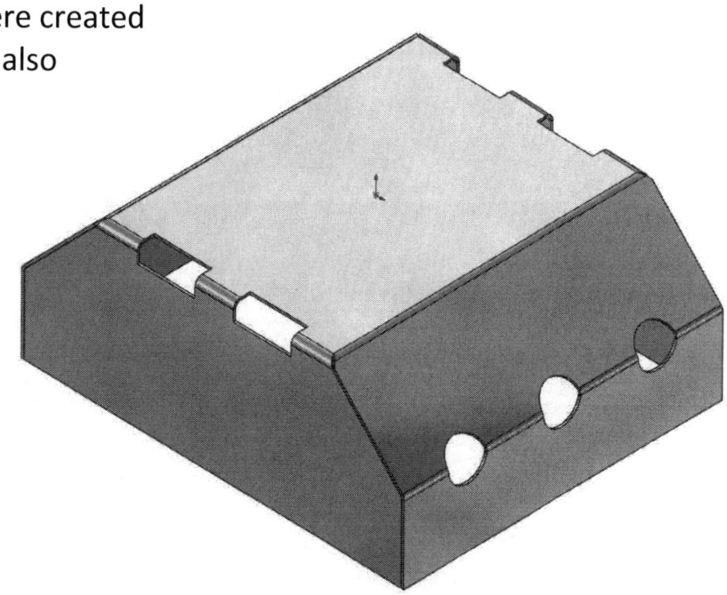

Rotate to different orientations and inspect the cuts from all sides. Make sure they were cut and folded correctly.

8. Viewing the flat pattern:

Right-click anywhere on the part and select: **Toggle Flat Pattern**.

The flat pattern is projected on the top of the fold pattern.

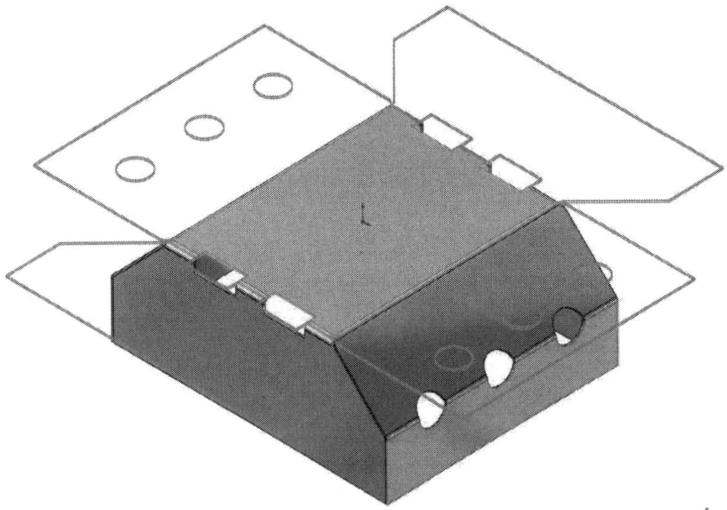

To view the flat pattern and the bounding-box, use the **Flatten** tool instead.

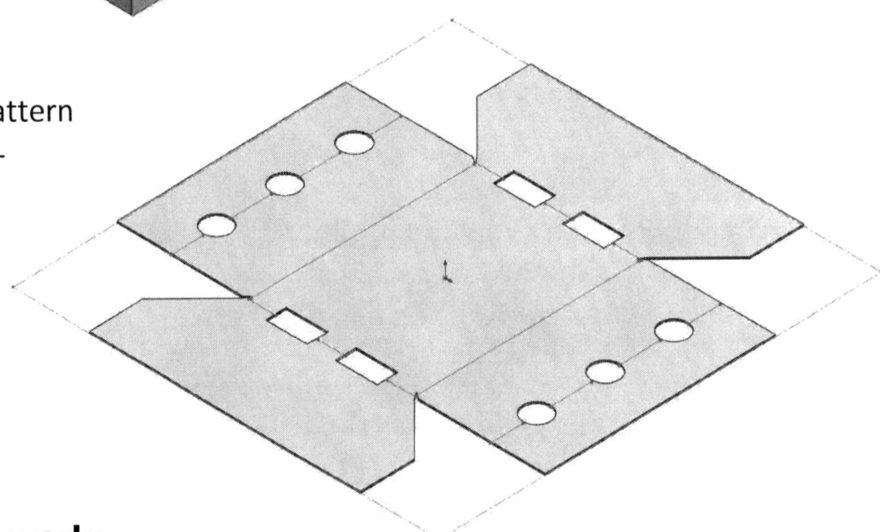

9. Saving your work:

Select **File, Save As.**

Enter **Fold & Unfold Exe_Completed** for the file name.

Click **Save**.

Lesson 6: Curved Flanges & Joggles

Curved flanges can be added to edge flanges that are created off of a planar base and on nonlinear (circular) edges of nonplanar faces.

When flattened, if an edge flange is created on a curved edge that is based on another edge flange, you must select both bends to unflatten or flatten the nonlinear edge flange.

1. Opening a part document:

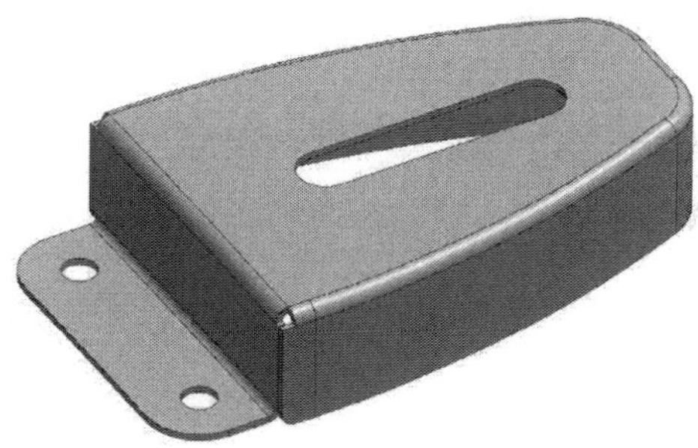

Browse to the Training Folder and open a part document named: **Curved Flanges.sldprt**

This model contains 1 Base flange and all sheet metal parameters have been assigned to it.

2. Creating a tab:

Select the <u>face</u> as noted and open a new **sketch**.

Sketch the profile shown here.

Add the dimensions and relations needed to fully define the sketch.

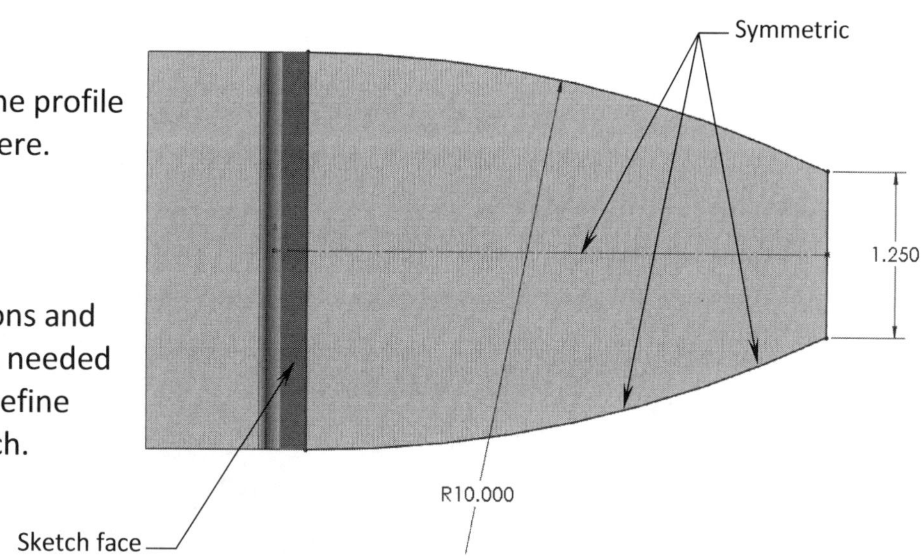

A Tab is a dependent feature in a sheet metal part. The depth of a tab feature is automatically linked to the thickness of the sheet metal part. The direction of the depth automatically coincides with the sheet metal part to prevent a disjointed body.

Click **Base Flange/Tab** on the **Sheet Metal** toolbar.

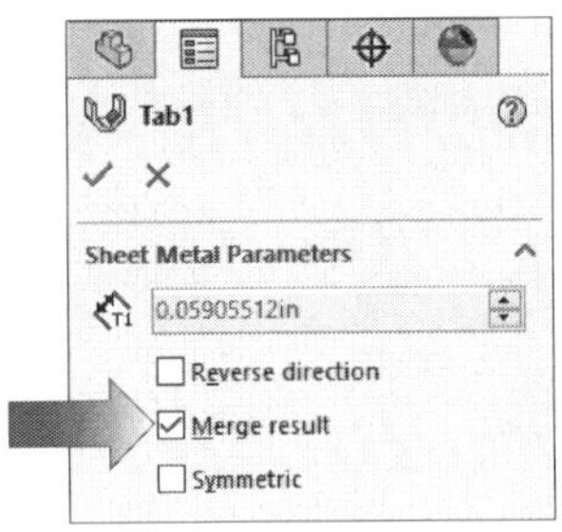

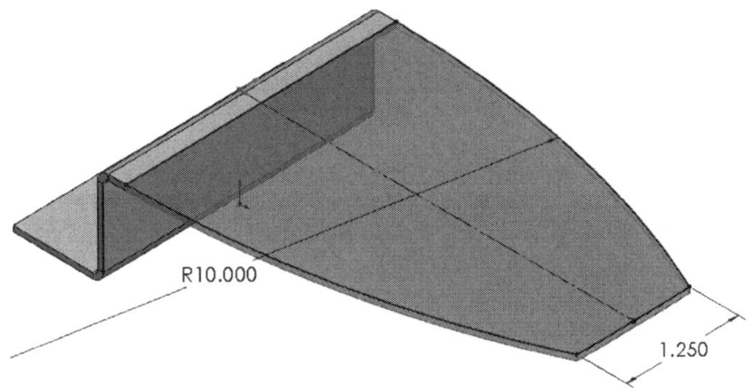

Click the **Merge Result** checkbox.

The sheet metal parameters from the Base Flange such as Thickness, Bend Radius, K-Factor, Auto Relief, etc., are automatically populated to the Tab feature.

Click **OK**.

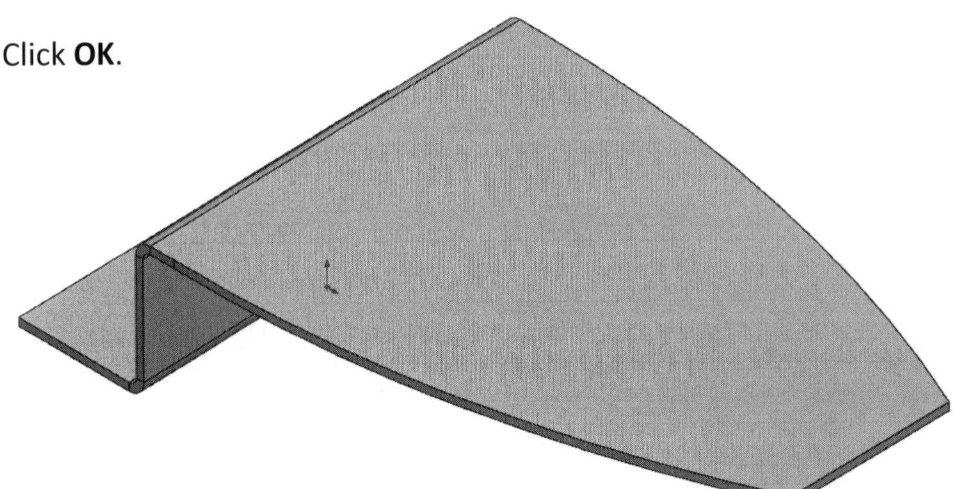

3. Breaking the corners:

Select: **Corners, Break Corners** on the **Sheet Metal** tab.

Click the **Fillet** button.

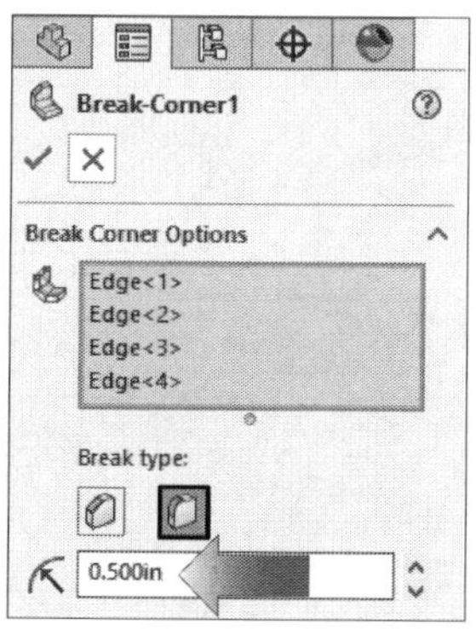

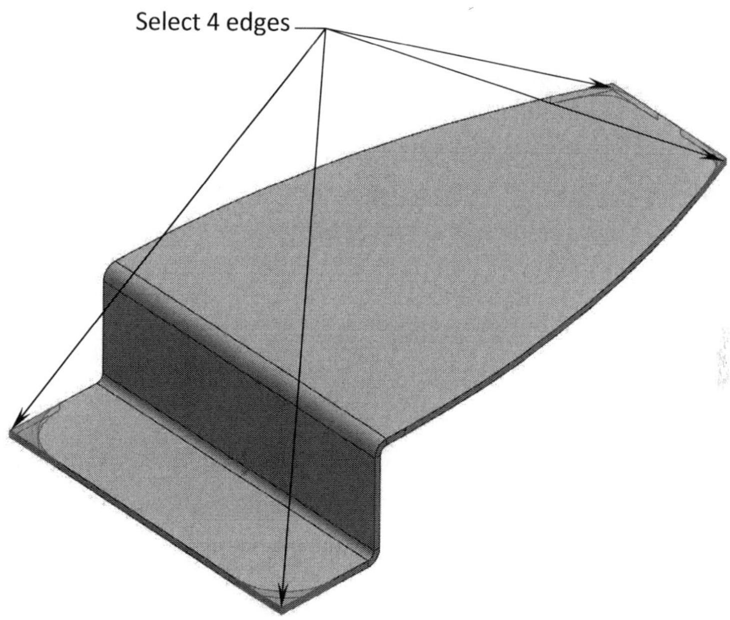

For Radius, enter **.500in**.

For Edges to Fillet, select the **4 small vertical edges** as shown in the image above.

Click **OK**.

The curved edges on the right side of the part will be used to create the curved flanges.

4. Creating the Curved Flanges:

Click **Edge Flange** on the **Sheet Metal** tab.

First, select on of the **curved edges**, then select the other **6 edges** as shown in the image below.

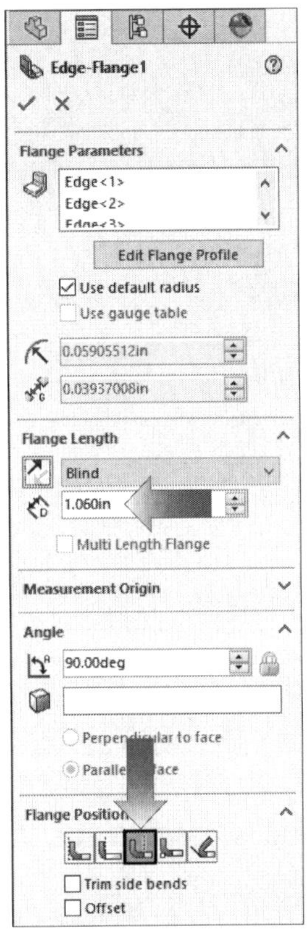

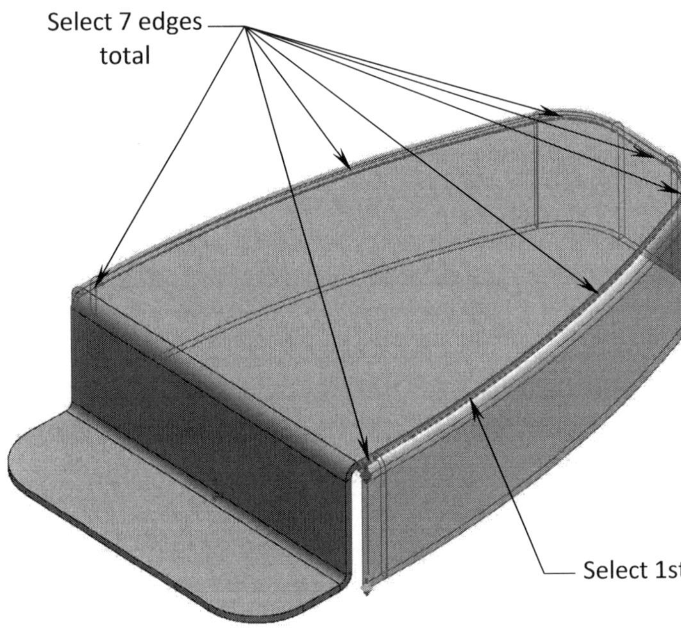

For Flange Length, select the **Blind** option and enter: **1.060in**.

Keep the Bend Angle at the default **90.00deg**.

For Flange Position, select **Bend Outside**.

Click **OK**.

Inspect your model against the image shown here.

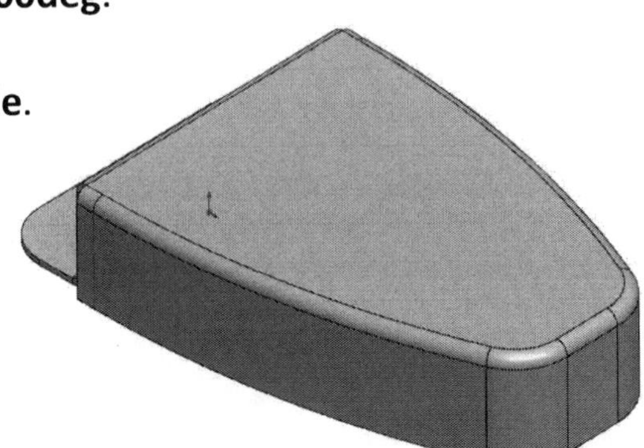

5. Closing the corners:

Click **Corners, Closed Corner**.

For Face to Extend, select the **2 faces** on both sides, as indicated.

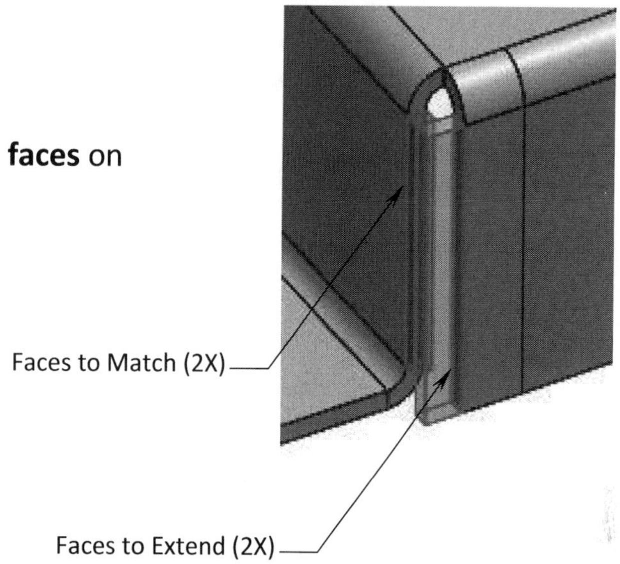

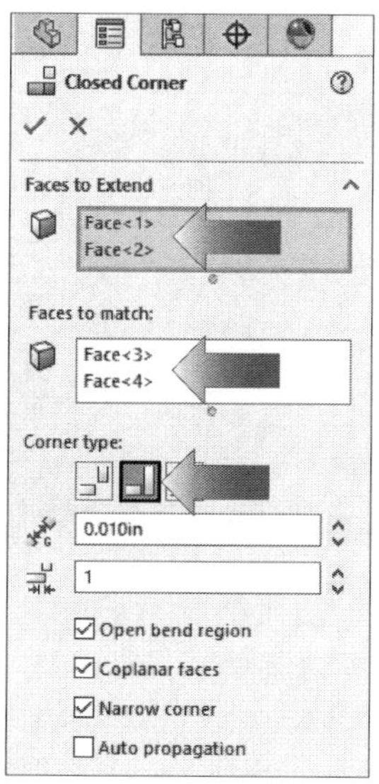

For Faces to Match, select the **2 adjacent faces** as noted in the image.

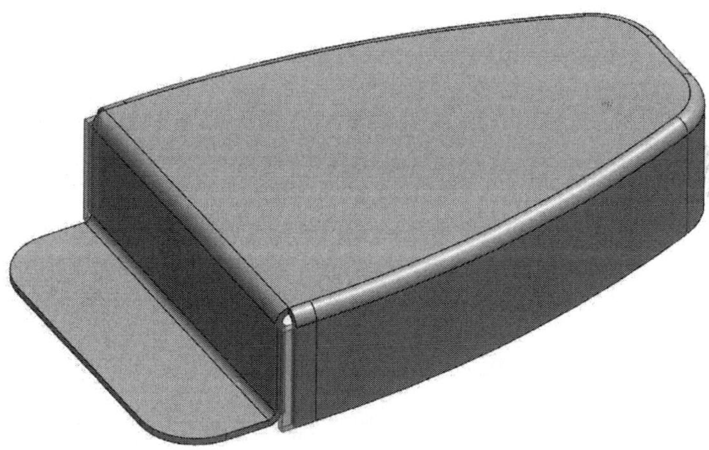

For Corner Type, select **Overlap**.

Enable the **Open Bend Region** checkbox to keep the corners open. Keep all other parameters at their default values.

Click **OK**.

6. Adding the cut features:

Select the upper face of the model and open a **new sketch**.

Sketch the **Slot** profile and **2 Circles**. The 2 circles are **symmetric** about the horizontal centerline.

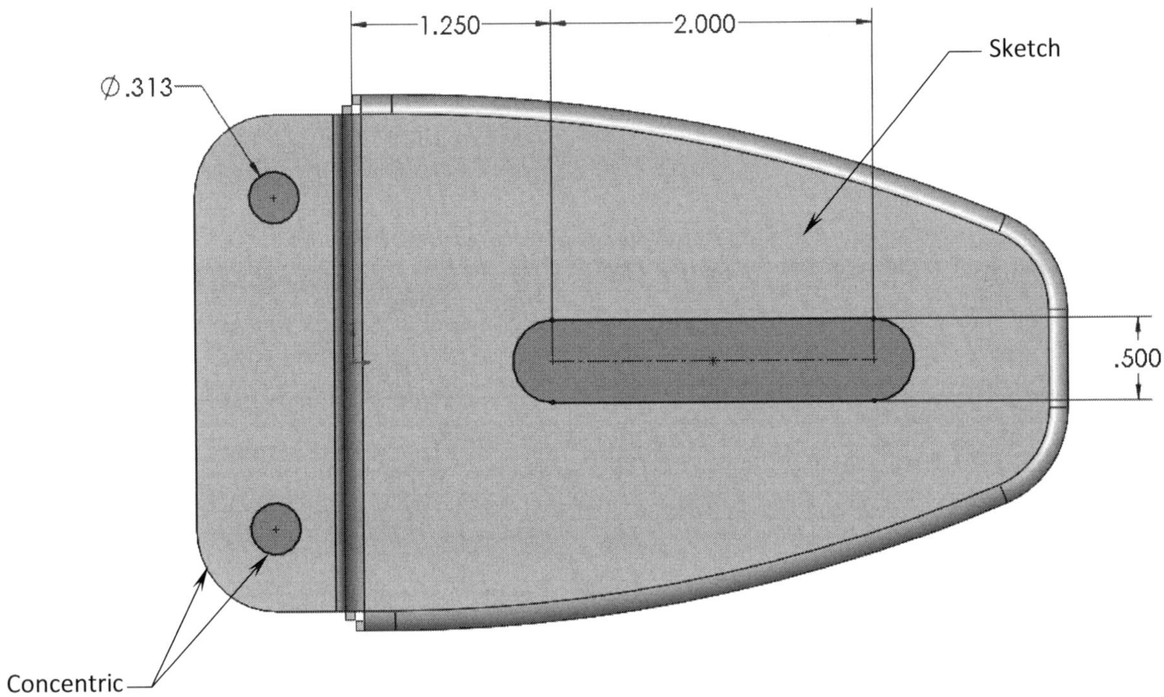

Add the dimensions and relations shown above to fully define the sketch.

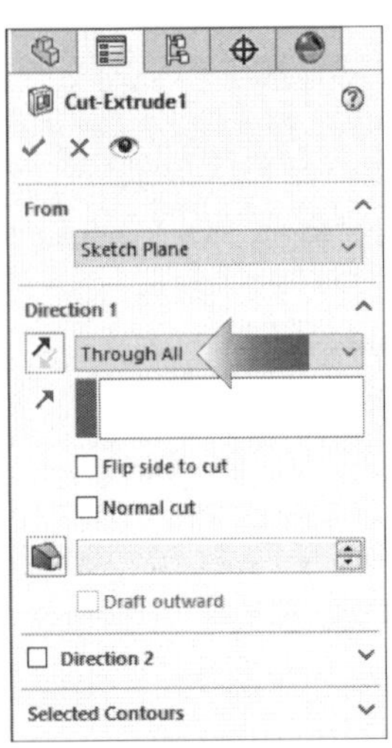

Switch to the **Sheet Metal** tab and click **Extruded Cut**.

For Direction 1, select: **Through All**.

Click **OK**.

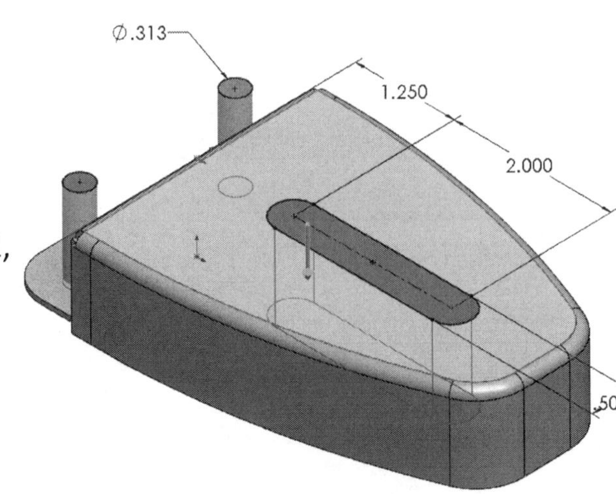

7. Removing the sharp corners:

Select **Corners, Break Corner**.

For Break Type, select the **Fillet** option.

For Radius size, enter **.125in**.

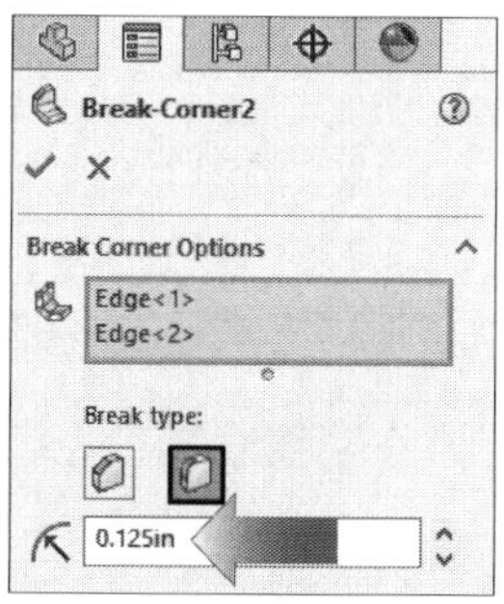

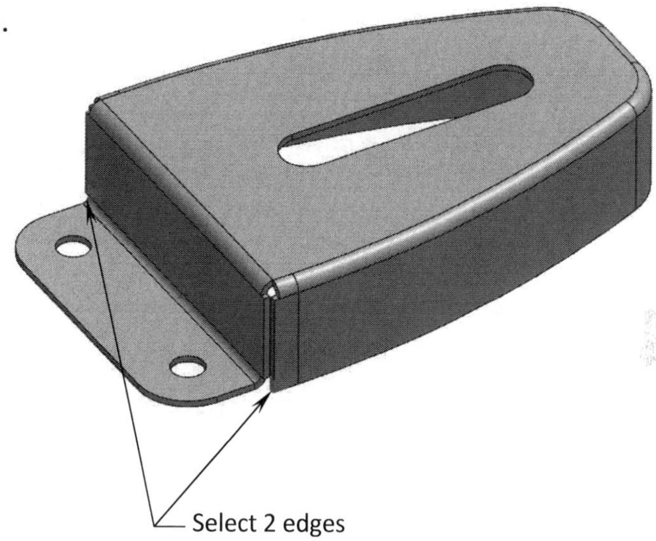

For Corners to Fillet, select the **2 edges** as indicated.

Click **OK**.

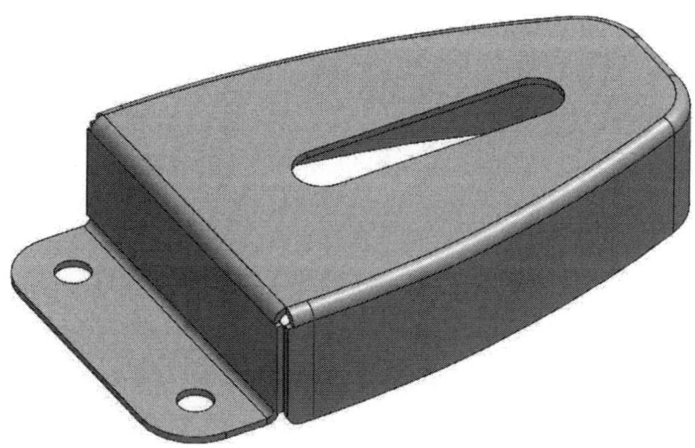

8. Saving your works:

Select **File, Save As**.

Enter: **Curved Flanges_Completed** for the file name.

Click **Save**.

Sheet Metal Jogs 1

A Jog or joggle is a small, controlled offset or step in the edge of a metal piece. This offset, often in the form of two opposite bends, allows one sheet to overlap another while maintaining a flush, smooth surface at the joint. It is commonly used for creating overlapping connections, like in aircraft or automotive body panels, where a strong, secure connection is needed without an unsightly step or bump.

1. Opening a part document:

Browse to the Training Folder and open a part document named: **Sheet Metal Jog1.sldprt**

2. Making the 1st jog:

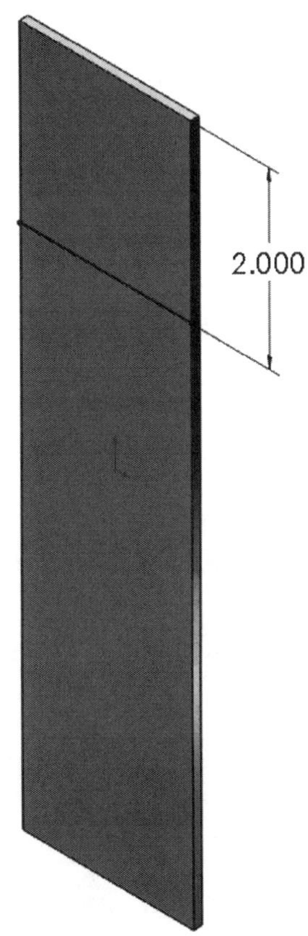

Select the face indicated and open a **new sketch**.

Sketch a horizontal **Line** and add the **2.00in.** location dimension.

The sketched line does not have to be coincident to the side edges, but it is good practice to always fully define your sketch to prevent it from shifting or moving away from the part without your knowledge.

Add a Coincident relation between the endpoint of the line and the vertical edge of the part. Add the same relation to both sides of the line.

Switch to the **Sheet Metal** tab and click **Jog** .

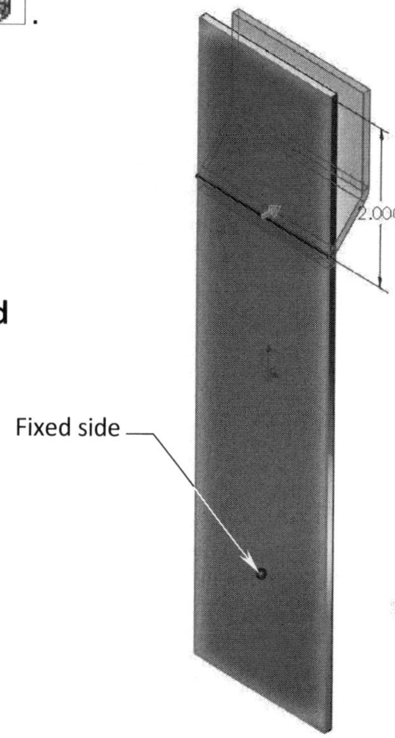

For Fixed Face, click anywhere below the Line.

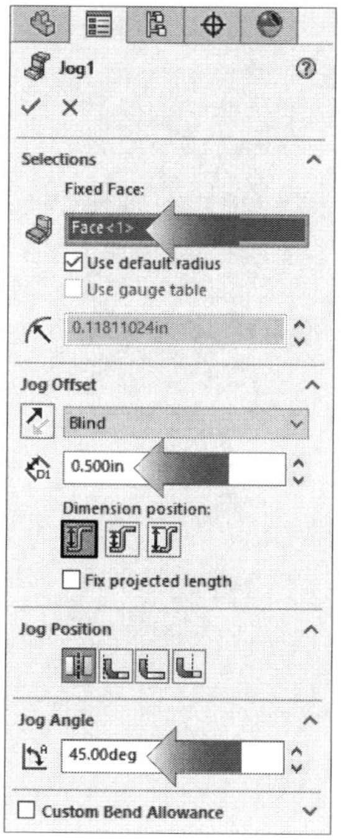

Enable the checkbox: **Use Default Radius.**

For Jog Offset, select **Blind** and enter **.500in**.

For Dimension Positions, select **Outside Offset**.

For Jog Position, select **Bend Centerline**.

For Jog Angle, enter **45.00deg**.

Click **OK**.

3. Making the 2nd jog:

Select the front face of the part and open a **new sketch**.

Sketch a horizontal **Line** and add the **2.00in**. location dimension.

Once again, it is good practice to always fully define your sketch.

Add 2 Coincident relations to the left and right sides of the line to keep it from shifting.

Switch to the **Sheet Metal** tab and click **Jog** .

For Fixed Face, click anywhere <u>below</u> the Line.

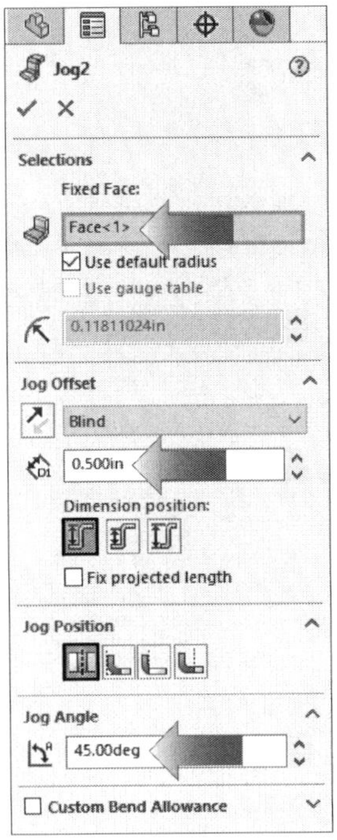

Enable the checkbox: **Use Default Radius**.

For Jog Offset, select **Blind** and enter **.500in**.

For Dimension Positions, select **Outside Offset**.

For Jog Position, select **Bend Centerline**.

For Jog Angle, enter **45.00deg**.

Click **OK**.

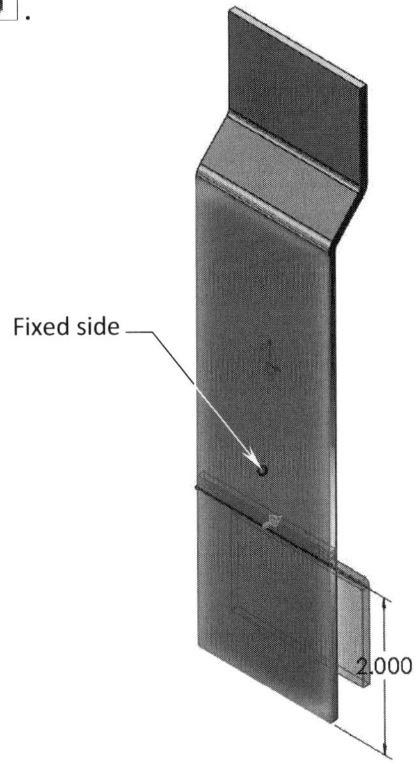

<u>Notes:</u>

1. The Fix Projected Length option will keep the overall length of the part from changing while adding the additional materials needed to accommodate the jog length. Clear this option.

2. The default direction for the jog is **Inward**. To jog **outward**, simply click the **Reverse** button next to the Blind condition.

4. Adding the cuts:

Select the face as noted and open a **new sketch**.

Sketch a **Slot** in the middle and **2 Circles** on top of the part.

Sketch a horizontal centerline to mirror the circles and a vertical centerline to make the slot symmetry.

Add the dimensions shown in the image to fully define the sketch.

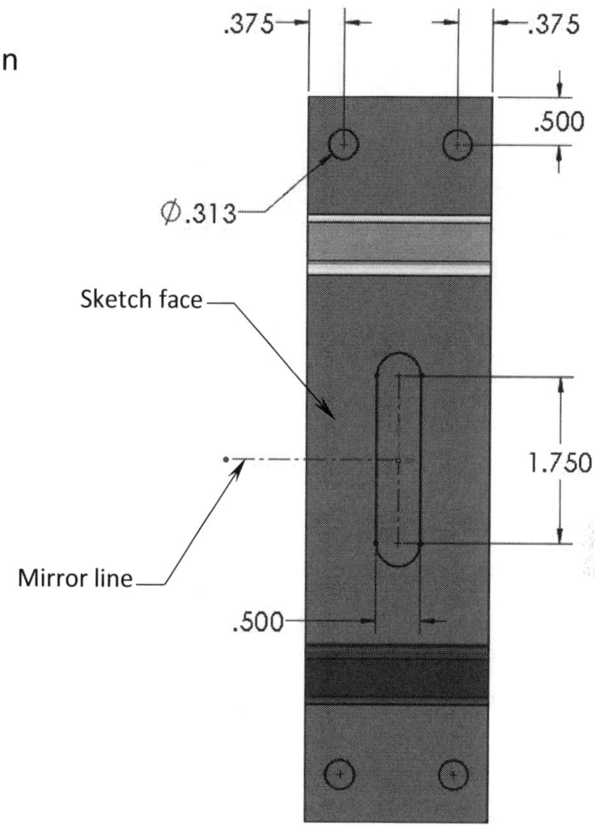

Switch to the **Sheet Metal** tab and click: **Extruded Cut**.

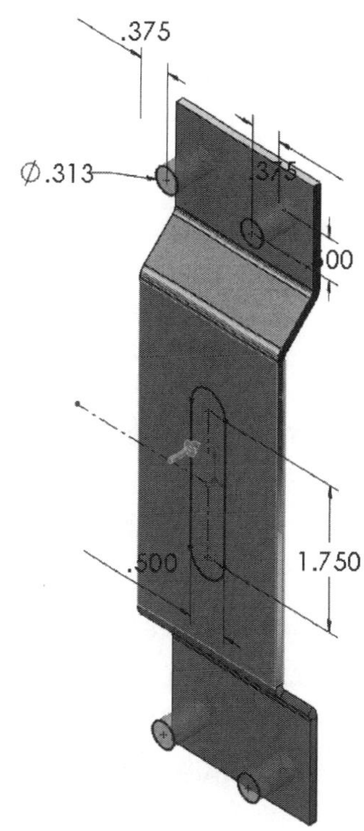

For Direction 1, select: **Through All**.

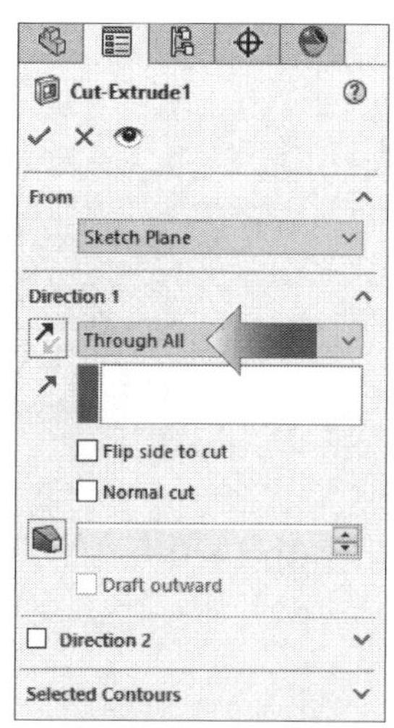

Click **OK**.

Since the slot and the holes are through cuts, it is all right to create them in the same sketch.

5. Adding fillets:

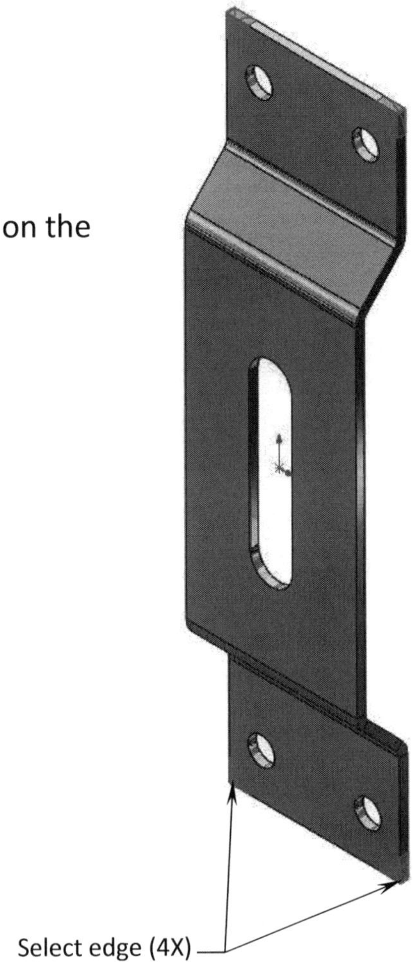

Select **Corners, Break Corner**.

For Corners to Fillet, select 4 edges, 2 on the top of the part and 2 on the bottom.

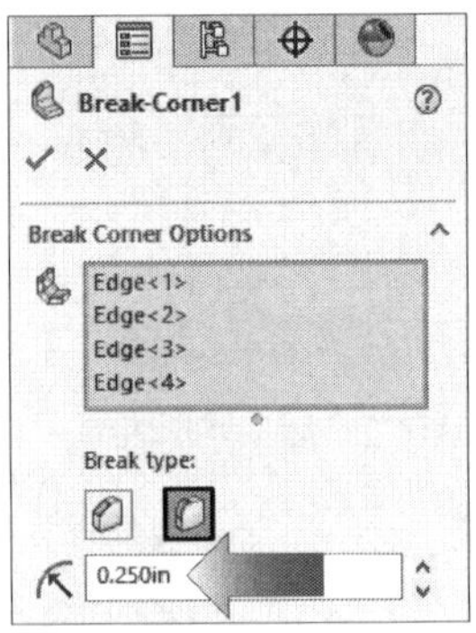

For Break Type, click the **Fillet** button and enter **.250in**. for Radius.

Click **OK**.

6. Saving your work:

Select **File, Save**.

Enter **Sheet Metal Jog1_Completed** for the file name.

Click **Save**.

Sheet Metal Jogs 2

The exercises in this textbook are intended to give you an opportunity to explore and to apply what you have learned from the previous chapters, at your own pace.

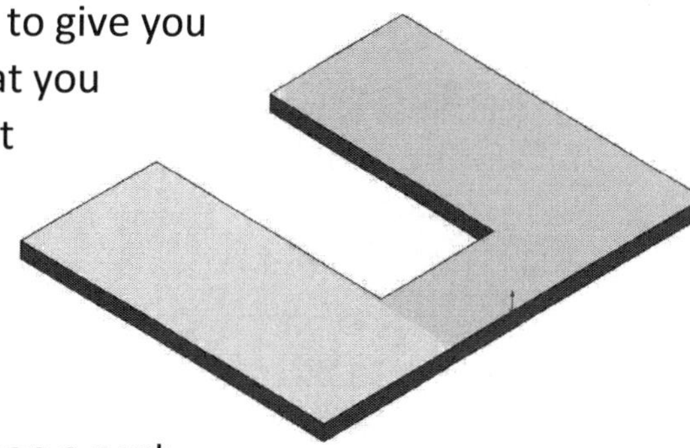

1. Opening a part document:

Browse to the Training Folder and open a part document named: **Sheet Metal Jog2.sldprt**

The jog features in this part are symmetrical about the right plane. After the features are created, we will mirror the jogs to maintain the relationships between them.

2. Creating a jog feature:

Select the upper <u>face</u> of the part and open a **new sketch**.

Sketch a vertical **Line** and add the **.125in**. location dimension.

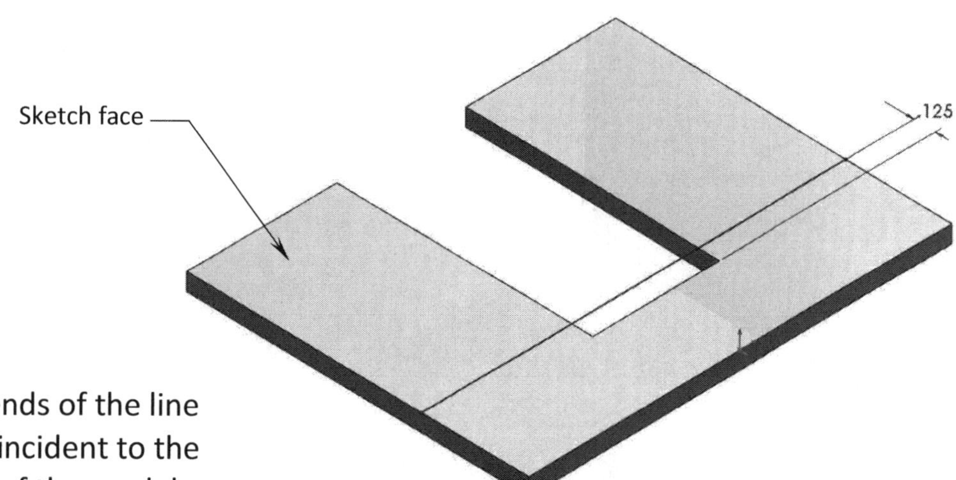

Both ends of the line are coincident to the edges of the model.

Switch to the **Sheet Metal** tab and click **Jog**.

For Fixed Face, click anywhere on the <u>right side</u> of the line.

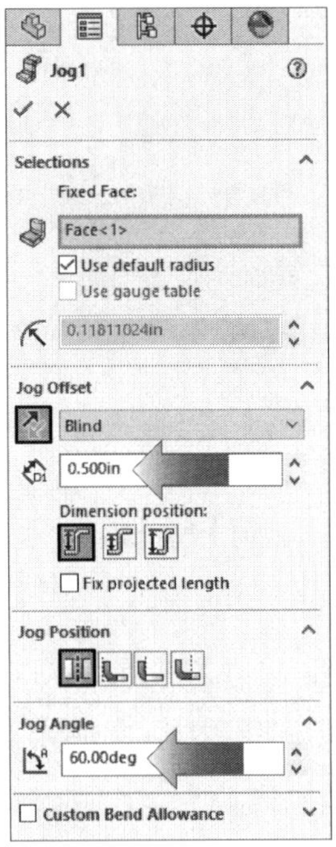

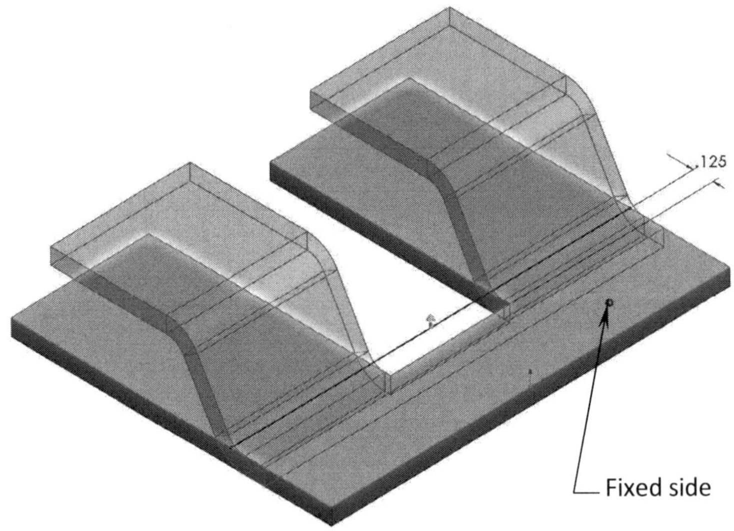

For Jog Offset, select **Blind** and enter **.500in**.

Click **Reverse** to jog upwards.

For Dimension Position, select **Outside Offset**.

For Jog Position, select **Bend Centerline**.

For Jog Angle, enter **60.00deg**.

Click **OK**.

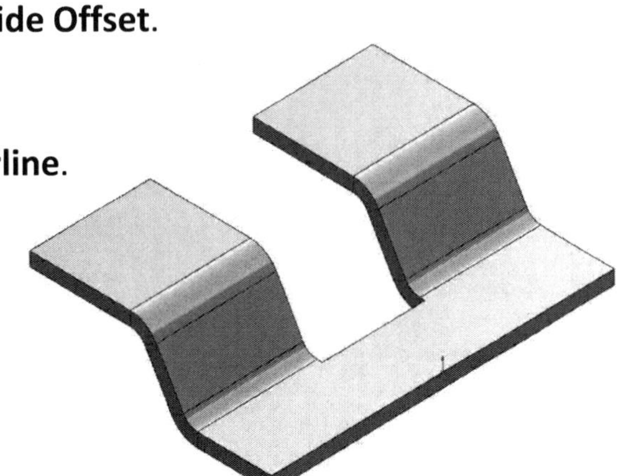

3. Adding the cuts:

Select the face indicated and open a **new sketch**.

Sketch a **Circle** and a **Corner Rectangle**.

Sketch a **horizontal Centerline** to mirror the circle and the rectangle.

Add dimensions to fully define the sketch.

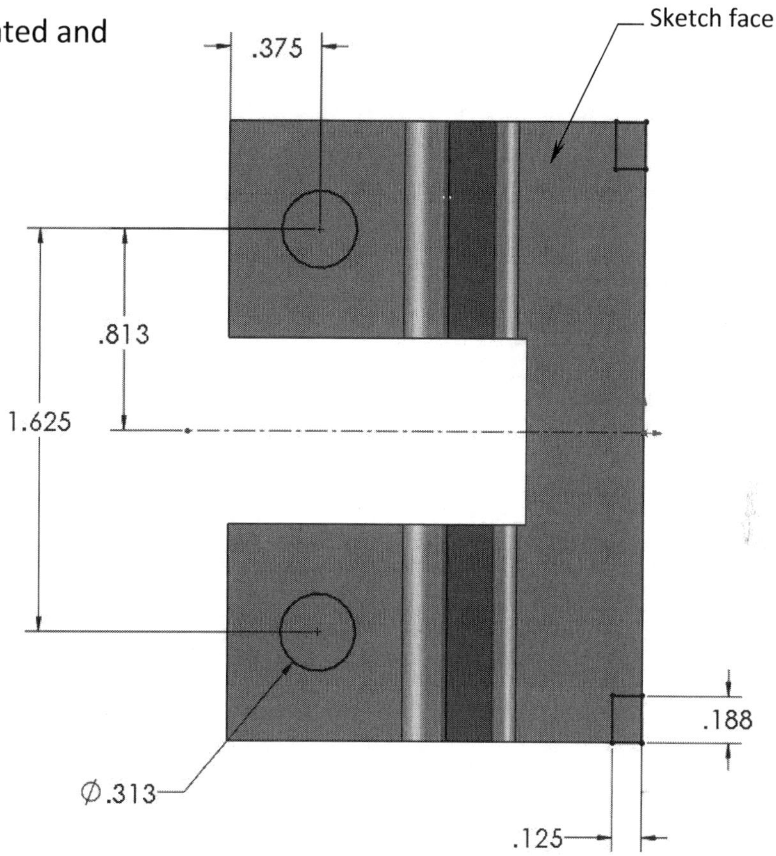

Switch to the **Sheet Metal** tab and click **Extruded Cut**.

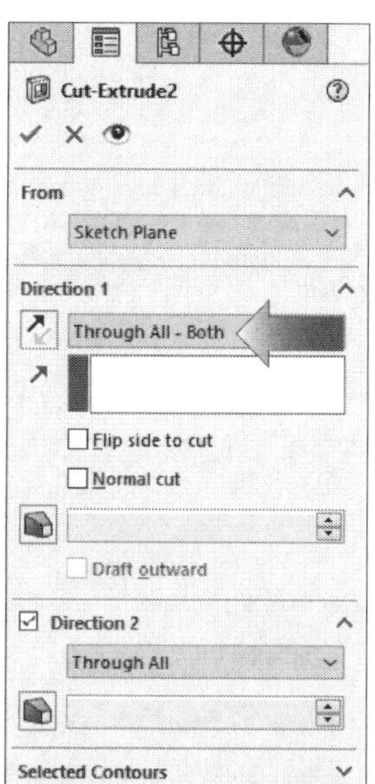

For Direction 1, select **Through All Both**.

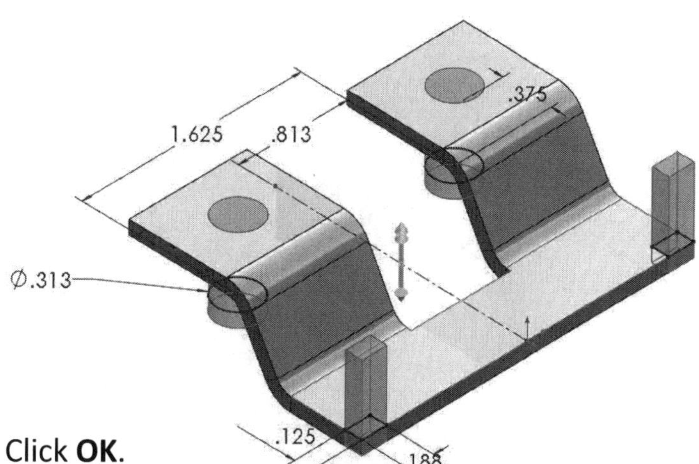

Click **OK**.

4. Mirroring a body:

Switch to the **Features** tab and click **Mirror**.

For Mirror Face/Plane, select the **face** as noted in the image.

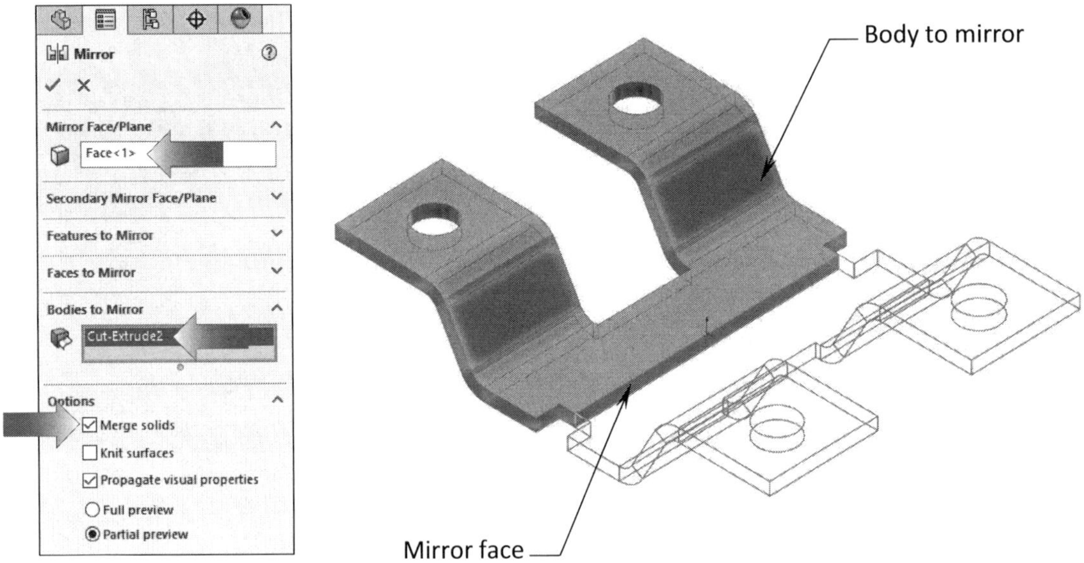

Expand the Bodies to Mirror section and select <u>the part</u> from the graphics area.

Enable the **Merge Solids** checkbox.

Click **OK**.

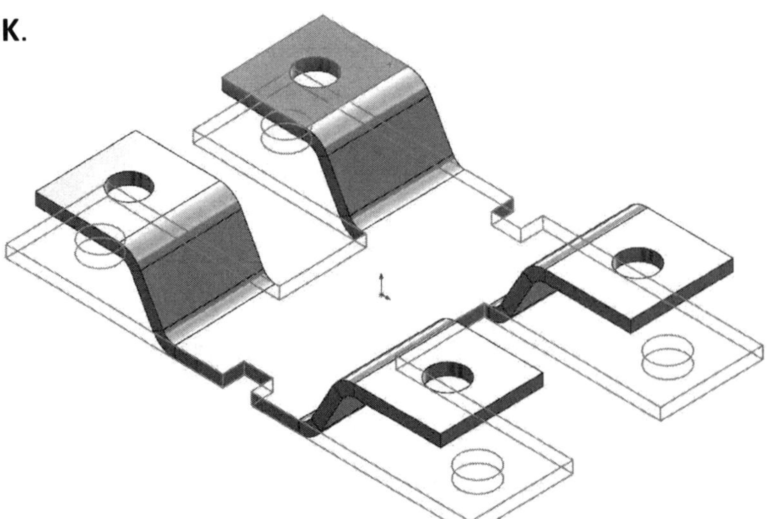

5. Adding fillets:

Switch back to the **Sheet Metal** tab and select: **Corners, Break Corner**.

For Edges to Fillet, select **8 edges** as indicated, 4 on each side.

For Break Type, select the **Fillet** button.

For radius, enter **.250in**.

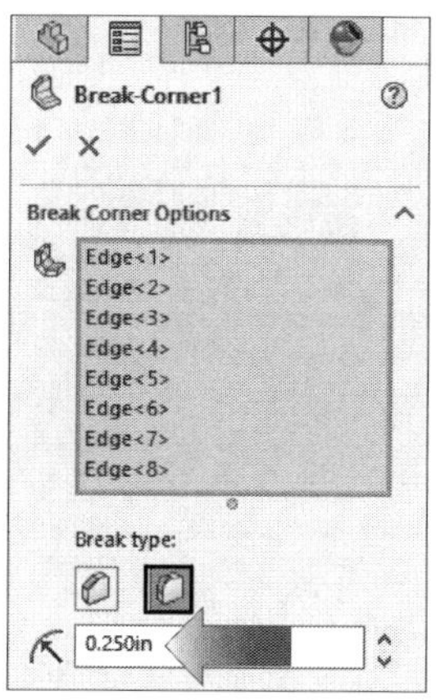

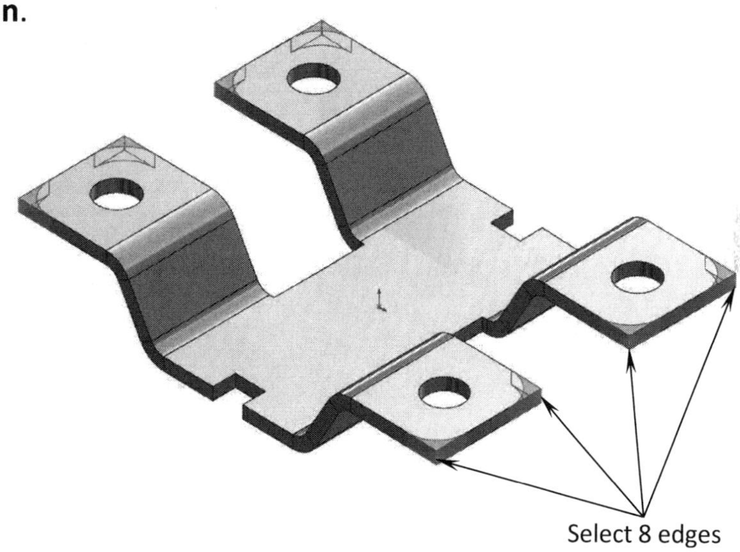

Click **OK**.

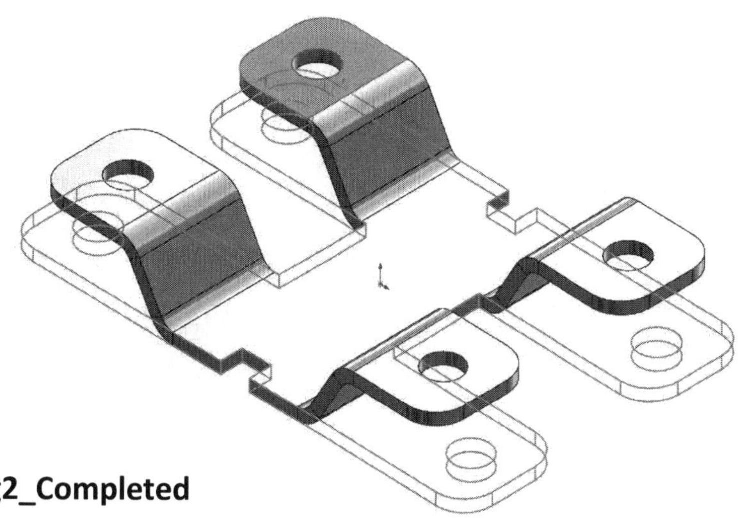

6. Saving your work:

Select **File, Save**.

Enter **Sheet Metal Jog2_Completed** for the file name.

Click **Save**.

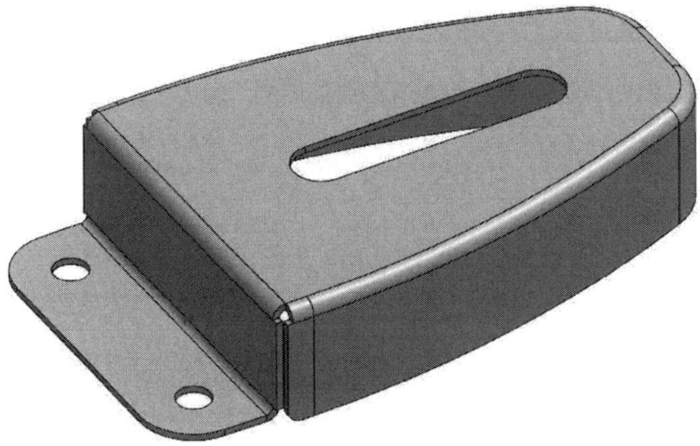

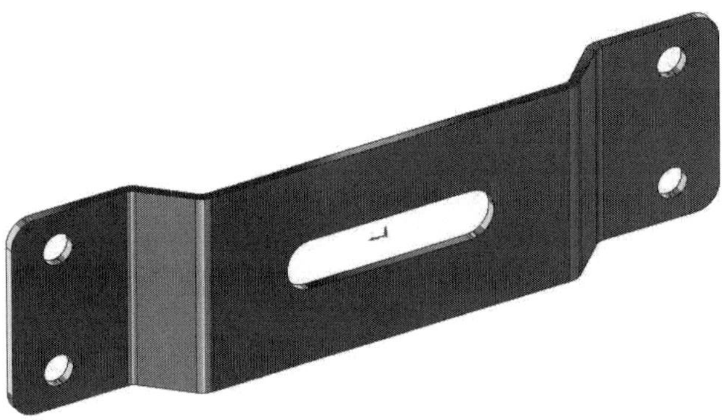

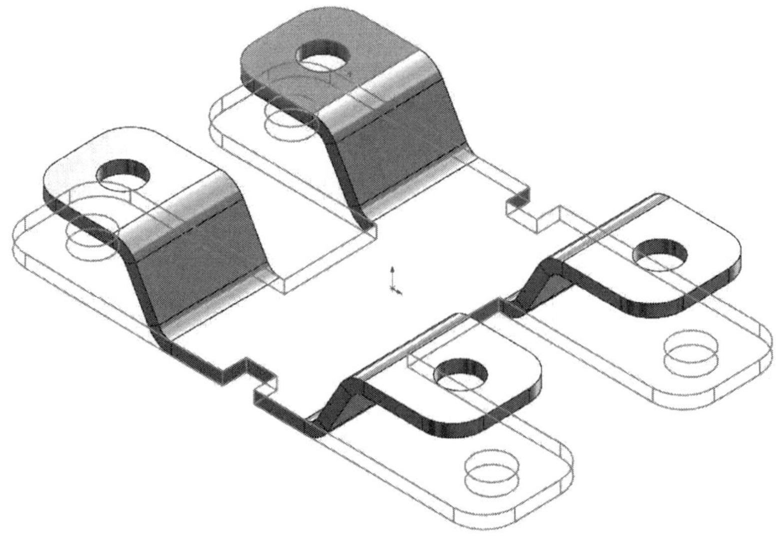

Lesson 7: Sheet Metal Tab/Slot & Multibody

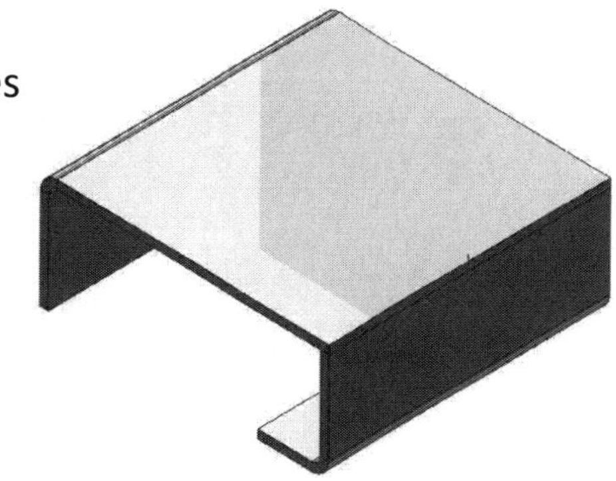

In SOLIDWORKS, the Tab and Slot feature creates tabs on one body and slots on another body to interlock the two bodies.
There are options to allow how the tabs and slots look and how they are distributed along the selected entities.
Tabs and slots make it easier to weld parts together and minimize the requirement to build complicated fixtures because you can interlock several sheet metal parts.

1. Opening a part document:

Browse to the Training Folder and open a part document named:
Sheet Metal Tab & Slot.sldprt

2. Creating the Tab & Slot feature:

Some of the options available for Tab & Slots are:

Length, Height, Thickness
Star/End Offsets
Fillet, Sharp, Chamfer
and Round corners.

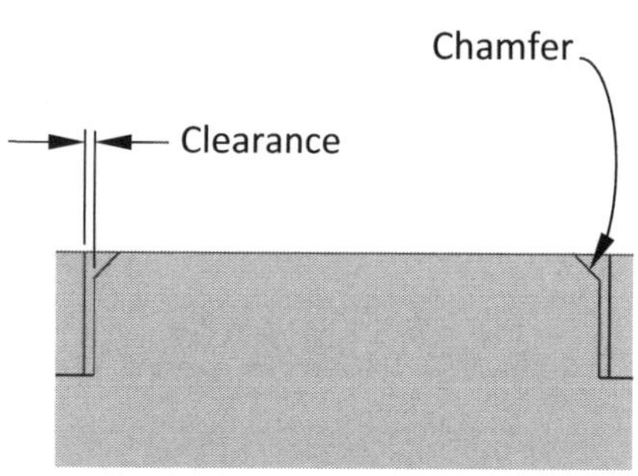

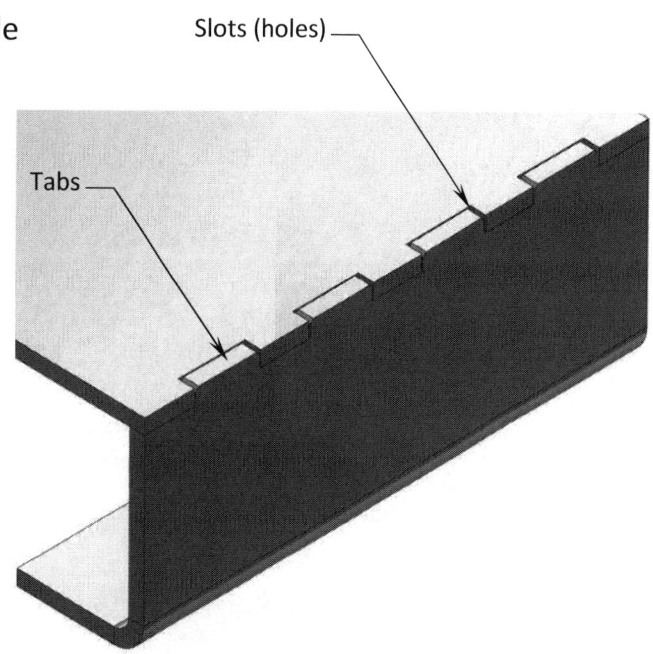

Switch to the **Sheet Metal** tab and click **Tab & Slot** .

Click the **New Group** button and enable **Link Groups Together** checkbox.

Click the **edge** as indicated with balloon 1.

Select the **face** balloon 2.

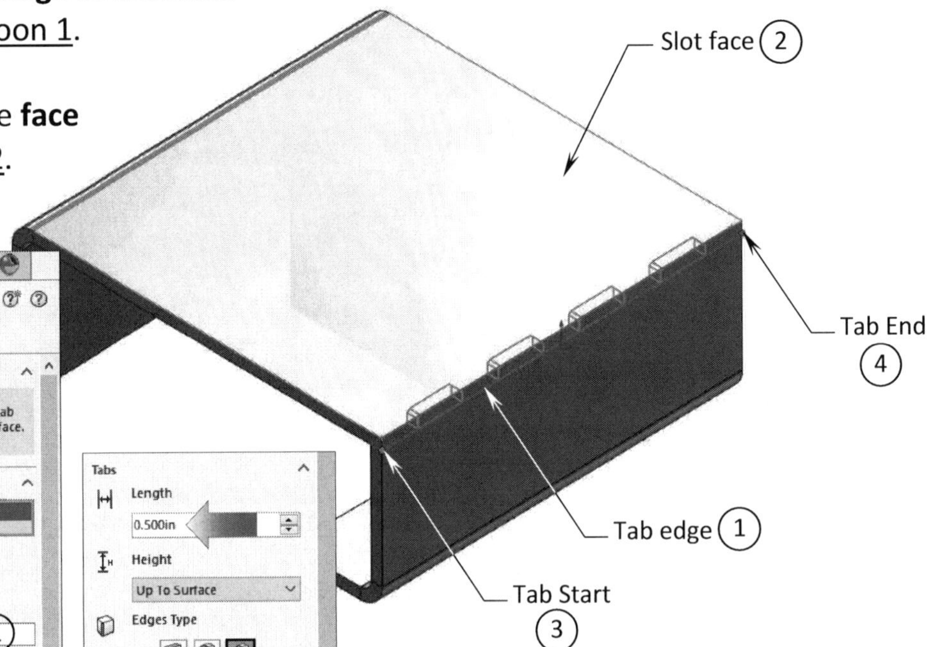

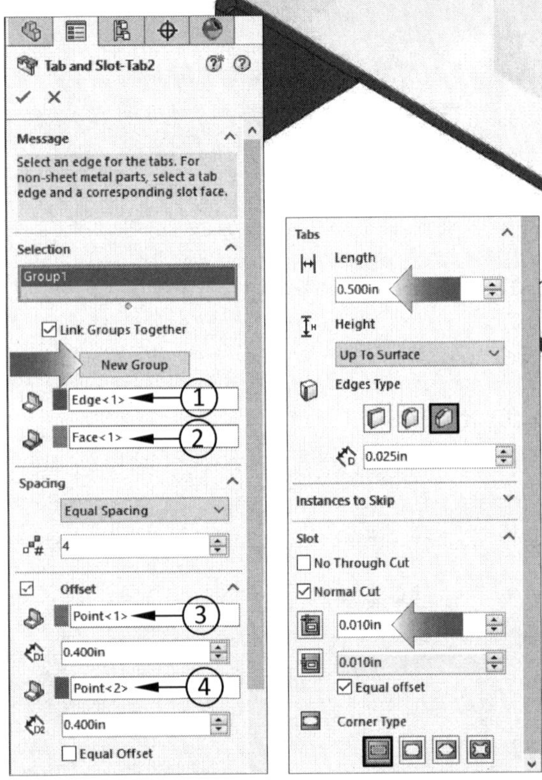

For Spacing, Select: **Equal Spacing - 4**

For Offset Tab Start, select the **vertex** as indicated with balloon 3.

For Offset Tab End, select the **vertex** labeled with balloon 4.

For Tab Length, enter **.500in**. and select **Up to Next** for Tab Height.

For Edges Type, click **Chamfer Edges** and enter **.025in**.

For Slot Length Offset, enter: **.010in**.

Select **Slot Sharp Corner** for Corner Type.

Click **OK**.

The Tab & Slot feature is created.

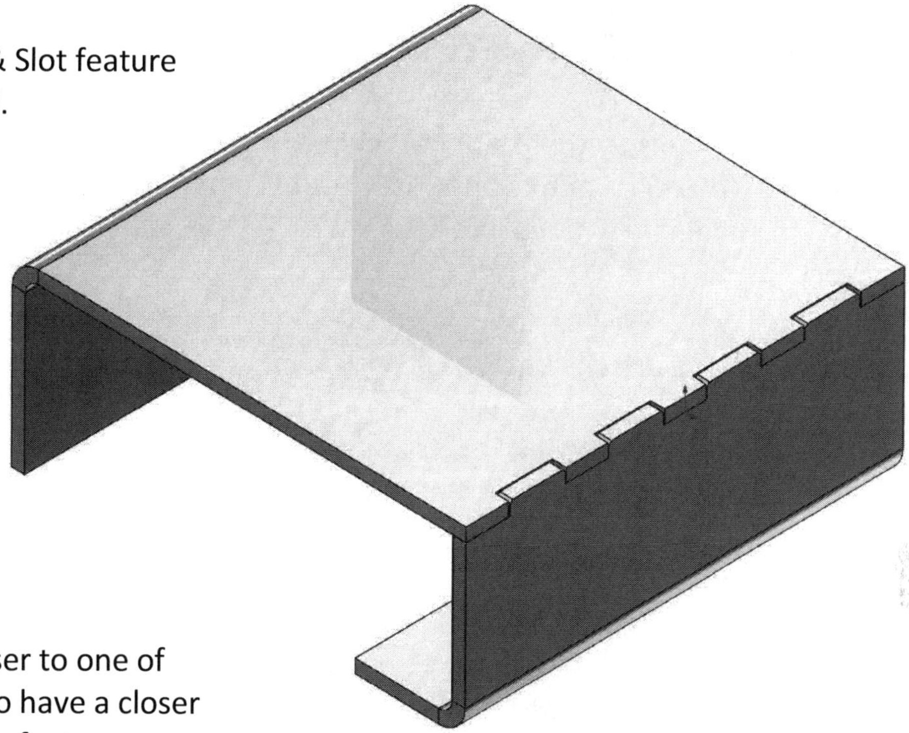

Zoom closer to one of the tabs to have a closer look at the feature.

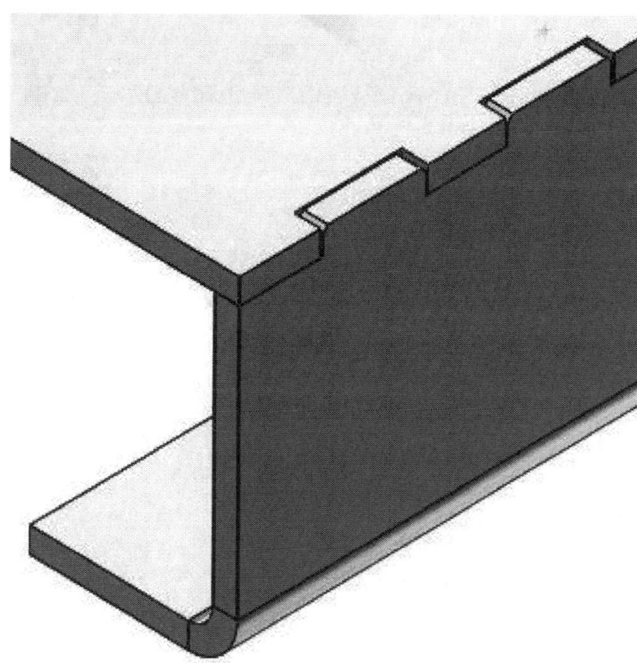

3. Saving your work:

Select **File, Save As**.

Enter: **Tab & Slot_Completed** for the file name.

Click **Save**.

Sheet Metal - Multibody Parts

The exercises in this textbook are intended to give you an opportunity to explore and to apply what you have learned from the previous chapters, at your own pace.

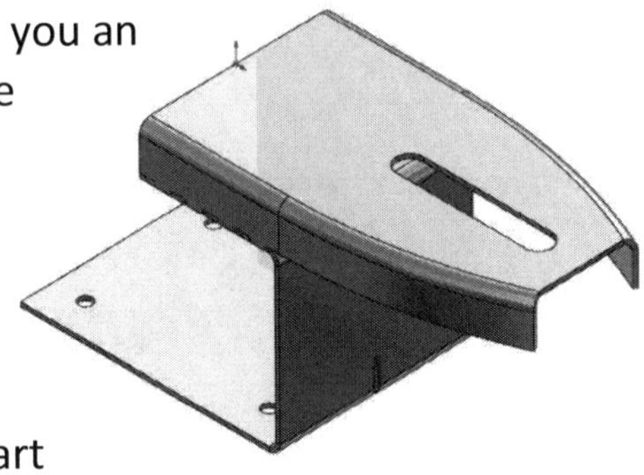

1. Opening a part document:

Browse to the Training Folder and open a part document named: **Sheet Metal_Exe2_Multibody.sldprt**

2. Creating the 1st body:

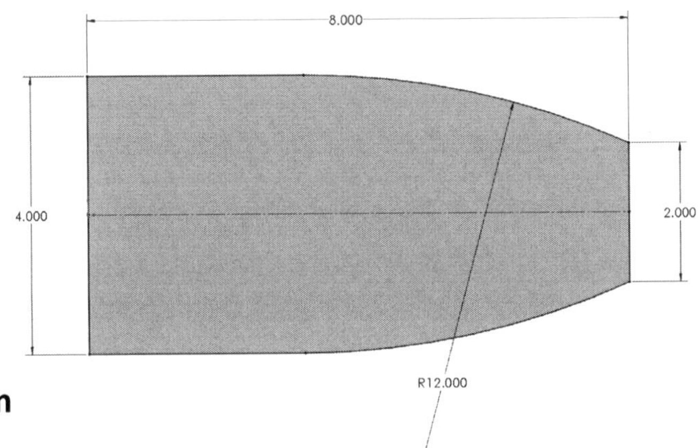

Select **Sketch1** and click **Base-Flange** on the **Sheet Metal** tab.

Enable the **Use Gauge Table** checkbox.

Select **Sample Table - Aluminum**

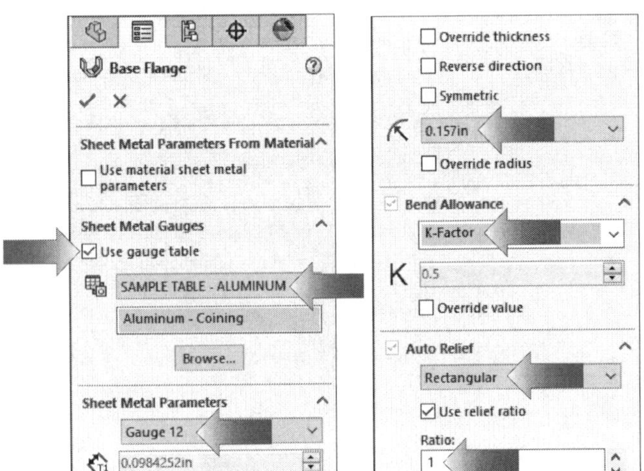

Thickness: **12 Gauge**.

Bend Radius: **.157in**.

K-Factor: **0.5**

Auto Relief: **Rectangular**

Ratio: **1**

Click **OK**.

3. Creating a curved flange:

Note: In order for the Curved Flange to work the curved edge must be selected first.

Click **Edge Flange** on the **Sheet Metal** tab.

Select the **curved edge** (1st), move the cursor downward and click the mouse to lock the direction, then select the **linear edge** (2nd).

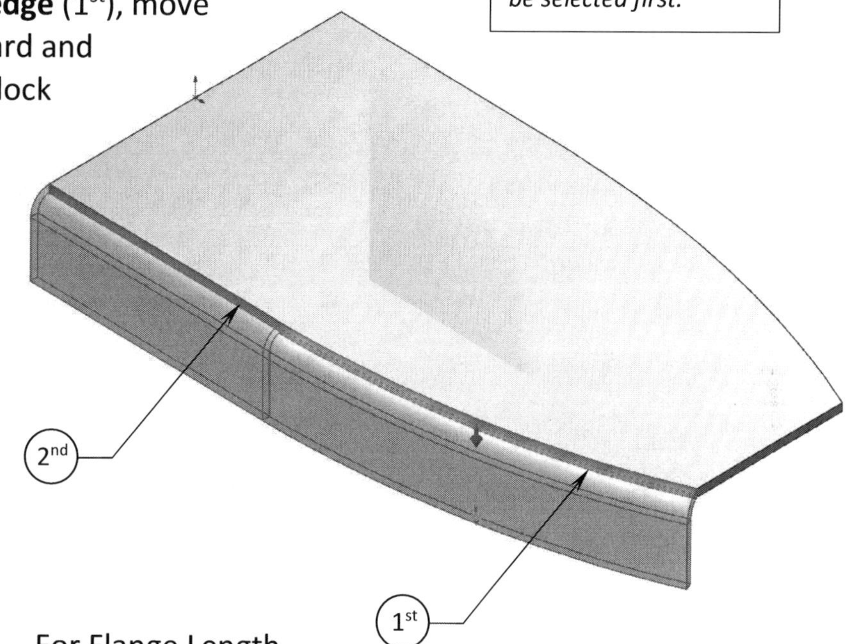

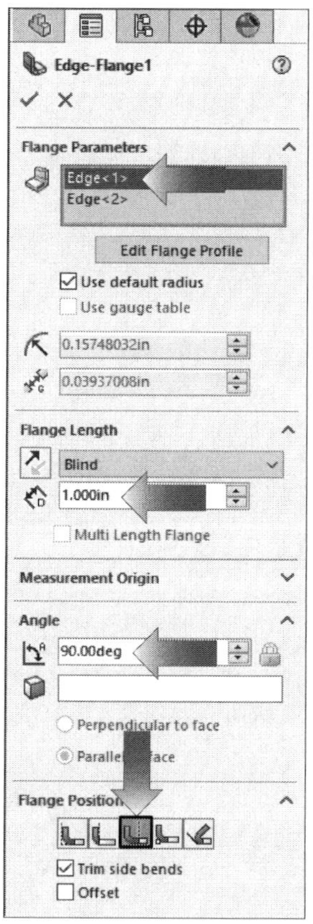

For Flange Length, select the **Blind** type and enter: **1.00in**.

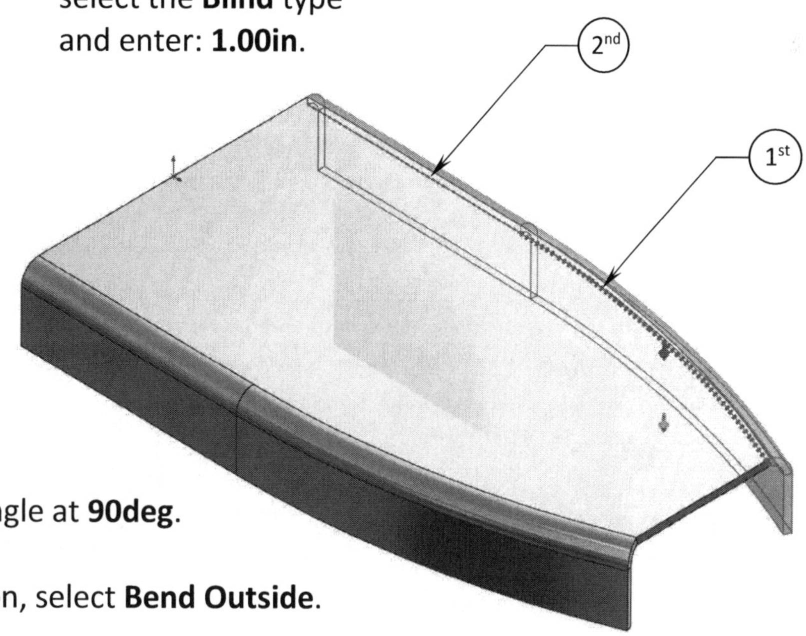

Keep the Bend Angle at **90deg**.

For Flange Position, select **Bend Outside**.

Click **OK**.

Repeat step 3 and create the same curved flange on the opposite side.

4. Creating the 2nd body:

Select the Front plane and open a **new sketch**.

Sketch 3 lines and add the relations and dimensions needed to fully define the sketch.

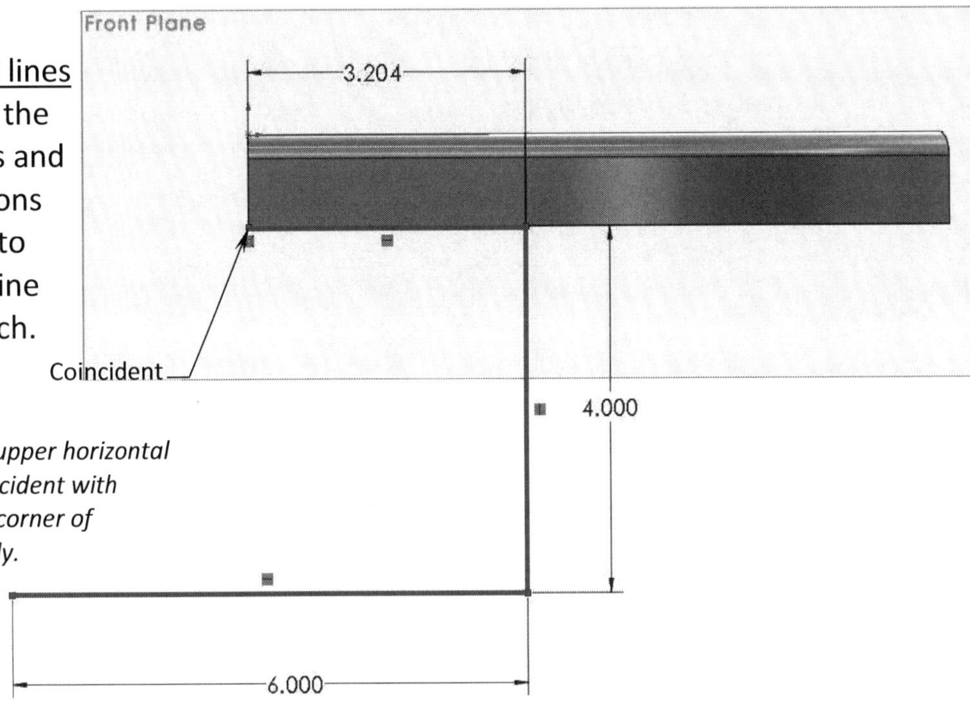

Note: the upper horizontal line is coincident with the lower corner of the 1st body.

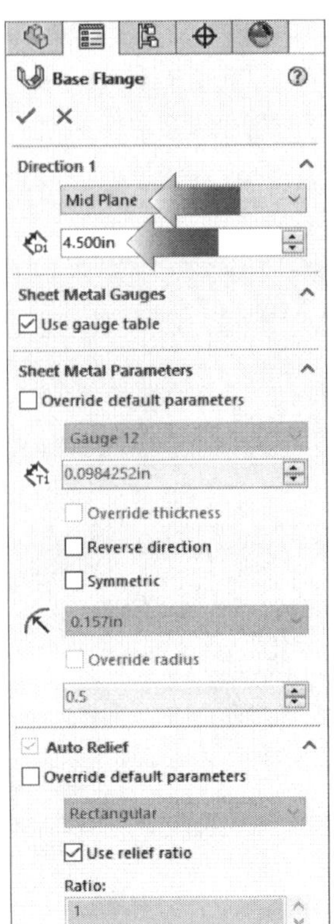

Switch to the **Sheet Metal** tab and click **Base Flange**.

For Direction 1, select the **Mid Plane** type.

For Depth, enter **4.500in**.

Enable the **Use Gauge Table** checkbox.

Keep all other parameters at their defaults.

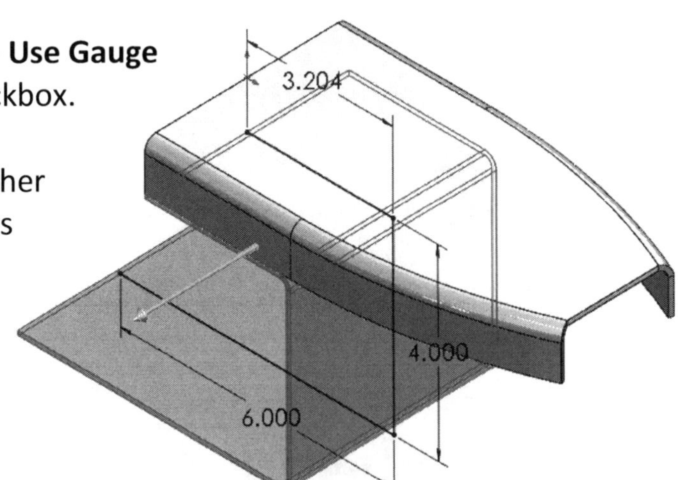

Click **OK**.

5. Adding the Tab & Slot feature:

Click **Tab and Slot** on the **Sheet Metal** tab.

For Selection of Group 1, select the **edge** as indicated.

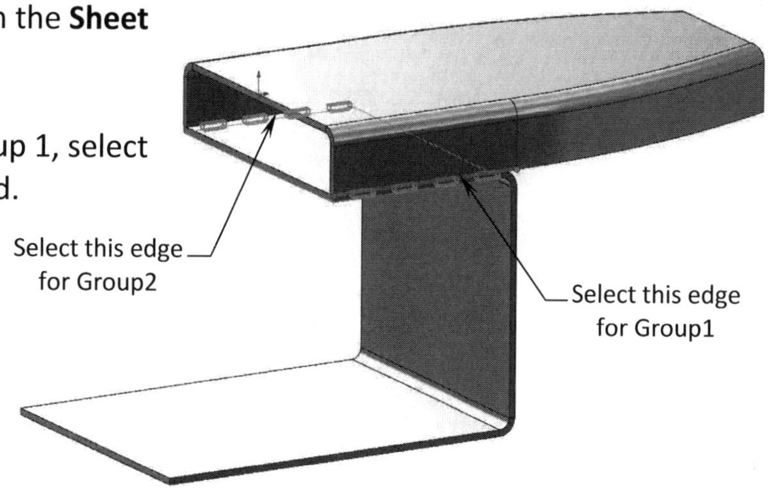

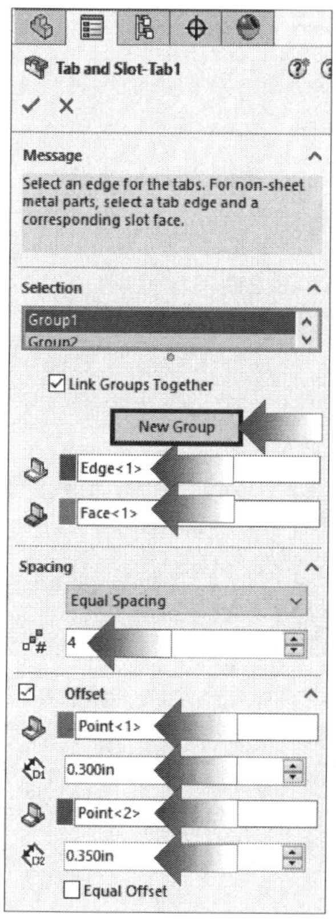

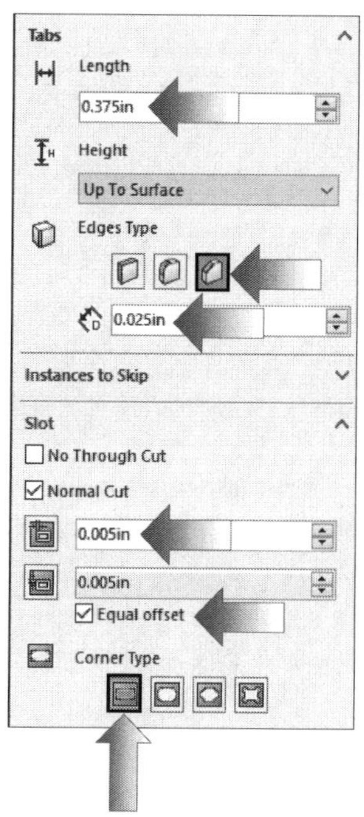

Enable **Link Groups Together** box.

Click the **New Group** button and select the **same edge** but on the opposite side.

For Spacing, enter **4**.

For Offset 1, enter: **.300in**.

For Offset 2, enter **.350in**.

For Tab Length, enter: **.375in**.

For Tab Height, select: **Up To Surface**.

Enable **Normal Cut** under the Slot section.

For Edges Type, click **Chamfer** and enter **.025in**.

For Slot Length and Width, enter **.005in**.

For Corner Type, select **Slot Sharp Corner**.

Click **OK**.

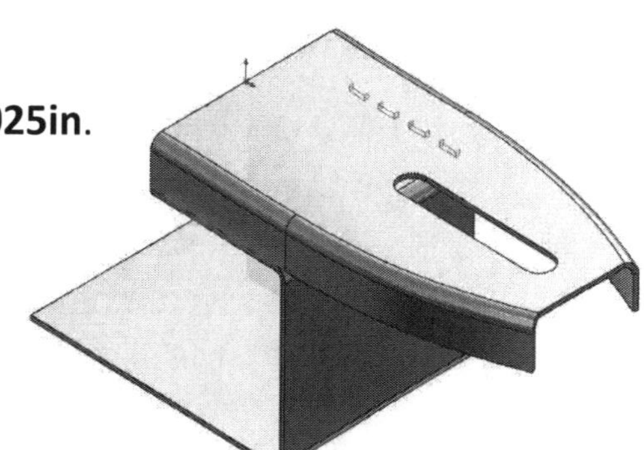

6. Adding the 5/16" holes:

Switch to the **Features** tab and click **Hole Wizard**.

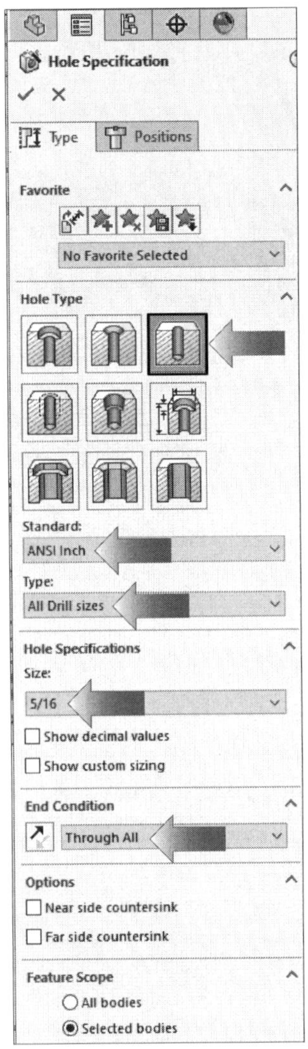

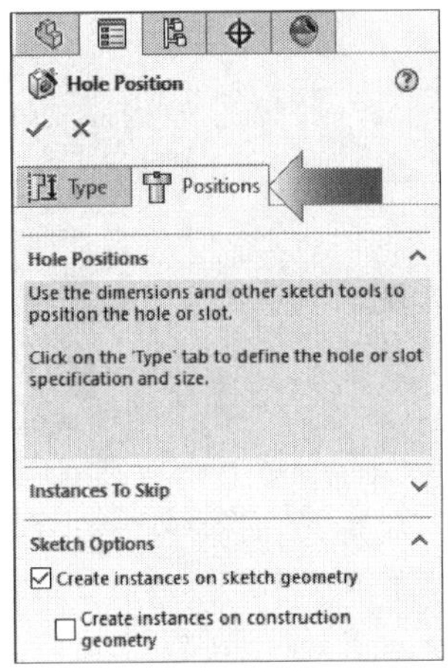

Select / set the following:

Simple Hole	**ANSI Inch**
All Drill Sizes	**5/16"**
Through All	**Selected Body**

Click the **Position** tab and select the **face** as noted below to rotate the view normal to you.

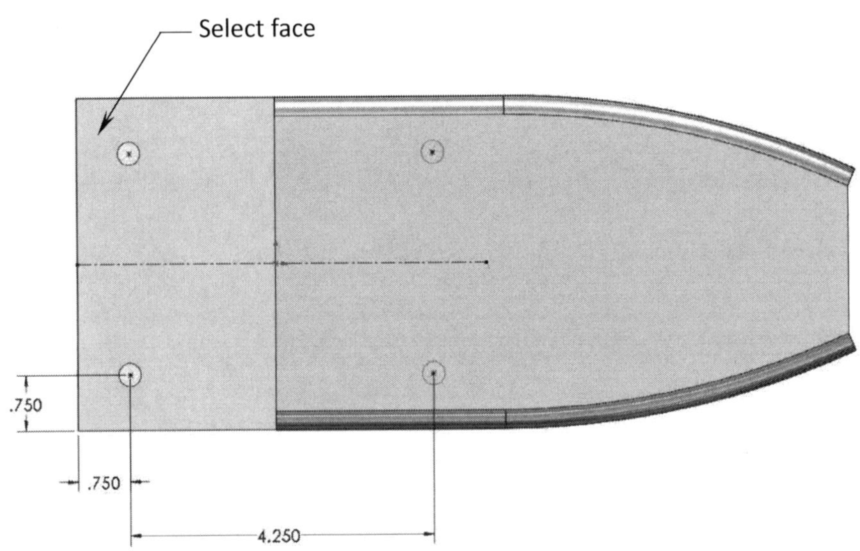

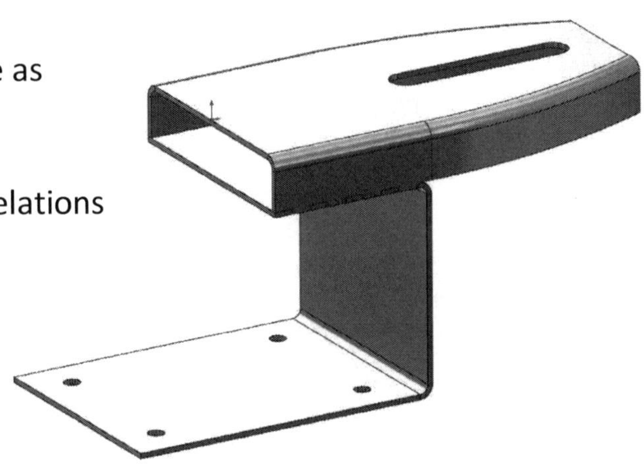

Place **4 points** (holes) on the face as shown in the image above.

Add the vertical and horizontal relations to align the holes.

Add the location dimensions to fully define the sketch.

Click **OK**.

7. Adding the lower gusset:

Click **Gusset** on the **Sheet Metal** tab.

For Position, select the **2 faces** as indicated below.

For Gusset Location, right-click the <u>lower edge</u> of the bend radius and pick: **Select Midpoint**.

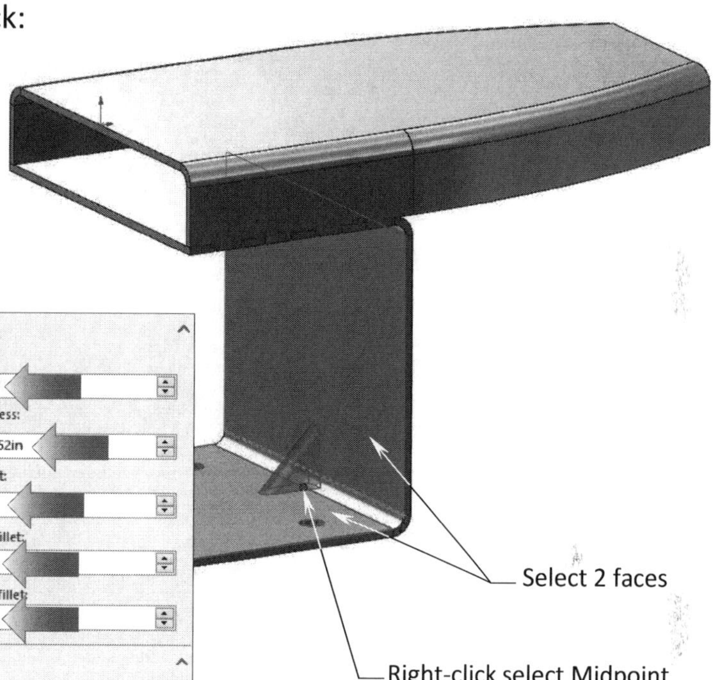

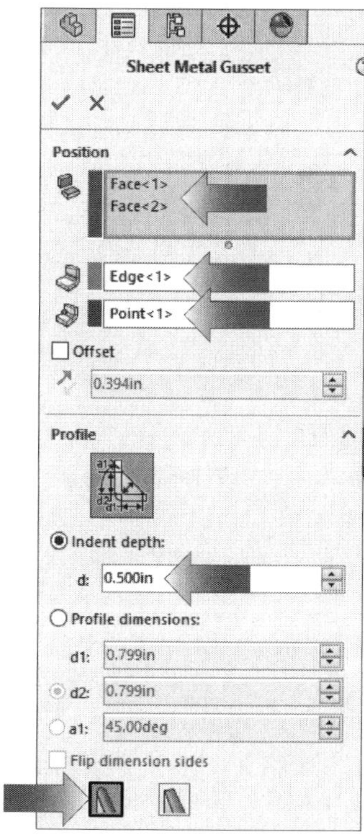

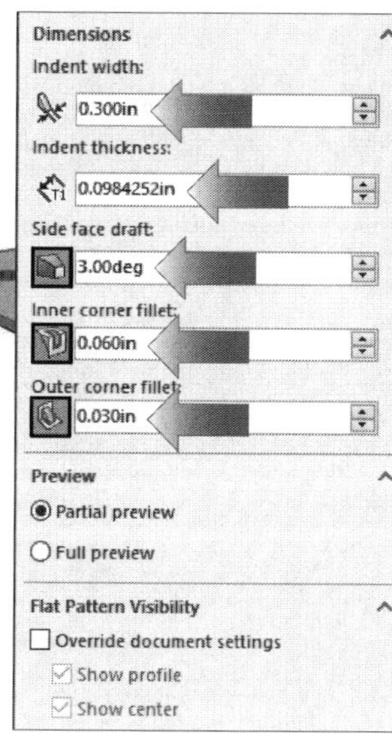

For Indent Depth, enter **.500in.**

Select the **Rounded Gusset** button.

For Indent Width, enter **.300in.**

For Indent Thickness, enter **.098in.**

Enable **Side Face Draft** and enter **3.00deg.**

Inner Corner Fillet: **.060in.**

Outer Corner Fillet: **.030in.**

Click **OK.**

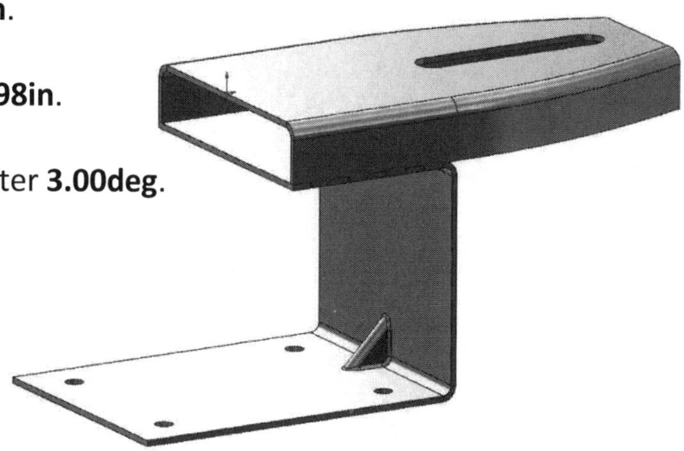

8. Adding the upper gusset:

Rotate the model to see the inside of the upper area, as shown in the image below.

Click **Gusset** on the **Sheet Metal** tab.

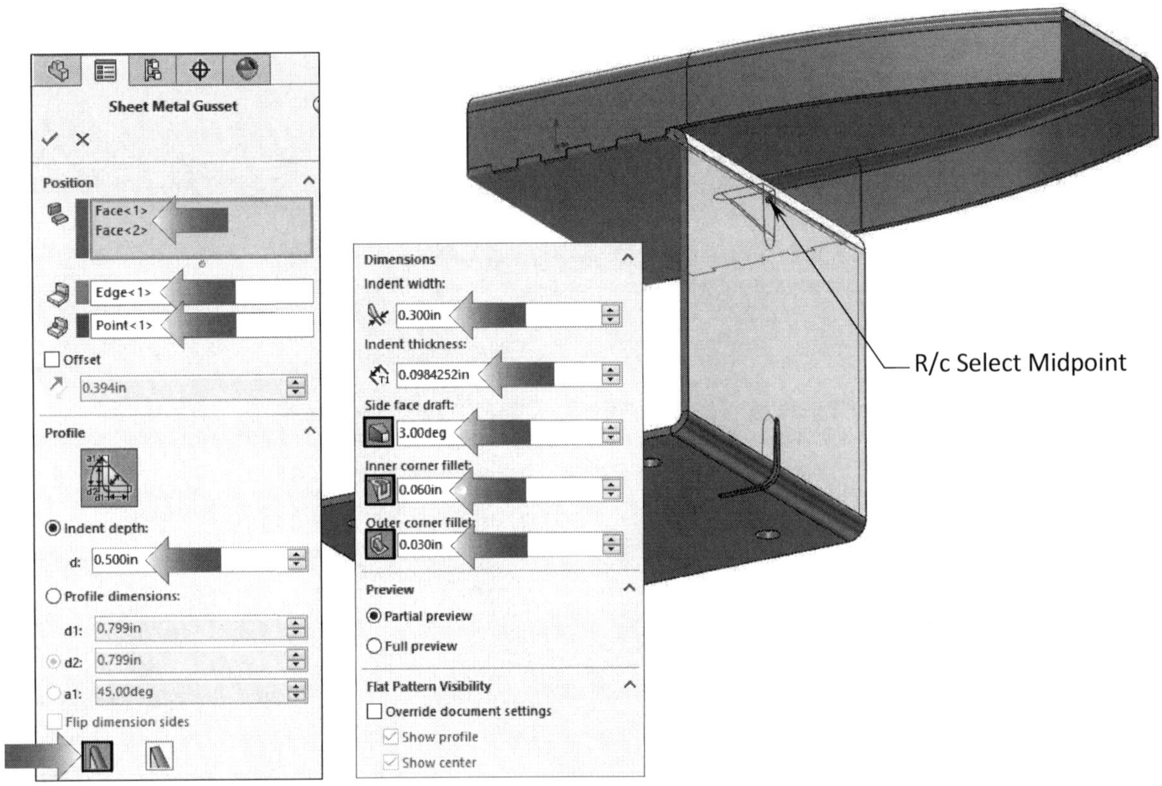

For Gusset Position, select the **2 faces** of the 2nd body as shown in the image below.

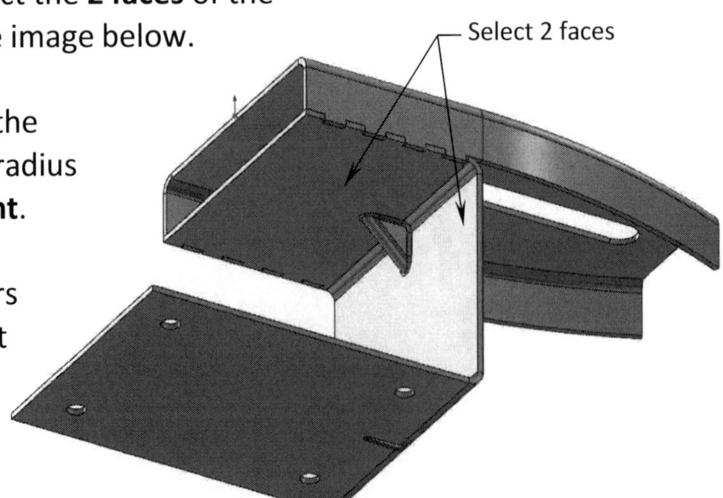

For Location, right-click the <u>lower edge</u> of the bend radius and pick: **Select Midpoint**.

Use the same parameters from the previous gusset to make the 2 gussets identical to each other.

Click **OK**.

9. Adding a slot to the 1st body:

Select the top surface of the 1st body and open a **new sketch**.

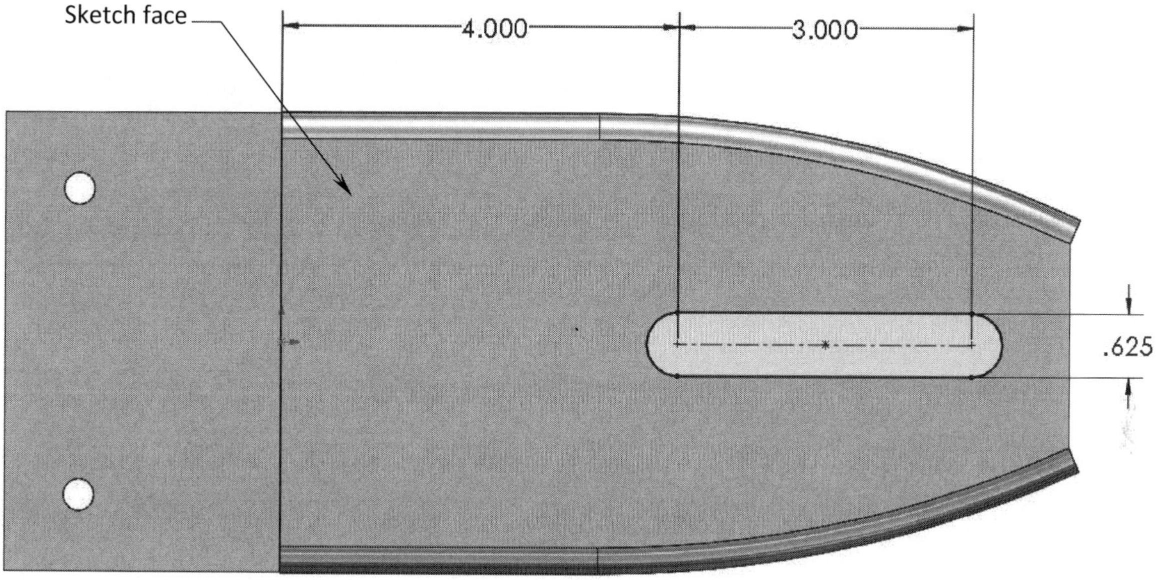

Sketch the **slot profile** and add the dimensions shown above to fully define the sketch.

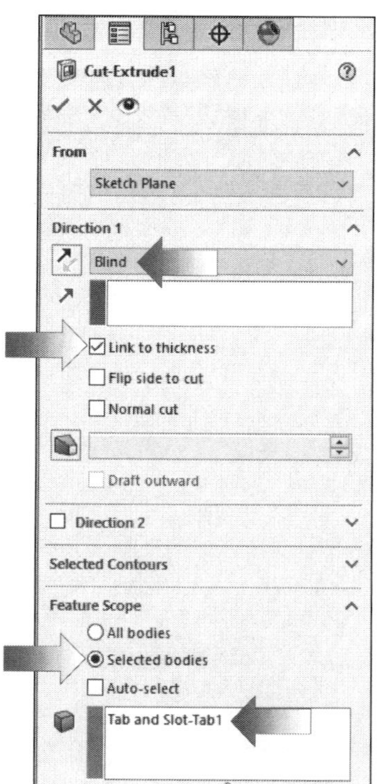

Switch to the **Sheet Metal** tab and click **Extruded Cut**. Use the default **Blind** type and click **Link To Thickness**.

Click **Selected Bodies** and select the **1st body** from the graphics to cut.

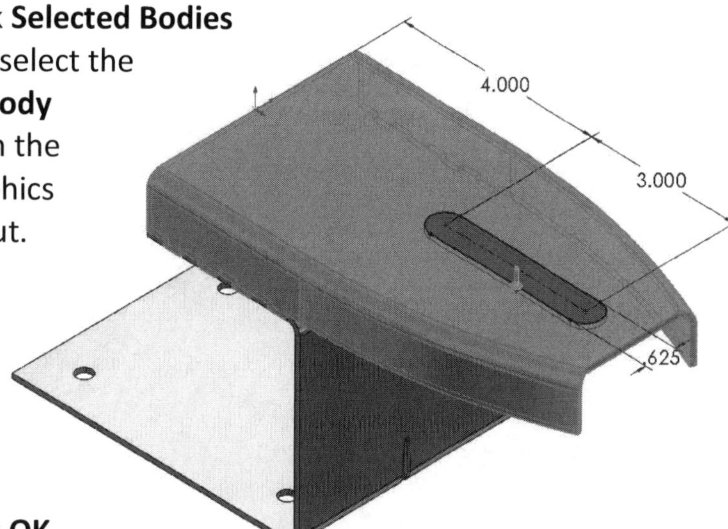

Click **OK**.

10. Toggling the Flat Display:

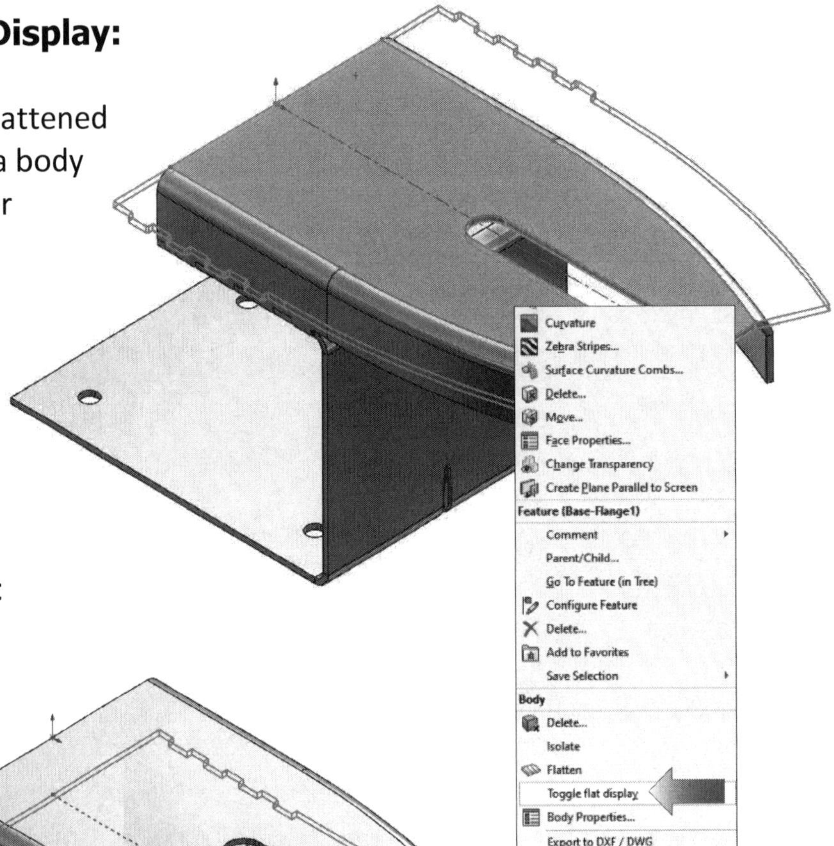

Only 1 body can be flattened at a time, and while a body is flattened, the other bodies are hidden.

To work around the hidden issues, let us try the option called: **Toggle Flat Display**.

Right-click on the **1st body** and select: **Toggle Flat Display**.

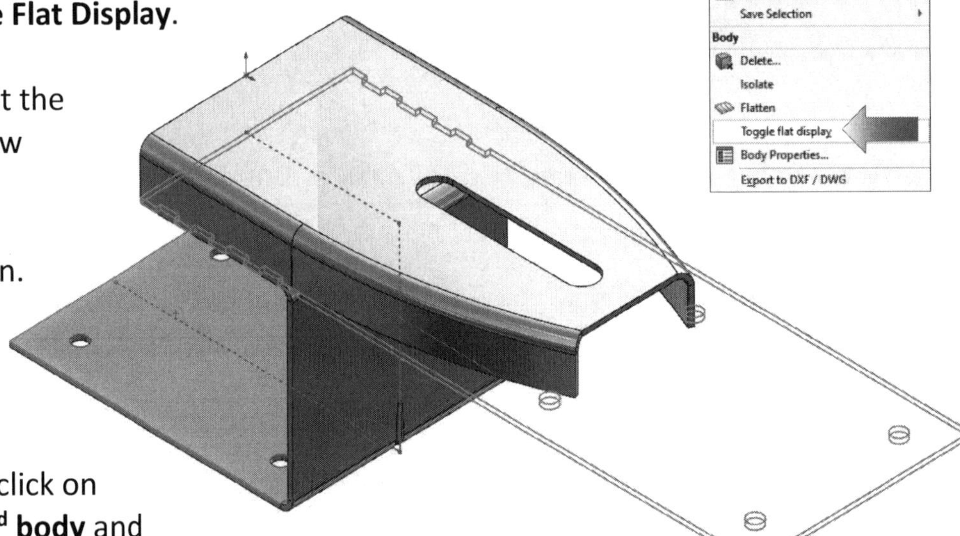

Inspect the preview of the flat pattern.

Right-click on the 2nd **body** and select: **Toggle Flat Display**. Inspect the flat pattern that is superimposed over the fold pattern.

11. Saving your work:

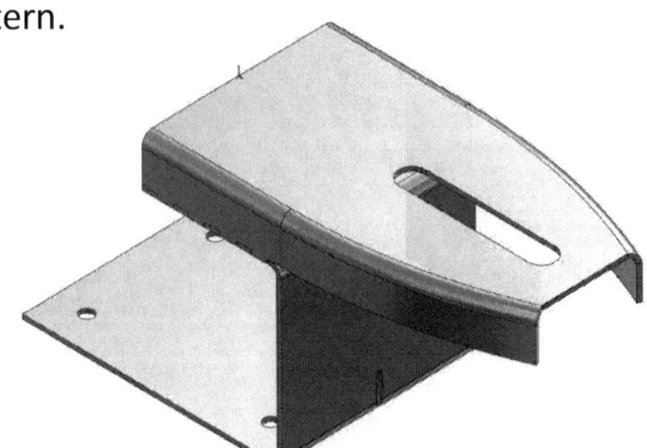

Select **File, Save As**.

Enter **Tab-Slot & Multibody_ Completed** for the file name.

Click **Save**.

Lesson 8: Sheet Metal Lofted Bends & Swept Flanges

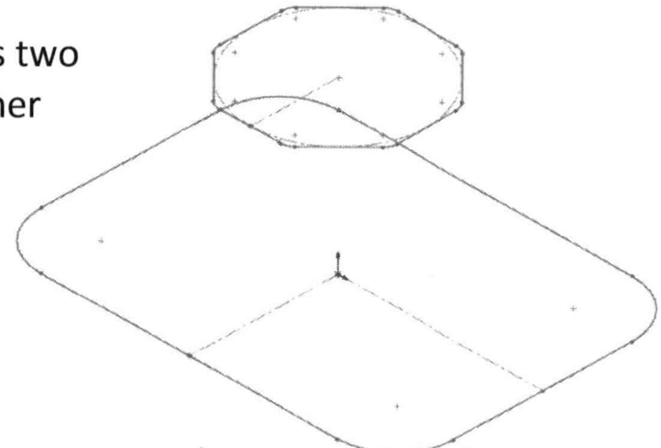

In SOLIDWORKS the Lofted bend tool uses two open-profile sketches to connect each other in a loft. Each profile should have a small gap in order for the sheet metal part to be flattened. The Base-Flange feature is not used with the Lofted Bend feature.

1. Opening a part document:

Browse to the Training Folder and open a part document named:
Sheet Metal Lofted Bends.sldprt

2. Creating a Lofted Bend feature:

Switch to the **Sheet Metal** tab and click **Lofted Bends** .

For Manufacturing Method, select the **Bent** option.

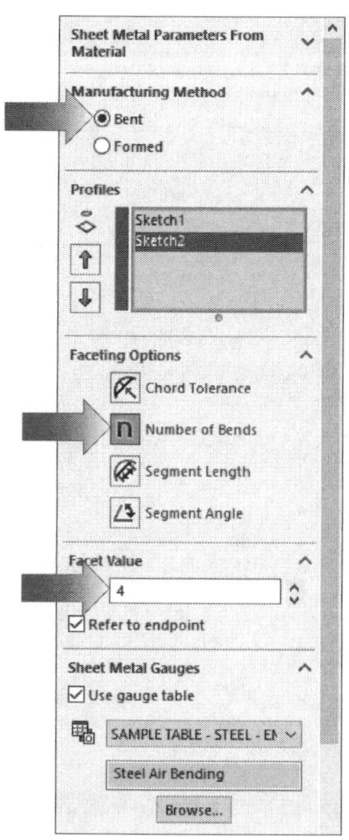

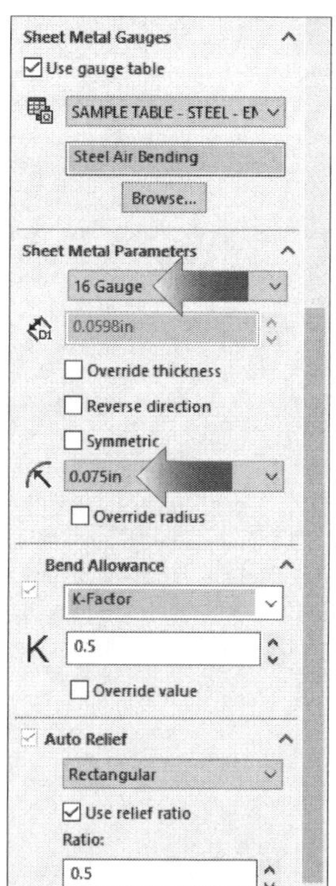

Select the **2 sketch profiles**.

Enter/select the following:
Number of Bends Facet Value: **4.**
Refer to Endpoint checked
Use Gauge Table – Steel – 16 Gauge
Bend Radius: **.075in**. Rectangular: **0.5**
K-Factor: **0.5**

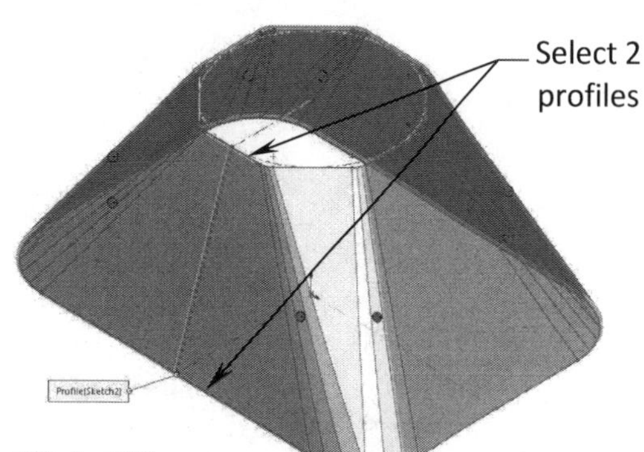

Click **OK**.

The Bent method creates a realistic transition between two profiles to facilitate instructions for press brake manufacturing.

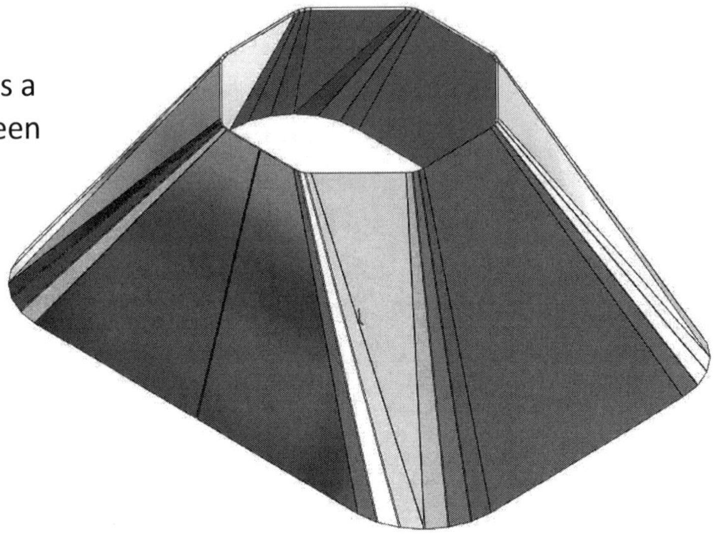

3. Viewing the Flat Pattern:

Click **Flatten** on the **Sheet Metal** tab.

The bend lines are visible in the flat pattern.
(The image below is shown in black & white to be able to see the bend lines more clearly.)

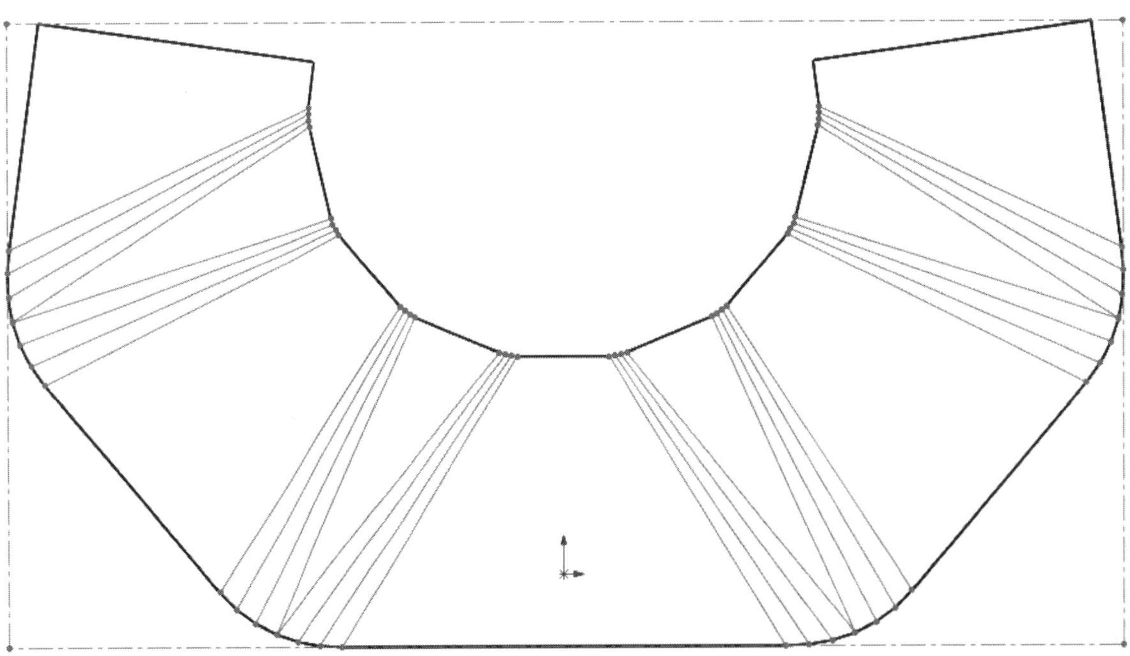

4. Creating a Formed Lofted Bend feature:

The last step was done using the manufacturing method called **Bent**. Let us take a look at the 2nd option call **Formed** at this time.

Delete the **Sheet Metal** feature as well as the **Lofted Bend1** feature.

Your screen should only show the 2 sketched profiles.

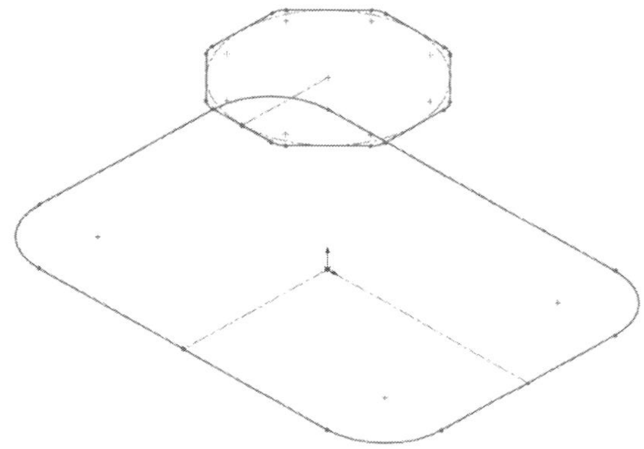

Click **Lofted Bends** again.

For Manufacturing Method, click the **Formed** option.

For Profiles, select the **2 sketch profiles** by clicking on the common sides.

For Thickness, enter: **.0598in**.

Click **OK**.

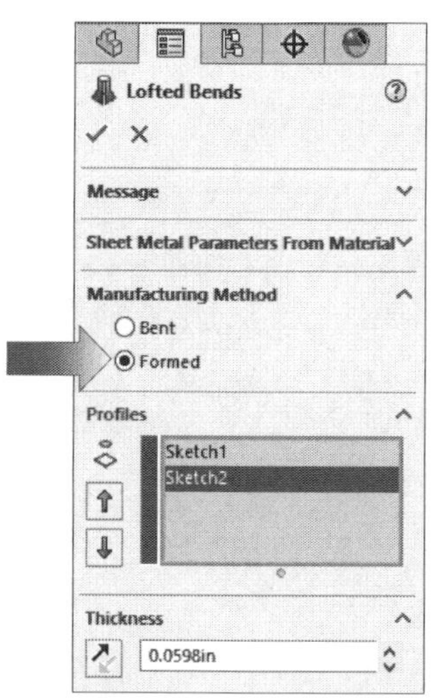

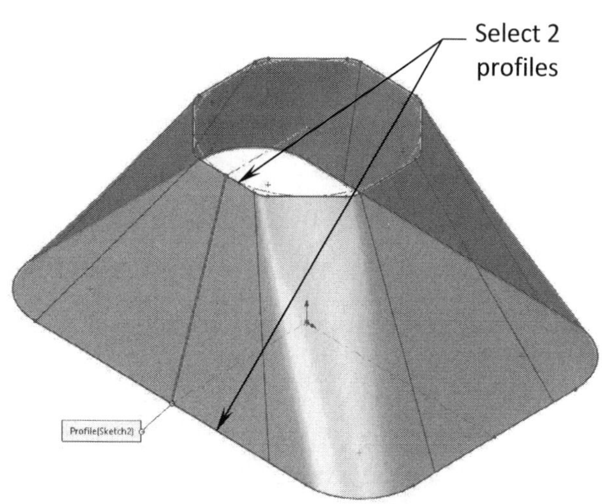

The Form method creates a smooth transition between the profiles, but requires a set of dies to form the shape, and can cost significantly more than the bent method.

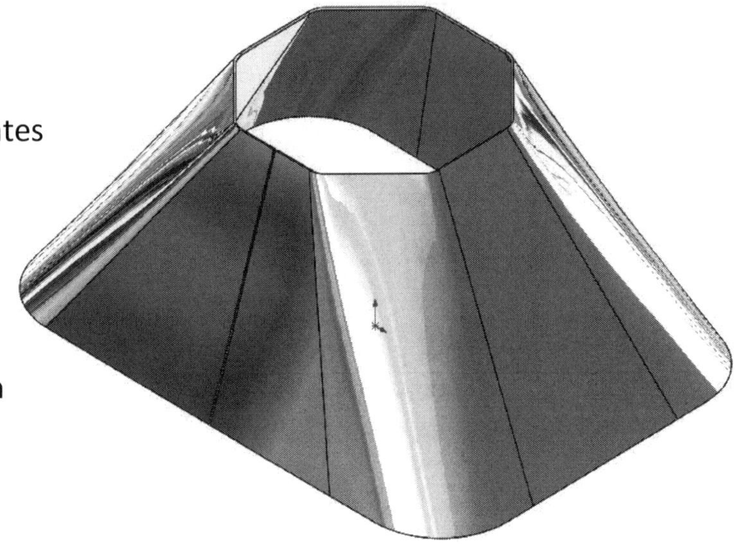

5. Viewing the Flat Pattern:

Click **Flatten** on the **Sheet Metal** tab.

(The view below was rotated and changed to black & white for clarity.)

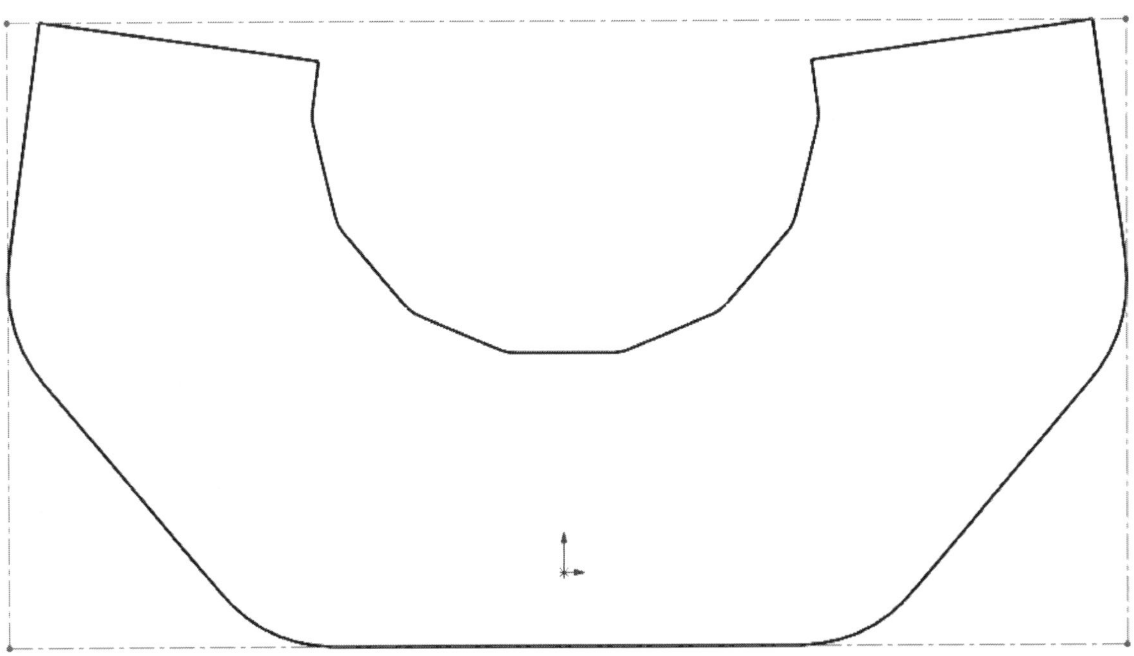

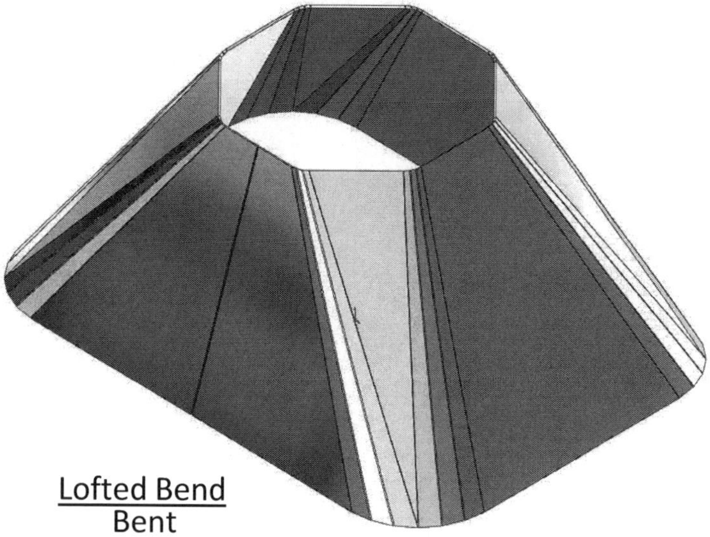
Lofted Bend
Bent

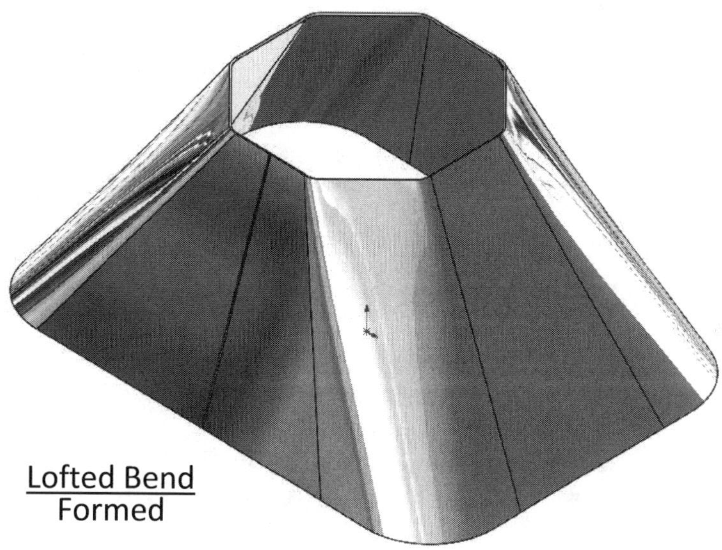
Lofted Bend
Formed

6. Saving your work:

Select **File, Save As**.

Enter: **Lofted Bends_Completed** for the file name.

Click **Save**.

Sheet Metal Swept Flanges

The sheet metal Swept Flange tool is similar to the Sweep tool; a profile and path are needed to create the flange.

The profile must be an open-sketch in order for the flange to be flattened. The path can be a sketch or a series of existing model edges.

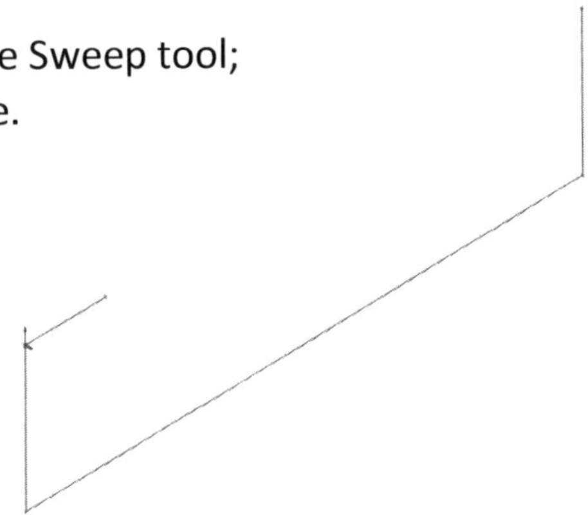

1. Opening a part document:

Browse to the Training Folder and open a part document named:
Sheet Metal Swept Flanges.sldprt

2. Creating a Swept Flange feature:

Switch to the **Sheet Metal** tab and click **Swept Flange** .

For Profile select **Sketch2** either from the graphics area or from the Feature-Manager tree.

For Path, select **Sketch1**.

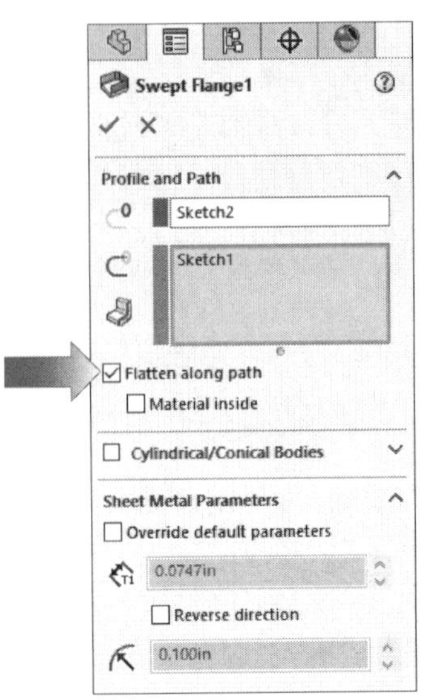

Enable the checkbox:
Flatten Along Path.

Keep the Thickness and Bend Radius at their default values.

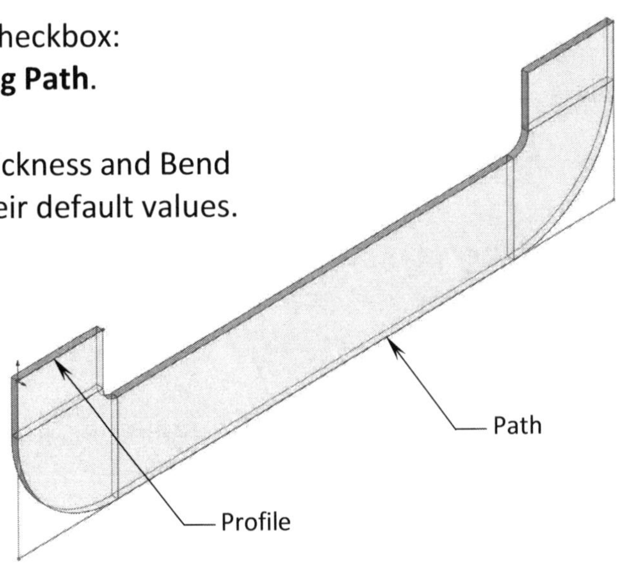

Click **OK**.

3. Creating the rolled hem:

The Hem tool adds a hem feature to the sheet metal part at a selected edge or edges. The selected edge must be linear.

Click **Hem** .

For Edges, select the **2 edges** as indicated in the image below.

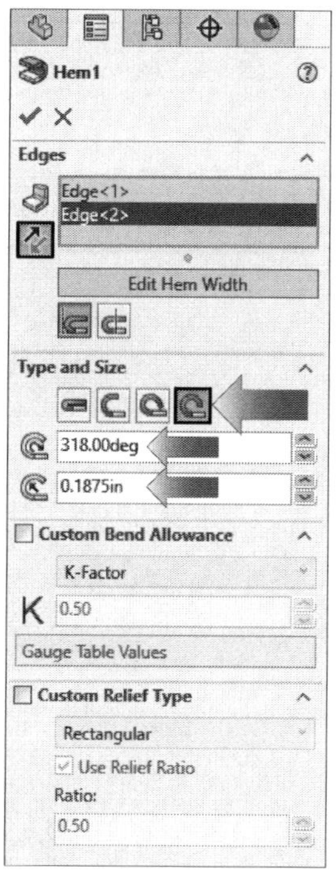

Click **Reverse** if needed to roll inwards.

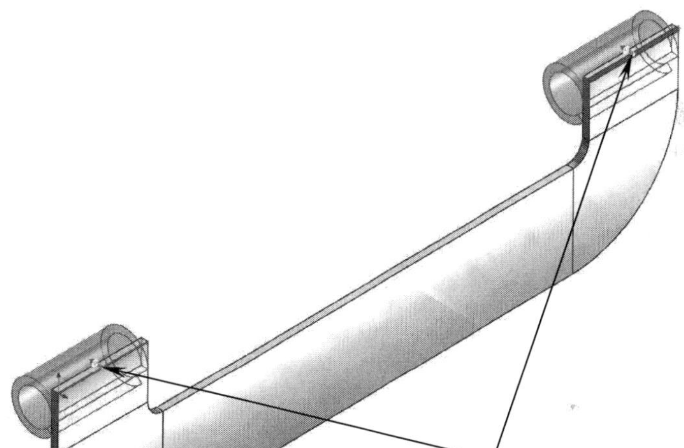

For Type and Size, select **Rolled**.

For Angle, enter: **318.00deg**.

For Radius, enter: **.1875in**.

Keep all other parameters at their default values.

Click **OK**.

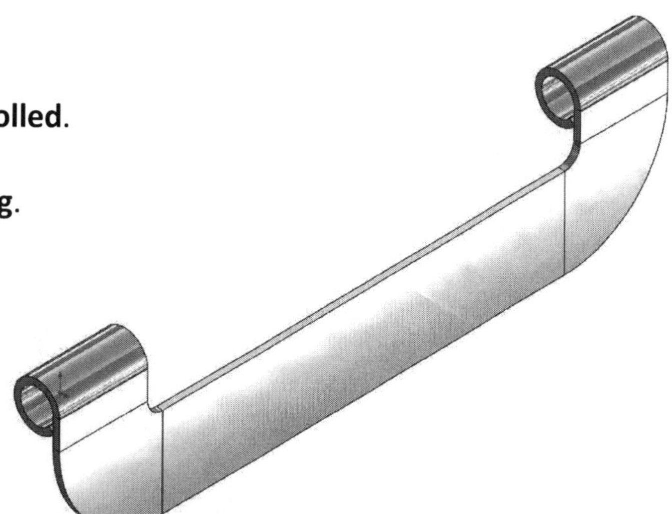

4. Adding the 1st jog:

Select the face as noted and open a **new sketch**.

Sketch a vertical **Line** and add the location dimension.

Switch to the **Sheet Metal** tab and click **Jog**.

For Fixed Face, select the lower left side of the part as indicated.

For Jog Offset, select **Blind** and enter **.750in**.

For Dimension Position, click: **Outside Offset**.

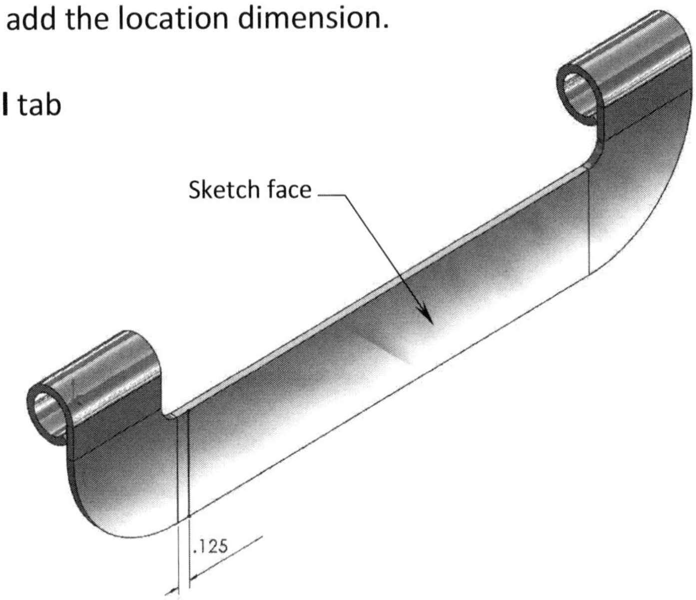

Clear the **Fixed Projected Length** checkbox.

For Jog Position, click **Bend Centerline**.

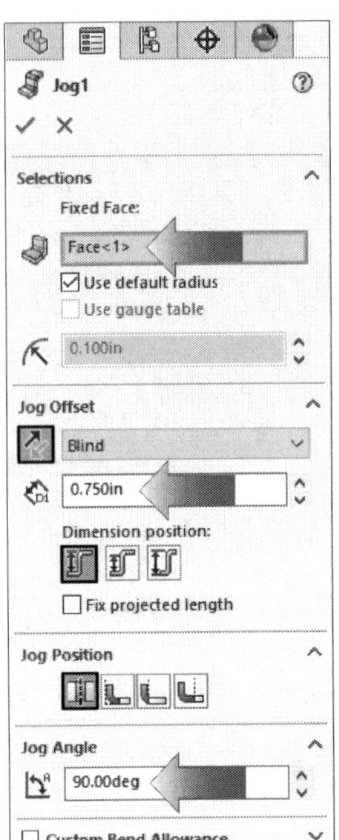

For Jog Angle, enter **90.00deg**.

Keep all other parameters at their defaults.

Click **OK**.

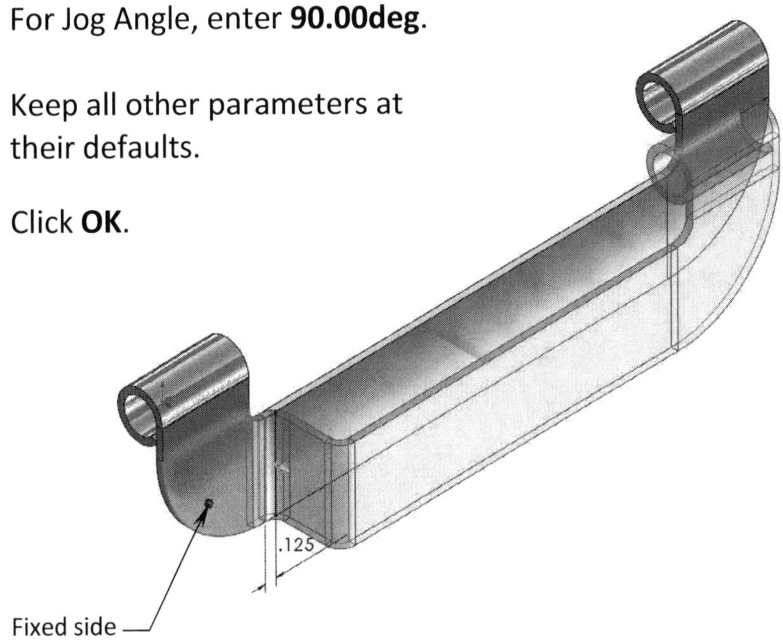

5. Adding the 2nd jog:

Select the face as noted and open a **new sketch**.

Sketch a vertical **Line** and add the location dimension.

Switch to the **Sheet Metal** tab and click **Jog**.

For Fixed Face, select the lower left side of the part as indicated.

For Jog Offset, select **Blind** and enter **.750in**. (Click Reverse if needed to jog inwards.)

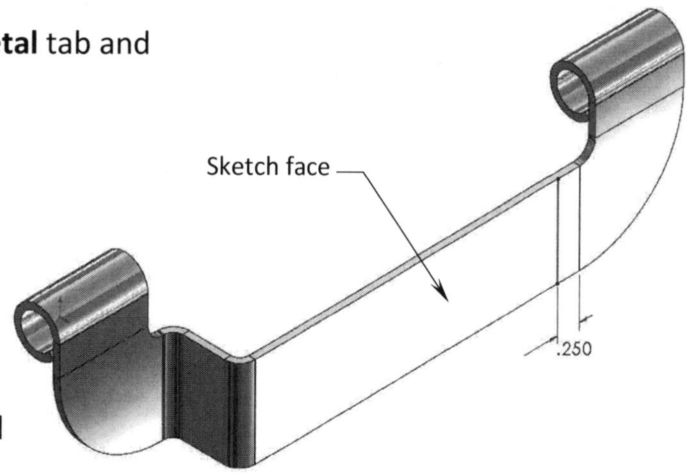

For Dimension Position, click: **Outside Offset**.

Clear the **Fixed Projected Length** checkbox.

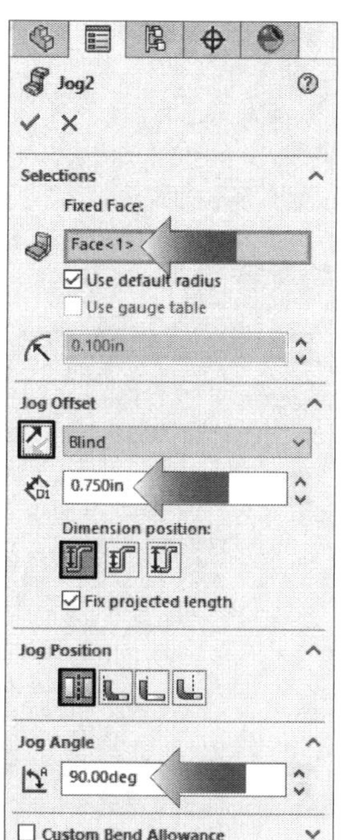

For Jog Position, click **Bend Centerline**.

For Jog Angle, enter **90.00deg**.

Keep all other parameters at their defaults.

Click **OK**.

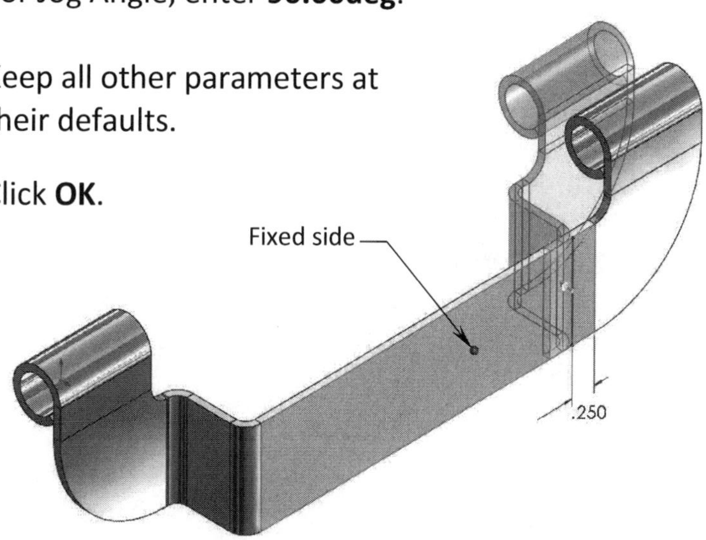

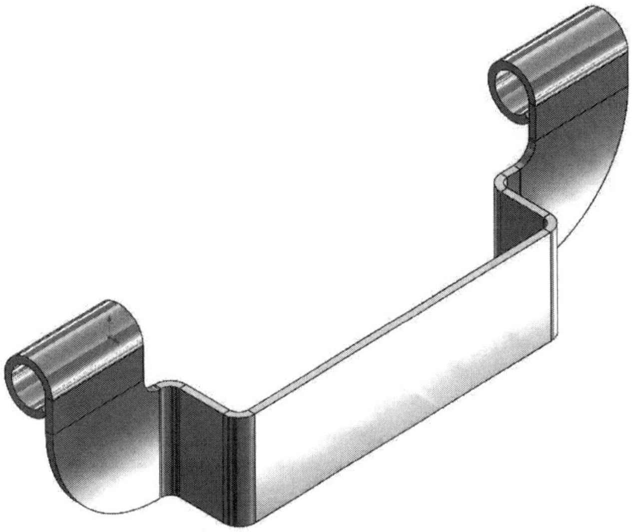

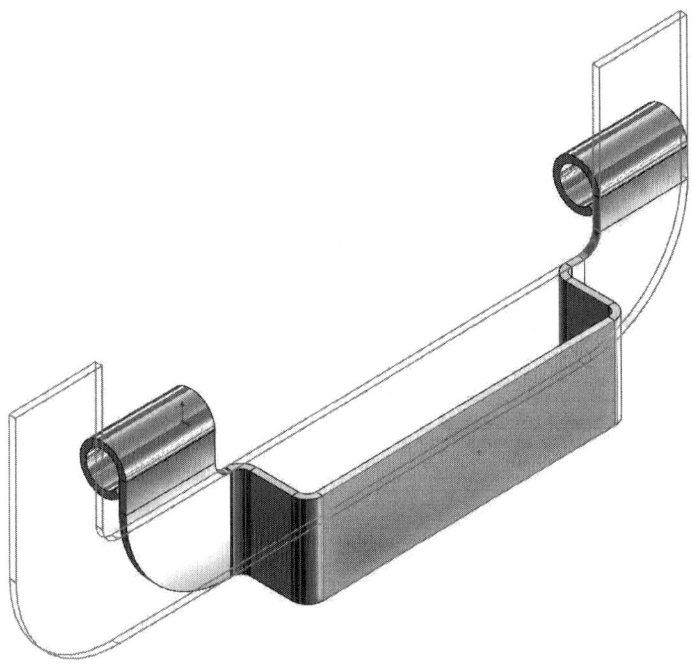

6. Saving your work:

Select **File, Save As**.

Enter: **Swept Flanges_Completed** for the file name.

Click **Save**.

4 Common Types of Sheet Metal Hems

Common types of sheet metal hems include rolled hems, open hems, teardrop hems, closed hems, and double hems. These hems serve various purposes in sheet metal fabrication, providing reinforcement, edge protection, and aesthetic finishes.

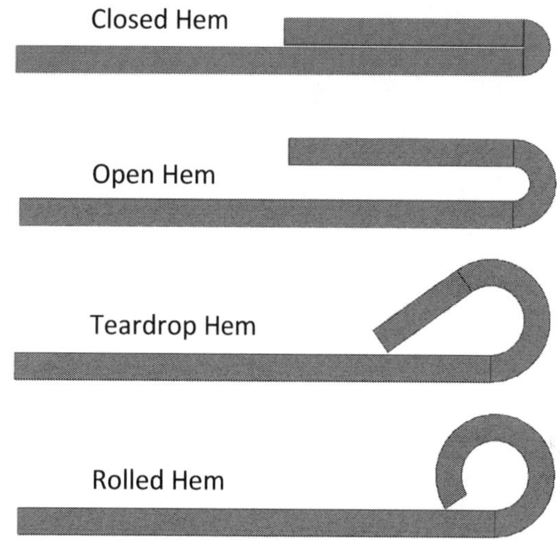

These different types of hems are often used in conjunction with each other and with other fabrication techniques like laser cutting and traditional die hemming.

This lesson will walk us through the creation of the 4 common sheet metal hems using SOLIDWORKS.

1. Opening a part document:

Browse to the Training Folder and open a part document named:
Sheet Metal Hems.sldprt

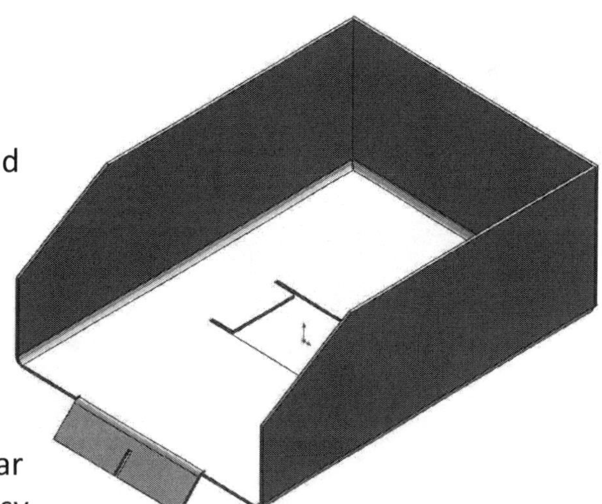

2. Creating a Closed Hem:

Closed hems are the most popular type of hem because they are easy to make; the sheet metal is simply flattened onto itself.

Most Sheet Metal shops usually do not use closed hems on aluminum parts, as this type of material is highly susceptible to cracks and fractures.

Closed hems works best with material thicknesses of .040”-.125”.

Switch to the **Sheet Metal** tab and click **Hem**.

For Edges to Hem, select 2 edges on each side for a total of **4 edges** as noted.

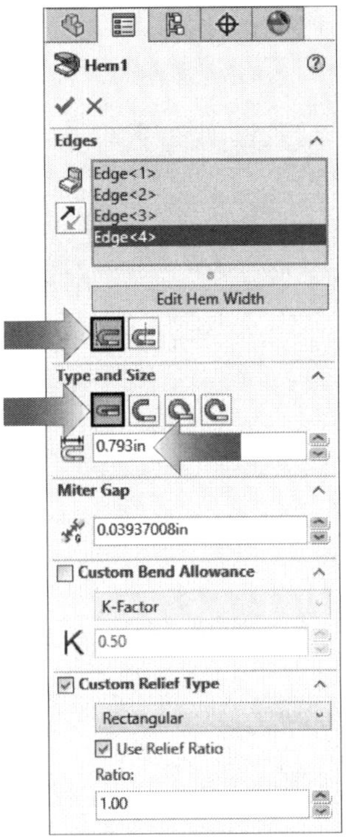

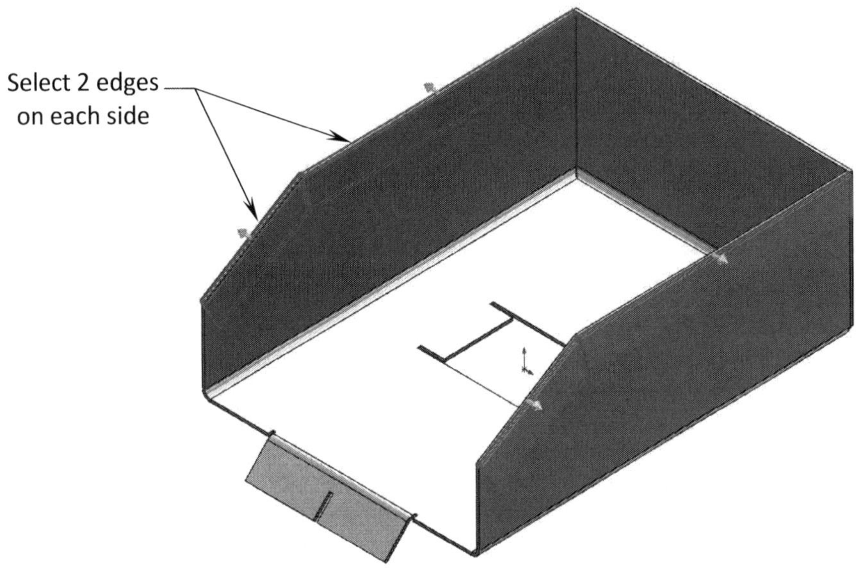

Use the default **Material Inside**.

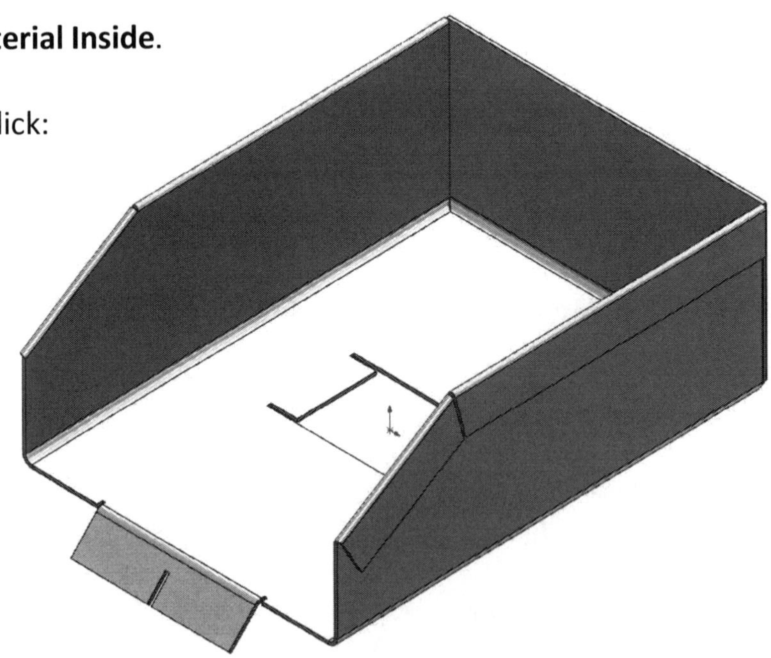

For Type and Size, click: **Closed Hem**.

For Length enter: **.703in**.

Use the default Miter Gap and K-Factor.

Select **Rectangular** Relief, **1.0** ratio.

Click **OK**.

3. Creating an Open Hem:

An open hem features a soft, curved outer edge and an air pocket in its bend. It is ideal for handles and other applications that come into contact with people.
Open hem works best with material thicknesses of .040”-.125” and a flat length that is a minimum of 4x the material thickness and the common gap sizes are 060”, .090”, .125”, .187”, and .250”.

Click the **Hem** tool again.

For Type and Size, select: **Open Hem**.

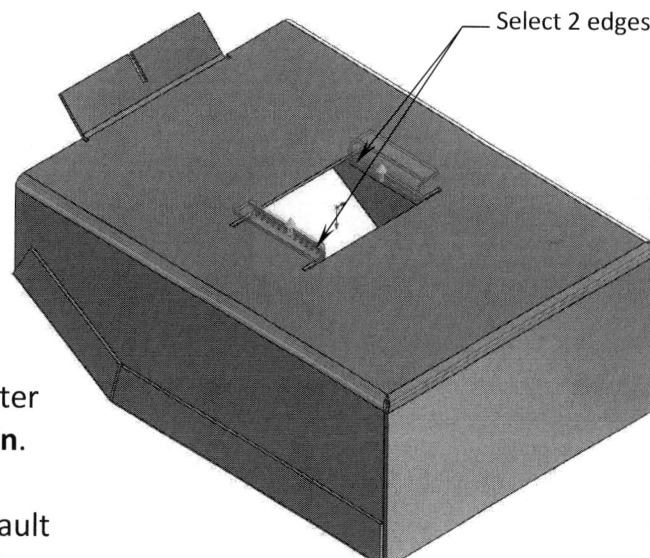

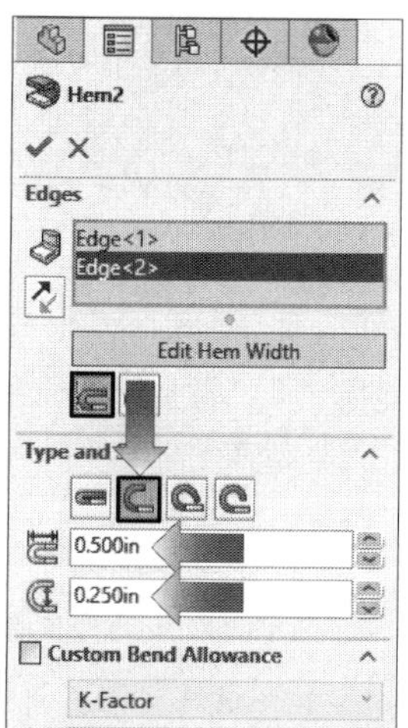

For Length enter: **.500in**.

For Gap, enter enter: **.250in**.

Use the default K-Factor value **0.50**.

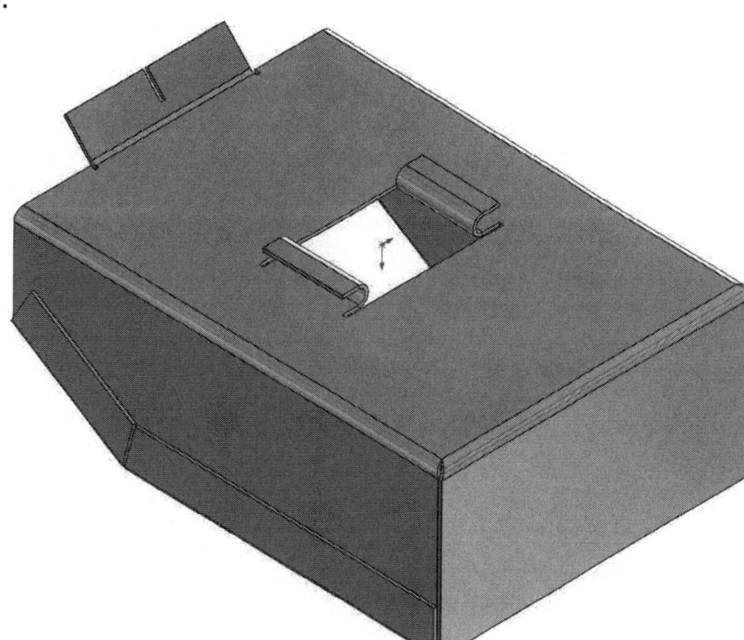

For Custom Relief, select **Rectangular** Ratio: **1.0** (1 thickness).

Click **OK.**

4. Creating a Teardrop Hem:

A tear drop hem is a flange that has been bent more than 180 degrees. Teardrop hems are used for materials that lack the flexibility required of closed hems. This type of hem is perfect for aluminum and other fragile metals.

Click the **Hem** tool on the Sheet Metal tab.

For Type and Size, select: **Teardrop**.

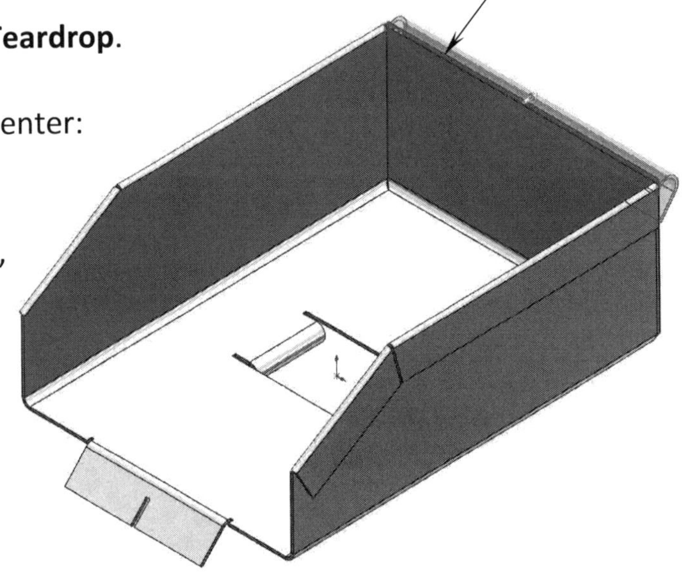

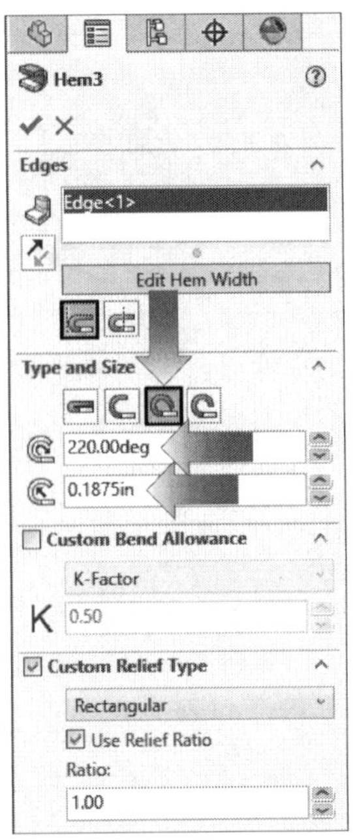

For Angle, enter: **220deg**.

For Radius, enter: **.1875in**.

Use the default K-Factor **0.50**.

For Custom Relief, use **Rectangular** Ratio: **1.0**.

Click **OK**.

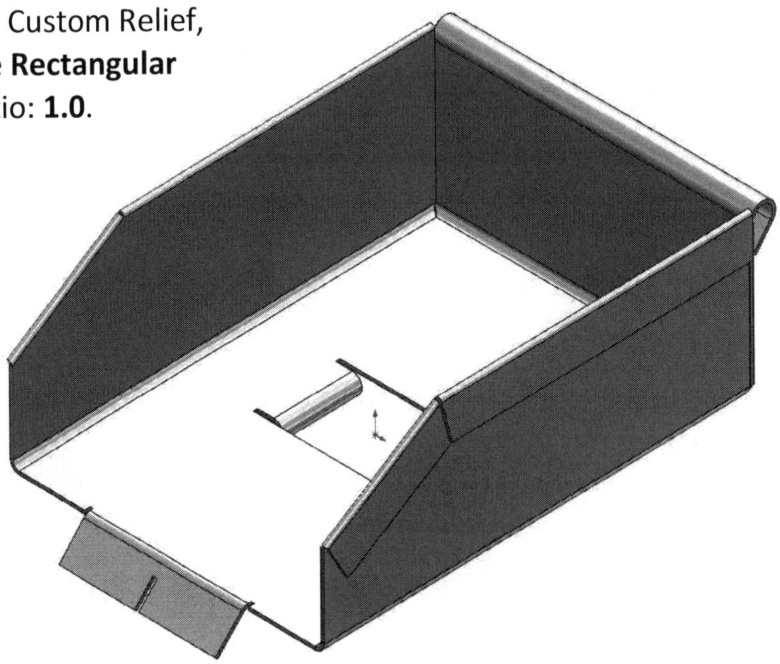

Change to different view orientations to inspect the hem results.

5. Creating a Rolled Hem:

The purpose of a rolled hem is to eliminate raw sheet metal edges from a part. This type of hem is common for door and hinges—they look nice, clean, and easy to handle.

Click the **Hem** tool once again.

For Type and Size, select **Rolled**.

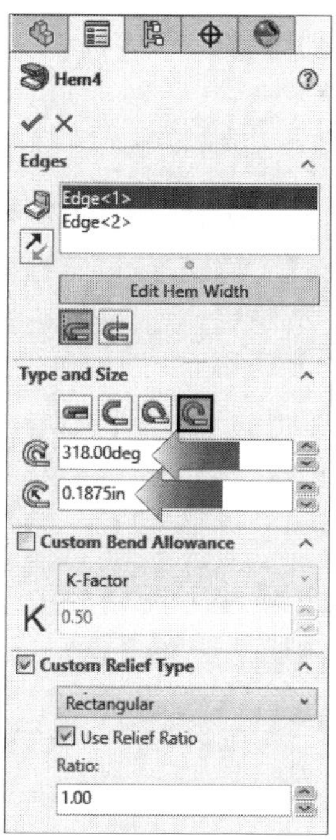

For Angle, enter: **318.00deg**.

For Radius, enter: **.1875in**.

Use the default K-Factor **0.50**.

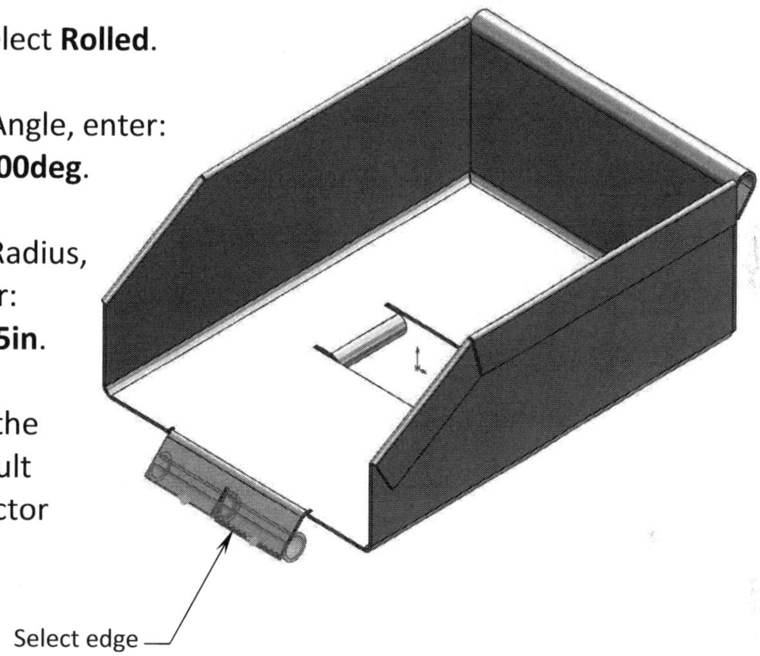

For Custom Relief, select **Rectangular**, Ratio **1.0**.

Click **OK**.

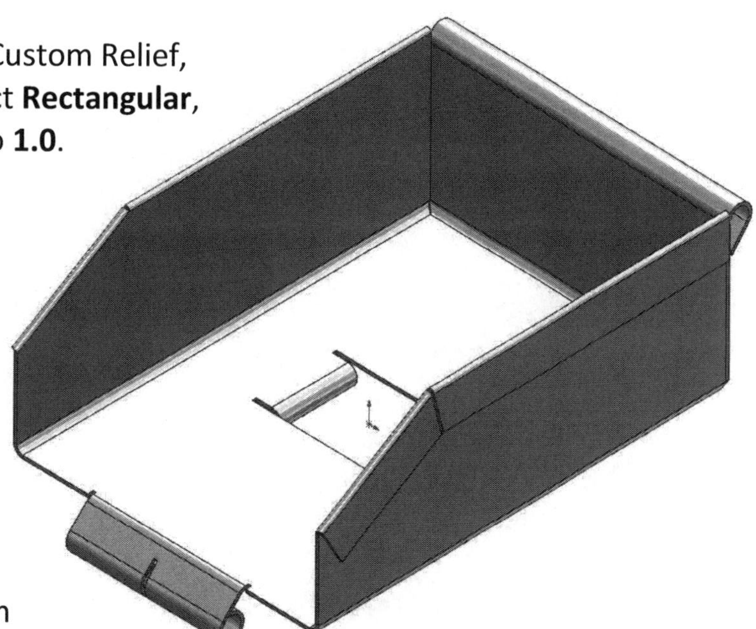

The 4 commonly used hems for sheet metal parts are created. Change to the Front, Top, Right views and zoom closer to inspect them.

6. Toggling the Flat Display:

Right-click on one of the faces of the sheet metal part and select: **Toggle-Flat-Display**.

There are several options for displaying the sheet metal flat pattern: Fold & Unfold, Toggle Flat Display, and Flat Pattern.

Each option was designed for different tasks but they all serve the same purpose, to flatten the sheet metal part.

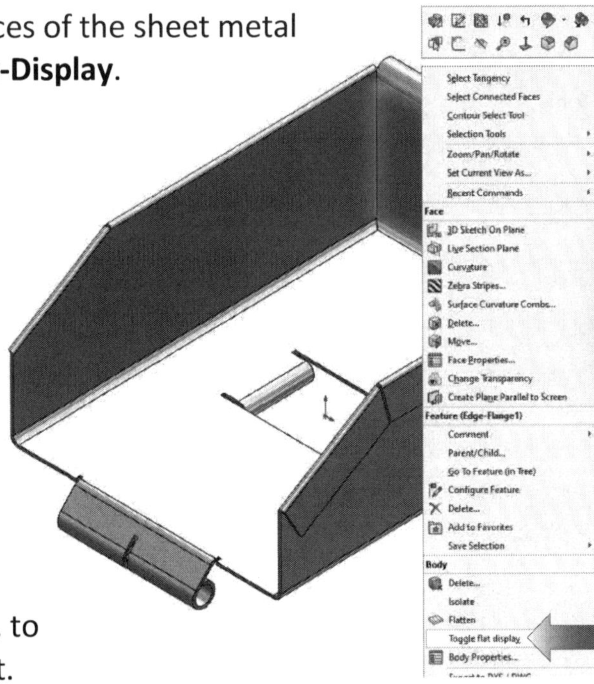

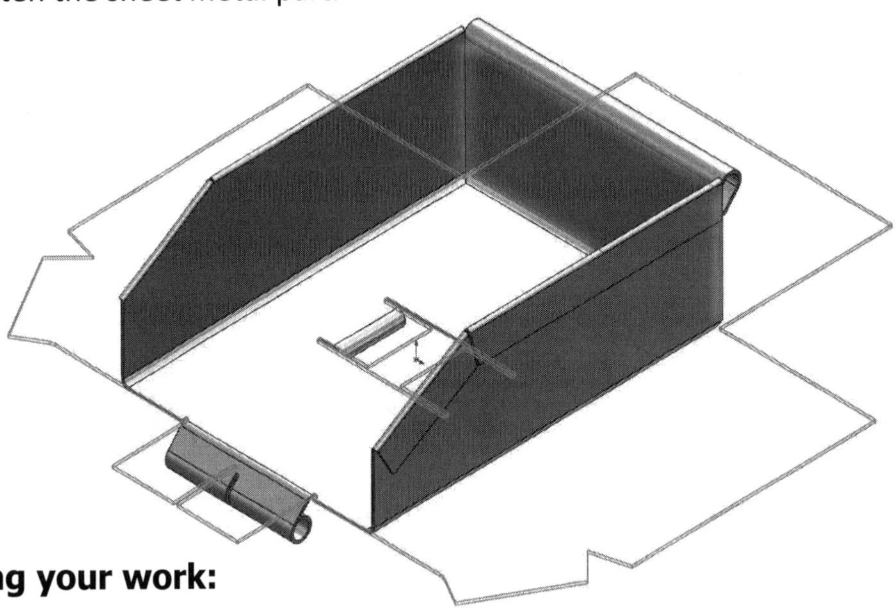

7. Saving your work:

Select **File, Save As**.

Enter: **Sheet Metal Hems_Completed** for the file name.

Click **Save**.

Lesson 9: Sheet Metal Gussets & Vents

A sheet metal gusset is an indented feature that forms a gusset to stiffen a bend in sheet metal parts.

Sheet metal gussets are formed with special tooling which has a ridge going across the V opening. The punch is split to the left and right of the ridge as not to be damaged while forming.

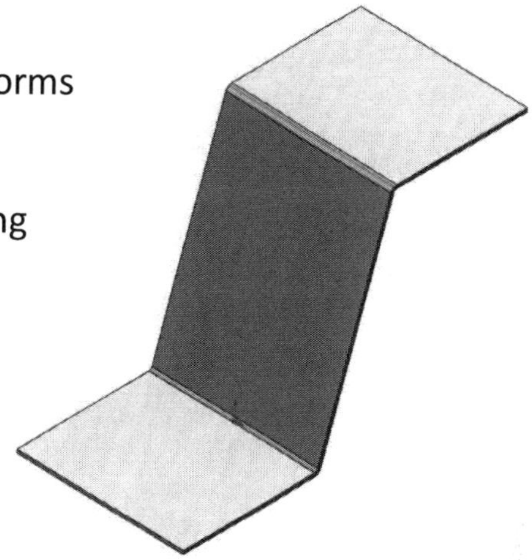

1. Opening a part document:

Browse to the Training Folder and open a part document named:
Sheet Metal Gusset. Sldprt

2. Creating the 1st gusset:

Switch to the **Sheet Metal** tab and click **Gusset** .

For Gusset Position, select the **2 faces** as noted in balloon 1.

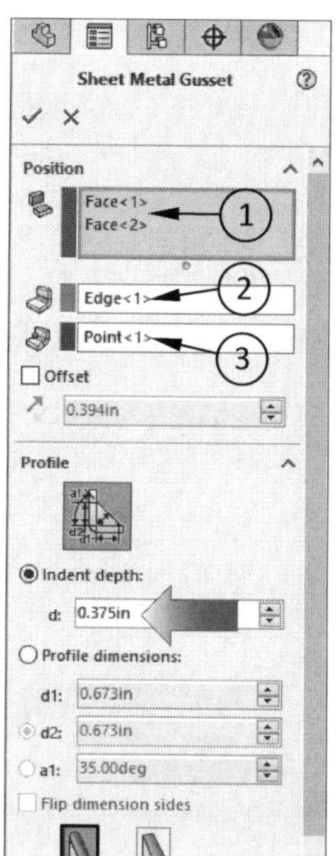

Select the **Edge** for Ref. Line (balloon 2).

Select the **Mid-Point** for Reference Point (right-click select Mid-Point, balloon 3).

For Indent Depth, enter **.375in**.

Click the **Rounded Gusset** button.

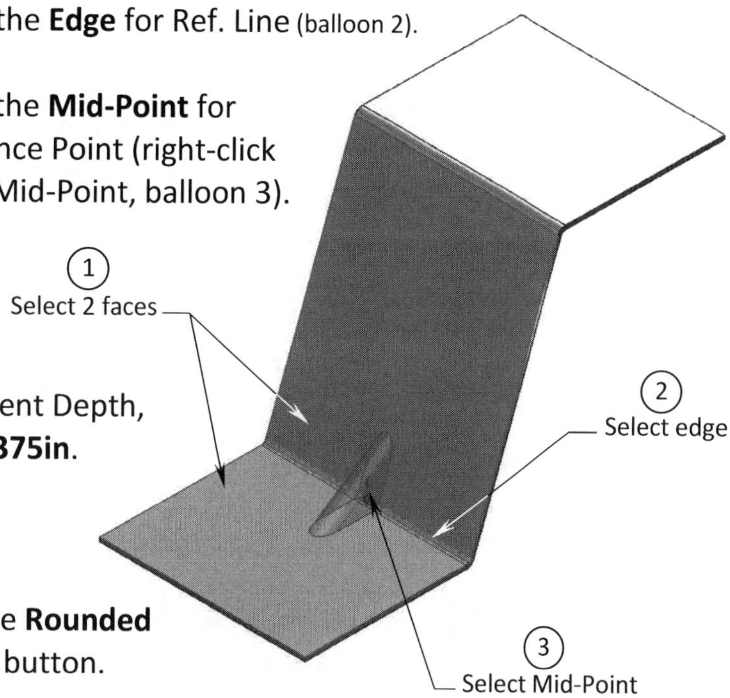

Under the Dimensions section, enter the following:

Indent Width: **.250in.**

Indent Thickness: **.0478in.**

Side Face Draft: **3.00deg.**

Inner Corner Fillet: **.060in.**

Outer Corner Fillet: **.030in**.

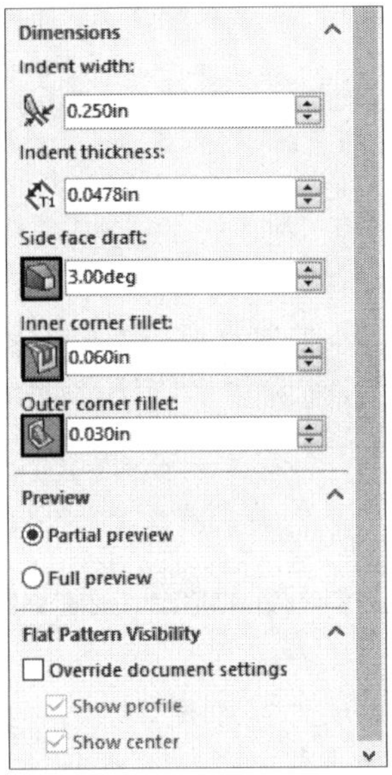

Click **OK**.

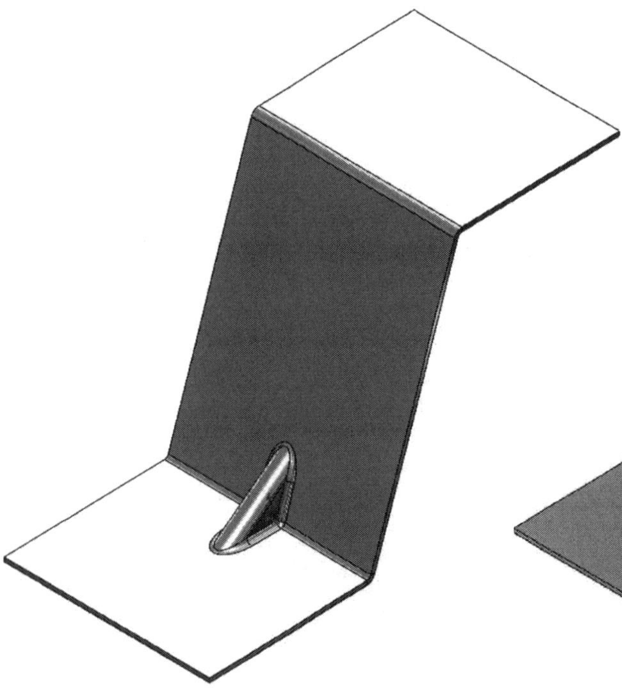

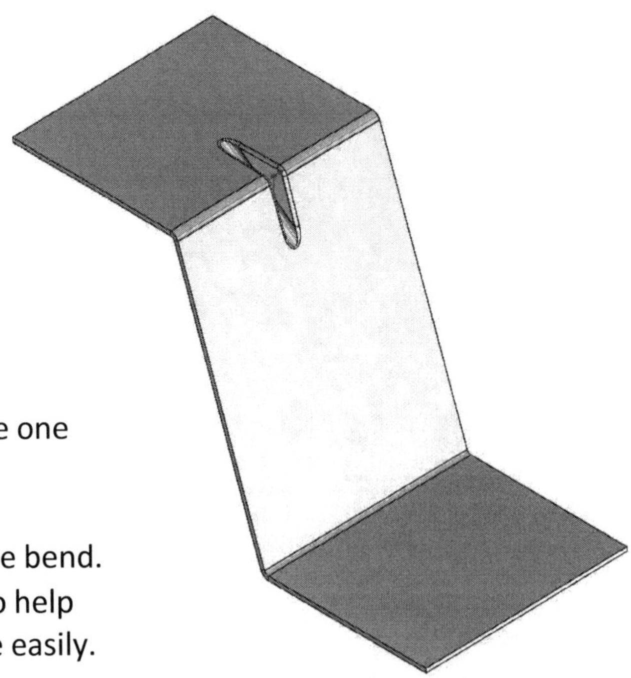

Inspect your gusset against the one shown here.

The gusset is formed across the bend. It has a 3° draft on the sides to help pulling the form tool out more easily.

3. Creating the 2nd gusset:

Click **Gusset** again, on the **Sheet Metal** tab.

For Gusset Position, select the **2 faces** as indicated with balloon 1.

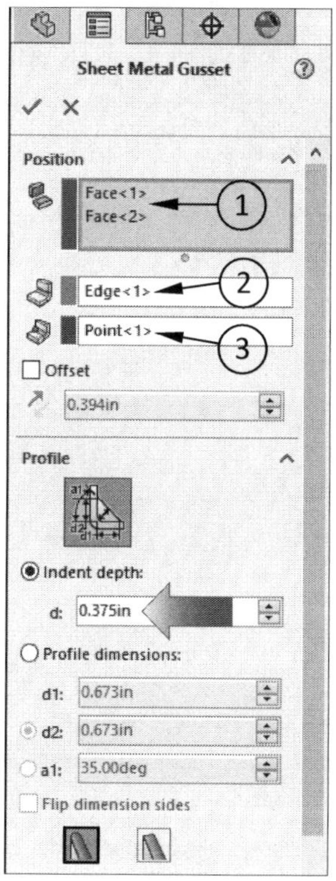

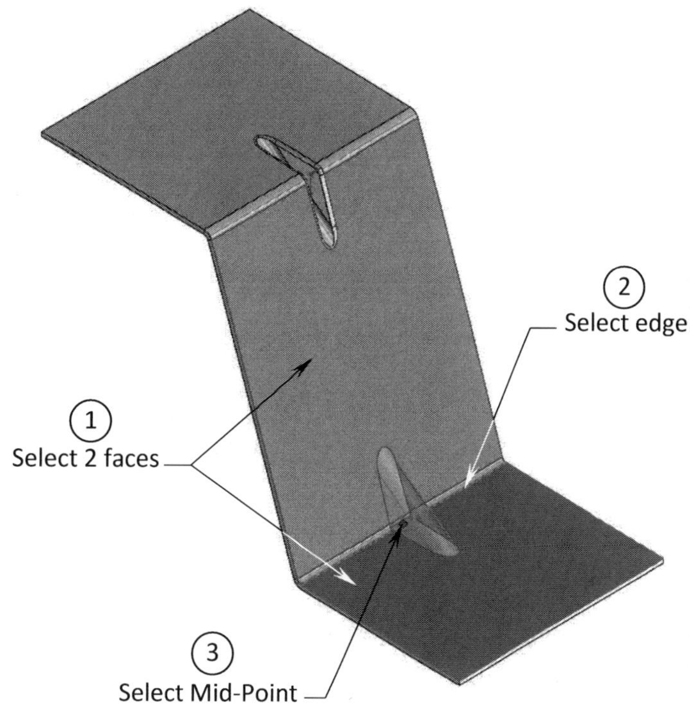

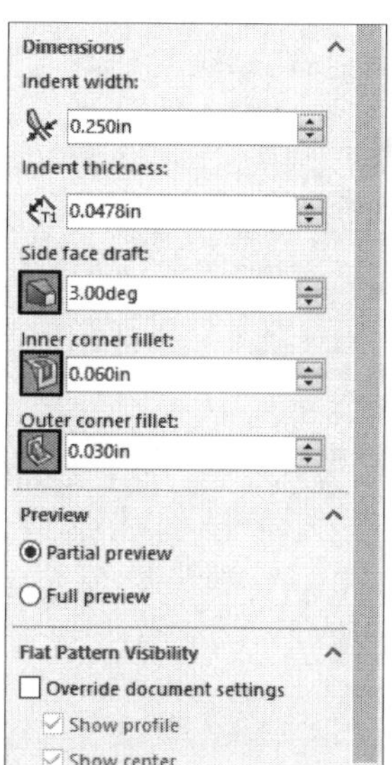

For Reference Edge, select the **edge** as note in balloon 2.

For Reference Point, select the **mid-point** as shown in balloon 3.

Enter the following dimensions:

Indent Width: **.250in** Indent Thickness: **.0478in.**

Side Face Draft: **3.0deg.** Inner Corner Fillet: **.060in.**

Outer Corner Fillet: **.030in**.

Click **OK**.

4. Adding fillets:

Select **Corners, Break Corner**.

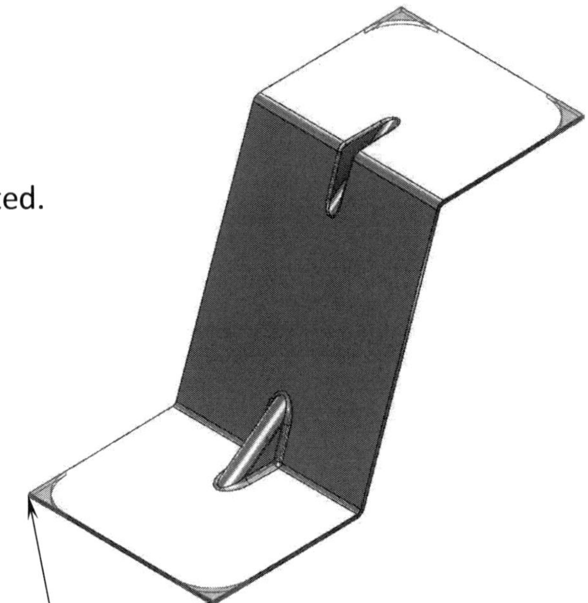

For Corners, select **4 edges** as noted.

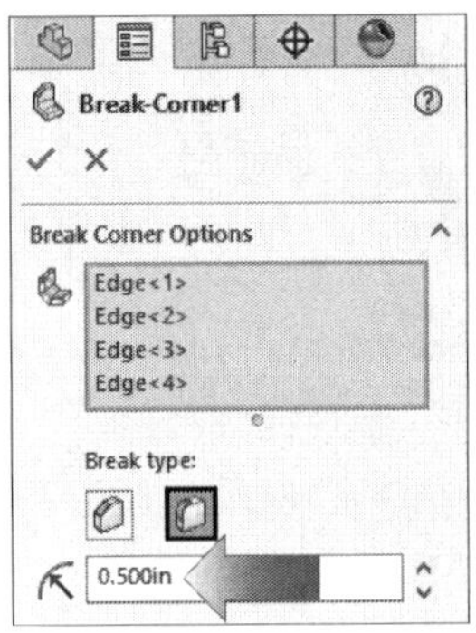

Select edges (4X)

For Break Type, select
the **Fillet** button.

For Radius, enter **.500in**.

Click **OK**.

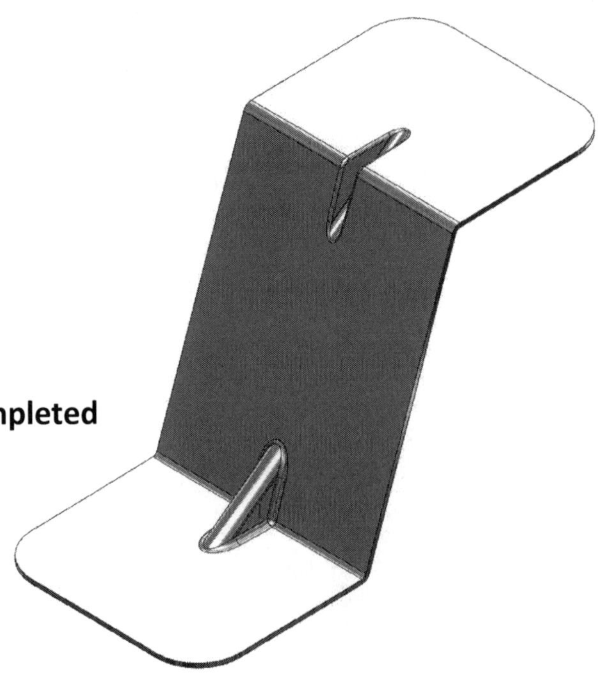

5. Saving your work:

Select **File, Save As**.

Enter **Sheet Metal Gussets_Completed** for the file name.

Click **Save**.

Sheet Metal Vents

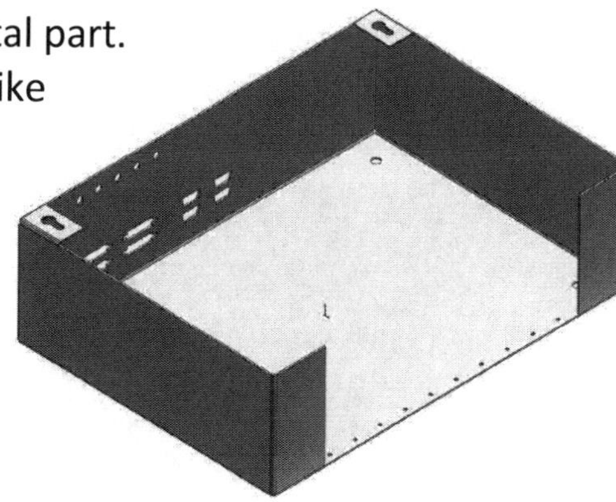

Sheet metal vents are openings in a sheet metal part. They are typically made of thin metal sheets, like galvanized steel or aluminum, and are an essential feature to allow air flow and for heat to exit the enclosed chassis.

This lesson will walk us through the creation of a Sheet Metal Vent using SOLIDWORKS.

1. Opening a part document:

Browse to the Training Folder and open a part document named:
Sheet Metal Vents.sldprt

This part document contains a basic sheet metal housing, some flanges, and some mounting features. The next step is to add the Vent feature to it.

2. Sketching the Vent profile:

Select the <u>face</u> in the back of the housing and open a **new sketch**.

Sketch the profile shown below.

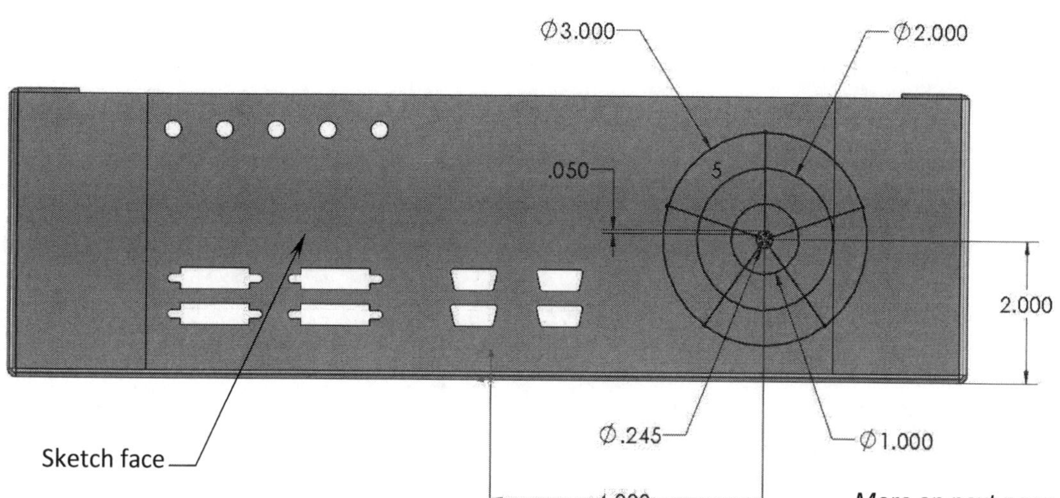

More on next page...

Sketch **4 Circles** and a **Vertical Line**.

Circular Pattern the vertical line **5 times**.

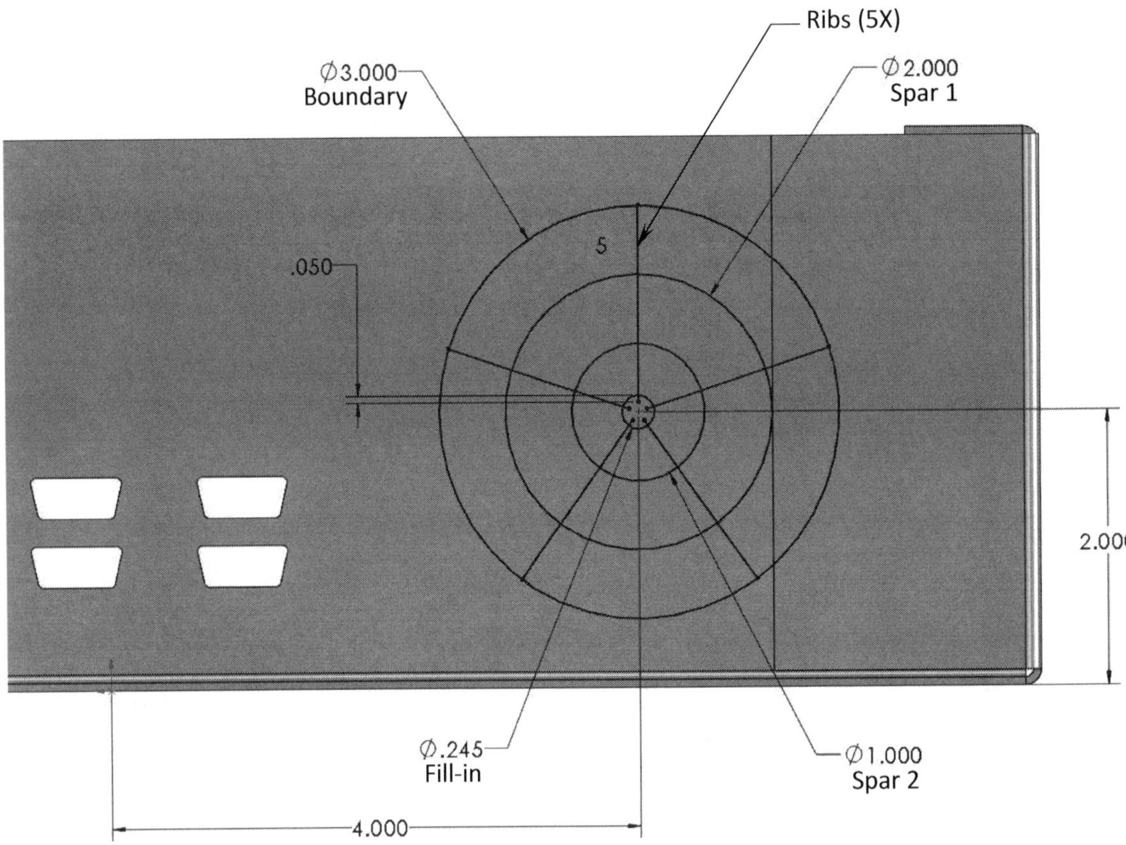

The vertical line should extend through the smallest circle by about .050".

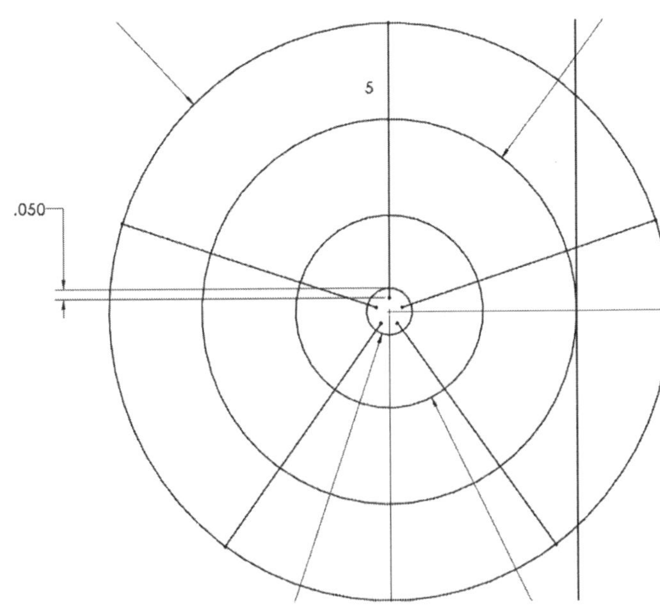

Add the dimensions shown in the image above to fully define the sketch.

3. Creating the Vent feature:

Switch to the **Sheet Metal** tab and click **Vent** .

For Boundary, select the **large circle** (balloon 1).

For Fillet between the Ribs and Spars, enter **.040in**.

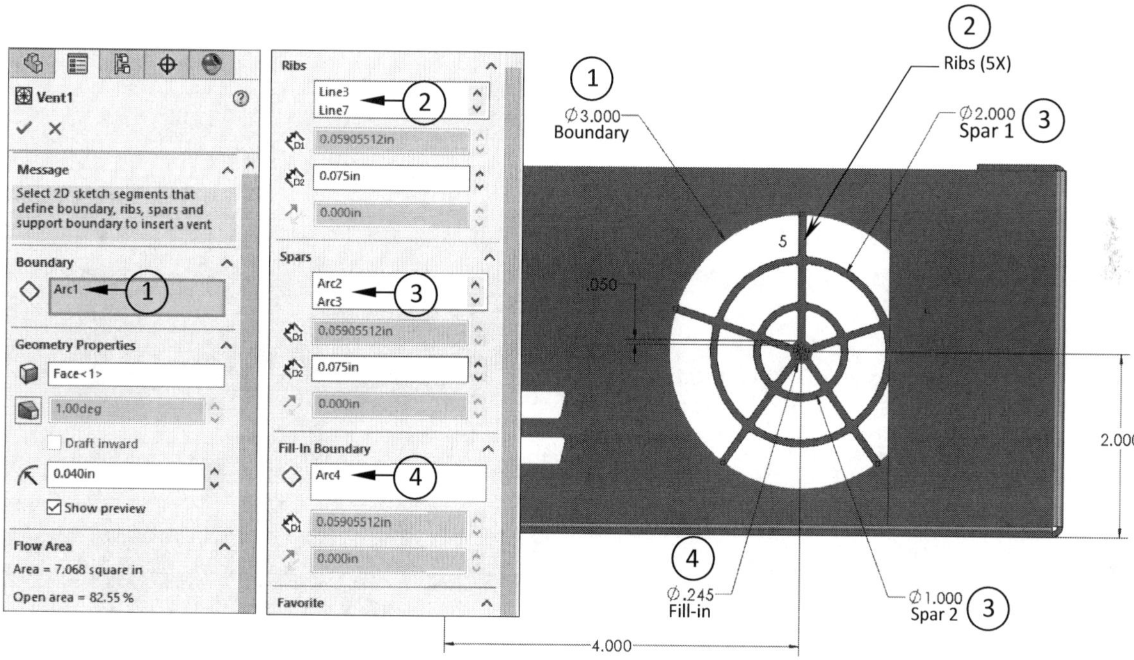

For Ribs, select the **5 lines** (balloon 2), Rib Thickness: **.075in**.

For Spars, select the next **2 circles** (balloon 3), Spars Thickness: **.075in**.

For Fill-In Boundary, select the **smallest circle** (Balloon 4).

Click **OK**.

Inspect your vent features against the image shown on the right.

4. Adding the mounting holes:

Select the face in the back of the part and open a **new sketch**.

Sketch a **Corner Rectangle** and convert it to **Construction Geometry**.

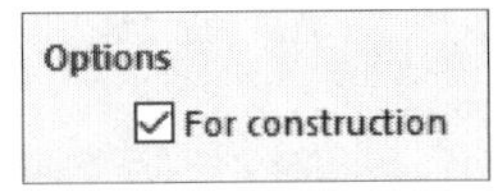

Add **4 Tangent relations** between each of the **construction line** and the **large circle** (Ø3.00) from the previous sketch.

Sketch **4 Circles** and add dimensions shown in the image below.

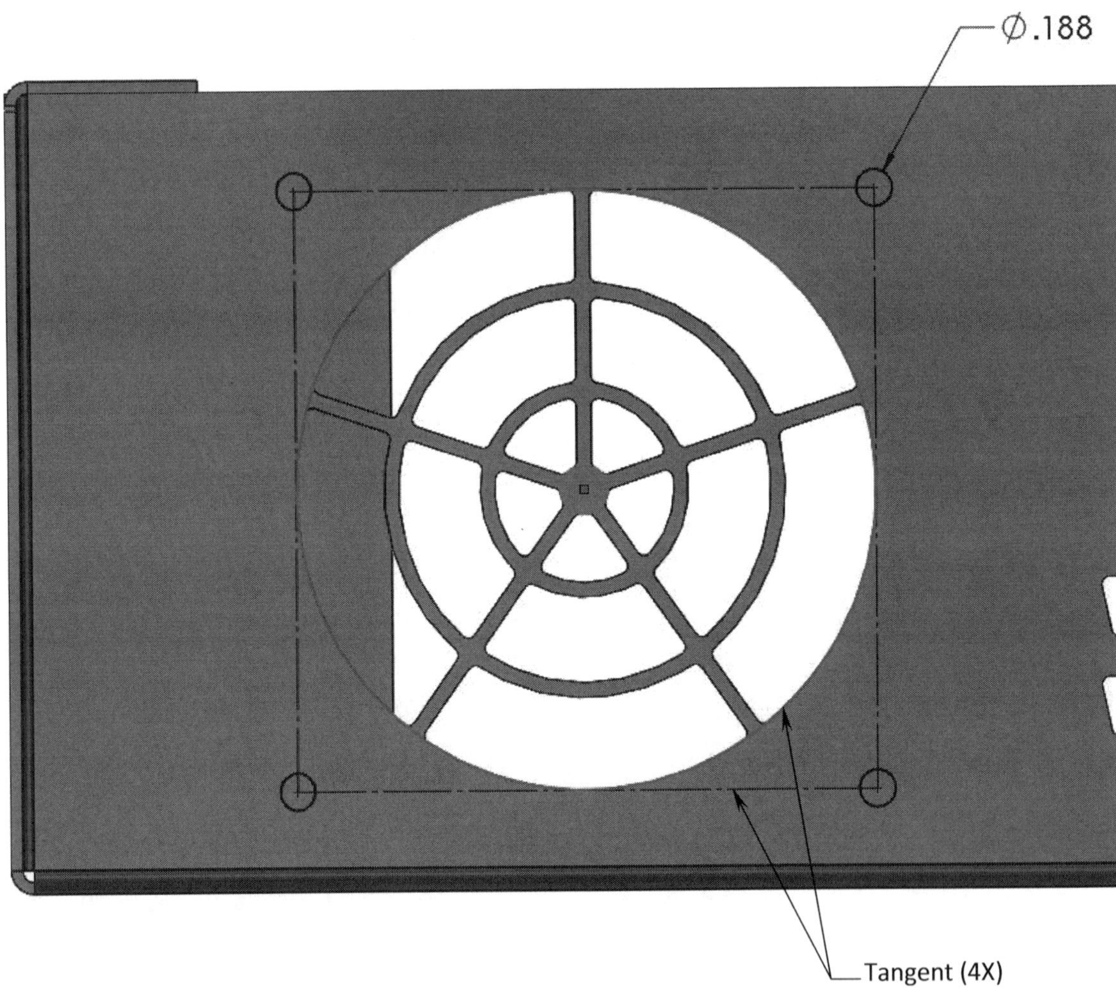

Add an **Equal relation** to the 4 circles.

The sketch should be fully defined at this time.

Switch to the **Sheet Metal** tab.

Click **Extruded Cut**.

Use the default **Blind** type and enable the **Link To Thickness** checkbox.

Click **OK**.

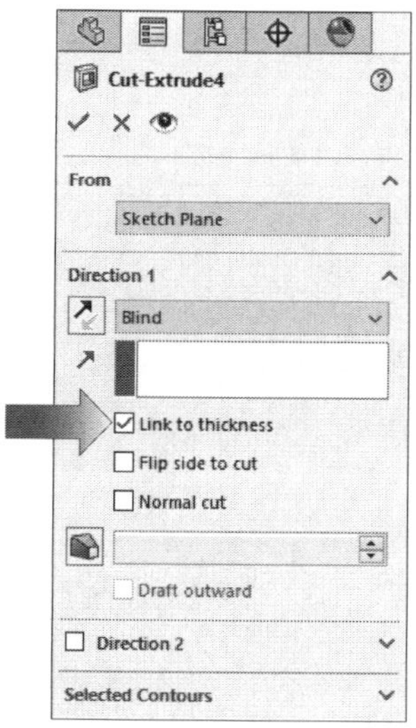

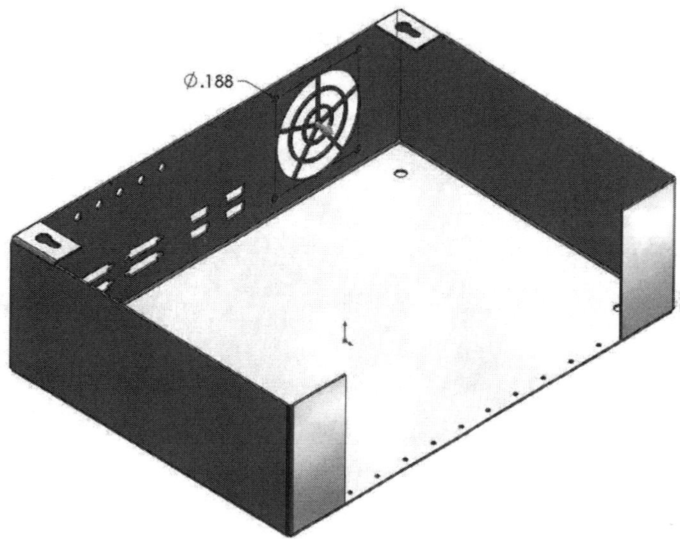

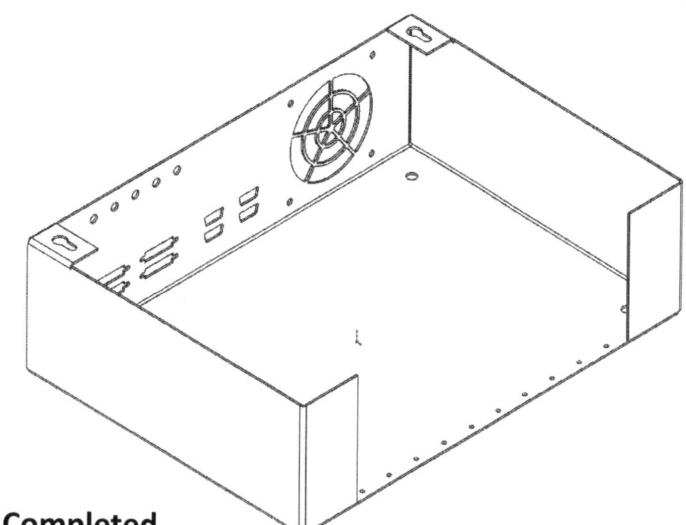

5. Saving your work:

Select **File, Save**.

Enter **Sheet Metal Vents_Completed** for the file name.

Click **Save**.

Exercise: Sheet Metal Vents

The exercises in this textbook are intended to give you an opportunity to explore and to apply what you have learned from the previous chapters, at your own pace.

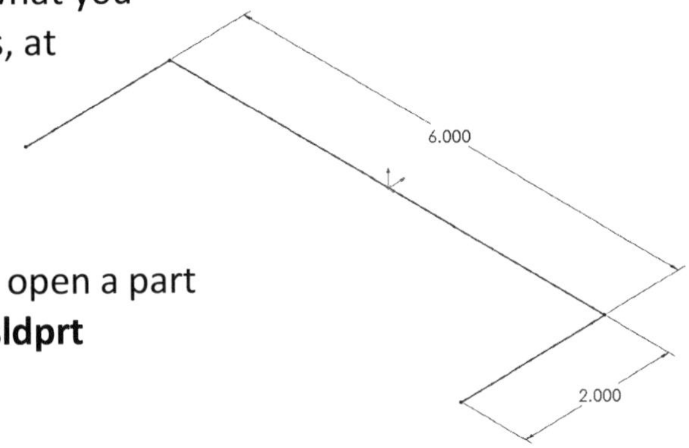

1. Opening a part document:

Browse to the Training Folder and open a part document named: **SM Vent_Exe.sldprt**

2. Creating the Base Flange:

Select **Sketch1** from the FeatureManager tree and click **Base Flange**.

Select the following:

Blind – 6.00in	**Use Gauge Table**	**Steel – 12 Gauge**
Bend Rad: **.125in**	K-Factor**: 0.5**	
Relief**: Rectangular** – Ratio: **0.5**		

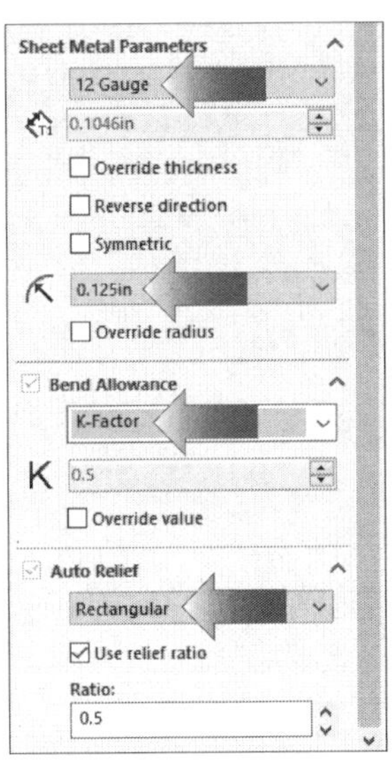

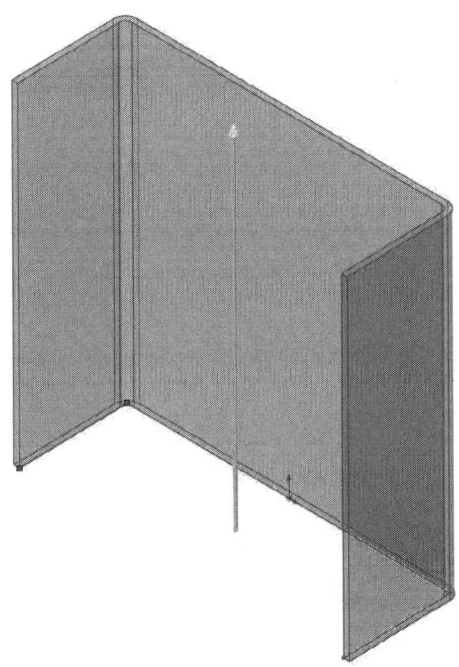

Click **OK**.

3. Adding a cut feature:

Select the Right plane and open a **new sketch**.

Sketch a **Circle**.

Add the diameter dimension and a Mid-Point relation as indicated in the image.

Switch to the **Sheet Metal** tab and click **Extruded Cut**.

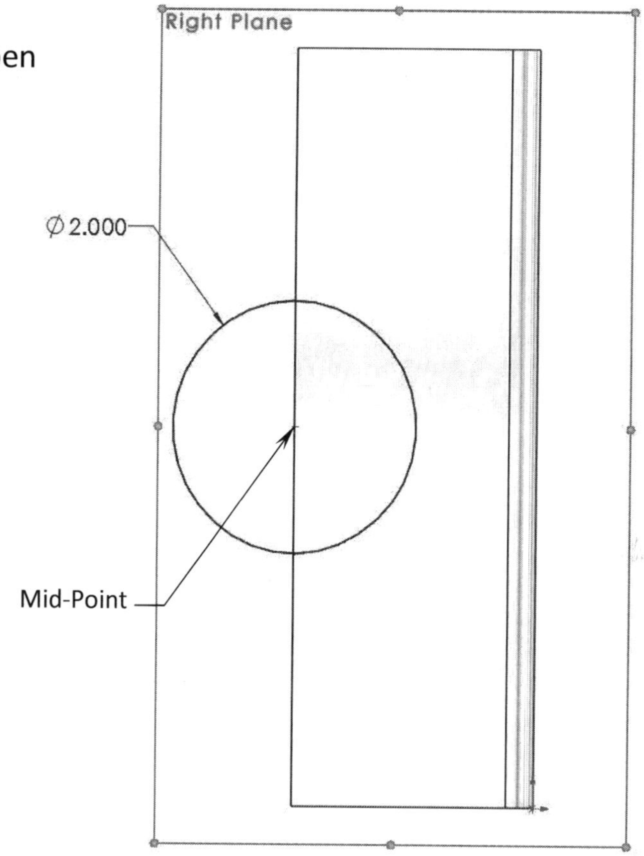

For Direction 1, select **Through All Both**.

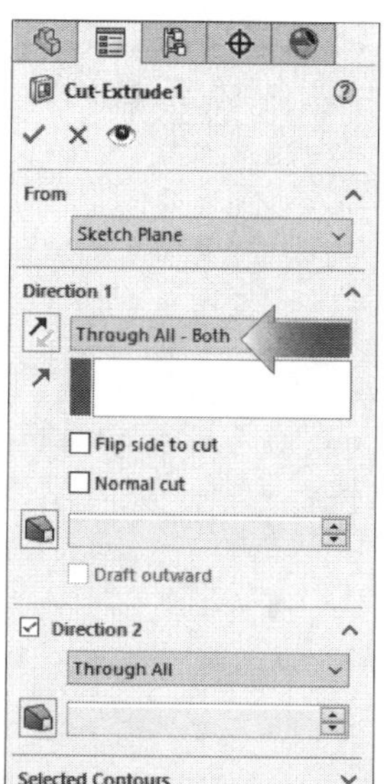

Click **OK**.

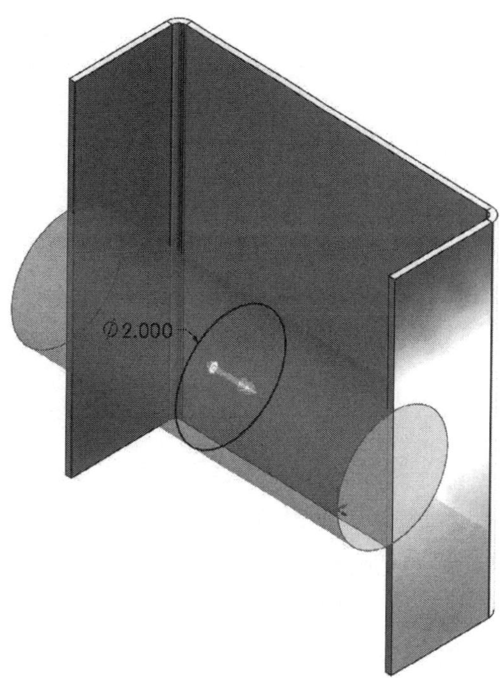

4. Adding fillets:

Add a Constant Size Fillet to **4 edges** of the circular cutout.

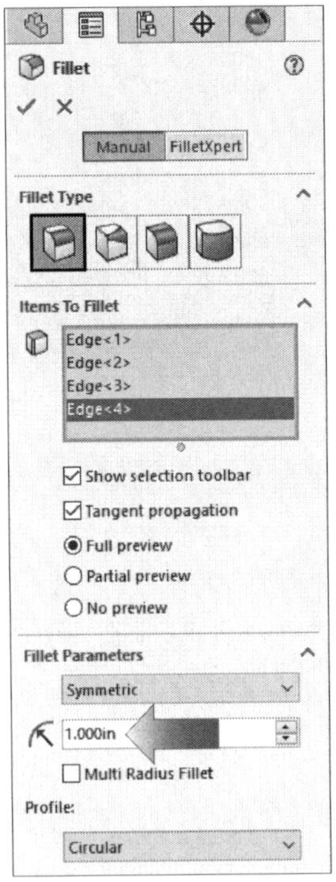

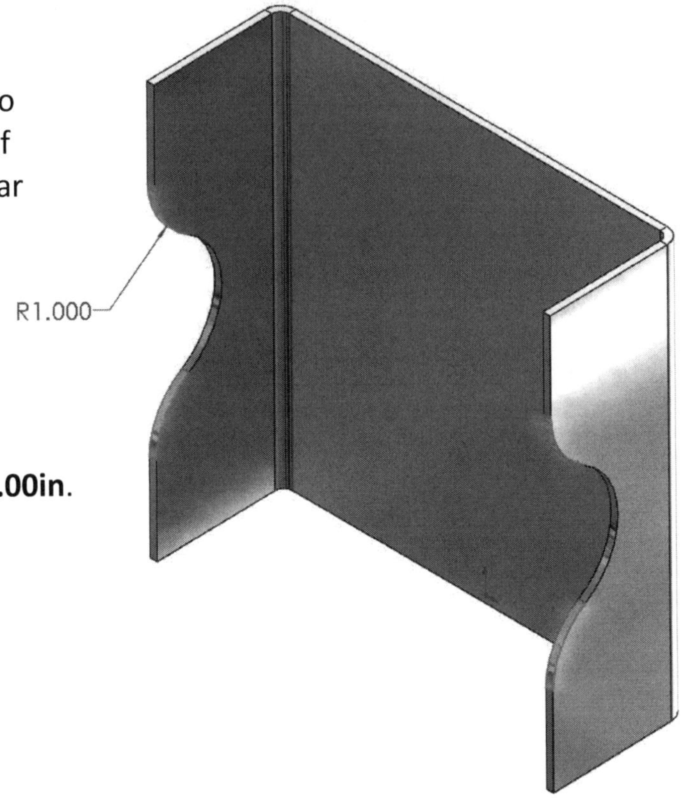

Radius: **1.00in**.

Click **OK**.

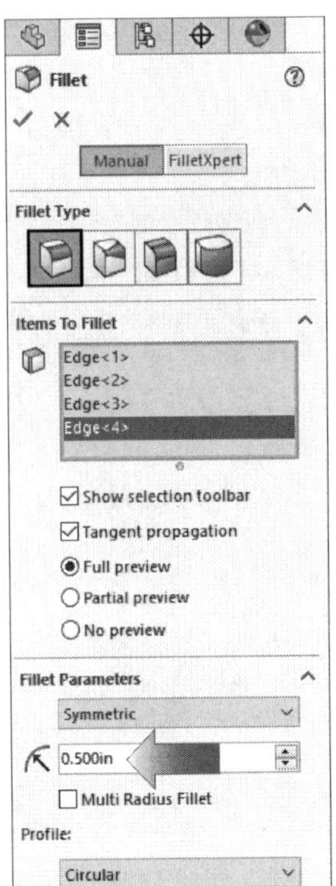

Add another Constant Size Fillet to the **4 corners** of 2 side flanges.

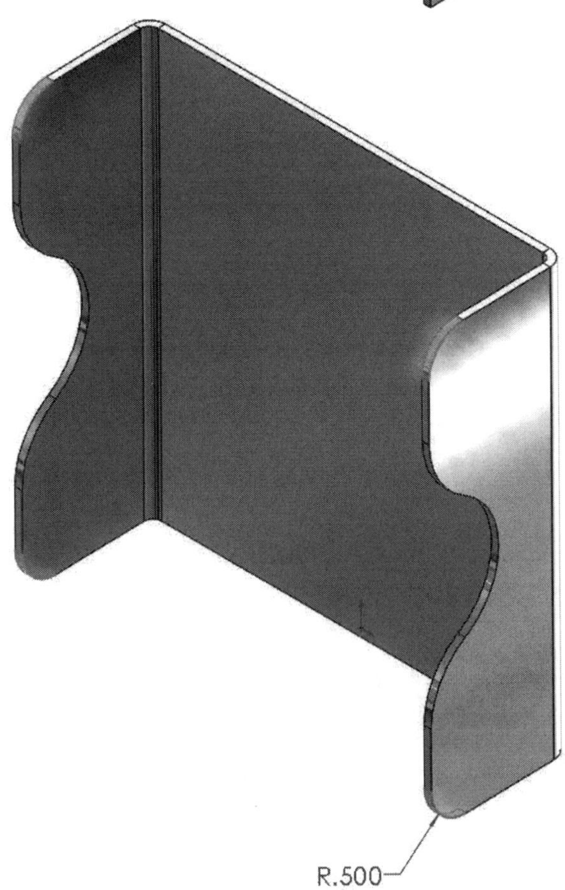

Radius: **.500in**.

Click **OK**.

5. Adding the 3/8" holes:

Switch to the **Features** tab.

Select the side face and click **Hole Wizard**.

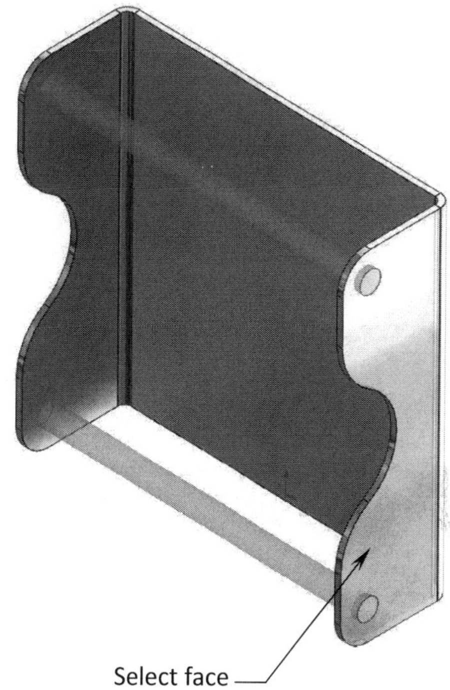

Select the following:

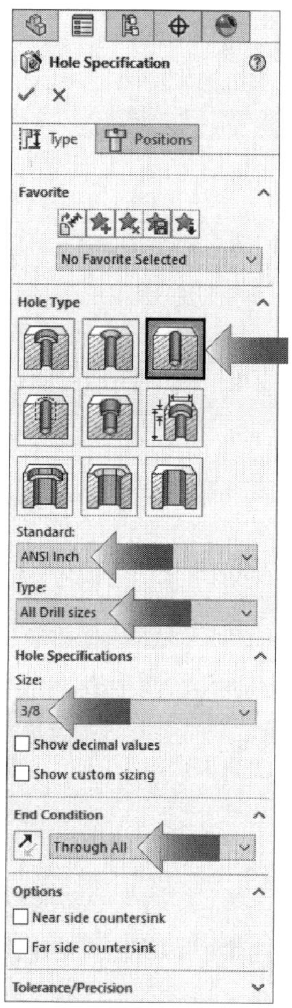

Hole Type: **Simple Hole**

Standard: **ANSI Inch**

Type: **All Drill Sizes**

Size: **3/8**

End Condition: **Through All**

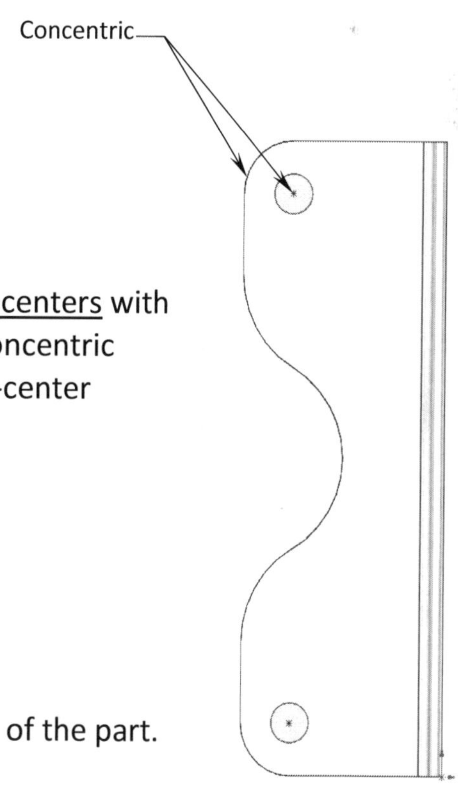

Click the **Position** tab.

Place **2 holes** on the same centers with the .500 fillets, or add a Concentric relation between the hole-center and the edge of the fillet.

Click **OK**.

The 2 holes should cut through both sides of the part.

6. Creating a Vent feature:

Select the inside face of the part and open a **new sketch**.

Sketch **4 circles** and **1 construction circle**.

Sketch a **vertical line** and circular pattern it **6 times**.

Switch to the **Sheet Metal** tab and click **Vent**.

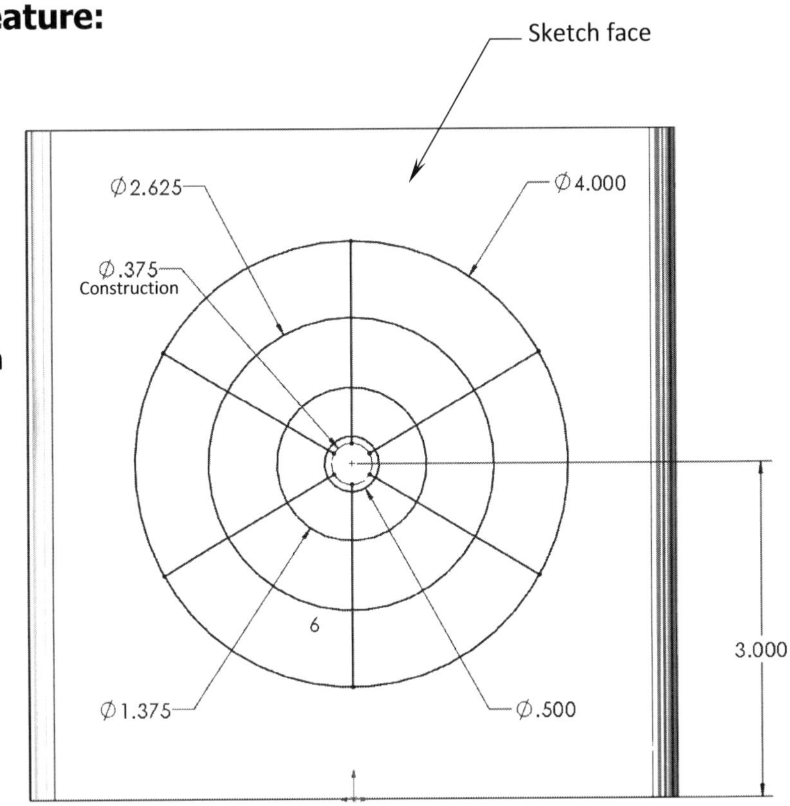

Select or enter the dimensions of the vent feature as shown in the dialog boxes below.

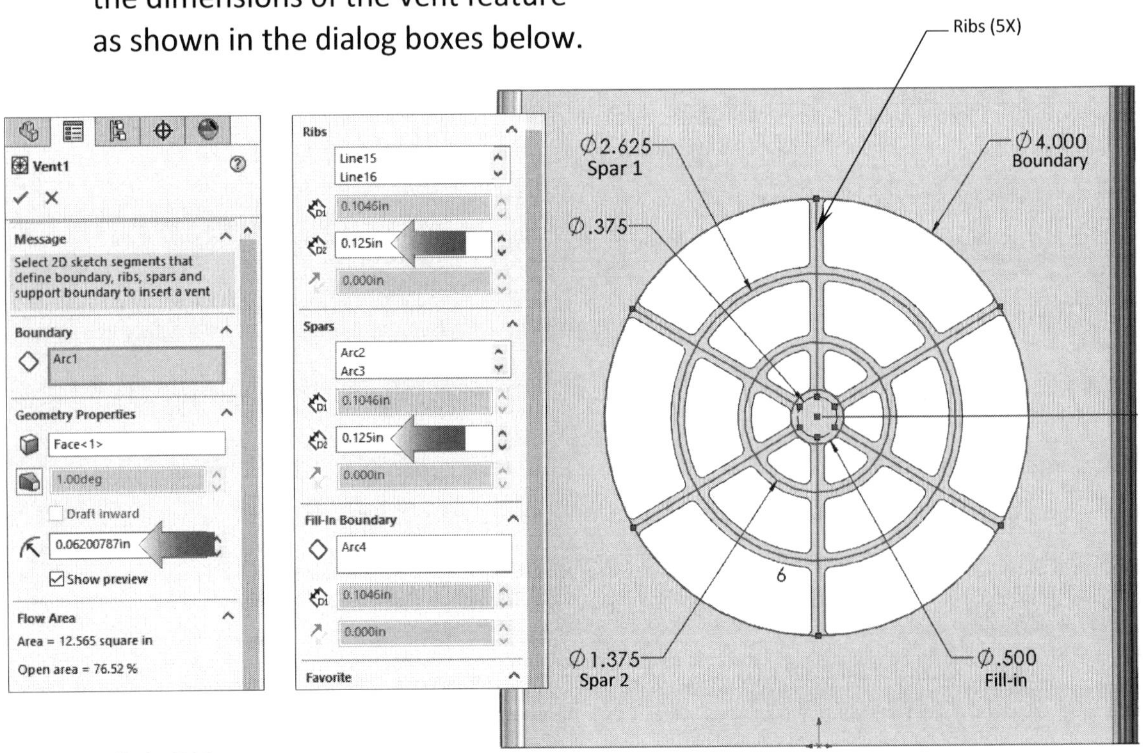

Click **OK**.

7. Adding the mounting holes:

Select the face as noted in the image and click **Hole Wizard**.

Select the following:

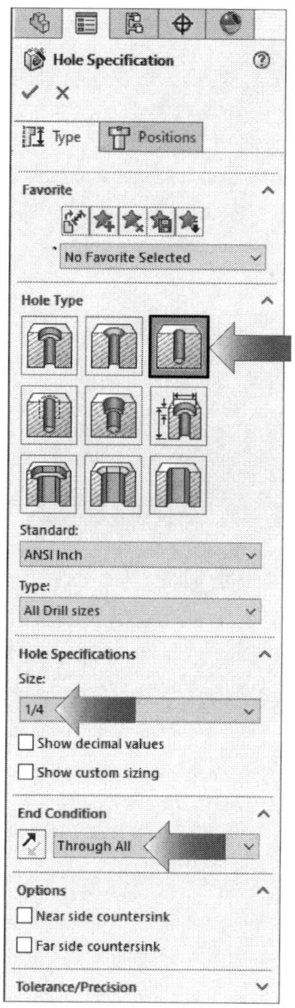

Hole Type: **Simple Hole**

Standard: **ANSI Inch**

Type: **All Drill Sizes**

Size: **1/4**

End Condition: **Through All**

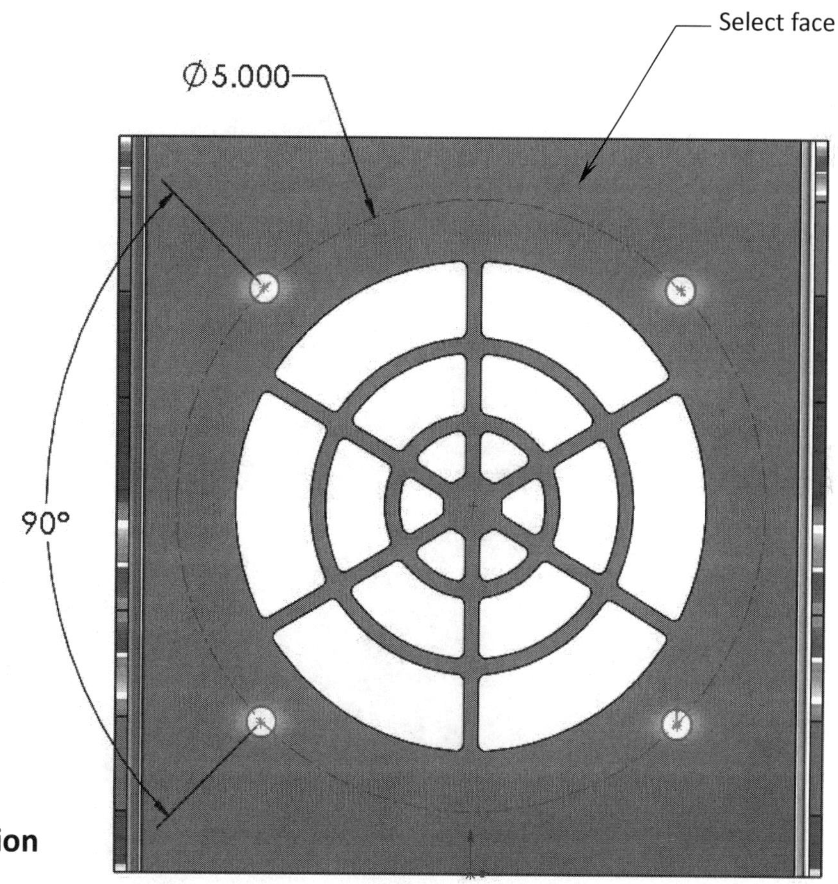

Click the **Position** tab.

Sketch a **Construction Circle** and place **4 points** on the circumference of this circle. The 4 points are on the same centers as the 4 holes.

Add dimensions and relations needed to fully define the sketch.

Click **OK**.

Click **Flatten** on the **Sheet Metal** tab.

Inspect your model against the image shown here.

Make any adjustments where needed.

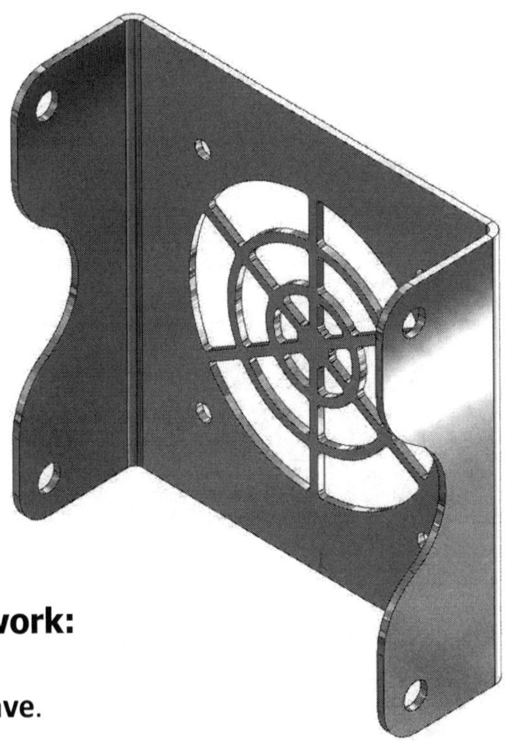

8. Saving your work:

Select **File, Save**.

Enter **SM Vent_Exe_Completed** for the file name.

Click **Save**.

Lesson 10: Convert To Sheet Metal

The Convert to Sheet Metal tool allows you to specify the thickness, bends, and rips necessary to transform a solid into a sheet metal component.
Let us try out this tool.

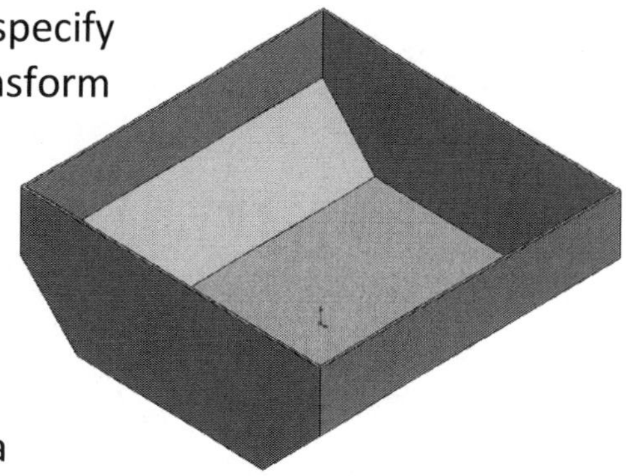

1. Opening a part document:

Browse to the Training Folder and open a part document named: **Convert to Sheet Metal**.

This model was created as a solid part and shelled to a uniform thickness. We need to convert the model to a sheet metal part with proper sheet metal parameters such as Bend Radius, Rip Edges, Corner Treatments, etc.

2. Converting to Sheet Metal:

Right-click the **Features** tab and select: **Tabs, Sheet Metal**.

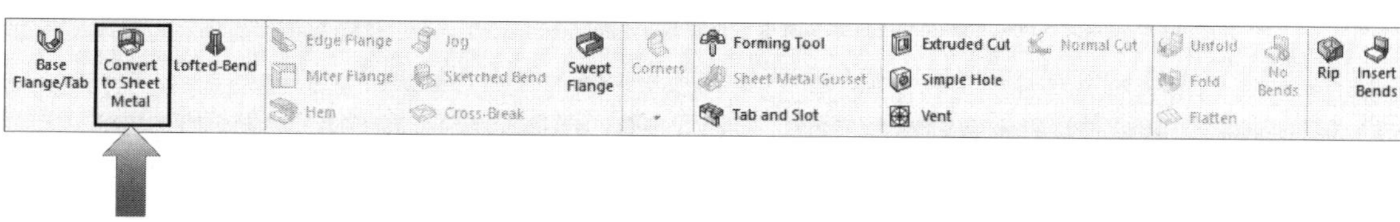

Click **Convert to Sheet Metal**.

The 1st Sheet Metal Parameter is the fixed face, or the face that will remain in place when the part is flattened.

Select the face as noted in the image on the right.

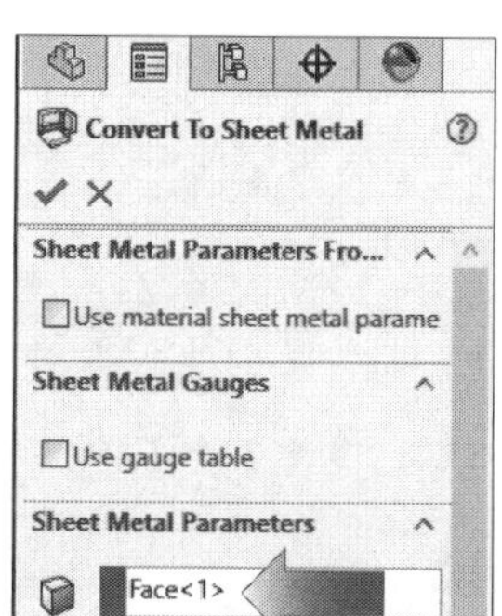

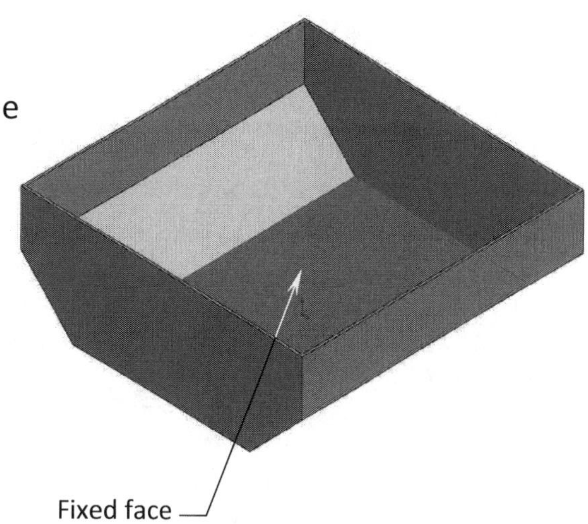

For Thickness, enter **.060in**. and set the Bend Radius to **.060in**.

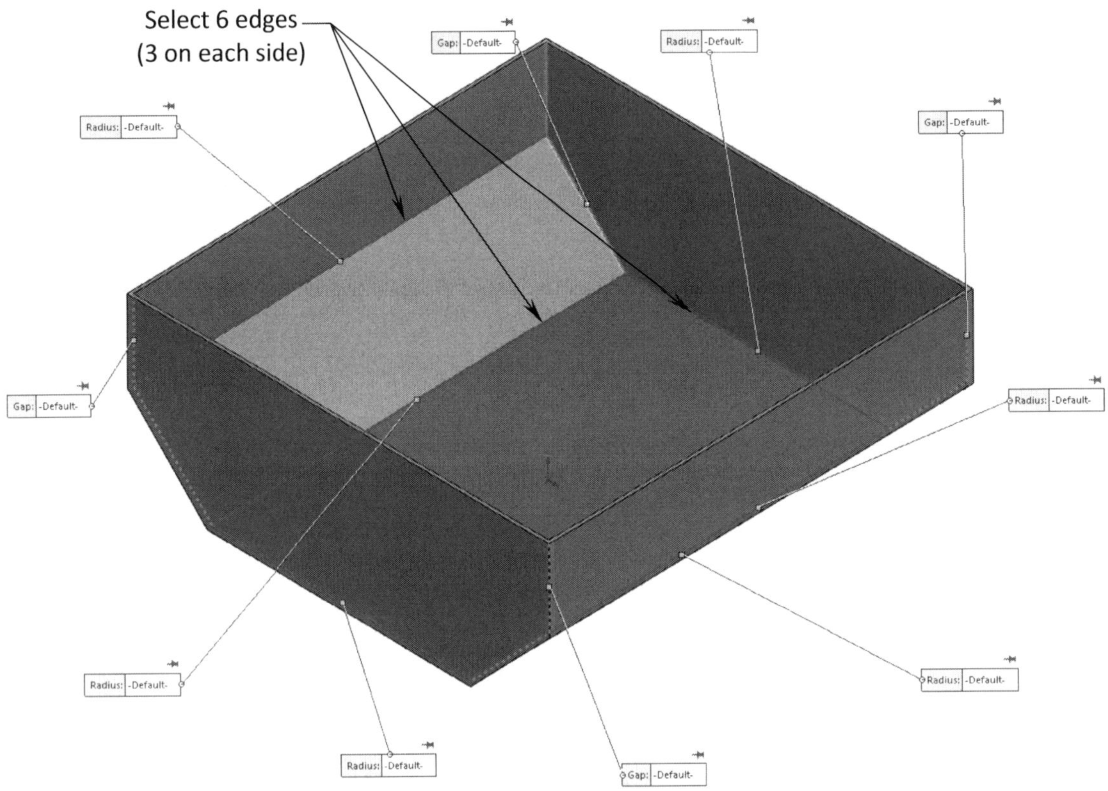

For Bend Edges, select **6 edges** on the inside of the model.

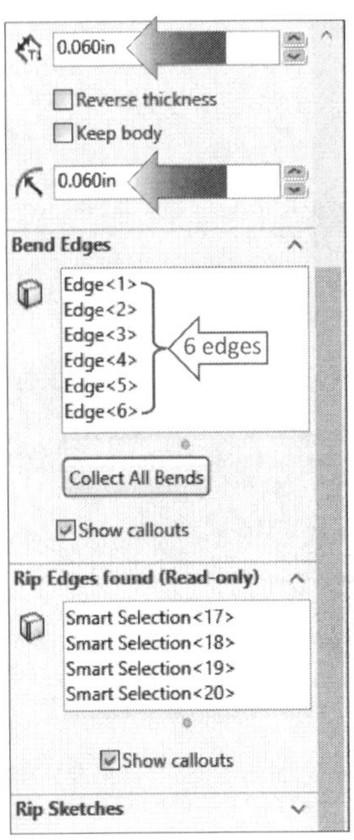

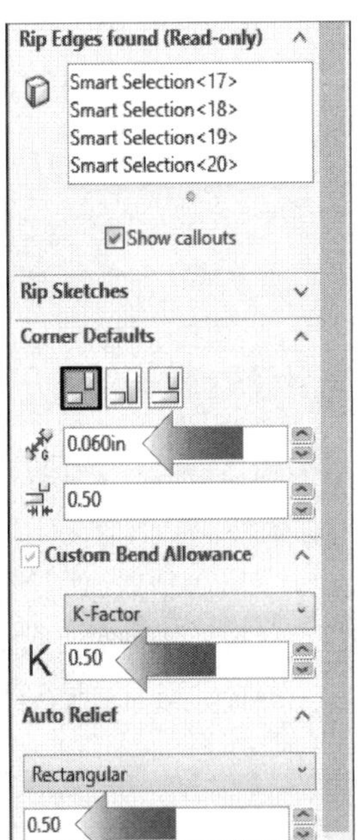

The Rip Edges should be selected automatically after the Bend Edges are selected.

For Corner Defaults, click **Open Butt**.

For Gap, enter **.060in**.

Keep the Overlap Ratio at **0.50**.

Use the default **K-Factor** and **0.50**.

Use **Rectangular Relief**, Ratio **0.50**.

Click **OK**.

3. Flattening the part:

The model is converted into a sheet metal part. It has all of the required parameters and is able to flatten at this point.

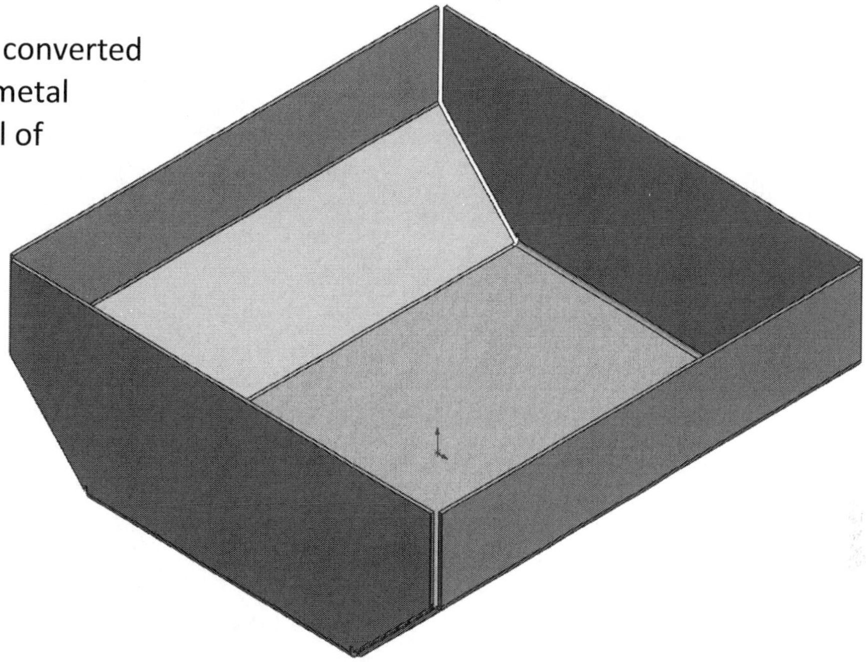

Click **Flatten** on the **Sheet Metal** tab.

The Bend Lines and the Bounding Box are visible in the flat pattern.

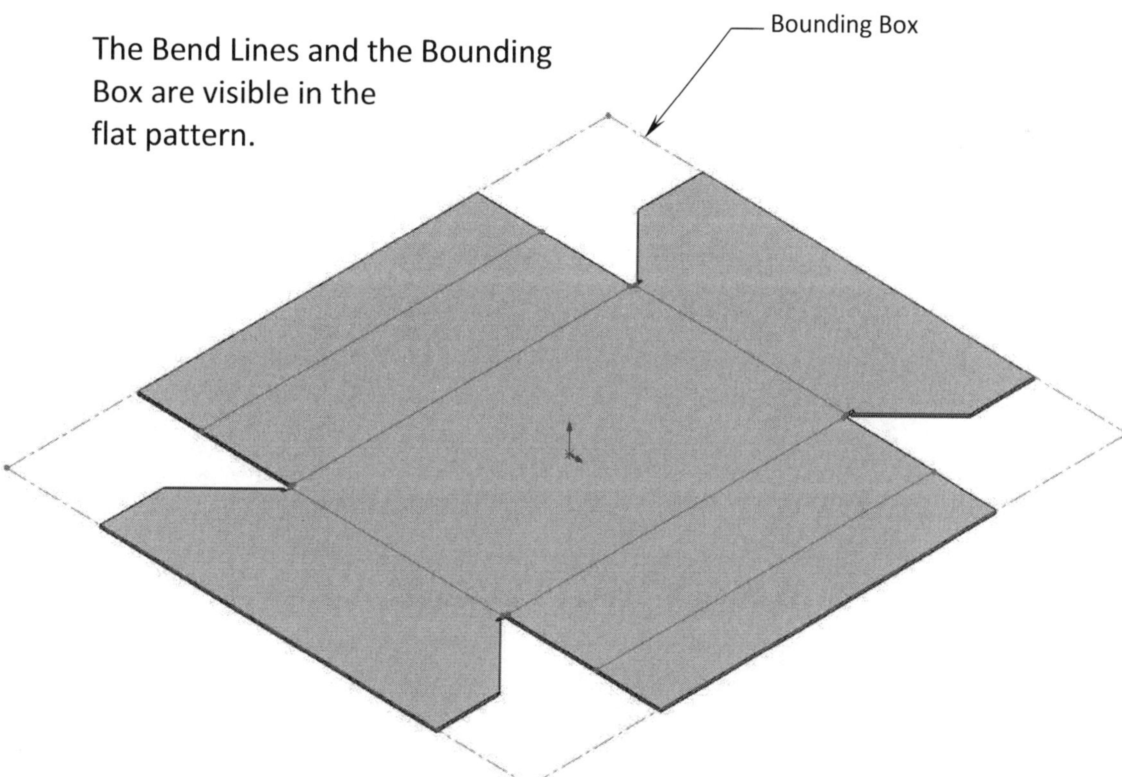

The bounding box is the smallest box in which the sheet metal fits.

4. Toggling the Flat Display:

Alternatively, the option Toggle Flat Display can be used to display the flat pattern on top of the fold pattern.

This is quite useful to be able to see both patterns on the same screen.

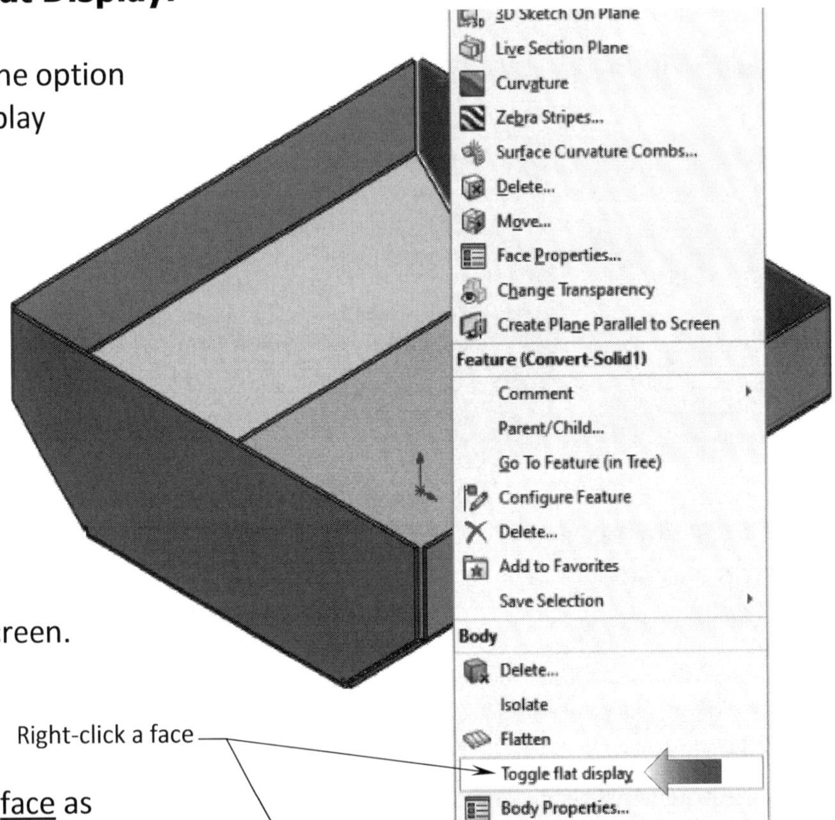

Right-click the <u>face</u> as indicated and select: **Toggle Flat Display**.

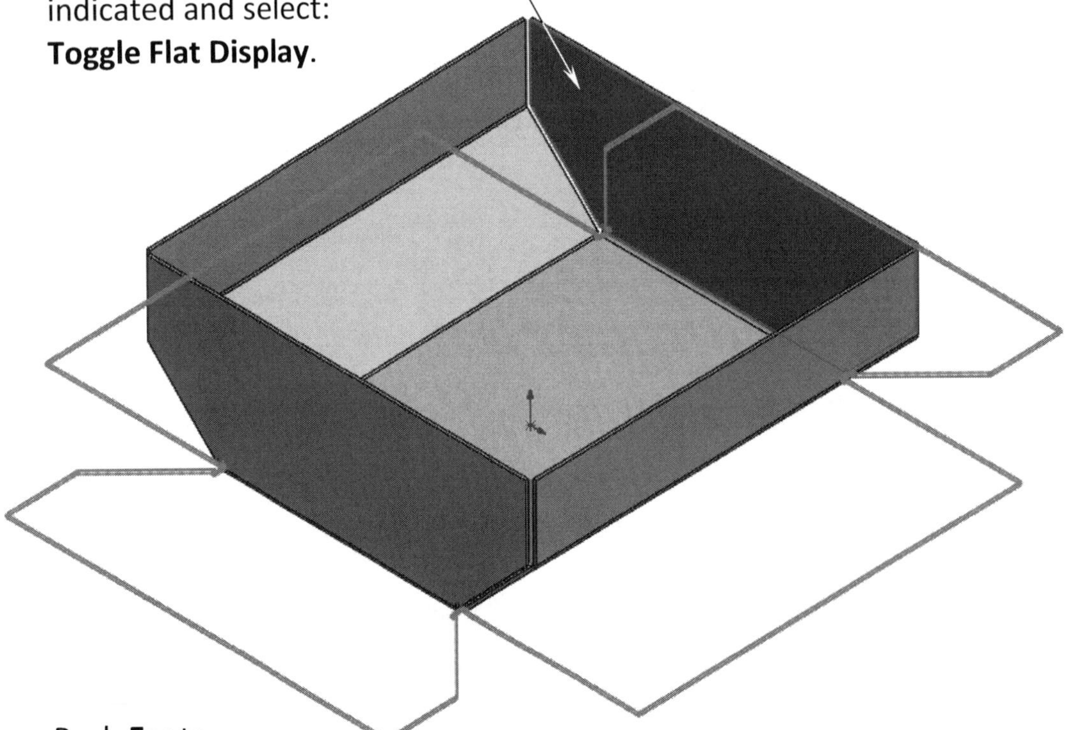

Push **Esc** to cancel the Flat Display.

Toggle between the Flat and the fold patterns to compare your model against the images shown here.

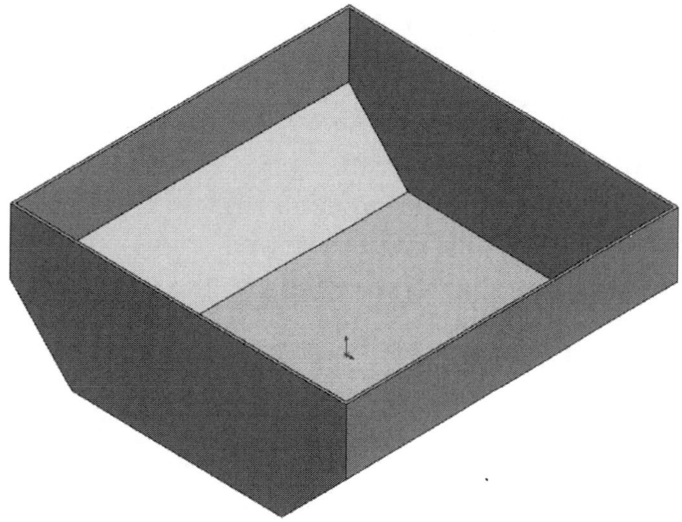

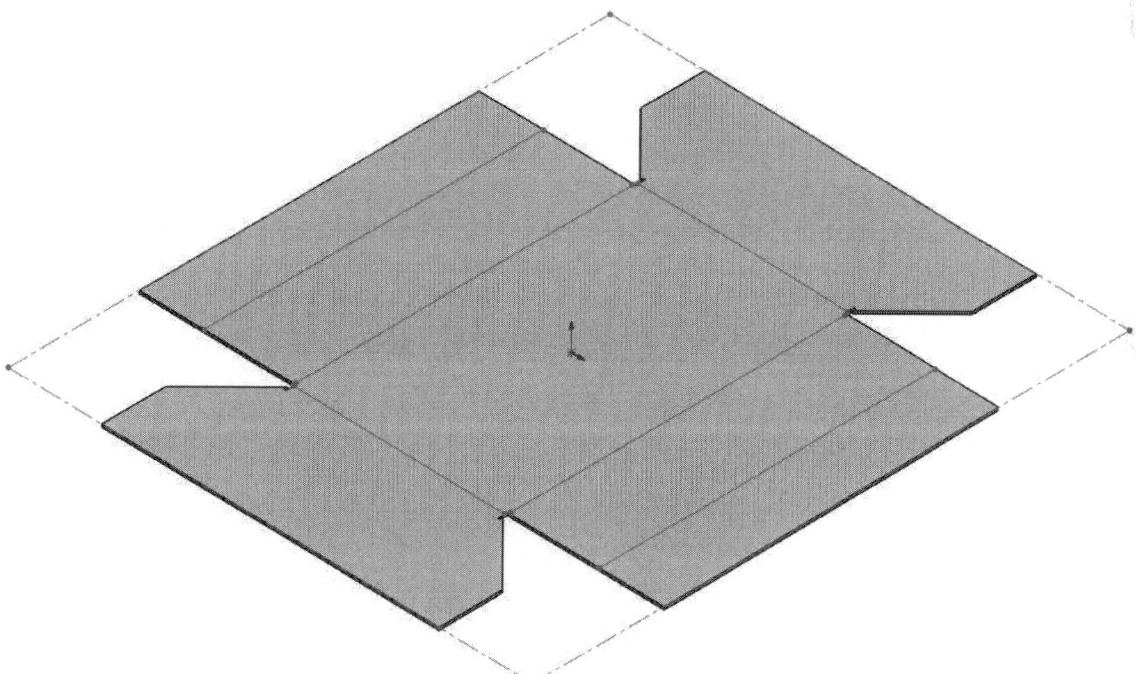

5. Saving your work:

Select **File, Save As**.

Enter: **Convert to SM 1_Completed.sldprt** for the file name.

Click **Save**.

Convert To Sheet Metal 2

1. Opening a part document:

Browse to the Training Folder and open a part document named: **Convert to SM 2.**

This model was created as a solid part and has not been shelled. Let us take a look at another method for converting a solid part into a sheet metal model. The sheet metal parameters such as Bend Radius, Rip Edges, Corner Treatments, etc. can be added during the conversion process.

2. Shelling the model:

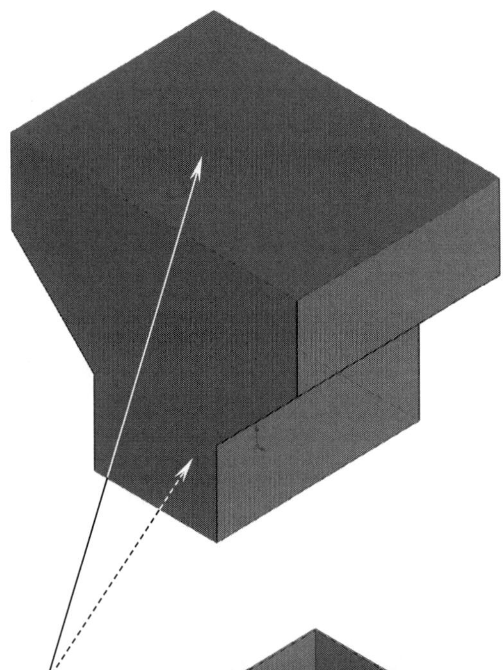

Switch to the **Features** tab.

Click **Shell**.

For Wall Thickness, enter **.1045in**.

For Faces to Remove, select the **top face** and the **bottom face** of the model.

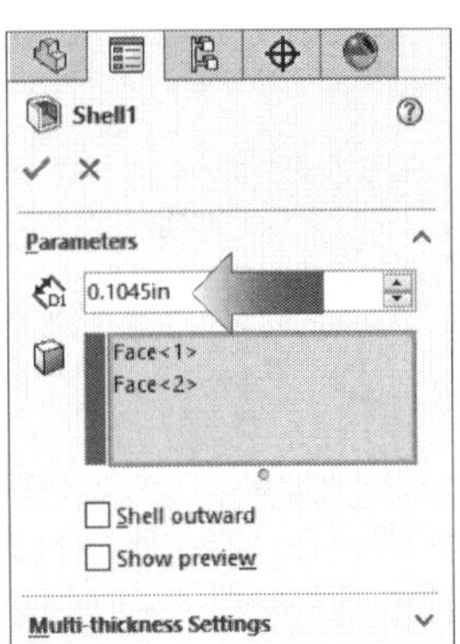

Click **OK**.

3. Creating the rip edges:

Switch to the **Sheet Metal** tab.

Click **Rip**.

The Rip tool creates rips in the thin-walled part so that it can be converted to sheet metal part and be flattened.

For Rip Selections, select **3 inside edges** on one side, and **2 inside edges** on the other 3 sides.

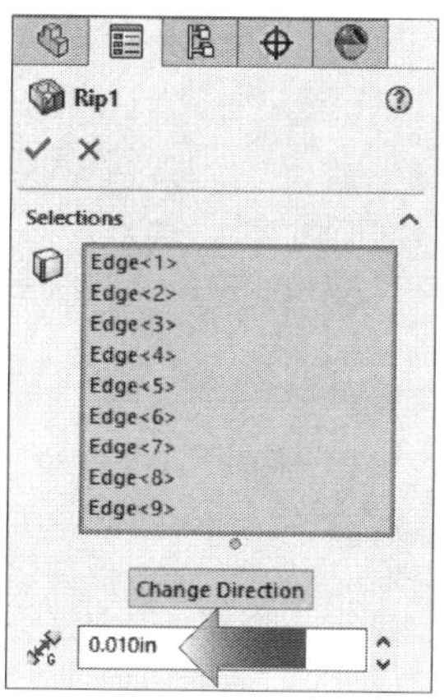

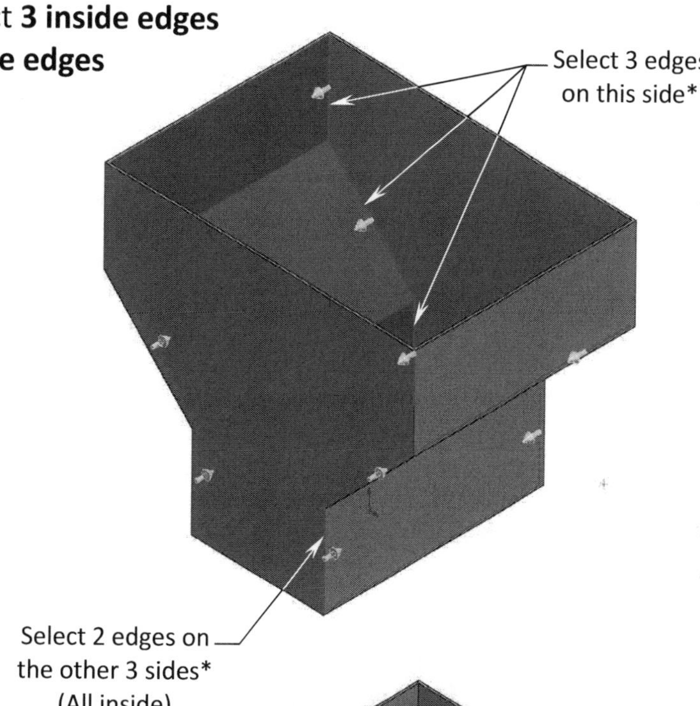

* After selecting an edge, click on the yellow arrow that represents the Rip Direction.

Notice all arrows are pointing inward, that simply means one side will be ripped and one material thickness will be subtracted for that side.

Two arrows means one material thickness will be subtracted for both sides.

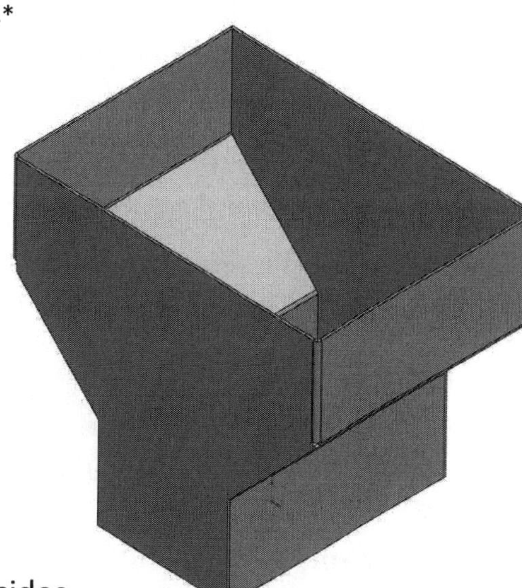

4. Converting to Sheet Metal:

Click **Insert Bends** on the **Sheet Metal** tab.

For Fixed face, select the **face** as indicated.

For Bend Radius, enter **.105in**.

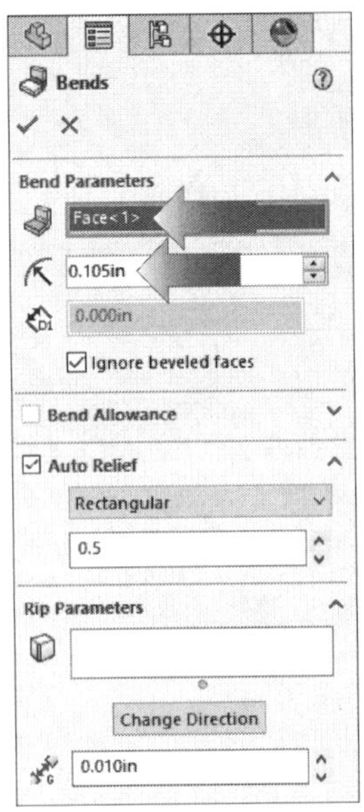

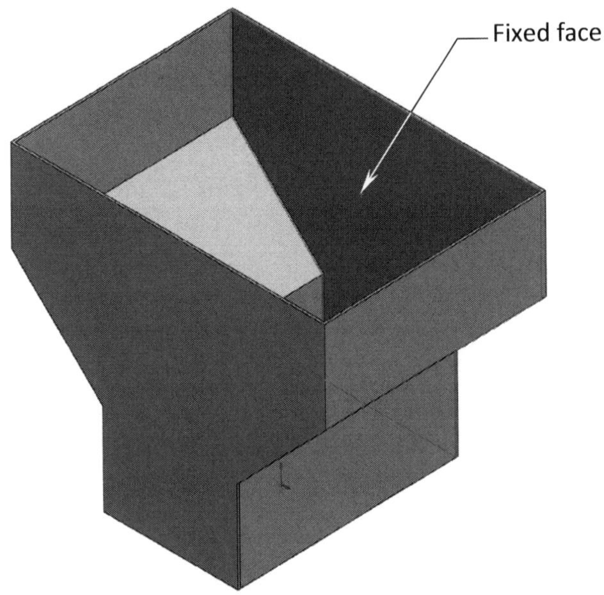

Enable the Auto Relief checkbox and select:

Rectangular
Ratio: **0.50**

Keep the Gap at the default **.010in**.

Click **OK**.

Auto Relief cuts were added to some of the corners. Click **OK** to accept and close out of the message dialog box.

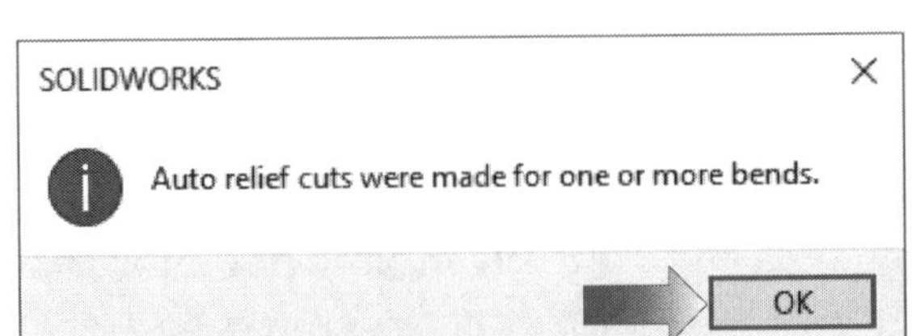

5. Flattening the sheet metal part:

The model has been converted into a sheet metal part and it can be flattened at this time.

Click **Flatten** on the **Sheet Metal** tab.

The image below shows Bend Lines in the flat pattern.

To toggle the bend lines on or off, expand the Flat-Pattern feature at the bottom of the FeatureManager tree and <u>Show</u> the **Bend-Lines1**.

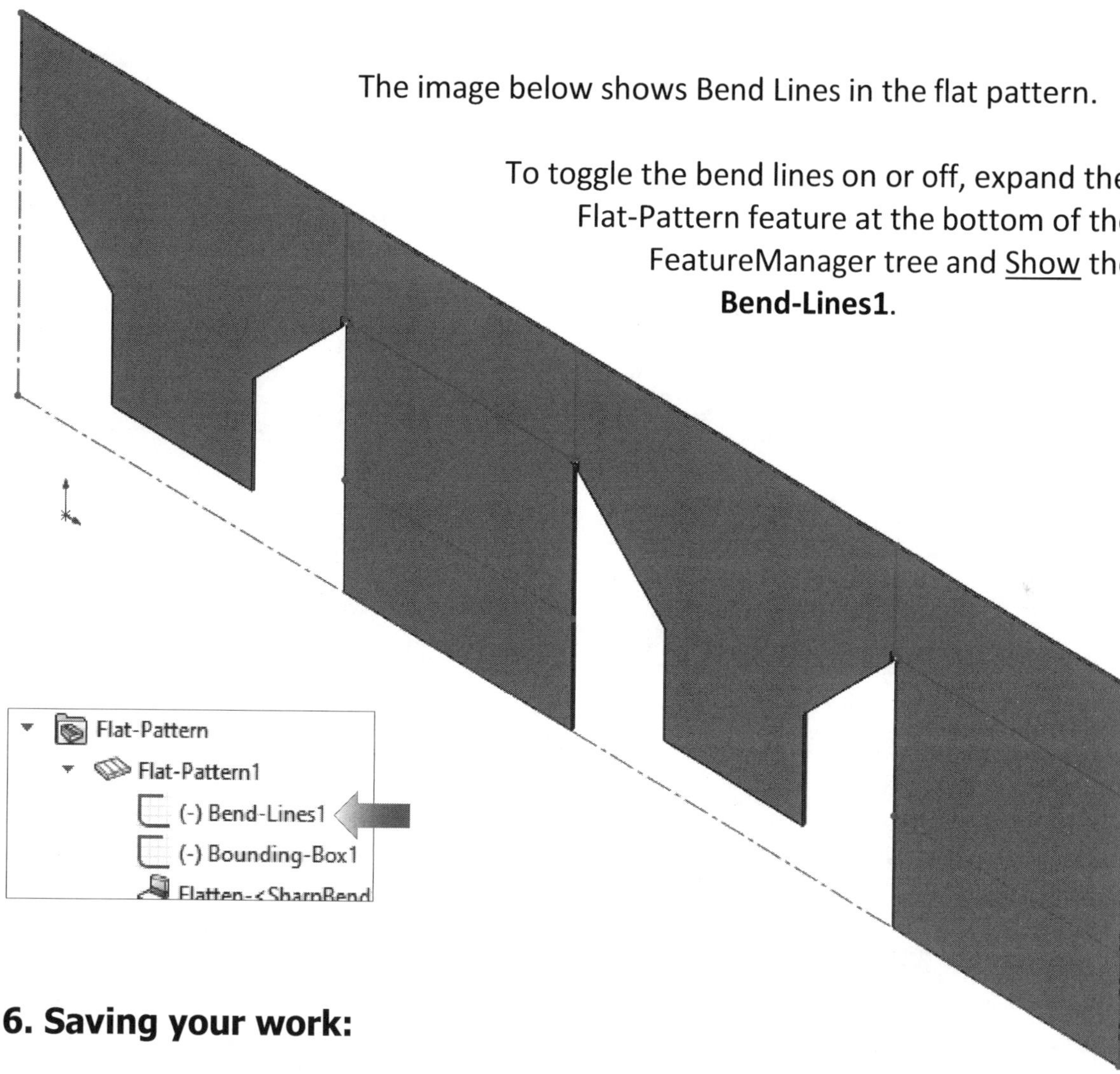

6. Saving your work:

Select **File, Save As.**

Enter: **Convert to SM 2_Completed.sldprt** for the file name.

Click **Save.**

Sheet Metal Costing

The Sheet Metal Costing tool helps you calculate how much it costs to manufacture sheet metal, machined, multibody parts, and assemblies as well as plastic molded, cast, 3D printed parts, and multibody weldments by automating the cost estimation and quotation process.

You can set the model material for a part from the material you select in the Costing Task Pane. You can save Costing data such as CAD files, Costing templates, and Costing reports locally as a package, with the Costing Pack and Go tool.

1. Opening a part document:

Browse to the Training Folder and open a part document named: **Sheet Metal Costing.**

The Sheet Metal Costing operations include the following:

* Flattened sheet cutting operations (such as laser, water jet, and plasma cutting)
* Library features (such as punches and forming tools)
* Bends
* Custom operations (such as painting, anodizing, and heat treat)
* Machine or process setup operations (such as brake setup costs)

The Costing tool automatically recognizes a sheet metal part as a part that contains sheet metal features such as flanges, bends, or forming tools. Features such as holes and cuts are recognized as manufacturing cut paths for operations such as laser, water jet, and plasma cutting.

The costs calculated by the Costing tool are as accurate as the data in your templates. Although SOLIDWORKS provides prepopulated templates, it is best to create custom templates based on your manufacturing costs. You may need to work with your manufacturing vendors to create custom templates that reflect actual costs.

2. Launching the Costing program:

Switch to the **Evaluate** tab and click **Costing** 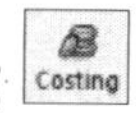.

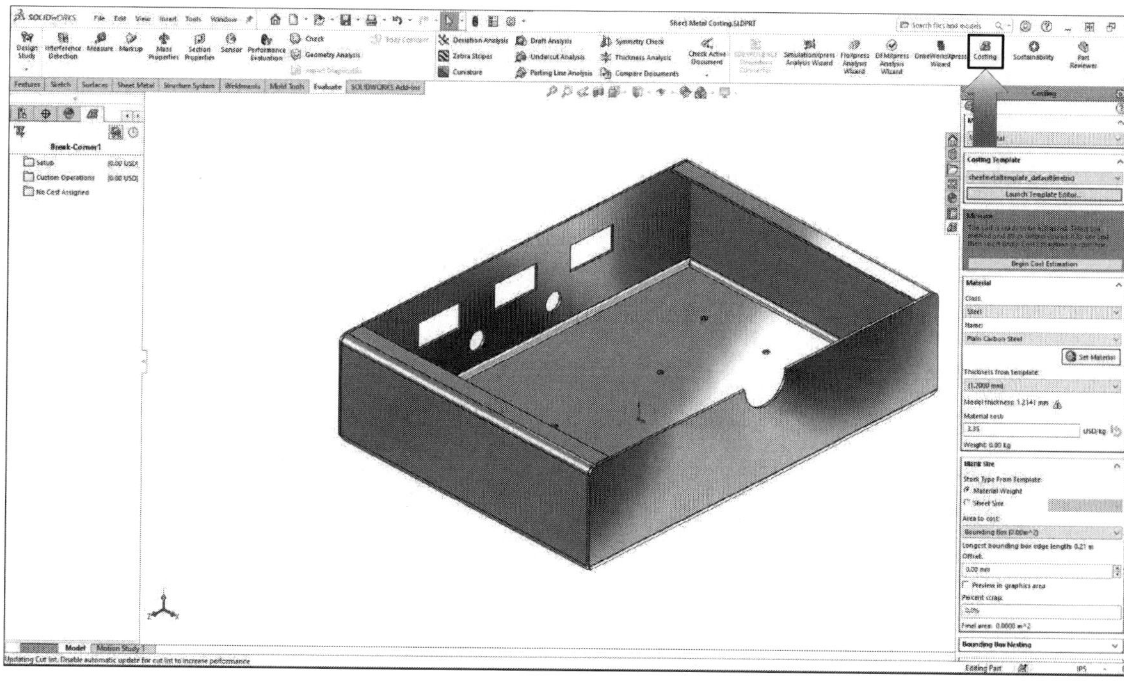

Let us take a minute and get familiar with the layout of the Sheet Metal Costing program.

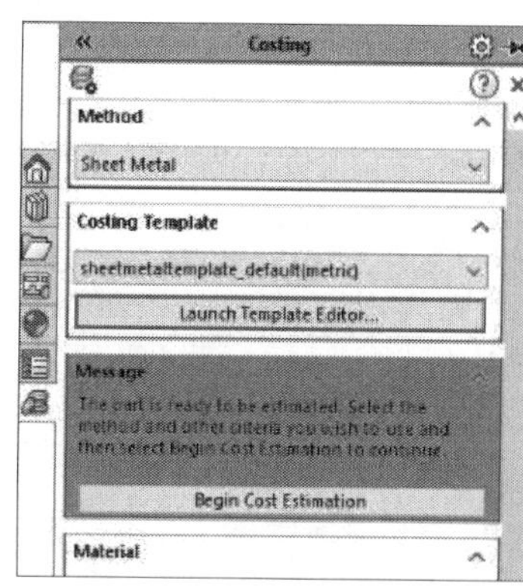

The Sheet Metal Costing program is loaded on the right side of the screen, in the **Task Pane**.

The manufacturing operations in the Costing template are displayed on the left side of the screen or in the **CostingManager**.

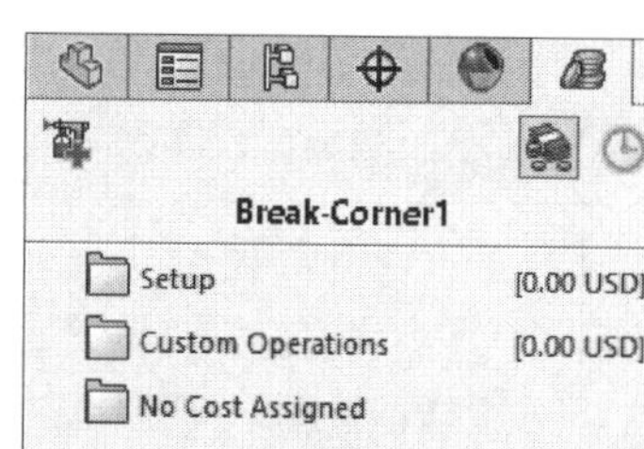

3. Filling out the Costing info:

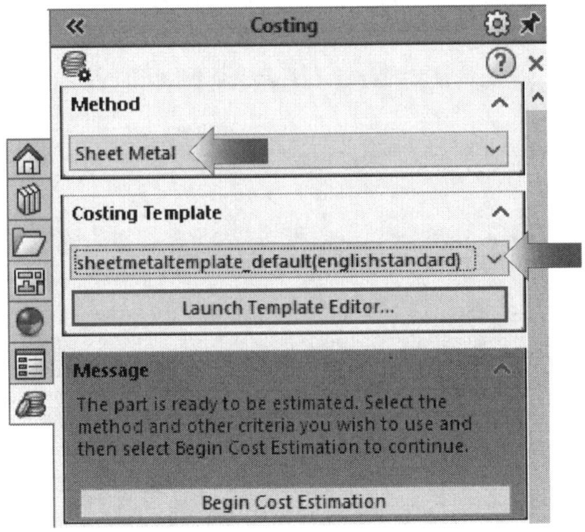

For Manufacturing Methods, on the upper right side of the screen, under the **Methods** section, select: **Sheet Metal**.

For **Costing Template**, select: **Sheetmetaltemplate_default (Englishstandard).**

Note: You can customize the template and specify rates and costs for the procedures required to manufacture a sheet metal part or body in the sheet metal template. You can include customized information in the template, such as material cost and thicknesses, cost of manufacturing, and manufacturing setup costs.

You can determine how manufacturing operations affect the cost of your design. For example, you can set up templates for vendors that use different manufacturing operations.

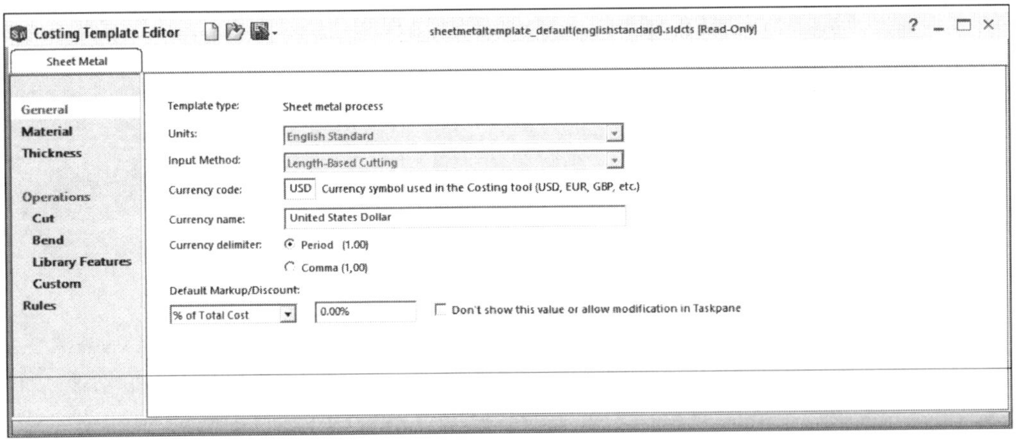

The sample Costing Template Editor window is shown above, but for this lesson, we will use the default values that have been preset and saved in the Sheet Metal Costing template.

Filling out the material information.

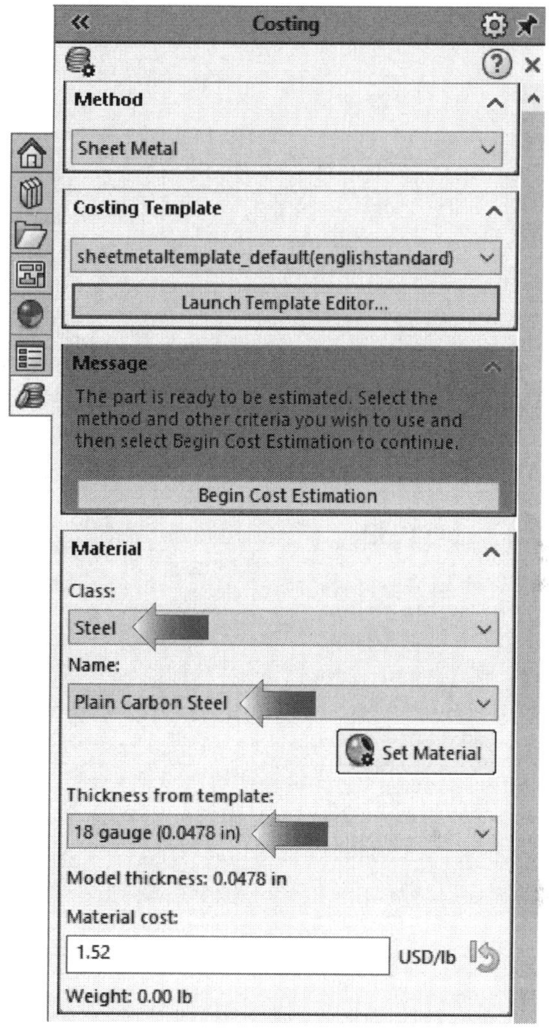

Change the Material Class to:
Steel.

For Material Name, select:
Plain Carbon Steel.

Material Thickness:
18 Gauge (0.0458in).

The **Material Cost** is selected from the Costing Template automatically. It is preset to **$1.52 USD/lb**.

Click **Begin Cost Estimation**.

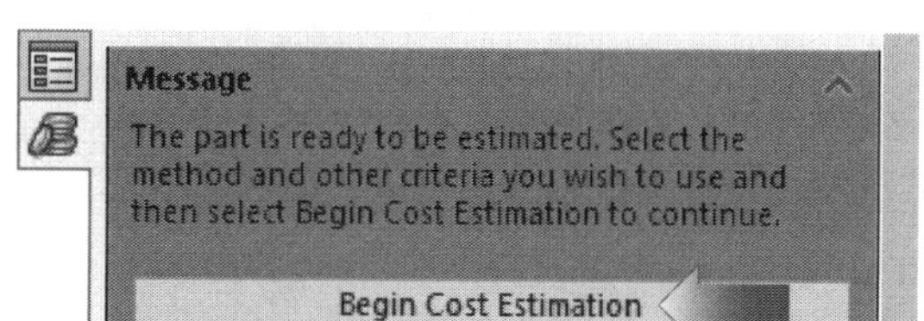

The Sheet Metal Costing program starts analyzing the costs based on the input values and the selected material. The default quantity is set to 100; we will make some modifications to those options in the next few steps.

Based on the information provided, the cost-per-part is **$9.54** in the quantity of **100**.

The cost break down is also displayed on the left side, in the **CostingManager**.

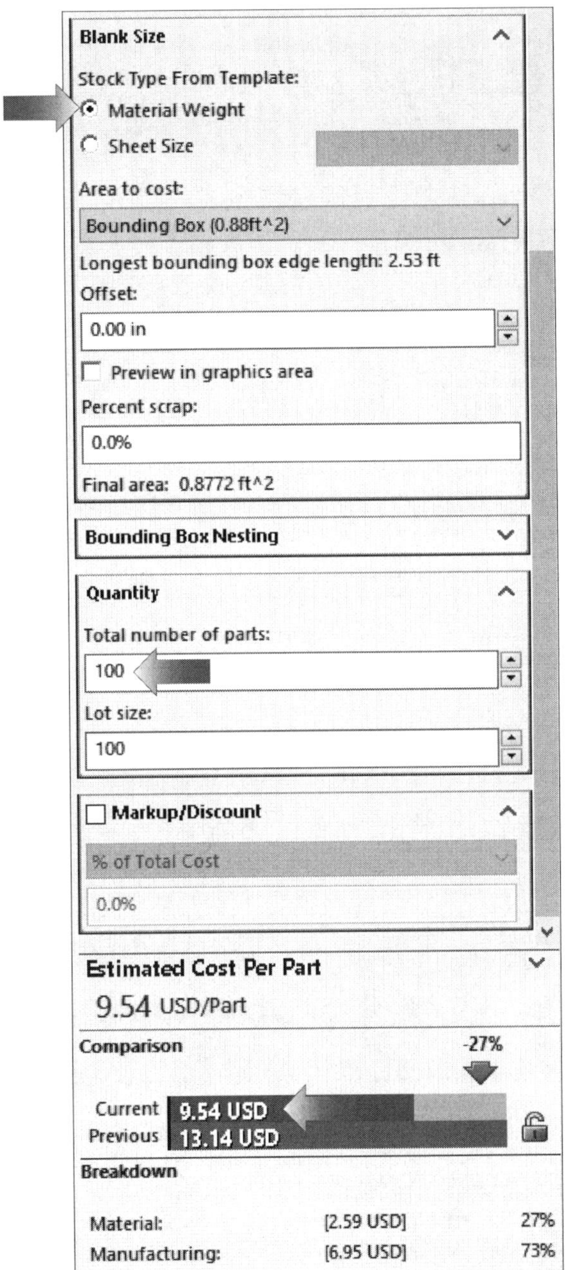

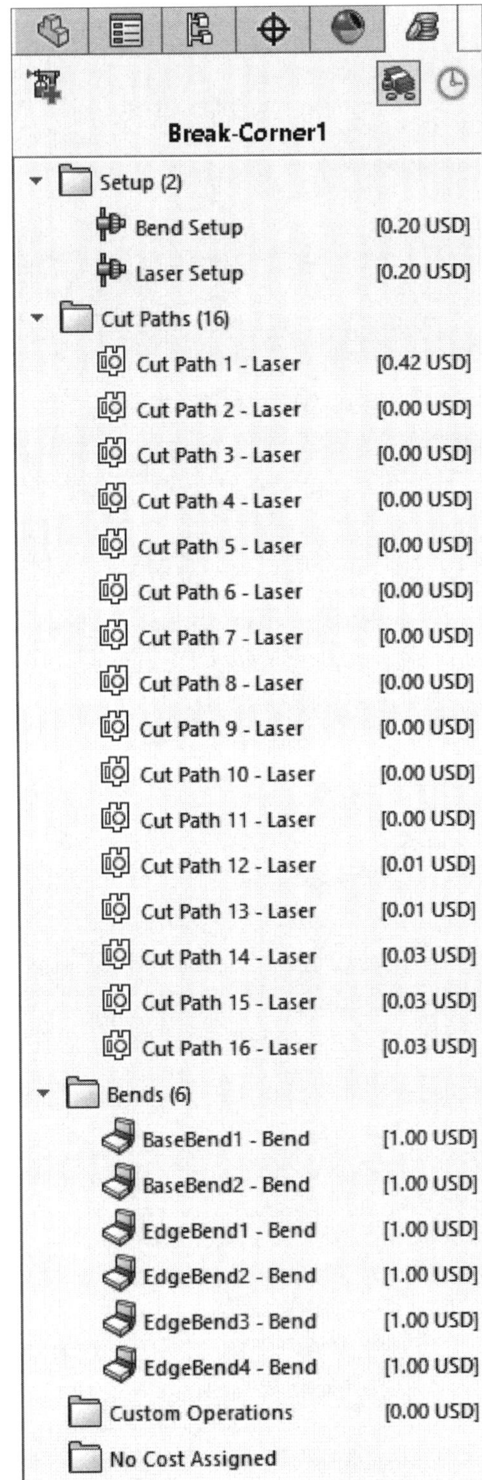

4. Changing the quantity:

For learning purposes, let us make some adjustments to see if the cost-per-part will increase or decrease.

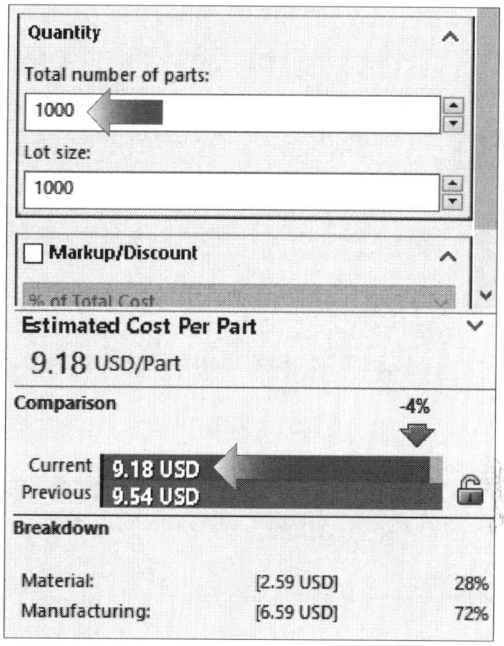

Locate the Quantity section and change the **Total Number of Parts** to **1000**.

The Sheet Metal Cost program recalculates and displays the cost-per-part in the quantity of 1000 is **$9.18 USD**.

The difference between 100 quantity and 1000 quantity is **.36 cents** per part.

Let us try a larger quantity to see the difference in cost-per-part.

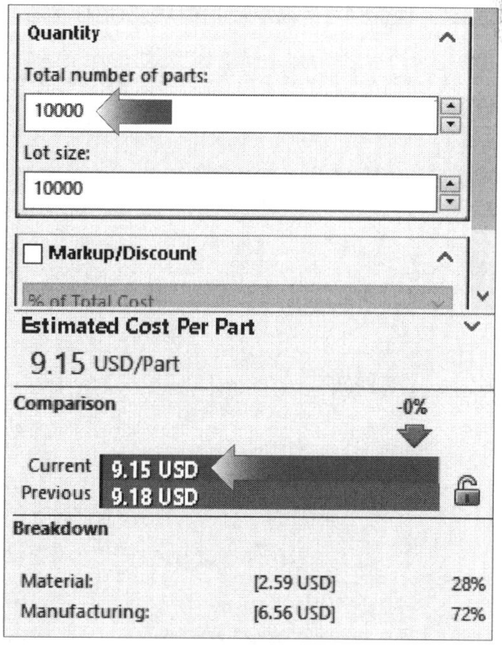

Change the Quantity to **10,000**.

The Sheet Metal Cost program recalculates and displays the cost-per-part in the quantity of 10,000 is **$9.15 USD**.

The difference is **.3 cents** per part.

5. Changing the material:

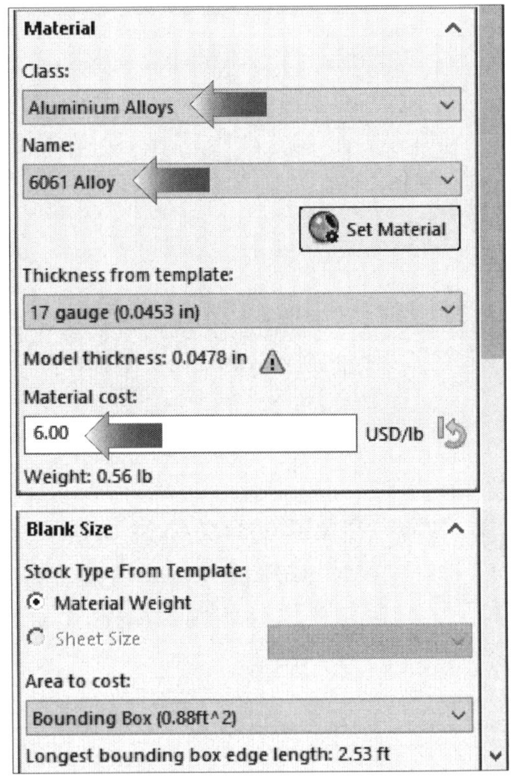

It would be interesting to see how changing the material can greatly increase or decrease the costs, let us change the material of the part to a close substitute for aluminum.

In the **Material** section, change the Class to: **Aluminum Alloys**.

Change the **Material Name** to: **6061 Alloy**.

The preset value for this material is **$6.00 USD/lb**. which is much higher than the Plain Carbon Steel that was selected earlier.

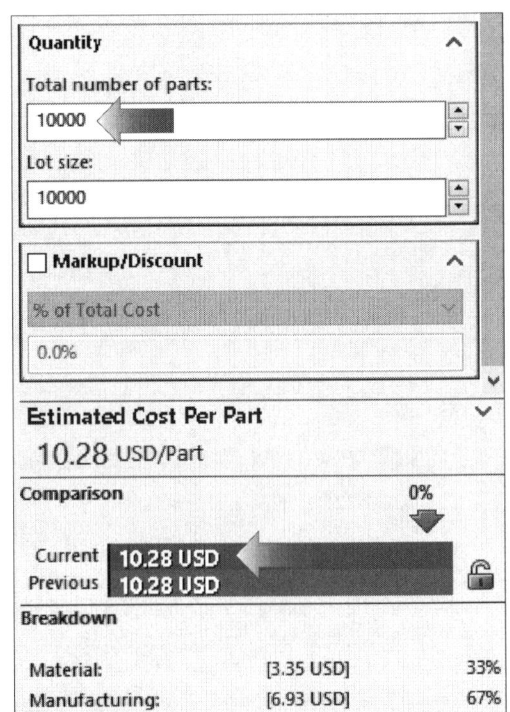

The Sheet Metal Costing program recalculates the costs based on the material changes.

The cost-per-part is now at: **$10.28 USD** in the same quantity of 10,000 pieces.

We are going to change the material back to **Plain Carbon Steel** as shown on page 10-14, and then generate a report to capture the details of the sheet metal cost estimate.

The report is for the **Plain Carbon Steel** material, quantity **10,000** parts.

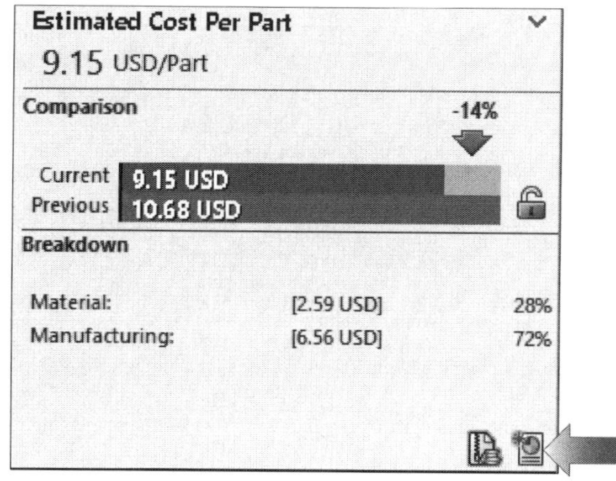

Click **Generate Report**  at the lower right corner of the Task Pane.

In the Report Options dialog box, select the File Type: Word (.docx) or Excel (.xlsx).

Enter a **name** for the report.

Select a **location** to save the report.

Click **Publish**.

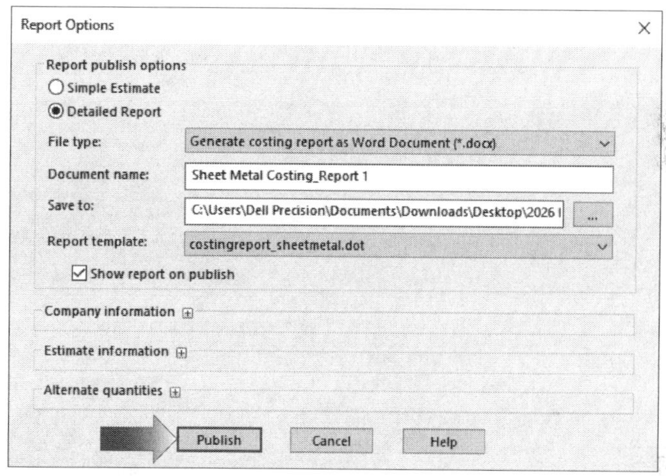

Note:
It may take several minutes for the report to be created.

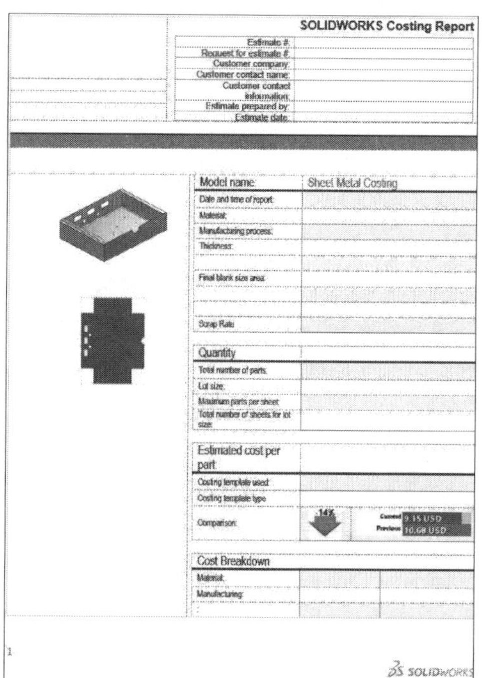

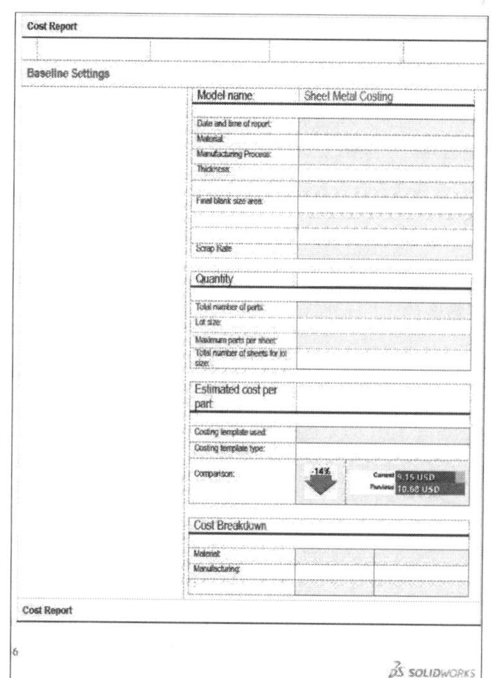

6. Saving your work:

Select **File, Save As**.

Enter: **Sheet Metal Costing_Completed** for the file name.

Click **Save**.

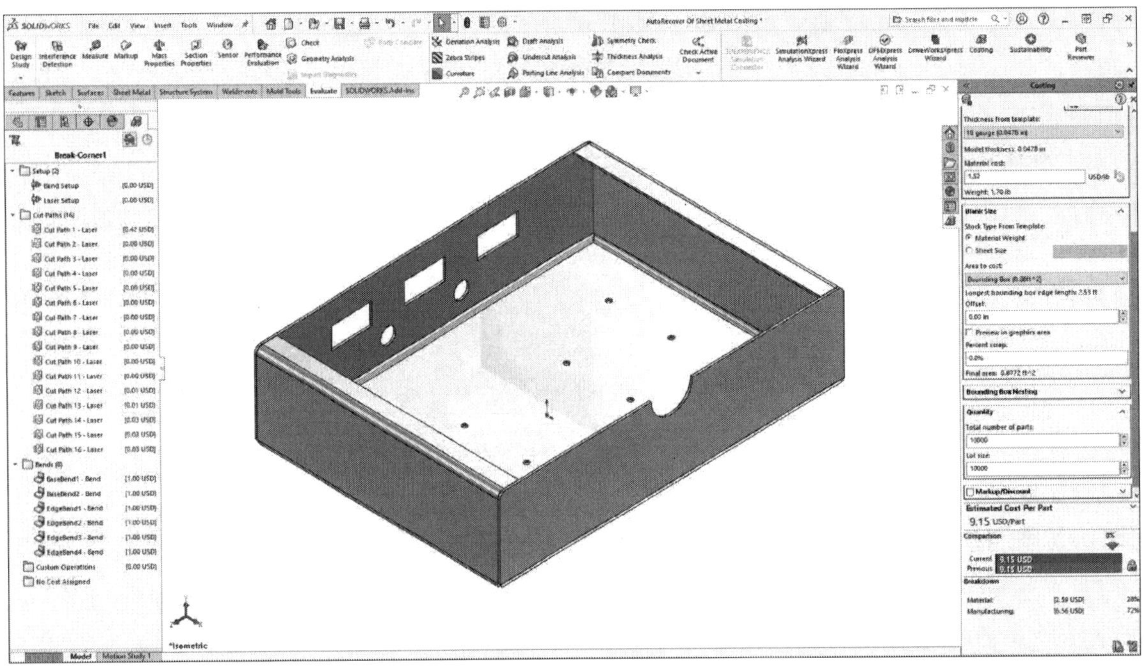

Close all documents.

Lesson 11: Sheet Metal Assemblies

Most of the time, sheet metal parts are designed as a single or as multibody parts, but if you prefer to develop them in the assembly level so that assembly features such as Hole Series and toolbox fasteners can be used, this would be a great alternative.

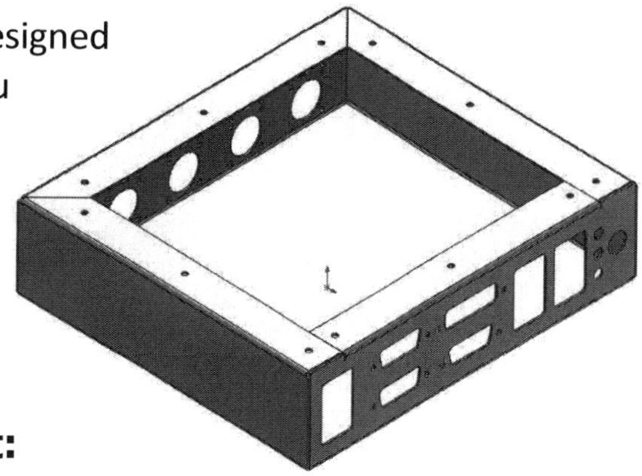

1. Opening an assembly document:

Browse to the Training Folder and open an assembly document named: **Sheet Metal Assembly.sldasm**.

There is only 1 component in this assembly document at this time. We will insert another component and create the matching holes for both.

2. Inserting a component:

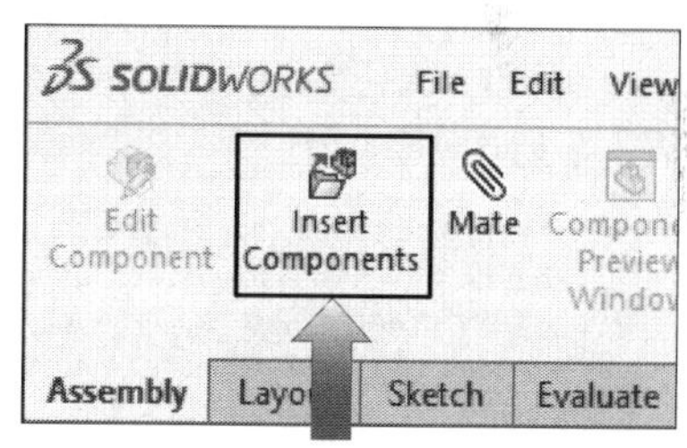

Switch to the **Assembly** tab and select: **Insert Components**.

Browse to the Training folder and select the component name: **Chassis Cover**.

Place the Chassis Cover above the Housing approximately as shown.

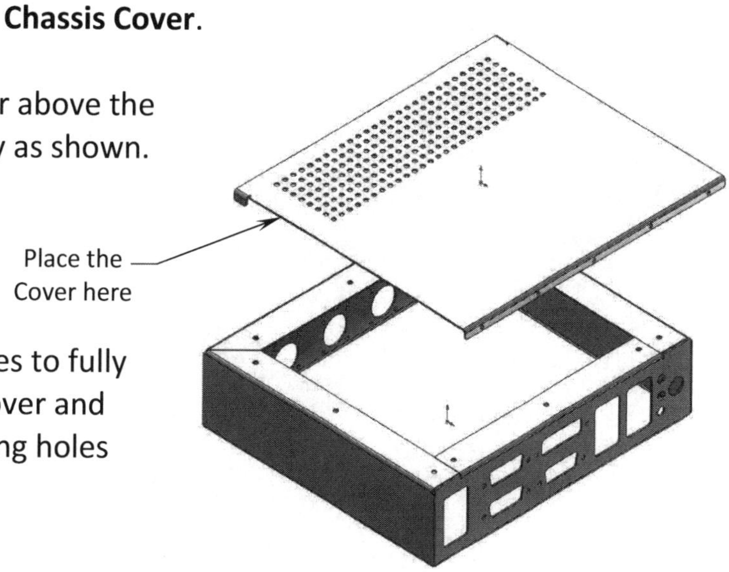

We will add some mates to fully position the Chassis Cover and then add some matching holes to both components.

3. Adding a Width mate:

The Selection Filters are commonly used in the assembly environment when mating the components together. The filters will assist us with selecting the right type of entities for mating, quickly and easily.

Press the <u>**F5**</u> function key to enable the **Selection Filters**.

Select the **Filter Faces** button as indicated below.

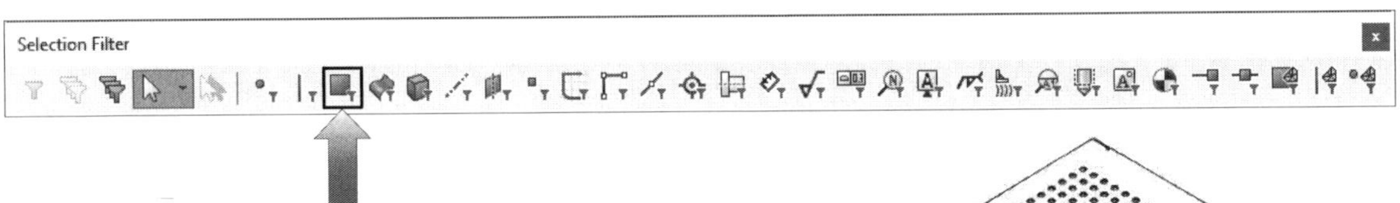

A funnel symbol is attached to the mouse cursor indicating a filter is active.

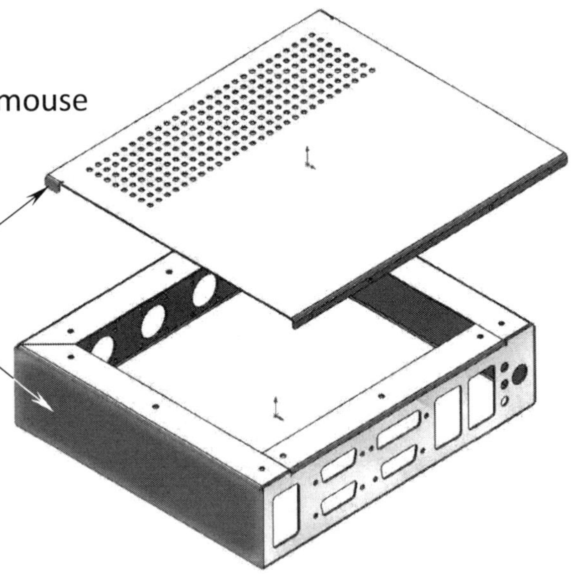

Let us try out a shortcut called: **Quick-Mate**.

Control + select 2 faces on the left side

Hold the **Control** key and select **2 faces** on the left side as noted.

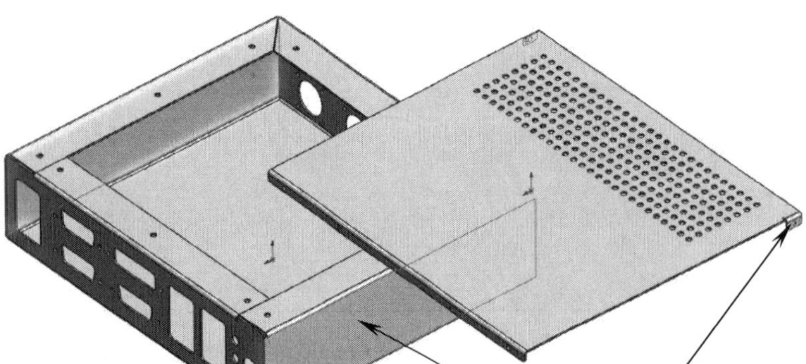

Release the Control key and rotate the assembly to the opposite side.

Hold the **Control** key and select **2 faces** of the 2 components as indicated. Total of <u>4 faces</u> are selected.

Control + select 2 faces on the right side

Click the **Width** button.

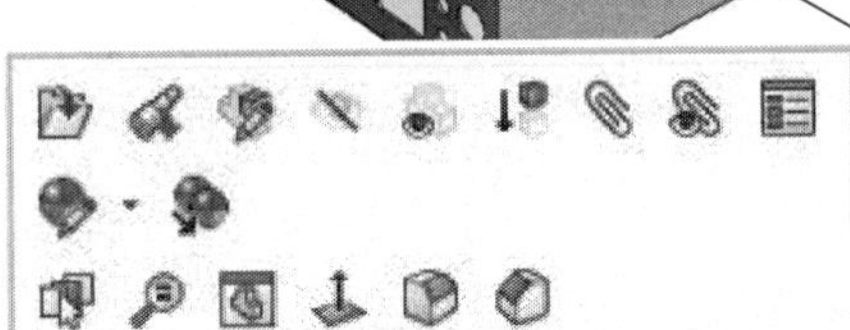

Click **OK**.

4. Adding a Coincident mate:

Continue with using the Quick-Mate shortcut.

Hold the **Control** key and select the **front face** of the Chassis, release the control key, and rotate the assembly to the opposite side.

Hold the **Control** key and select the **inside face** of the small tab, represented by the dotted line.

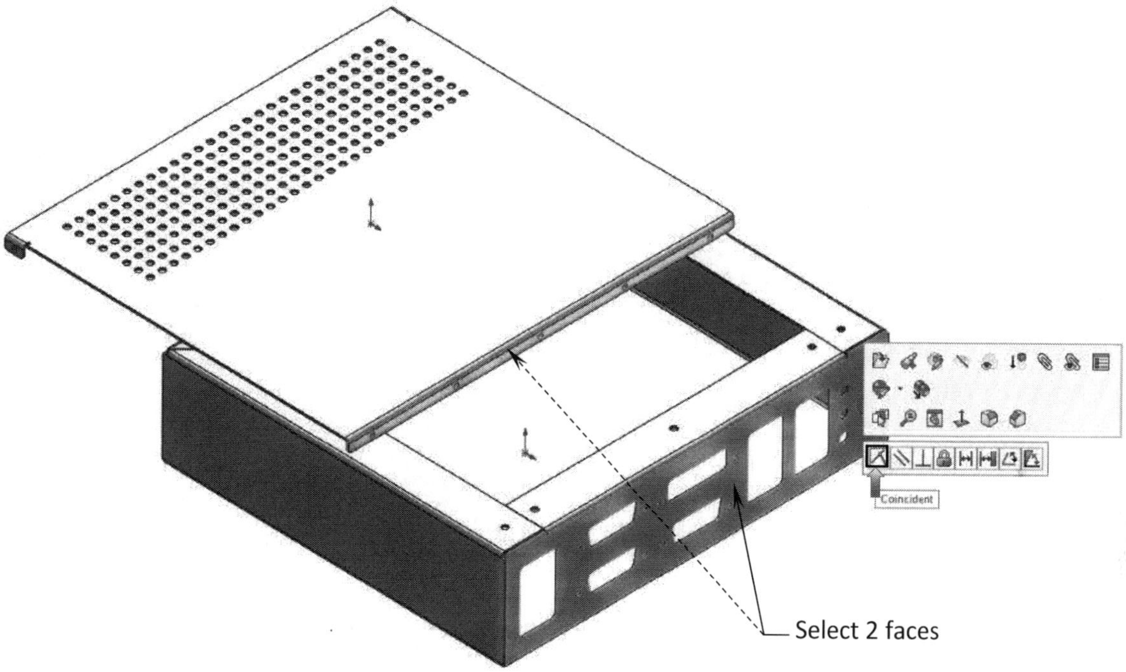

Release the Control key and select the **Coincident** button from the flyout shortcut menus.

Note: when using the Quick-Mate shortcuts, do not move the mouse after selecting the 2 faces or the flyout shortcut menus will be canceled.

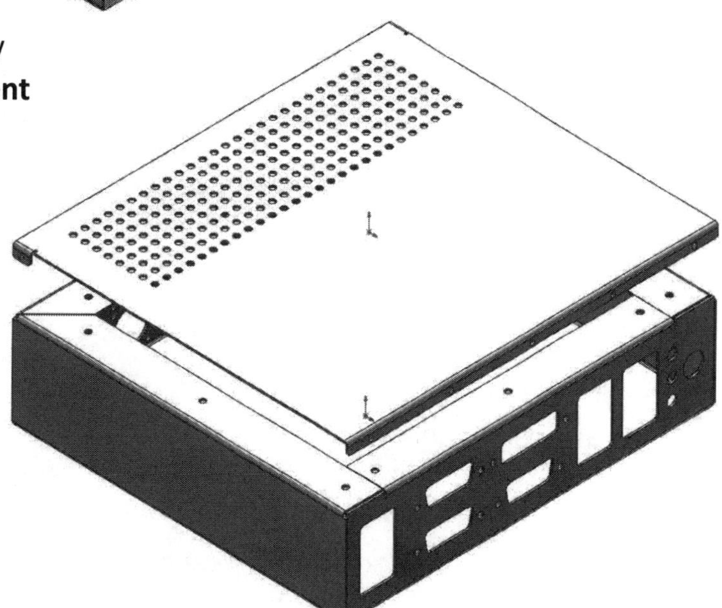

5. Adding another Coincident mate:

Hold the **Control** key and select the **top face** of the Chassis, release the control key, rotate the model until you can see the bottom of the cover.

Hold the **Control** key and select the **bottom face** of the Cover.

Click **Coincident** on the pop-up shortcut menus.

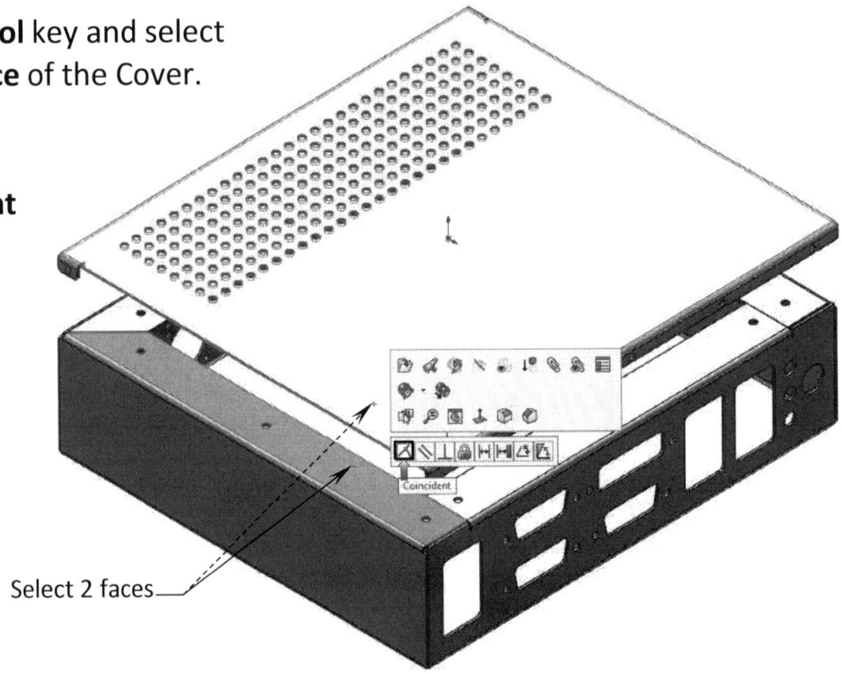

The 2 components are fully defined.

On the FeatureManager tree, there should be no **Plus** or **Minus** symbols next to the name of each component.

The **Minus** sign appears next to the name of the component means it is under defined.

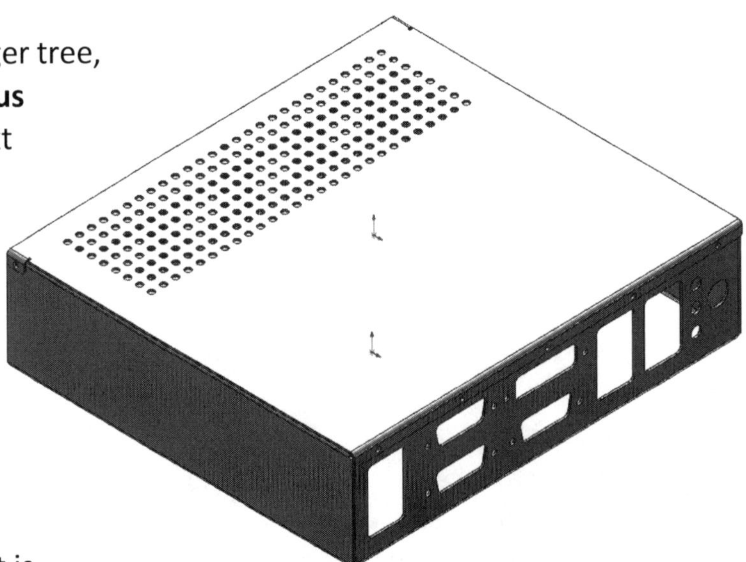

The **Plus** sign means it is over defined (either some wrong mates were used, or too many mates have been assigned to the component).

6. Enabling the Toolbox library:

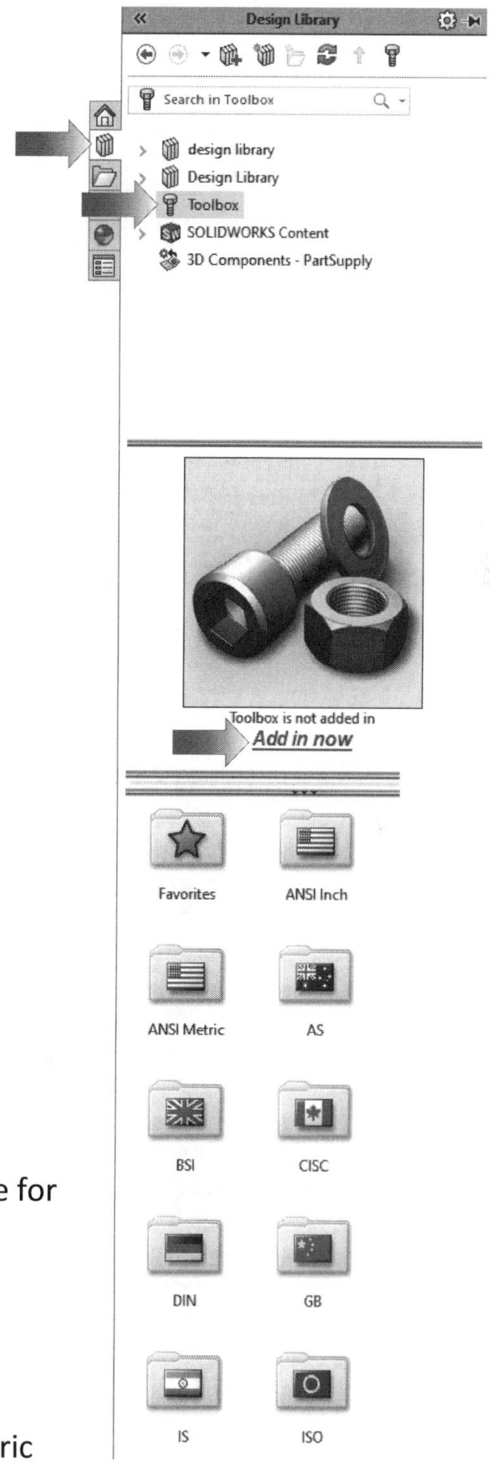

This is an optional step; you need to have Toolbox installed in your computer in order to work with step 6 and step 7.

The tree on the right hand side of the screen is called the **Task-Pane**.

Click the **Design Library** tab on the Task-Pane to expand it.

Click on the **Toolbox** icon to expand it.

Click **Add In Now** to load this library into the memory.

Once loaded, the fasteners and hardware for different standards are displayed on the lower right side of the Task-Pane.

We will use either ANSI Inch or ANSI Metric in the next couple of steps.

7. Using the Hole Series:

Switch to the **Assembly** tab and select:
Assembly Features, Hole Series.

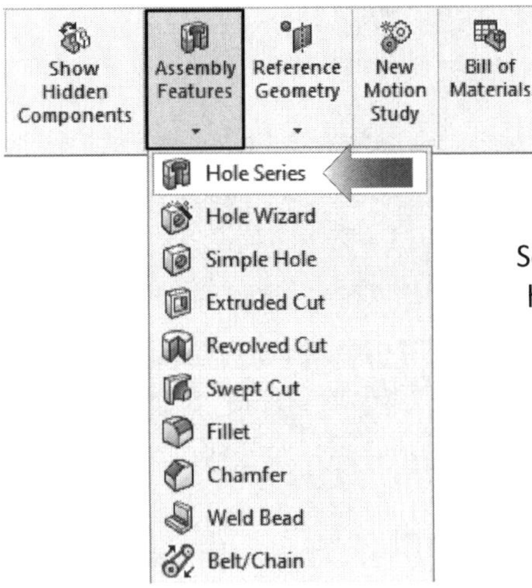

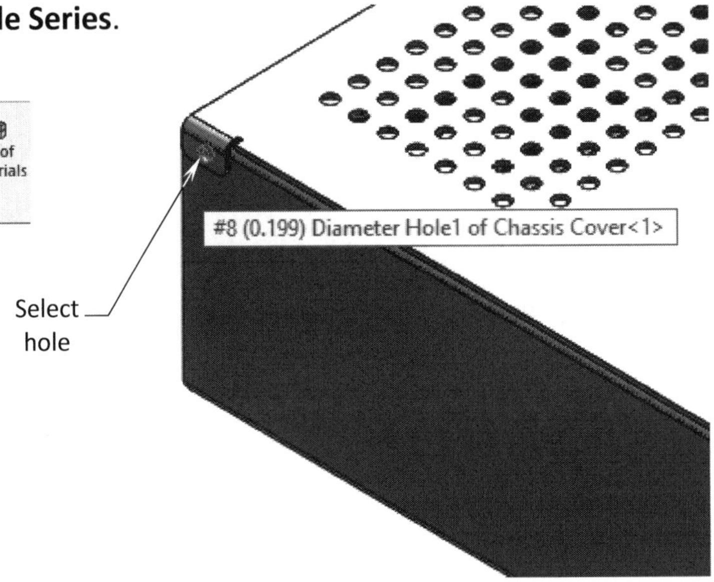

On the 1st screen, click **Use Existing Hole(s)** and select one of the side holes.

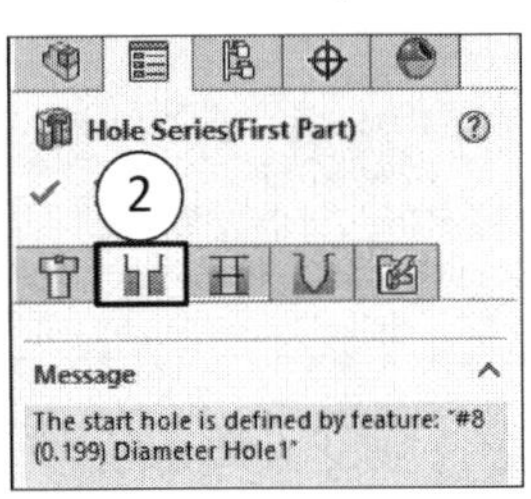

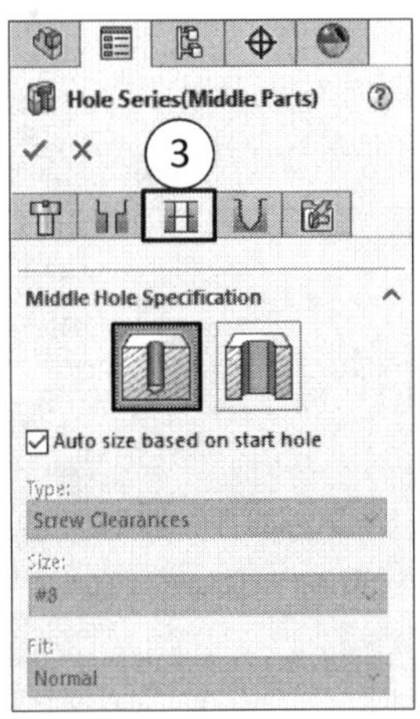

Skip the 2nd screen, because the new hole has already been defined by the existing holes.

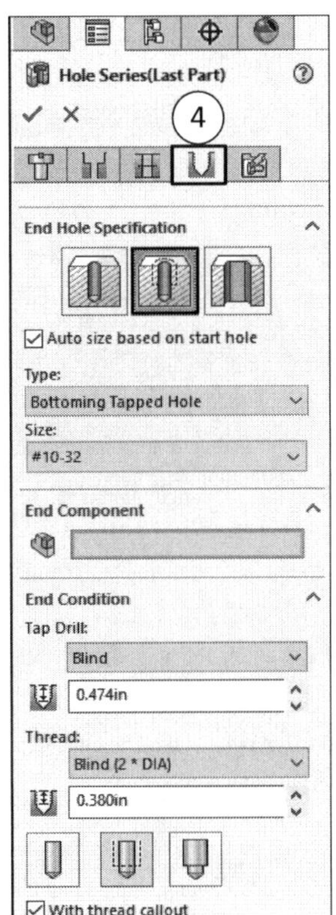

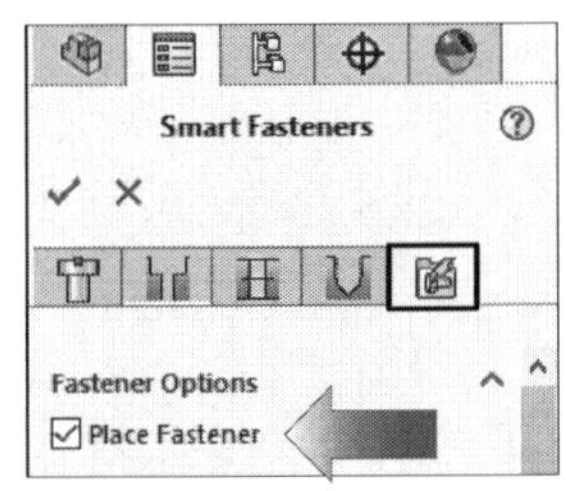

On the 3rd screen, select the **Hole** option.

On the 4th screen, select **Straight Tap** and accept all the default values.

Click screen no. 5 to add the fasteners.

On the 5th screen, click the **Place Fastener** checkbox.

Also enable the checkboxes:

Auto Size

Auto Update

The matching screw size is found and placed over the hole, but it may not be the right type.

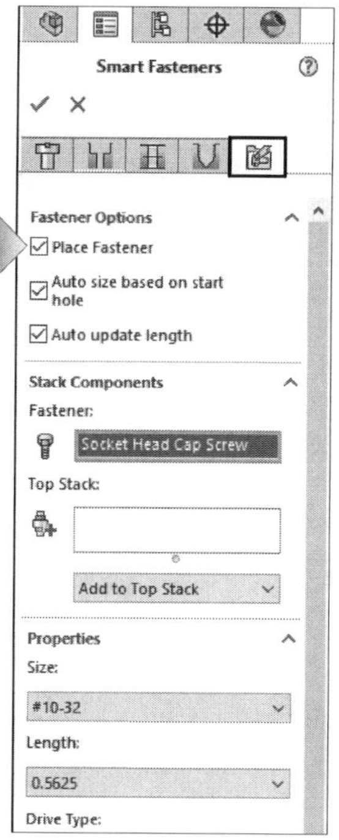

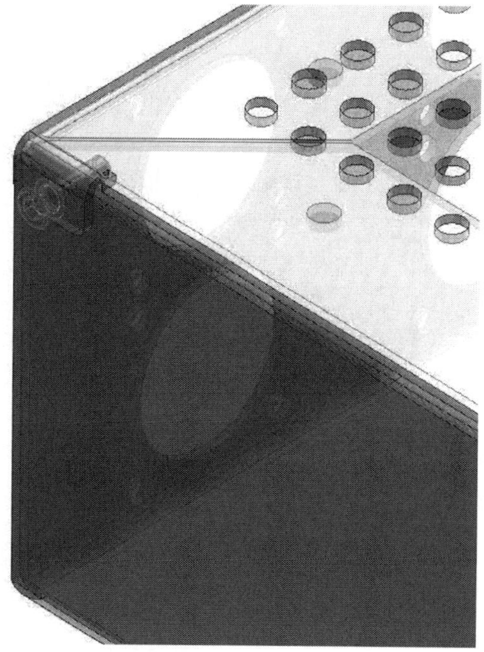

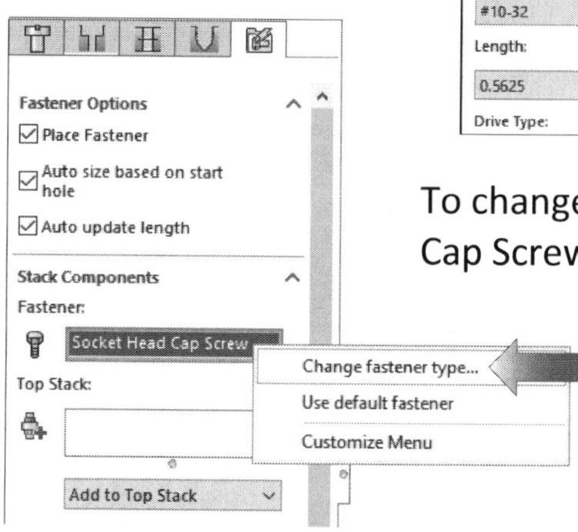

To change the screw type, right-click on the Socket Head Cap Screw and select: **Change Fastener Type**.

Expand the Round Head Bolts group and select: **Round Head Bolt**.

Size: **#10-24** - Length **.375in**.

Click **OK**.

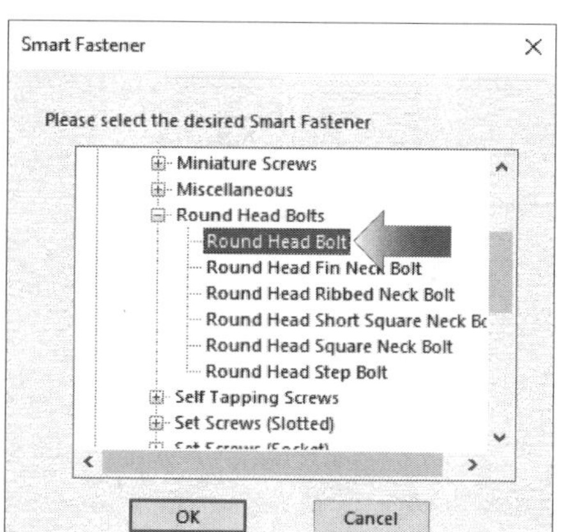

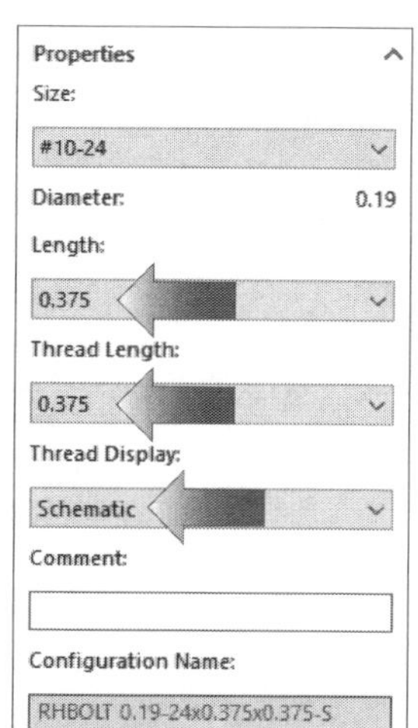

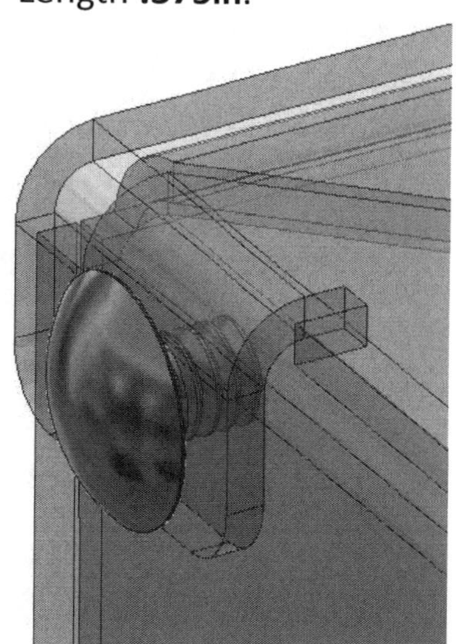

Select **Assembly Features, Hole Series** again.

Screen 1: select <u>one</u> of the holes in the front of the **Cover** component.

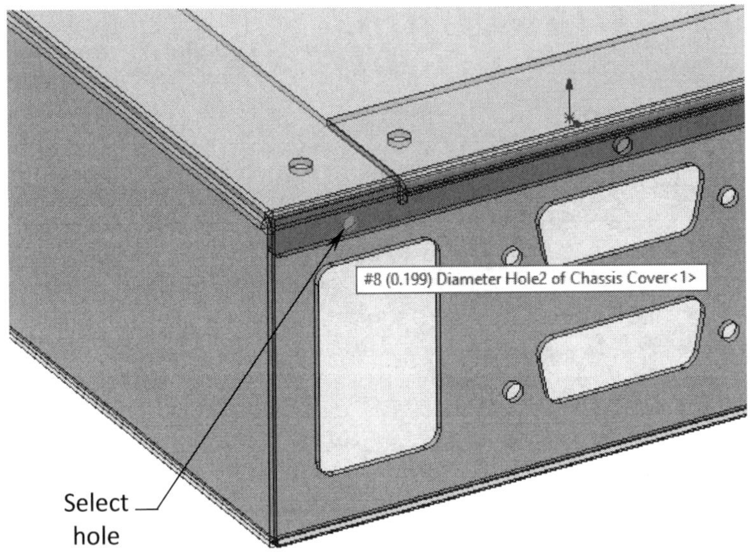

Screen 2: **skip**. - Screen 3: select **Hole**. - Screen 4: click **Straight Tap**.

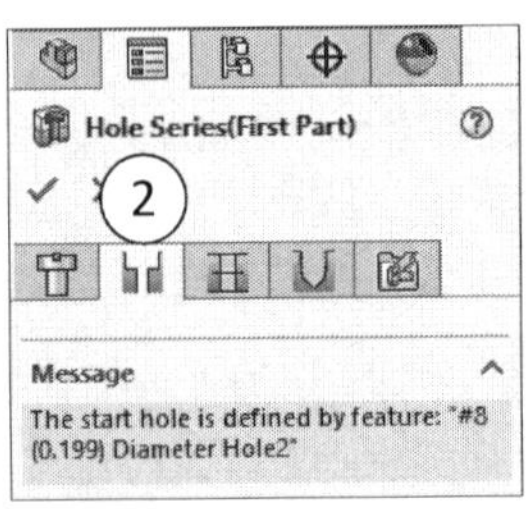

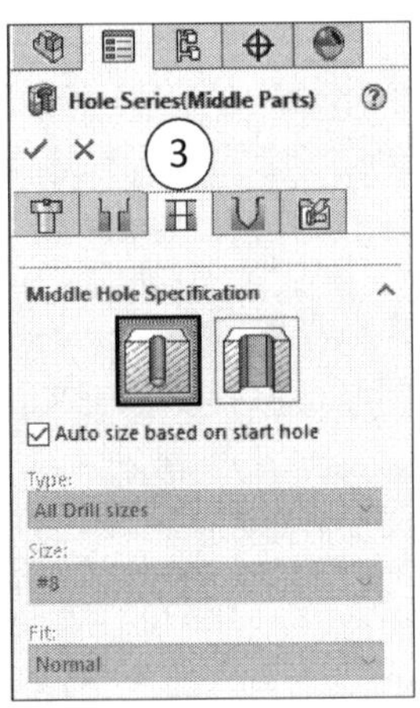

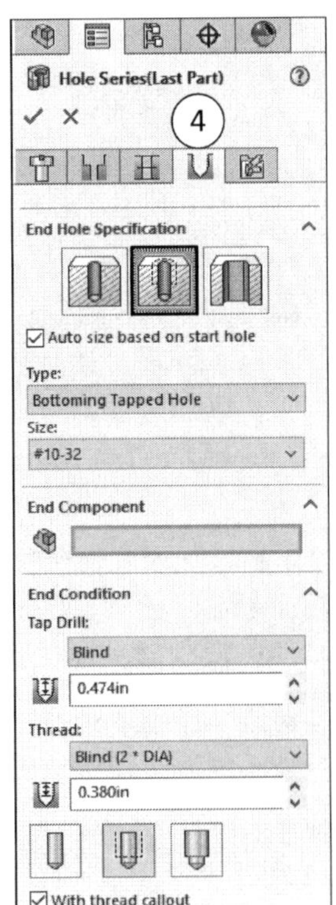

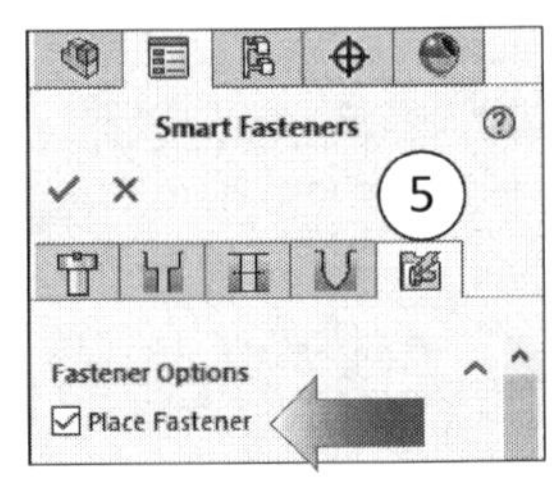

Screen 5: click **Place Fastener**.

Right-click on Socket Head Cap Screw and select: **Change Fastener Type**.

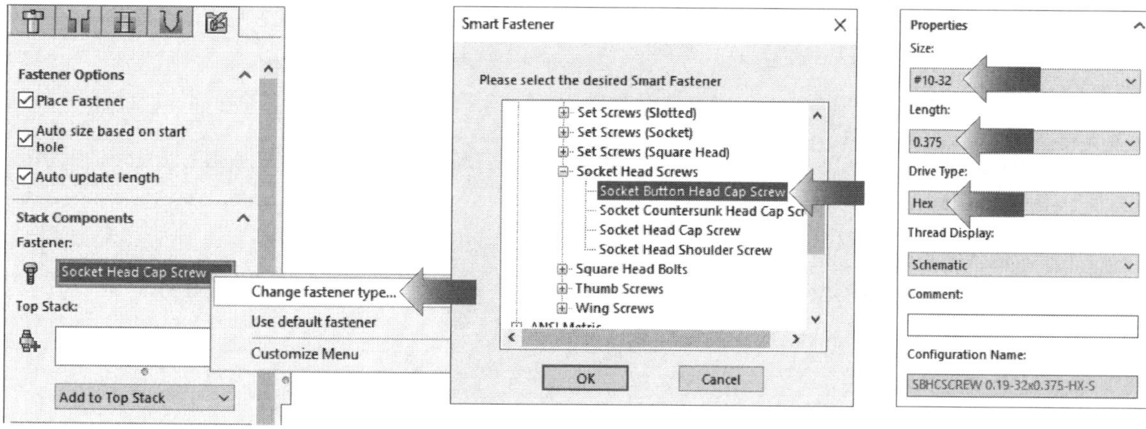

Expand the Socket Head Cap Screw group and select:
Socket Button Head Cap Screw.

Size: **#10-32** - Length" **.375in**. - Drive Type: **Hex**

Click **OK**.

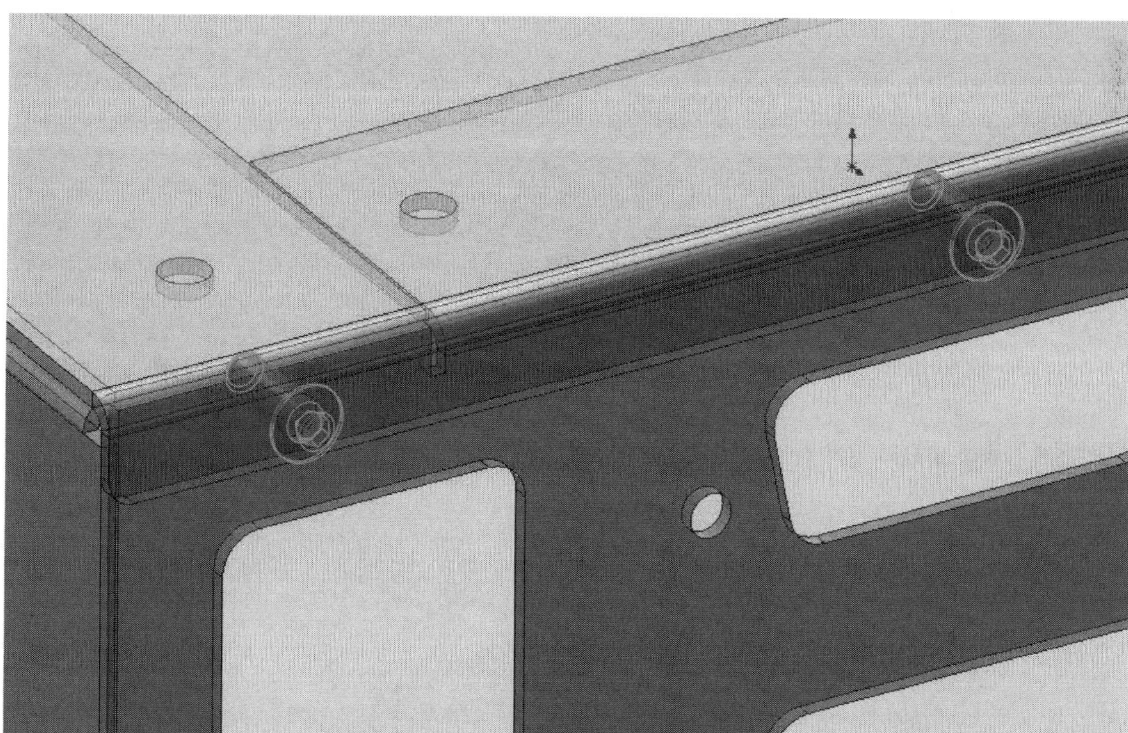

8. Mirroring a screw:

We can repeat the last step and add another screw on the far side, but we will just mirror the screw instead.

Switch to the **Assembly** tab. Expand the **Linear Component** drop-down and select: **Mirror Components**.

Use the assembly's <u>Front</u> plane and mirror the **1st screw** (#10-24).

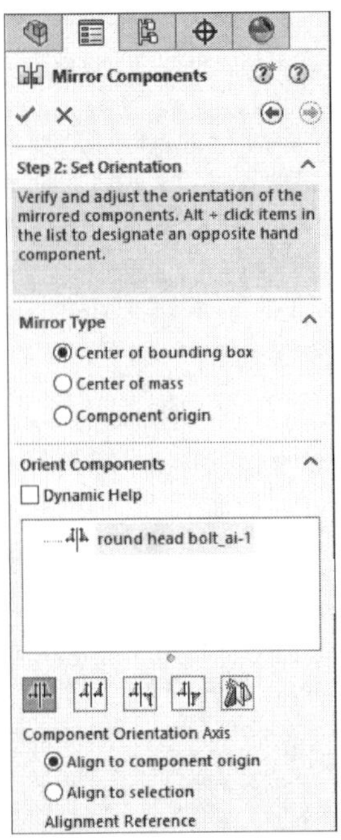

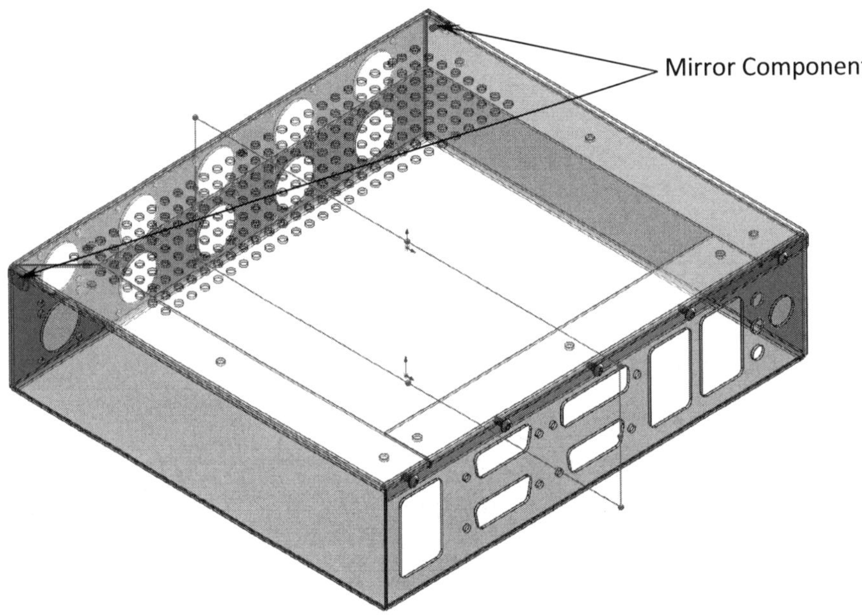

Click **OK**.

9. Saving your work:

Select **File, Save As**.

Enter: **Sheet Metal Assembly _Completed.sldprt** for the file name.

Click **Save**.

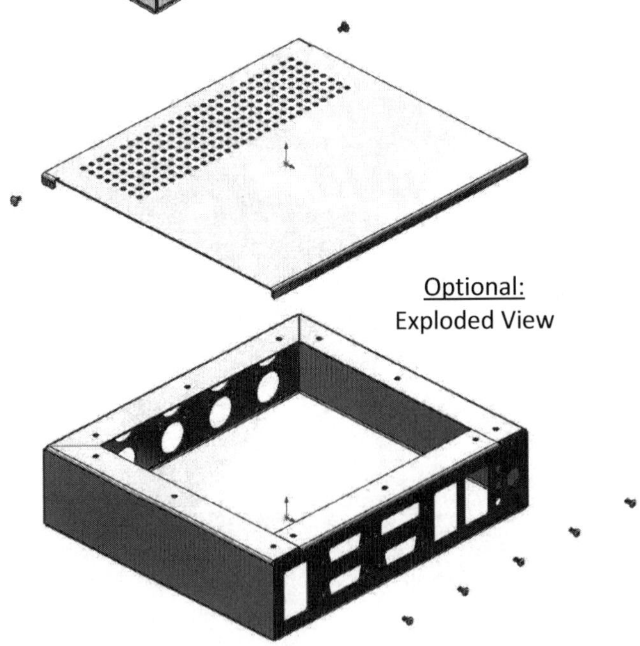

Lesson 12: Sheet Metal Drawings

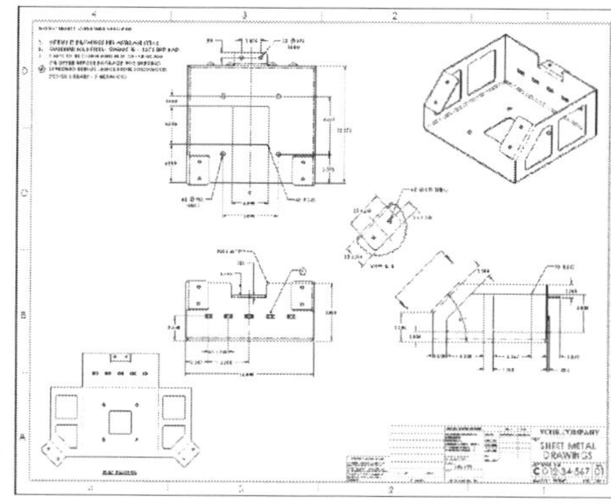

When a drawing is made from a sheet metal part, a flat pattern is automatically created. Drawings of sheet metal parts can also contain views of the bent sheet metal part, as well as the flat patterns.

DXF files of the sheet metal flat patterns also can be generated for use in manufacturing.

1. Opening a drawing document:

Browse to the Training Folder and open a drawing document named: **Sheet Metal Drawings.slddrw**

2. Examining the drawing views:

This drawing has 5 drawing views that were dragged/dropped from the **View Palette**; they are Front view, Top view, Right view, Isometric view, and a Flat Pattern view. There is also a General Notes added to the upper left corner of the drawing.

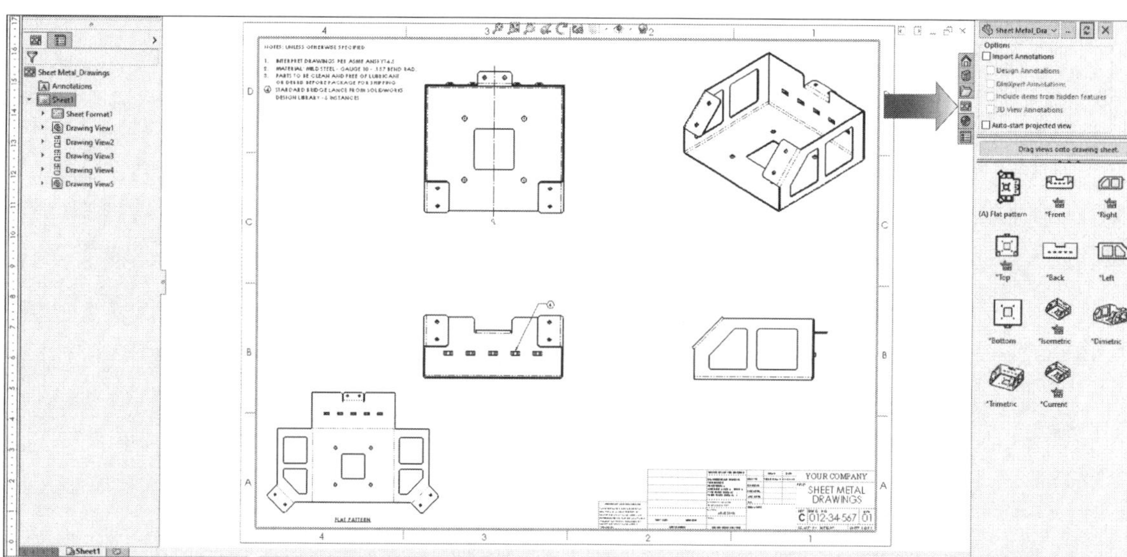

3. Adding an Auxiliary drawing view:

Depending on your company's standards and/or requirements, you may need to create a flat-pattern drawing for manufacturing and inspection purposes, but for this lesson, we will focus on making the drawing to document the finished products, or As-Folded.

Switch to the **Drawings** tab.

Select the edge as indicated and click **Auxiliary** .

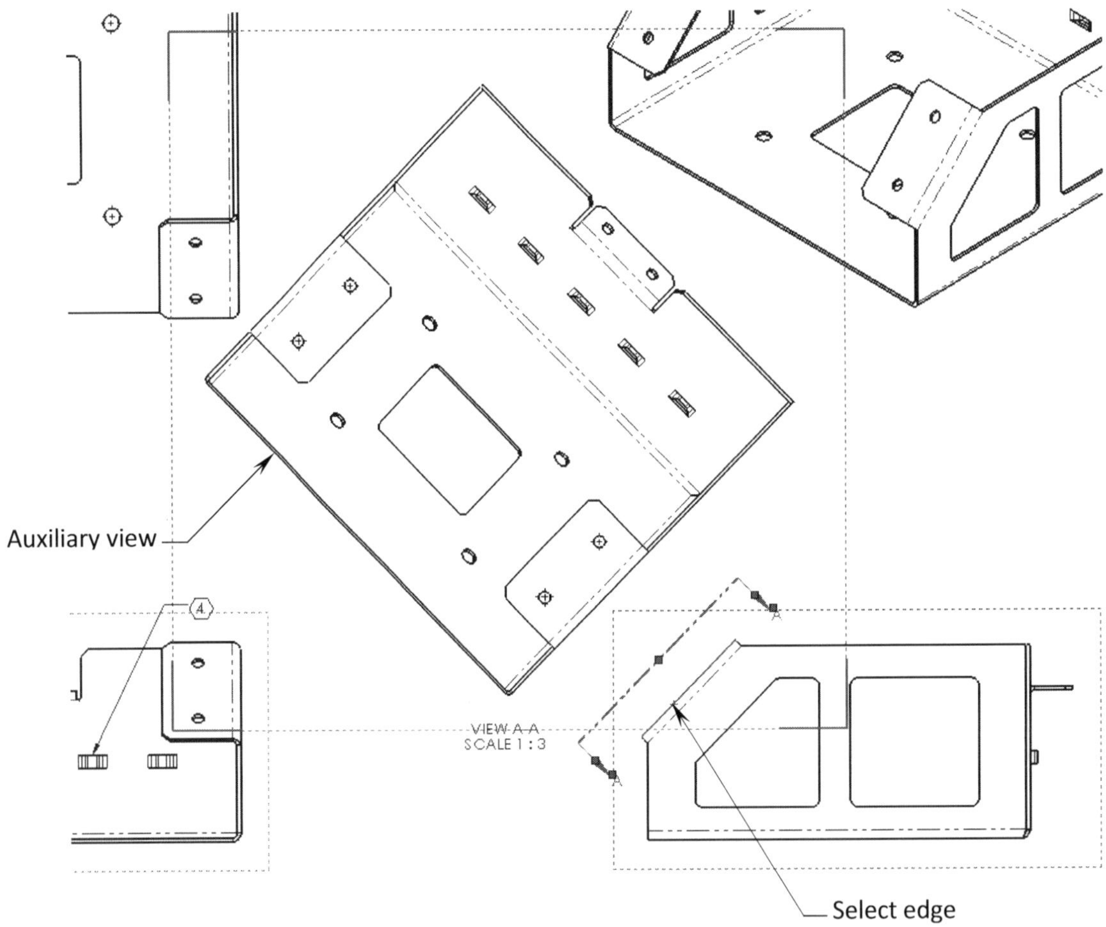

Place the Auxiliary view on the upper left side of the Right view.

Next, we will create a Crop view to show only the 2 holes on the tab.

4. Creating a Crop view:

Double-click on the dotted border of the Auxiliary view to lock the view focus.

Switch to the **Sketch** tab and sketch a **Circle** around the tab, as shown in the image on the right.

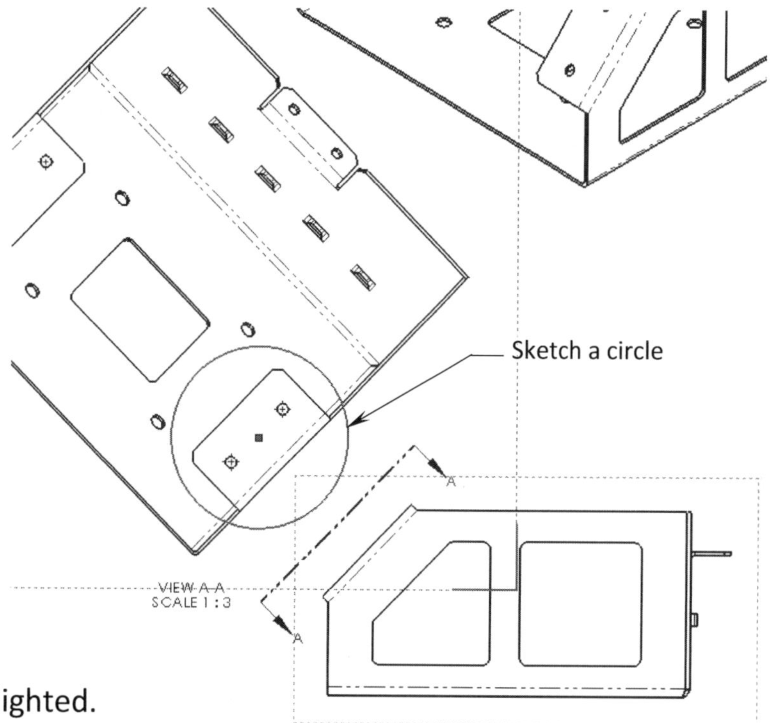

Keep the Circle highlighted.

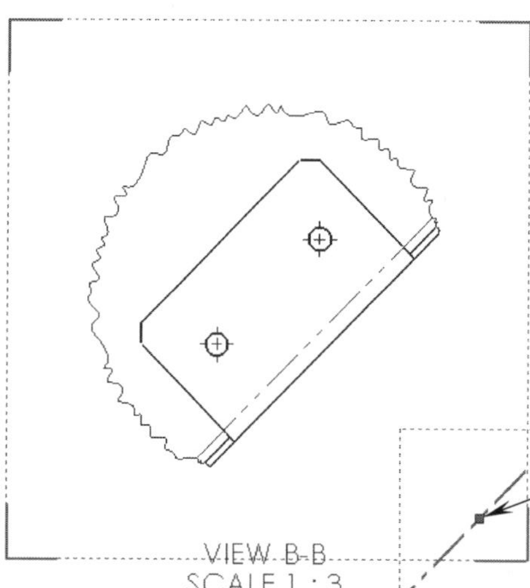

Switch to the **Drawings** tab and click **Crop View**.

The details on the outer portions of the circle are cropped and the inside details are kept.

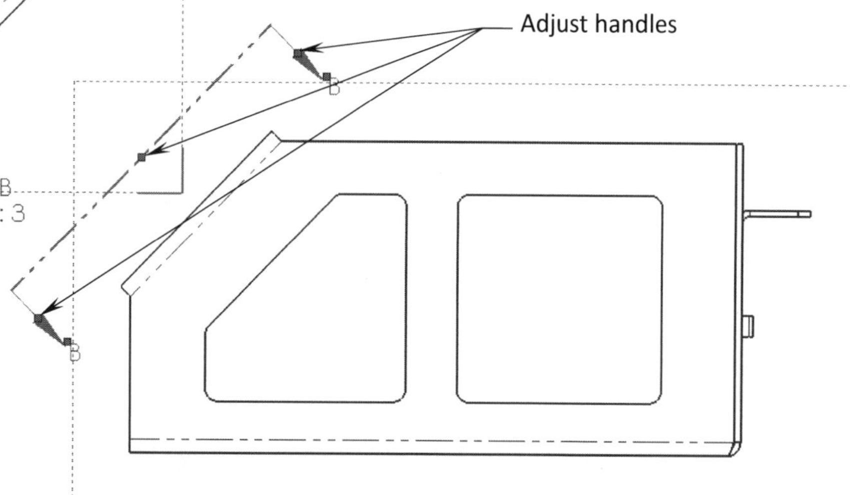

Drag the handles on the arrows and the phantom line to move and to shorten it.

5. Adding the Model Dimensions:

Switch to the **Annotation** tab.

Select the dotted border of the **Front** drawing view and click: **Model Items**.

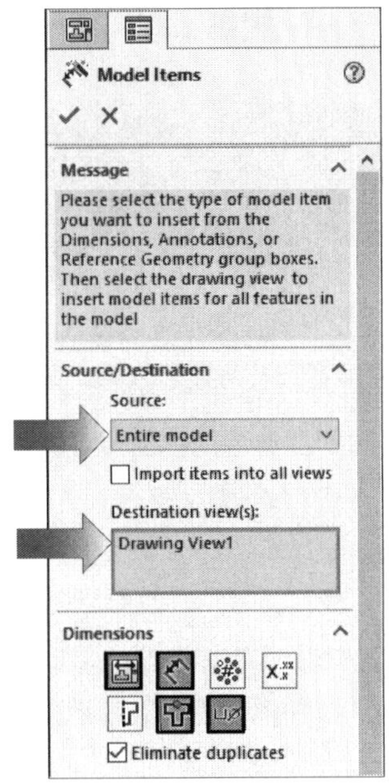

Select the following:

Source: **Entire Model**

Destination View(s): **Drawing View1 (Front)**

Dimensions: **Marked for Drawings**
Not Marked for Drawings
Hole Wizard Locations
Hole Callout

Click **OK**.

Rearrange the dimensions and add the missing ones, if needed.

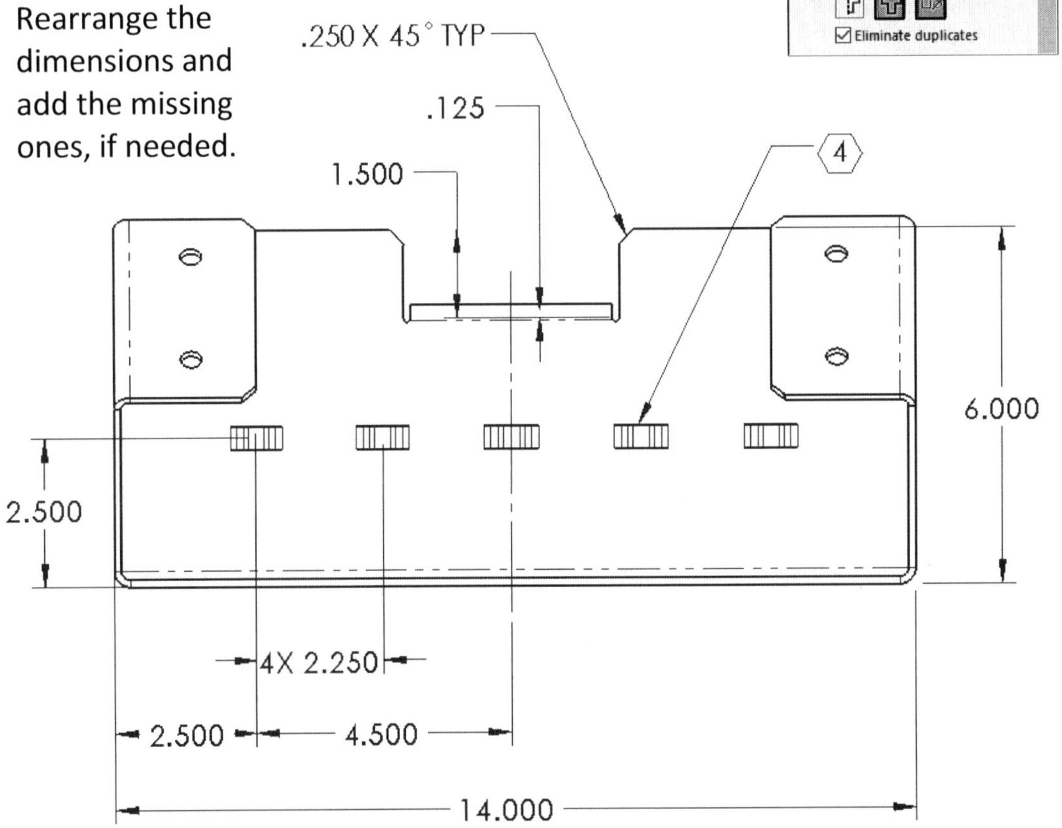

Select the dotted border of the **Top** drawing view.

Click **Model Items** .

Use the same settings as the last step, but this time, the dimensions will only be inserted into the Top drawing view.

Click **OK**.

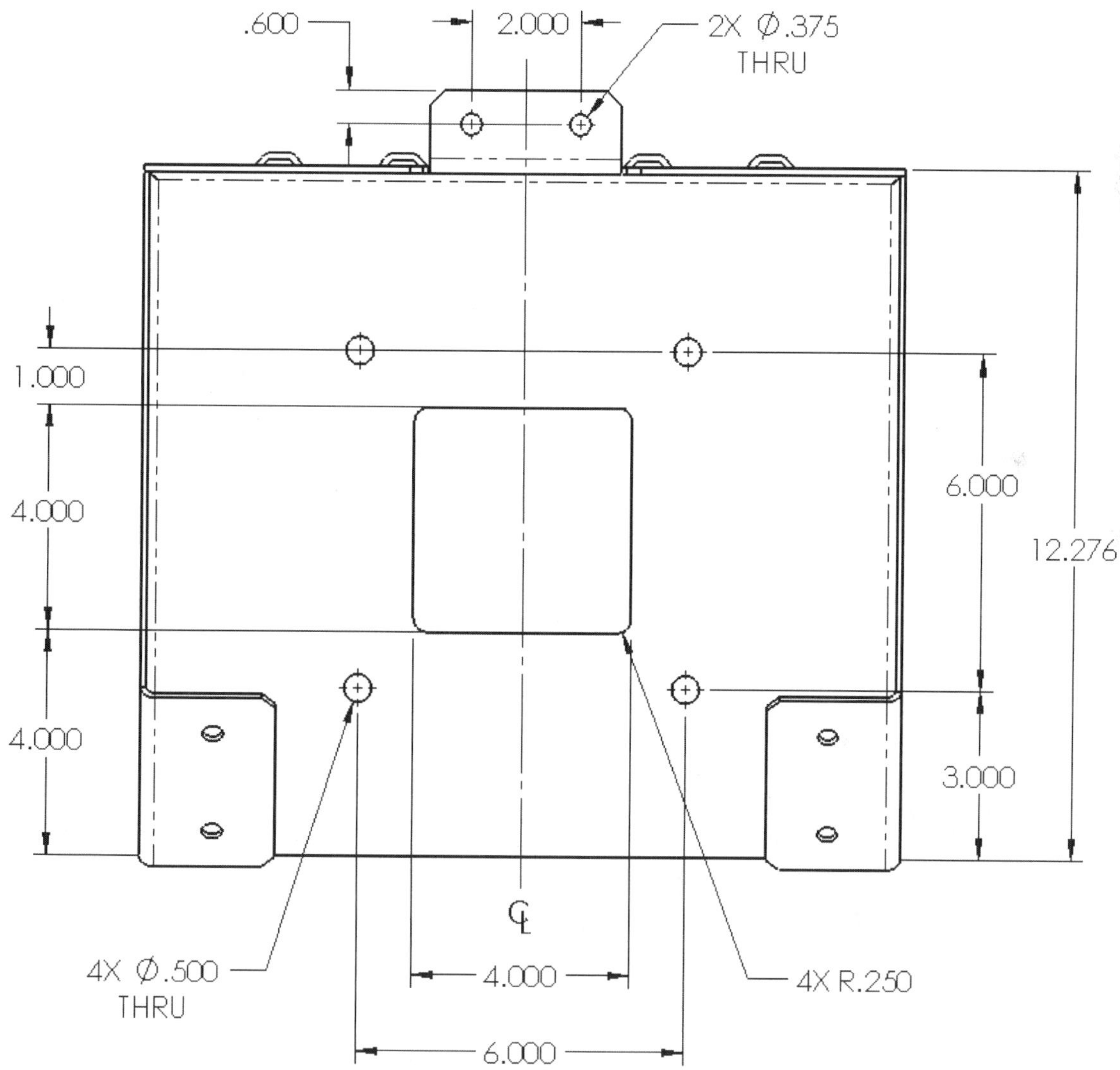

Rearrange the dimensions to make them clean and easy to read. Add any missing dimensions where needed.

Select the dotted border of the **Right** drawing view.

Click **Model Items** Model Items.

All settings and parameters should be kept the same as the last step.

Click **OK**.

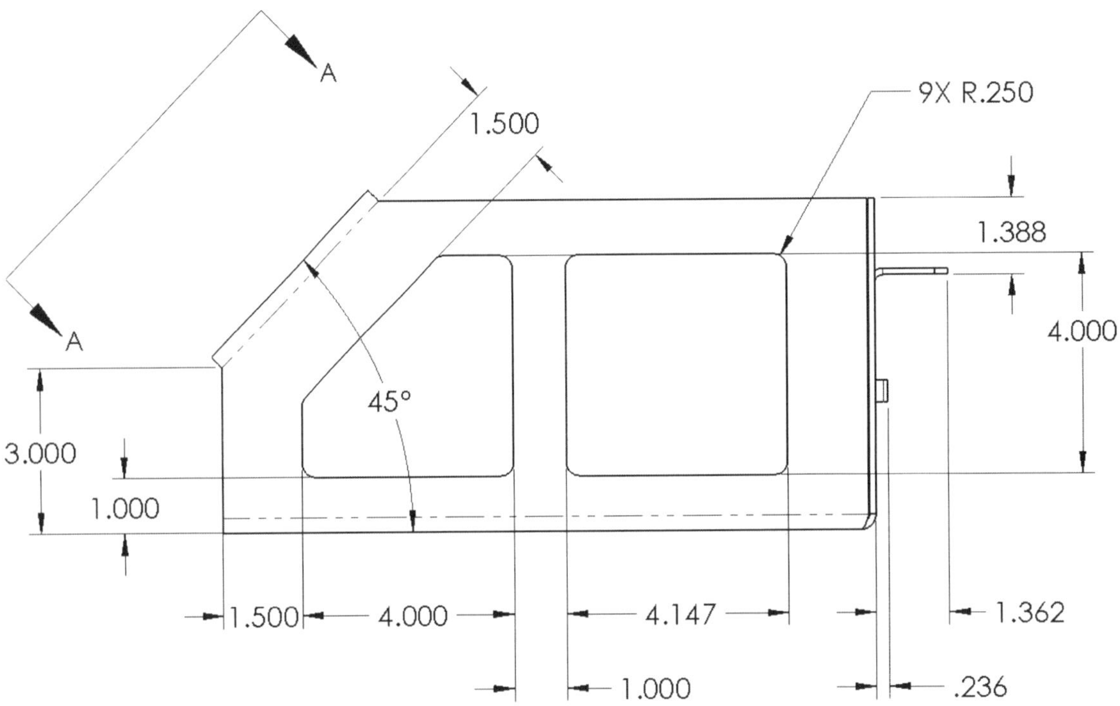

Repeat the same step and insert the model dimensions into the Cropped view.

Add the Number of Instances and the depth callouts as shown in each drawing view (4X, THRU, etc.).

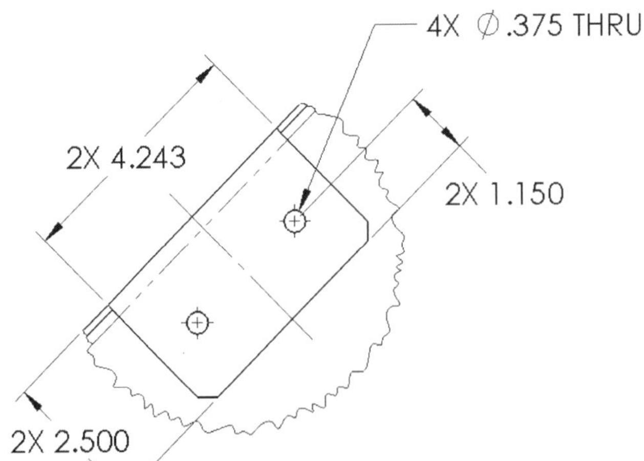

VIEW A-A

6. Filling out the Title Block:

Zoom closer to the Title Block area.

Right-click anywhere within the Title Block area and select:
Edit Sheet Format.

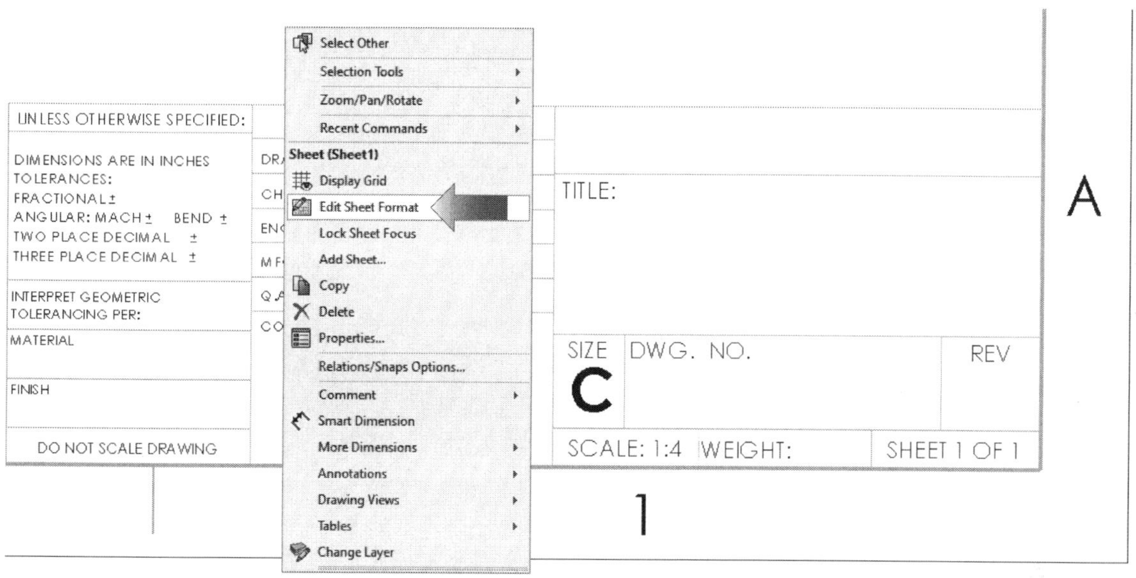

Fill out the information shown below; also add your name and date.

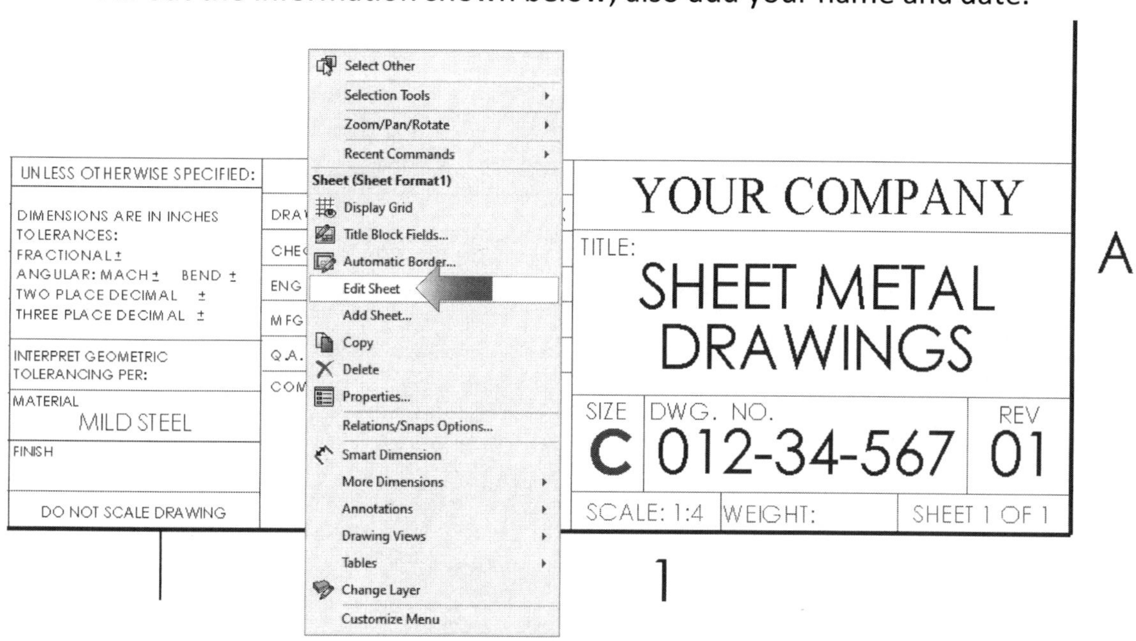

Right-click, select **Edit-Sheet** to exit the format and return to the drawing.

7. Saving your work:

Select **File, Save As**.

Enter **Sheet Metal Drawings_Completed** for the file name.

Click **Save**.

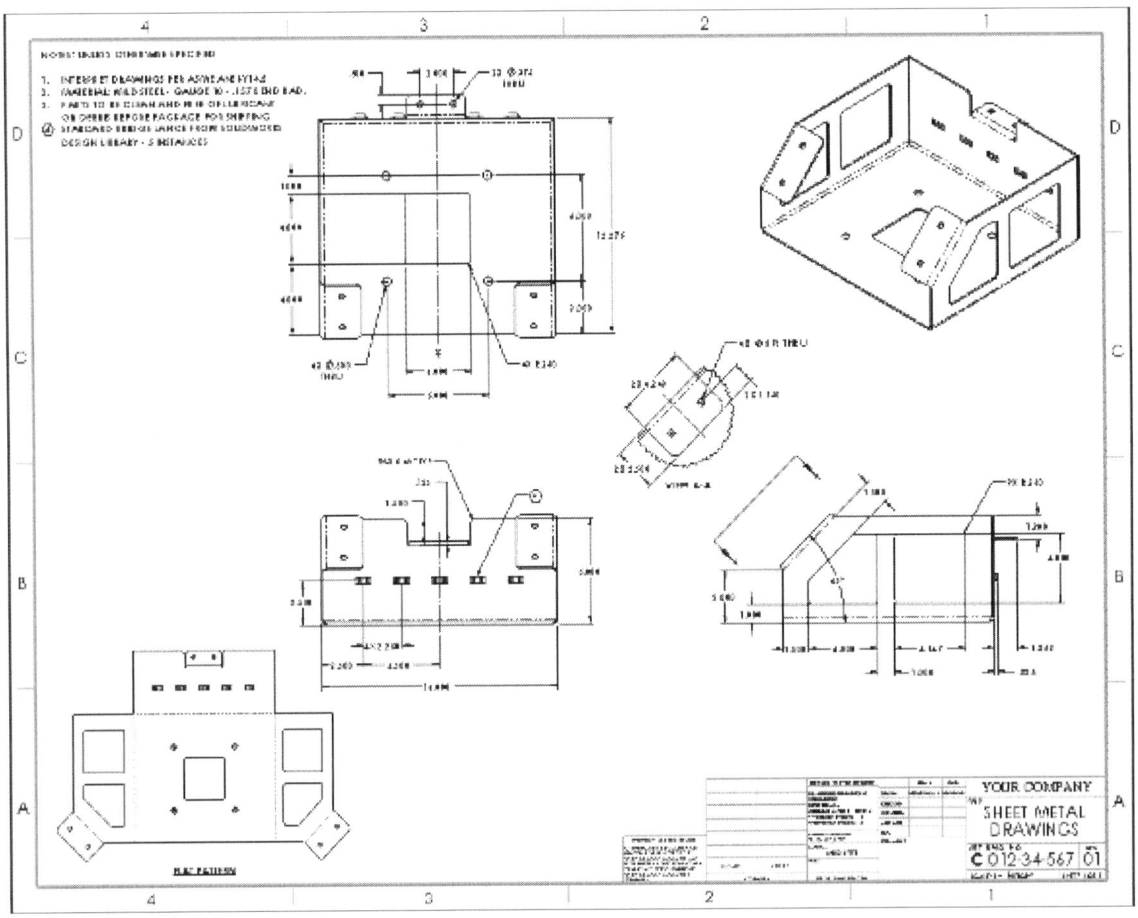

Continued on next page...

8. Adding the Flat Pattern drawing view:

For clarity, we will create the Flat Pattern drawing view in a separate sheet.

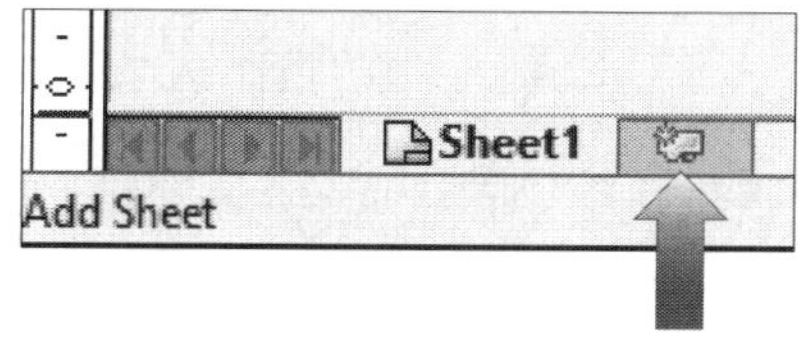

Click **Add-Sheet**, the icon at the lower left corner of the drawing.

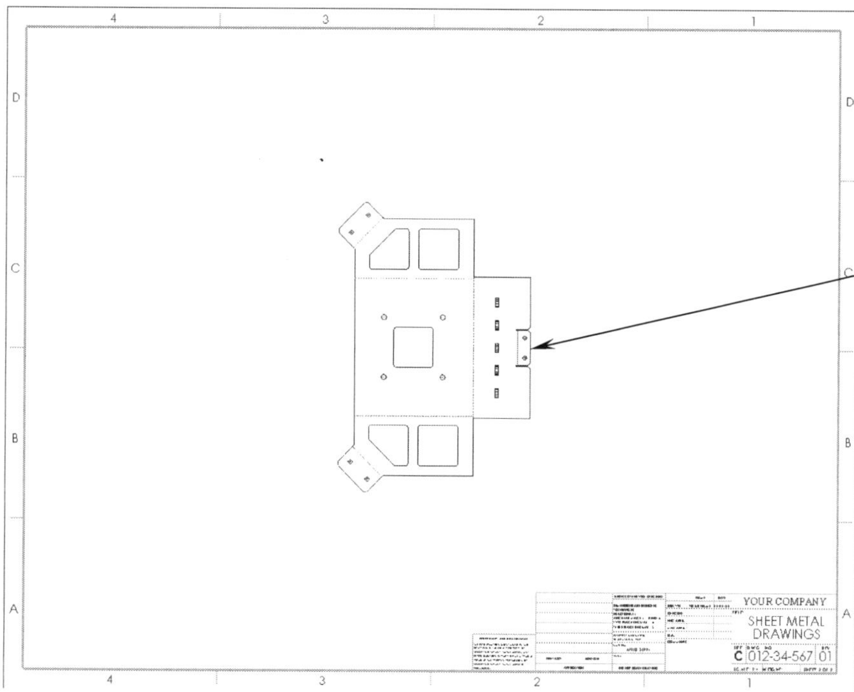

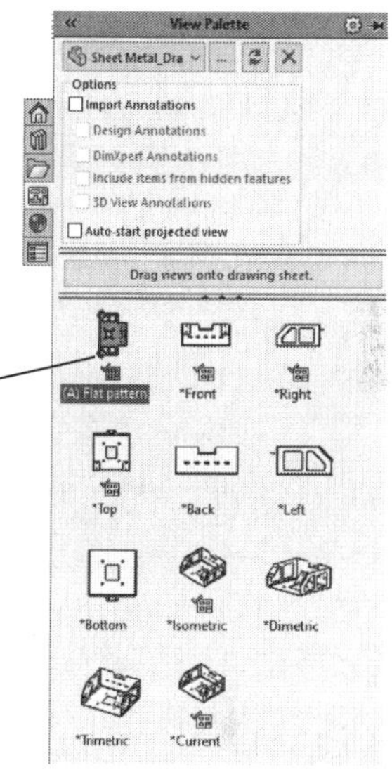

Drag the **Flat Pattern** view into the sheet.

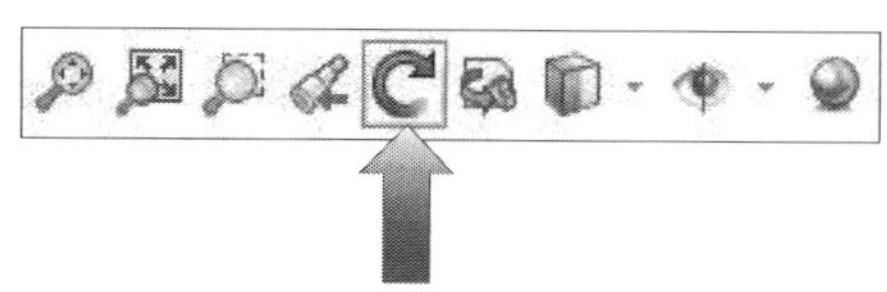

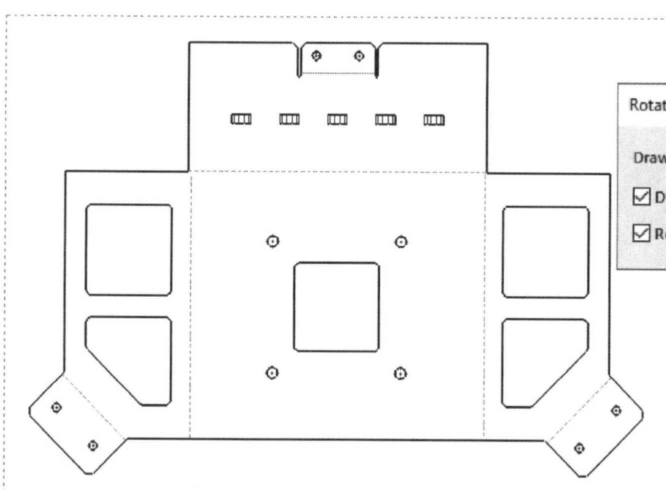

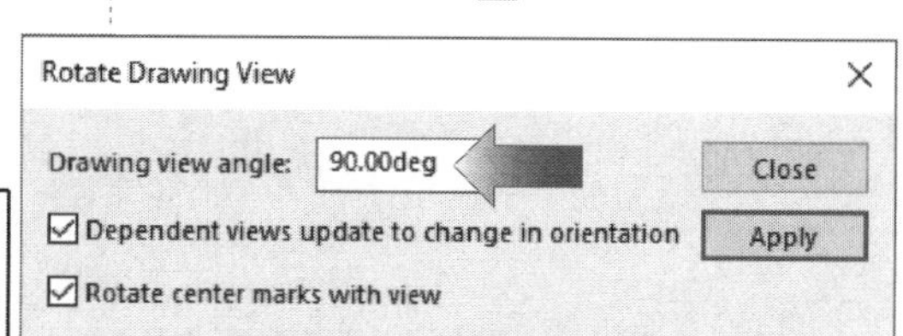

Click **Rotate View** on the Heads Up View toolbar.

Enter 90.00deg and click **Apply** and **Close**.

9. Adding centerlines:

For parts with symmetrical features, a centerline is used to define the symmetry of the features on either side of the centerline.

Switch to the **Annotation** tab and click **Centerline**.

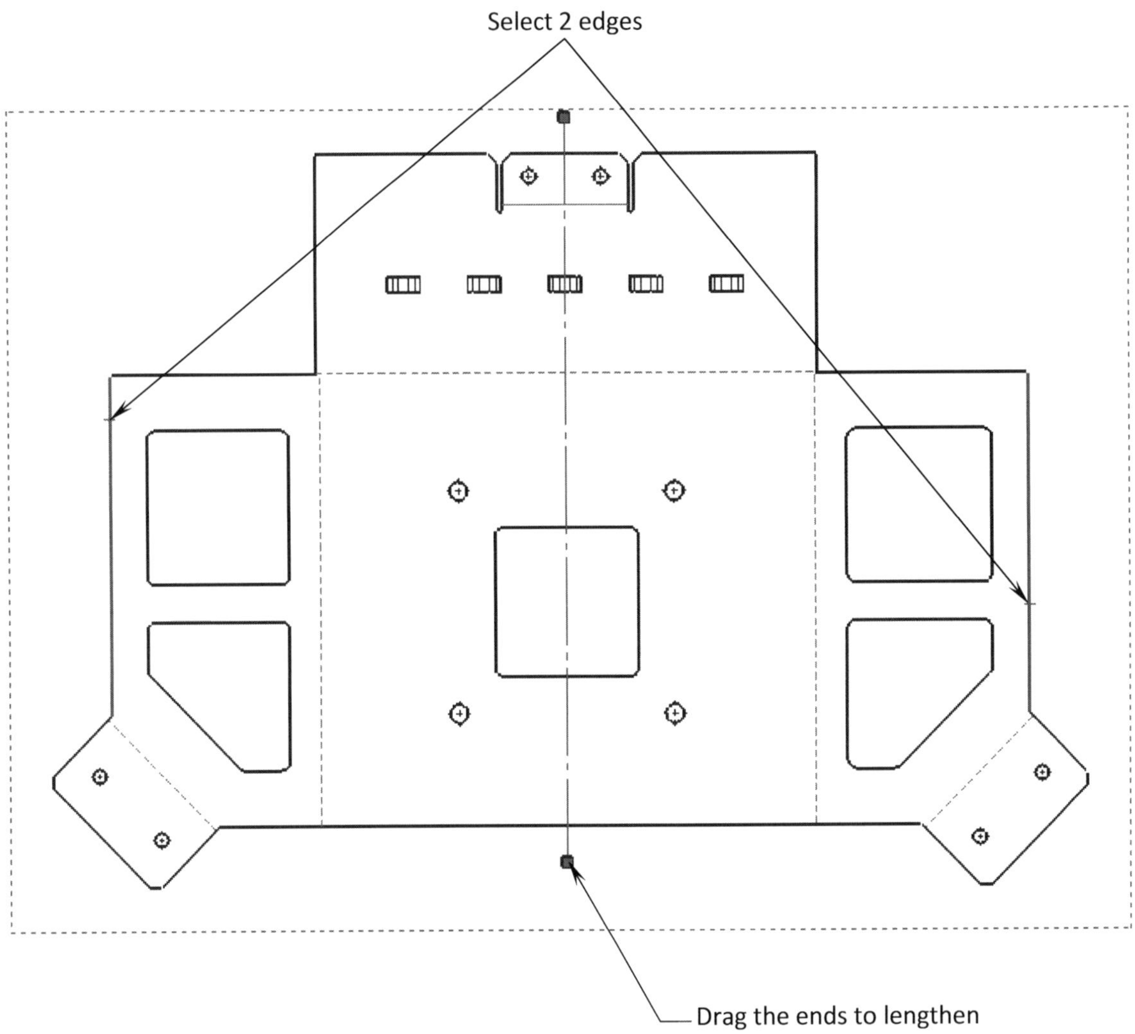

Select the left and right edges of the sheet metal part as indicated.

A Centerline is added to the middle of the 2 selected edges.

Drag the handles at the 2 ends of the centerline to lengthen it.

10. Adding the centerline symbol:

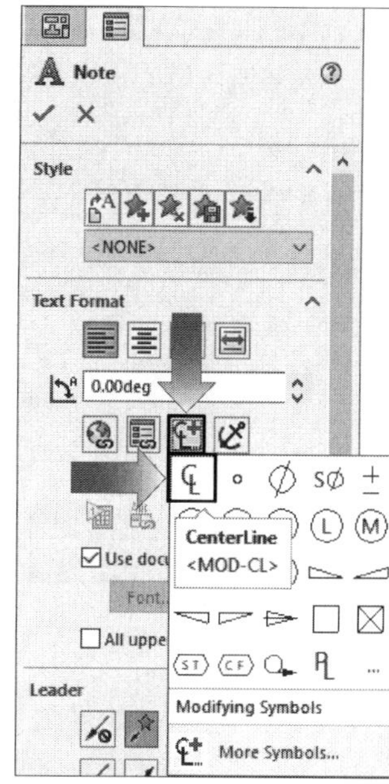

Click **Note** on the **Annotation** tab.

Click the **Add Symbol** button to access the Symbol Library.

Select the **Centerline** symbol.

Place the Centerline symbol <u>below</u> the centerline as shown in the image below.

Using the Formatting toolbar, change the font size to **14** – **Bolt** and click **OK**.

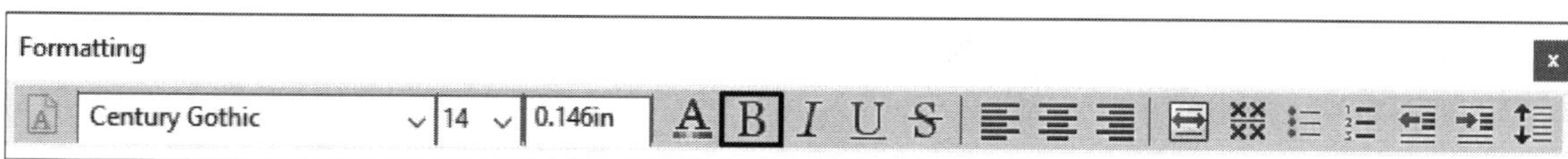

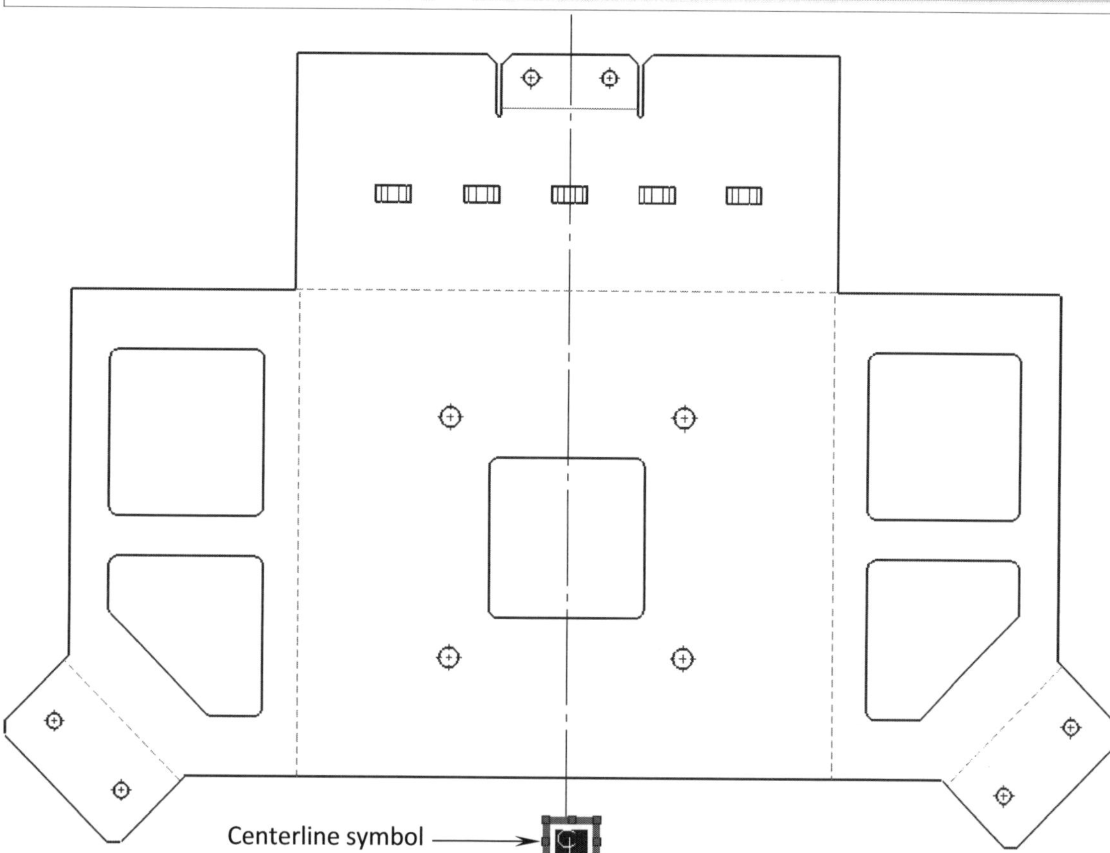

11. Adding dimensions:

Expand the **Smart Dimension** drop-down and select **Horizontal Ordinate Dimension**.

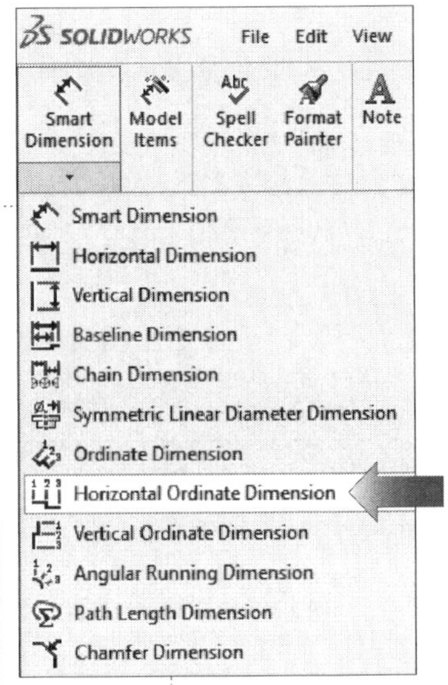

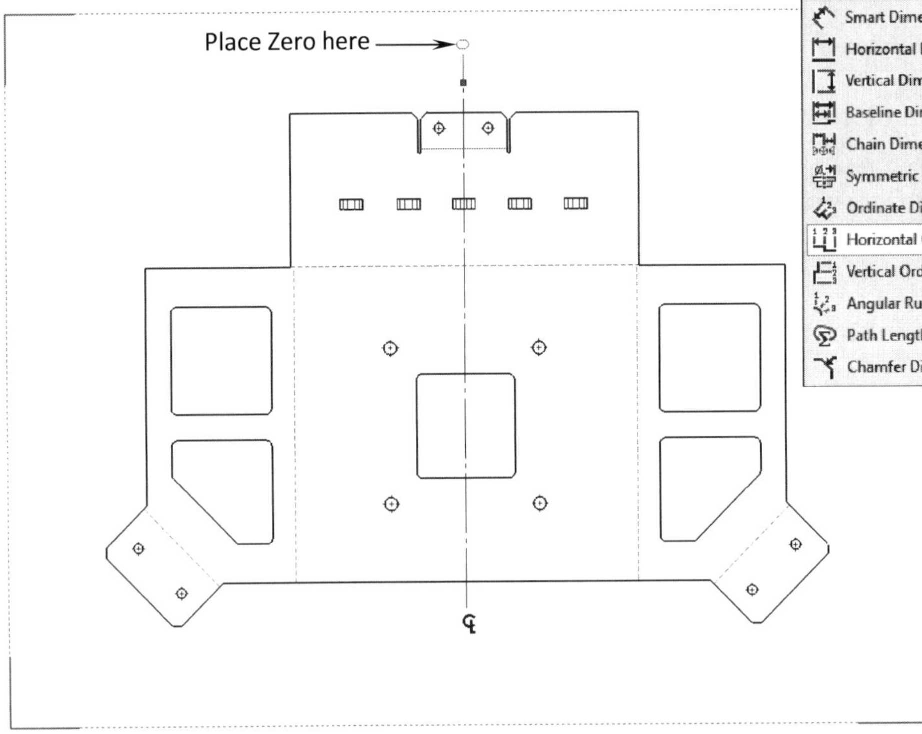

After the Zero dimension is created, move horizontally and select all other feature edges or vertices as shown.

The jog extensions are added to the dimensions automatically when they are too close to each other.

To find a mid-point, right-click a line (or an arc) and select Mid-Point.

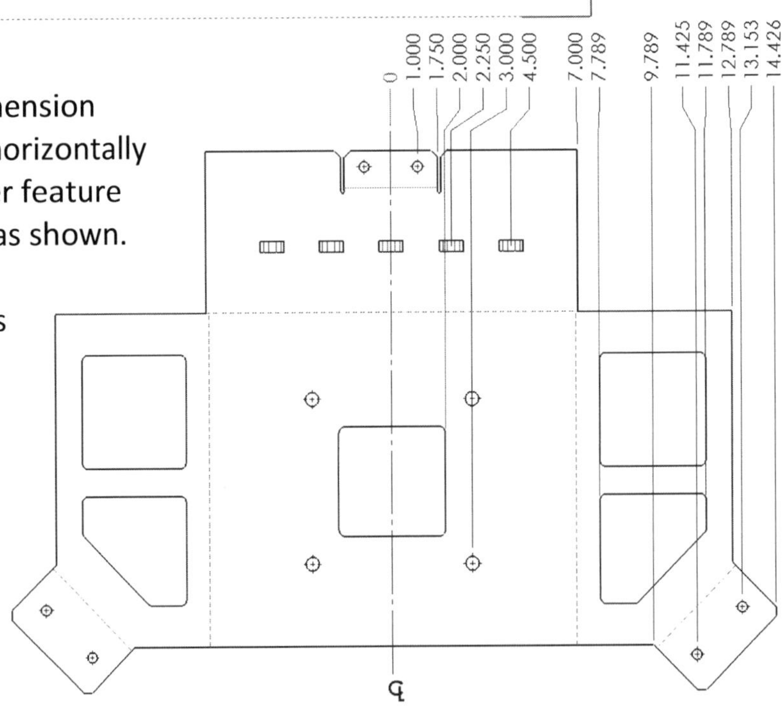

Expand the **Smart Dimension** drop-down and select **Vertical Ordinate Dimension**.

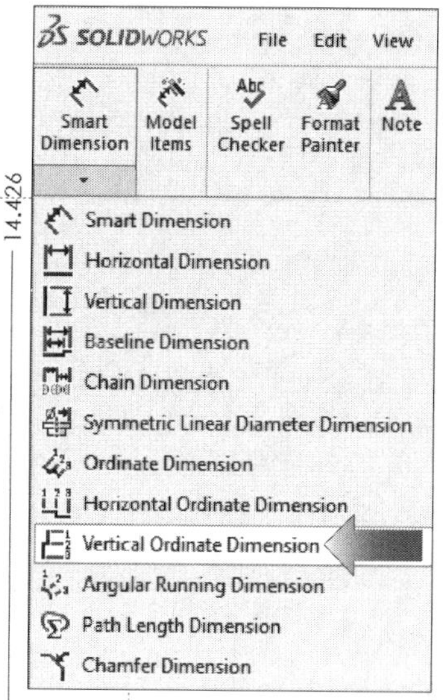

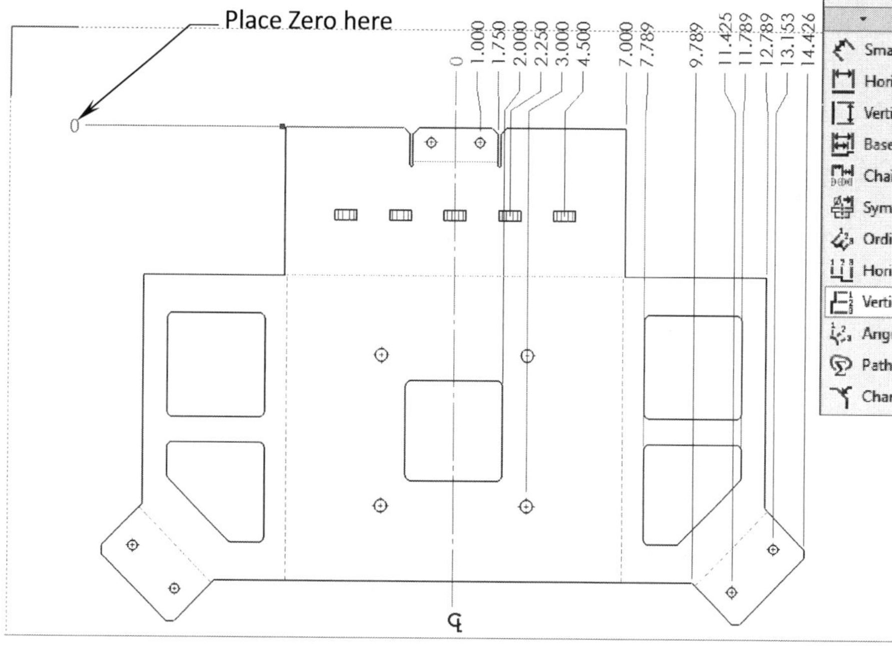

Select the top-most line and place the Zero dimension as indicated above.

Move vertically and click each feature's edge or vertex to add a dimension to locate it.

Right-click an edge or an arc and select Mid-Point, when needed.

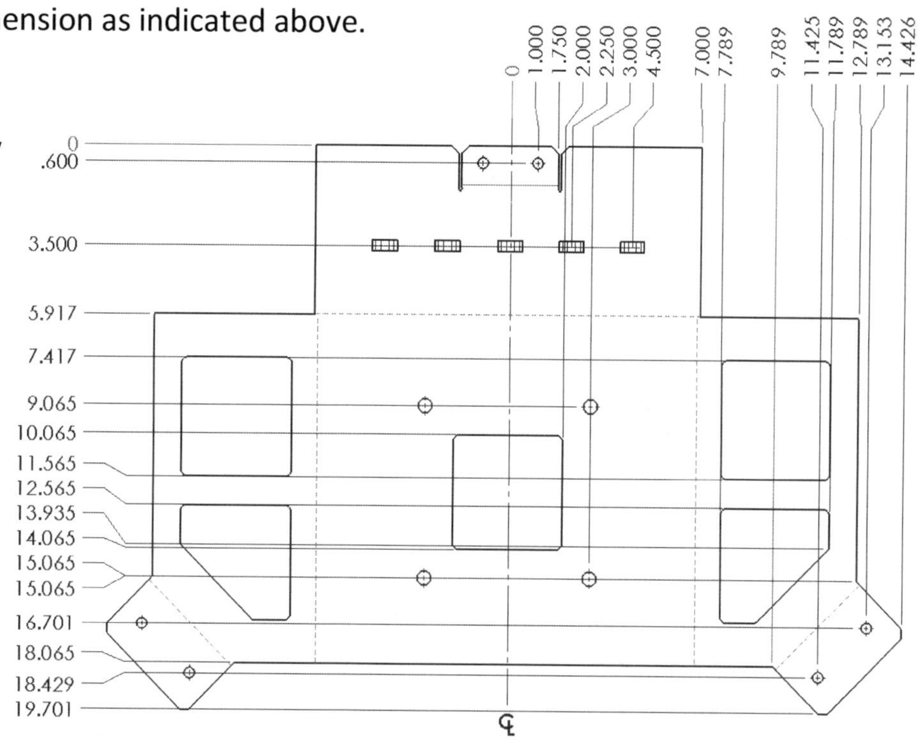

12. Adding other callouts:

Use the combination of the following tools: **Hole Callout**, **Smart Dimension**, and **Note** and add the dimensions circled below.

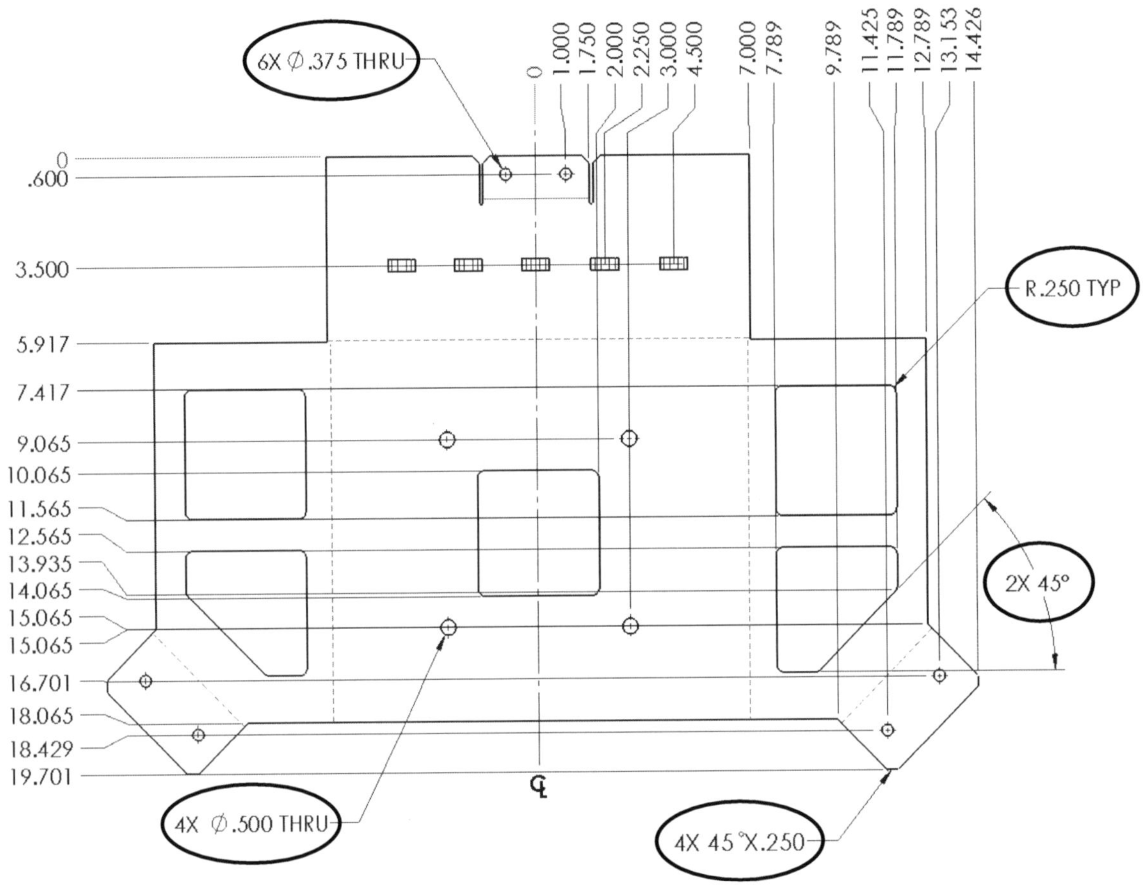

Add the number of instances using the options in the **Dimension Text**.

Change the **Grey** color dimensions to **Black**, using the Color options in the **Line Format** toolbar (View, Toolbars, Line Format).

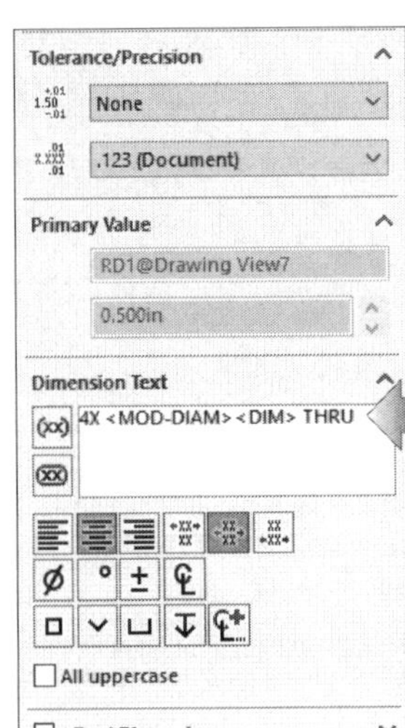

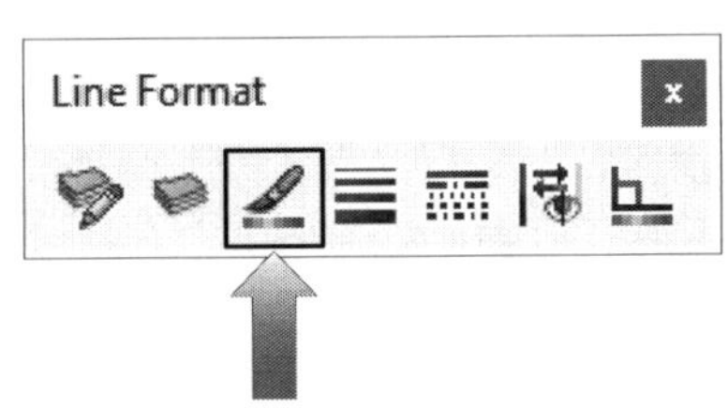

To add a missing dimension to the groups of Horizontal or Vertical Ordinates, right-click the Zero dimension and select: ***Add To Ordinate****.*

13. Saving your work:

Select **File, Save**.

Click **Save**.

Click **Yes** to save and over-write the existing drawing with this updated one.

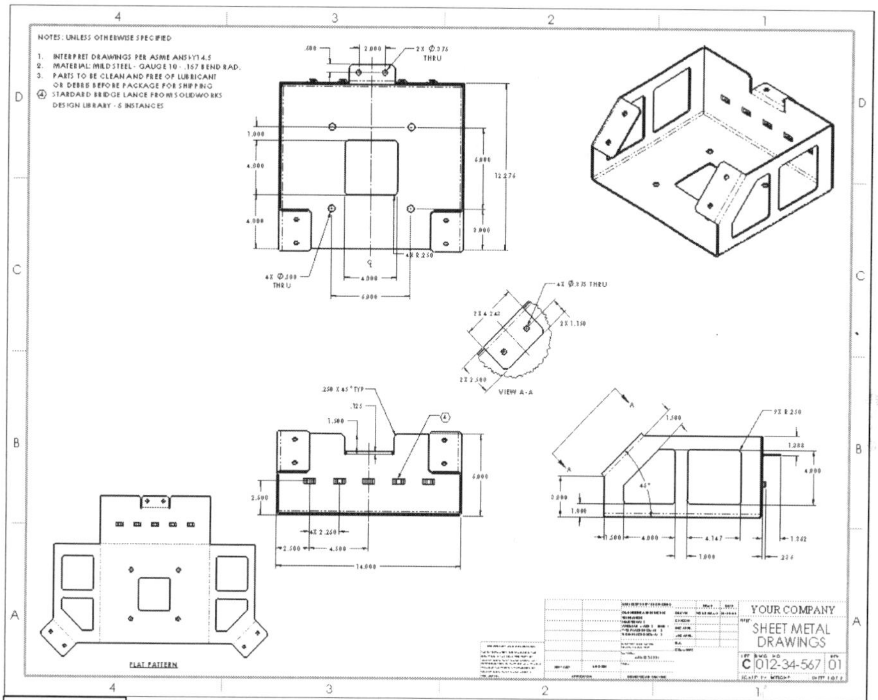

Sheet 1

Both drawing sheets are shown here.

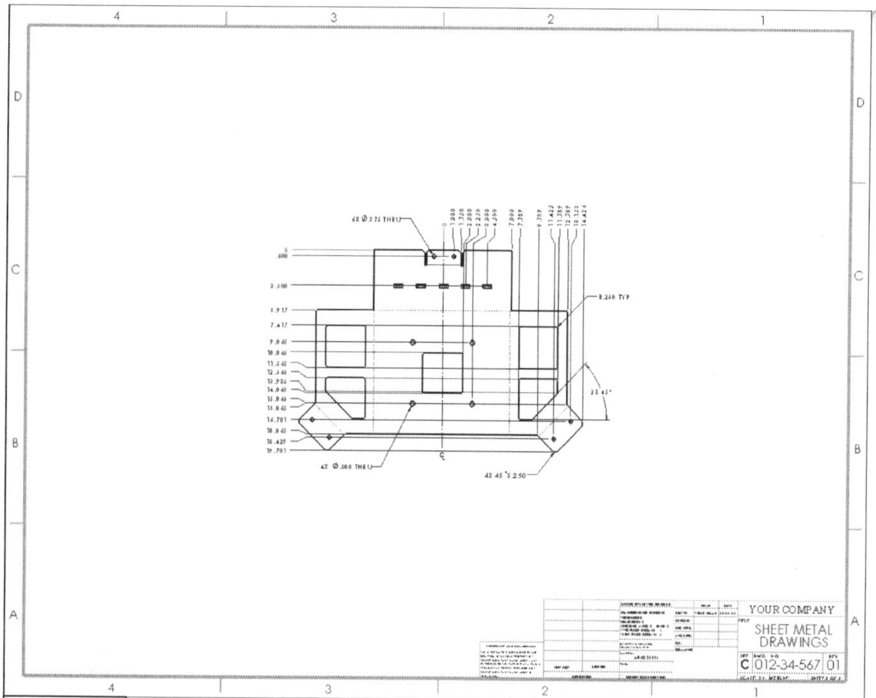

Sheet 2

Close the drawing document after done saving.

Export to DXF (or DWG)

DXF files (**D**rawing e**X**change **F**ormat) are used to represent flat patterns of sheet metal parts, which are then used to program CNC machines like laser cutters and punch presses. This allows for the creation of finished parts by cutting or punching the flat pattern from sheet metal.

Several types of software are used in sheet metal brakes, primarily for design, simulation, and programming. Popular choices include Almacam, Fabriwin, Vision, Delem, etc.

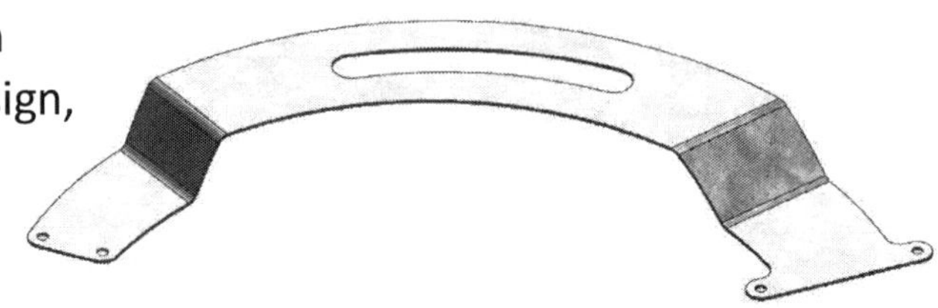

This lesson will walk us through the few simple steps of converting a sheet metal part to DXF format for sheet metal fabrication.

1. Opening a part document:

Browse to the Training Folder and open a part document named: **Export to DXF**.

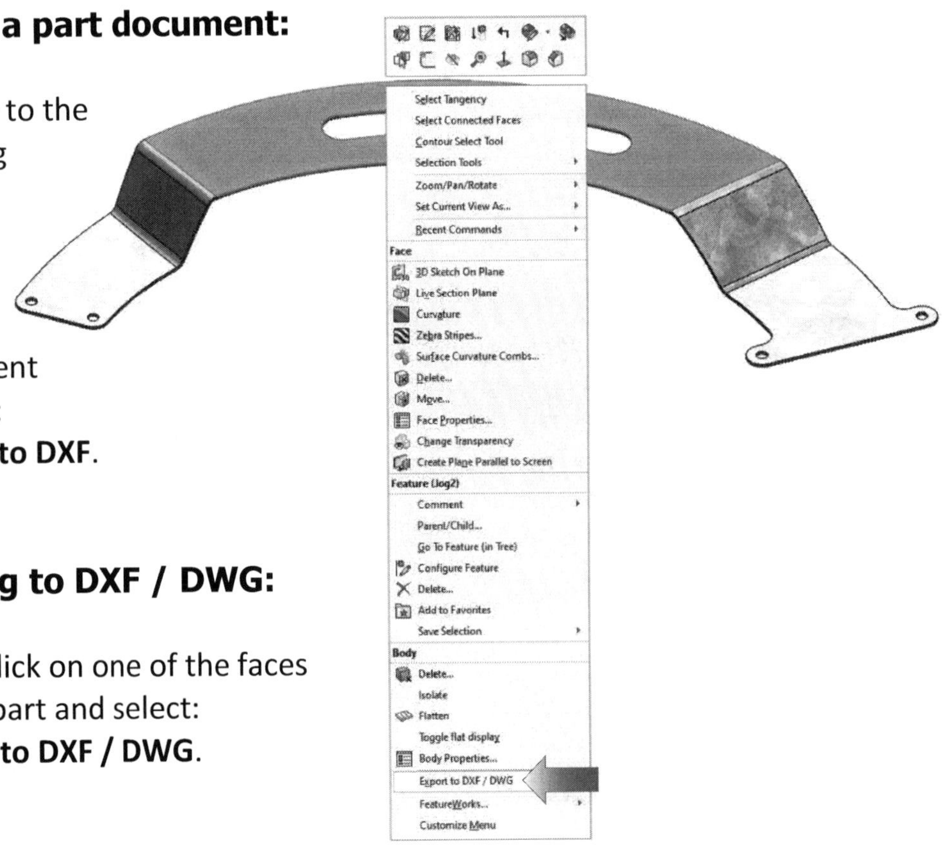

2. Exporting to DXF / DWG:

Right-click on one of the faces of the part and select: **Export to DXF / DWG**.

In the **Save As** dialog box enter the file name: **Export to DXF.dxf**

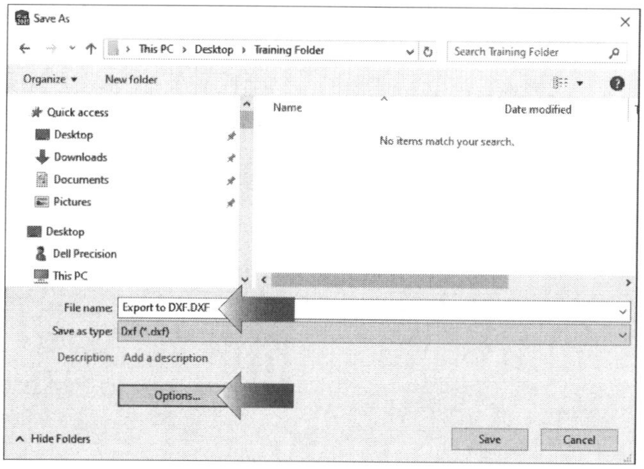

Select a location to save the DXF file.

Click the **Options** button.

In the File Format section select the option: **DXF/DWG**.

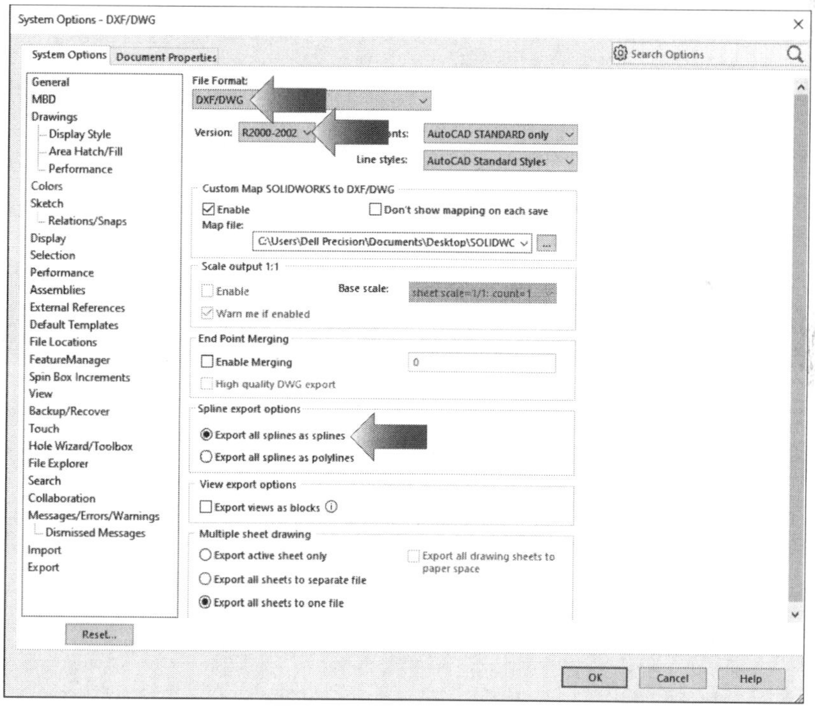

For Version, select: **R2000-2002**.

For Spline Export Options, select: **Export All Splines As Splines**.

Keep all other parameters at their default settings.

Click **Save**.

The **DXF / DWG Output** dialog box appears on the FeatureManager tree.

Use the **DXF/DWG Output PropertyManager** to export any planar face or named view from a part file to one or more DXF or DWG files. A preview lets you remove entities. An expanded set of geometric entities is available when you export a sheet metal flat pattern.

Under the Export section, select the **Sheet Metal** option.

For Entities to Export, enable the checkboxes:

Geometry
Bend Lines
Bounding Box

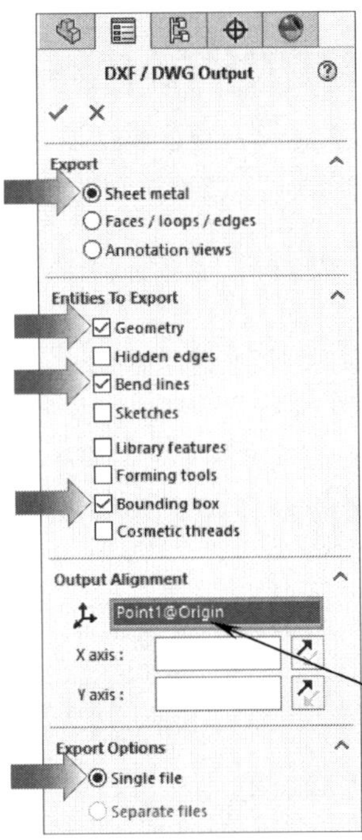

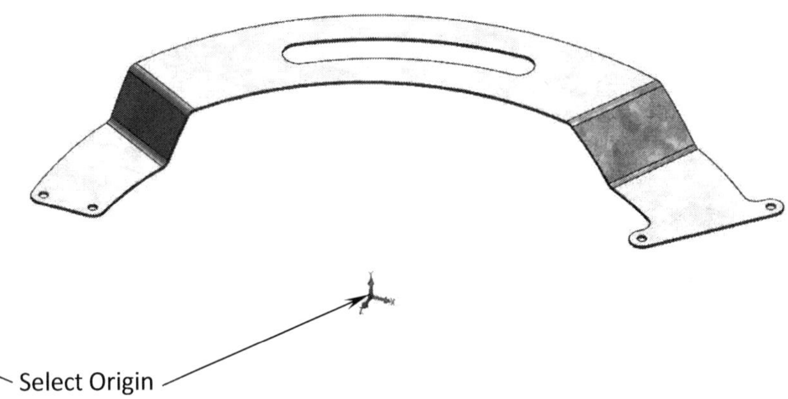

For Output Alignment, select the **Origin** from the graphics area.

For Export Options, click **Single File**.

Click **OK**.

Click OK again to close the SolidWorks To DXF DWG Mapping dialog box.

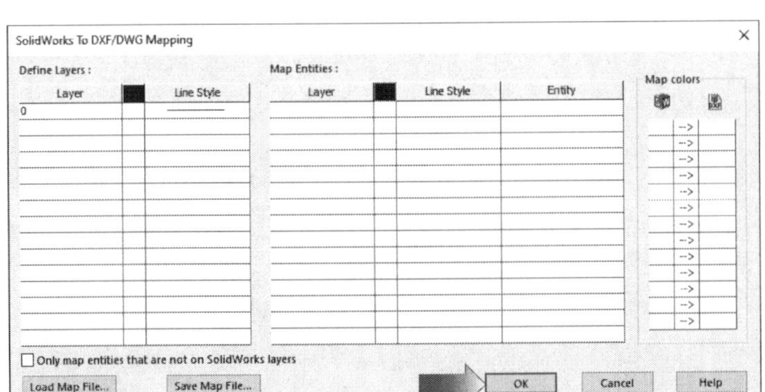

The **DXF/DWG Cleanup** dialog box appears to preview the exported model.

The option **Remove Entities** allows any unwanted entity to be erased.

There are tools for Zoom & Pan available in this window.

We will leave everything the way it is without changing anything.

Click **Save**.

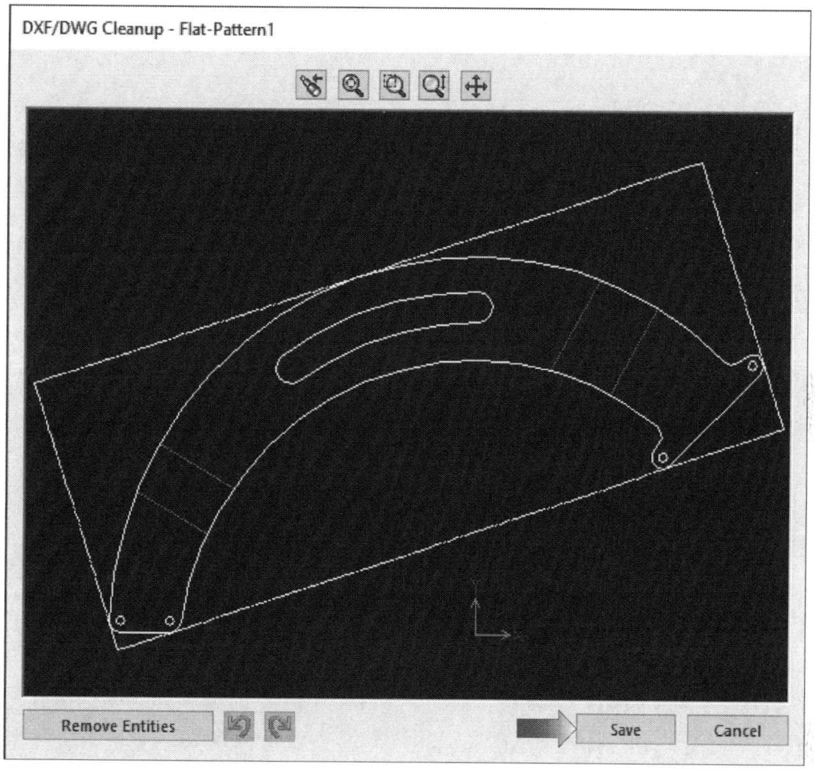

3. Testing the DXF file:

In SOLIDWORKS, select **File, Open**.

Change to the location where the DXF file was saved in step 2, page 12-17.

Locate the DXF file named:
Export To DXF
and click **Open**.

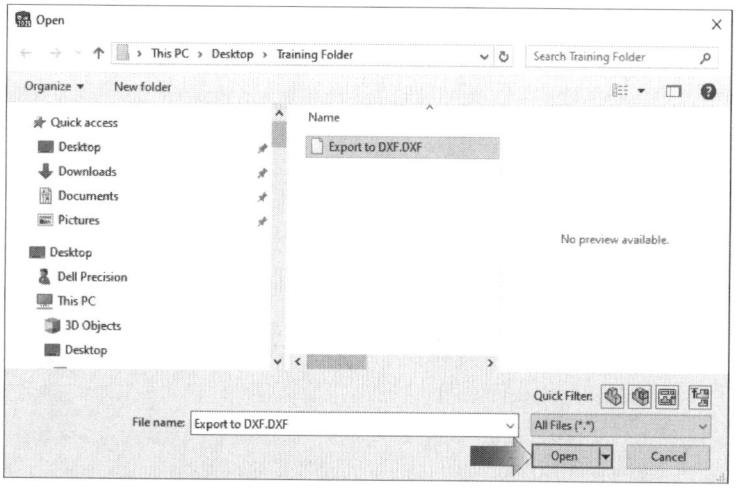

The **SOLIDWORKS DXF/DWG Import** dialog box appears.

In this dialog box select: **Create New** SOLIDWORKS **Drawing**.

Click: **Convert to SOLIDWORKS Entities**.

Click **Next**.

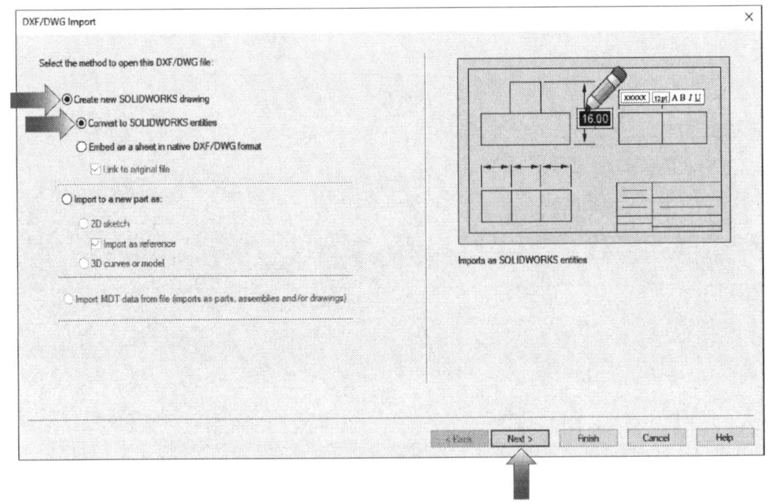

In the Drawing Layer Mapping dialog box select: **All Selected Layers**.

Click **Next**.

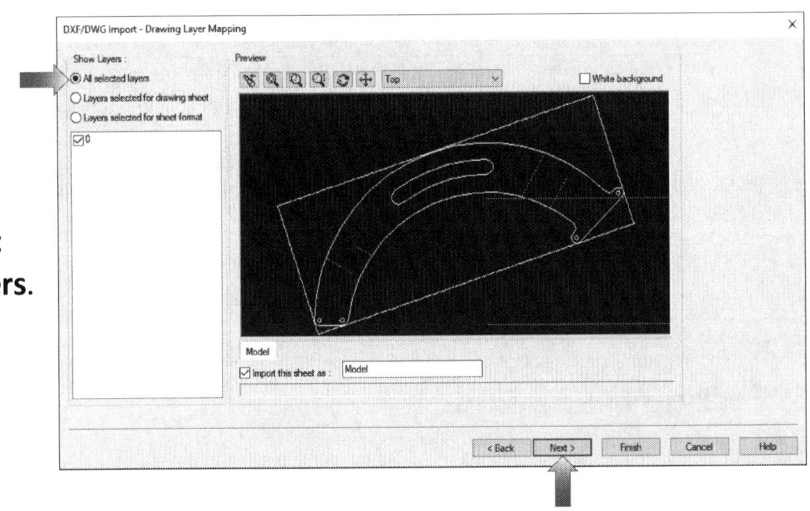

In the Document Settings dialog box select:

D-Landscape
Sheet Scale 1:1
Center in Sheet

Click **Finish**.

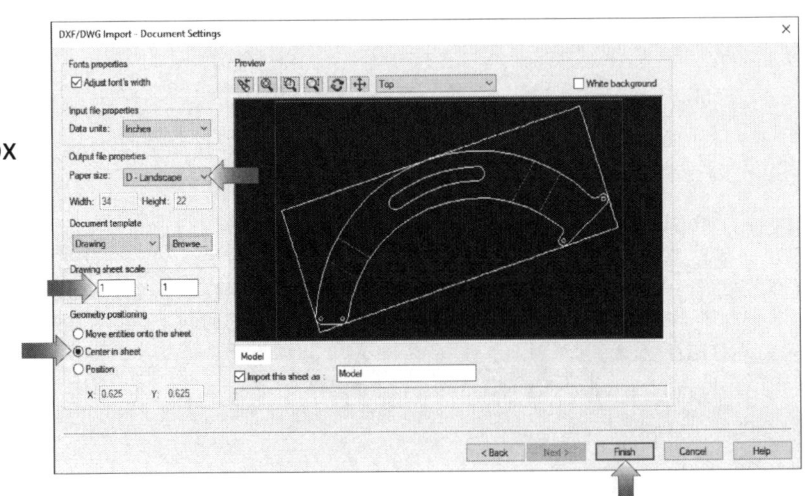

The DXF file is imported into a SOLIDWORKS drawing document.

The Flat Pattern, the Bend Lines, and the Bounding Box are all displayed correctly.

To hide the Title Block and display only the sheet metal flat pattern, right-click anywhere inside the drawing and select: **Properties**.
Clear the checkbox: **Display Sheet Format**.

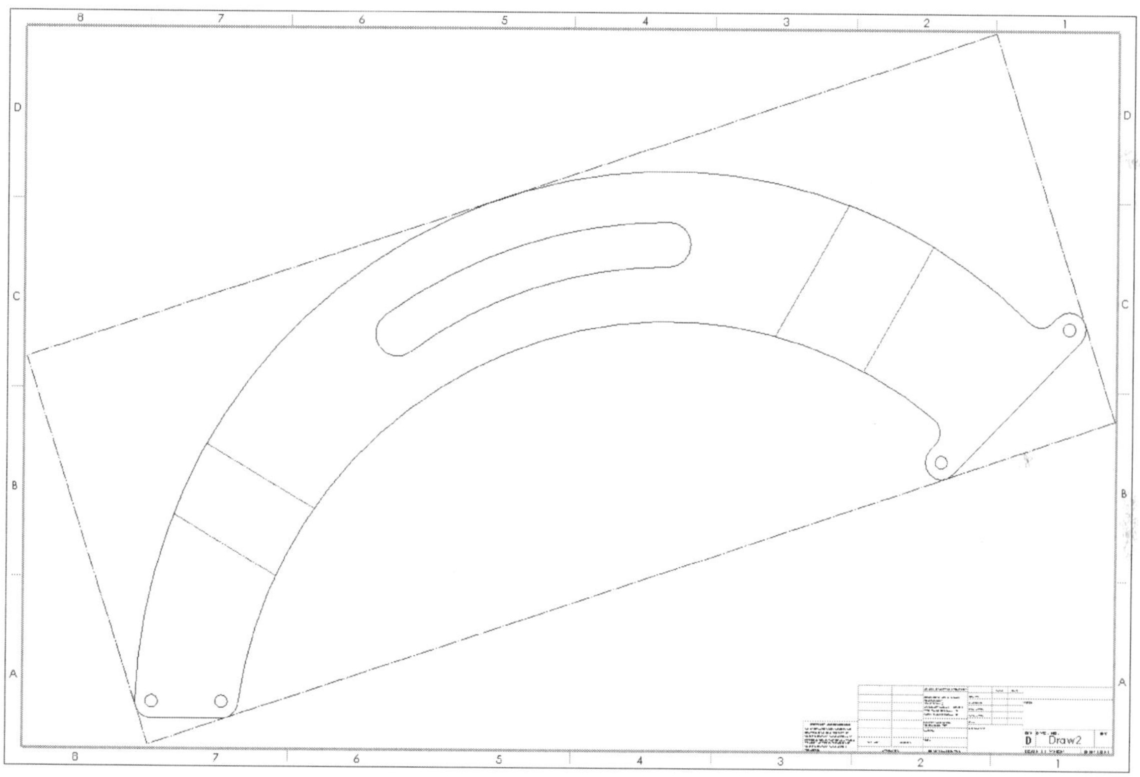

4. Saving your work:

Select **File, Save As**.

Enter **Export To DXF_Completed** for the file name.

Click **Save**.

(Use the same file name to save both Part and drawing documents.)

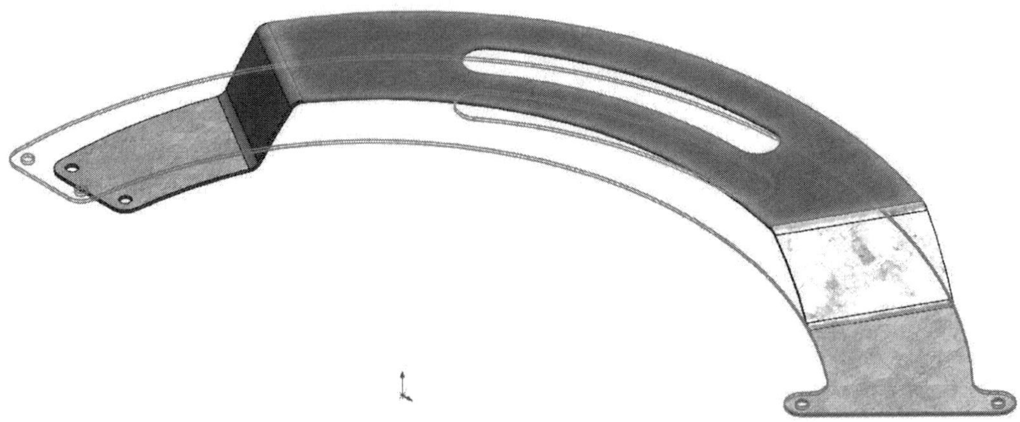

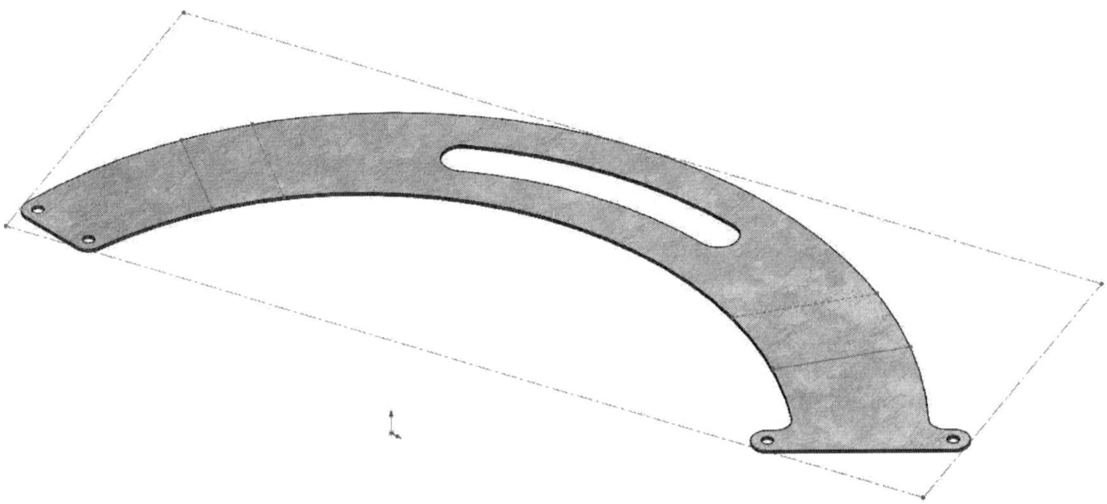

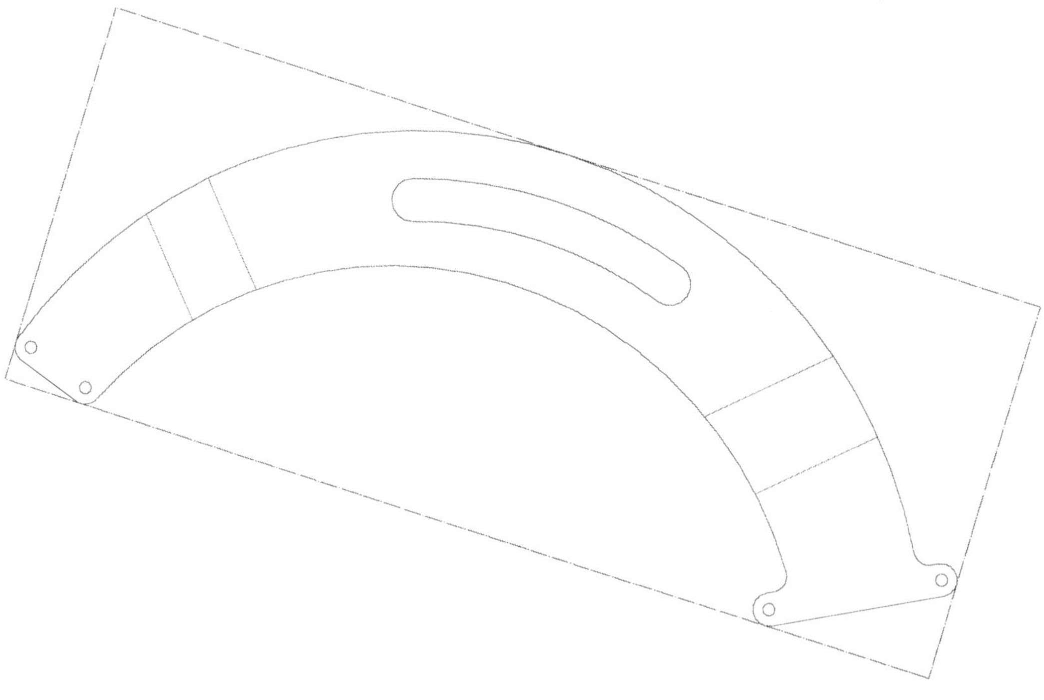

Lesson 13: SOLIDWORKS Weldments

A weldment is an assembly or structure created by welding together multiple metal pieces to form a single, unified part. It is a common method in manufacturing, particularly for creating large or complex structures that may be difficult or uneconomical to produce in a single piece.

A weldment is essentially a welded assembly. It involves joining two or more metal parts using welding processes like MIG, TIG, or stick welding.

A weldment includes the base metals (the original metal pieces), the weld metal (the filler metal added during welding), and the heat-affected zone (the area around the weld that has been affected by the heat of welding).

Weldments are used to create strong, lightweight, and often cost-effective structures. They are commonly used in industries like manufacturing, construction,

and shipbuilding. Common examples include metal frames, machine bases, and structural components in buildings and bridges.

Proper weldment design involves considering factors like weld type, weld size, material compatibility, and the resulting stresses in the welded structure.

The process of assembling parts to form a weldment involves several steps, including layout, measuring, cutting, grinding, fitting, and potentially tack welding. These steps prepare the components for welding and ensure proper alignment and fit before the final welding process is applied.

1. Layout and Measuring: Accurately defining the dimensions and positioning of each part within the weldment is crucial. This step ensures that the final assembly meets the required specifications and dimensions.

2. Cutting and Shaping: Metal parts are cut to the desired size and shape using various tools like laser cutters, water jet cutters, or plasma cutters. Forming techniques like bending, folding, or rolling may also be used to achieve the required shape.

3. Grinding: Grinding is used to smooth edges and ensure proper fit between parts, particularly in areas where welding will occur.

4. Fitting: This involves aligning and joining the prepared parts to form the weldment. This may involve using clamps or other temporary fixtures to hold the parts in place during the welding process.

5. Tack Welding (Optional): Tack welding is a preliminary welding process used to temporarily hold the parts together before the final welding is performed. This ensures that the parts remain securely joined during the main welding operation.

6. Welding: The final welding process fuses the prepared parts together, creating a permanent joint. Various welding techniques and parameters are used depending on the materials being welded and the desired strength and appearance of the weld.

7. Finishing: After welding, the weldment may undergo finishing processes like grinding, polishing, or painting to achieve the desired surface appearance and protect the welded joint.

In general, Weldments are either made from steel or aluminum. Each of these materials has its advantages and disadvantages. Steel is an incredibly versatile material with a wide range of alloys available to fit almost any use case.
Weld metal is the metal in a welded joint which has been molten in the welding process and then solidified. It is usually a mixture of any filler metal and the parent metal, as well as any additions from the flux in the consumables, and will have an as-cast metallurgical structure.

Weldments - Aluminum Frame

1. Opening a part document:

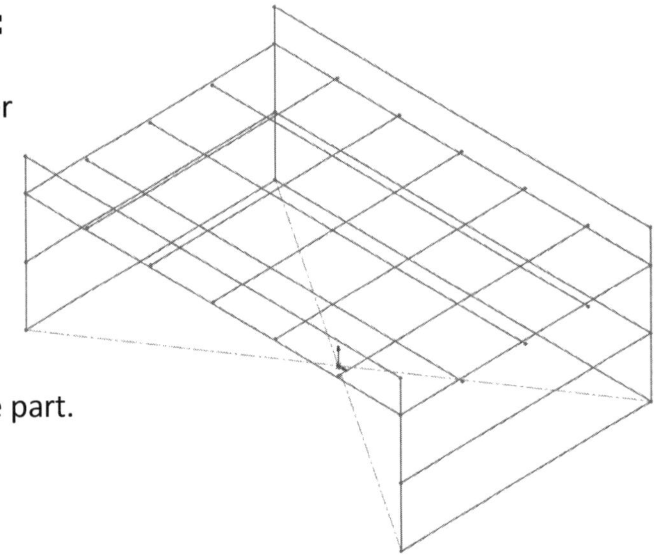

Browse to the Training Folder and open a part document named: **Aluminum Frame.**

There is a 3D-Sketch in this model and the material **Aluminum5052-H2** has already been assigned to the part.

2. Weldment Groups:

A group is a collection of related segments in a structural member.

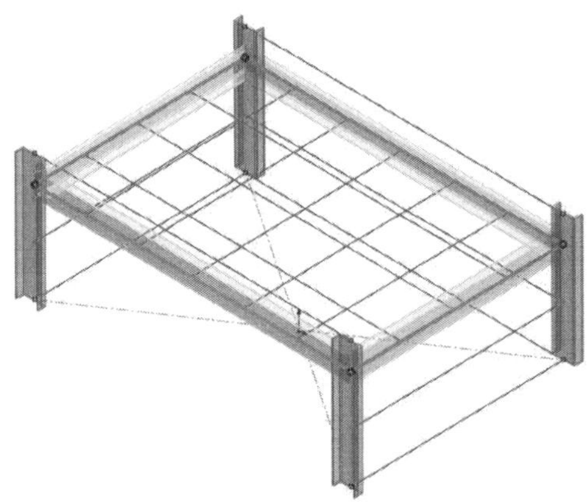

You configure a group to affect all its segments without affecting other segments or groups in the structural member.

There are 2 types of groups:

Contiguous Group: A continuous contour of segments joined end-to-end. You can control how the segments join to each other.
The end point of the group can optionally connect to its beginning point.

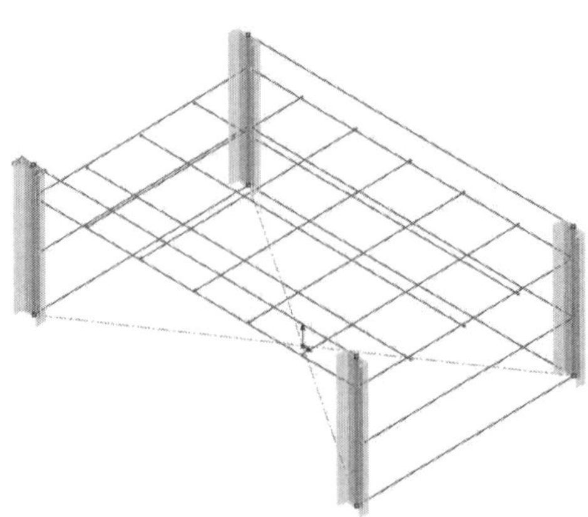

Parallel Group: A discontinuous collection of parallel segments.
Segments in the group cannot touch each other.

3. Adding the Structural Members:

Structural members are the individual components that form the skeletal structure of a weldment. They are created by inserting pre-defined profiles, like tubes, pipes, or beams, onto a sketch that outlines the desired framework. These members are then trimmed, extended, and connected to create the final weldment structure.

This lesson will teach us how to insert the weldment profiles to the framework, change the corner treatments, and trim/extend the structural members to the desire angles and lengths.

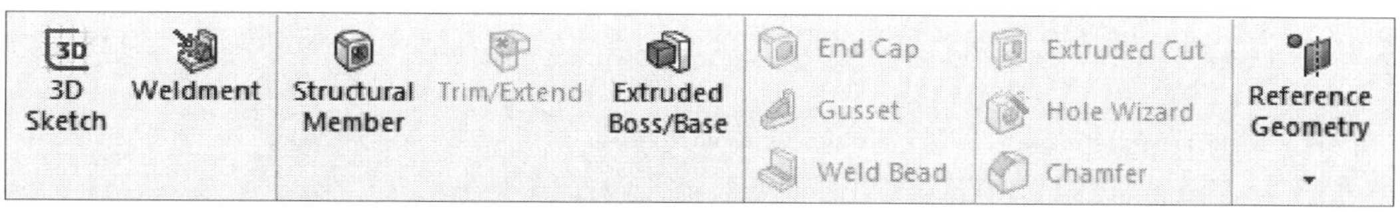

WELDMENT TOOLBAR

Switch to the **Weldments** tab and click: **Structural Member** .

The **Cut list** and **Weldment** features are added to the FeatureManager tree.

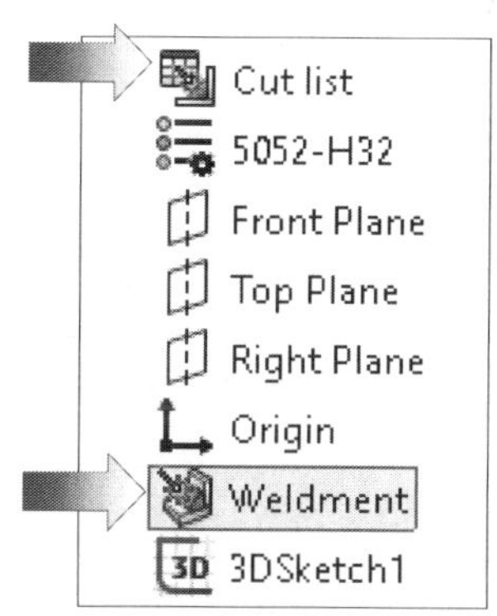

SOLIDWORKS also creates two default configurations in the Configuration-Manager:
A parent configuration Default<**As Machined**>
and a derived configuration Default<**As Welded**>.

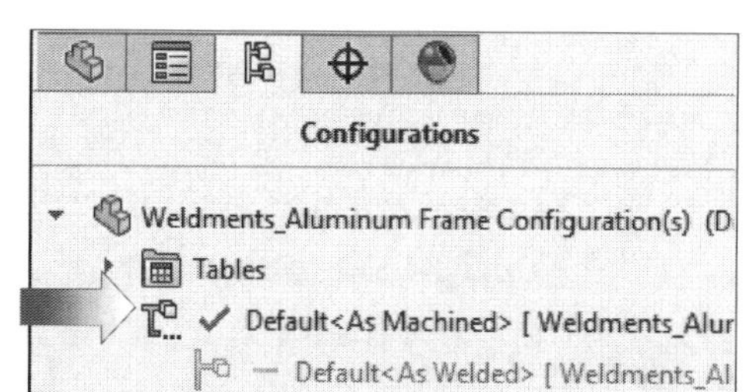

Select the following from the list:

Standard: **ANSI**
Type: **C Channel**
Size: **C5x9**

Click **New Group**.

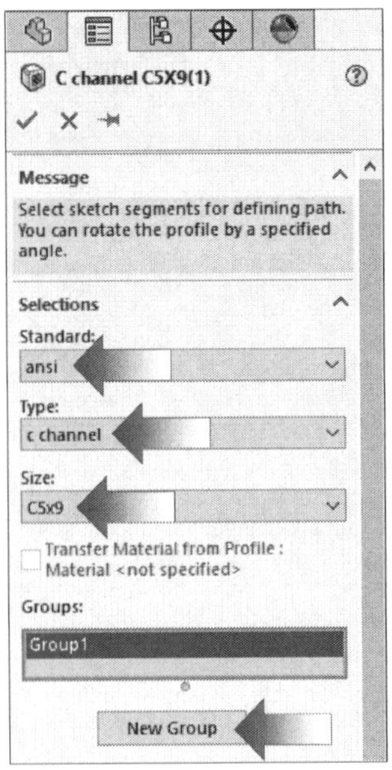

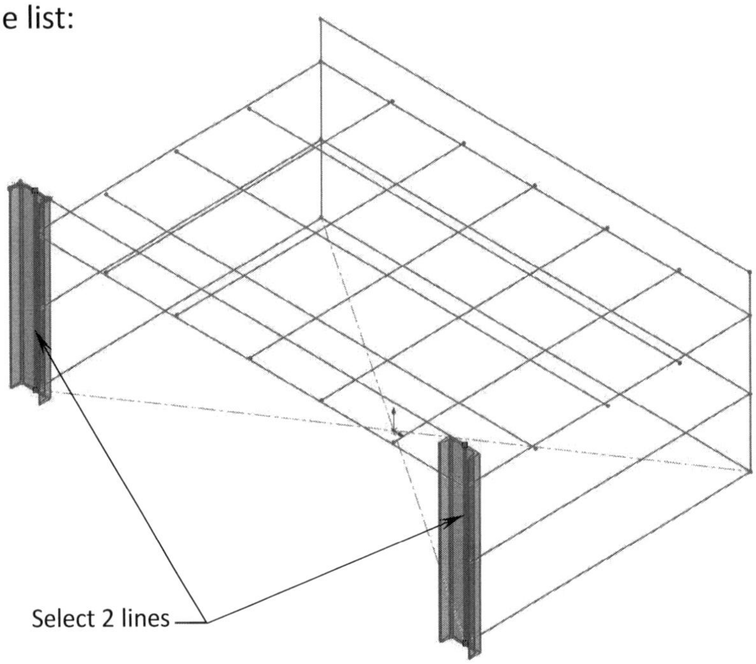

For **Group 1**, select the **2 vertical lines** as indicated.

The C-Channel Profile is attached to the selected lines and extruded automatically to match the length of the lines.

A Weldment Profile is a SOLIDWORKS sketch that is saved as a library feature part, then filed in a defined location so it is available for selection.

Weldment Profiles are identified by Standard, Type, and Size. You can:

- Create your own profiles and add them to the existing library of weldment profiles.
- Specify the orientation and pierce point of the profile relative to the sketch segment.
- Weldment profiles are located in ***C:\Program Files\SOLIDWORKS Corp\SOLIDWORKS\Lang\English\Weldment Profiles***.

You can add or change locations for weldment profiles in: ***Tools > Options > System Options > File Locations***.

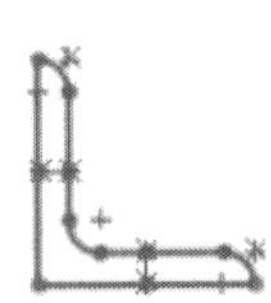
Angle Iron

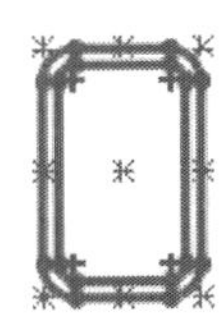
Rectangular Tube

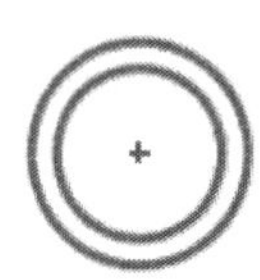
Pipe

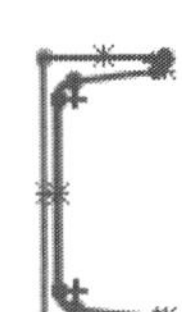
C-Channel

Click the **New Group** button.

For **Group 2**, select the **2 vertical lines** on the back side of the frame as noted.

Use the same C-Channel and parameters as the previous group.

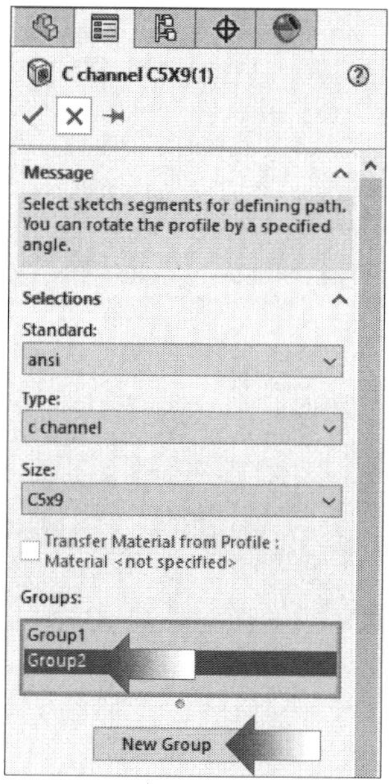

The 4 Legs are created,
2 in group 1 and
2 in group 2.

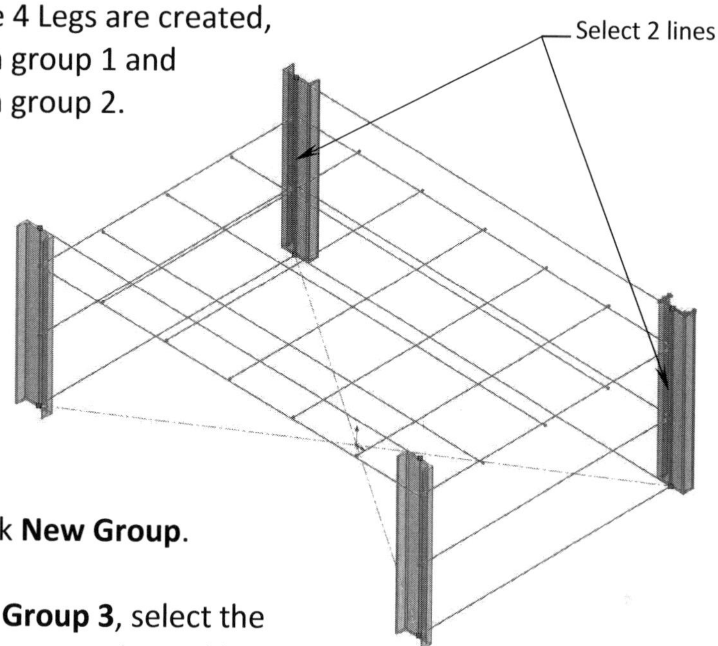

Click **New Group**.

For **Group 3**, select the **4 lines** as indicated below.

Enable the **Apply Corner Treatment** checkbox and select the End **Miter** option.

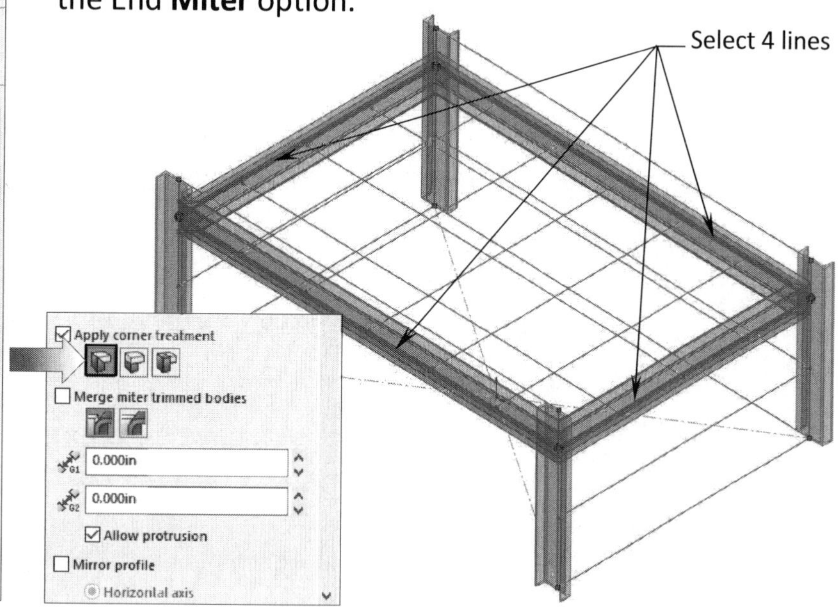

Click the **New Group** button.

For **Group 4**, select the **2 lines** at the bottom of the frame as shown below.

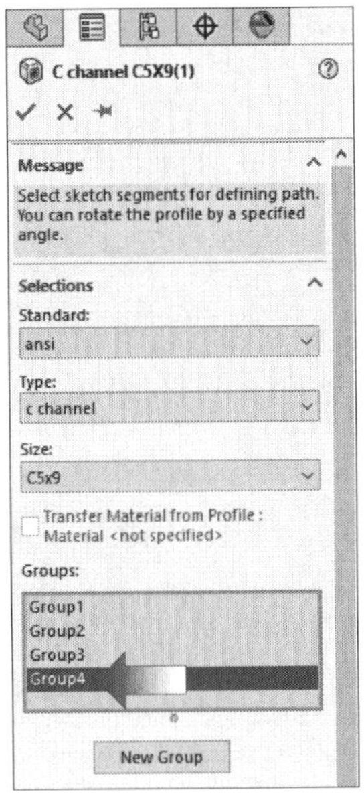

Keep the parameters the same as the other groups.

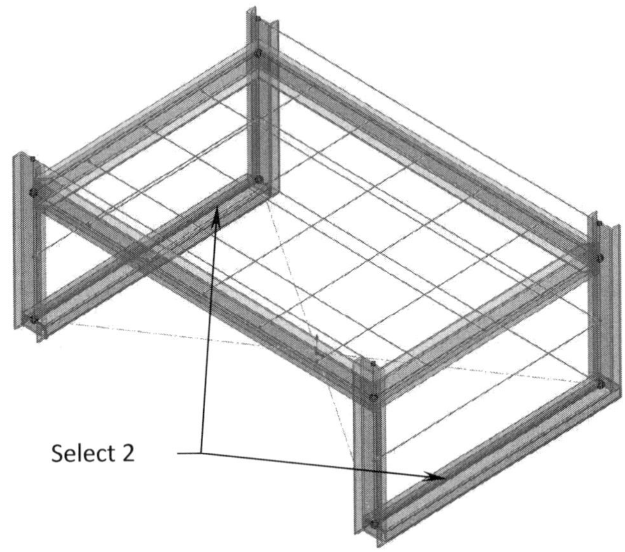

Click **New Group** again.

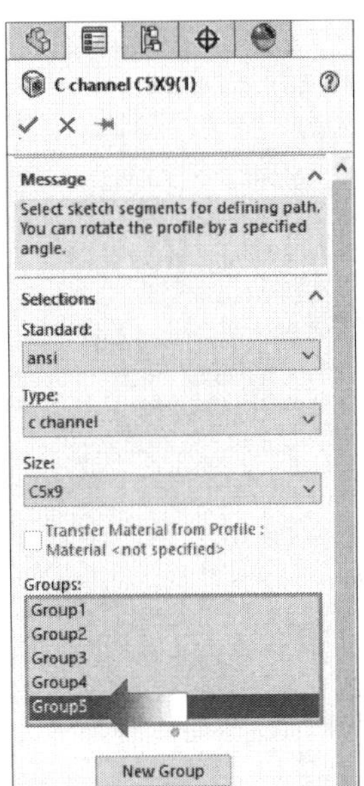

For **Group 5**, select the **line** as indicated below.

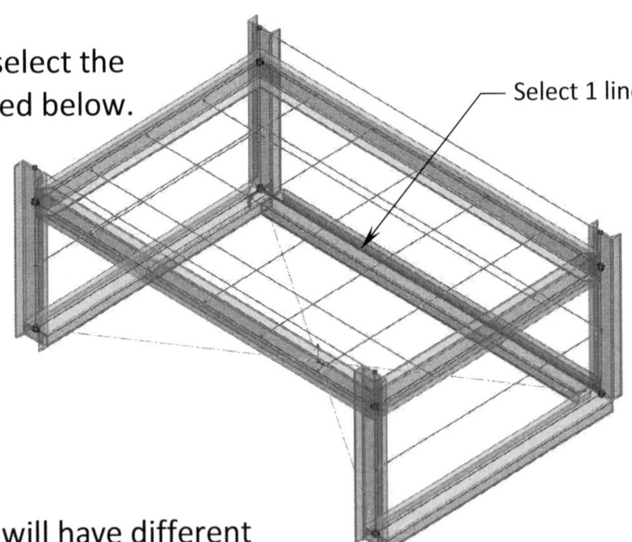

Click **OK**.

Other groups will have different structural members assigned to them in the next step.

4. Adding other Structural Members:

Click **Structural Member**  .

Change the Type to **Tube Square**.

Change the Size to **TS2x2x0.1875**

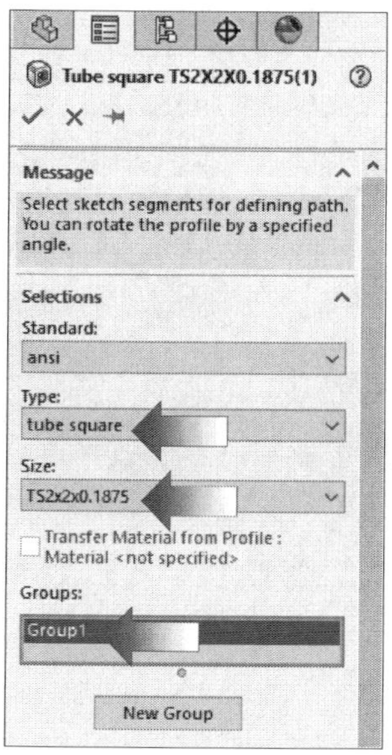

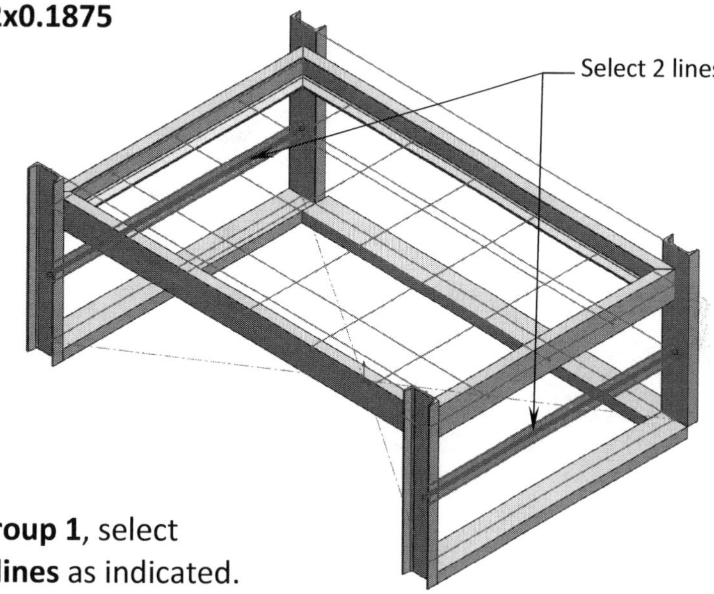

For **Group 1**, select the **2 lines** as indicated.

Click the **New Group** button.

For **Group 2**, select the **3 lines** as noted below.

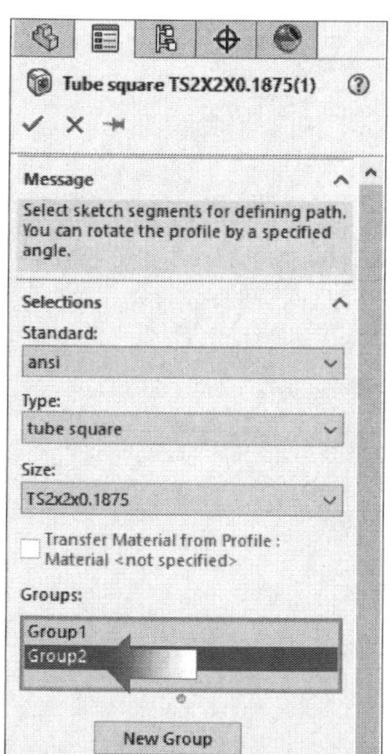

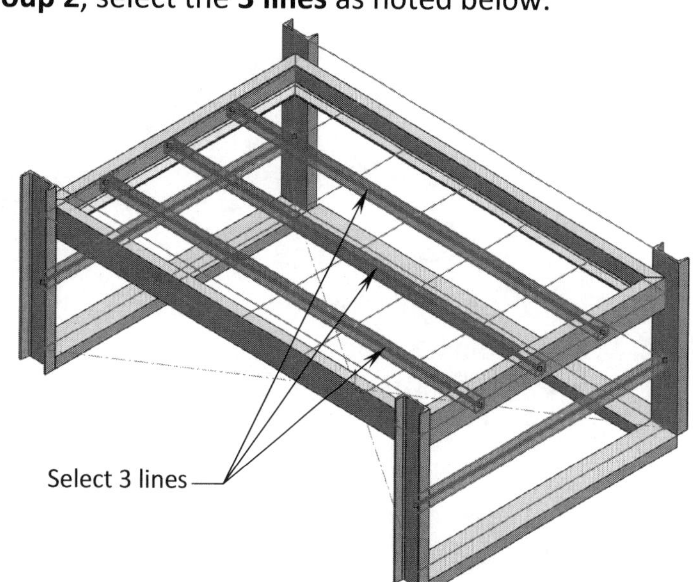

Click the **New Group** button again.

For **Group 3**, select the **line** as noted below.

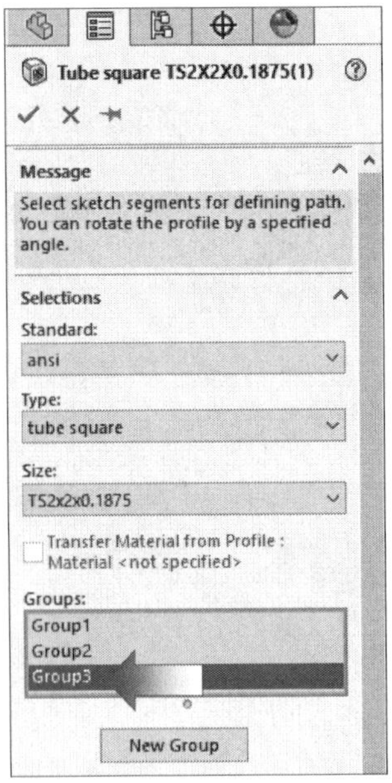

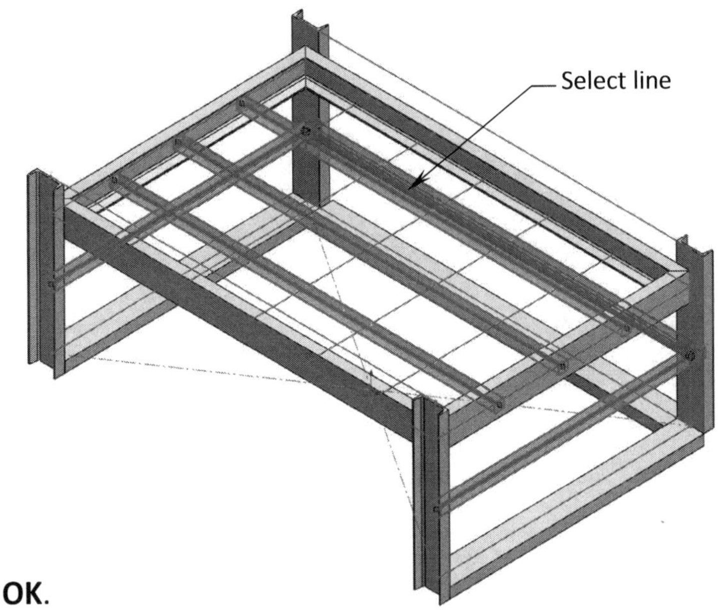

Click **OK**.

Inspect your Weldments part against the one shown here.

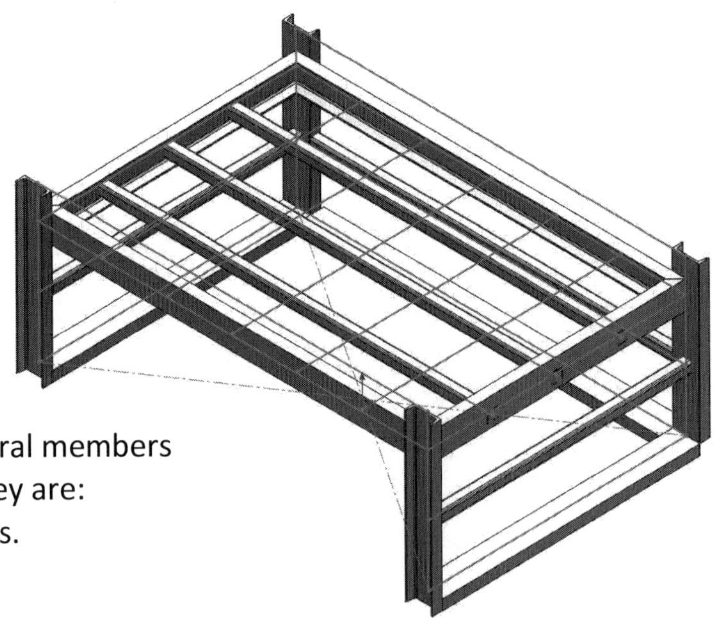

The next group's structural members will be smaller tubes; they are: 1x1x0.083" Square Tubes.

5. Adding the 1.0" Square Tubes:

Click **Structural Member**  .

Change the Type to **Al Tube Square**.

Change the Size to **Al Tube 1 SQR 0.083 Wall**.

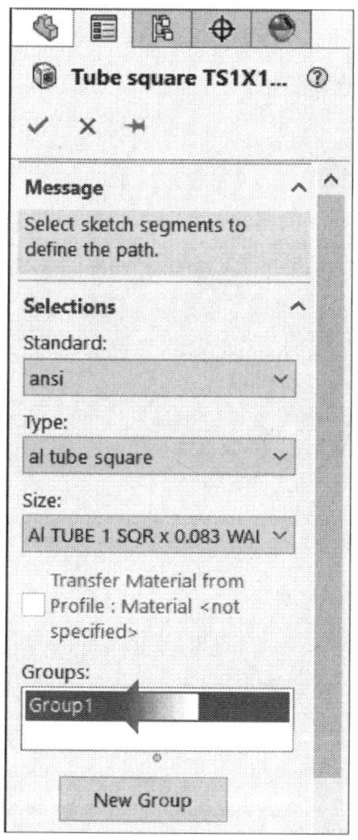

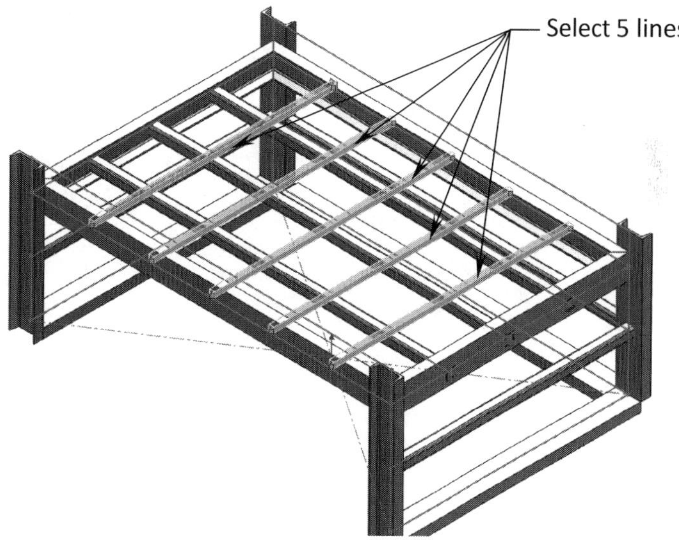

Click **OK**.

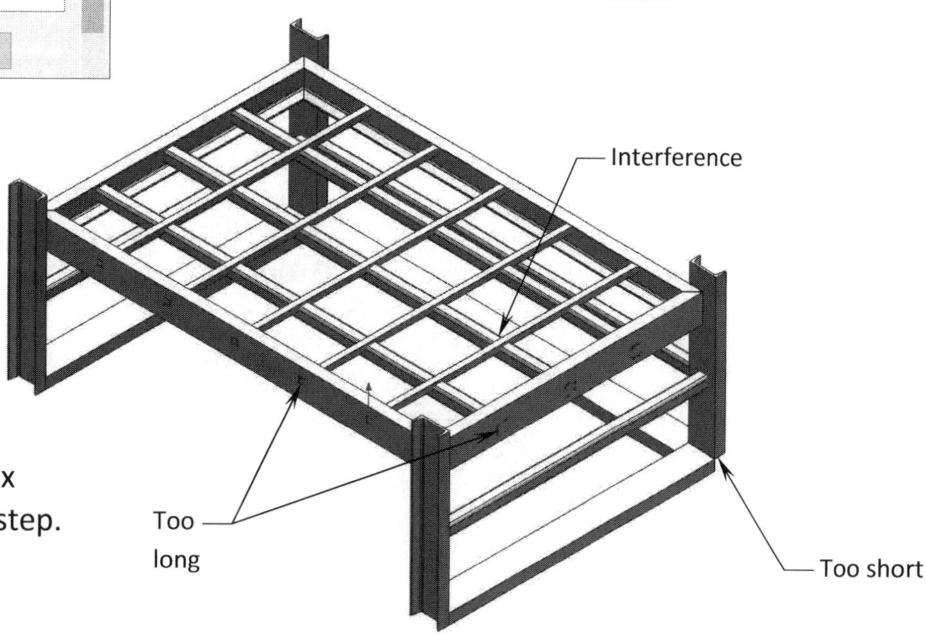

Some of the tubes are too long or too short. We will need to fix them in the next step.

6. Extending the structural members:

Click **Trim/Extend** on the **Weldments** tab.

For Corner Type, select **End Miter**.

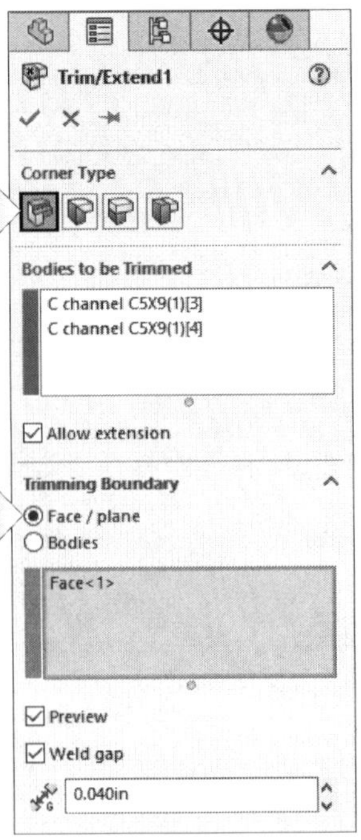

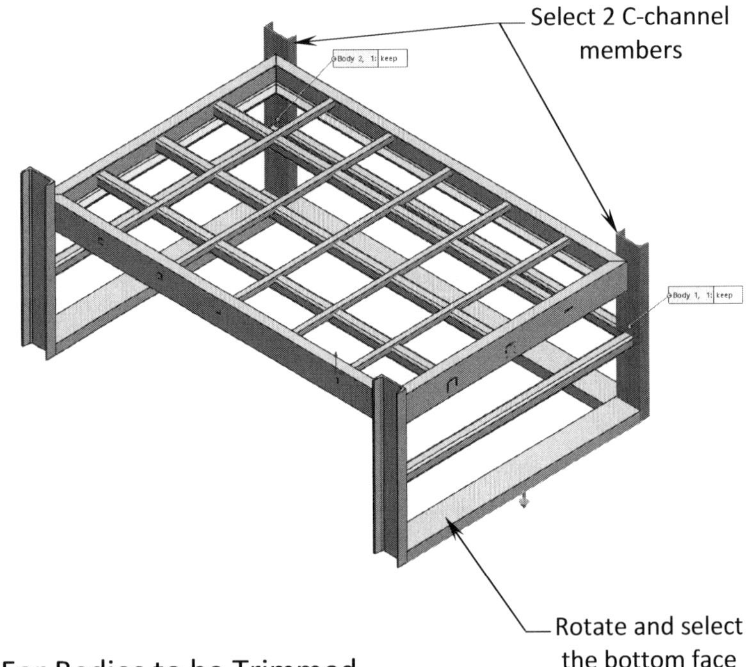

For Bodies to be Trimmed, select the **2 vertical C-Channel** members in the back of the frame.

For Trimming Boundary, click the **Face / Plane** option. Rotate the model and select the **bottom face** to extend the C-channel members up to that surface.

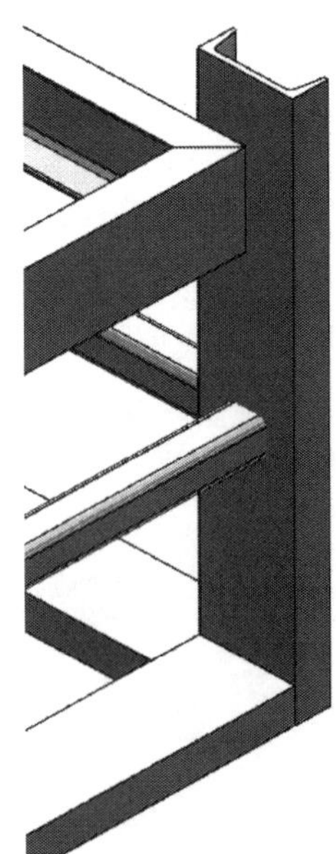

Rotate and zoom closer to inspect the 2 C-channel members. Make sure the bottom faces lined up with the bottom of the frame.

7. Trimming the structural members:

Click **Trim/Extend** on the **Weldments** tab .

For Corner Type, select **End Miter**.

For Bodies to be Trimmed, select the **3 Square Tubes TS2x2x0.1875** and the **5 Al Tube Square x .083 Wall**.

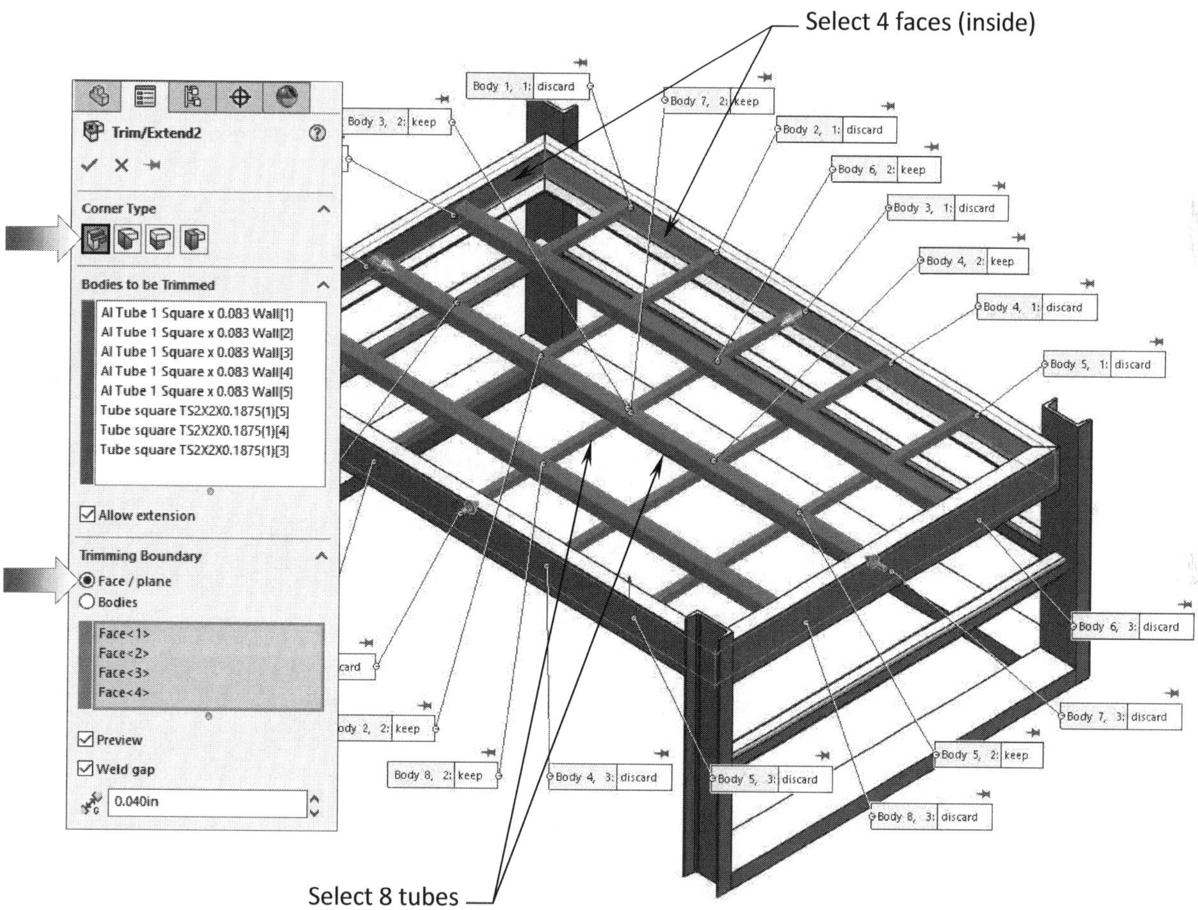

For Trimming Boundary, click the **Face / Plane** option and select the **4 inside faces** of the C-Channels, as indicated in the image.

Enable the **Weld Gap** checkbox and enter **.040in** for gap.

Click **OK**.

8. Moving a structural member:

Press **Control+4** to change to the **Right** view orientation.

One of the C-channel members needs to move inward and be flushed with the back side of the frame, and 3 of the 2x2x0.1875" members still need to be trimmed.

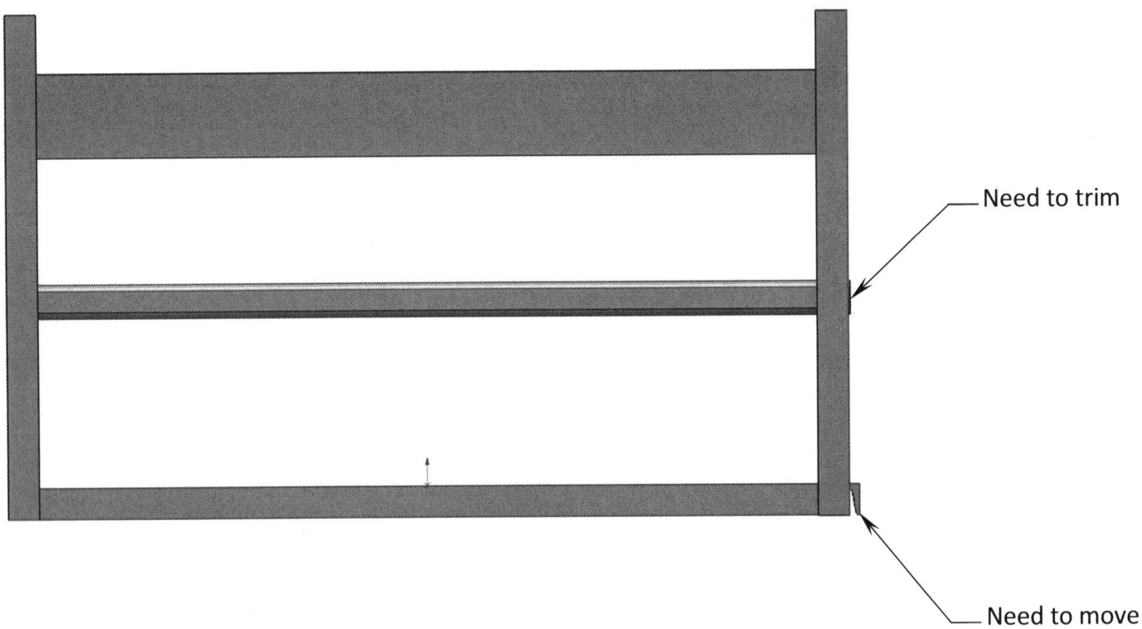

Select: **Insert, Features, Move/Copy Bodies**.

For Bodies to be Move/Copy, select the **C-channel member** on the lower right.

For distance, enter: **.620in**. in the **Delta Z** field.

Click **OK**.

The C-channel is now flushed with the weldment frame.

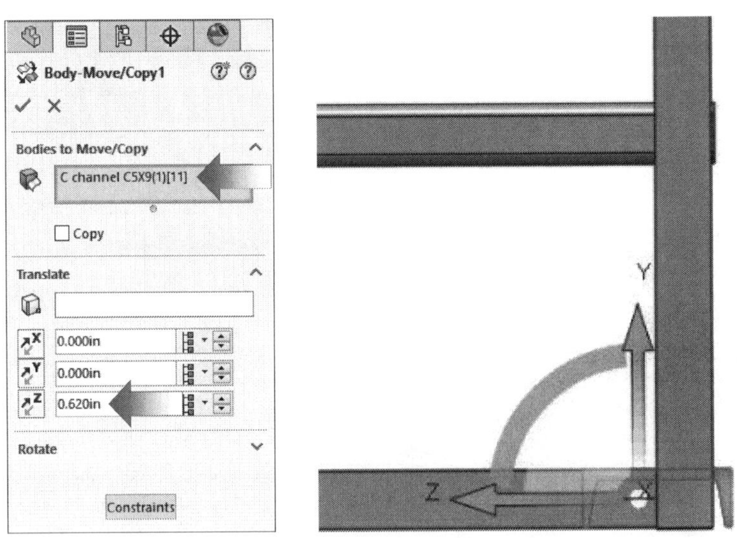

9. Trimming the 2x2x0.1875 tubes:

Rotate the weldment frame to see the back side of the bodies to be trimmed.

Click **Trim/Extend** .

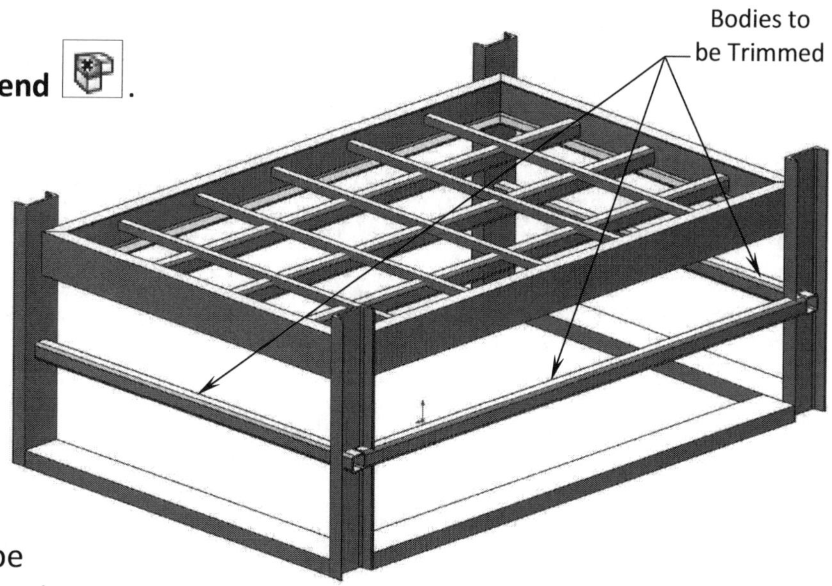

For Corner Type, use the same **End-Miter** as last time.

For Bodies to be Trimmed, select the **3 Tube Square TS2x2x0.1875** members as indicated above.

For Trimming Boundary, select the **2 vertical faces** on the left and right sides of the C-channel member, and also the **inside face** of the same part.

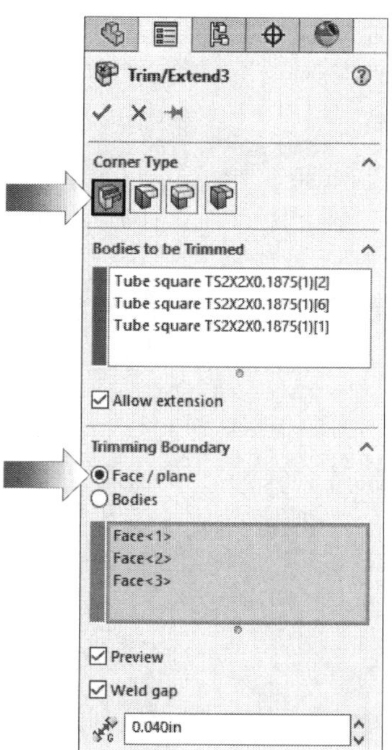

Keep all other parameters at their defaults.

Click **OK**.

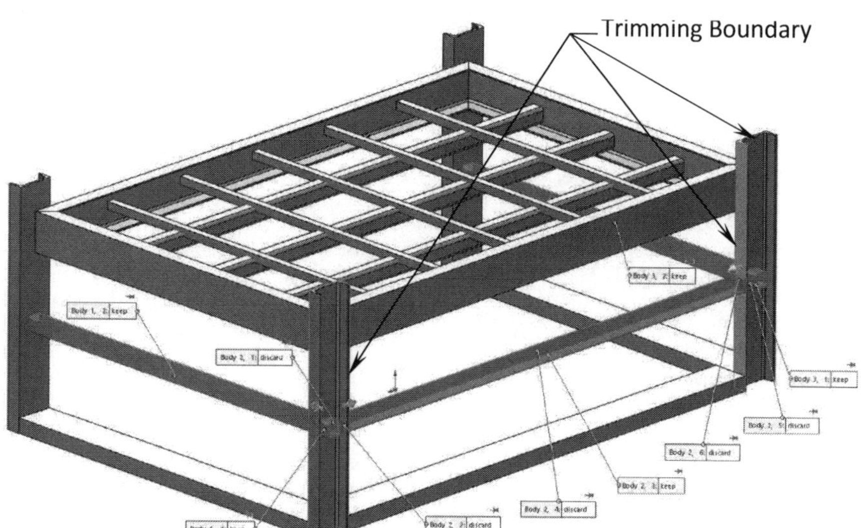

10. Deleting Bodies:

If the Trim tool did not remove all the unwanted bodies, we can delete them after the fact.

Right-click on one of the bodies that needs to be removed and select **Delete**.

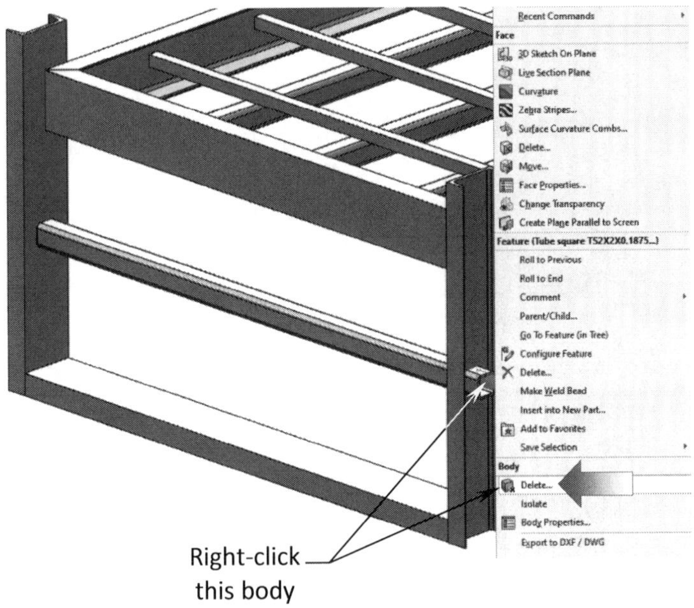

For Body-Delete/Keep dialog box, click the **Delete Bodies** option.

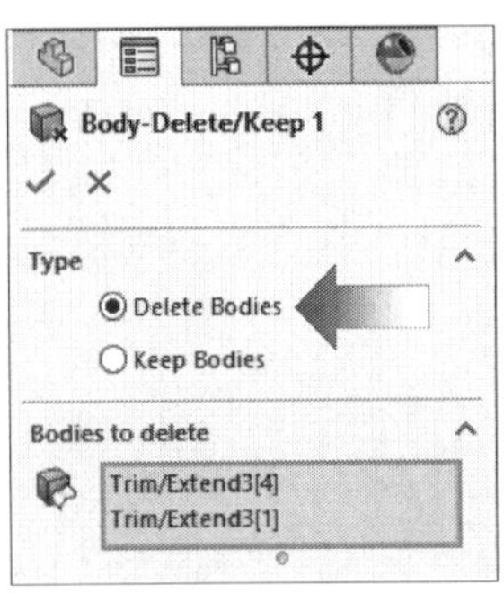

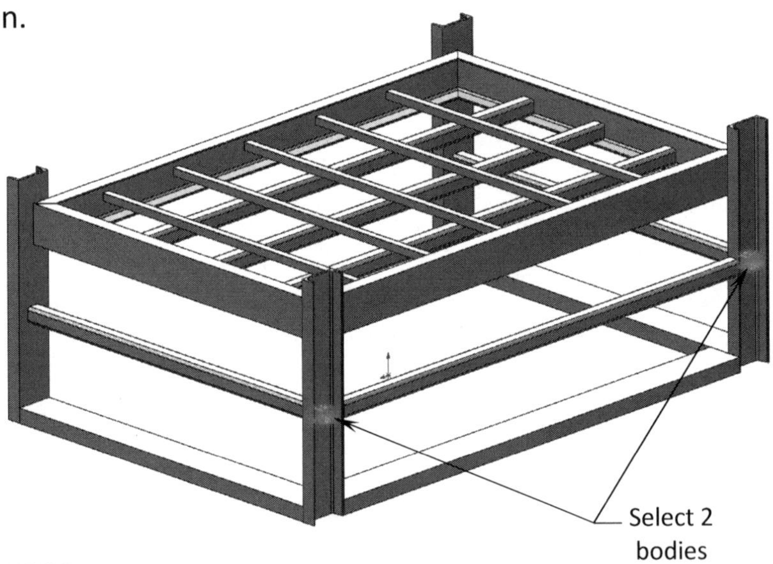

For Bodies to Delete,
select the **2 bodies** as indicated in the image.

Click **OK**.

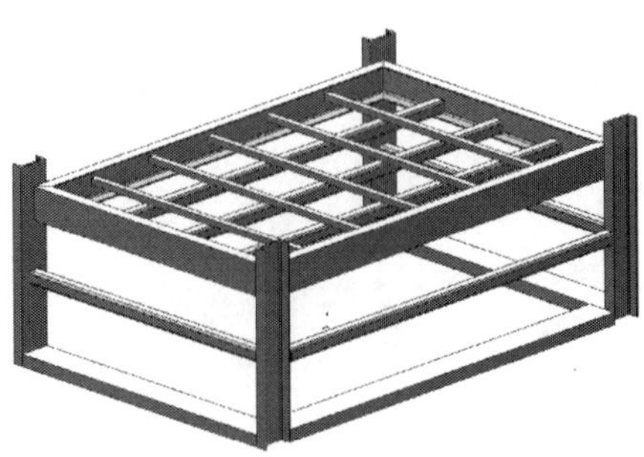

The 2 selected bodies are deleted.

11. Removing the interference:

There are interferences between the **TS2x2x0.1875** and the **Al Tube 1 Square**.

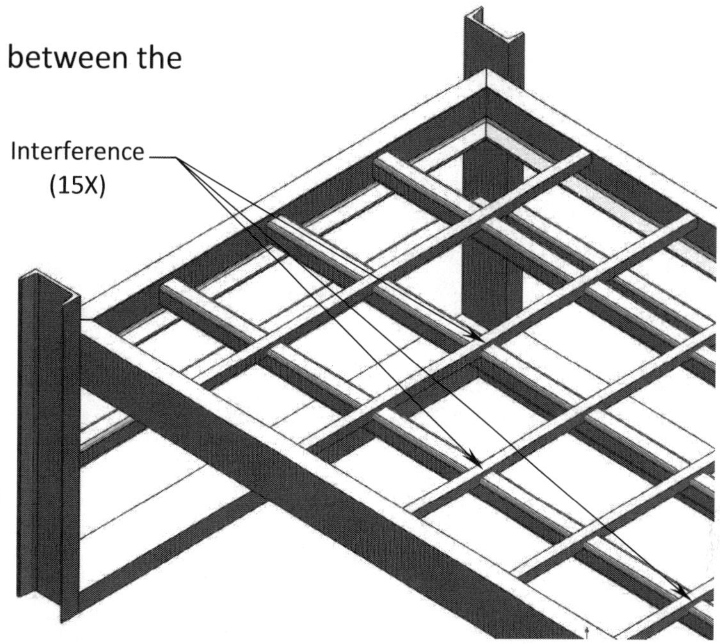

One quick way to resolve this issue is to move the **TS2x2x0.1875** downward.

Select: **Insert, Features, Move, Copy Bodies.**

For Bodies to Move, select the **3 tubes TS2x2x0.1875** from the graphics area.

For distance, enter **.502in.** in the **Delta Y** field.

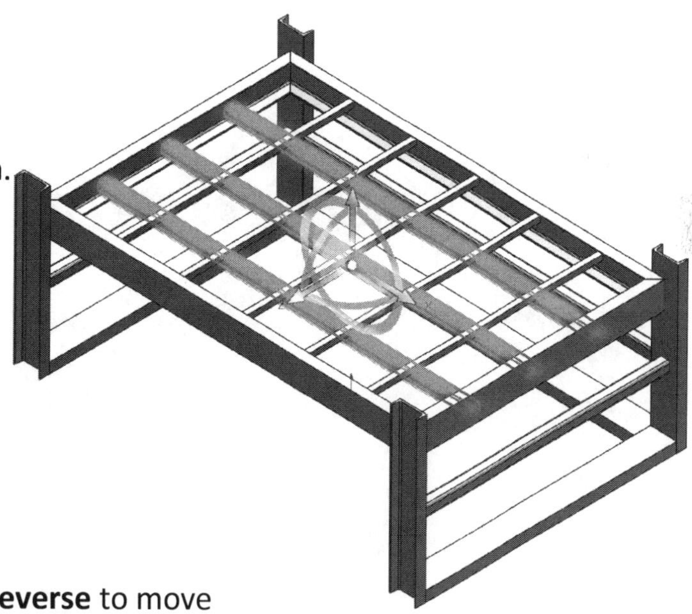

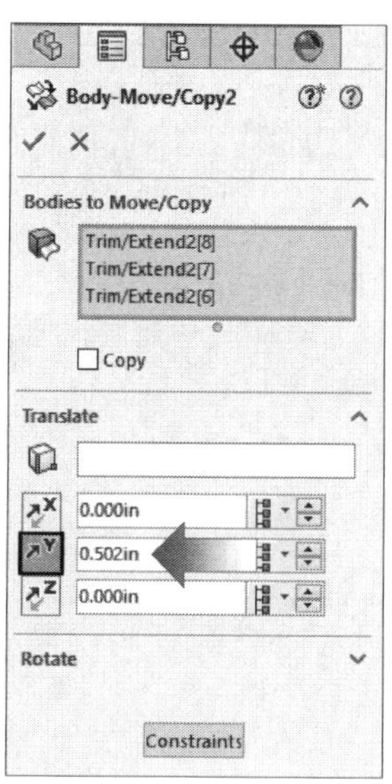

Click **Reverse** to move the tubes downward.

Click **OK**.

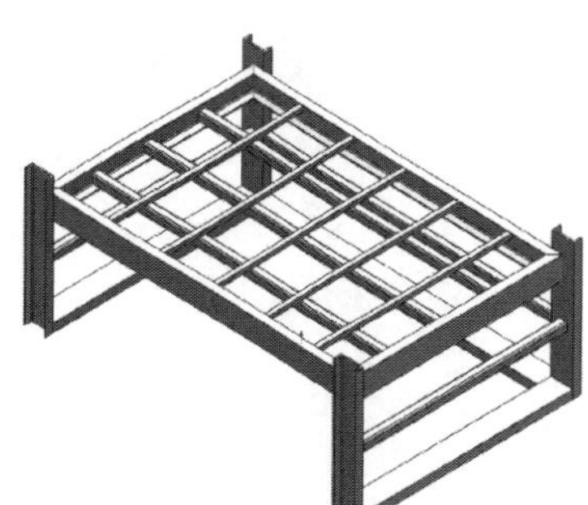

There should be no interference in the weldment part.

12. Saving your work:

Select **File, Save As**.

Enter: **Aluminum Frame_Completed.sldprt** for the file name.

Click **Save**.

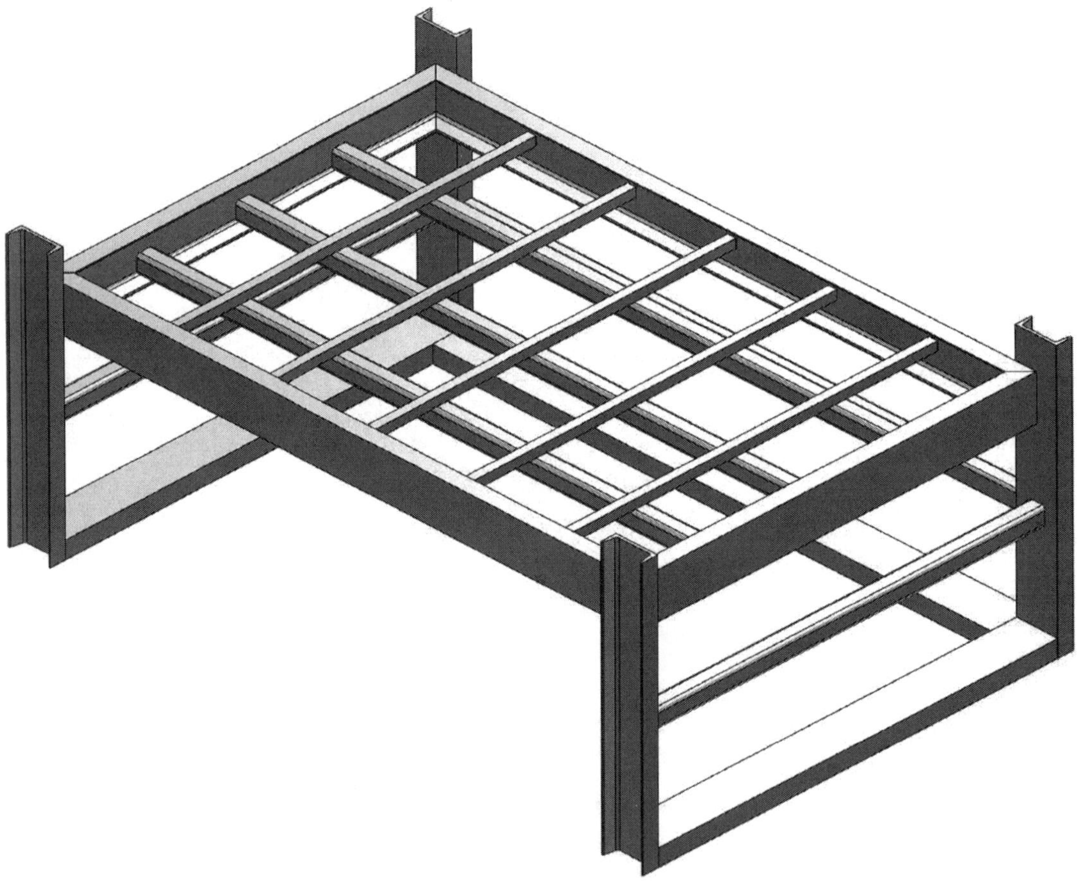

Lesson 14: Weldments Steel Frame

In this lesson, we will take a closer look at the following: Adding the structural members, changing the corner treatments, adding end caps, gussets, and mirroring the solid bodies.

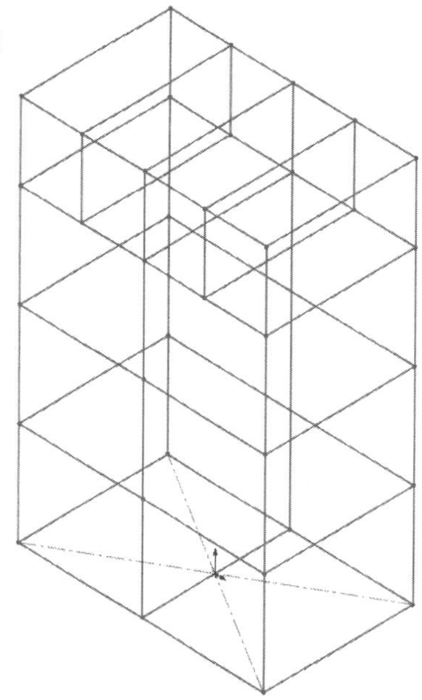

1. Opening a part document:

Browse to the Training Folder and open a part document named: **Weldments Steel Frame**.

There is a 3D Sketch that has been created for this exercise to help us focus on adding the Structural Members and treating the Corners.

2. Enabling the Weldment tab:

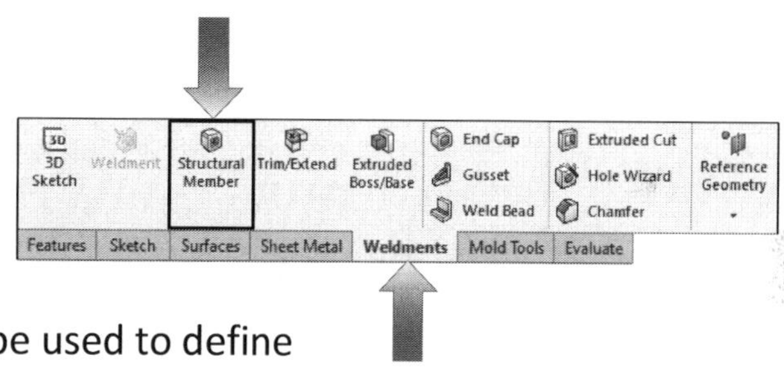

Right-click one of the existing tabs (Sketch or Features) and select: **Tabs, Weldments**.

Either 2D or a 3D sketches can be used to define the basic framework of a weldment structure, then create structural members containing groups of sketch segments.

A group is a collection of related segments in a structural member. You configure a group to affect all its segments without affecting other segments or groups in the structural member.

There are 2 types of Groups: **Contiguous** and **Parallel**.

Contiguous Group is a continuous contour of segments joined end-to-end. You can control how the segments join to each other. The end point of the group can optionally connect to its beginning point.

Parallel Group is a discontinuous collection of parallel segments. Segments in the group cannot touch each other.

After the framework is created, add items such as gussets and end caps using tools on the Weldments toolbar.

3. Adding the Structural Members:

Click **Structural Member** on the **Weldments** tab.

Select the following:

Standard: **ANSI**

Type: **Tube Square**

Size: **TS4x4x0.1875**

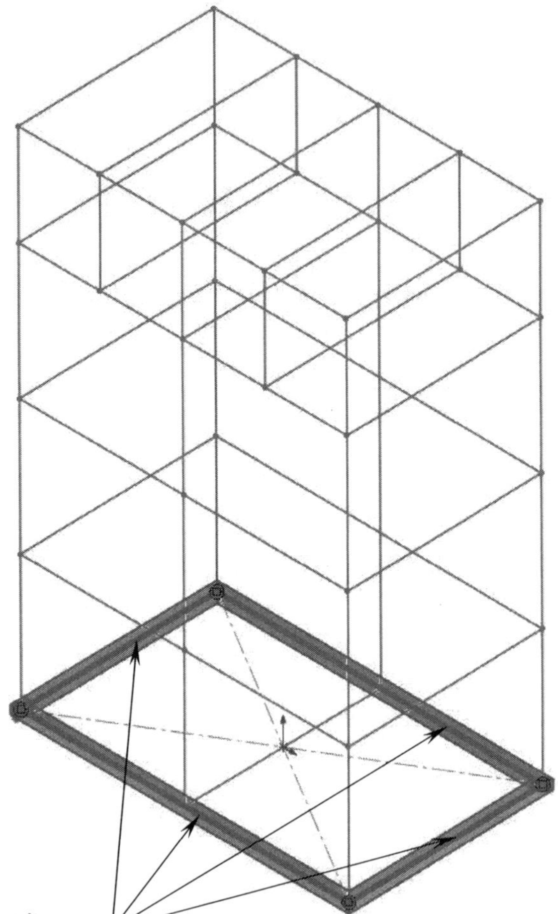

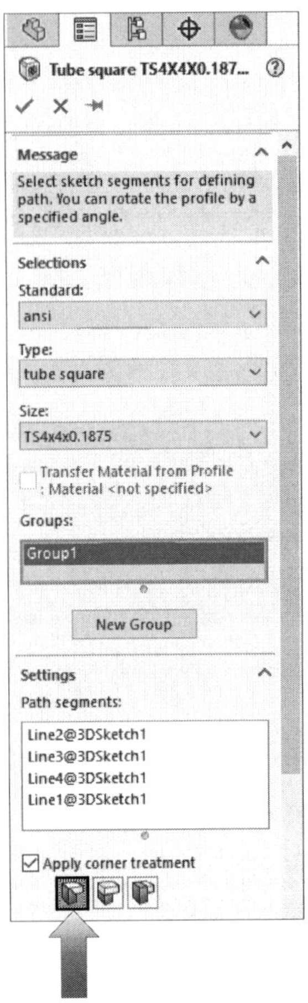

First, we will select the **Contiguous Groups**.

Click **New Group**.

Select the **4 lines** at the bottom of the frame as indicated.

Select the **End Miter** option.

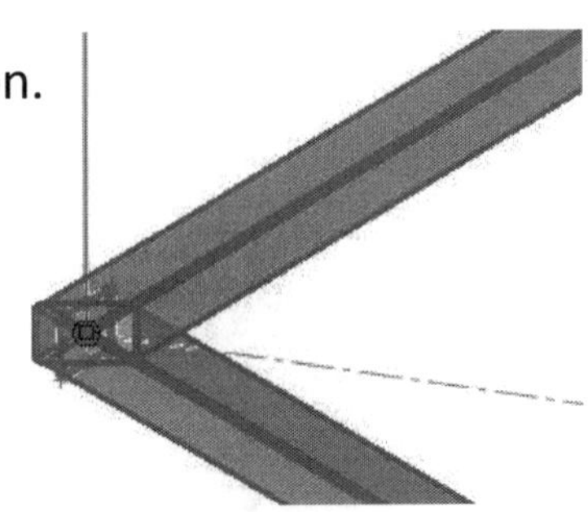

Zoom closer to inspect the corners.

Click the **New Group** button.

For **Group 2**, select the **4 lines** as noted in the image.

Keep all parameters the same as the last group.

Both Group 1 and Group 2 are called **Contiguous Group** because their lines are joined end-to-end.

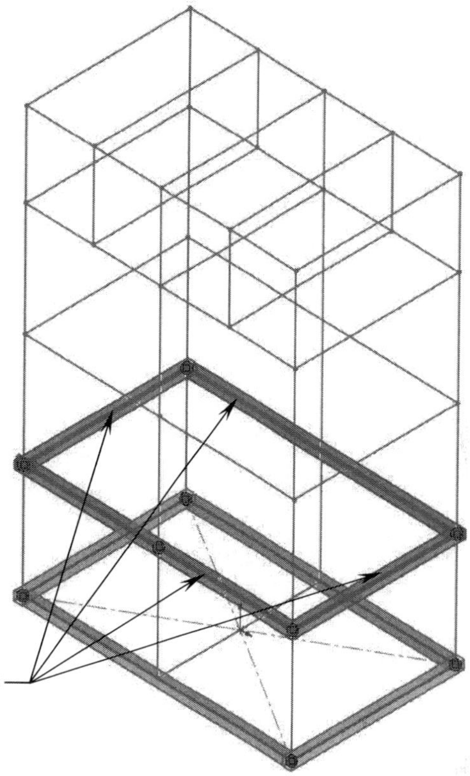

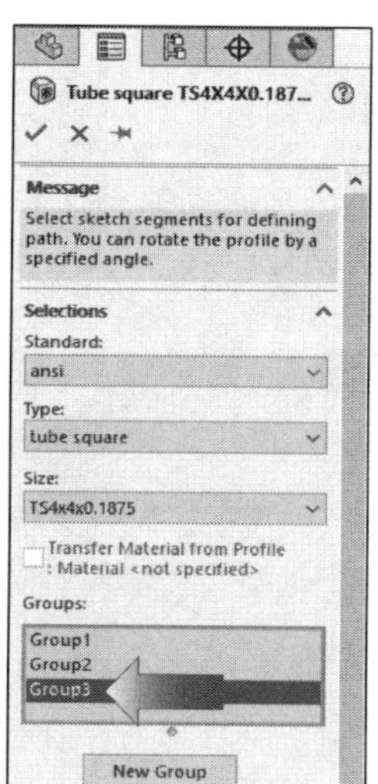

Click **New Group**.

For **Group 3**, select the **4 lines** shown in the image on the right.

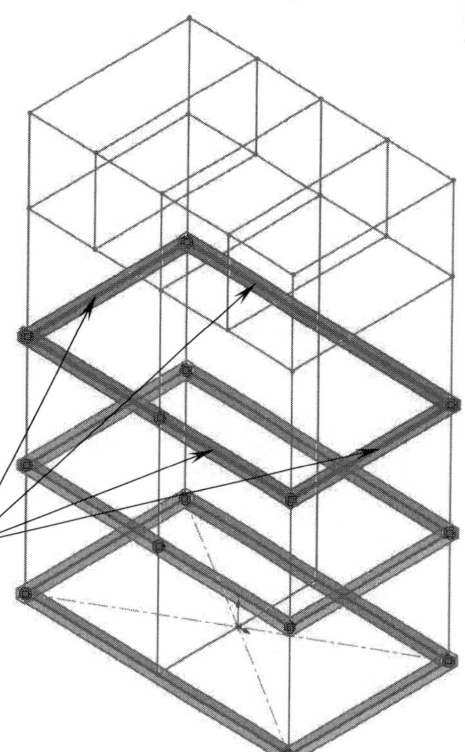

Keep all parameters the same as the previous groups.

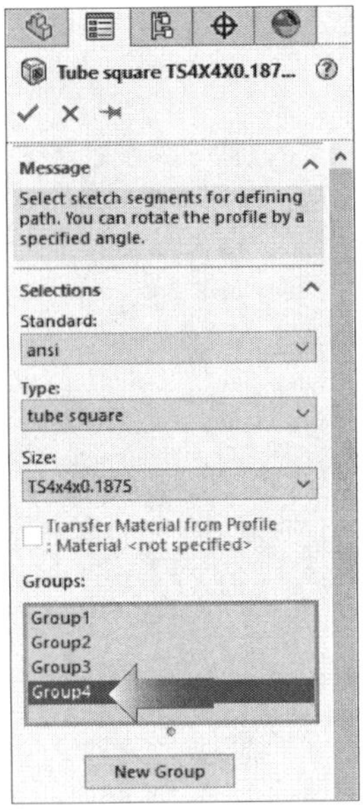

Click **New Group**.

For **Group 4**, select the **4 lines** shown in the image on the right.

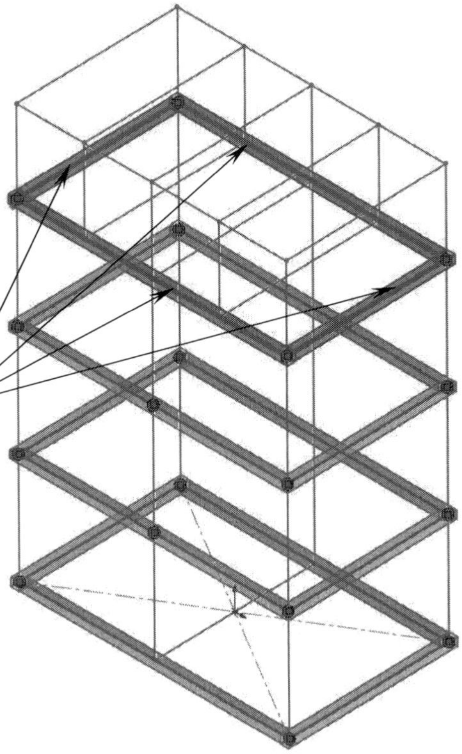

Keep all parameters the same as the previous groups.

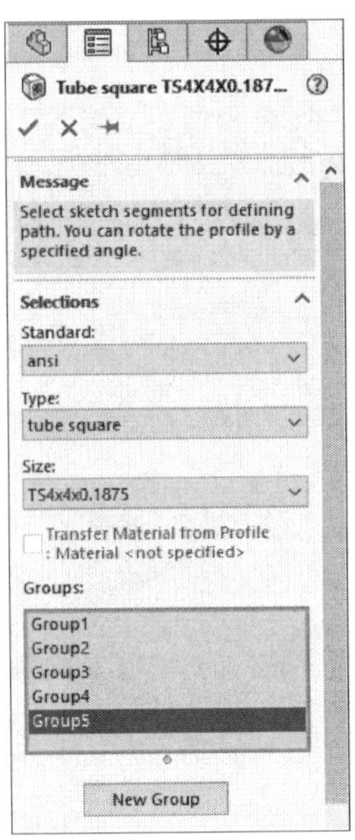

Click **New Group**.

For **Group 5**, select the **4 lines** shown in the image on the right.

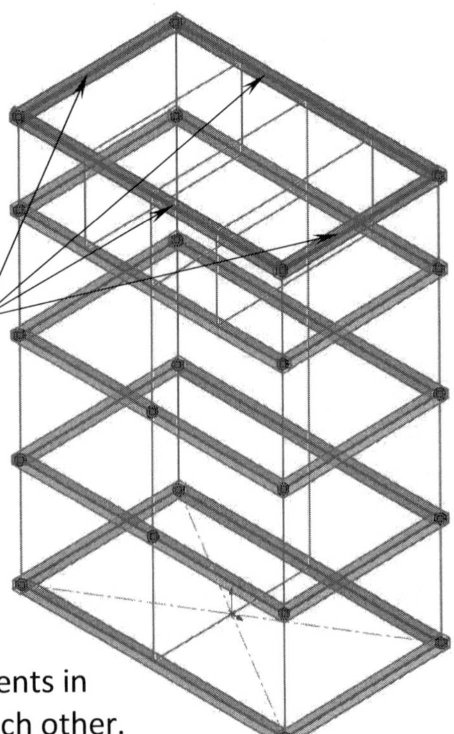

Keep all parameters the same as the previous groups.

Next, we will select the **Parallel Groups.** The segments in this group cannot touch each other.

Selecting the **Parallel Groups**.

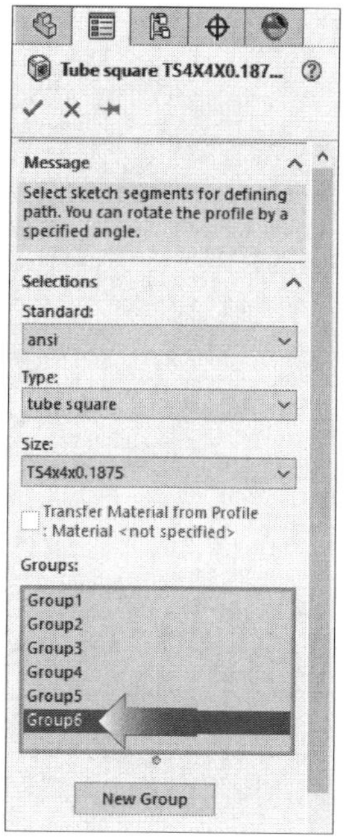

Click the **New Group** button again.

For **Group 6**, select the **6 vertical lines** shown in the image on the right.

Use the same tube settings as the last groups.

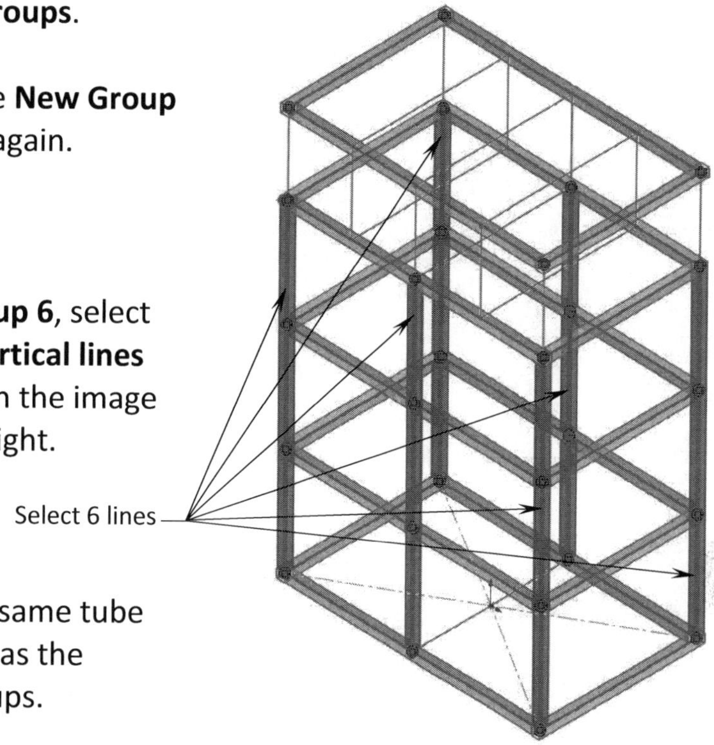

Click **New Group**.

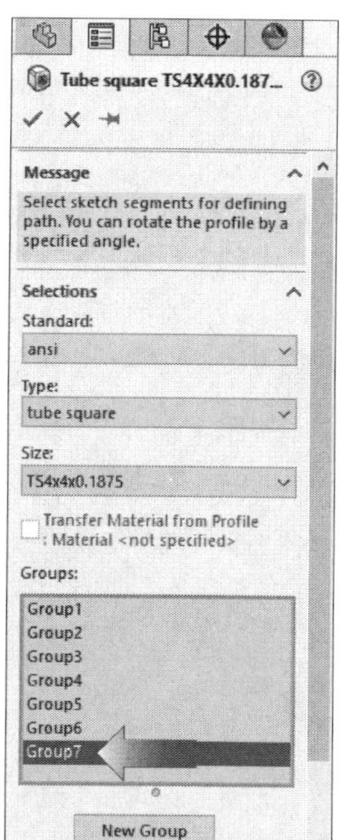

For **Group 7**, select the **10 vertical lines** shown in the image.

Keep all parameters the same as the previous groups.

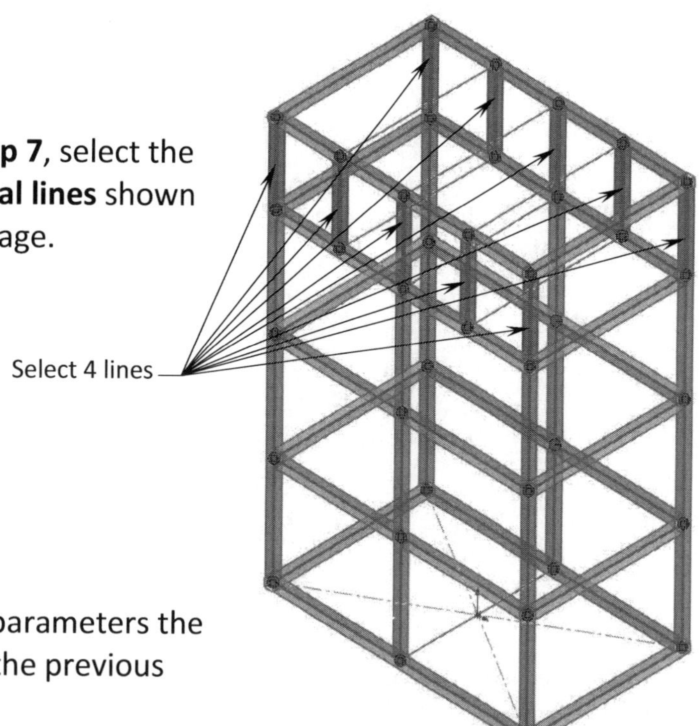

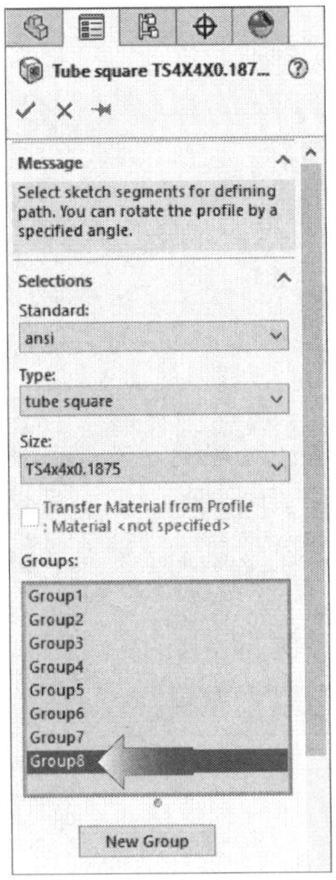

Click **New Group** once again.

For **Group 8**, select the **7 horizontal lines** as indicated.

We have selected 3 Parallel Groups.

The lines are not supposed to touch or connect with each other.

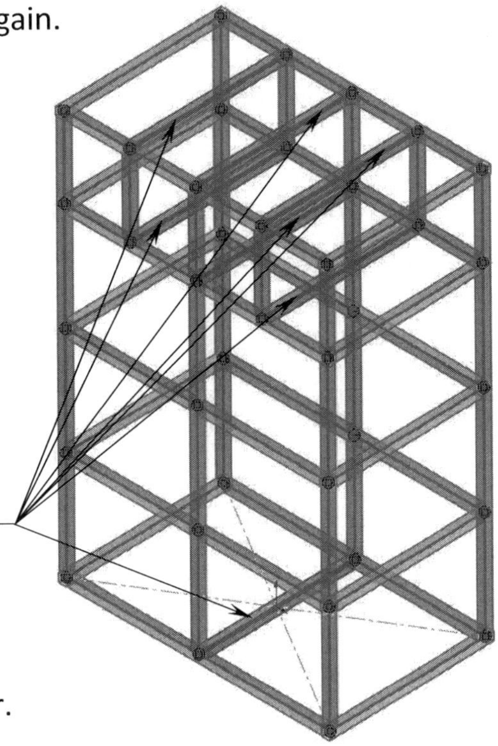

Click **OK**.

The corners of bottom tubes were set to End-Miter.

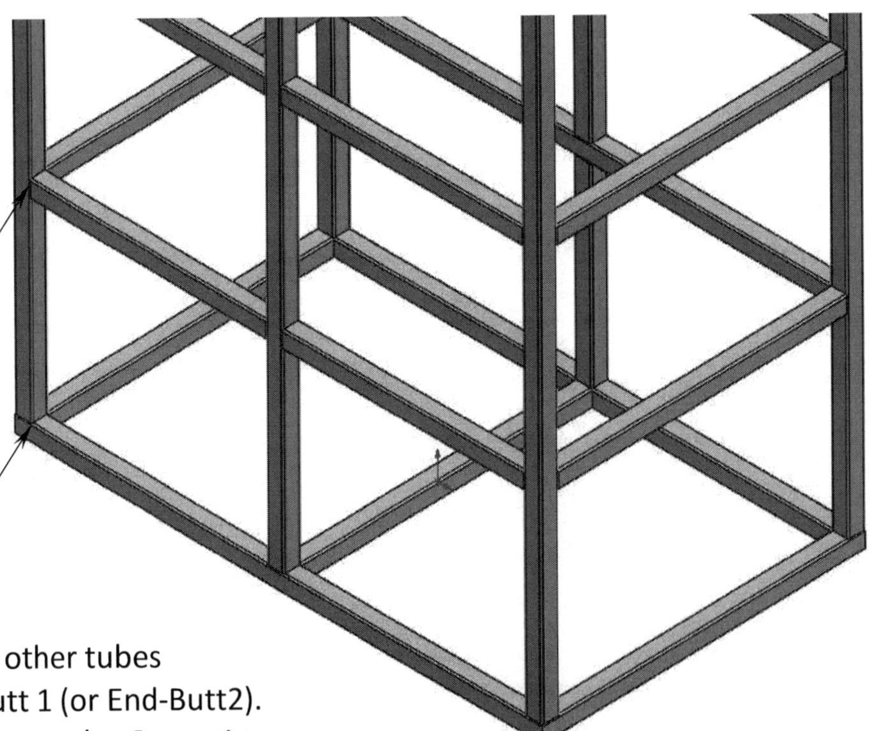

The corners of the other tubes were set to End-Butt 1 (or End-Butt2). We will need to change the Group 1 to End-Butt to match the rest of the tubes.

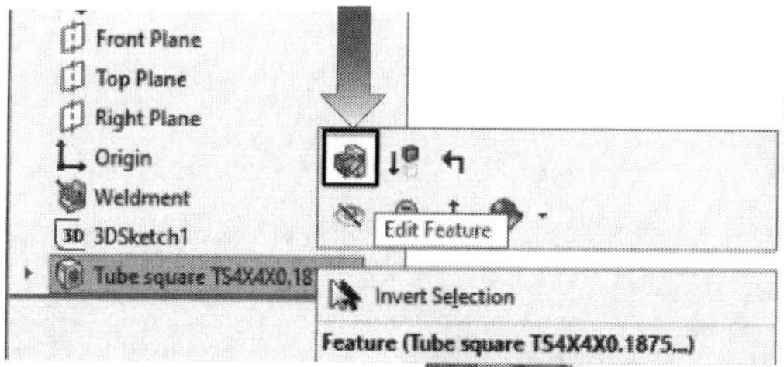

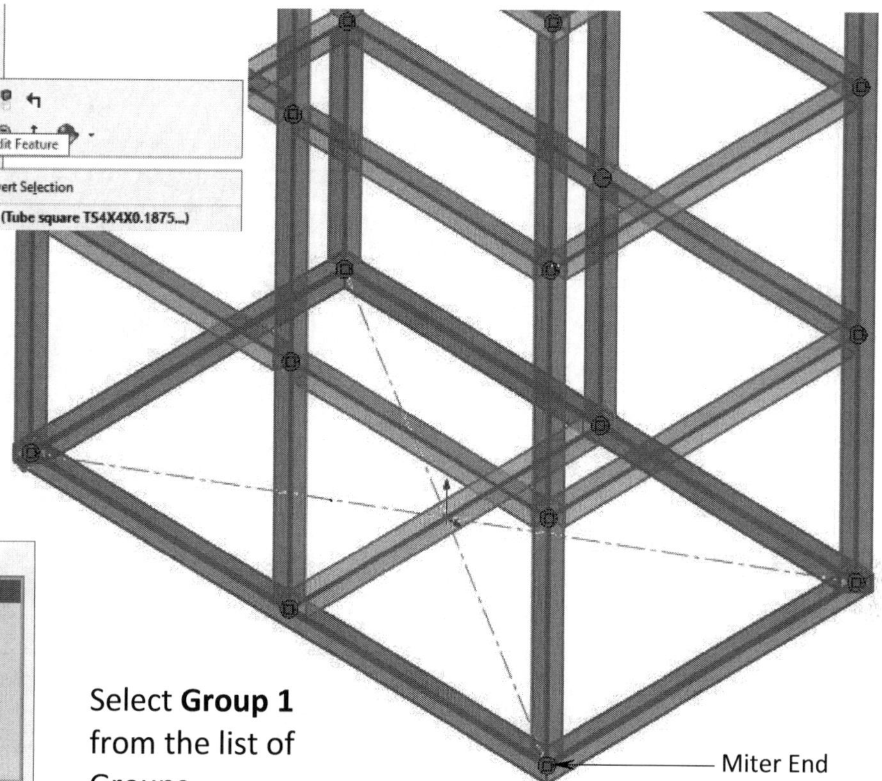

Right-click the **Tube Square-TS4x4x0.1875** and select: **Edit Feature**.

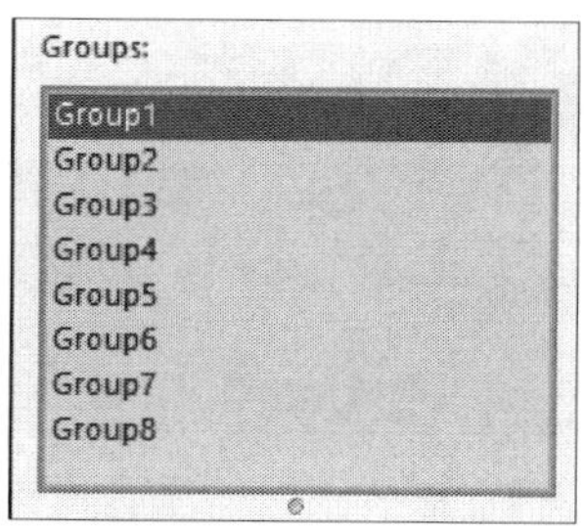

Select **Group 1** from the list of Groups.

Click the **"Pink-dot"** to access the Corner-Treatment dialog box.

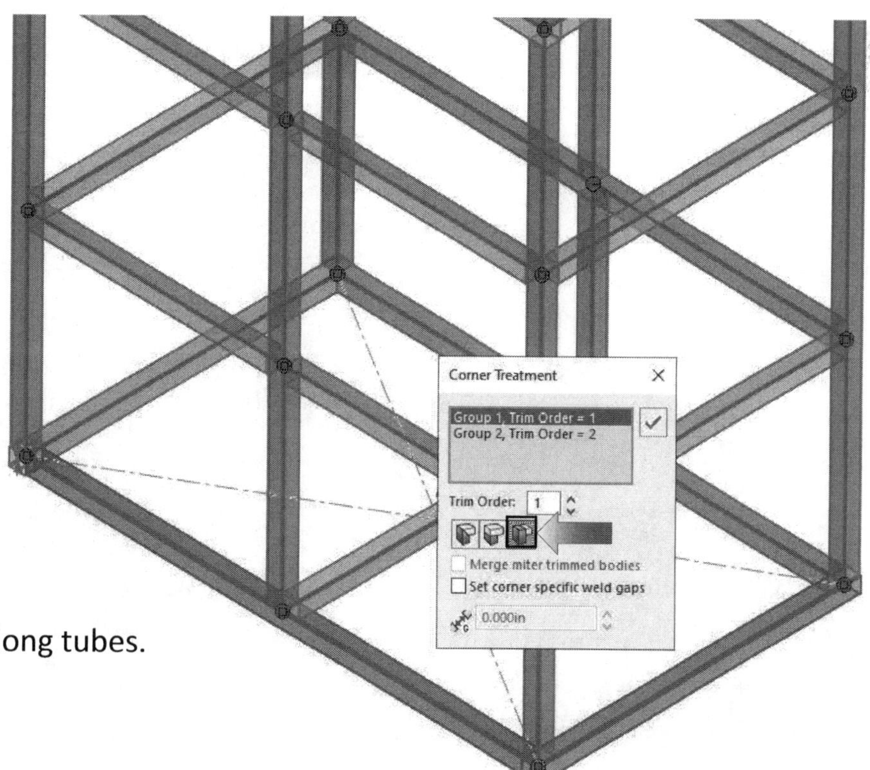

Under the Trim Order section, select either **End-Butt 1** or **End-Butt 2** so that the short tubes on the left and right sides are overlapped by the long tubes.

Click **OK**.

Switch back to the **Isometric** view (Control+7).

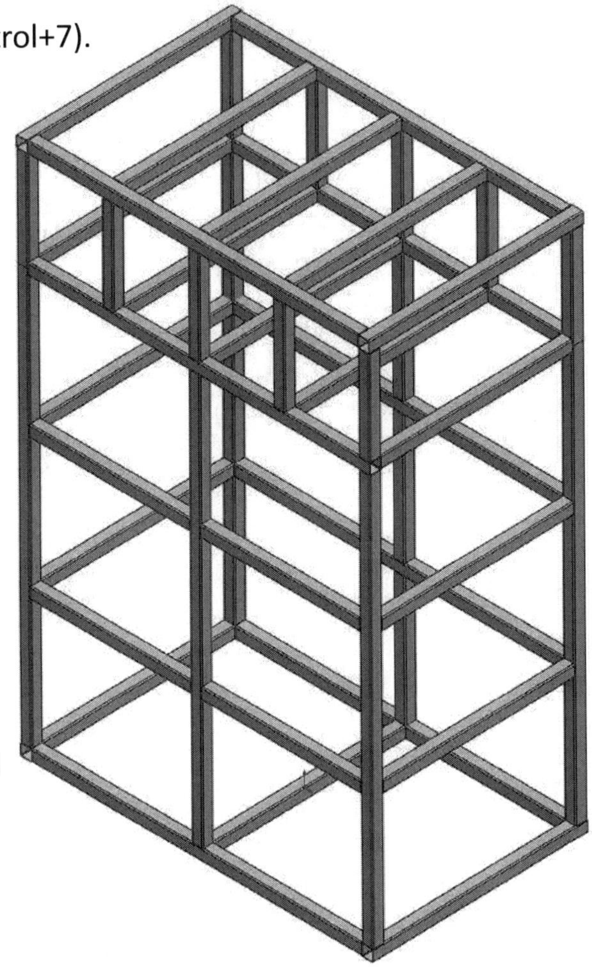

Inspect your weldment frame against the image shown on the right.

Make any corrections as needed.

Add the material **Plain Carbon Steel** to the model if it has not been assigned already.

Next, we will take a look at adding the end caps to close off the ends of the structural members.

End caps' overall size can be set to be smaller or larger than the structural member's outside dimension.

End caps can be added externally or internally, and the corners can have fillets or chamfers added.

External End Cap

Internal End Cap

4. Adding end caps:

Click **End Cap** on the **Weldments** tab.

For Thickness Direction, click **Outside**.

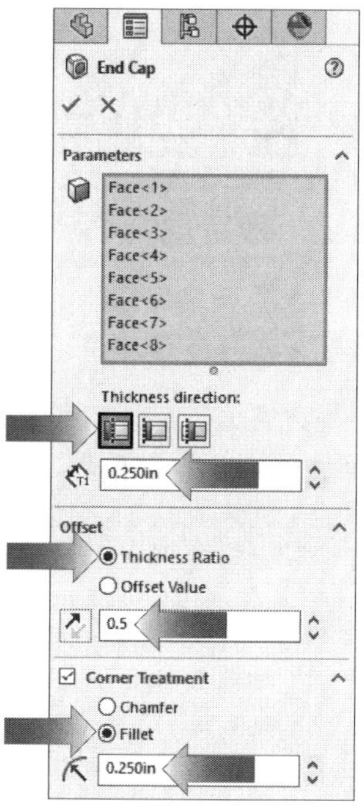

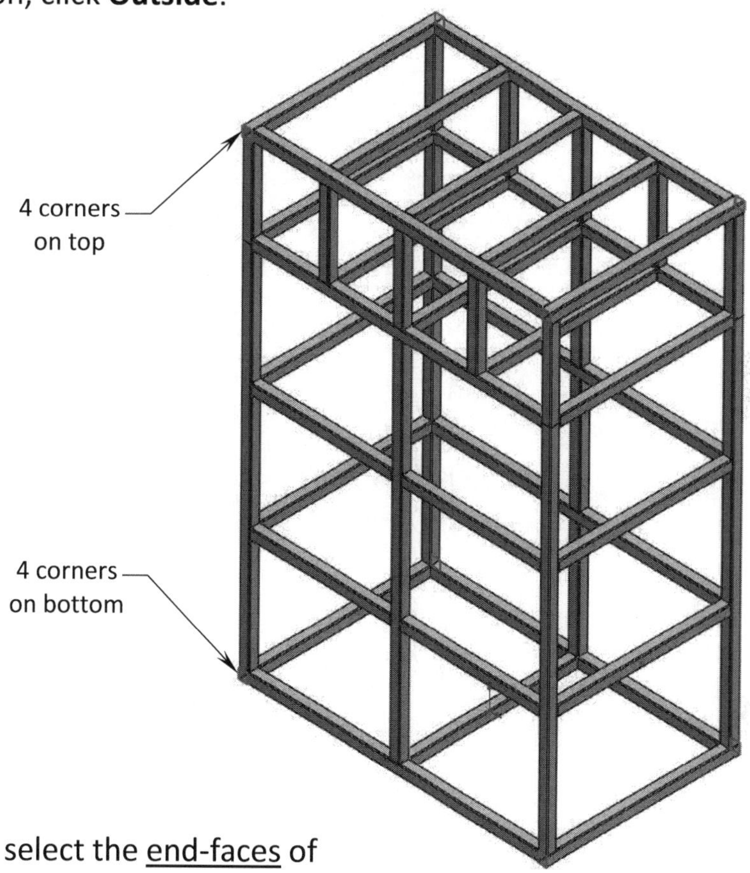

For End Cap Location, select the <u>end-faces</u> of the structure, **4 on top** and **4 at the bottom.**

For End Cap Thickness, enter **.250in**.

For Offset, click **Thickness Ratio** and enter: **0.5**.

Enable the **Corner Treatment** checkbox and select the **Fillet** option.

For corner fillet size, enter **.250in**.

Click **OK**.

5. Adding gussets:

Gussets are added to the weldments structure to reinforce the area between two intersecting structural members with planar faces.

There are two types of gussets available: Triangular and Polygonal.

Click **Gusset** on the **Weldments** tab.

For Supporting Faces, select the **2 faces** as noted.

For Profile, click **Triangular**. For Distance, enter **.500in**. for both distances.

For Thickness, select **Both Sides** and enter **.500in**.

For Profile Location, select: **At Mid Point**.

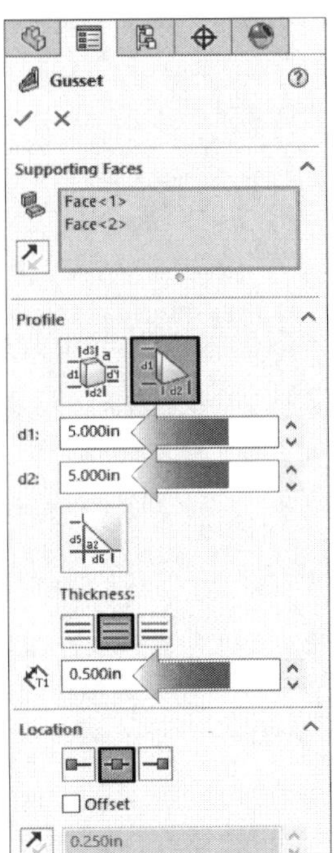

Click **OK**.

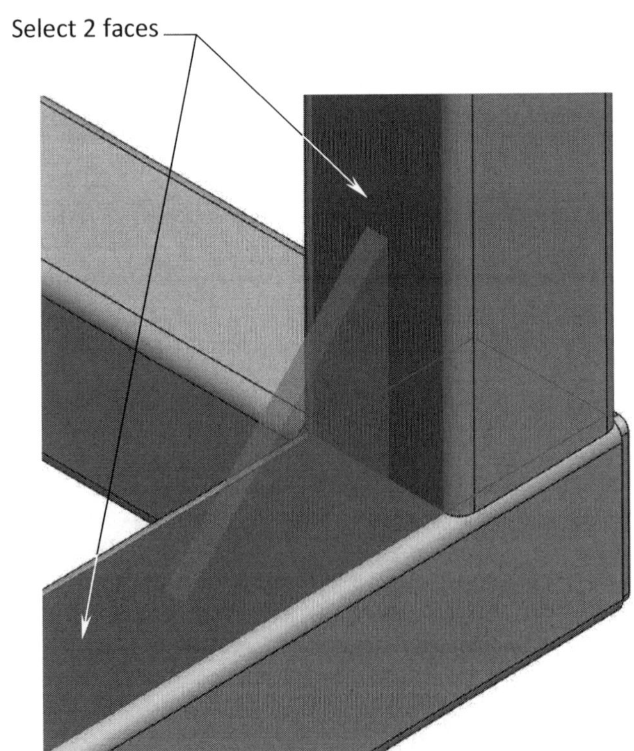

Add a total of 10 gussets to the right-rear side of the structure. We will mirror them to opposite sides in the next step.

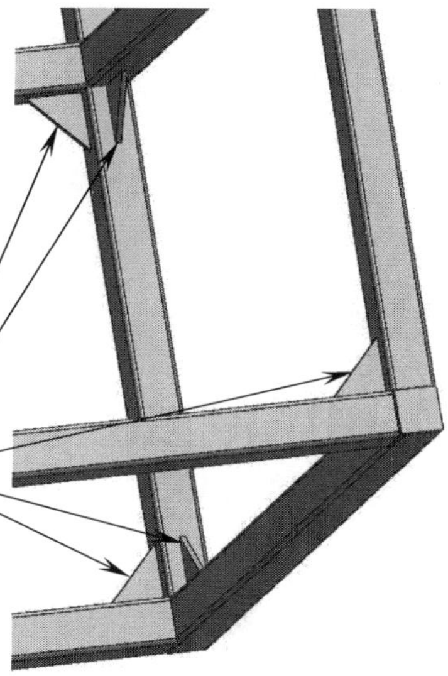

Add 10 gussets

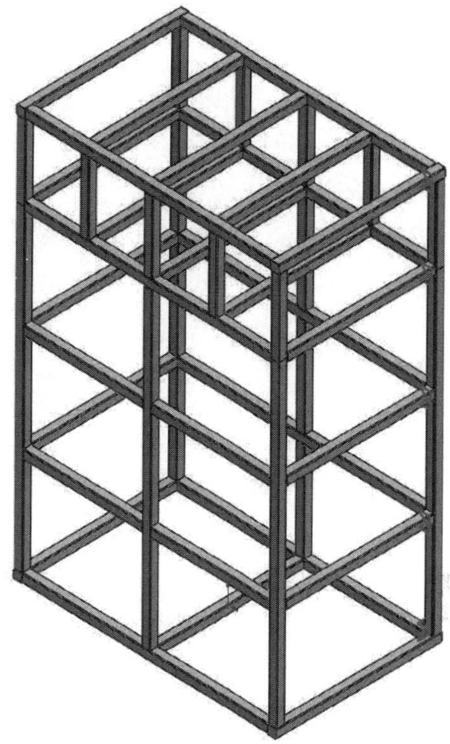

6. Mirroring the gussets:

Switch to the **Features** tab and click **Mirror**.

For the 1st Mirror Plane, select the **Front** plane from the FeatureManager tree.

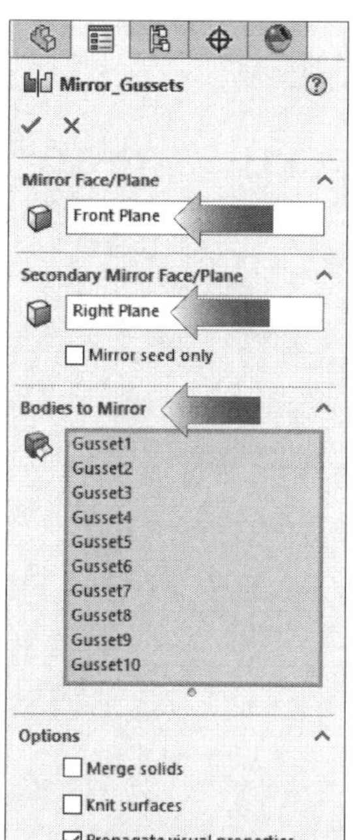

For the 2nd Mirror Plane, select the **Right** plane, also from the Feature-Manager tree.

Expand the Bodies-To-Mirror section and select all **10 gussets** from the **Cut-List-Items2** (inside the Cut List folder).

<u>Clear</u> the **Merge Solids** checkbox.

Click **OK**.

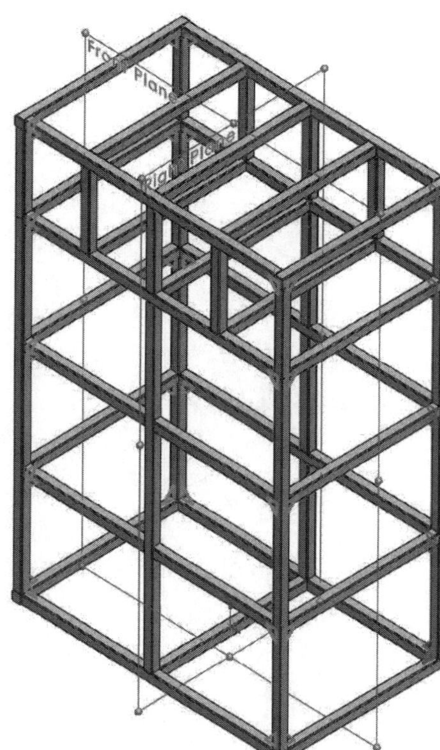

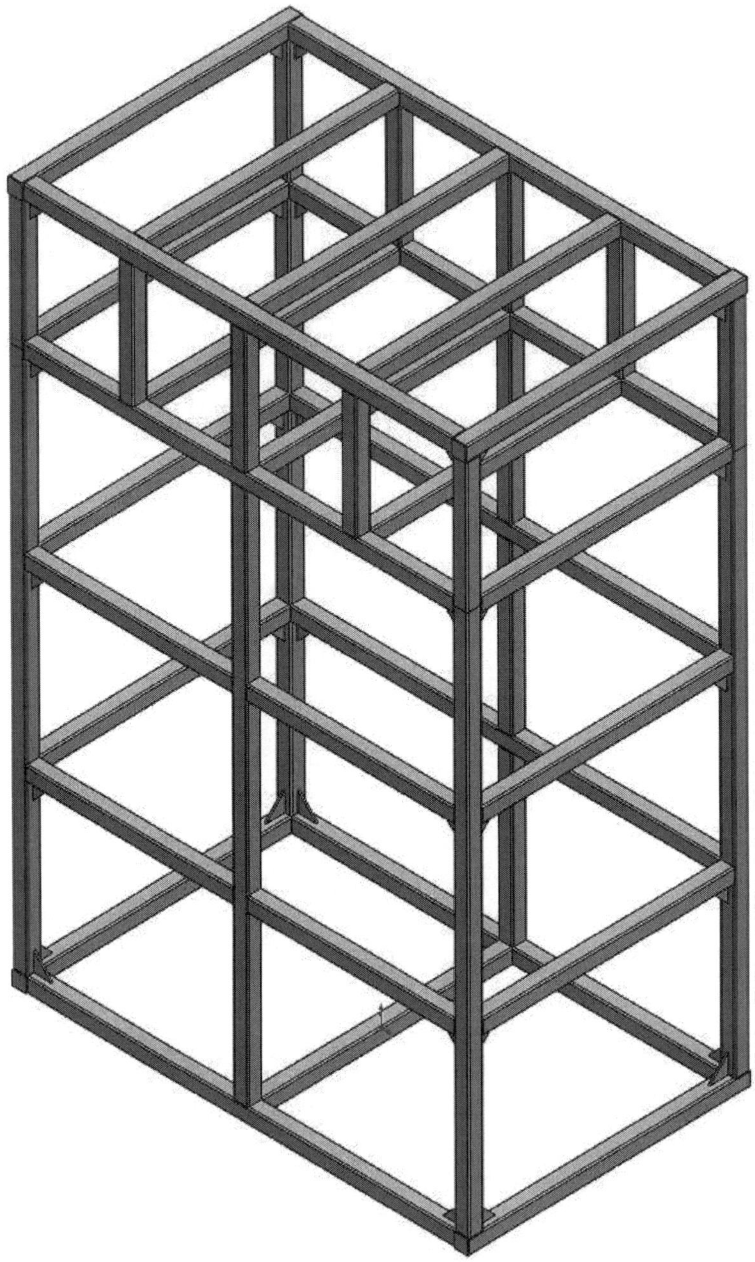

Inspect your weldments part against the image shown here.

Make any corrections as needed.

OPTIONAL:

Add more gussets to other locations of the structure.

7. Saving your work:

Select **File, Save As**.

Enter: **Weldments Steel Frame_Completed.sldprt** for the file name.

Click **Save**.

Lesson 15: Weldments Platform

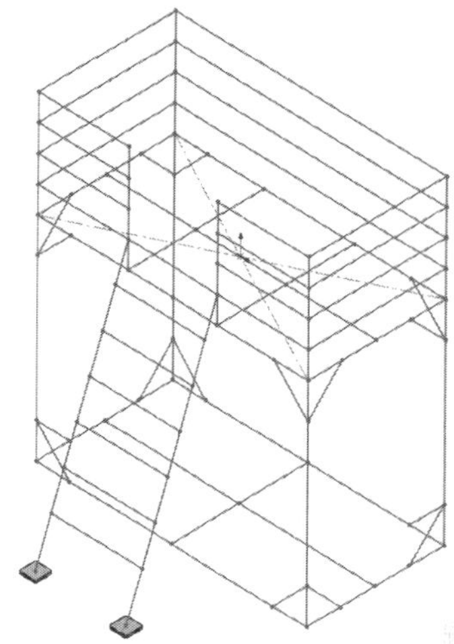

A weldment platform refers to a welded assembly that forms the base or support structure for a platform. It is a structure made by welding together multiple metal components to create a strong, unified platform.

1. Opening a part document:

Browse to the Training Folder and open a part document named: **Weldments Platform.sldprt**

There is a 3D Sketch that has been created for this exercise to help us focus on adding the Structural Members and treating the Corners.

2. Enabling the Weldment tab:

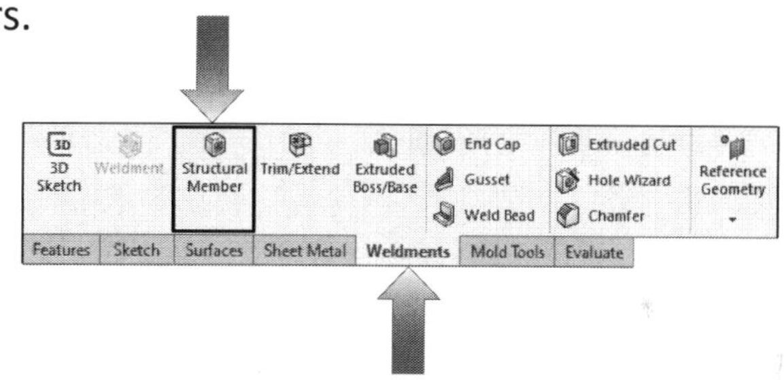

Right-click on one of the tabs (Sketch or Features) and select: **Tabs, Weldments**.

Click **Structural Member** .

Selecting the following:

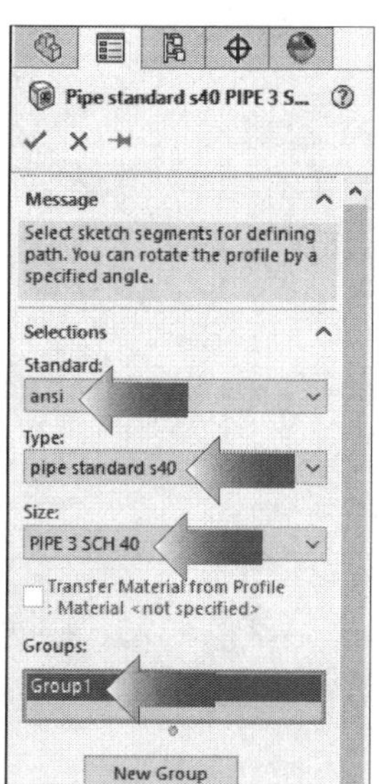

Standard: **ANSI**
Type: **Pipe STD S40**
Size: **Pipe 3 SCH 40 (Ø3.50in.)**
Click **New Group**.

For **Group 1**, select the **4 vertical lines** as indicated.

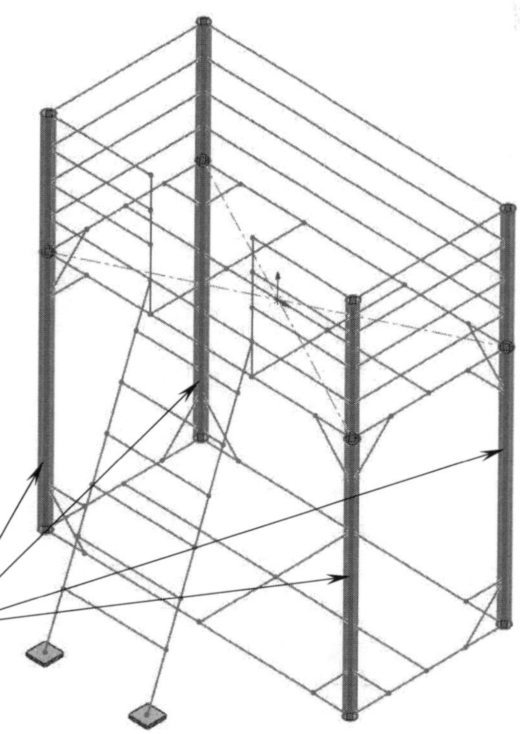

Select 4 lines

Group 1

Do not click OK.

3. Adding the Pipe 3 SCH 40* to the frame:

In a Parallel Group, all structural members must be parallel and must not be joined or connected to one another, but in a Contiguous Group, all structural members must be connected and joined end-to-end.

Click the **New Group** button.

Keep all parameters for this group the same as the last group.

For **Group 2**, select the **4 lines** at the bottom of the frame, as indicated.

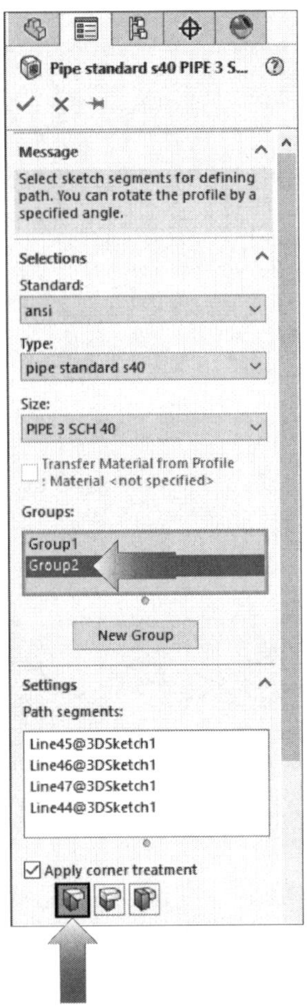

Enable the checkbox for: **Apply Corner Treatment**.

Select the option: **End Miter**.

Zoom closer to one of the 4 corners to inspect the End-Miter corner treatments.

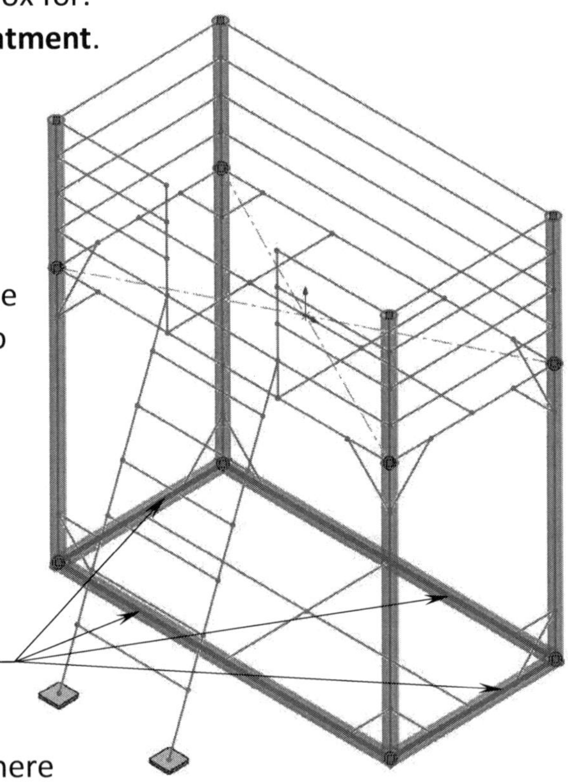

<u>Do not</u> click OK; there are several more structural members to add to the frame.

** Pipe Schedule 40 (Sch 40) refers to a specific standard for the wall thickness of a pipe, <u>not</u> a specific material. It indicates a standard wall thickness, meaning that pipes designated as "Sch 40" have a particular wall thickness for their given nominal pipe size (NPS).*

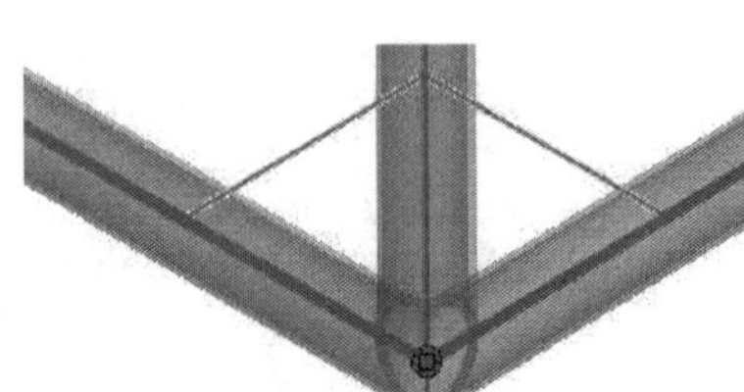

Click the **New Group** button again.

Keep all parameters for Group 3 the same as the last groups.

For **Group 3**, select the **4 lines** as indicated in the image on the right.

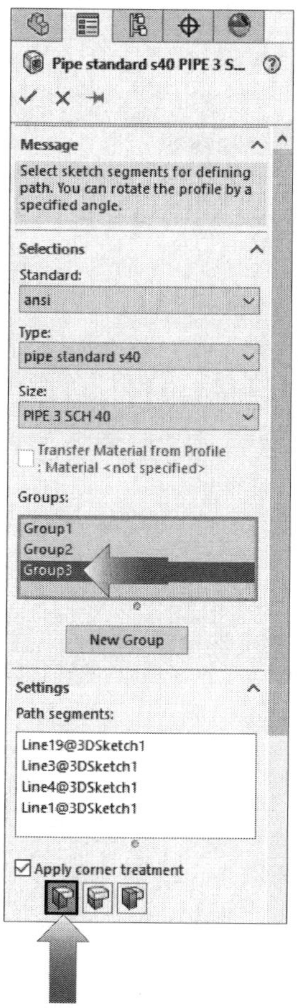

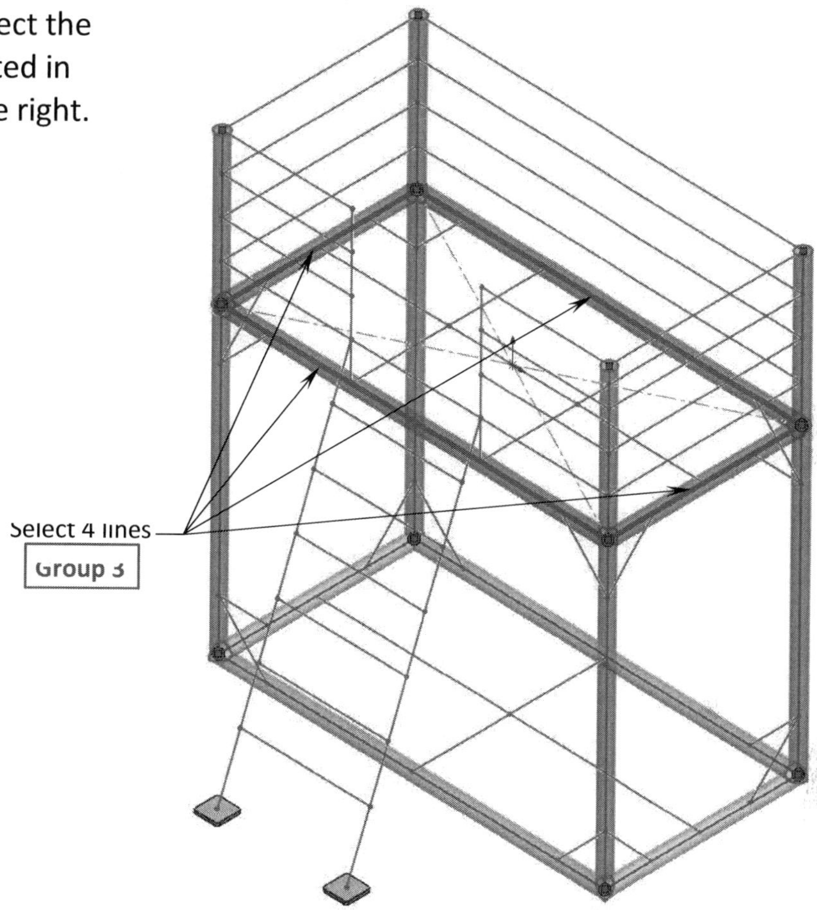

The End-Miter option automatically trims the side tubes to match the diameter of the vertical tubes.

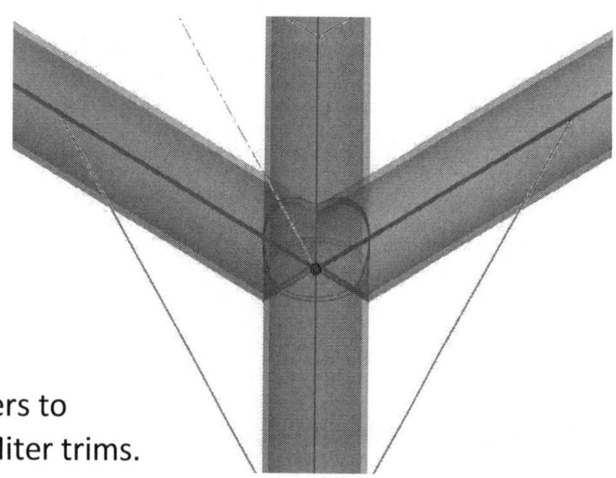

Zoom closer to one of the corners to inspect the results of the End-Miter trims.

Click **New Group**.

For **Group 4**, select the **vertical line** in the middle, at the bottom of the frame.

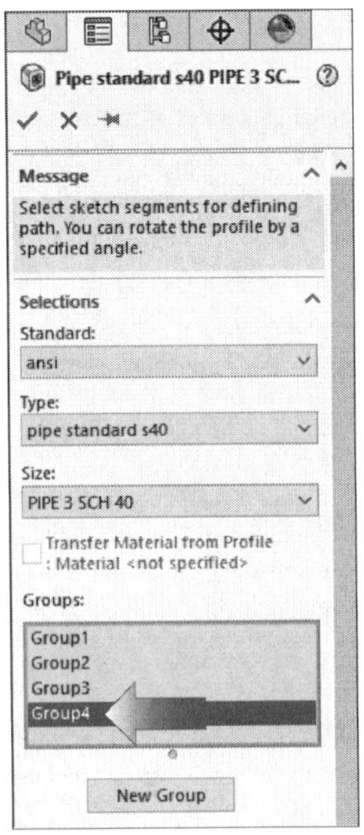

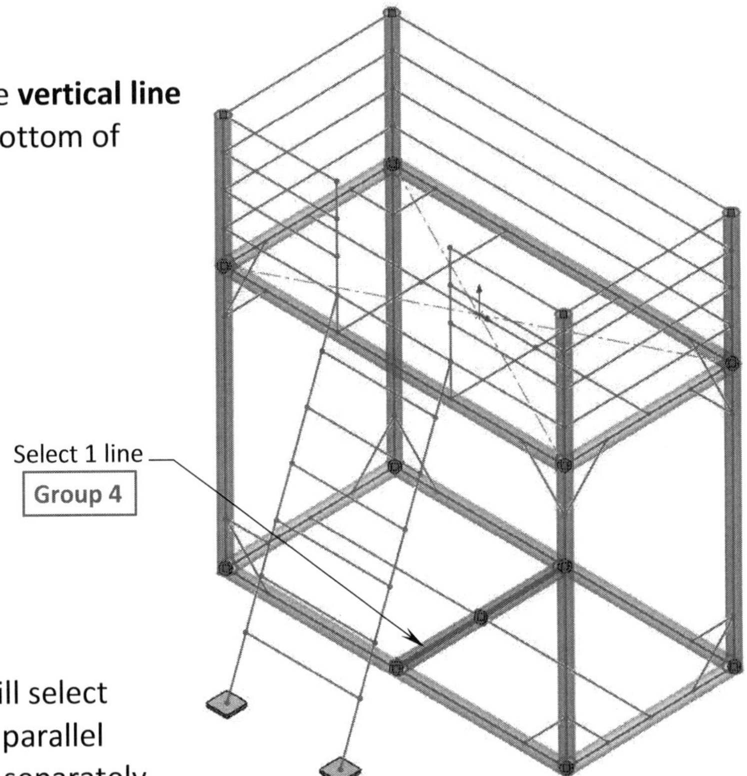

We will select these parallel tubes separately so that they will get trimmed individually.

Click **New Group**.

For **Group 5**, select the **horizontal line** in the middle, at the bottom of the frame.

The tube is trimmed at the intersection.

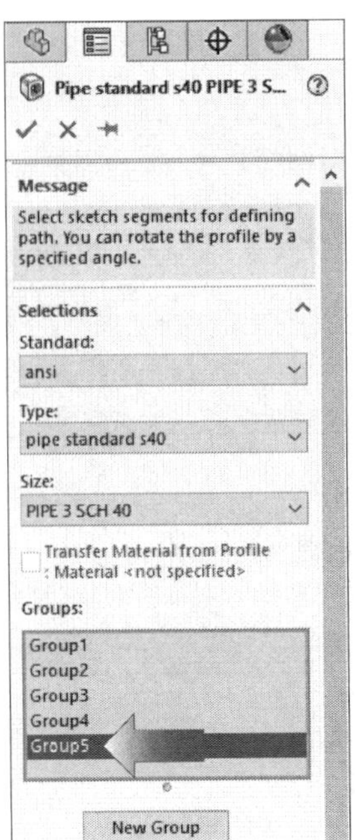

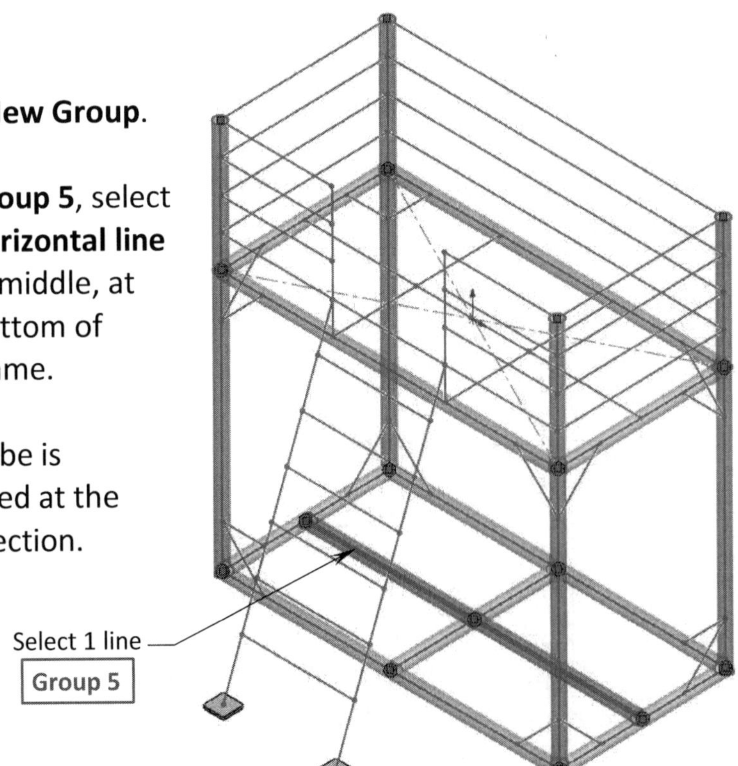

Click **New Group**.

For **Group 6**, select the **horizontal line** as shown in the image on the right.

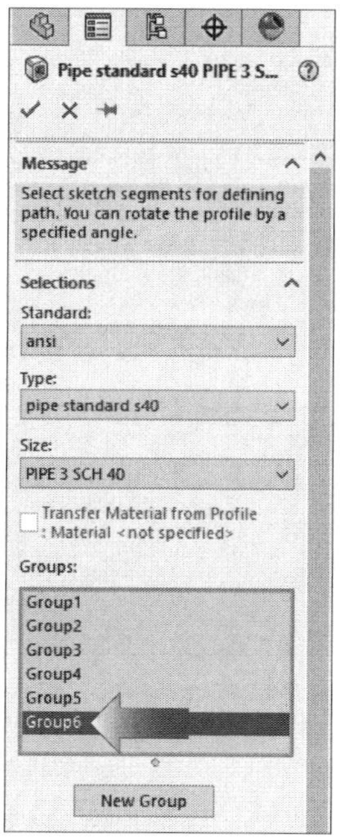

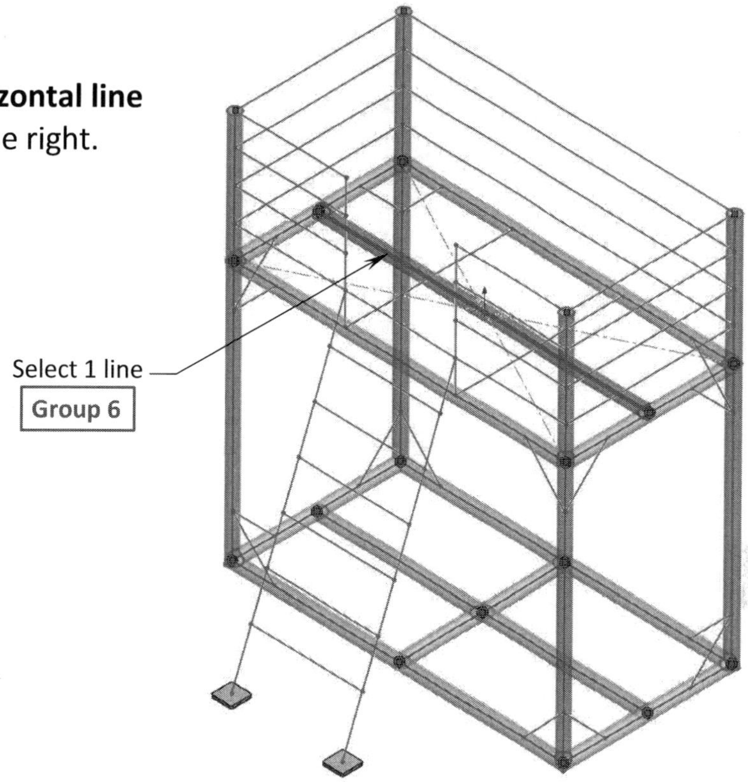

Click **New Group**.

For **Group 7**, select the **vertical line** as indicated.

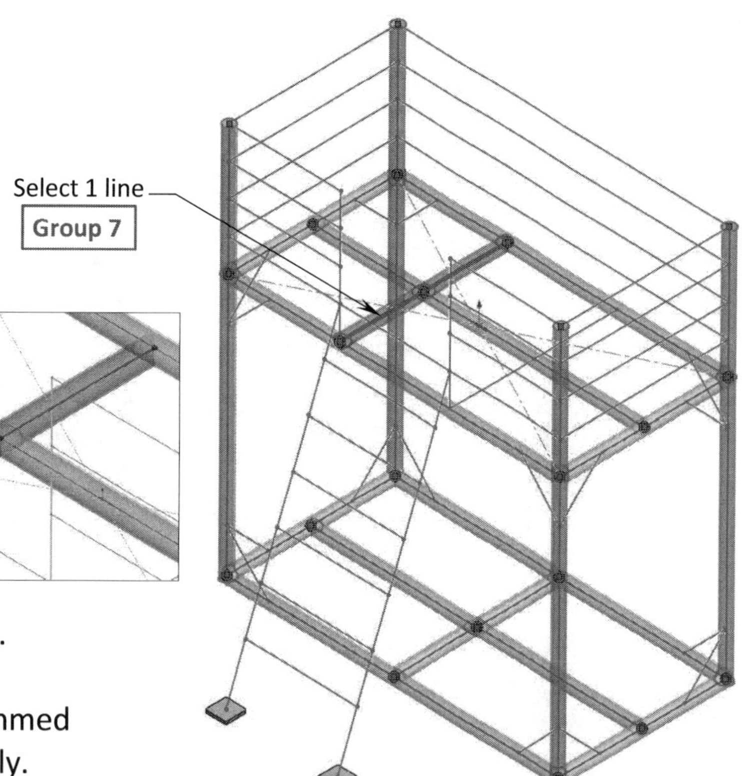

Again, we are selecting the parallel lines in their separate groups so that they will get trimmed individually.

The tube in Group 7 was trimmed into 2 segments automatically.

Click **New Group**.

For **Group 8**, select the **vertical line** as shown in the image on the right.

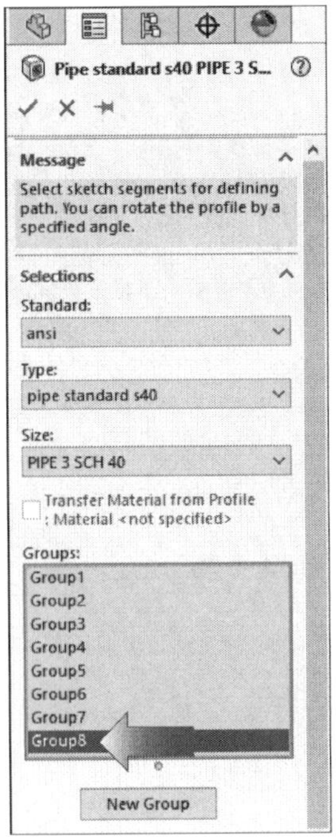

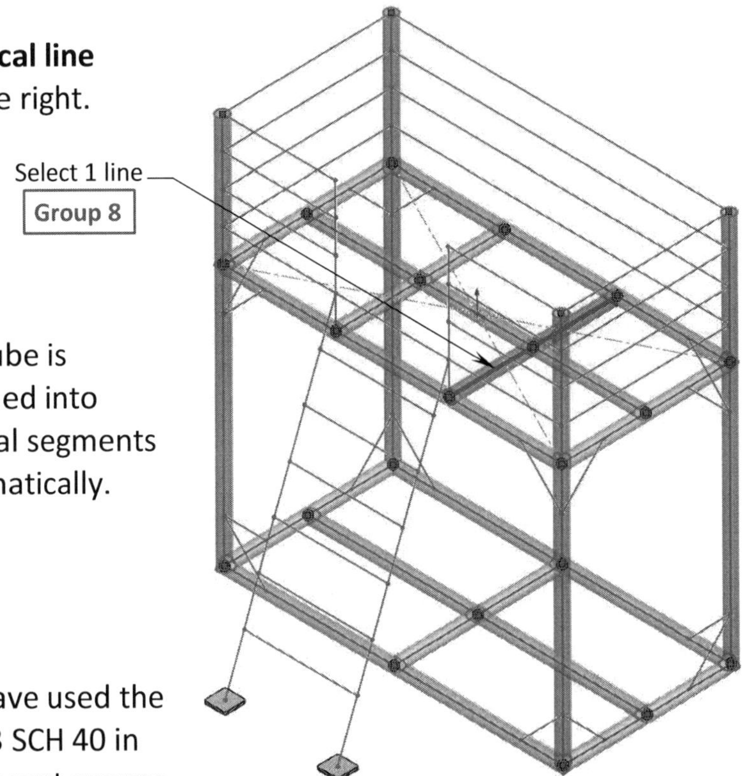

The tube is trimmed into 2 equal segments automatically.

We have used the Pipe 3 SCH 40 in 8 different groups. We will now switch to a smaller tube size and apply it to the rest of the the frame.

Click **OK**.

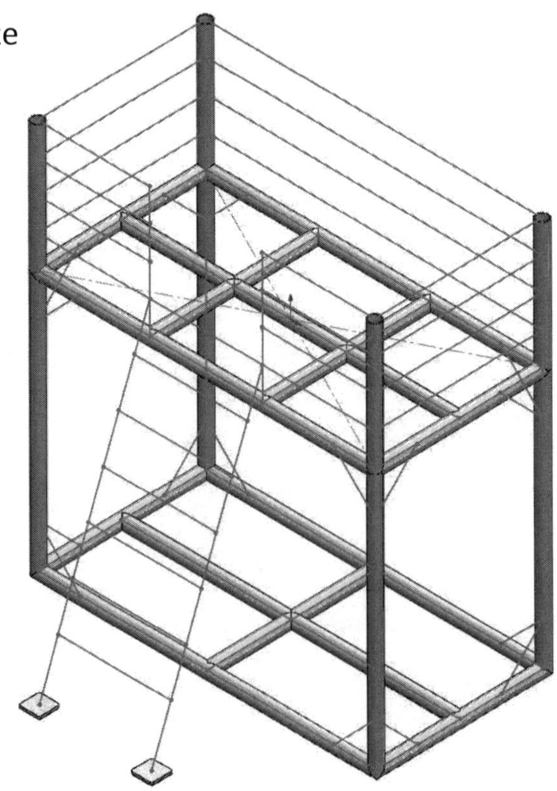

Inspect your weldment part against the image shown on the right.

Make any adjustments if needed prior to moving forward to the next steps.

4. Adding Pipe 2 SCH 40 to the frame:

Click **Structural Member** again .

Select the folowing:

Standard: **ANSI** Type: **Pipe Standard S40**

Size: **Pipe 2 SCH 40 (Ø2.375in.)**

Click the **New Group** button.

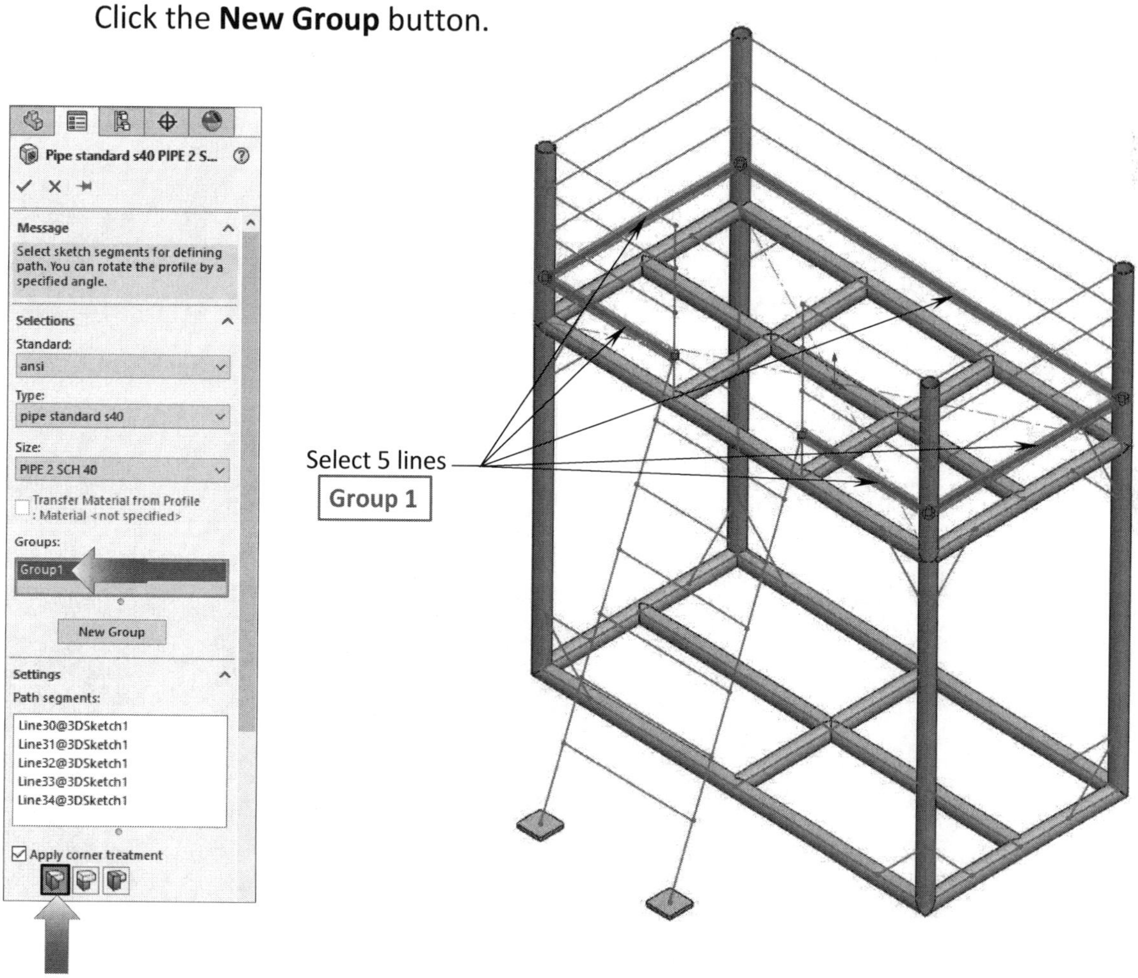

For the **first group** of the Pipe 2 SCH 40, select the **5 lines** that formed a Contiguous Group, as shown in the image above.

Enable the **Corner Treatment** checkbox and select the **End-Miter** option.

Click the **New Group** button.

For **Group 2**, select the **5 lines** as noted in the image.

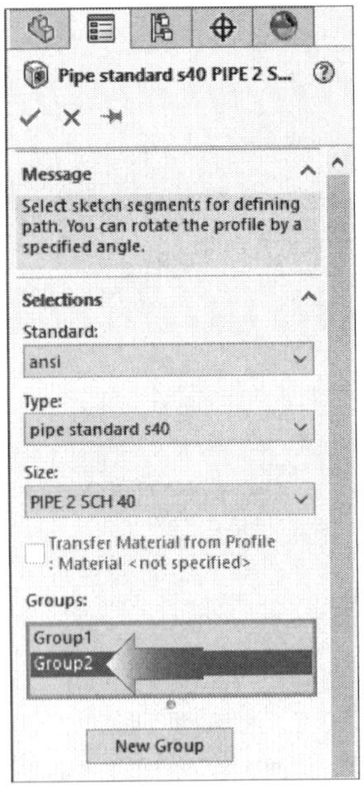

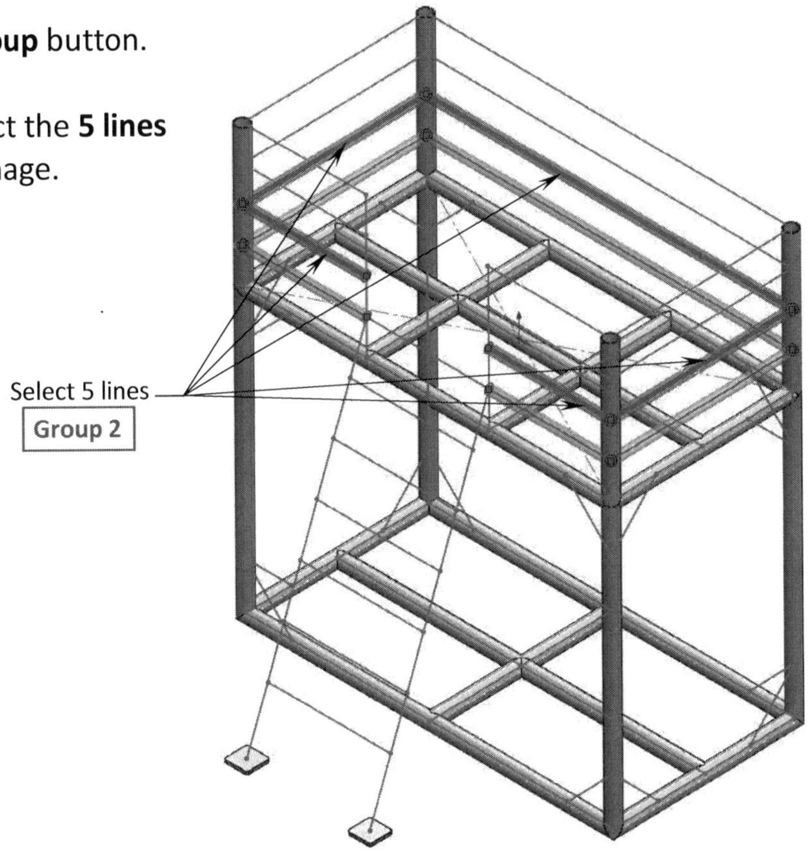

Click **New Group** again.

For **Group 3**, select the **5 lines** just above Group 2.

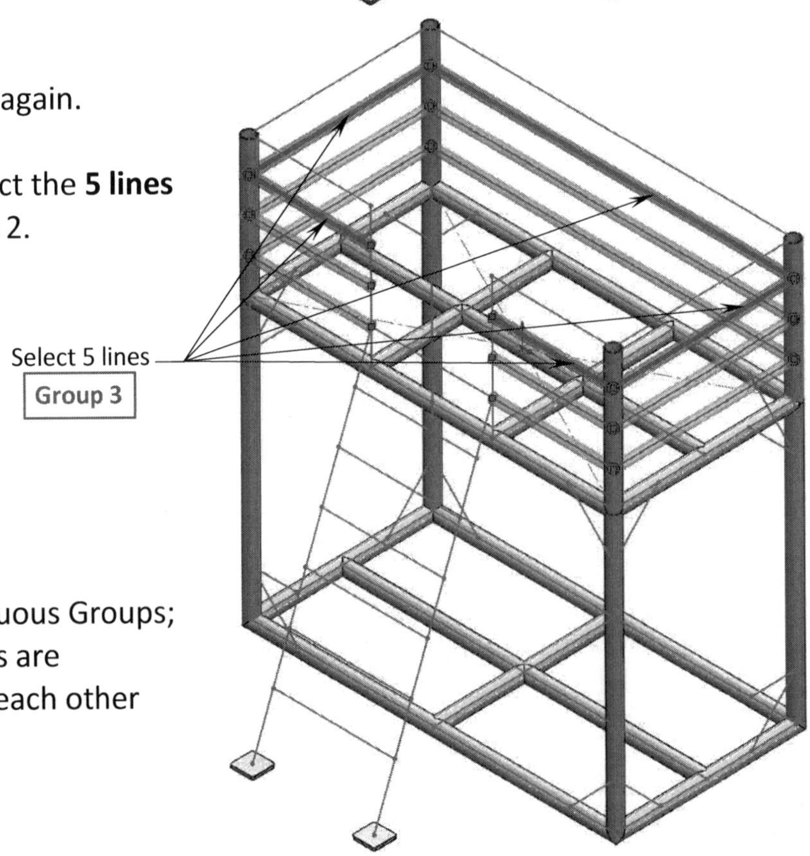

These are Contiguous Groups; the line segments are connecting with each other continuously.

Click **New Group** again.

For **Group 4**, select the **5 lines** just above Group 3.

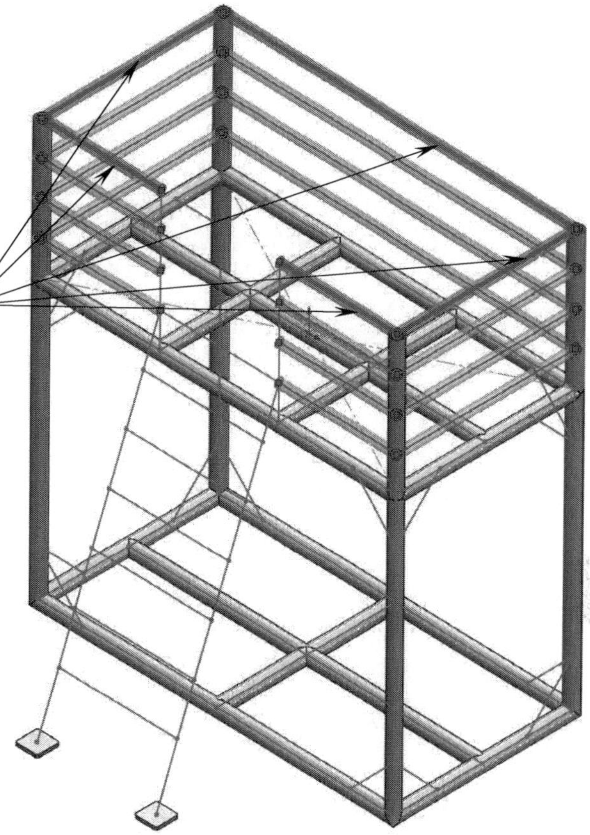

We have completed selecting the Contiguous Groups at this point. We will now begin to select the Parallel Groups.

Click the **New Group** button.

For **Group 5**, select the **2 vertical lines** as indicated in the image on the right.

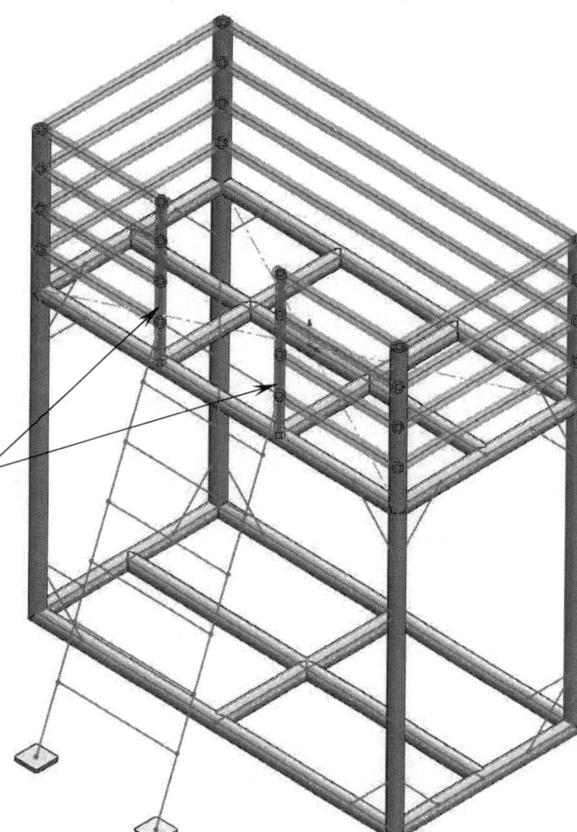

<u>Note:</u> Only the Groups that were selected in the same operation will be trimmed automatically; other groups must be trimmed manually.

Click the **New Group** button.

For **Group 6**, select the **2 lines** of the ladder.

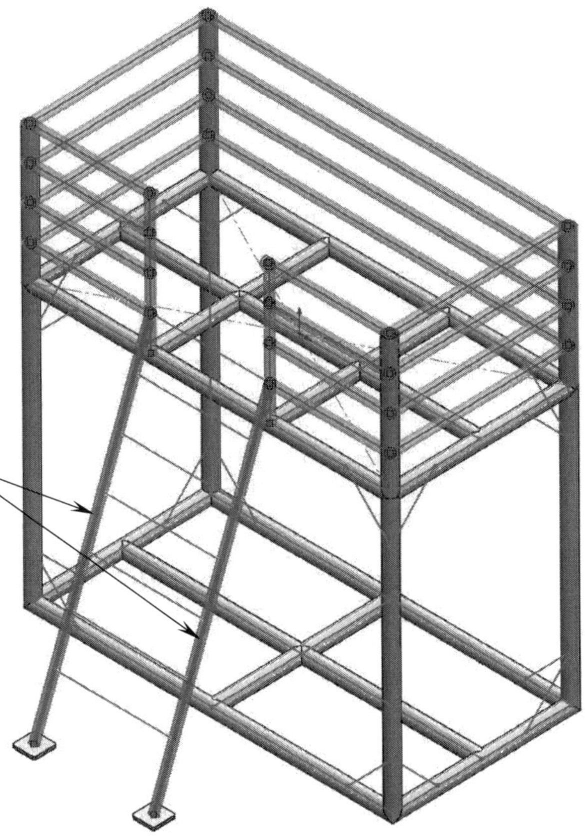

The 2 lines are parallel but but they do not touch or connect with each other; they belong to the Parallel Group.

Click **New Group** again.

For **Goup 7**, select the **7 lines** of the stairs as indicated.

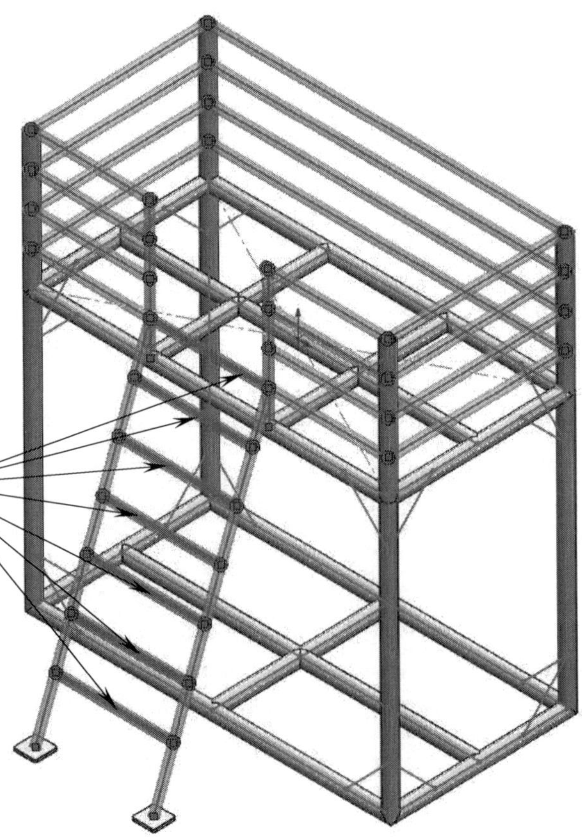

Again, those lines are parallel but do not connect with each other. They are called Parallel Group.

Click the **New Group** button.

For **Group 8**, select the **2 lines** that make up the angle braces at the upper left corner.

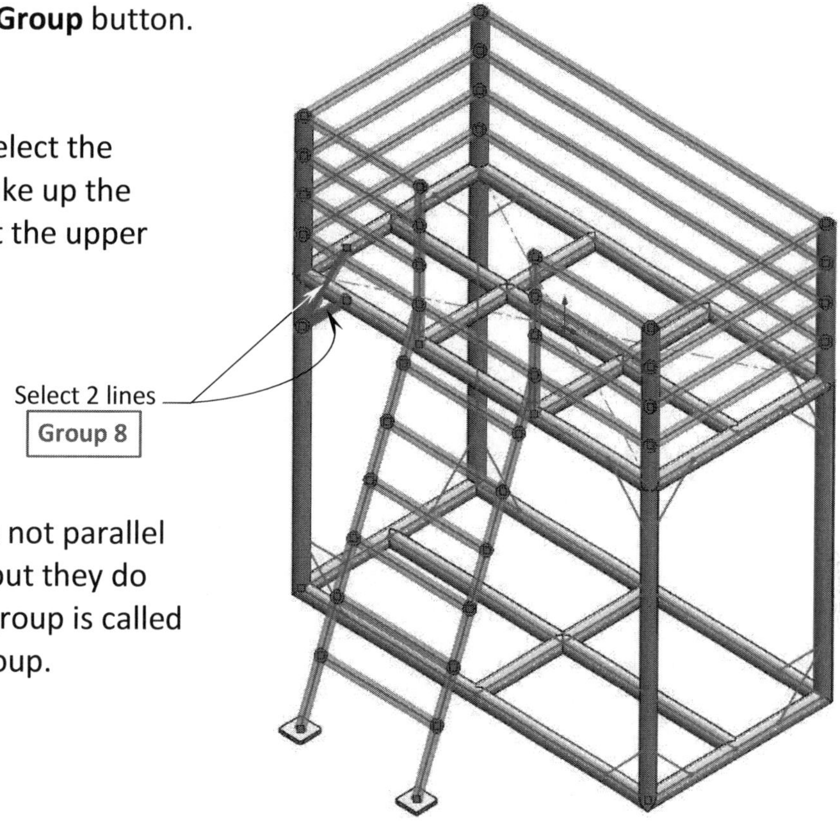

Those lines are not parallel to each other but they do connect. This group is called Contiguous Group.

Click **New Group** again.

For **Group 9**, select the **2 lines** at the bottom left corner as noted below.

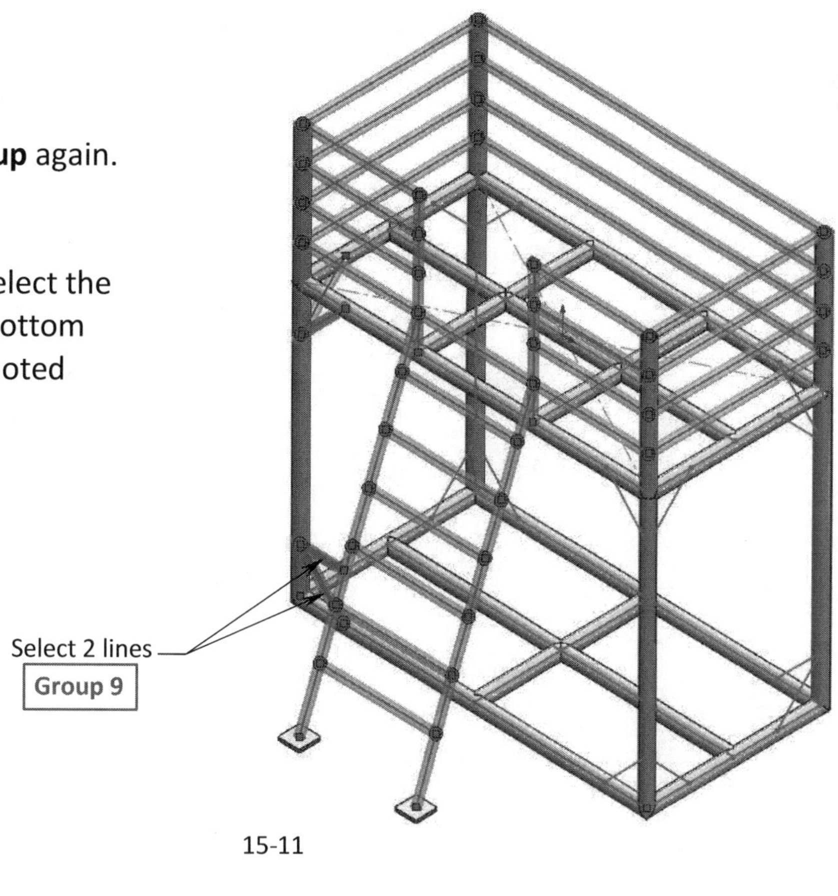

Click the **New Group** button.

For **Group 10**, select the **2 lines** at the upper left corner, on the back side of the frame.

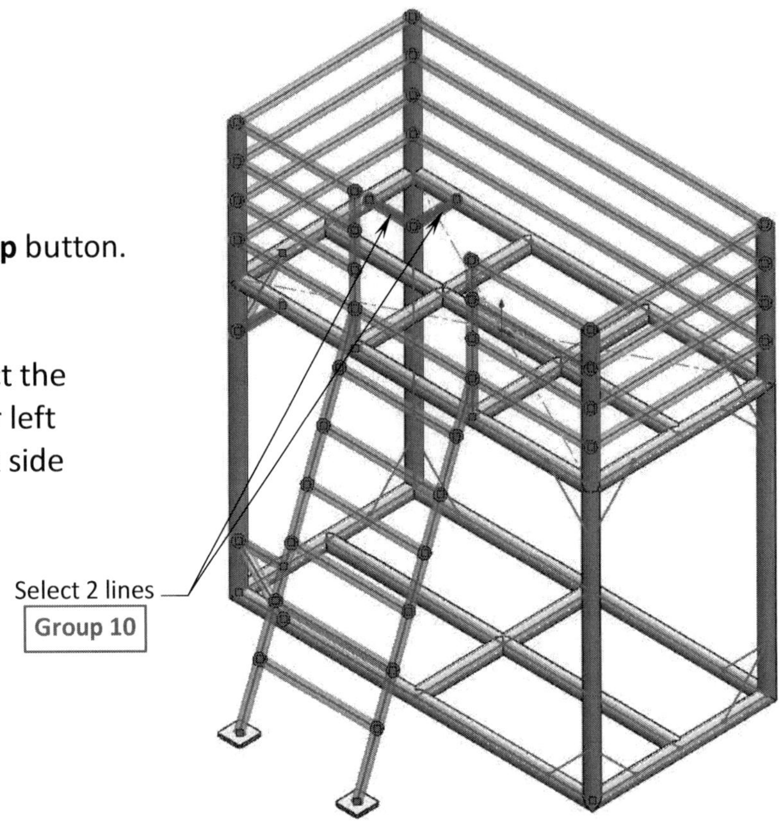

Click **New Group**.

For **Group 11**, select the **2 lines** at the upper right corner, on the back side.

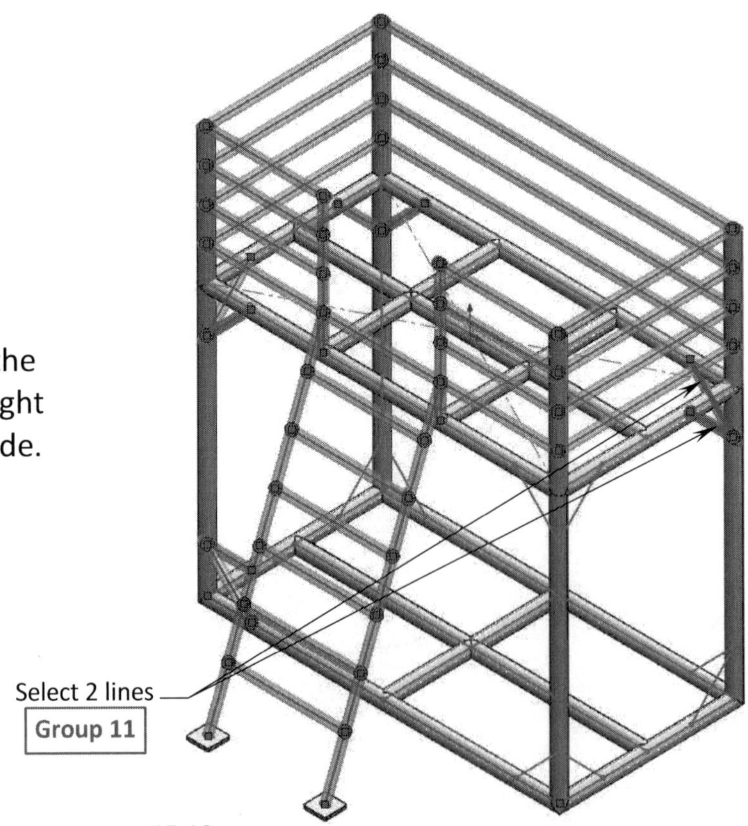

Click the **New Group** button.

For **Group 12**, select the **2 lines** at the bottom right corner, in the back of the frame.

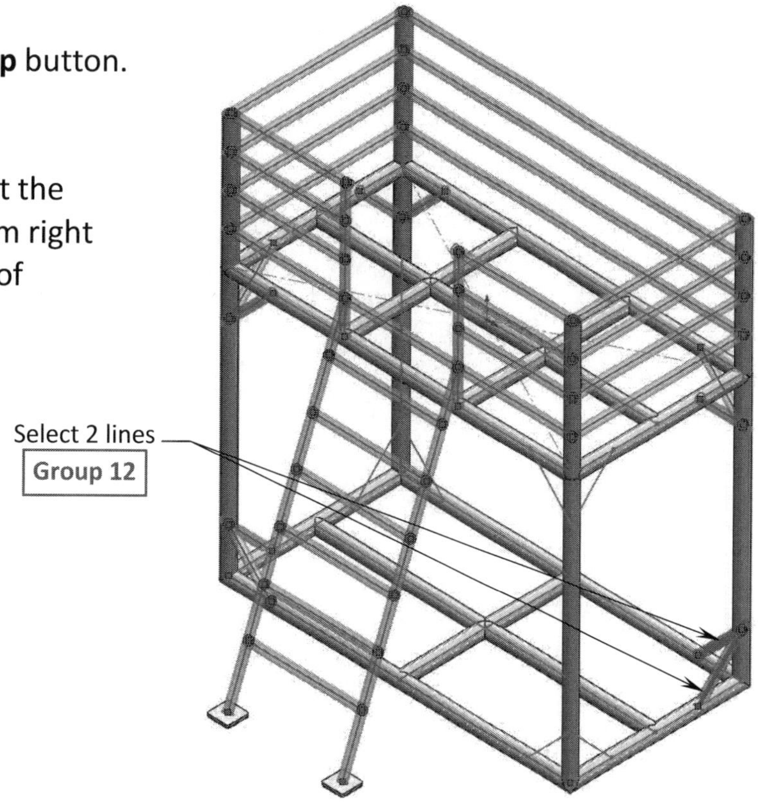

Click **New Group** again.

For **Group 13**, select the **2 lines** at the bottom right corner, in the front of the frame as indicated.

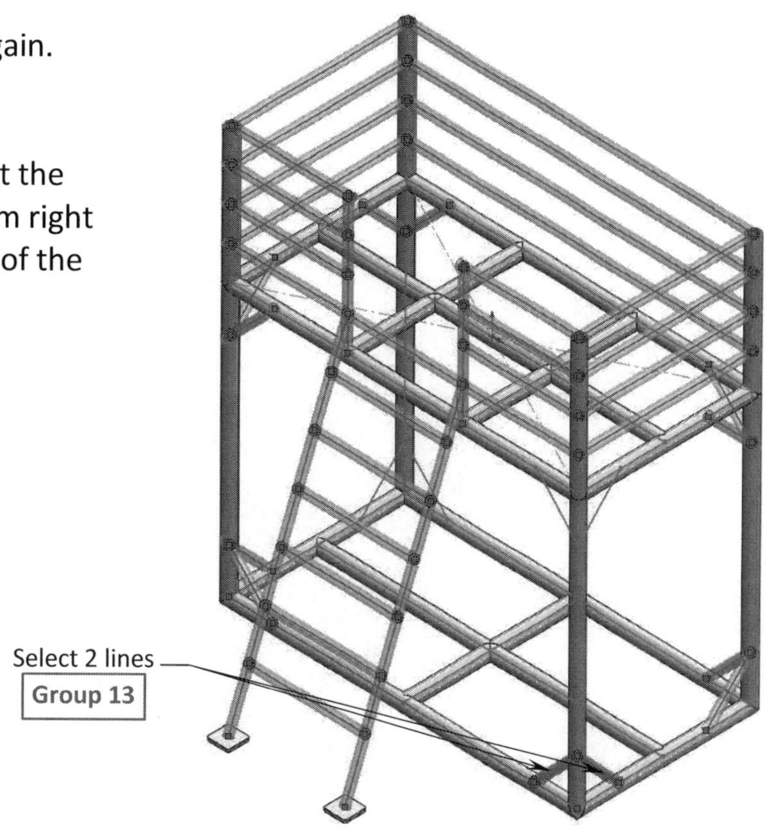

Click the **New Group** button.

For **Group 14**, select the **2 lines** at the lower left corner, in the back of the frame.

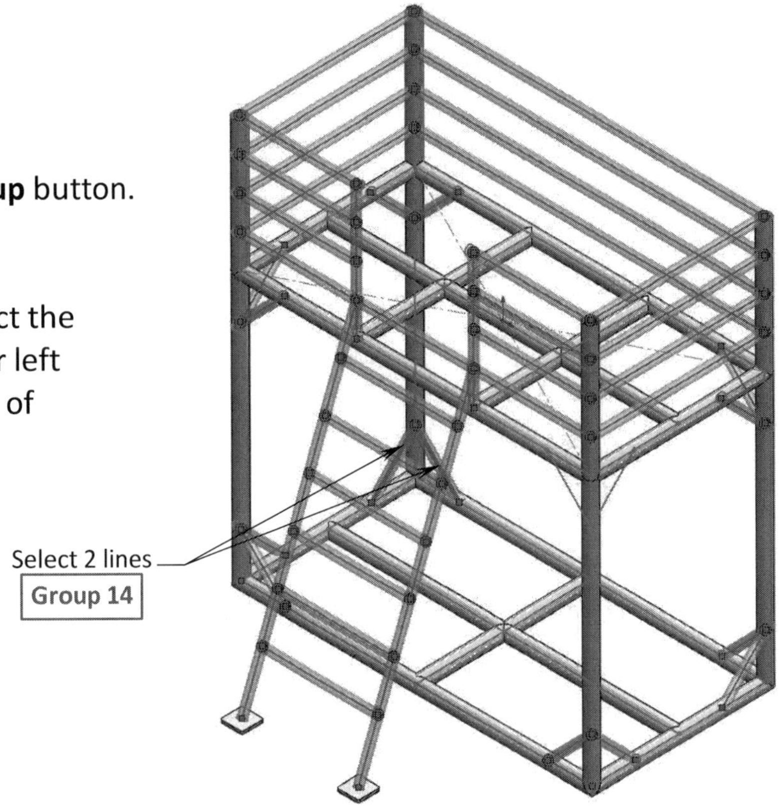

Click **New Group**.

For **Group 15**, select the **2 lines** at the upper right corner, in the front of the frame, as noted in the image.

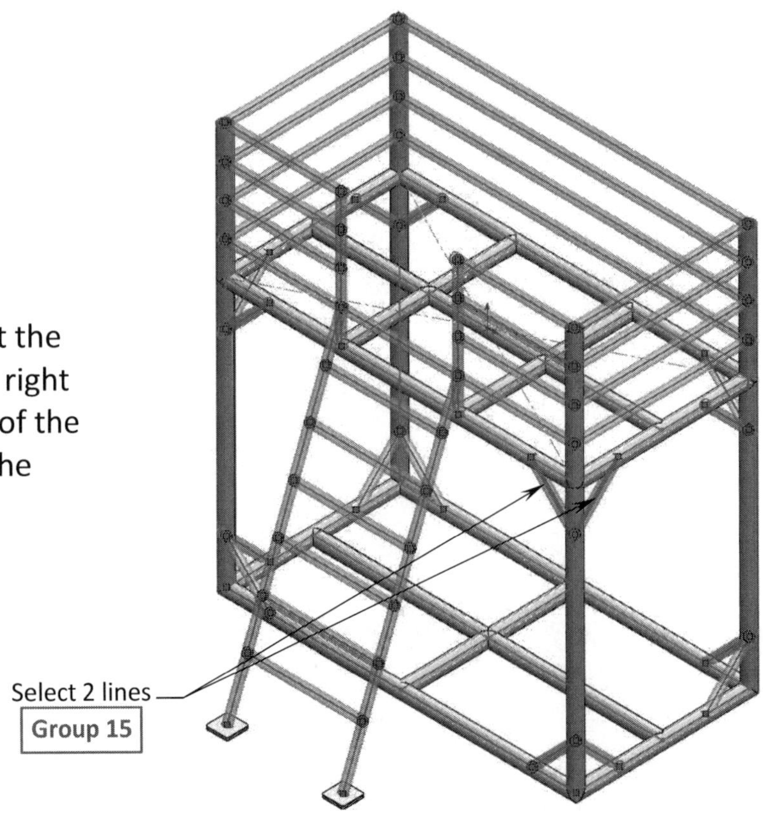

5. Trimming the structural members:

Click **Trim/Extend**.

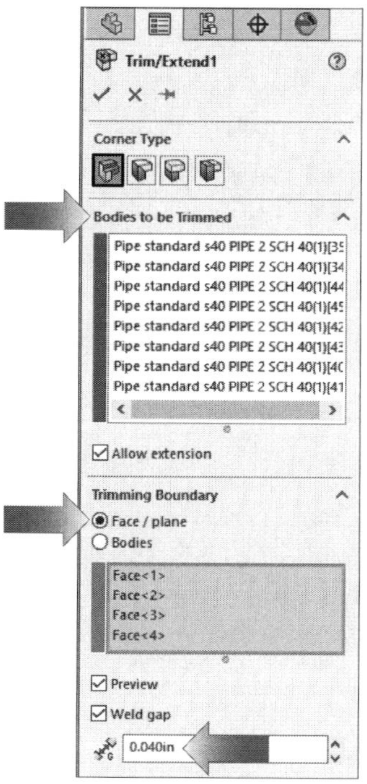

For Bodies to be Trimmed, select the **8 angled tubes** at the bottom of the frame.

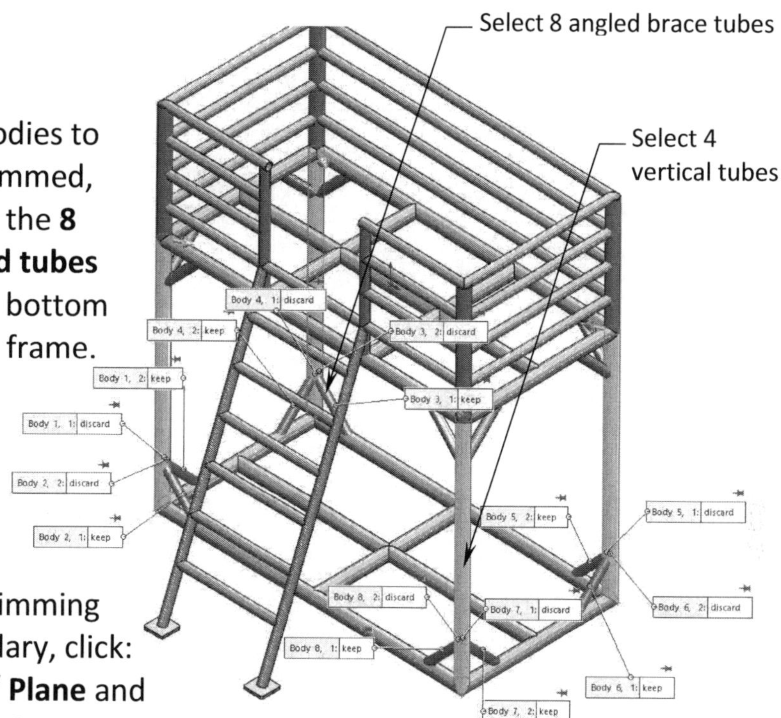

For Trimming Boundary, click: **Face / Plane** and select the **4 vertical tubes** as noted.

Enter **.040in**. for Weld Gap and Click **OK**.

Click **Trim /Extend**.

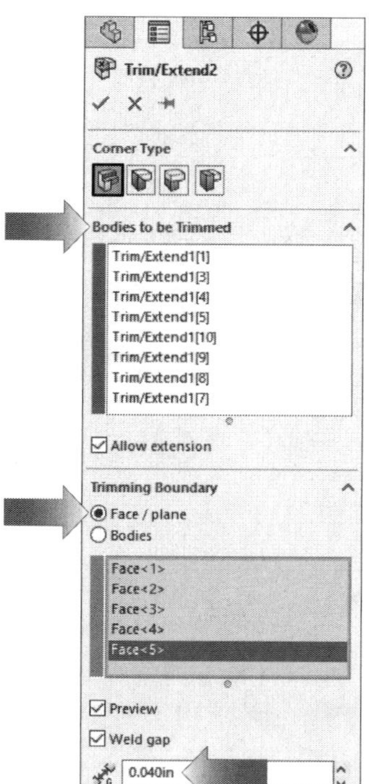

For Bodies to be Trimmed, select the **8 angled tubes** at the bottom of the frame.

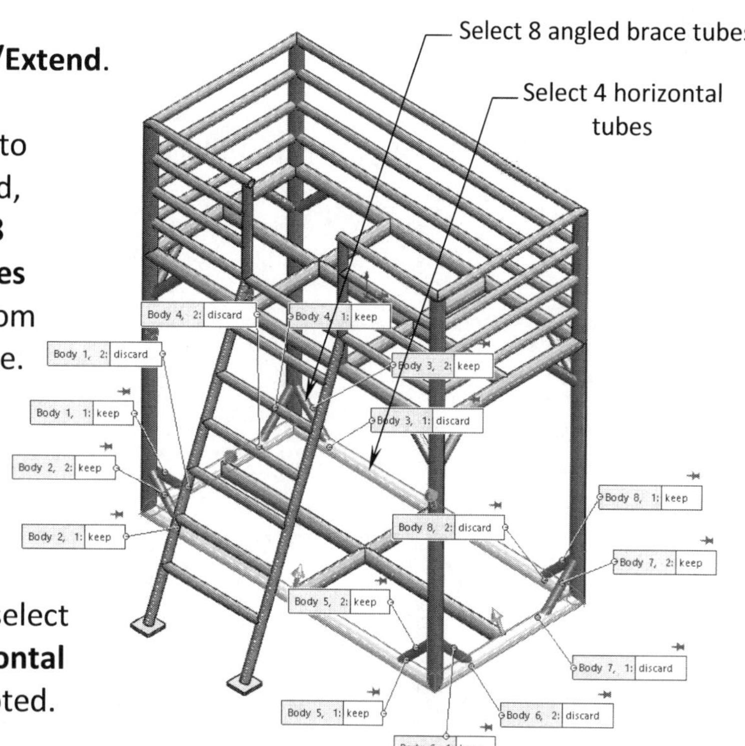

For Trimming Boundary, click **Face / Plane** and select the **4 horizontal tubes** as noted.

Keep the Weld Gap at **.040in**. and Click **OK**.
Click **Trim / Extend** again.

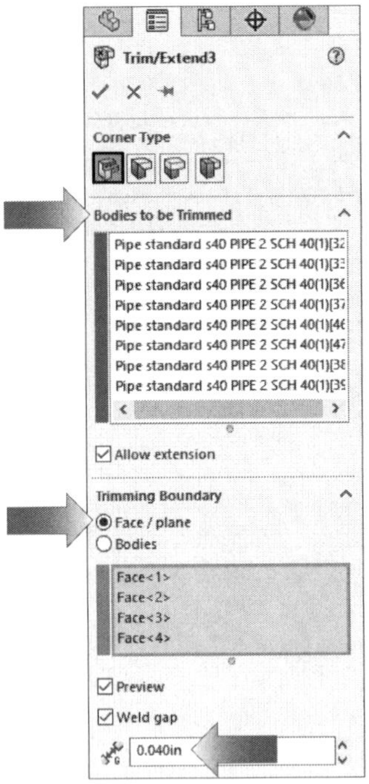

For Bodies to be Trimmed, select the **8 angled lines** on the top of the frame.

For Trimming Boundary, select the **4 vertical tubes** as indicated.

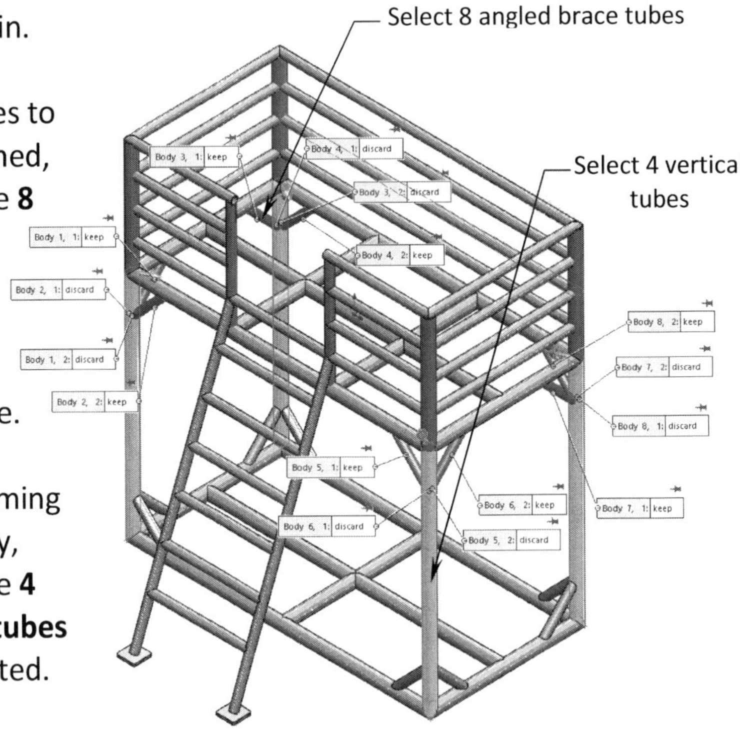

Click **OK**.

Click **Trim / Extend**.

Select the **8 angled lines** on the top of the frame, for Bodies to be trimmed.

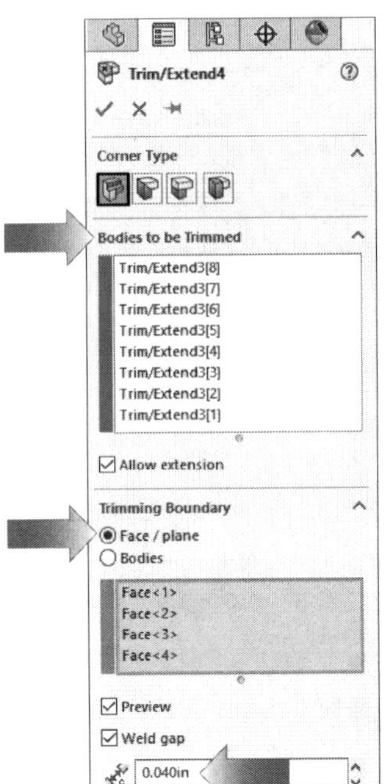

For Trimming Boundary, select the **4 horizontal tubes** in the middle of the frame.

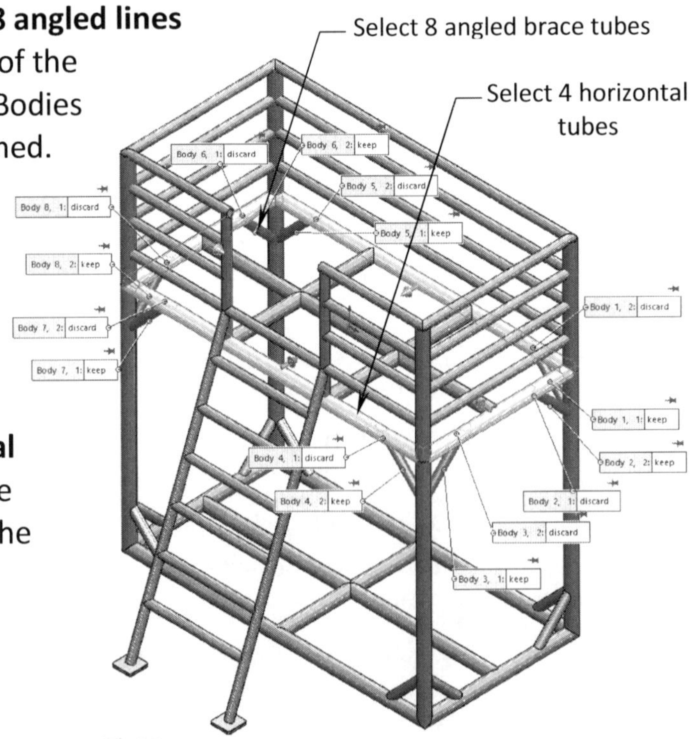

Click **OK**.

Click **Trim / Extend** again.

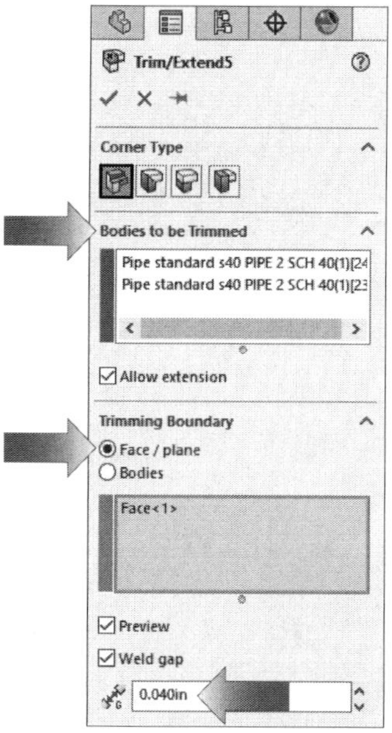

For Bodies to be Trimmed, select the **2 hand rails** of the ladder.

For Trimming Boundary, click Face / Plane and select the **upper face** of one of the foot plates.

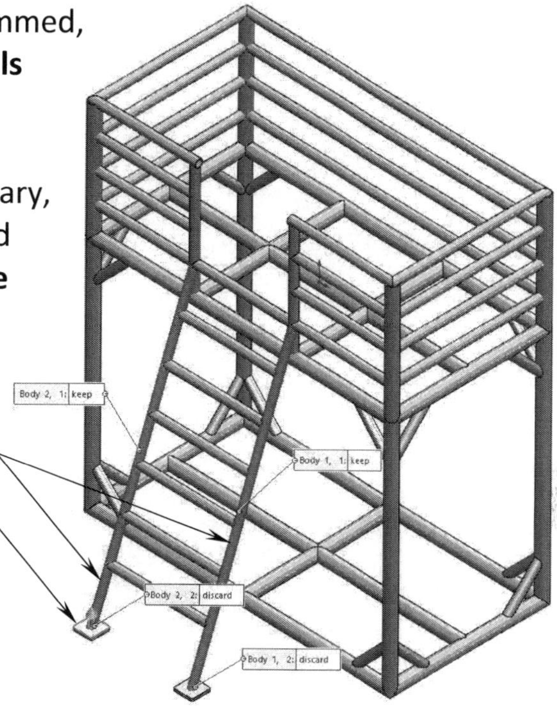

Click **OK**.

6. Adding a new plane:

Select **Reference Geometry, Plane**.

For First Reference, select the **Top** plane from the Feature tree.

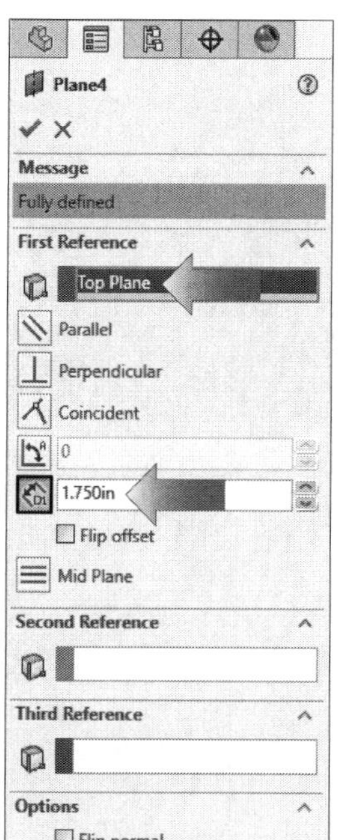

For Distance, enter: **1.750in**.

The new plane is placed above the Top plane.

Click **OK**.

Use this plane to create the floor on the upper deck.

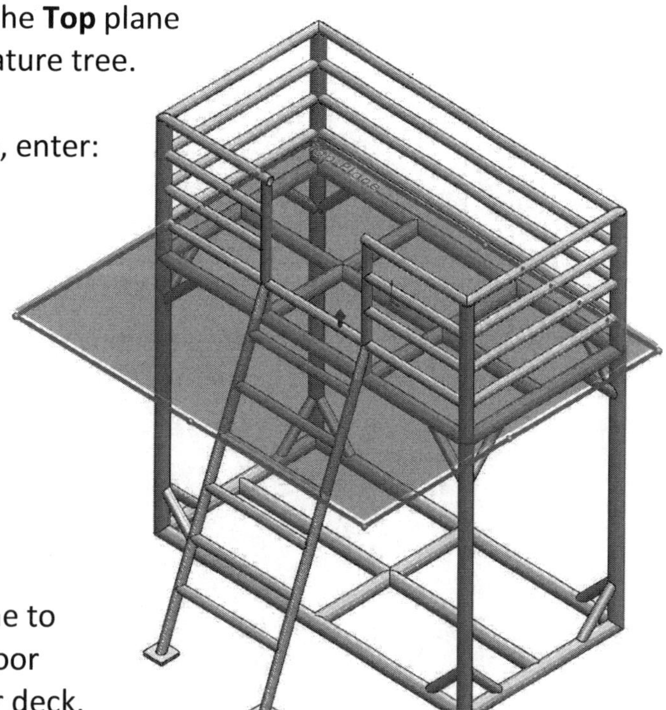

7. Creating the upper deck floor:

Select the new plane and open a **new sketch**.

Sketch the profile shown below. Use the **Sketch Mirror** tool to keep the sketch entities symmetric to each other.

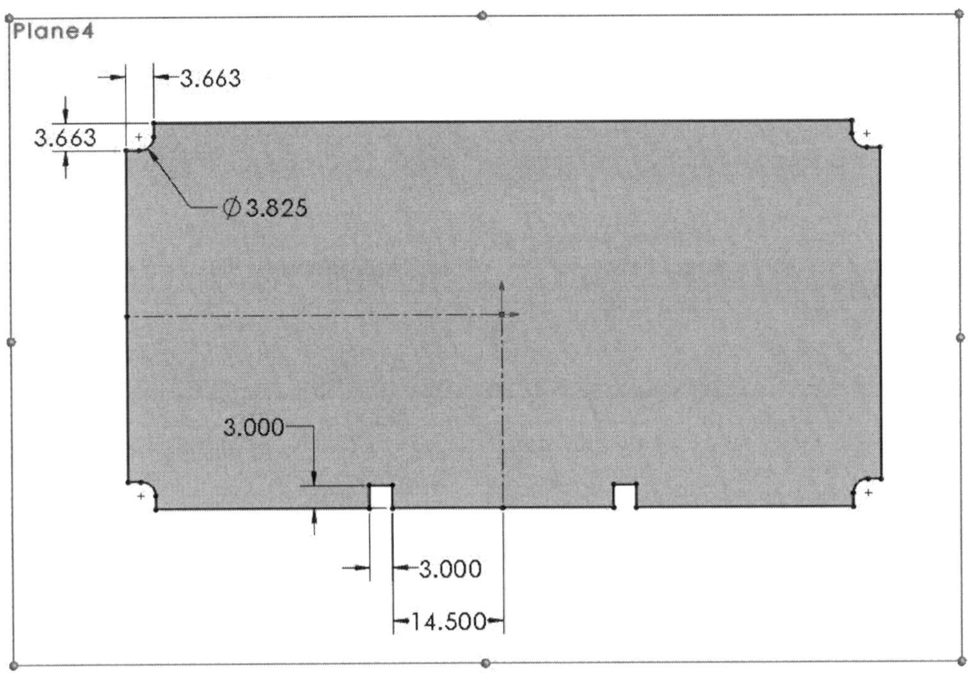

Switch to the **Sheet Metal** tab and click **Base Flange**.

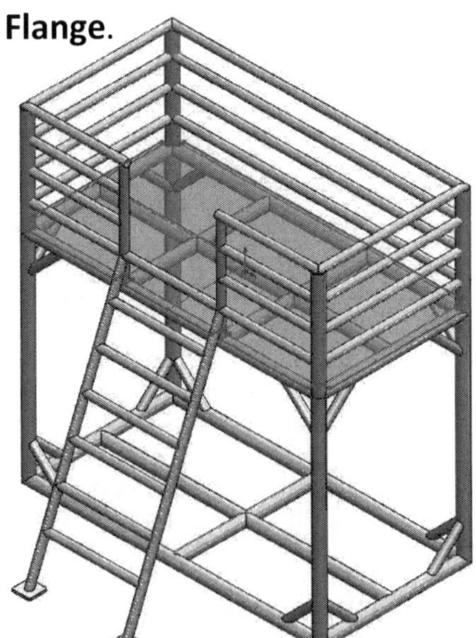

Select the parameters shown below.

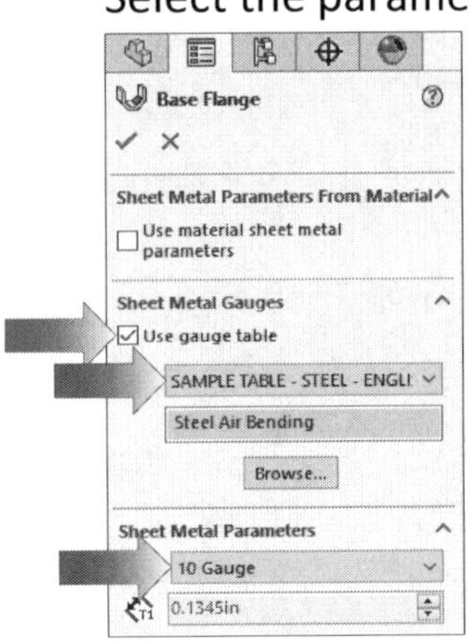

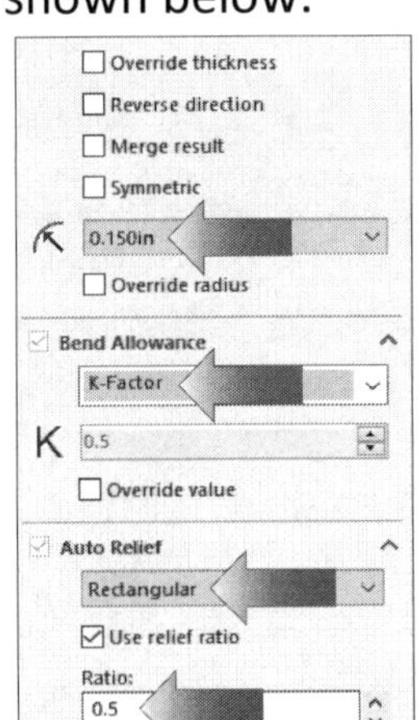

Click **OK**.

8. Adding fillets:

Select: **Corners, Break Corner** on the **Sheet Metal** tab.

For Break Type, select **Fillet**.

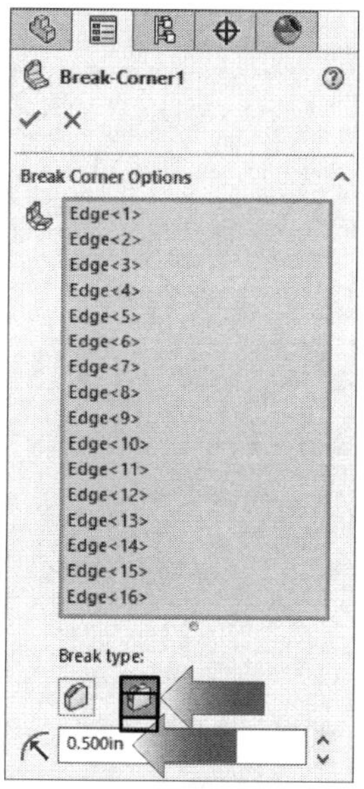

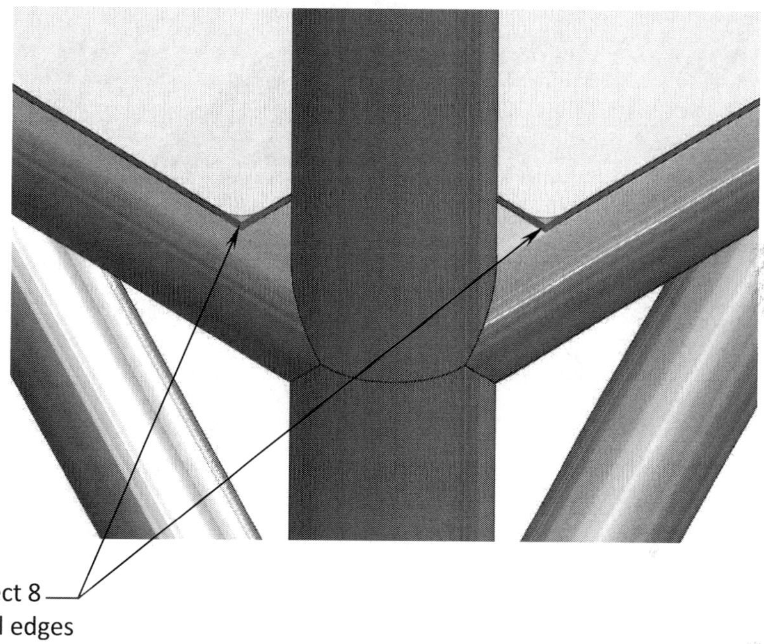

For Size, enter: **.500in**.

For Corners to Break, select the **8 vertical edges**, at the 4 corners of the Base Flange.

Click **OK**.

Inspect your Weldments model against the image shown here. Make adjustments if needed.

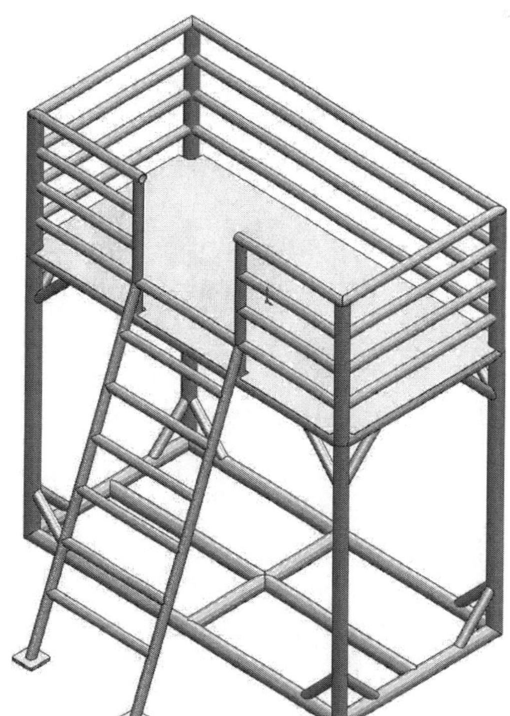

9. OPTIONAL:

Create an exploded view similar to the one shown below.

10. Saving your work:

Select **File, Save As**.

Enter: **Weldments Platform_Completed.sldprt** for the file name.

Click **Save**.

Lesson 16: Weldments - Playground Slide

The exercises in this textbook are intended to give you an opportunity to explore and to apply what you have learned from the previous chapters, at your own pace.

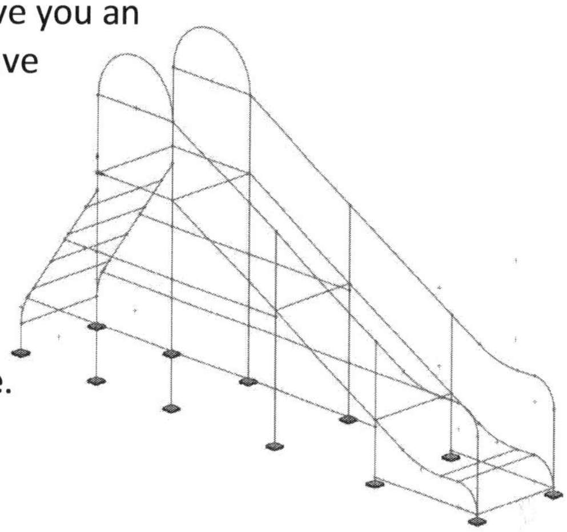

1. Opening a part document:

Browse to the Training Folder and open a part document named: **Playground Slide**.

The material **Galvanized Steel** has already been assigned to the weldment part.

2. Adding the Structural Members:

Switch to the **Weldments** tab and click **Structural Member**.

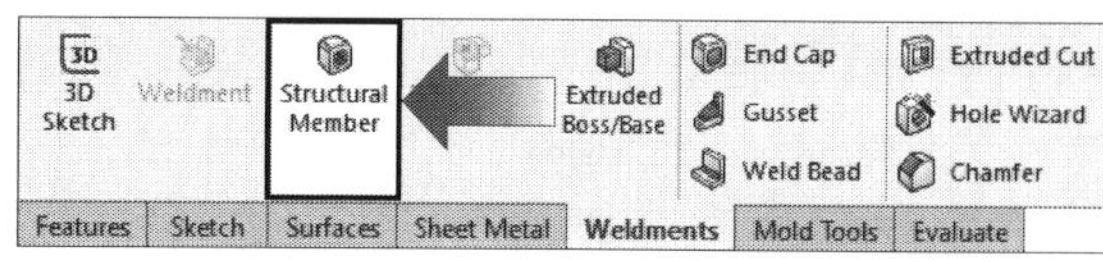

For Selections, select the following: Standard: **ANSI** Type: **Tube Square** Size: **TS2x2x0.1875** Click: **New Group**

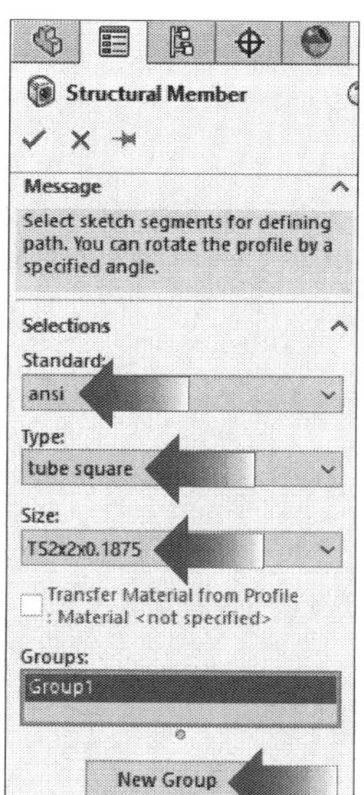

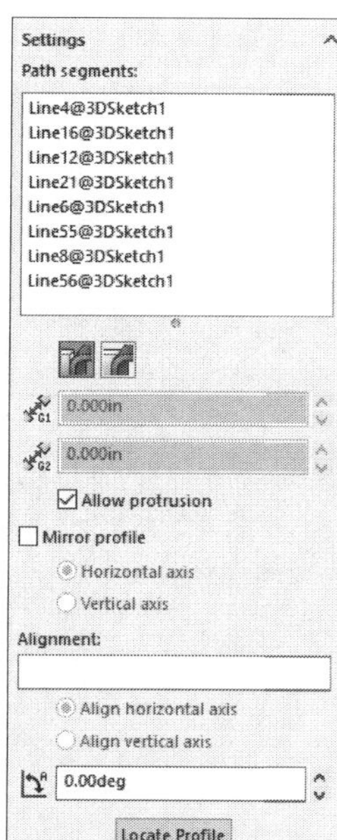

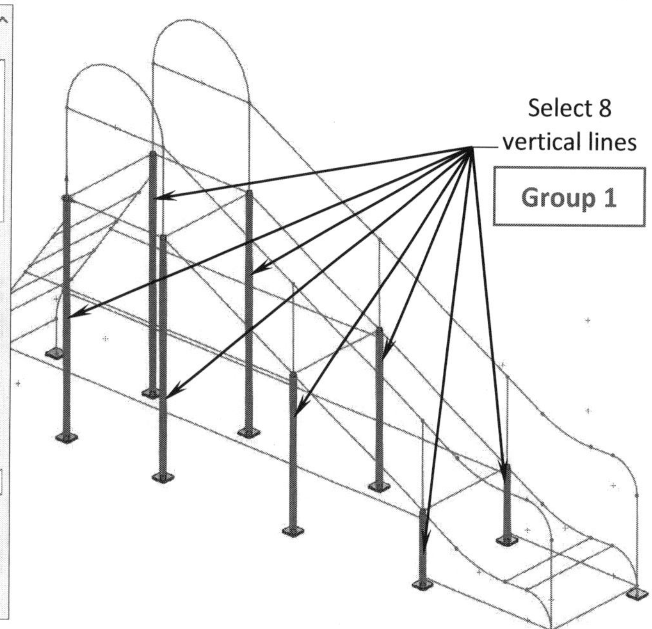

Select the **8 vertical lines** as indicated.

<u>Do not</u> click OK just yet.

3. Adding other Groups:

Keep all parameters the same as Group1, click the **New Group** button (Group 2).

For **Group 2**, select the **4 lines** as indicated in the image below.
We will work on correcting the corners later on, in another step.

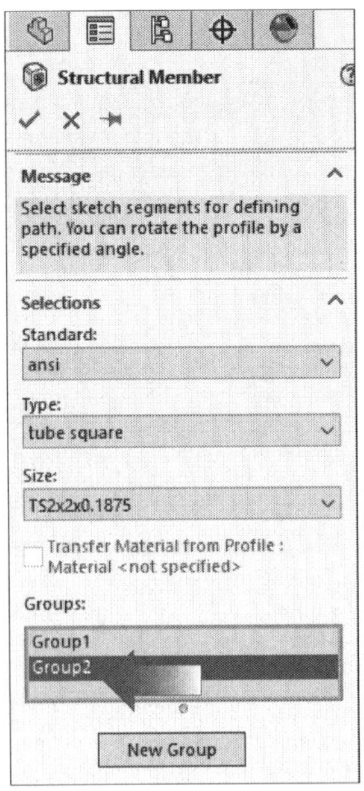

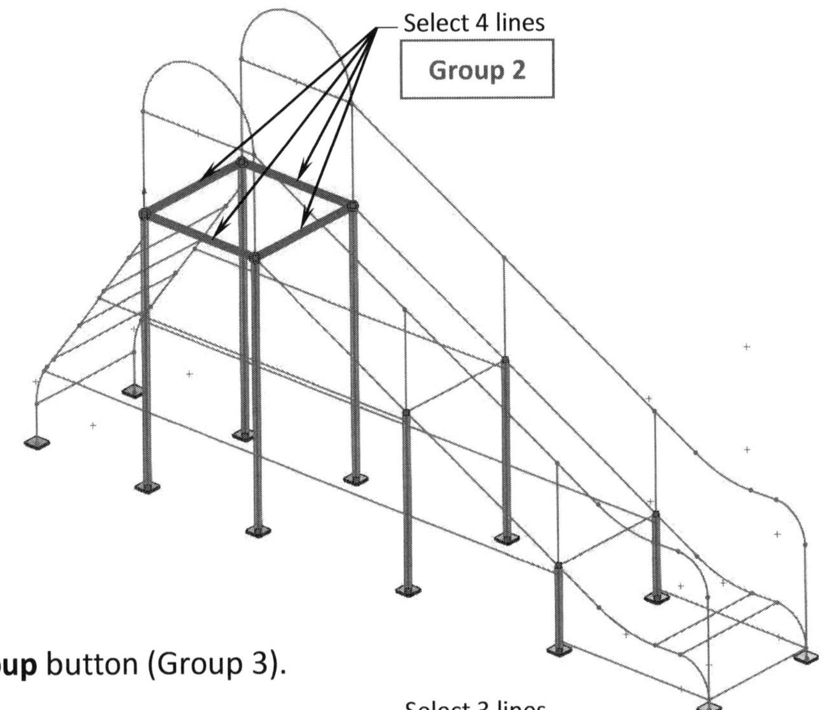

Click the **New Group** button (Group 3).

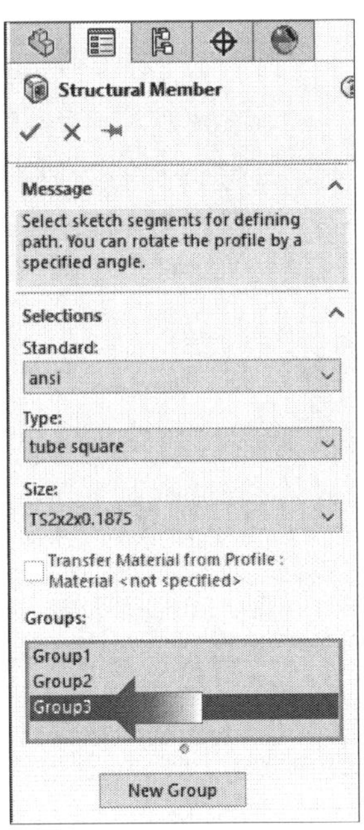

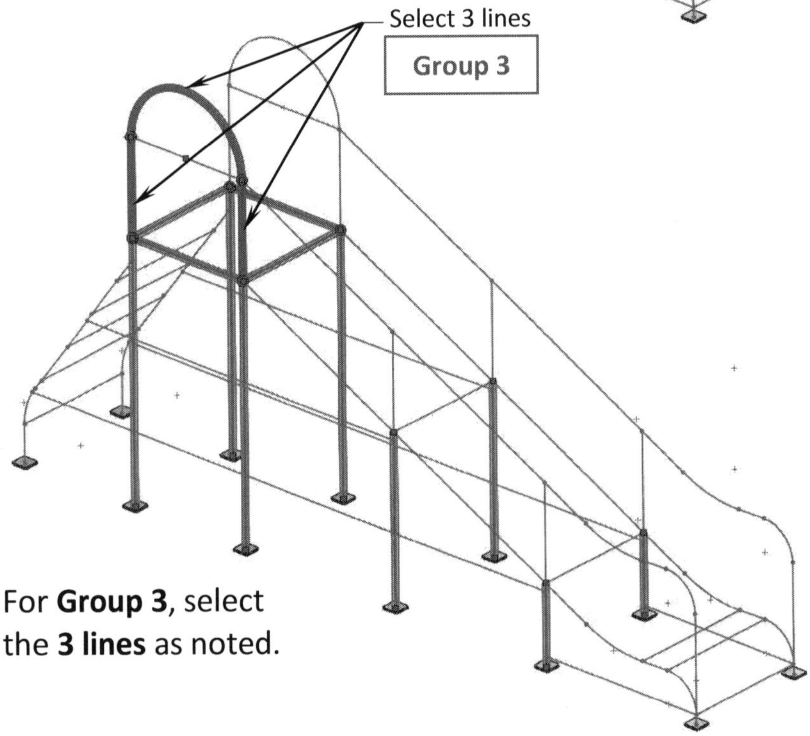

For **Group 3**, select the **3 lines** as noted.

Click the **New Group** button (Group 4).

Select the **2 vertical lines** and the **arc** as indicated.

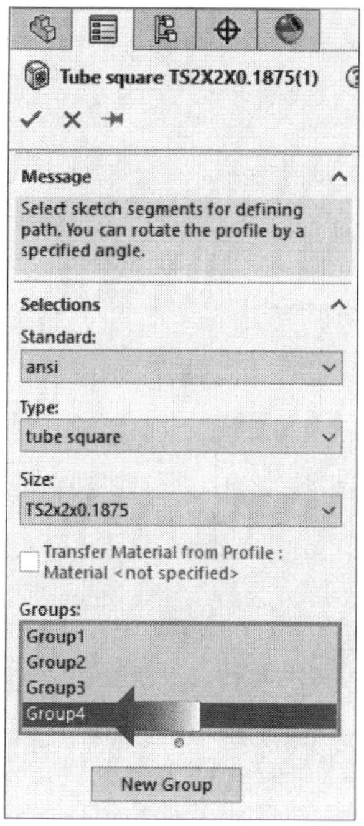

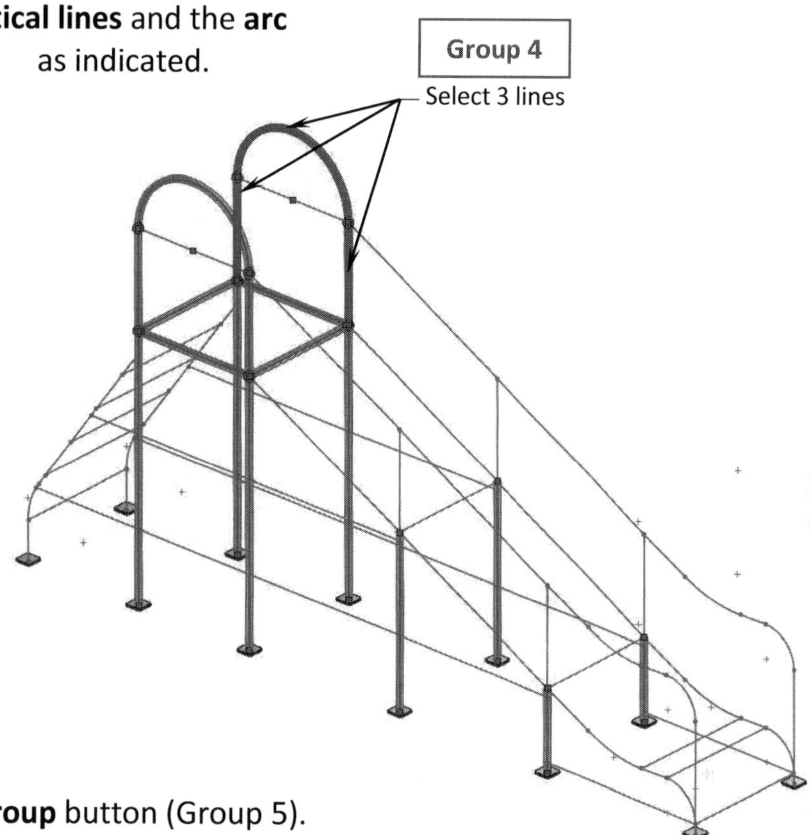

Click the **New Group** button (Group 5).

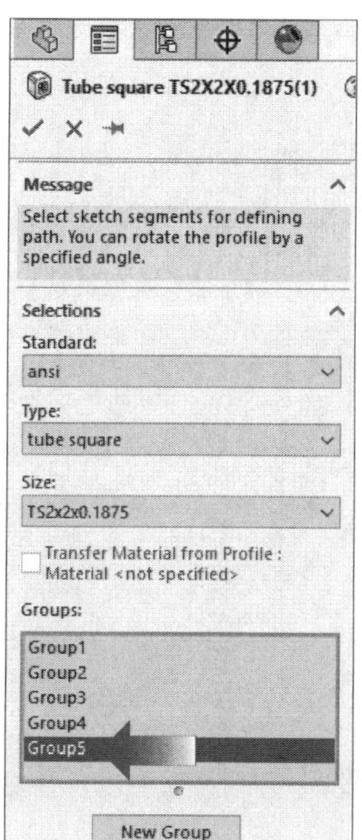

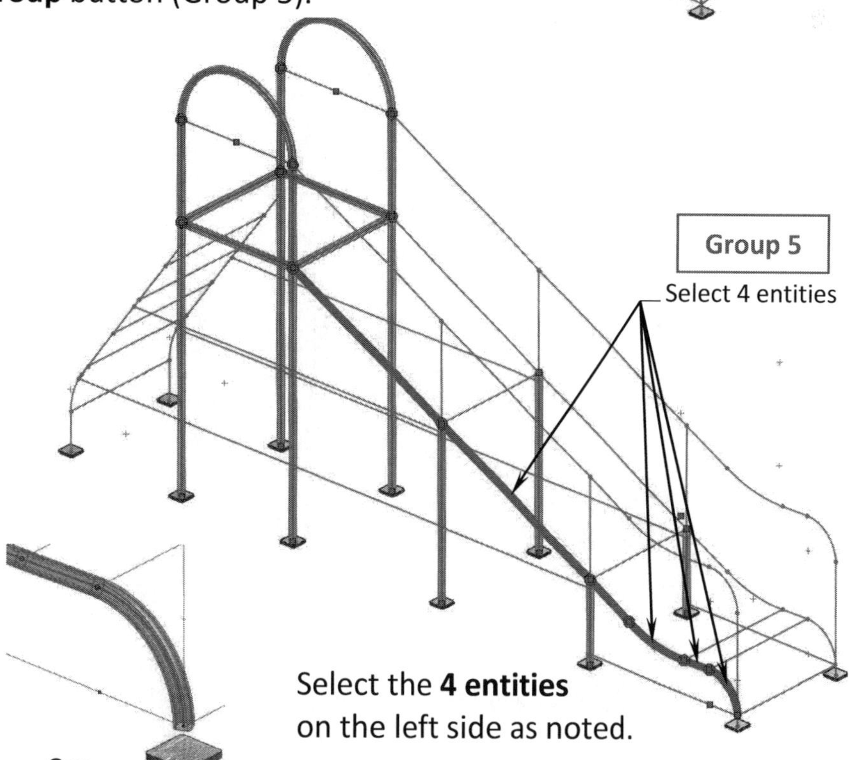

Select the **4 entities** on the left side as noted.

The gap at the bottom will be filled-in or extended later, in a separate step.

Click the **New Group** button (Group 6).

For Group 6, select the **4 entities** on the right side of the playground as indicated in the image.

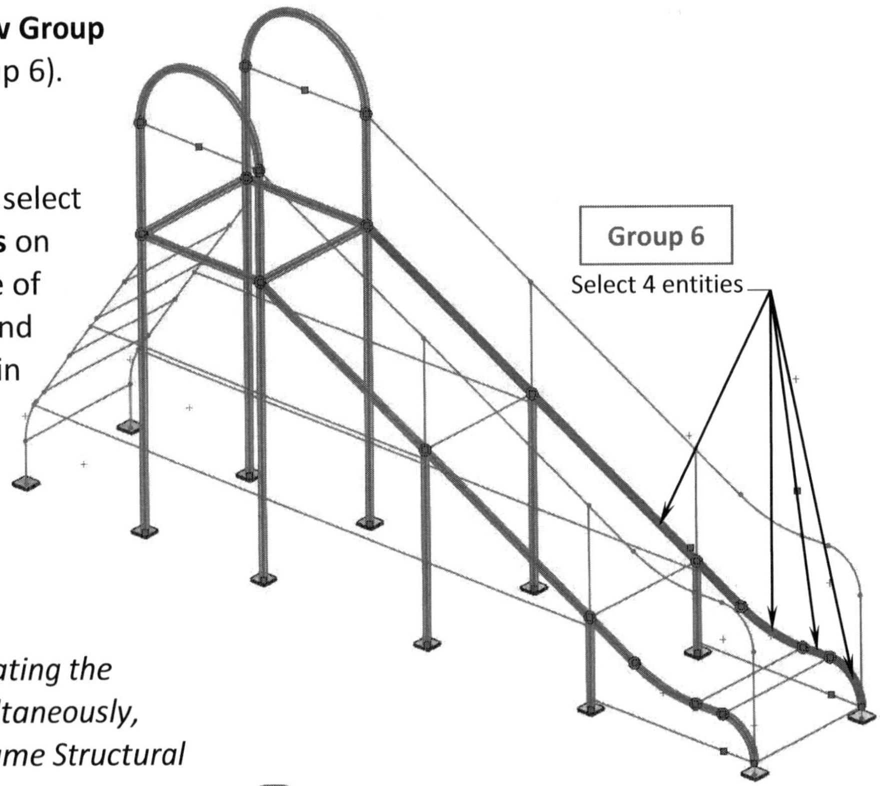

Note: by creating the groups simultaneously, within the same Structural Member feature, SOLIDWORKS automatically trims the tubes where they intersect.

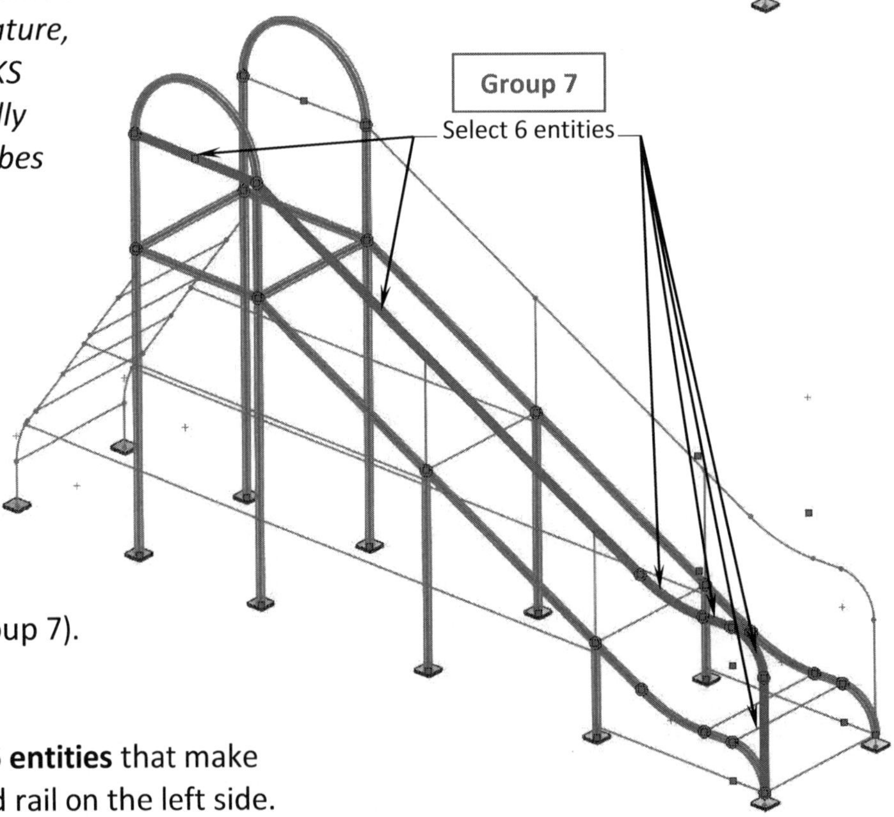

Click the **New Group** button (Group 7).

Select the **6 entities** that make up the hand rail on the left side.

The gap at the bottom will be extended later, in a separate step.

Click the **New Group** button (Group 8).

For Group 8, select the **6 entities** that make up the hand rail on the right side.

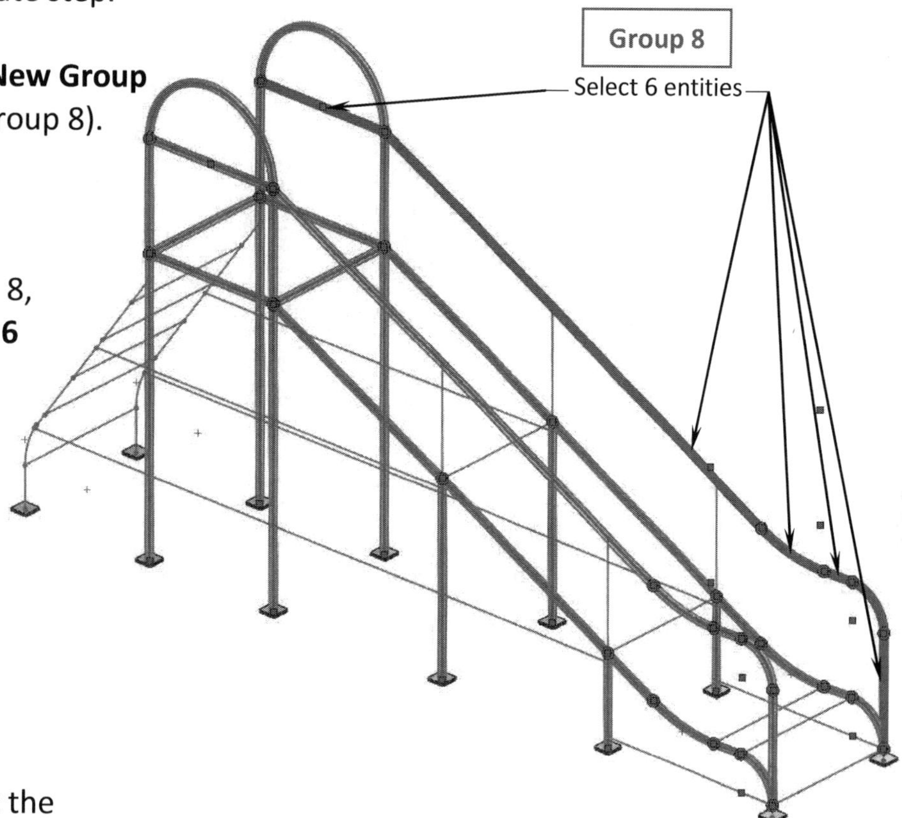

The gap at the bottom will be extended later on, in a separate step.

Click the **New Group** button (Group 9).

For Group 9, select the **4 horizontal lines** on the left side as noted.

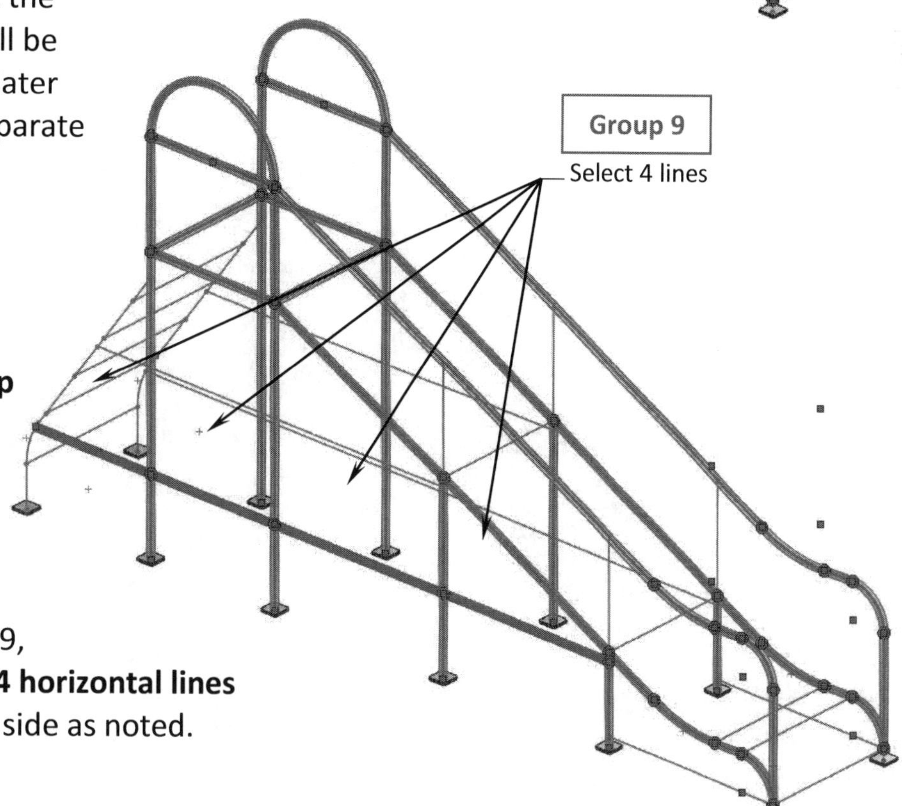

Do not click OK; there are more groups that need to be created.

Click the **New Group** button (Group 10).

For Group 10, select the **4 horizontal lines** as shown in the image.

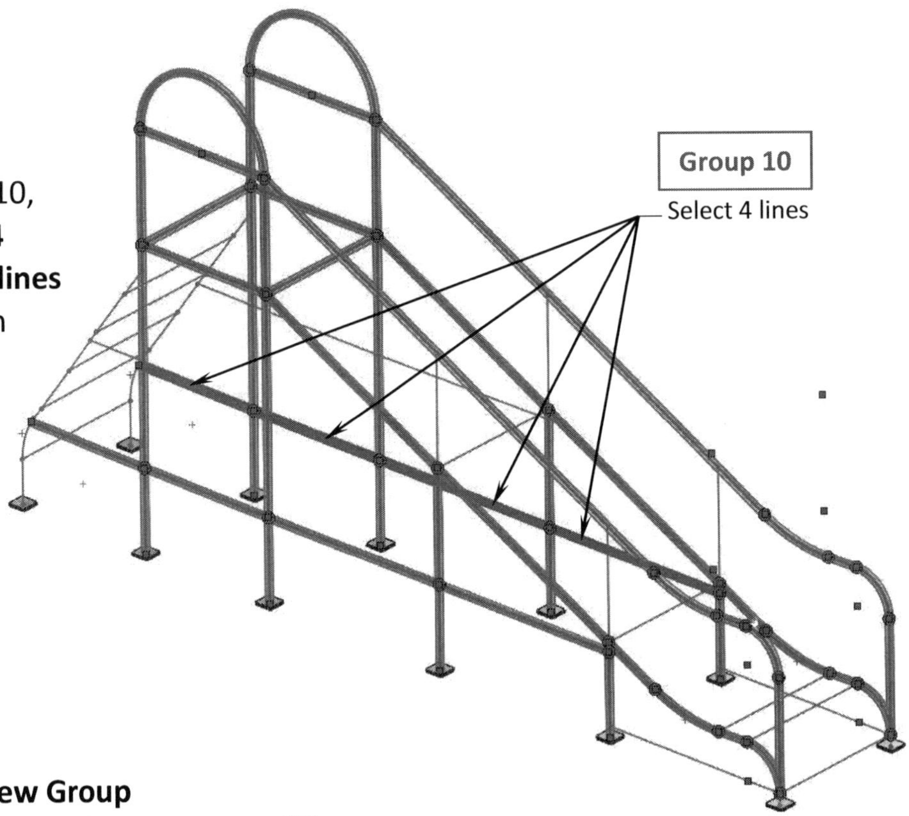

Click the **New Group** button (Group 11).

For Group 11, select the **3 horizontal lines** as shown on the right.

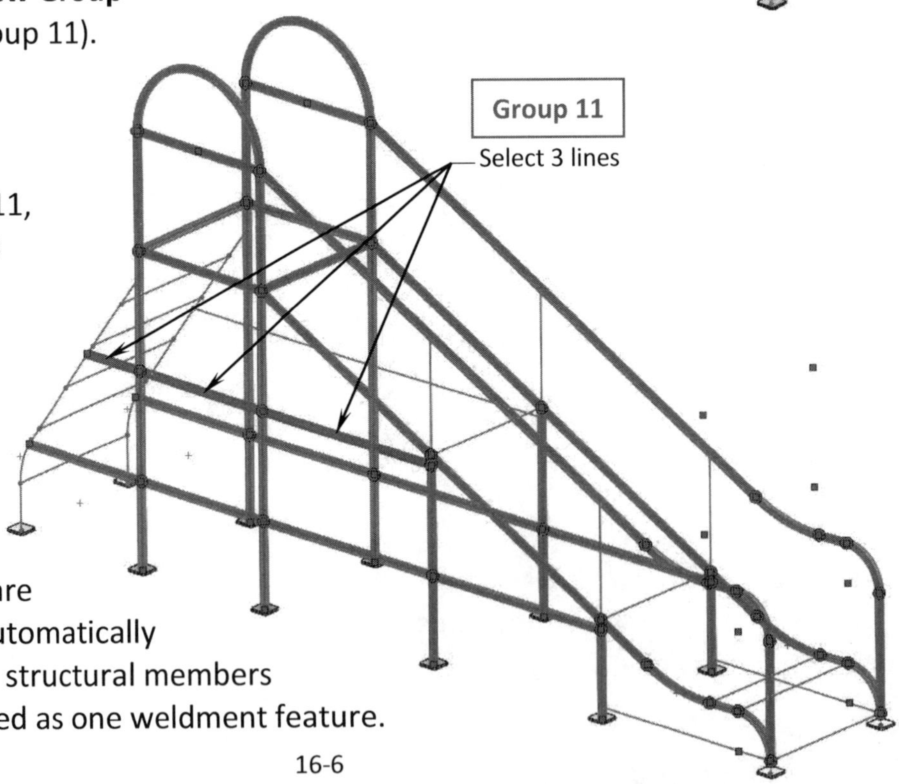

The tubes are trimmed automatically because all structural members were created as one weldment feature.

Click the **New Group** button (Group 12).

For Group 12, select the **3 horizontal lines** as shown in the image on the right.

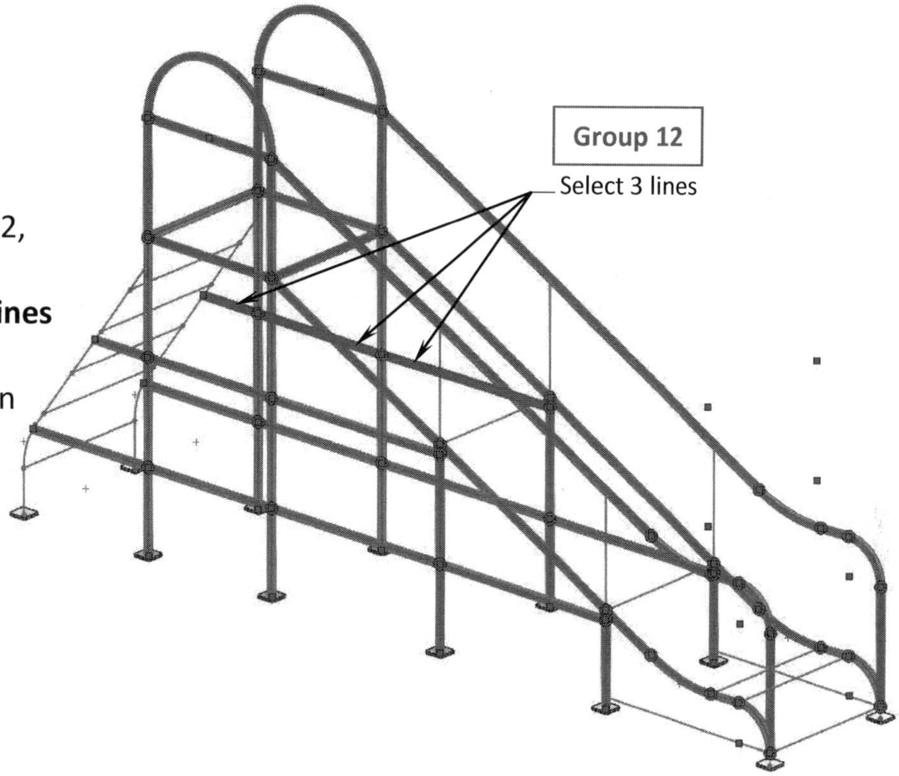

Click the **New Group** button (Group 13).

For Group 13, select the **5 horizontal lines** as indicated.

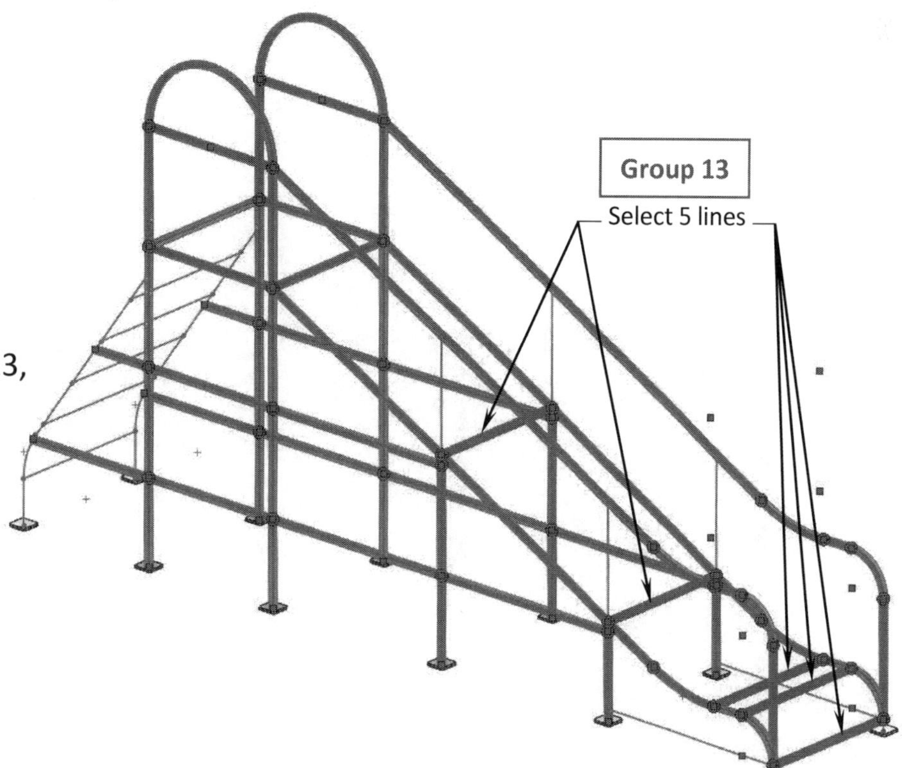

Click the **New Group** button (Group 14).

For Group 14, select the **2 horizontal lines** as shown in the image on the right.

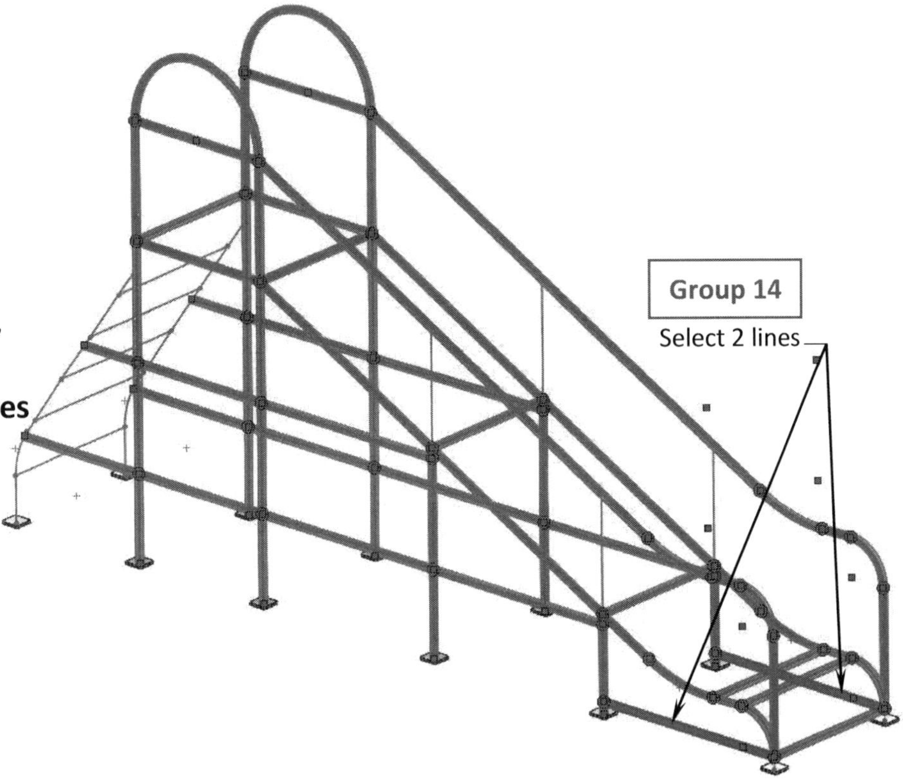

Click the **New Group** button (Group 15).

For Group 15, select the **4 horizontal Lines** as shown on the right.

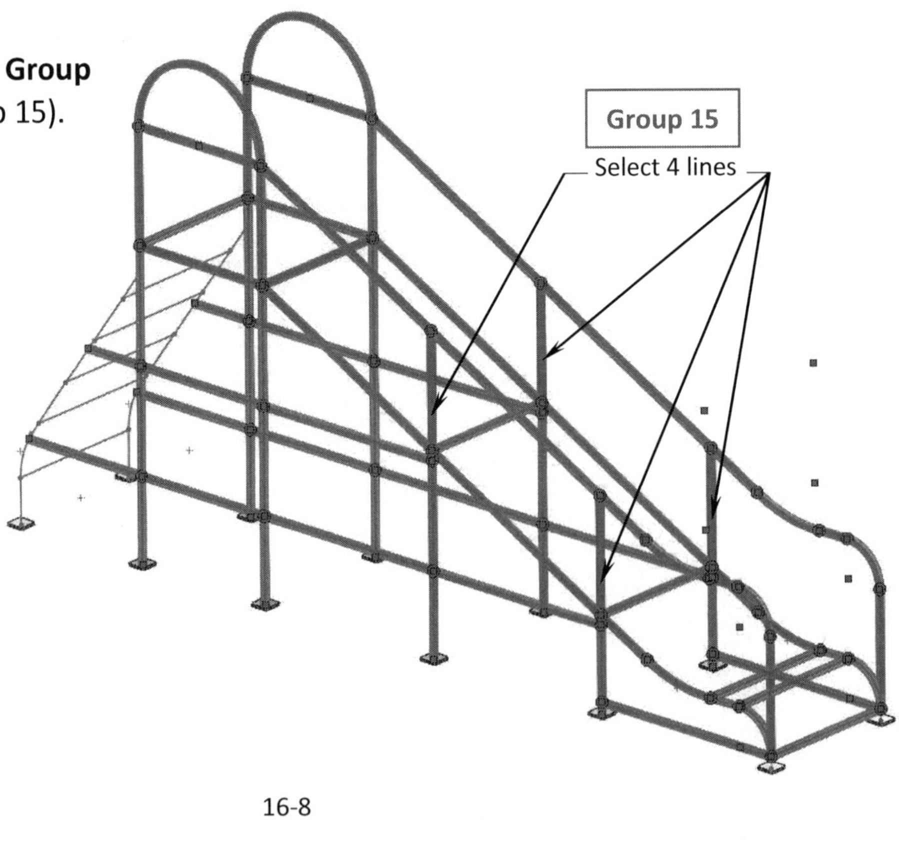

Click the **New Group** button (Group 16).

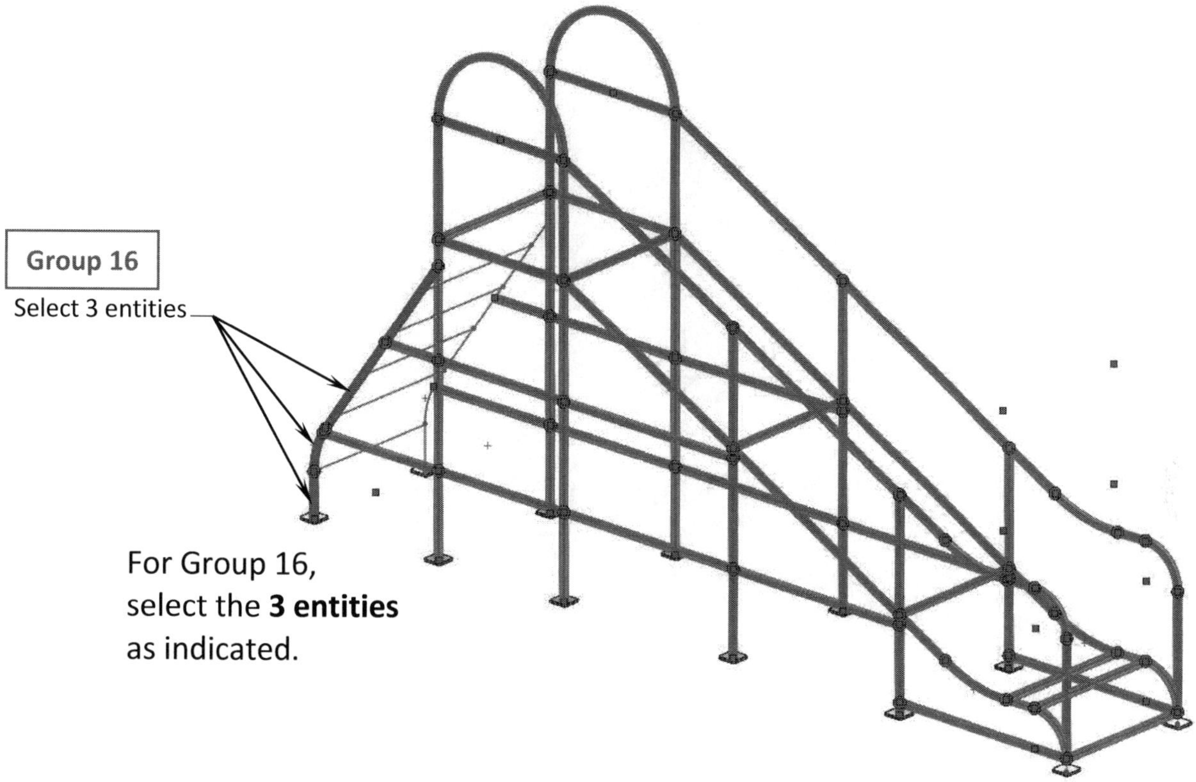

For Group 16,
select the **3 entities**
as indicated.

Click the **New Group** button (Group 17).

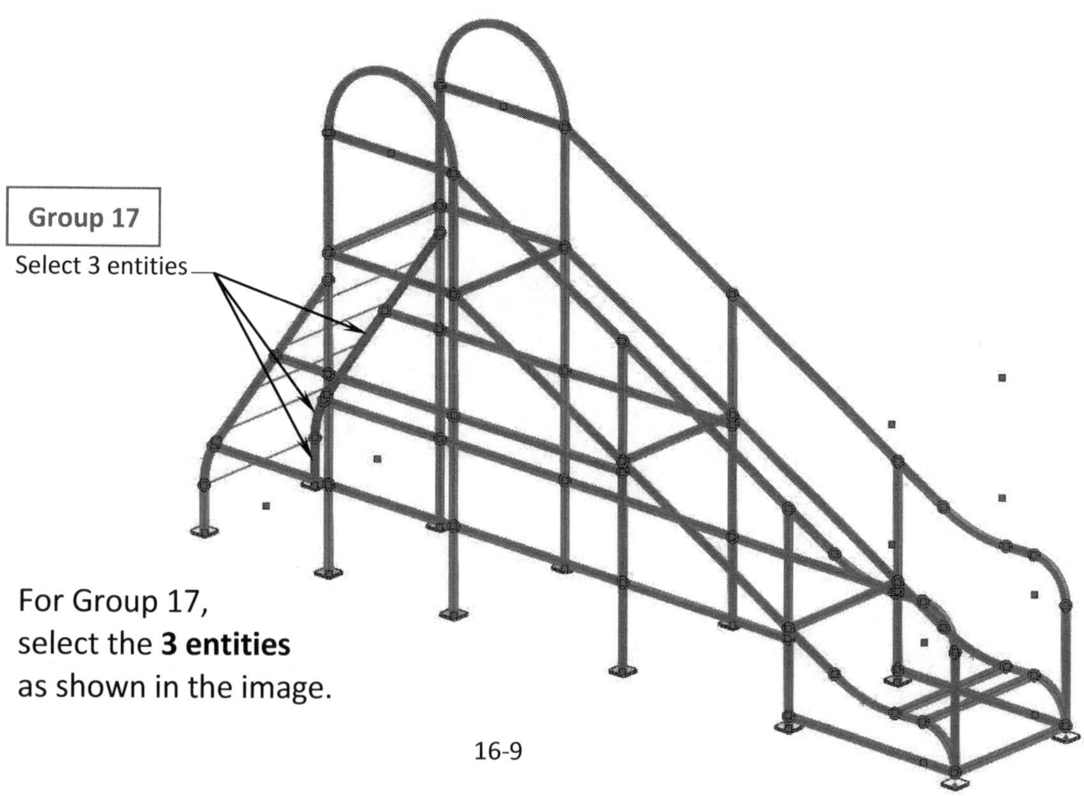

For Group 17,
select the **3 entities**
as shown in the image.

Click the **New Group** button (Group 18).

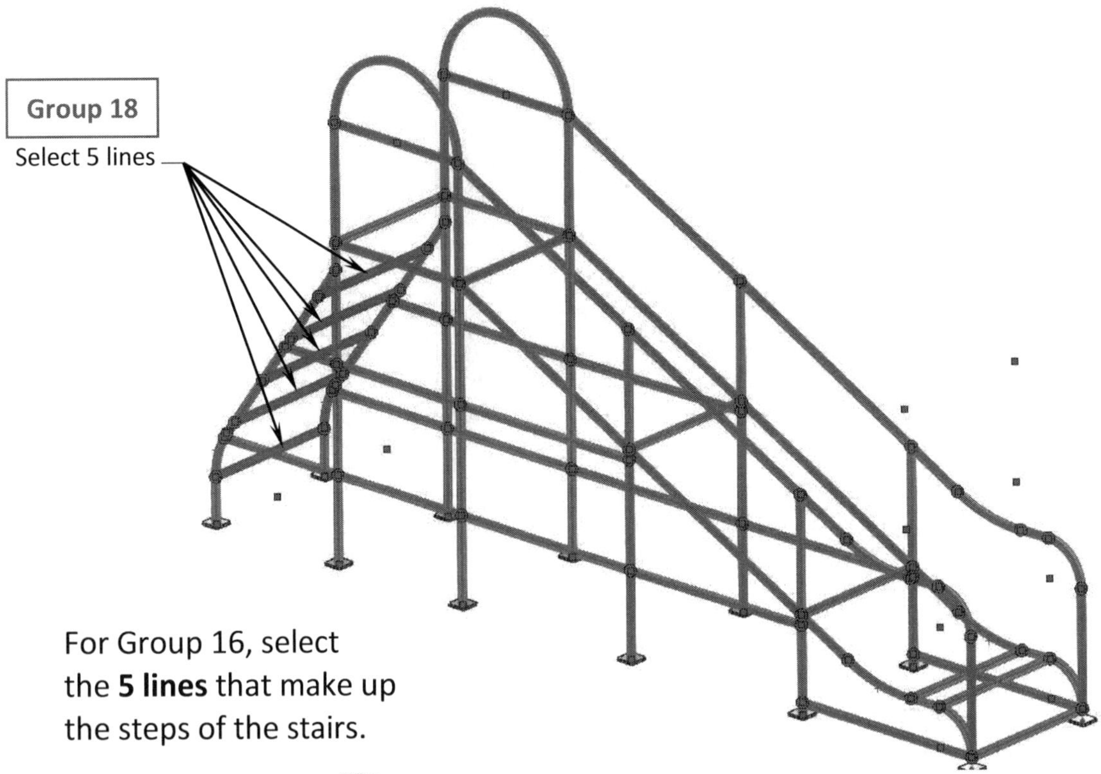

For Group 16, select the **5 lines** that make up the steps of the stairs.

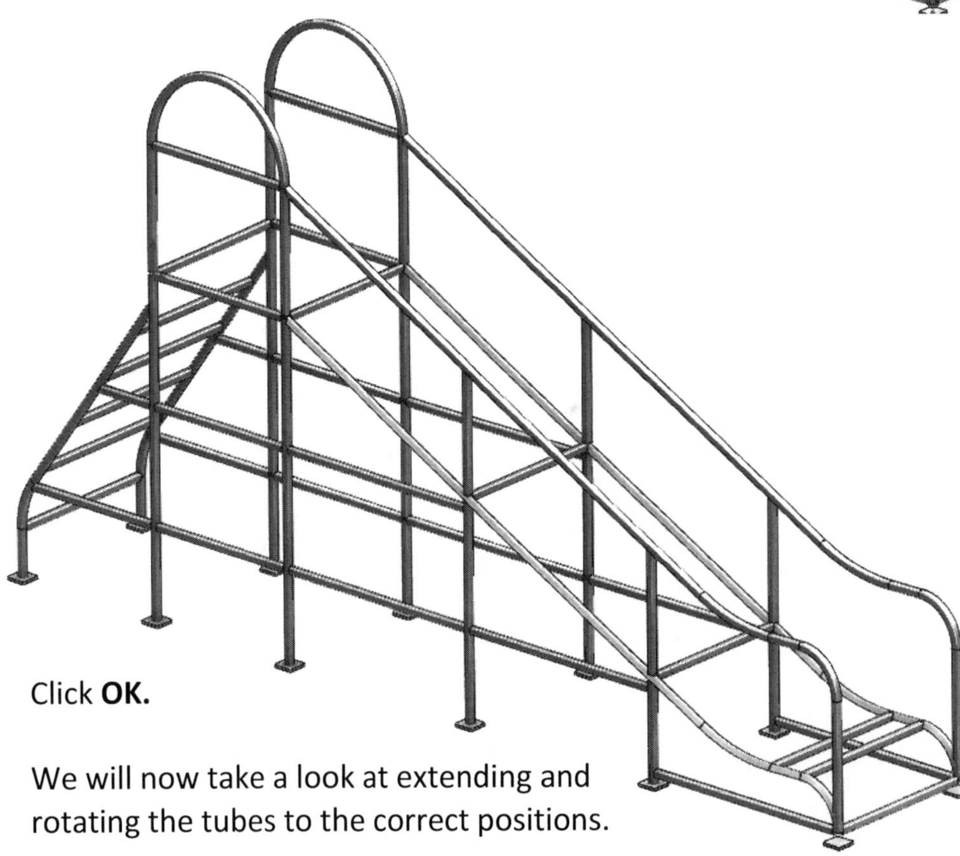

Click **OK.**

We will now take a look at extending and rotating the tubes to the correct positions.

4. Inspecting the Weldments:

Return to the **Isometric view** orientation (Control+7).

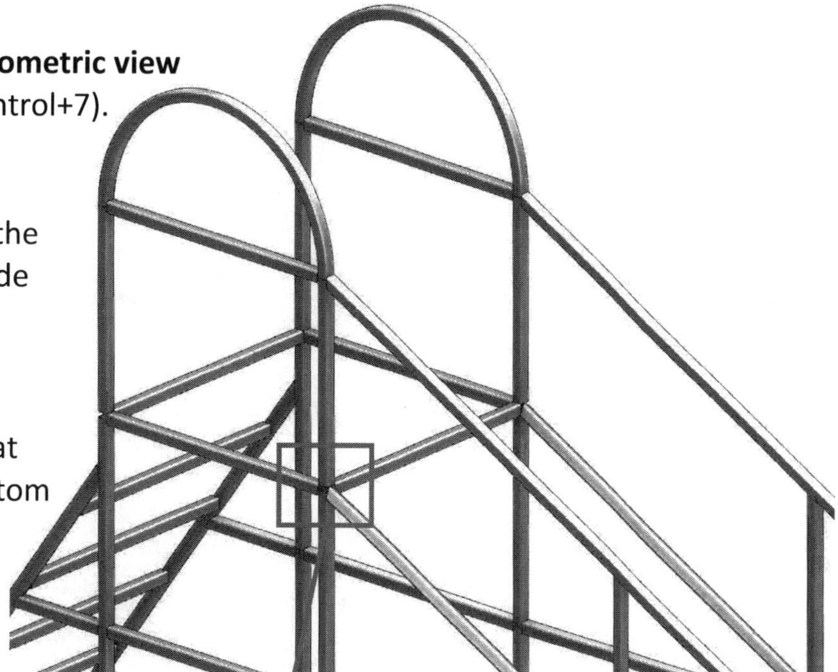

Zoom closer to the area shown inside the rectangle.

There are gaps at the top and bottom of the tubes.

The left and right lower rails are also positioned at a wrong angle. We need to correct them at this time.

5. Rotating a group:

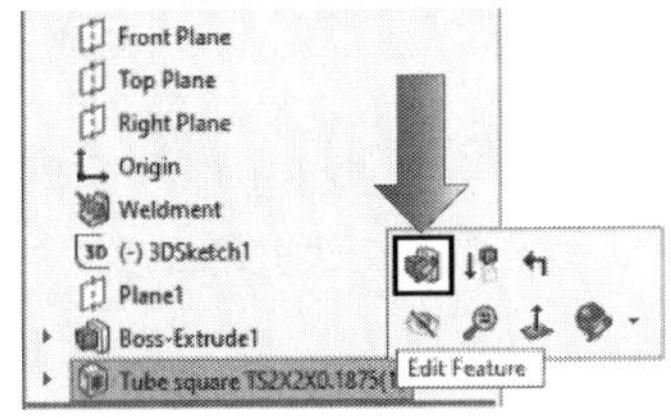

Click the weldment feature **Tube Square TS2x2x0x1875** and select **Edit Feature**.

In the Groups section, select **Group 5** (the group of the lower rail).

Zoom closer to the left end of the 1st tube. Notice the group is not aligned correctly.

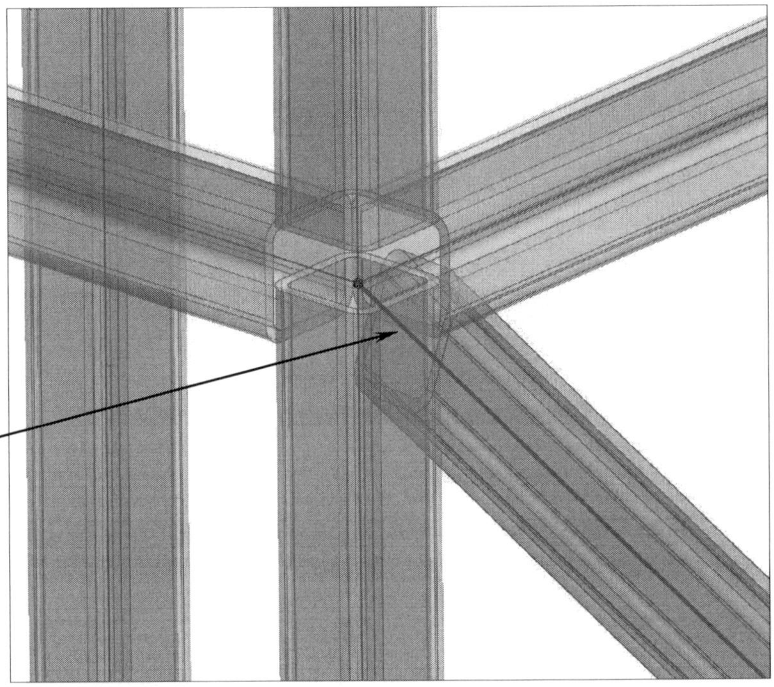

Not aligned

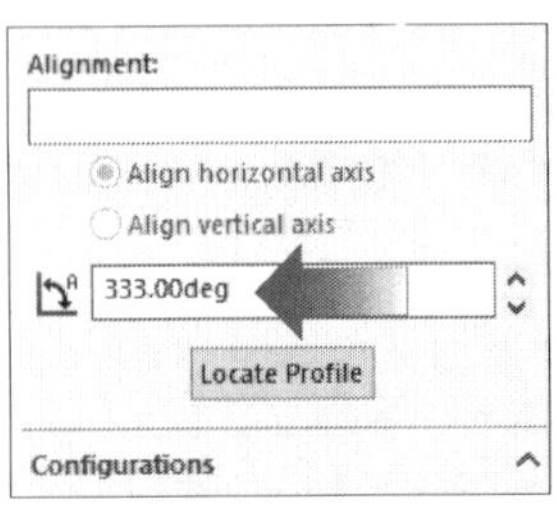

In the Rotate Angle cell, enter **333.00°** and press enter.

The group rotates to the correct position.

Aligned

Repeat the same step to correct the angle of the opposite rail.

Click **OK**.

6. Extending the structural members:

Zoom to the position similar to the image shown on the right.

Click **Trim/Extend**.

For Bodies to be Trimmed, select the **4 vertical tubes**.

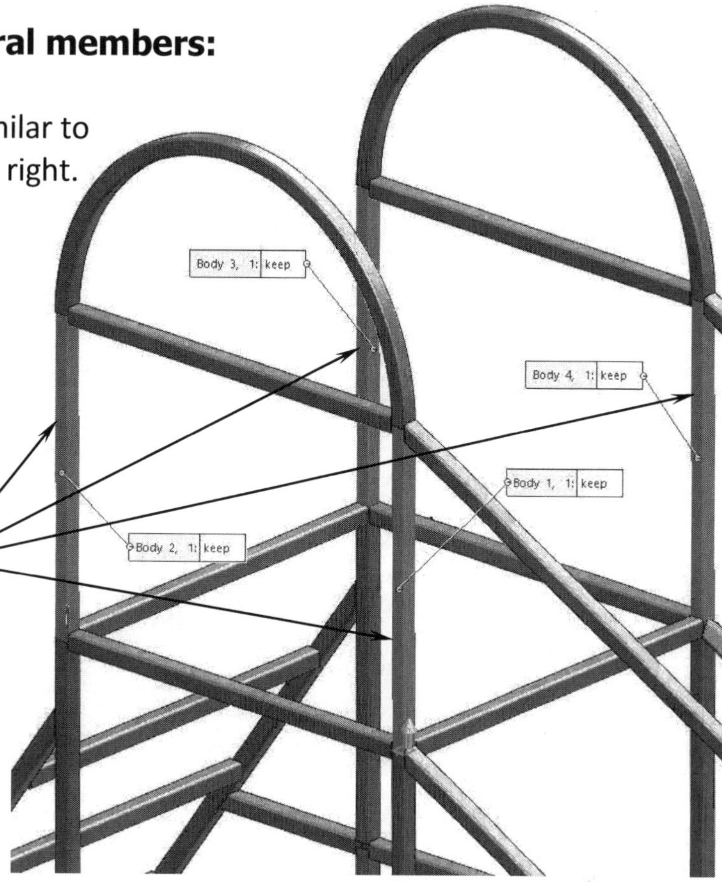

For Trimming Boundary, click **Face / Plane** and select the **upper face** of the tube shown in the image below.

Change the Weld Gap dimension to **.040in** and click **OK**.

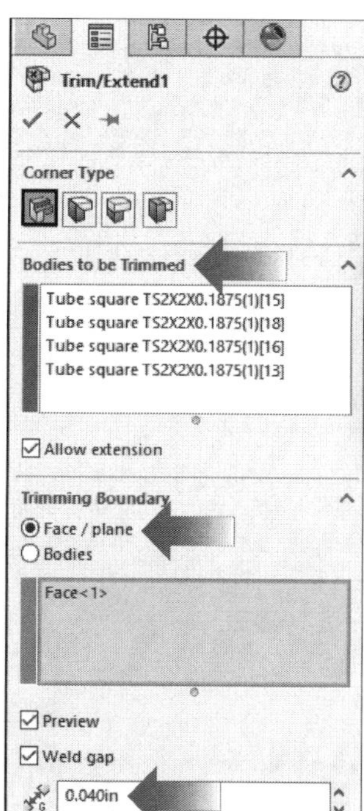

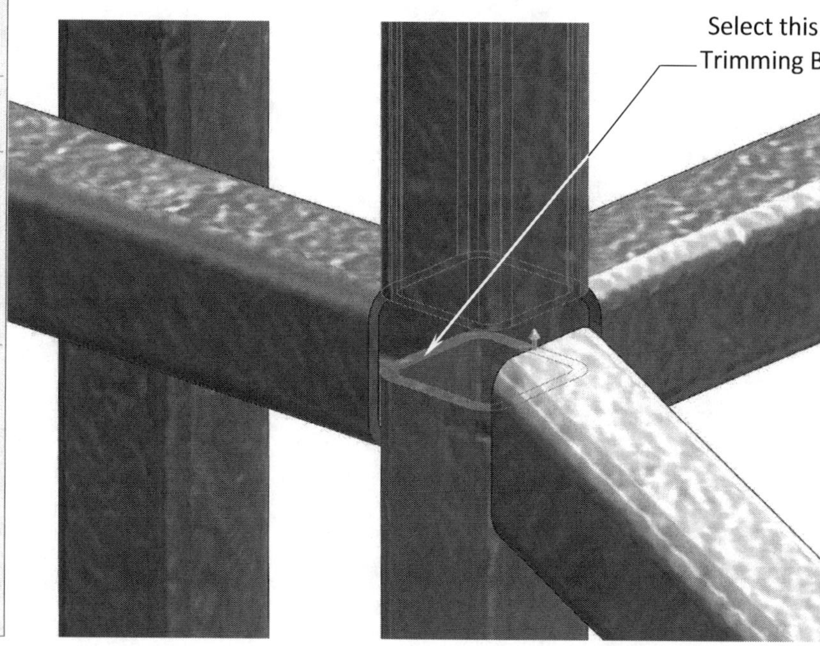

7. Modifying the corner treatments:

Click the weldment feature **Tube Square TS2x2x0x1875** and select: **Edit Feature**.

In the Groups section, select **Group 5**, (the group of the lower rail).

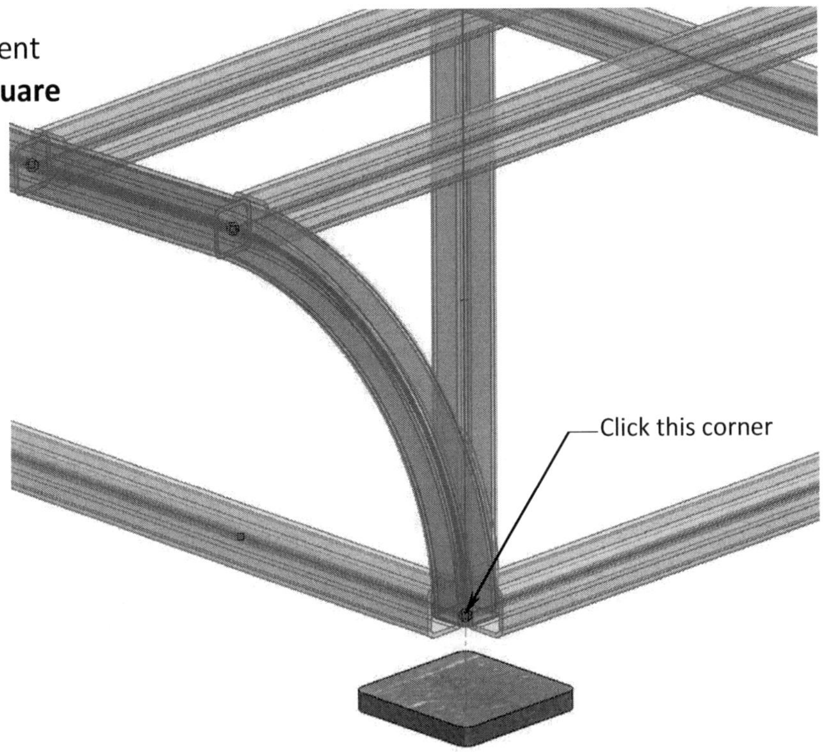

Click the corner handle to access the **Corner Treatment** dialog box.

Use the Up & Down arrows to see the different options for the corners.

Select the **Trim Order 4** as indicated.

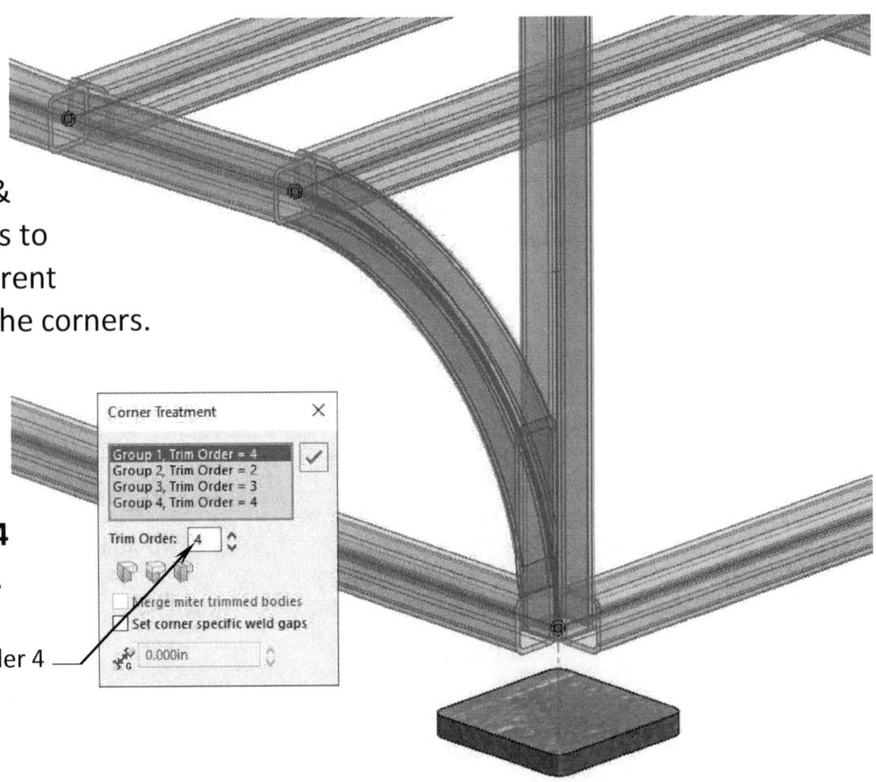

Use Trim Order 4

Click **OK**.

8. Extending other structural members:

Zoom closer to the position similar to the image shown below.

Click **Trim/Extend**.

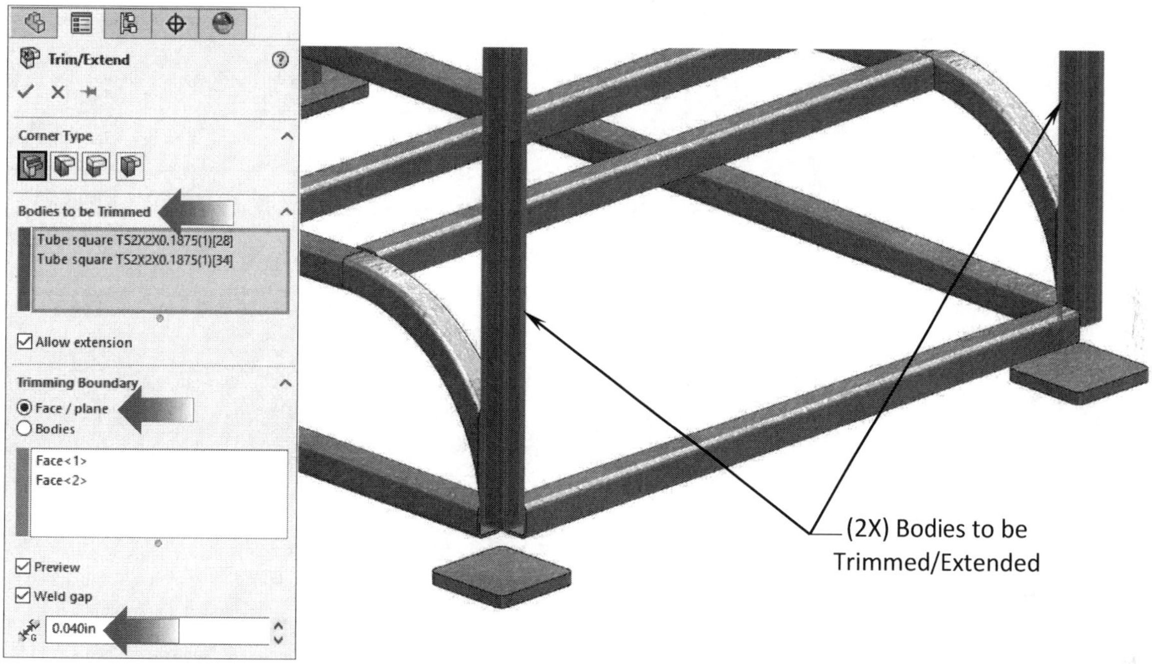

For Bodies to be Trimmed, select the **2 vertical tubes**.

For Trimming Boundary, click **Face / Plane** and select the **upper face** of one of the foot plates.

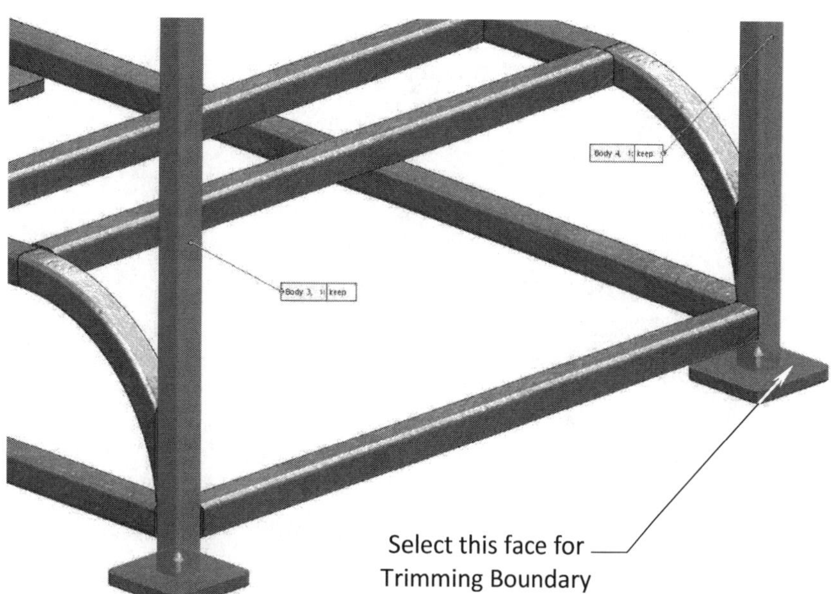

Click **OK**.

Inspect and compare your weldments frame against the one shown below.

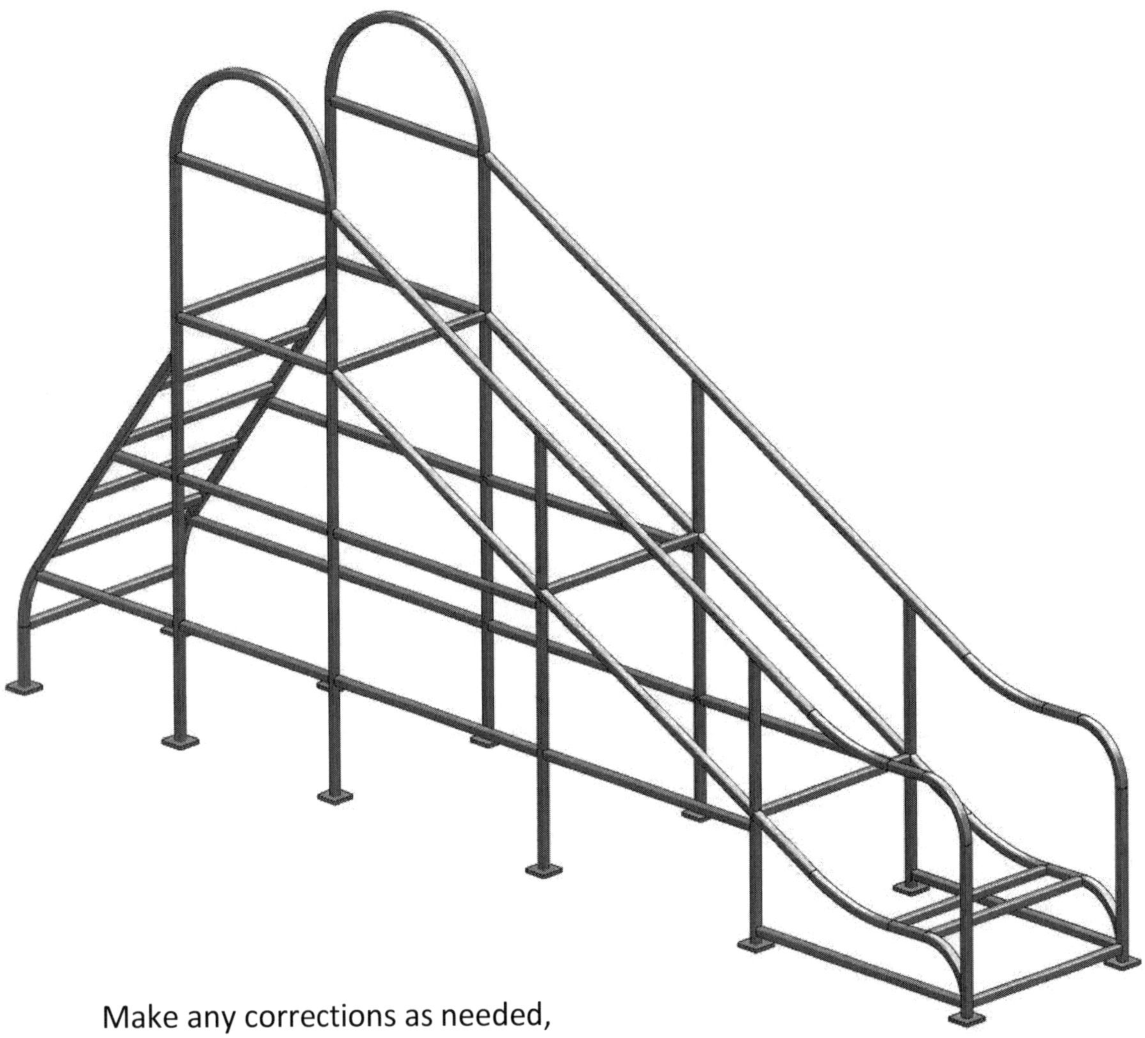

Make any corrections as needed, prior to saving the model.

9. Saving your work:

Select **File, Save As**.

Enter: **Playground Slide_Completed.sldprt** for the file name.

Click **Save**.

Lesson 17: Locating Profiles

The weldment profiles are 2D sketches that are used to sweep along the segments of the skeleton sketch. A button at the lower left corner of the screen called Locate Profile will allow a selected point in the weldment profile to be referenced as the insertion point for the structural member.

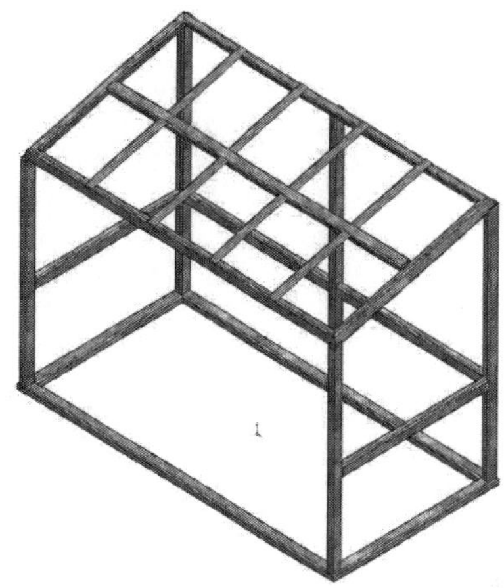

1. Opening a part document:

Browse to the Training Folder and open a part document named: **Weldments_Locate Profiles**.

The weldments part has been completed but interference issues existed in several locations. Also, the structural members on the top of the weldments part need to be rotated to the correct angles.

2. Using Interference Detection:

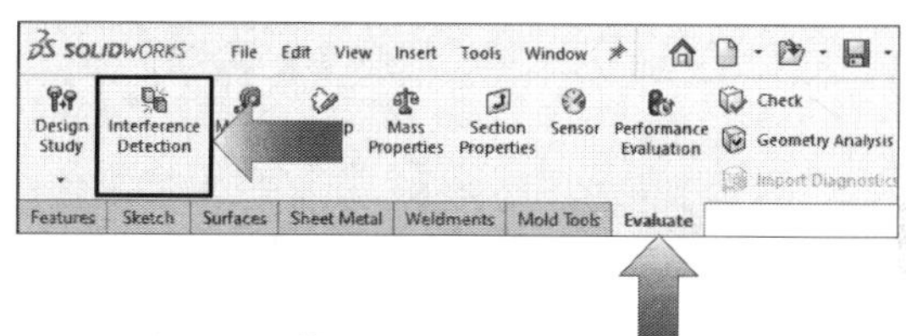

Right-click on the **Evaluate** tab and select: **Interference Detection**.

Click **Calculate.**

SOLIDWORKS found nearly two dozen interferences in the model.

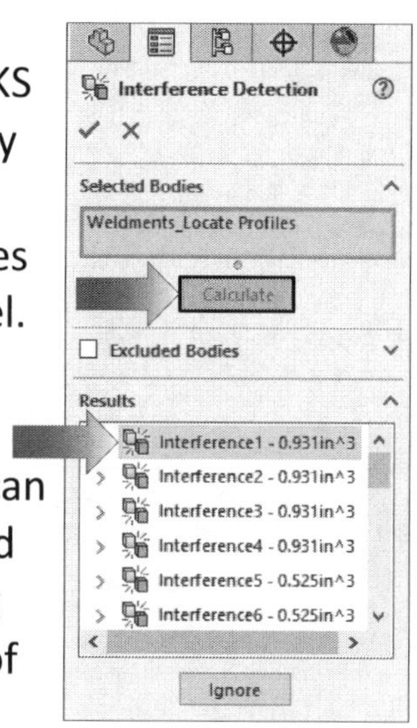

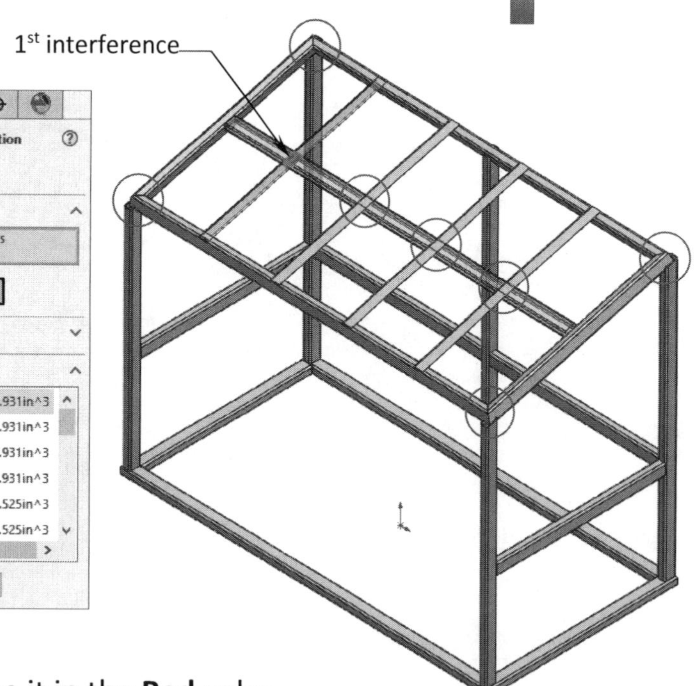

The errors can be corrected by changing the angles of the tubes.

Click on **Interference1** to see it in the **Red** color.

3. Changing the profile's angle:

Click the **Tube Rectangular TR3x2x0.1875** and select **Edit Feature**.

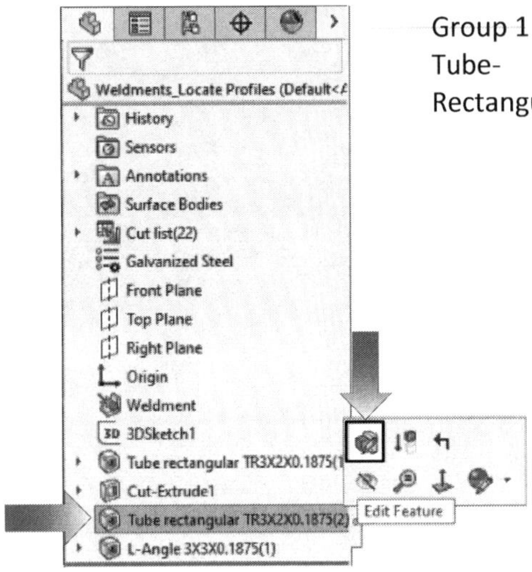

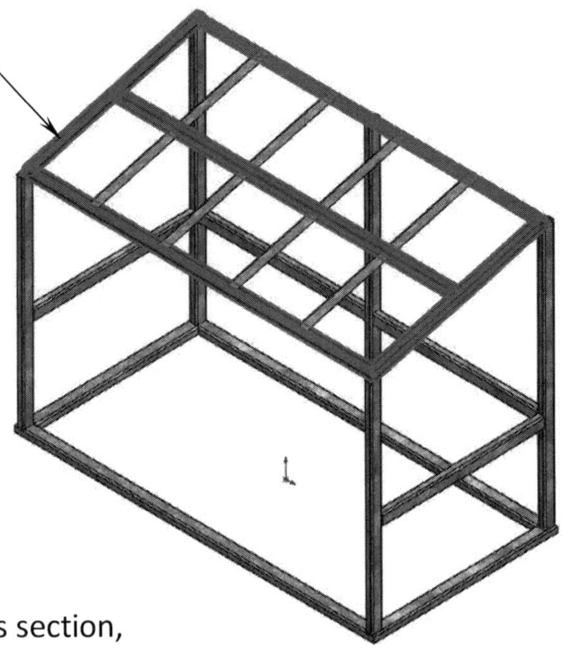

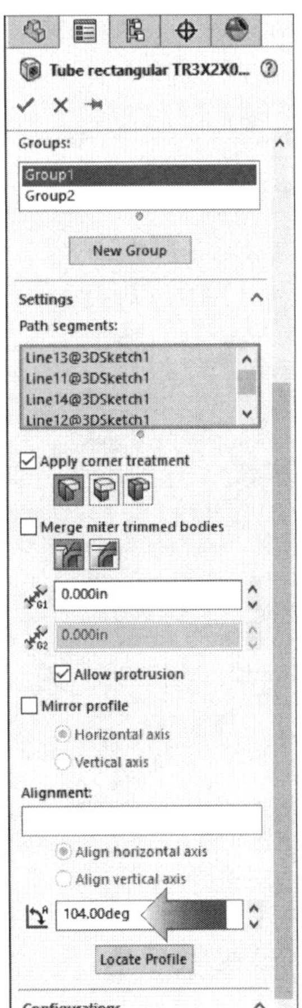

In the Groups section, select **Group 1**.

In the Rotation Angle field, change **0deg** to **104.0deg** and press **enter**.

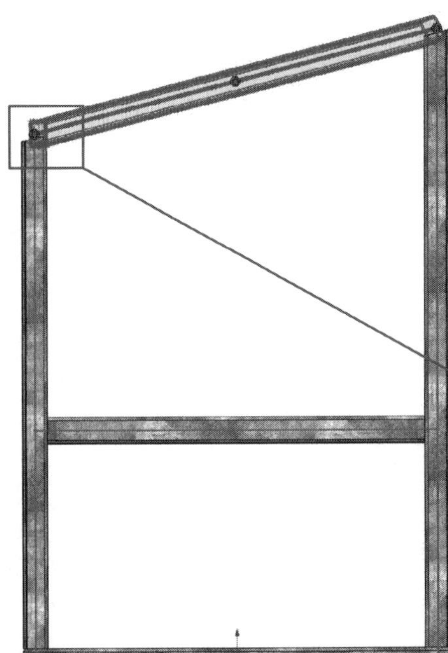

The tubes in Group 1 are rotated and matched up with the angles of the legs.

Click **OK**.

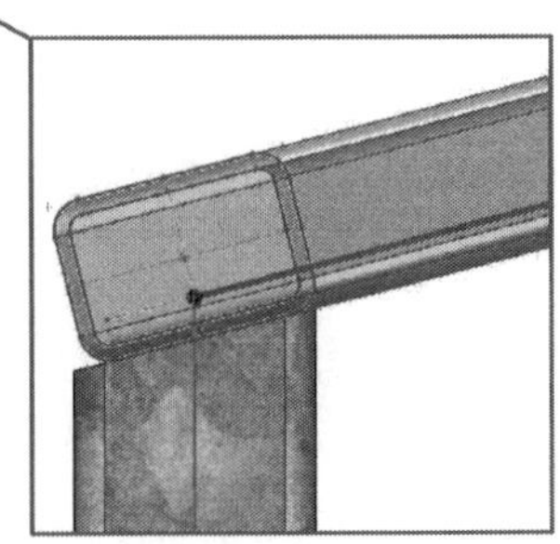

4. Changing the profile's angle:

Click the **L-Angle 3x3x0.1875** and select: **Edit Feature**.

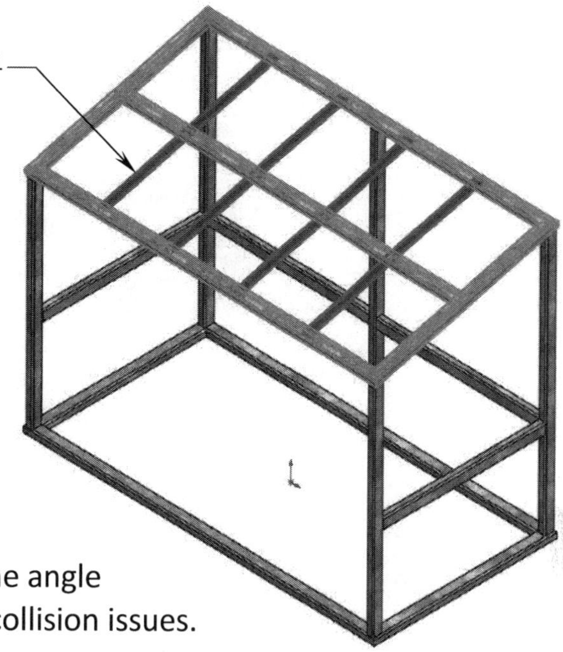

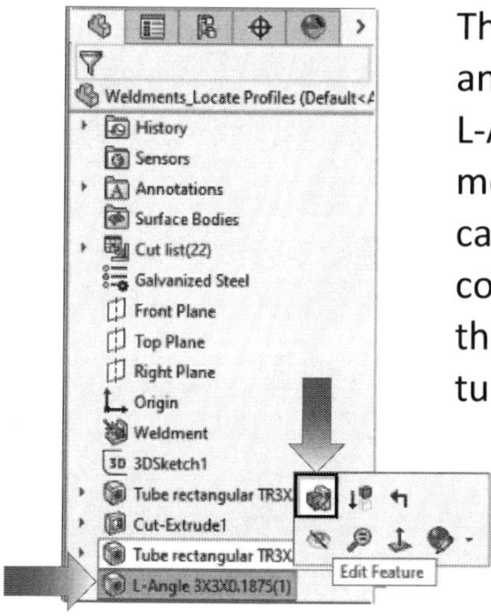

The current angle of the L-Angle members causes the collisions with the crossed tubes.

Changing the angle will fix the collision issues.

Select **Group 1** in the Groups section.

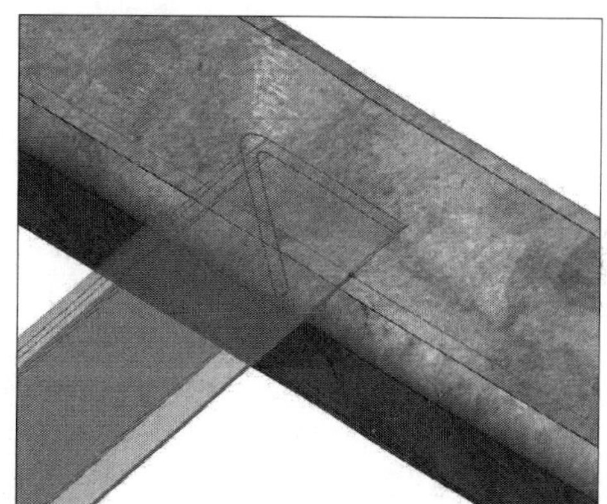
Current Angle

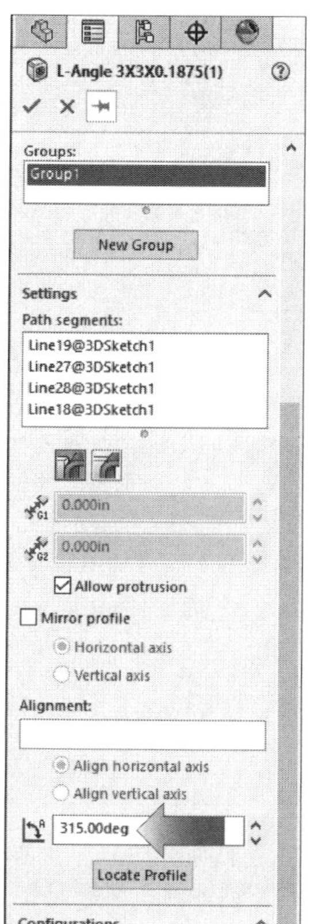

Scroll down to the **Rotation Angle** field and change the angle from:

0deg. to **315deg**.

Press **enter** to preview the change.

The interferences between the L-Angles and the crossed tubes should be cleared at this point.

Click **OK**.

New Angle

Inspect your weldments model against the image shown below.

Make adjustments as needed.

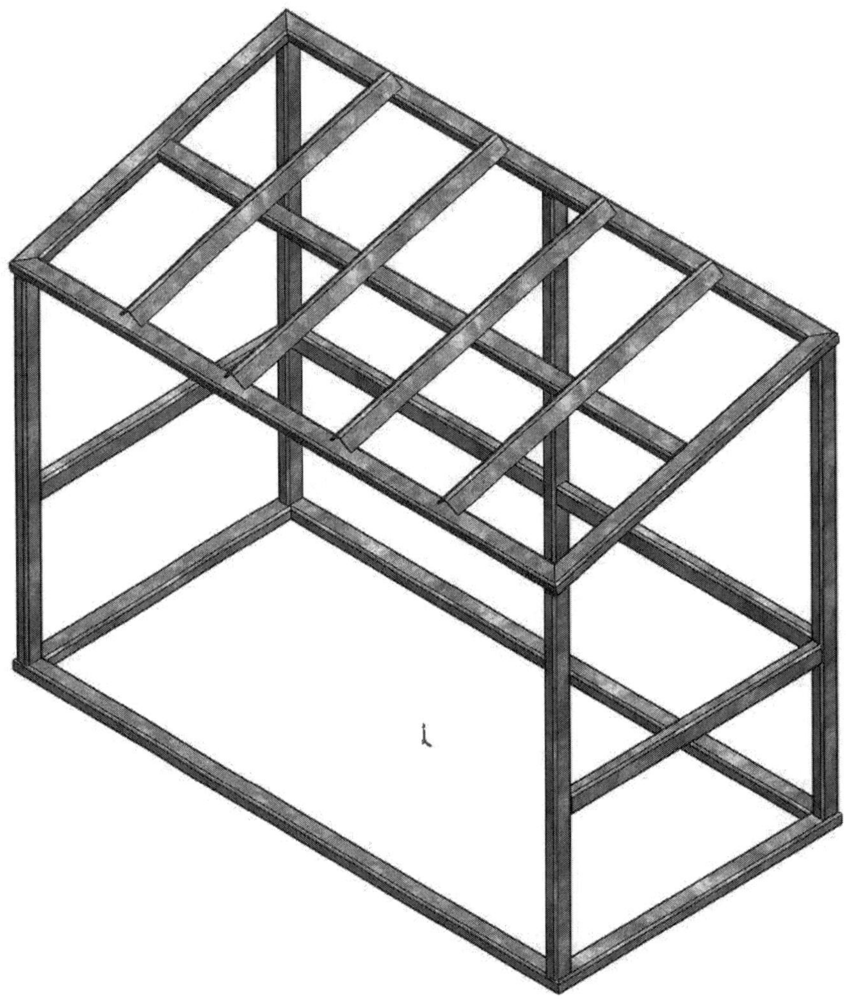

5. Saving your work:

Select **File, Save As**.

Enter: **Slide_Completed.sldprt**
for the file name.

Click **Save**.

Exercise: Weldments Fence

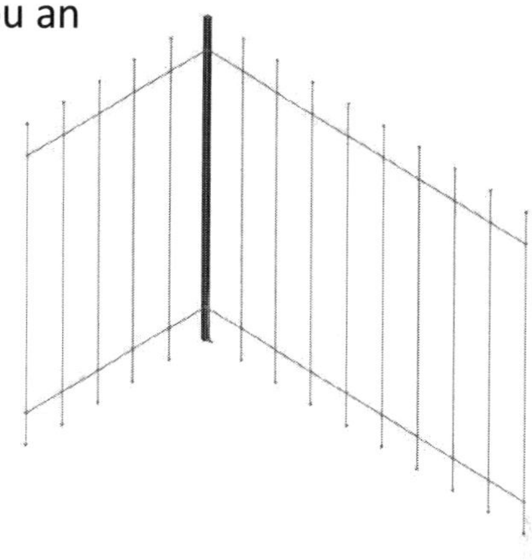

The exercises in this textbook are intended to give you an opportunity to explore and to apply what you have learned from the previous chapters, at your own pace.

1. Opening a part document:

Browse to the Training Folder and open a part document named: **Weldments_Fence.sldprt**

There is a 3D Sketch that has been created for this exercise to help us focus on adding the Structural Members and other solid bodies.

2. Enabling the Weldment tab:

Right-click on the **Features** tab and select: **Tabs, Weldments**.

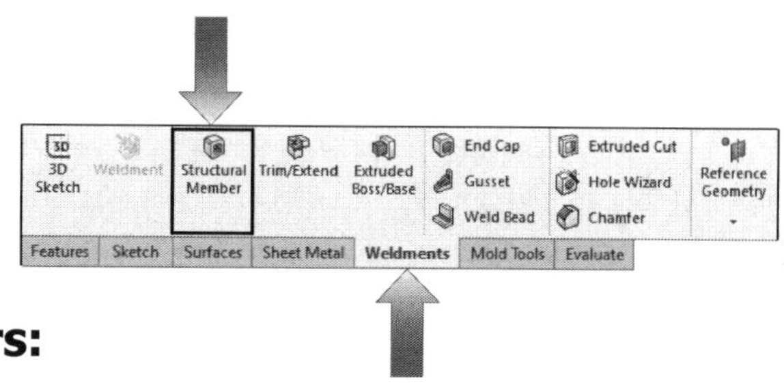

3. Adding the structural members:

Structural members should be added as weldment groups in order for the Cut-List to be parametrically created.

In this exercise, we will learn how to add the additional structural members to an existing weldments feature.

We will also learn how to insert an existing model into the current weldments part, and mate it to the structural members.

Using the FeatureManager tree, click the **Tube (Square) 1x1x0.125** feature and select **Edit Feature**.

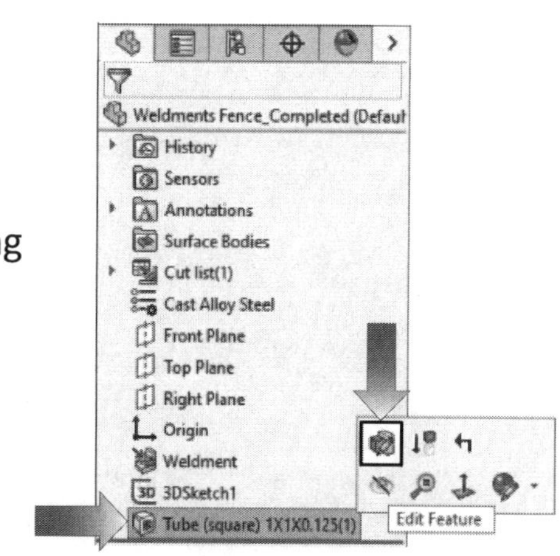

Group 1 should be the active group.

For **Group 1**, select the **15 vertical lines** as indicated below.

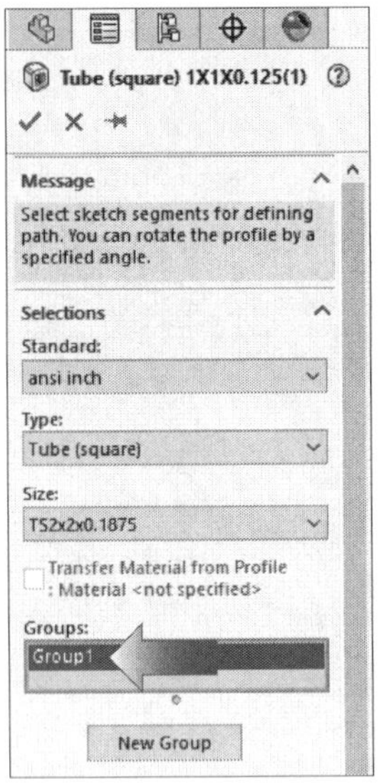

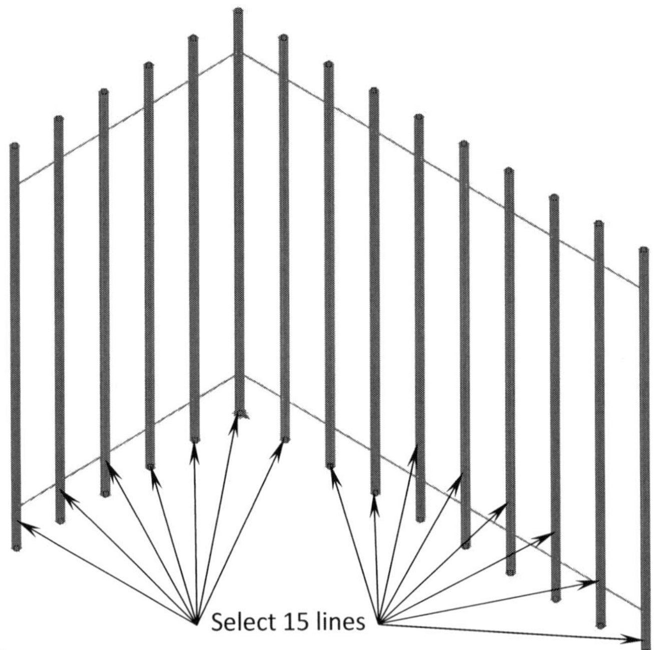

This is a **Parallel Group**. The lines are parallel but not connecting with each other.

Click the **New Group** button.

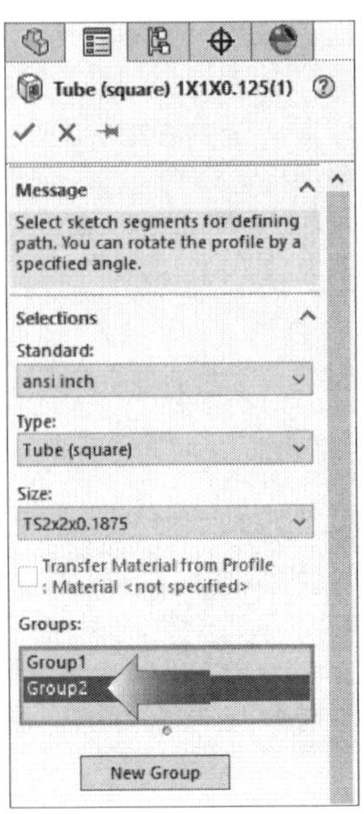

For Group 2 select the **14 horizontal lines** as indicated in the image.

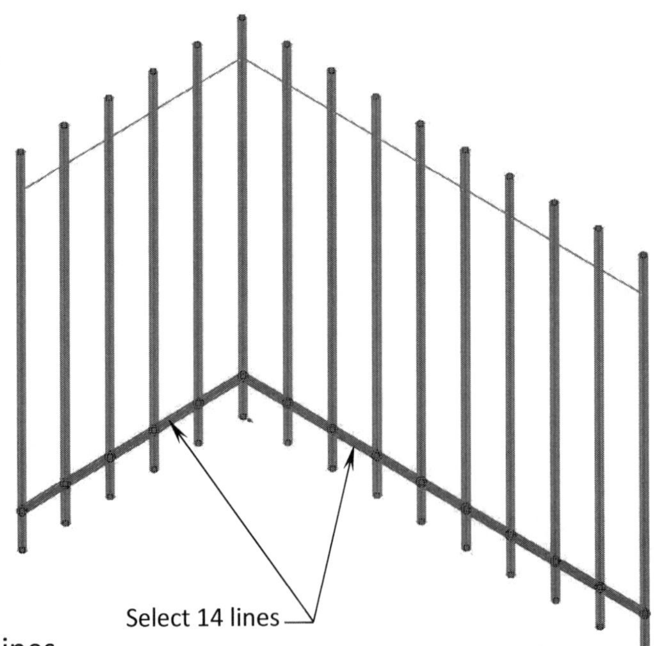

Group 2 is a **Contiguous Group**—the lines are connecting to each other.

Click **New Group** again.

For Group 3, select the **14 horizontal lines** on top of the fence.

This group is a **Contiguous Group**.

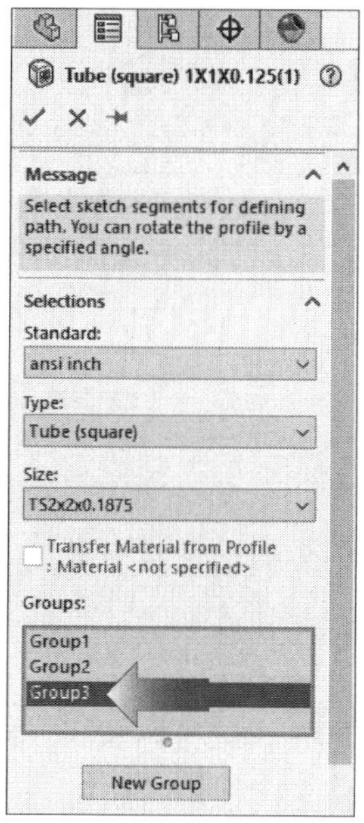

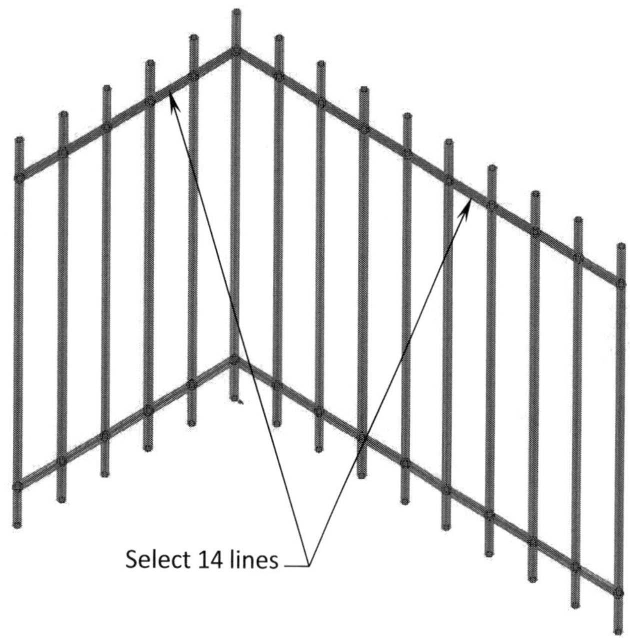

Click **OK**.

From the FeatureManager tree, click on **3DSketch1** and select **Hide**.

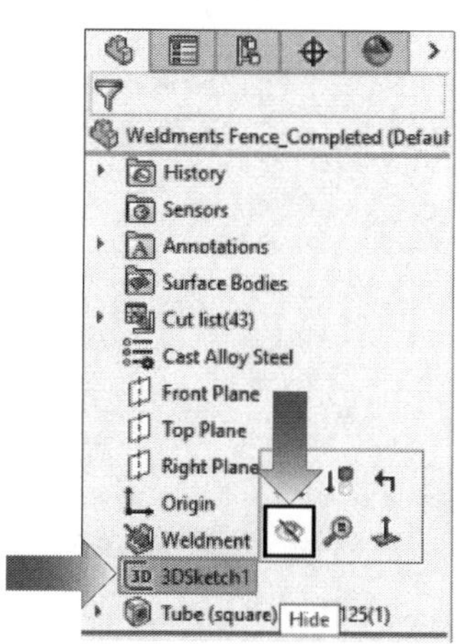

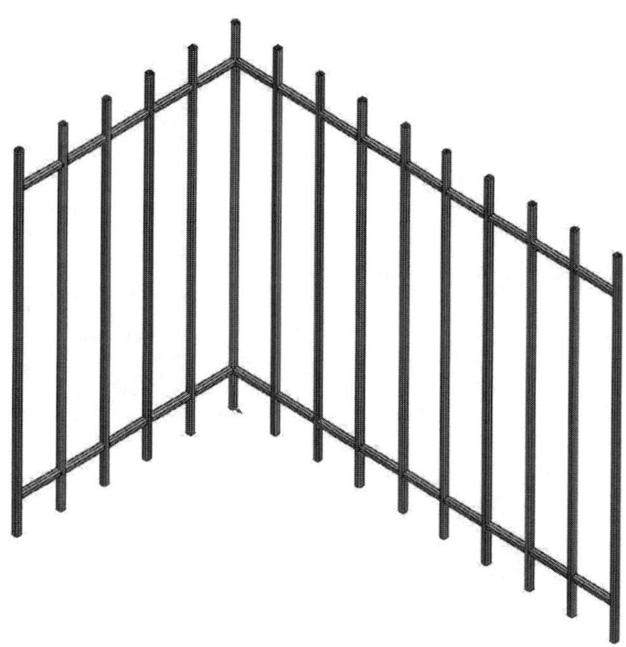

4. Inserting a solid model:

When another solid model is inserted into a part document, SOLIDWORKS recognizes more than one body exists in the document and treats it as a multibody part.

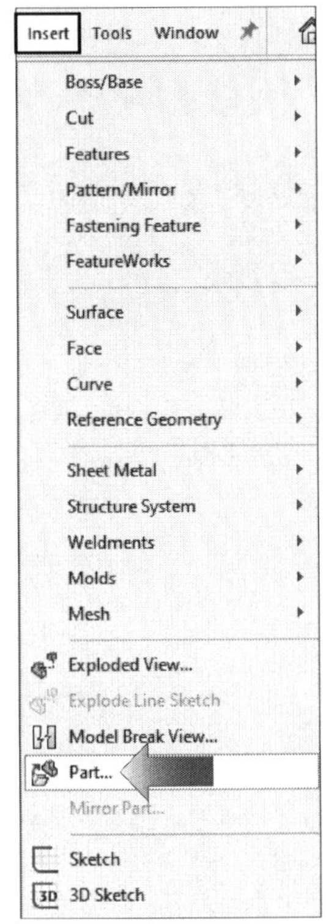

Select **Insert, Part**.

Browse to the Training Folder and select a part document named: **Fence Finial.sldprt**.

Enable the options shown in the 2nd dialog box at the bottom right.

Also enable the checkbox for: Locate Part with Move/Copy Feature.

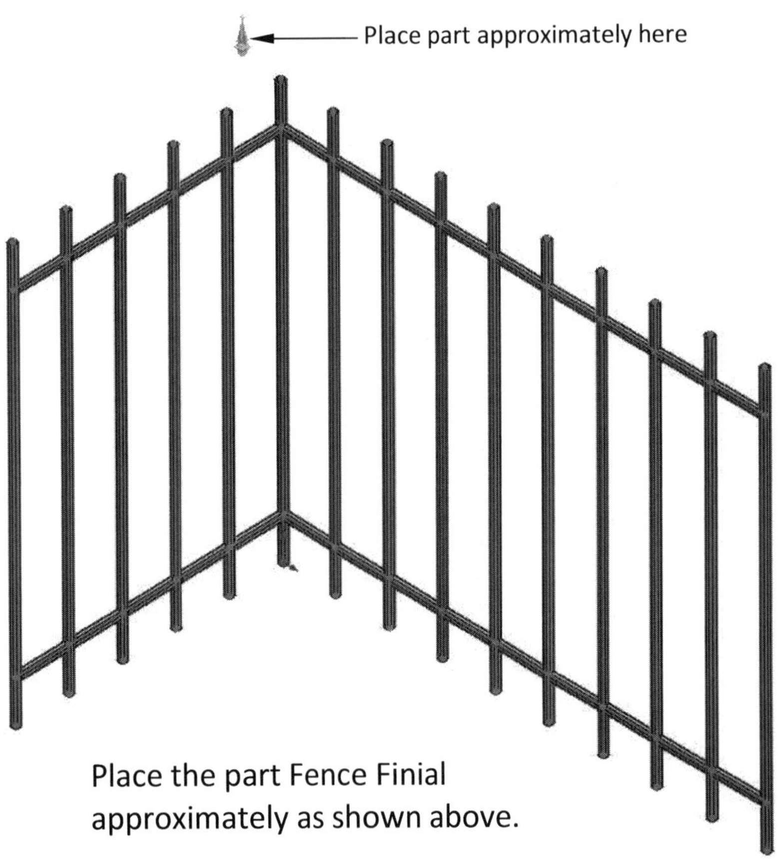

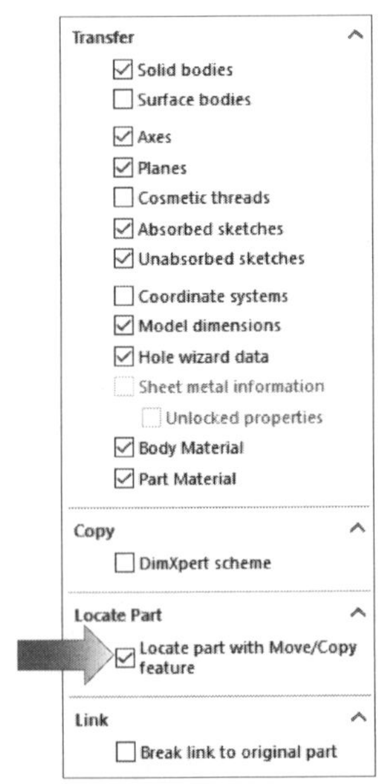

Place the part Fence Finial approximately as shown above.

Click **OK**.

Click **YES** to close the Material message.

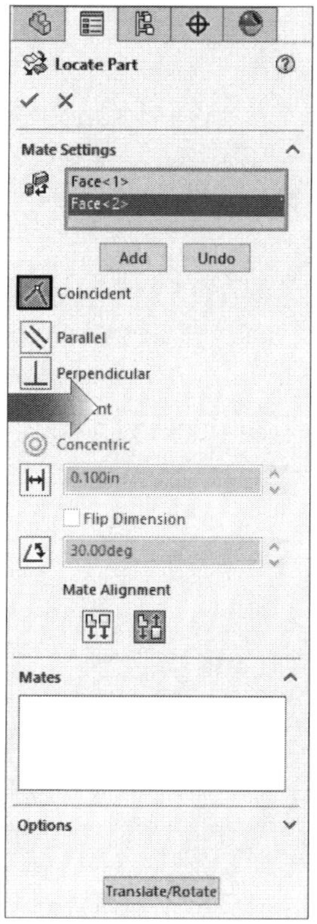

The **Mate** dialog box appears on the Properties tree.

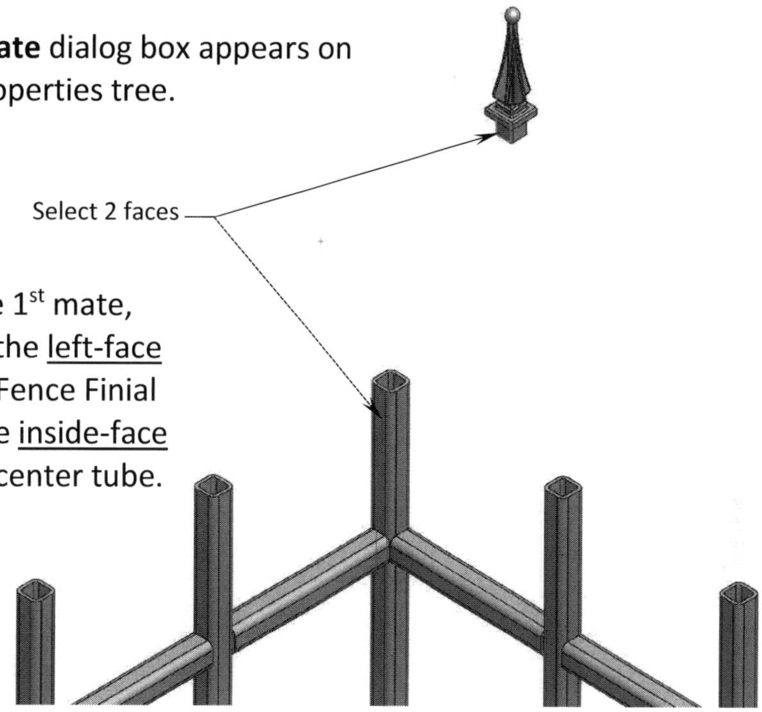

For the 1st mate, select the <u>left-face</u> of the Fence Finial and the <u>inside-face</u> of the center tube.

Click **Add**.

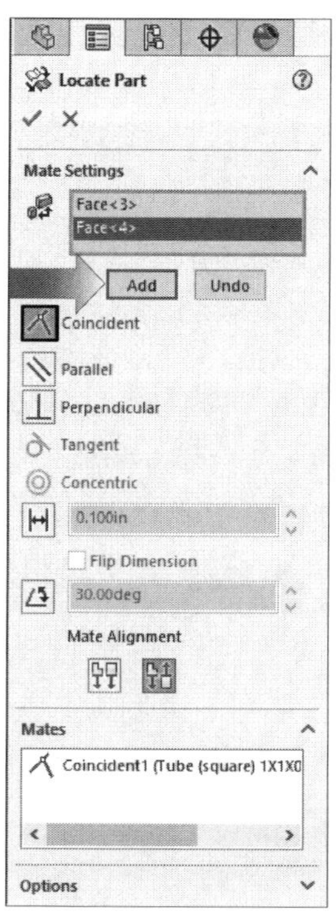

For the 2nd mate, select the <u>right-face</u> of the Fence Finial and the <u>inside-face</u> of the center tube.

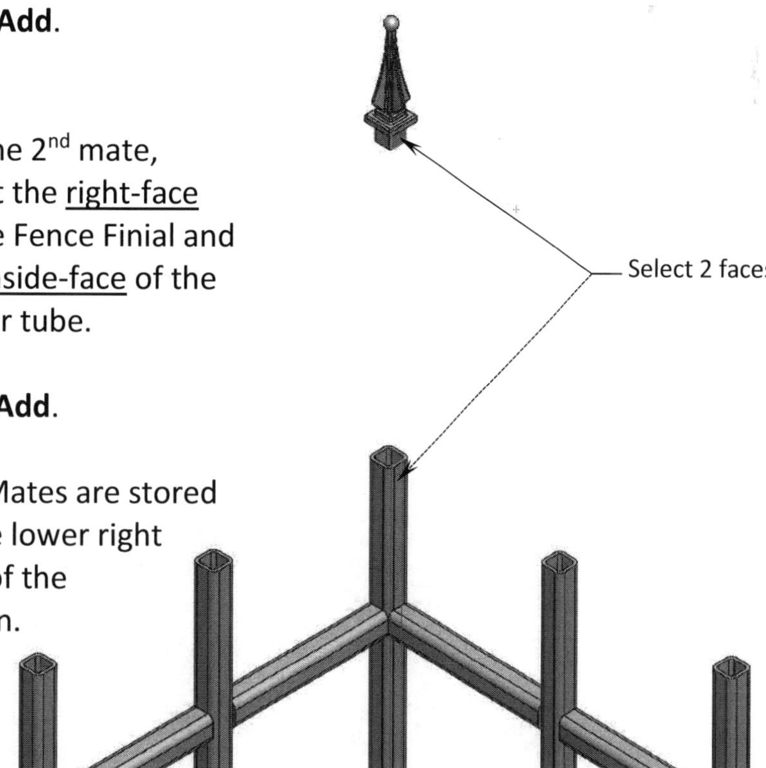

Click **Add**.

The Mates are stored at the lower right side of the screen.

For the 3rd mate, select the <u>bottom-face</u> of the Fence Finial flange and the <u>top-face</u> of the center tube.

The **Coincident Mate** is selected automatically.

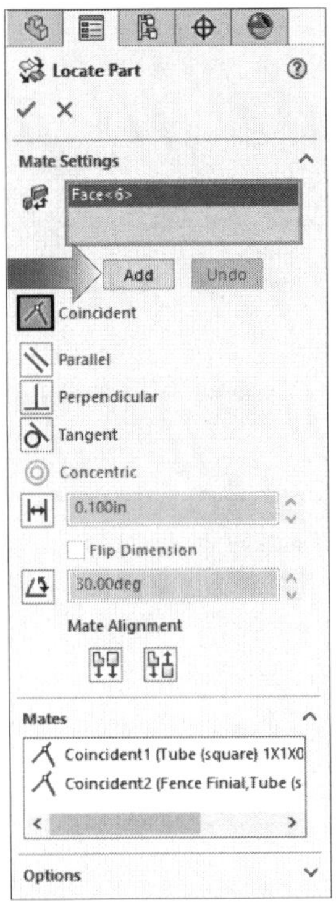

Click **Add**.

The Fence Finial is now fully positioned.
We can pattern it so that each tube will have one of its instances.

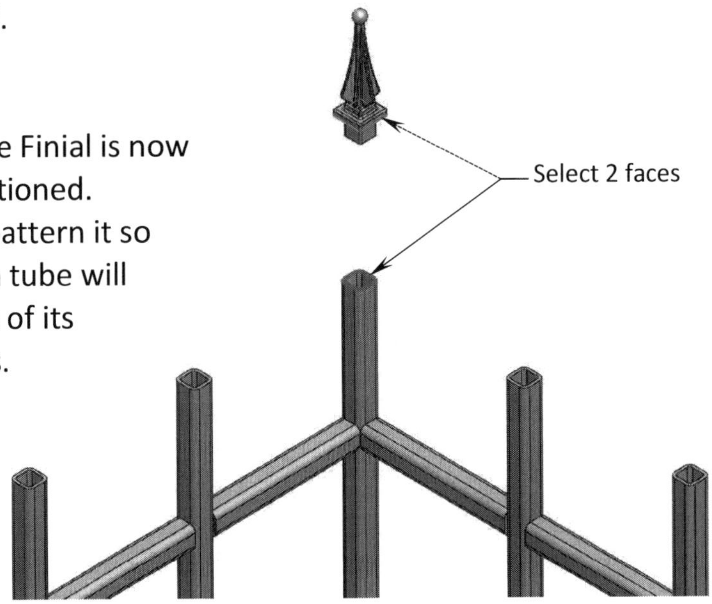

Inspect your weldments model against the image shown here.

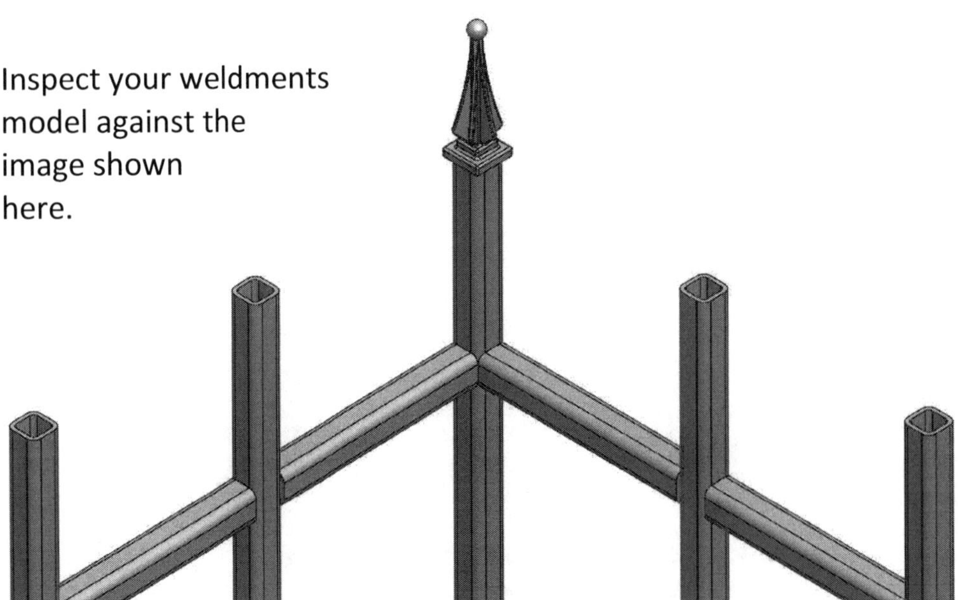

5. Patterning the Fence Finial:

The Fence Finial is a solid model, when insert into another part file it becomes a body of a multibody part.

Switch to the **Features** tab and click **Linear pattern**.

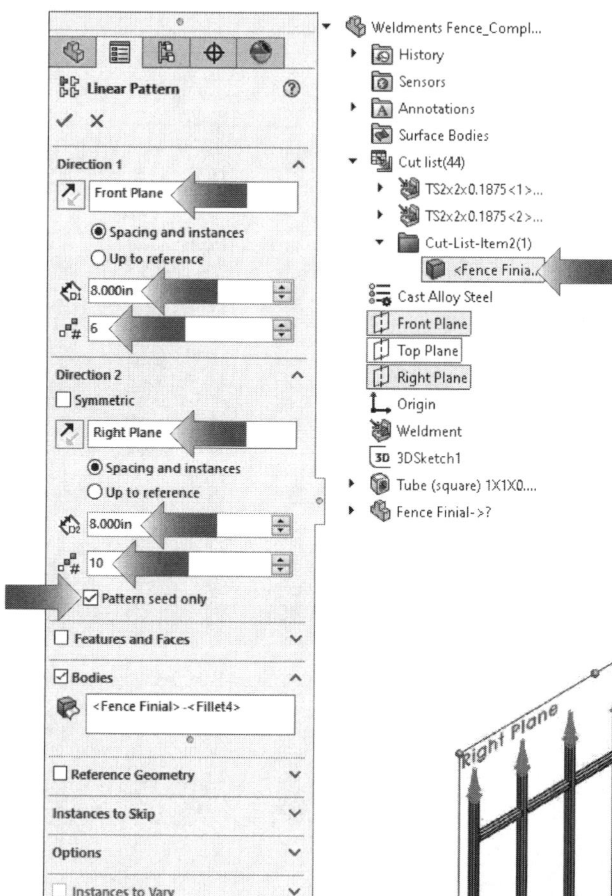

For Direction 1, select the **Front** plane from the FeatureManager tree.

For Spacing, enter **8.00in**.

For Number of Instances, enter **6**.

For Direction 2, select the **Right** plane from the FeatureManager tree.

For Spacing, enter **8.00in**.

For Number of Instances, enter **10**.

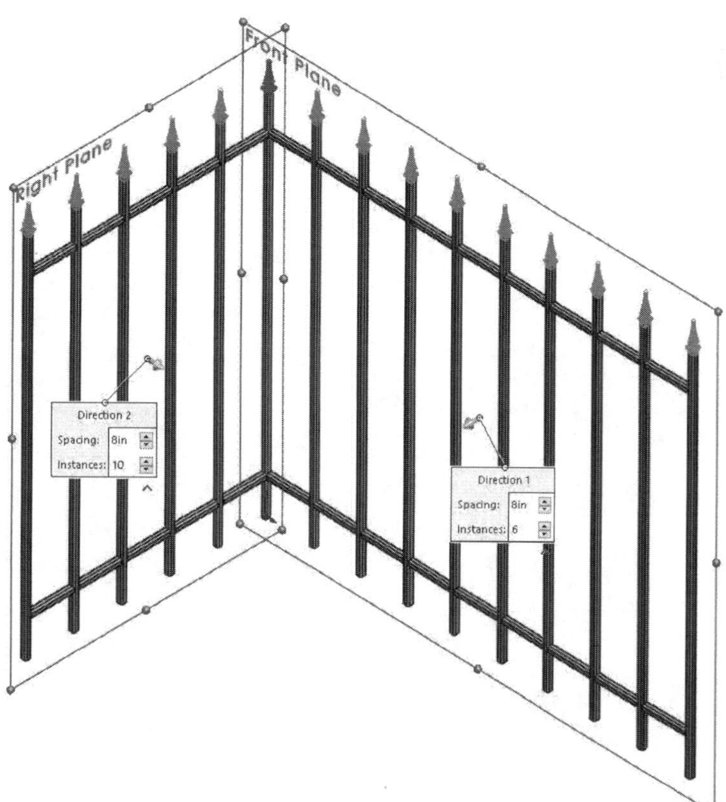

Enable the checkbox **Pattern Seed Only**.

For Bodies to Pattern select the **Fence-Finial** body from the Solid Bodies folder.

Click **OK**.

The multibody weldments part is completed.

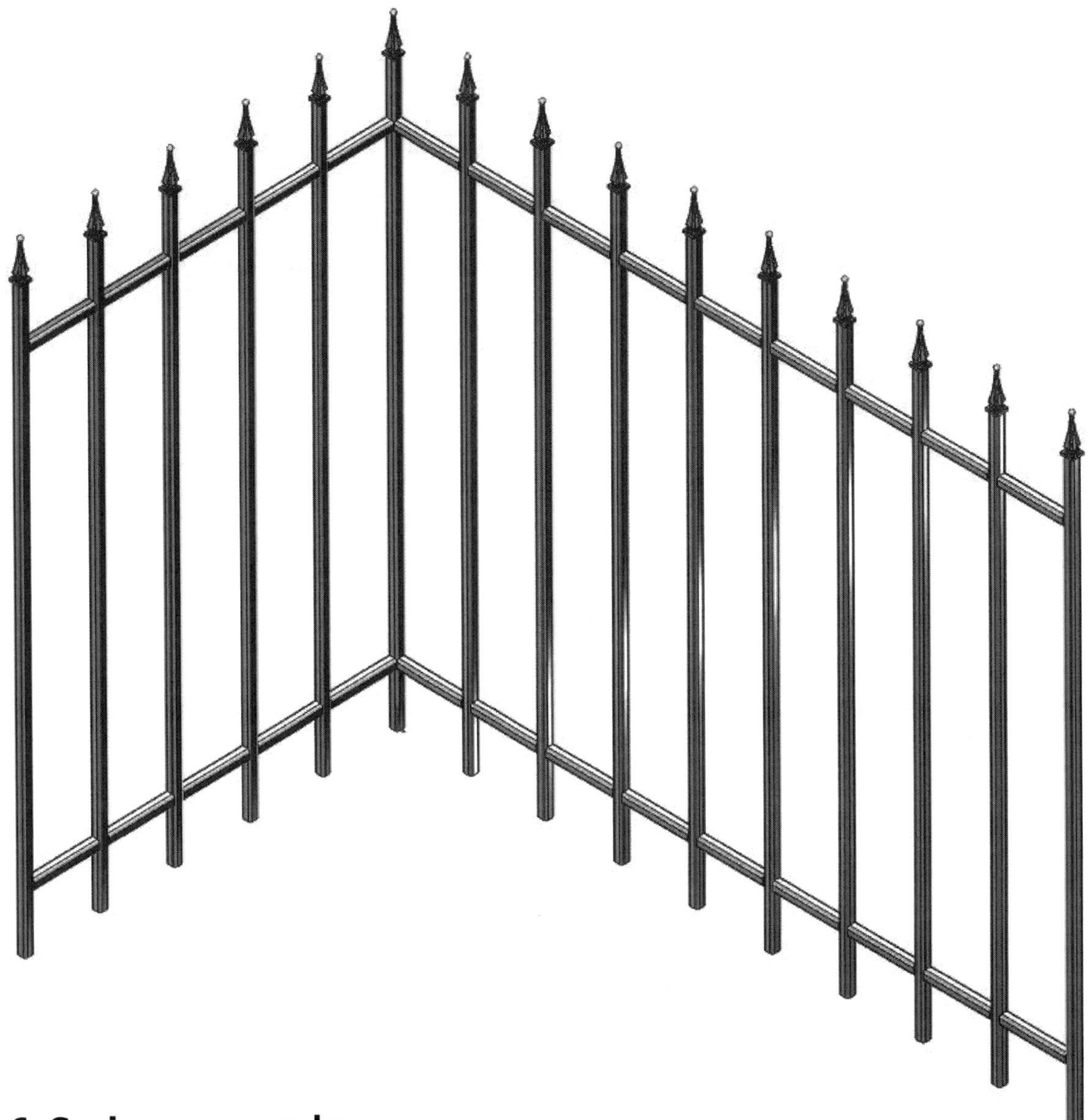

6. Saving your work:

Select **File, Save As**.

Enter: **Weldments Fence_Completed.sldprt**
for the file name.

Click **Save**.

Lesson 18: Weldment Cut List

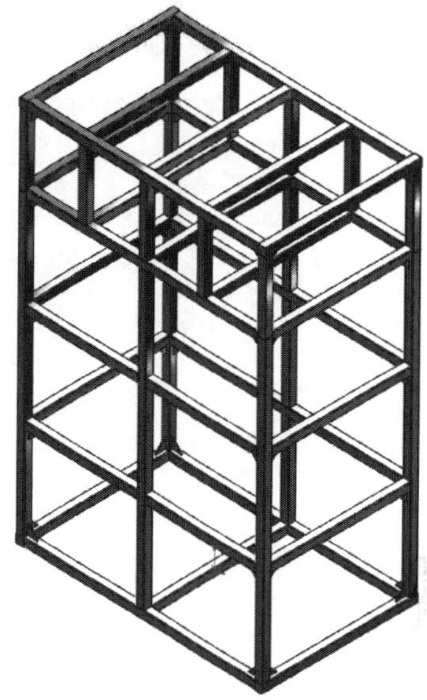

A weldment cut list table can be added to a drawing to display the cuts, or the welded structural shapes.

When the first weldment feature is inserted in a part, the **Solid Bodies** folder is renamed to **Cut List** to indicate the items to include in the cut list.

The icon next to the name Cut List indicates:

 This icon indicates that the cut list needs to be updated.

 This icon indicates that the cut list is up to date.

 This icon indicates Items that appear in the cut list must appear in the Cut list folder at the part level.

1. Opening a part document:

Browse to the Training Folder and open a part document named: **Weldments Cut List.sldprt**

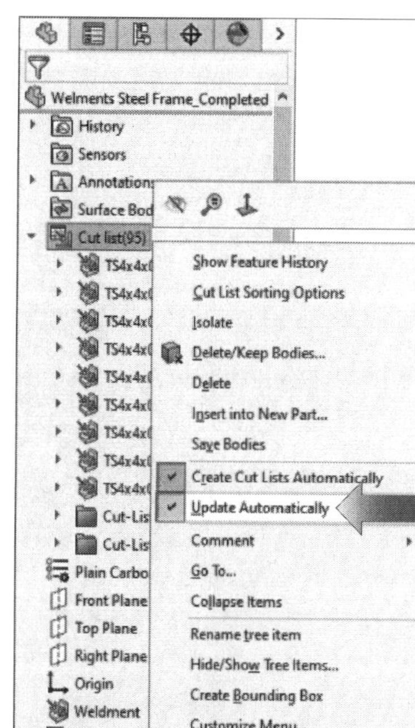

2. Updating the Cut List:

The Cut List can be preset to update automatically anytime a change occurs in the model.

Right-click the Cut List and enable: **Update Automatically**.

The icon next to the Cut List should change to **Up-To-Date** .

3. Viewing the structural member's properties:

Custom properties for cut lists are different from custom properties at the document level. In weldment parts, properties are included with cut list items created from structural members with library feature part profiles:

- LENGTH
- ANGLE1
- ANGLE2
- DESCRIPTION
- MATERIAL
- QUANTITY
- TOTAL LENGTH

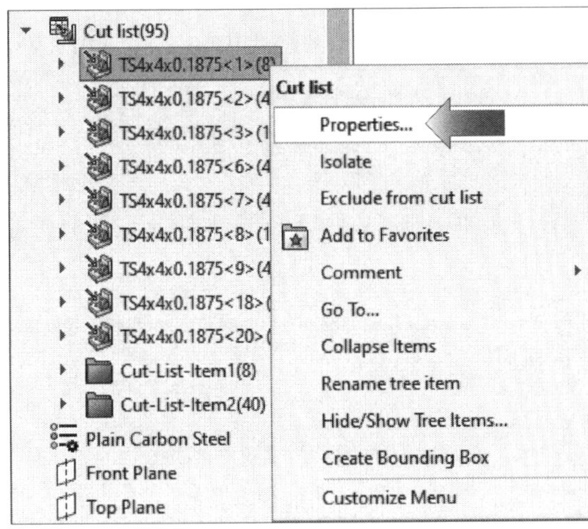

To view or edit any of the custom properties, right-click on one of the Weldment Items inside the Cut List and select **Properties**.

The existing Custom Properties for the selected item are displayed.

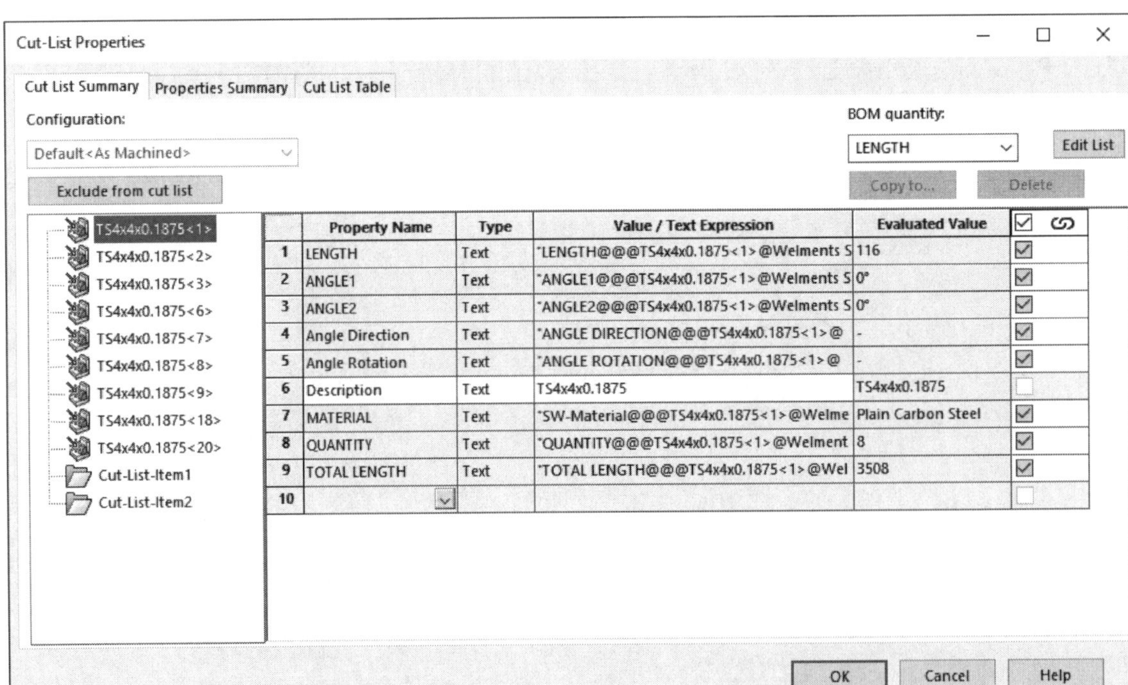

4. Renaming the folders:

The folders inside the Cut List should be renamed to what they hold inside of them.

The assigned names will be displayed in the Weldment Cut List Table later on, when a drawing is made from the weldment part.

For this lesson, we will only rename the last 2 folders to End Caps and Gussets. The others are just fine the way they currently are.

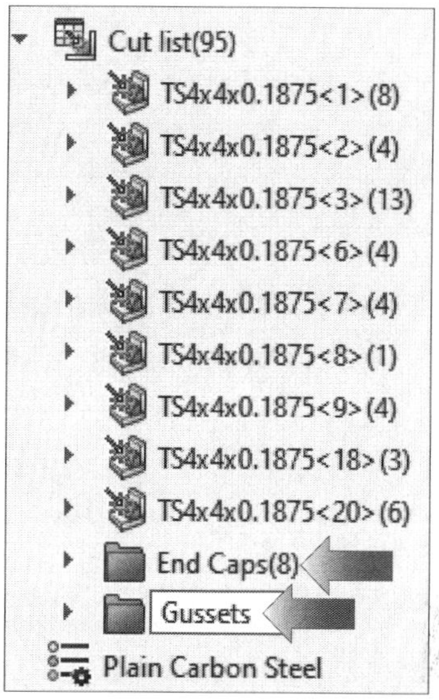

Slow-double-click on **Cut list Item1** and rename it to: **End Caps**.

Slow-double-click on **Cut list Item2** and rename it to: **Gussets**.

The number next to each cut list item represents the quantity, or number of items inside that folder.

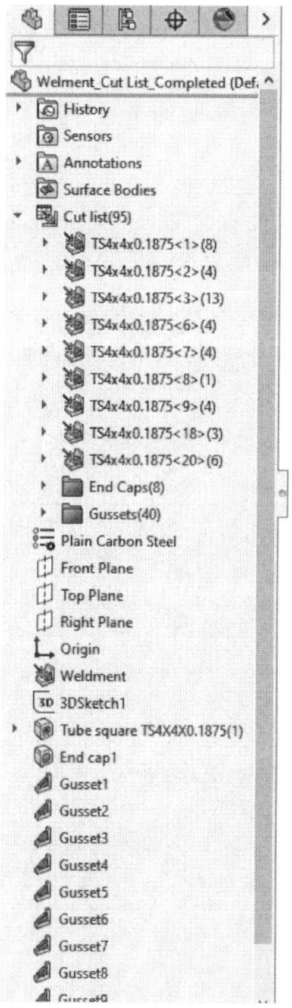

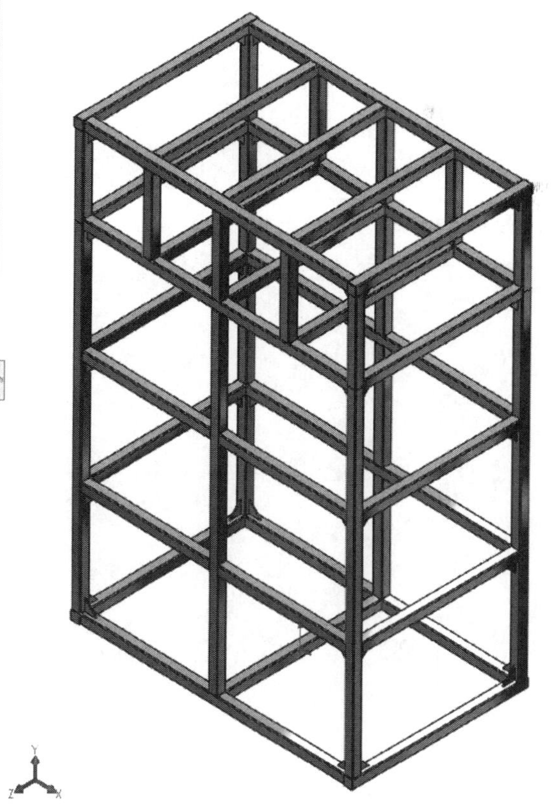

5. Viewing the End Cap's properties:

Right-click on the **End Caps** folder and select **Properties**.

There are only 2 Custom Properties that have been assigned to the End Caps so far.

The Material property was linked to the material of the part itself, and the Quantity property was linked to the number of items inside the folder.

We will add a couple more custom properties to this Cut List Item in the next few steps.

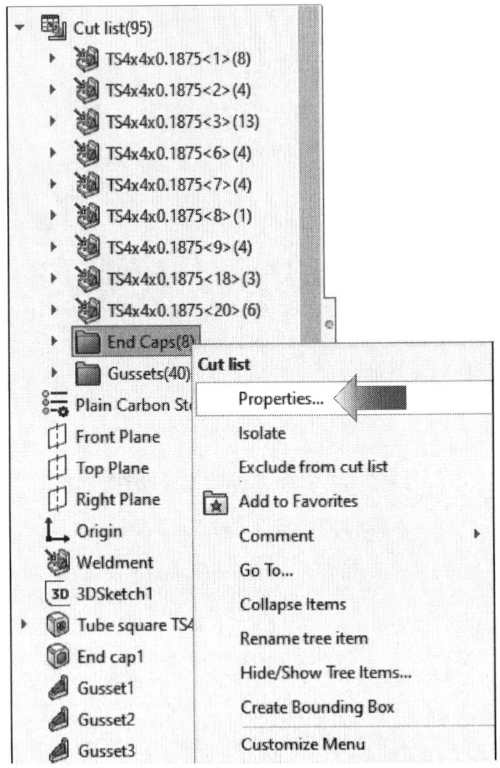

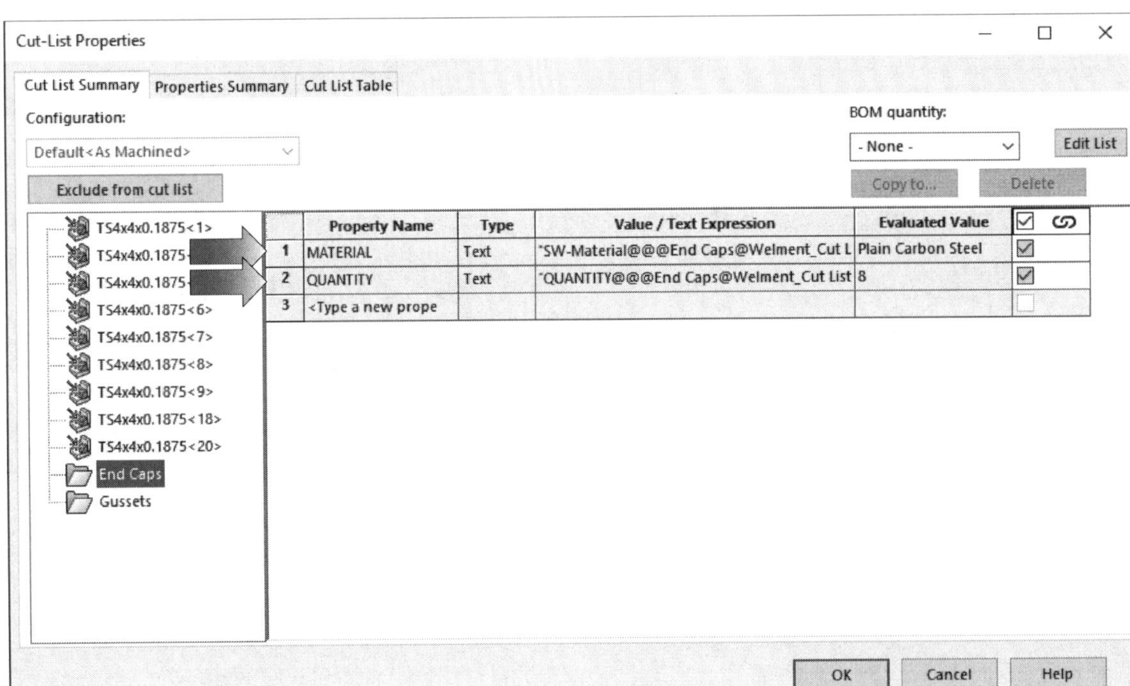

6. Generating a drawing from part:

Let us take a look at the Weldment Cut List Table in a drawing and review the information such as Description, Length, Quantity, Material, etc.

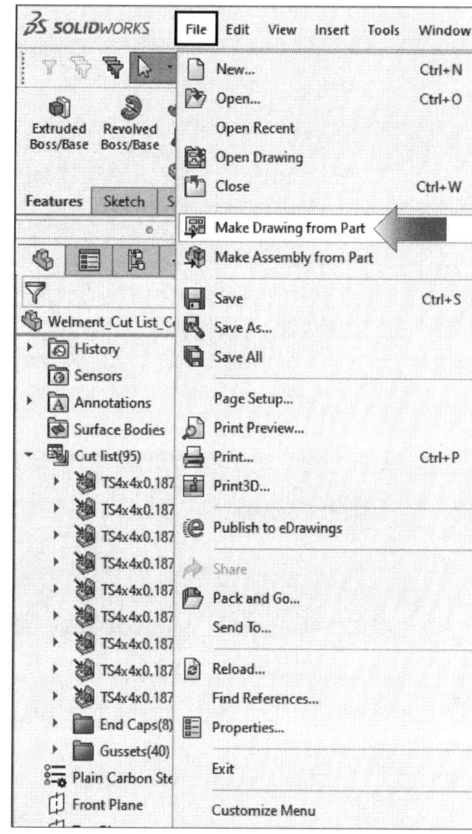

Select: **File, Make Drawing From Part**.

Select the following:

B-Size (ANSI) Landscape
3rd Angle Projection
Scale: 1:40

Click **OK**.

Drag/drop the **Isometric view** from the **View Palette**. This Weldment part already has an exploded view created.

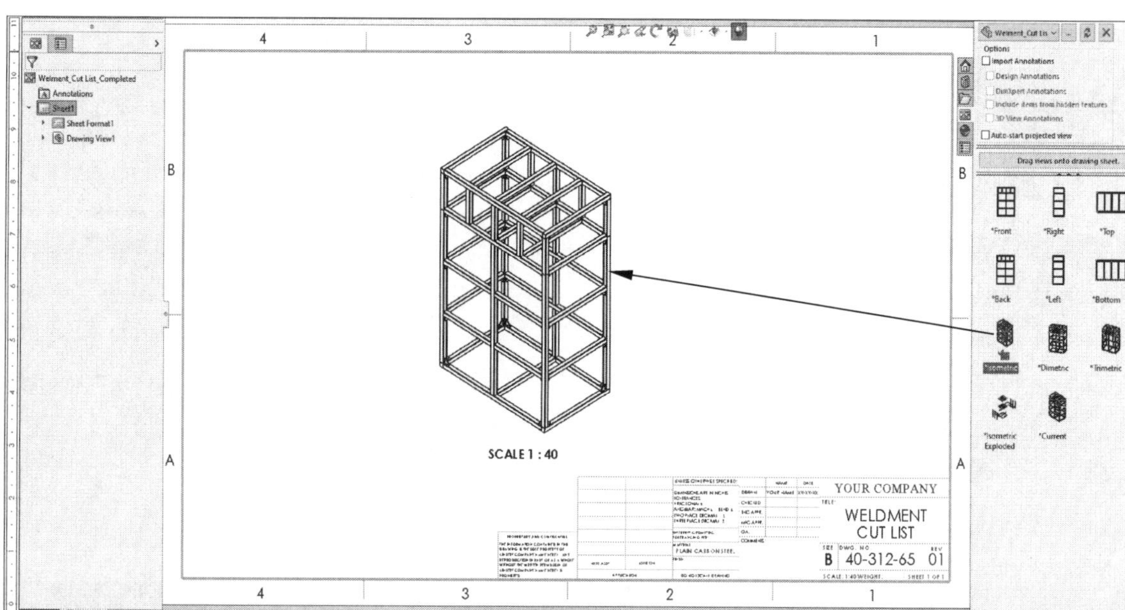

7. Inserting the Weldment Cut List:

Click the dotted border of the **Isometric** view and switch to the **Annotation** tab.

Select **Tables, Weldment Cut List**.

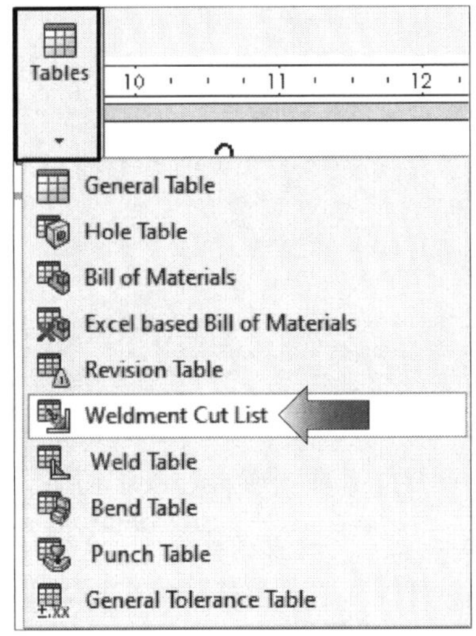

Click the **Green check** to accept the default Cut List Template and its parameters.

A Weldment Cut List table is inserted into the drawing.

Items 1 thru 9 are automatically filled with Quantity, Description, and Length, but Item 10 and 11 are missing the information for Description and Length. We will need to return to the part-level and fill them in.

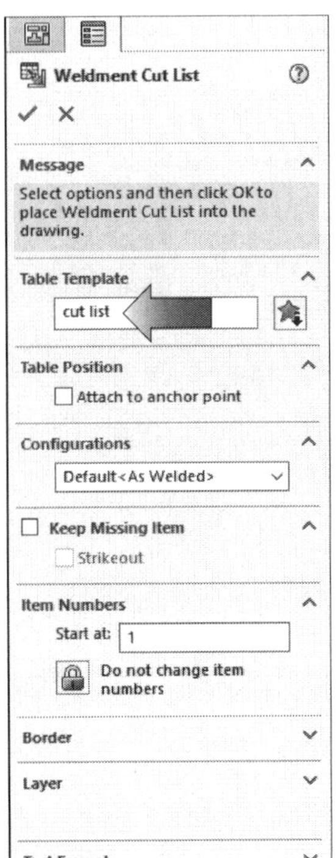

ITEM NO.	QTY.	DESCRIPTION	LENGTH
1	8	TS4x4x0.1875	116
2	4	TS4x4x0.1875	76
3	13	TS4x4x0.1875	68
4	4	TS4x4x0.1875	56
5	4	TS4x4x0.1875	142
6	1	TS4x4x0.1875	140
7	4	TS4x4x0.1875	34
8	3	TS4x4x0.1875	44
9	6	TS4x4x0.1875	32
10	8		
11	40		

Push **Control + Tab** to switch back to the Weldment part, or select: **Windows, Weldment Cut List**.

At the part-level, expand the Weldment Cut List.

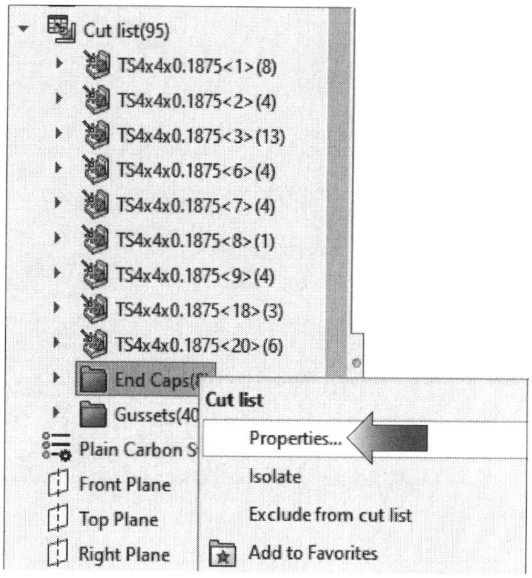

The Cut List contains 95 items and 11 folders. Each folder has the quantity number (XX) displayed next to its name.

Right-click the **End Caps** folder and select **Properties**.

For **Line 3**, under the Property Name, either select from the drop-down list, or enter: **DESCRIPTION**.

For Value, enter: **End Caps**.

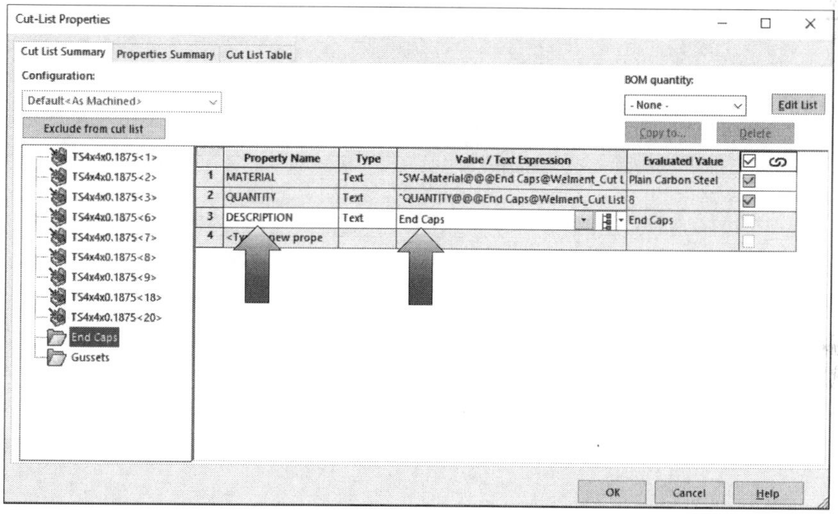

Move down to **Line 4**, under the Property Name, either select from the drop-down list, or enter: **LENGTH**.

For Value, enter: **3.8125x 3.8125x.25**

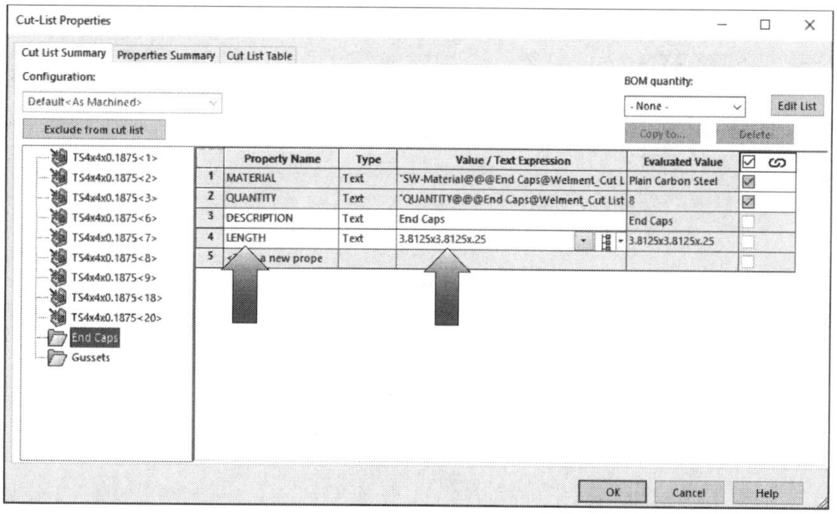

Click **OK**.

We will enter the same Custom-Properties for the Gussets.

Right-click the **Gussets** folder and select **Properties**.

For **Line 3**, under the Property Name, either select from the drop-down list, or enter: **DESCRIPTION**.

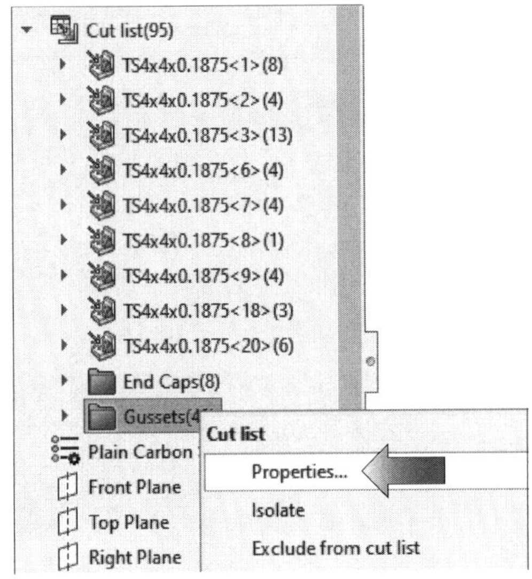

For Value, enter: **Gussets.**

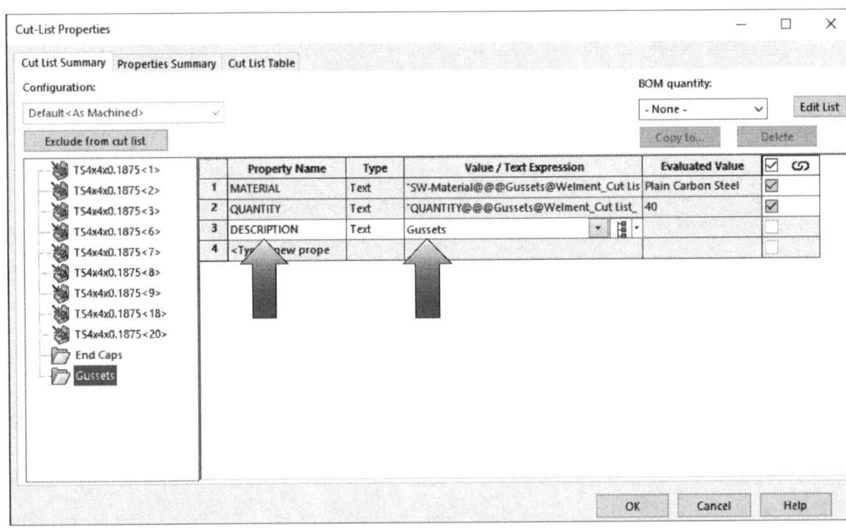

Move down to **Line 4**, under the Property Name, either select from the drop-down list, or enter: **LENGTH**.

For Value, enter: **5.0x5.0x.5**

Click **OK**.

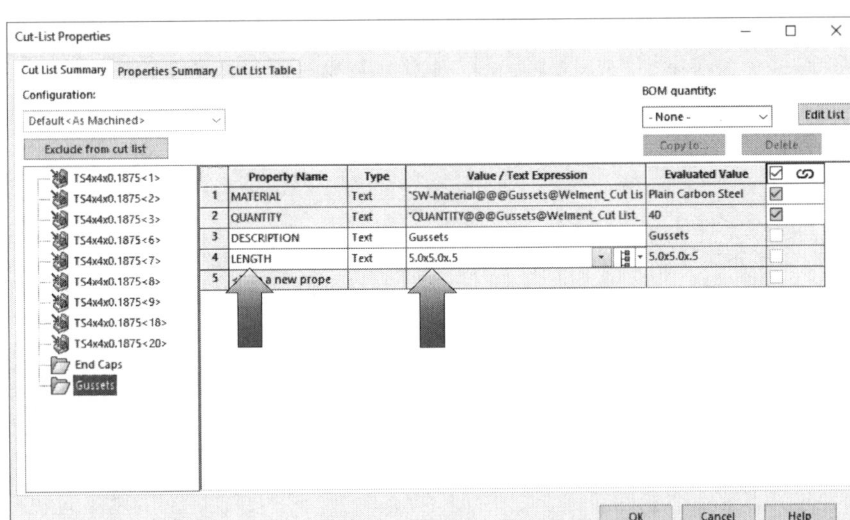

8. Populating the weldment cut list:

Push **<u>Control + Tab</u>** to switch back to the drawing (or select: Windows, Weldment Cut List.slddrw).

The Weldment Cut List Table is updated automatically and the information that was added to the End Caps and the Gussets are displayed in the table.

ITEM NO.	QTY.	DESCRIPTION	LENGTH
1	8	TS4x4x0.1875	116
2	4	TS4x4x0.1875	76
3	13	TS4x4x0.1875	68
4	4	TS4x4x0.1875	56
5	4	TS4x4x0.1875	142
6	1	TS4x4x0.1875	140
7	4	TS4x4x0.1875	34
8	3	TS4x4x0.1875	44
9	6	TS4x4x0.1875	32
10	8	End Caps	3.8125x3.8125x.25
11	40	Gussets	5.0x5.0x.5

Place the Weldment Cut List Table above the Title Block, as shown below.

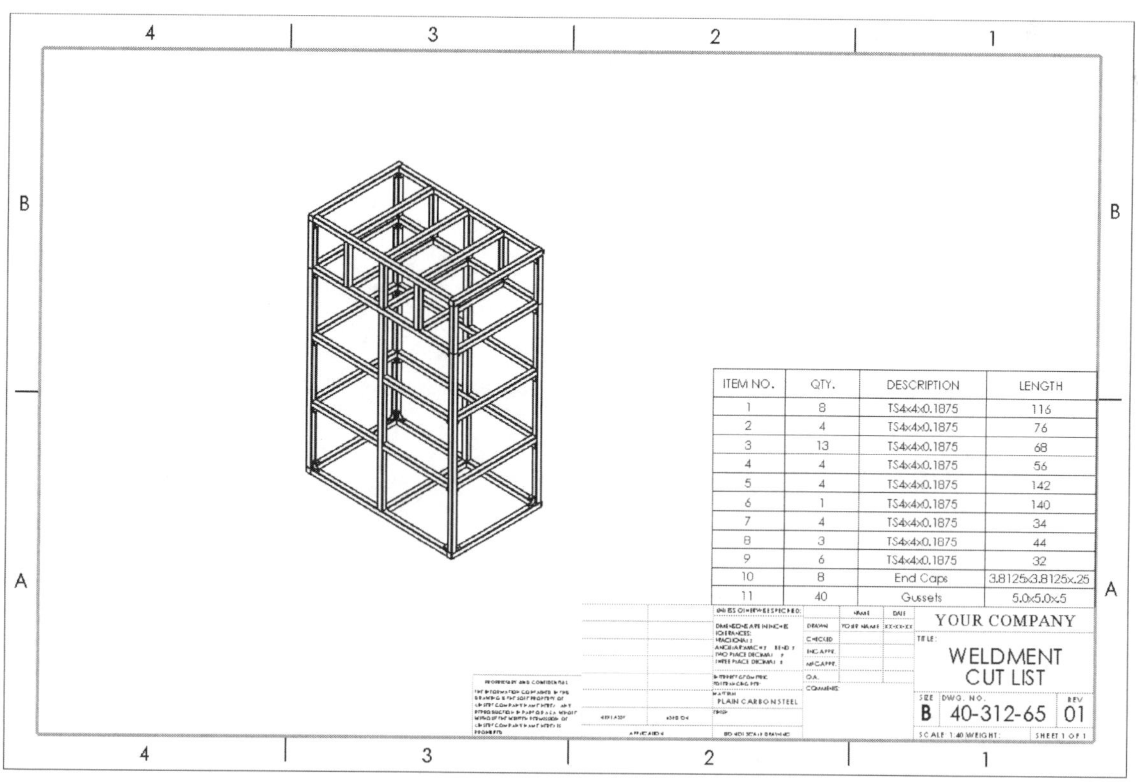

9. Showing the exploded view:

To enhance the clarity of the assembly drawing and also to help eliminate some of the confusion, we will show the exploded view and label the Weldment Items with the balloons that matched the items numbers in the Weldment Cut List Table.

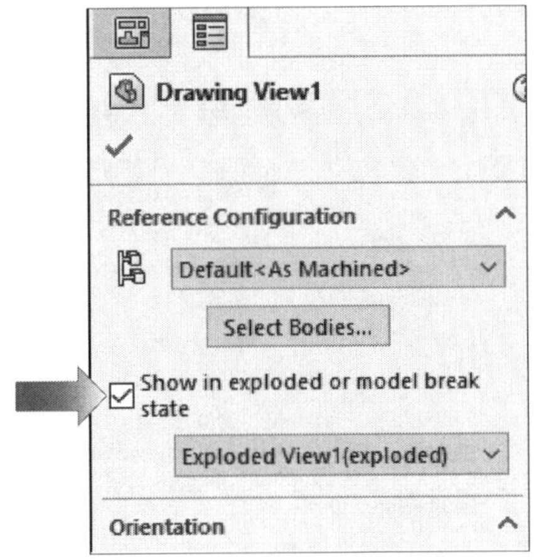

Click the dotted-border of the **Isometric view**.

Enable the checkbox: **Show in Exploded or Model Break State**.

Click **OK**.

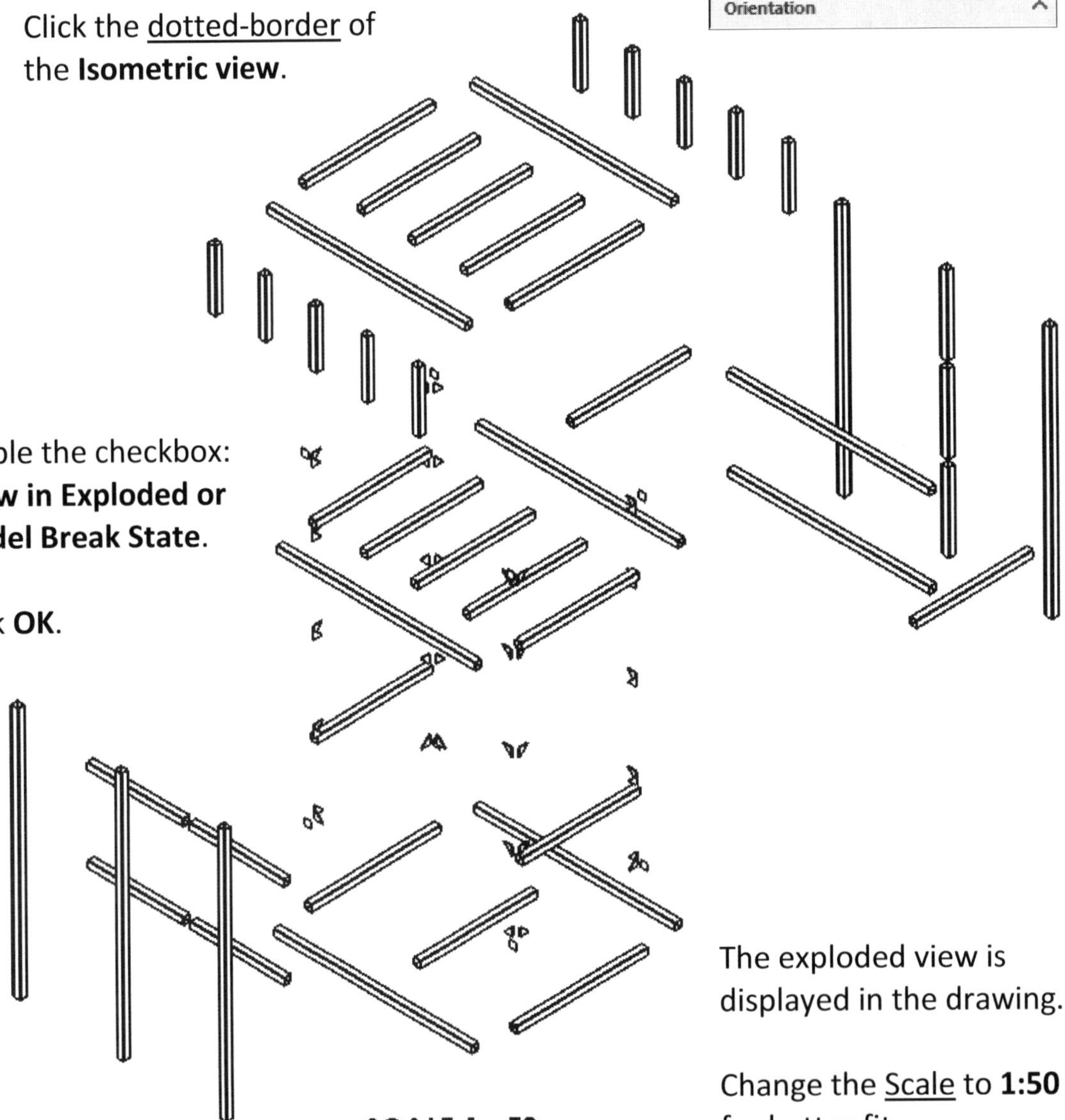

SCALE 1 : 50

The exploded view is displayed in the drawing.

Change the Scale to **1:50** for better fit.

10. Adding Balloons:

Click the dotted-border of the **Isometric view** and switch to the **Annotation** tab.

Click **Auto-Balloon**.

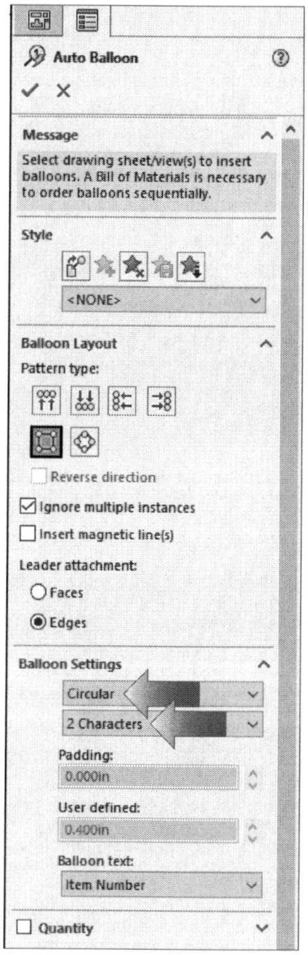

Select the following:

Square Layout **Circular** **2 Characters**

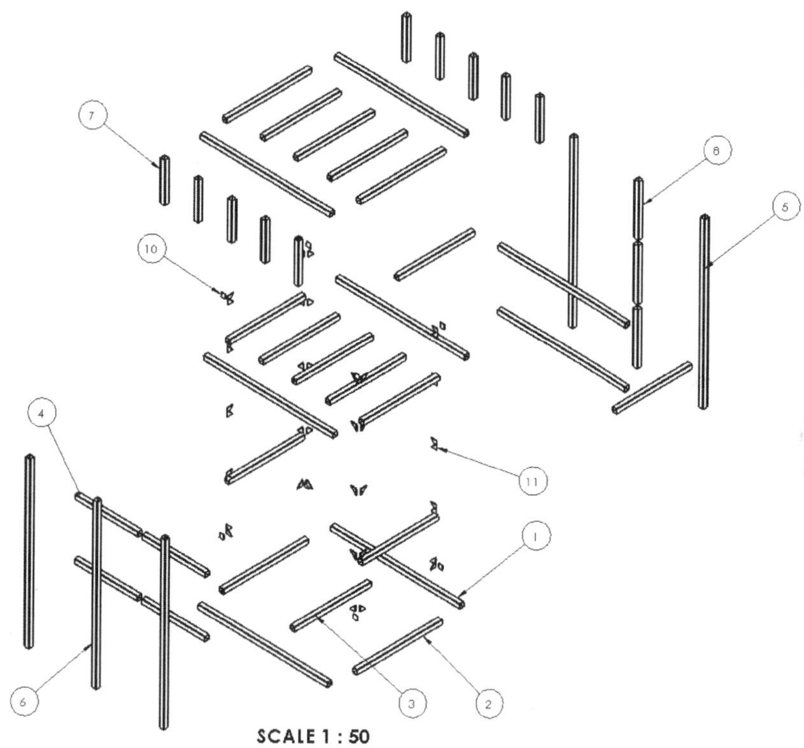

Click **OK**.

Rearrange the balloons so that they do not cross or overlap with each other.

Each item's quantity has already been displayed in the Weldment Cut List Table; we do not need to enable this option in the balloon's settings.

Drag/drop another instance of the **Isometric view** into the drawing.

Change the scale of this view to **1:60**.

This view will show how the structural members are put together.

In reality, these structural members will be welded together. The weld details are usually shown in a separate sheet of drawing, as a Configuration, where information such as weld type, material, location, etc., will be called out.

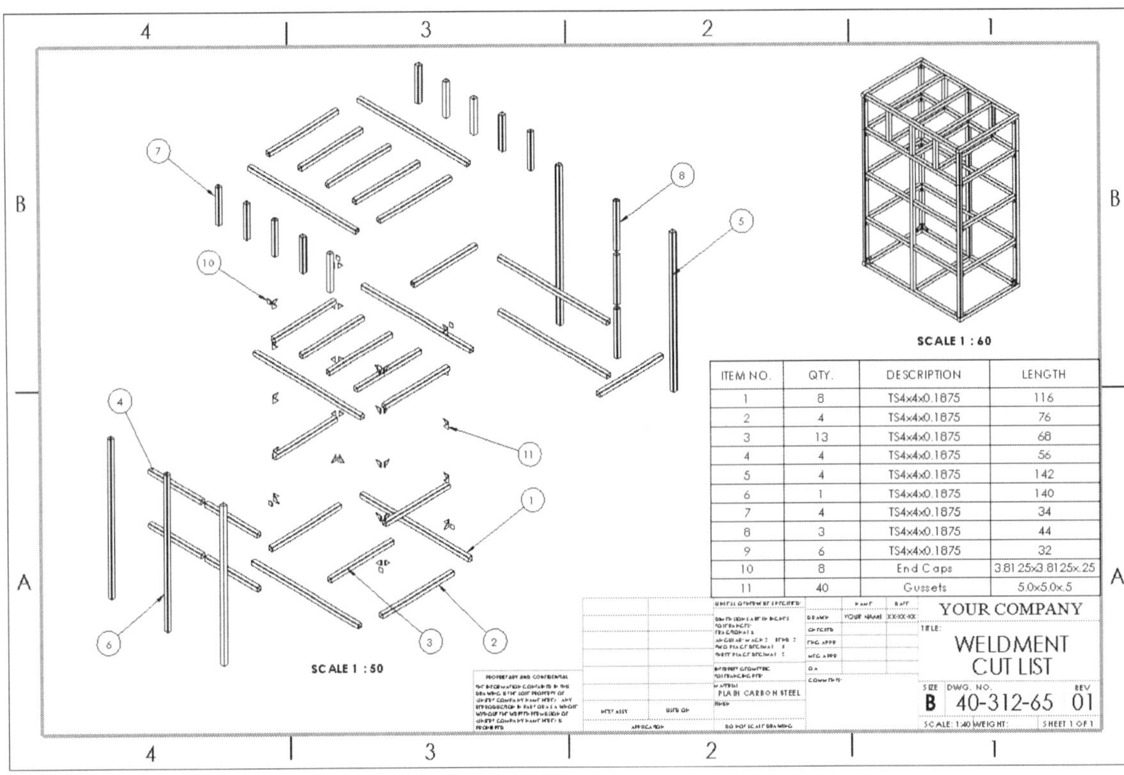

11. Saving your work:

Select **File, Save As**.

Enter: **Weldment Cut List_Completed** for the file name.

Click **Save**.

Lesson 19: Certified SOLIDWORKS Professional Sheet Metal Exam Preparation Materials

Challenge 1 – Convert to Sheet Metal

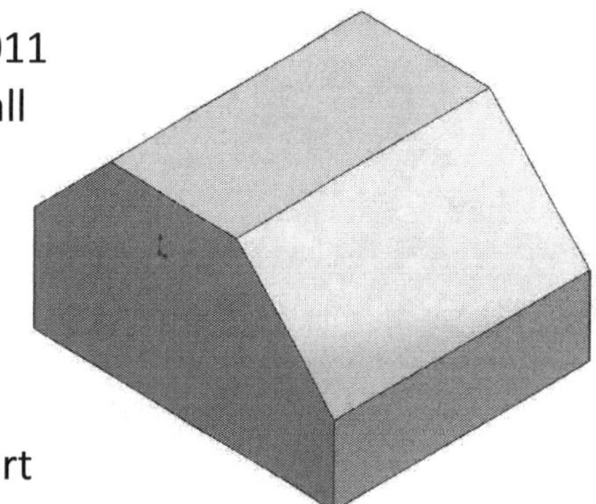

The CSWP-SM requires the use of SOLIDWORKS 2011 or newer. Exam length is 90 minutes to complete all 5 challenges. The minimum passing grade is 75%, and a 14 days waiting period for all re-tests.

1. Opening a part document:

Browse to the Training Folder and open a part document named: **Challenge 1_Convert to Sheet Metal**.

You will need to make a copy of this solid body and convert the copy into a sheet metal part that wraps perfectly around the original body.

2. Making a copy:

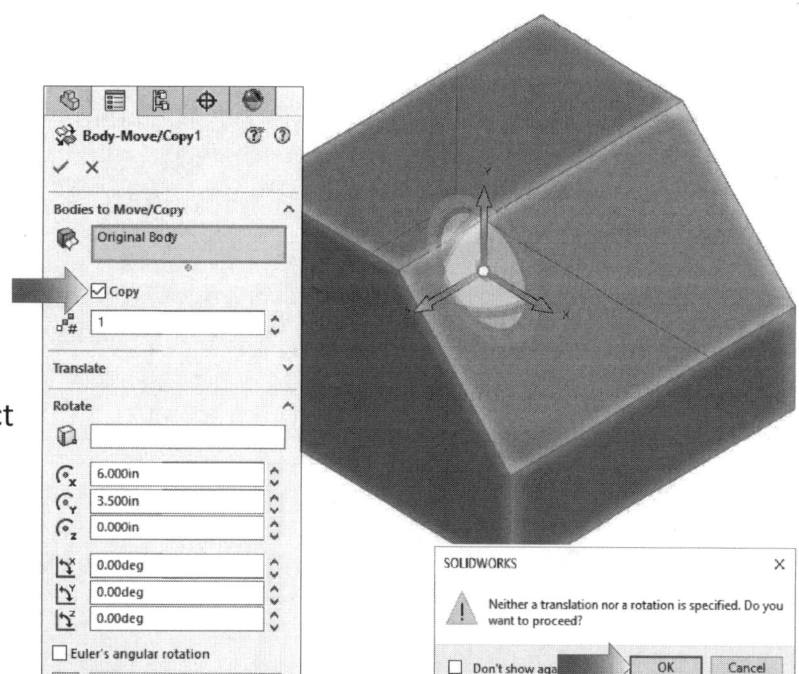

Click **Move/Copy Bodies** or select: Insert **Features, Move/Copy Bodies**.

For Bodies to Move/Copy, select the original body.

Enable the **Copy** checkbox

Click **OK** twice.

3. Converting to Sheet Metal:

For clarity, Hide the original body.

Switch to the **Sheet Metal** tab and click **Convert to Sheet Metal**.

For Fixed Face, select the Top face of the part.

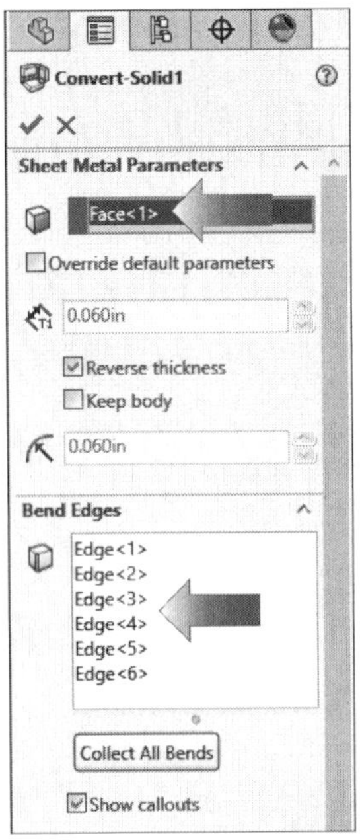

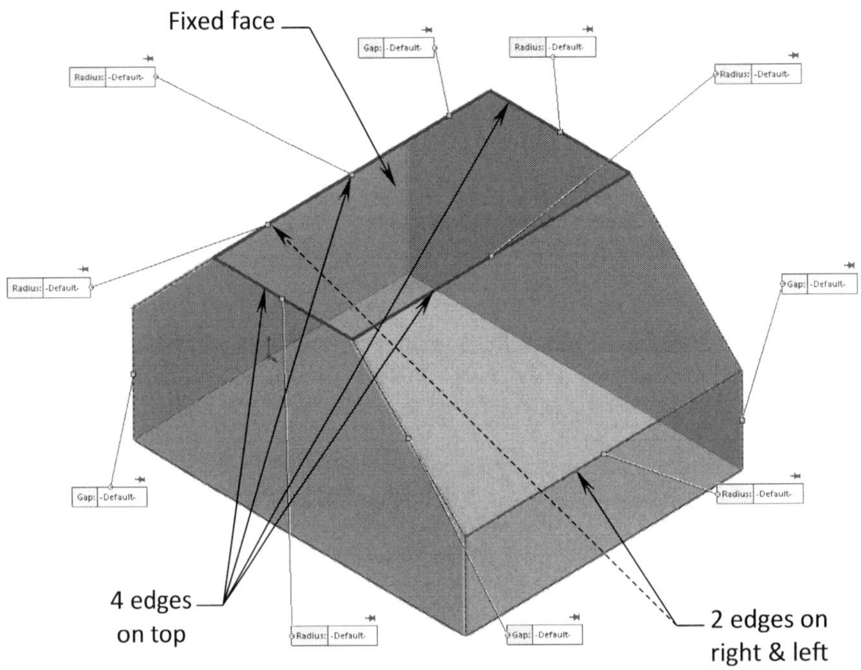

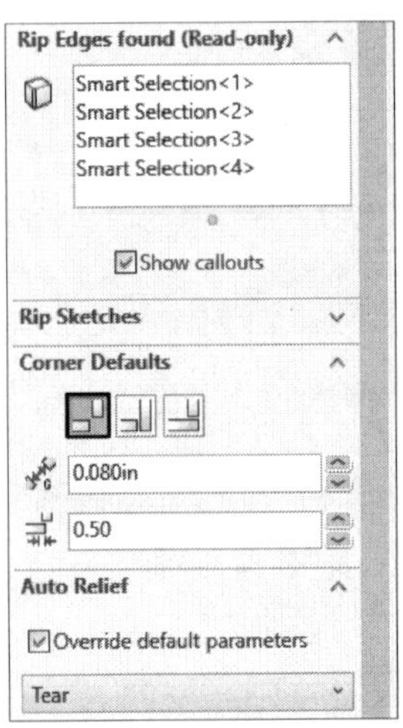

For Thickness, enter: **.060in.**, Bend Radius: **.060in**.

Click **Reverse Thickness**. (not overlap with original body).

For Bend Edges, select 4 edges on the **top** of the part and 2 edges on the **right** and **left** sides, or 6 edges total.

For Corner Defaults, click: **Open Butt**.

Gap: **.080in.**, Ratio: **0.50**

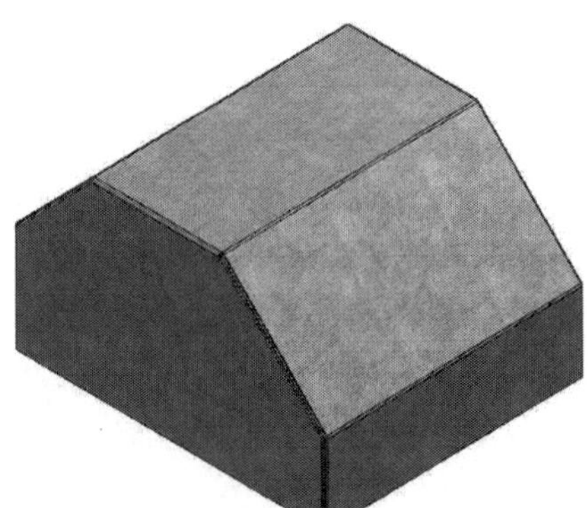

Auto Relief: **Tear**.

Click **OK**.

4. Measuring the horizontal length:

Show the Original body.

Select the Converted body and click **Flatten**.

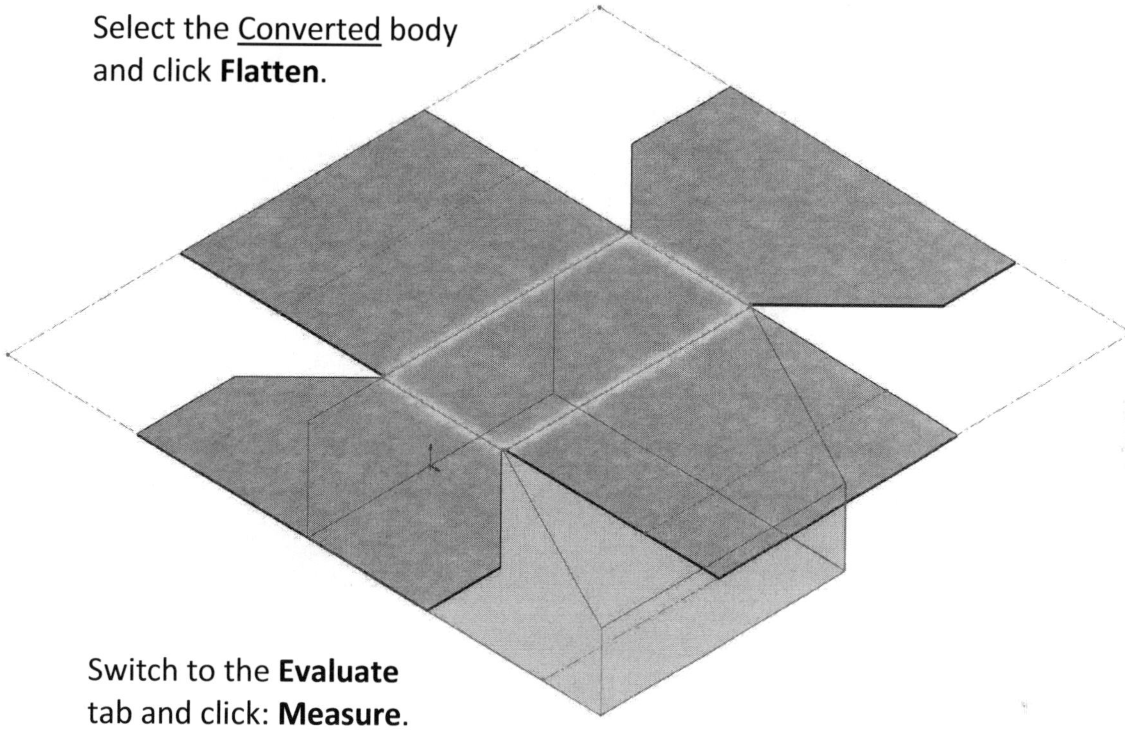

Switch to the **Evaluate** tab and click: **Measure**.

Select the horizontal line and enter the length here:

_______________ in.

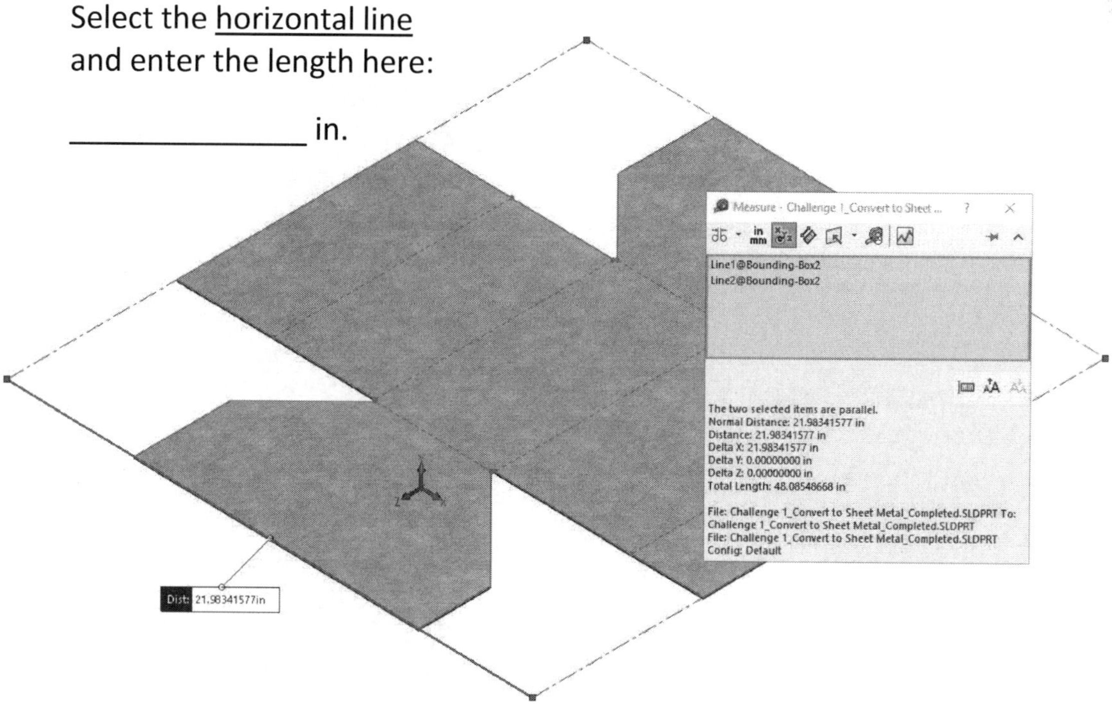

5. Calculating the mass:

The material **Galvanized Steel** has already been assigned to the part.

Select the <u>Converted</u> body and click:
Mass Properties on the **Evaluate** tab.

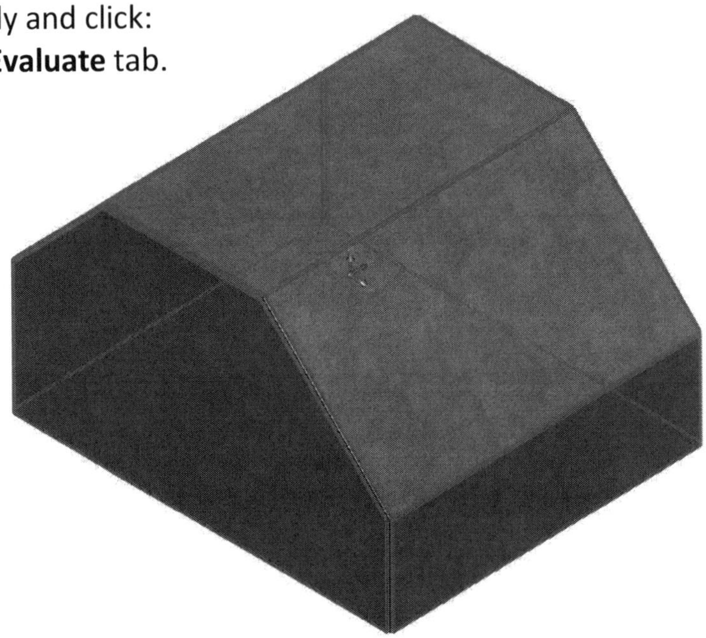

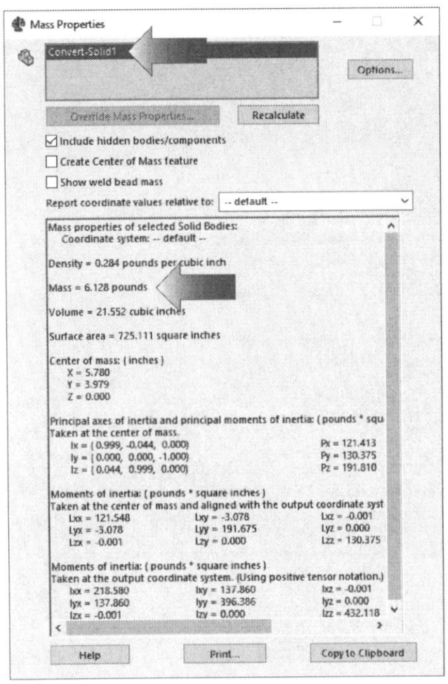

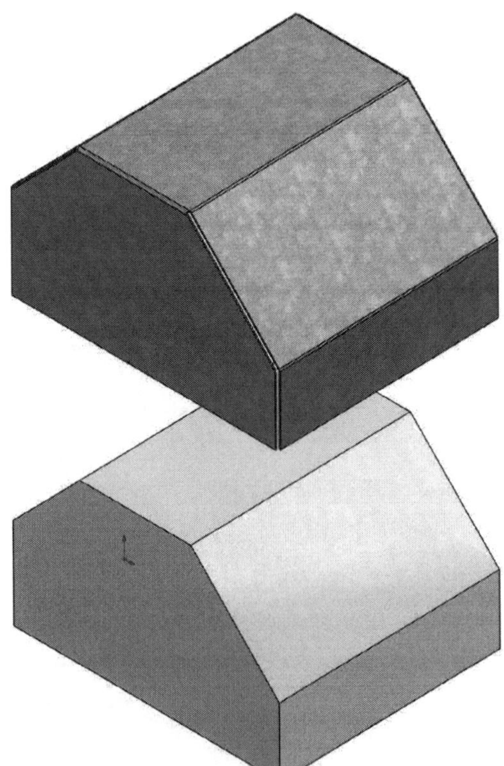

Locate the **mass** of the Converted body and enter it here:

____________________lbs.

6. Saving your work:

Select **File, Save As.**

Enter: **Challenge 1_Completed** for the file name.

Click **Save.**

CSWP-SM: Certified SOLIDWORKS Professional Sheet Metal Exam Preparation Materials

Challenge 2 – Sheet Metal Modifications

This challenge will test your skills on making changes to the sheet metal parts. You are expected to navigate through the design history to find the correct features and dimensions and apply the changes.

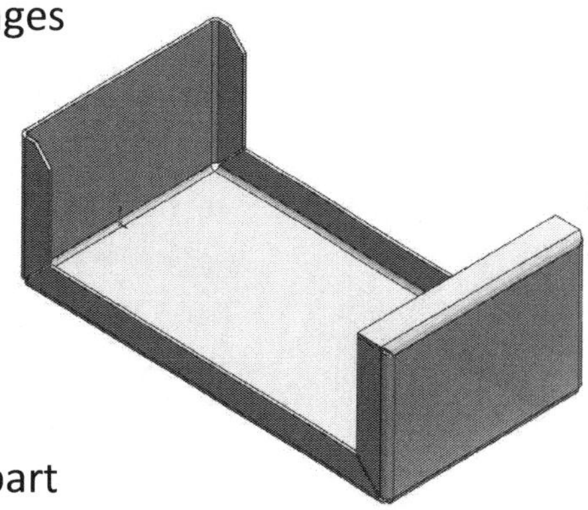

1. Opening a part document:

Browse to the Training Folder and open a part document named: **Challenge 2_Modifications**.

2. Showing the dimensions:

Right-click on the **Annotations** folder and enable:

* **Display Annotations**

* **Show Feature Dimensions**

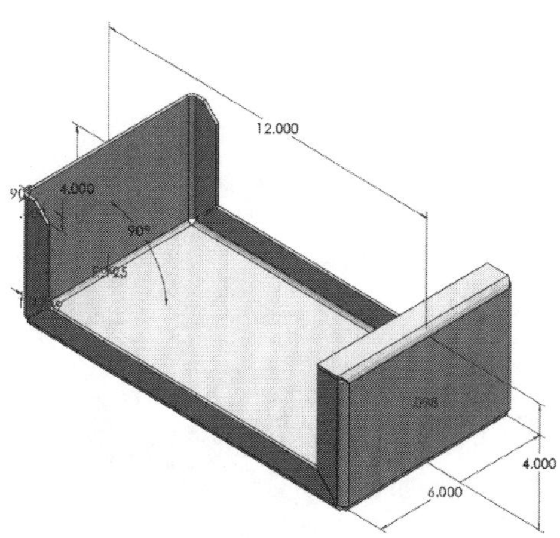

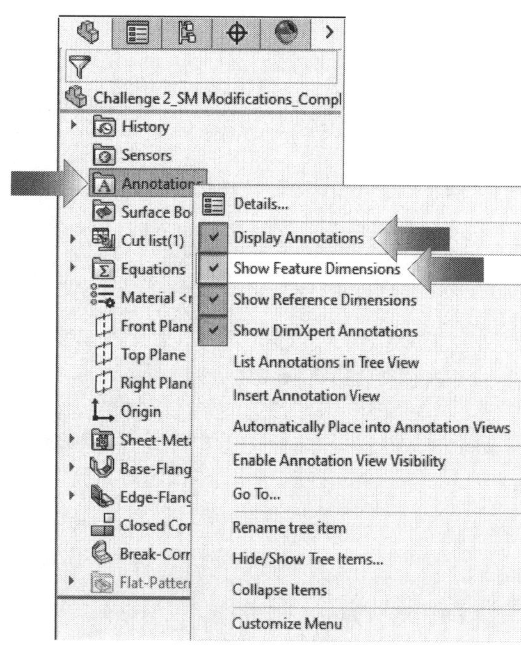

3. Modifying dimensions:

Change the circled dimensions as follows:

12.00 to **14.00**

90° to **120**°

4.00 to **3.00**

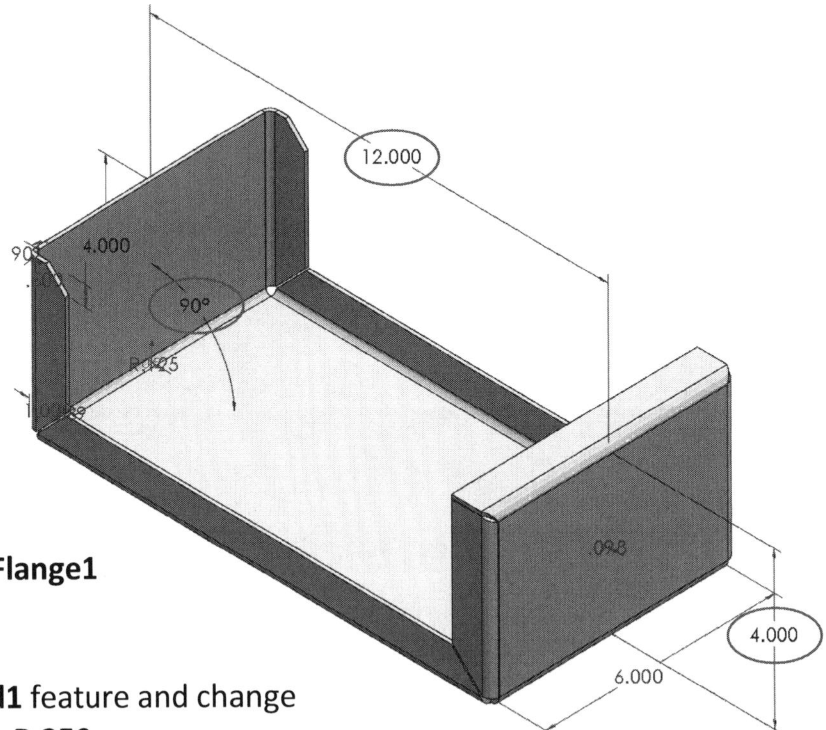

Click **Rebuild** to execute the changes and to refresh the model.

Expand the **Base-Flange1** feature.

Edit the **BaseBend1** feature and change the bend radius to **R.250**.

Edit the **BaseBend2** and change the bend radius to **R.250**.

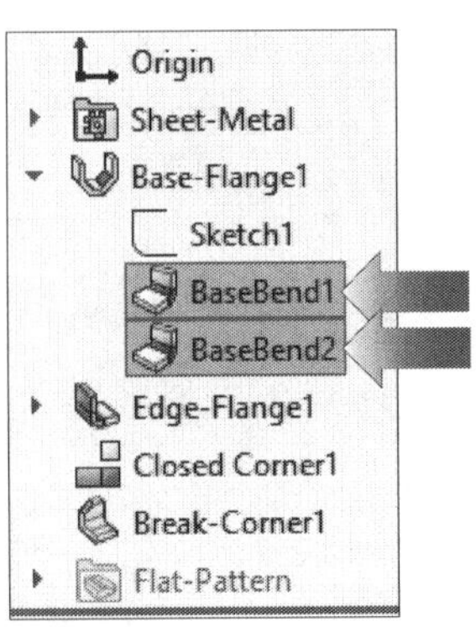

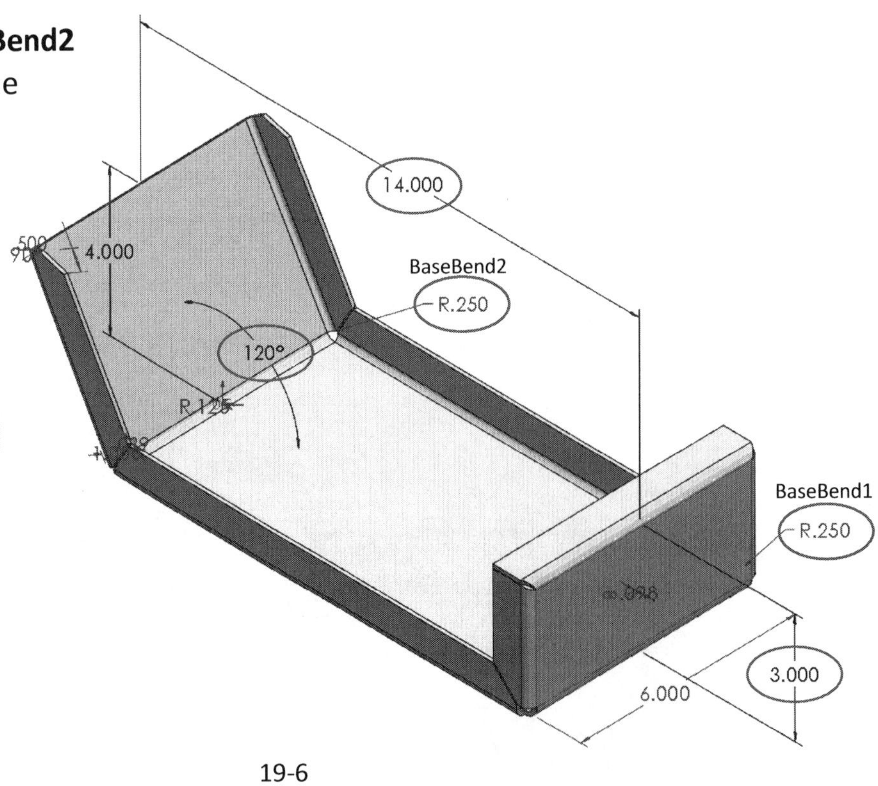

Click **OK**.
Click **Rebuild**.

Switch to the **Evaluate** tab.

Select **Mass Properties**.

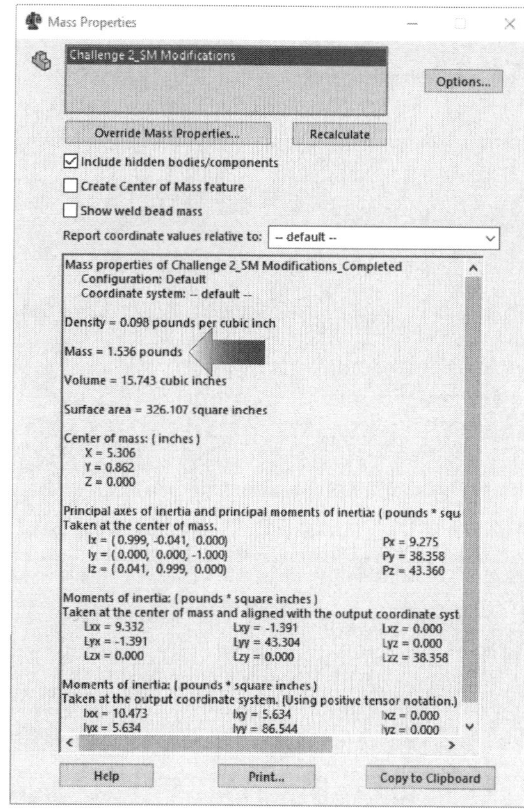

Locate the **mass** of the part and enter it below:

_______________ lbs.

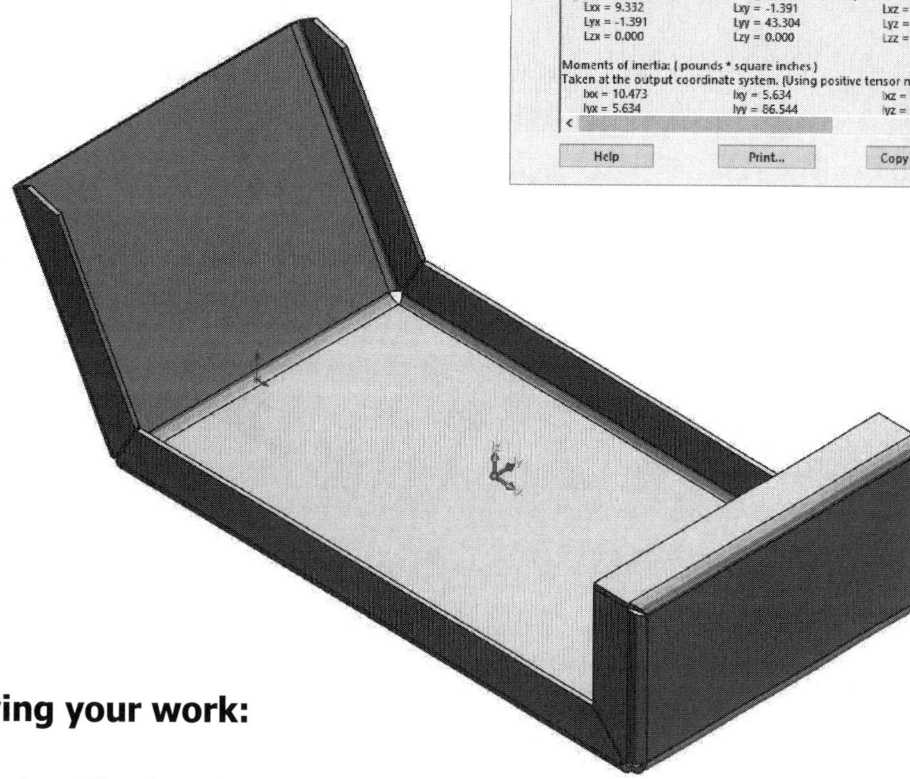

4. Saving your work:

Select **File, Save As**.

Enter: **Challenge 2_Completed** for the file name.

Click **Save**.

CSWP-SM: Certified SOLIDWORKS Professional Sheet Metal Exam Preparation Materials

Challenge 3 – Creating a Sheet Metal Part

This challenge will examine your skills on the creation of different flanges such as Base Flange, Miter Flange, Edge Flange, Hem, as well as applying one of the forming tools from the Design Library.

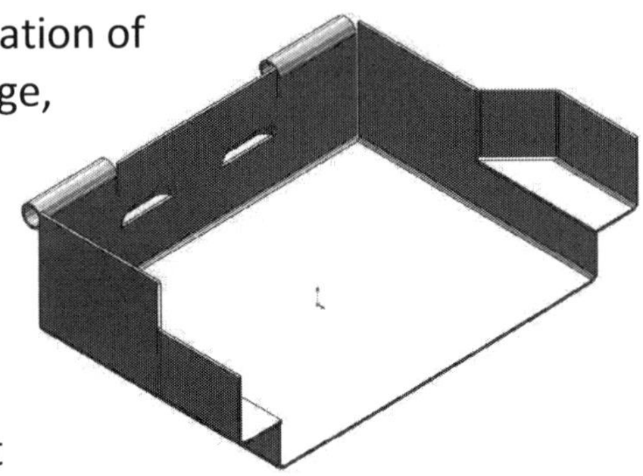

1. Creating a part:

This model is symmetrical about the Front plane. We will create the 1st half and mirror it towards the end of the design process.

Select the Top plane from the FeatureManager tree and open a **new sketch**.

2. Making the Base flange:

Sketch a **Corner Rectangle**.

Add the **Mid-Point** relation to center the line on top.

Add the vertical and horizontal dimensions to fully define the sketch.

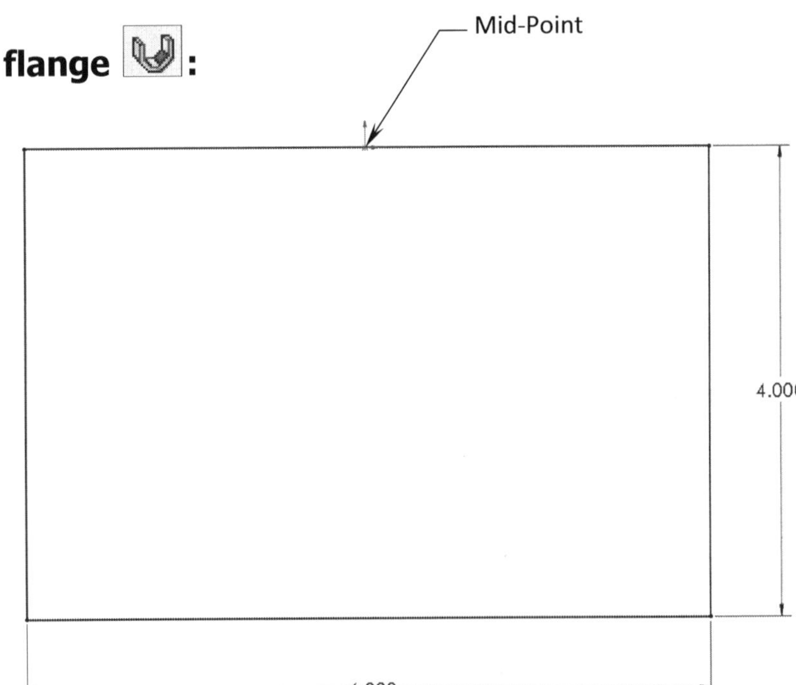

Switch to the **Sheet Metal** tab and click **Base Flange** .

Click **Use Gauge Table** and select **Sample Table – Aluminum.**

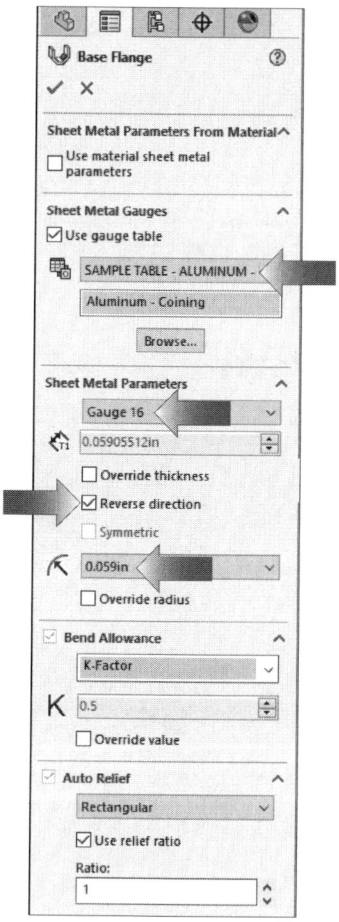

Gauge: **16** (.05905512in.)

Reverse Direction: **Enabled.**

Bend Radius: **.059in.**

K-Factor: **0.5**

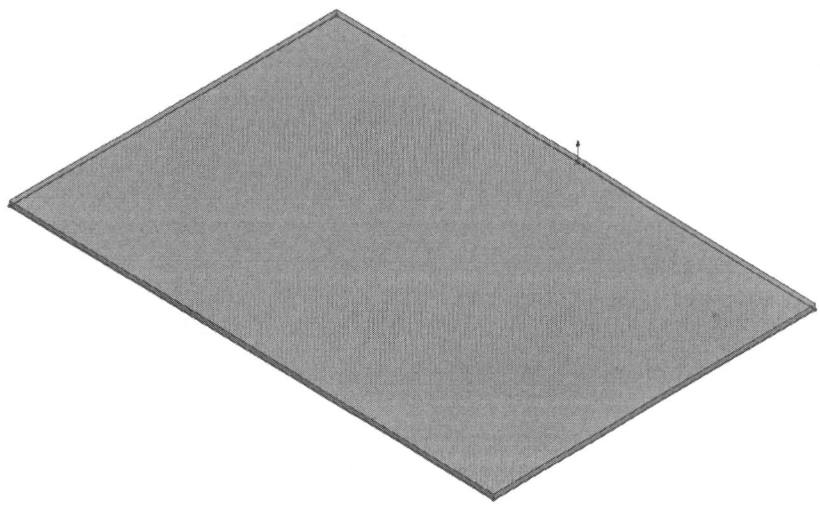

Auto Relief: **Rectangular**

Ratio: **1**

Click **OK.**

A base flange is the first feature in a new sheet metal part.

When a base flange feature is created, the part is marked as a sheet metal part. Bends are added wherever appropriate, and sheet metal specific features are added to the FeatureManager design tree.

3. Creating the Edge flanges :

Click **Edge Flange** on the **Sheet Metal** tab.

For Flange Parameters, select the **2 edges**, move the mouse cursor <u>upward</u> and click to lock the direction.

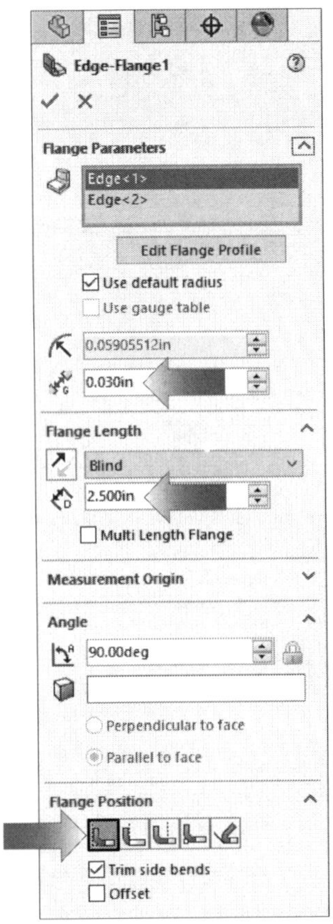

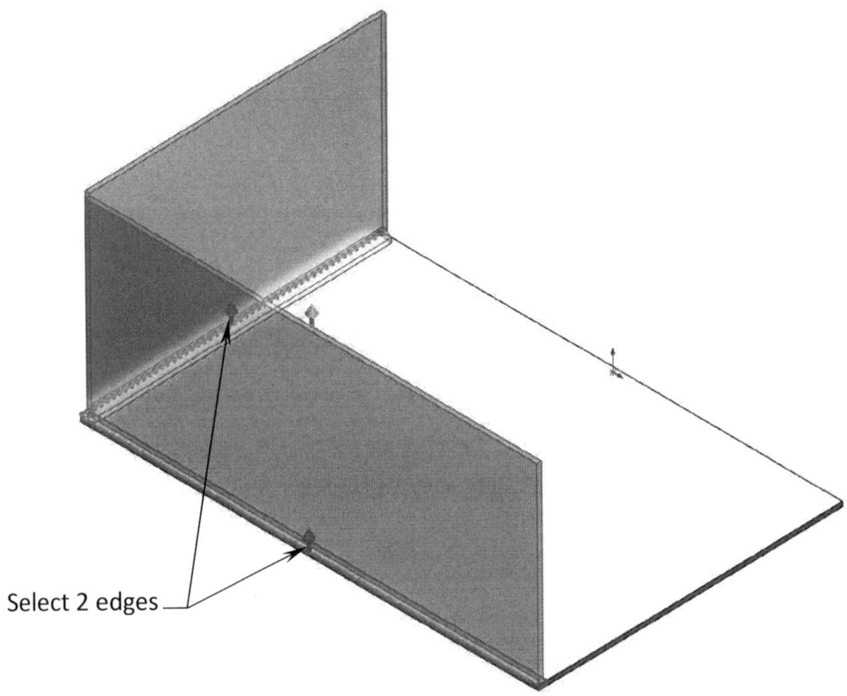

For gap, enter **.030in**.

For Flange Length, select **Blind** and enter **2.500in**.

Keep Bend Angle at **90.00deg**.

For Flange Position, select **Material Inside**.

Enable the **Trim Side Bends** checkbox.

Click **OK**.

4. Making a cut feature:

Select the <u>Front</u> plane and open a **new sketch**.

Sketch a **Rectangle**.

Add the **Coincident** relation as noted.

Add the height and width dimensions to fully define the sketch.

Switch to the **Sheet Metal** tab and click **Extruded Cut**.

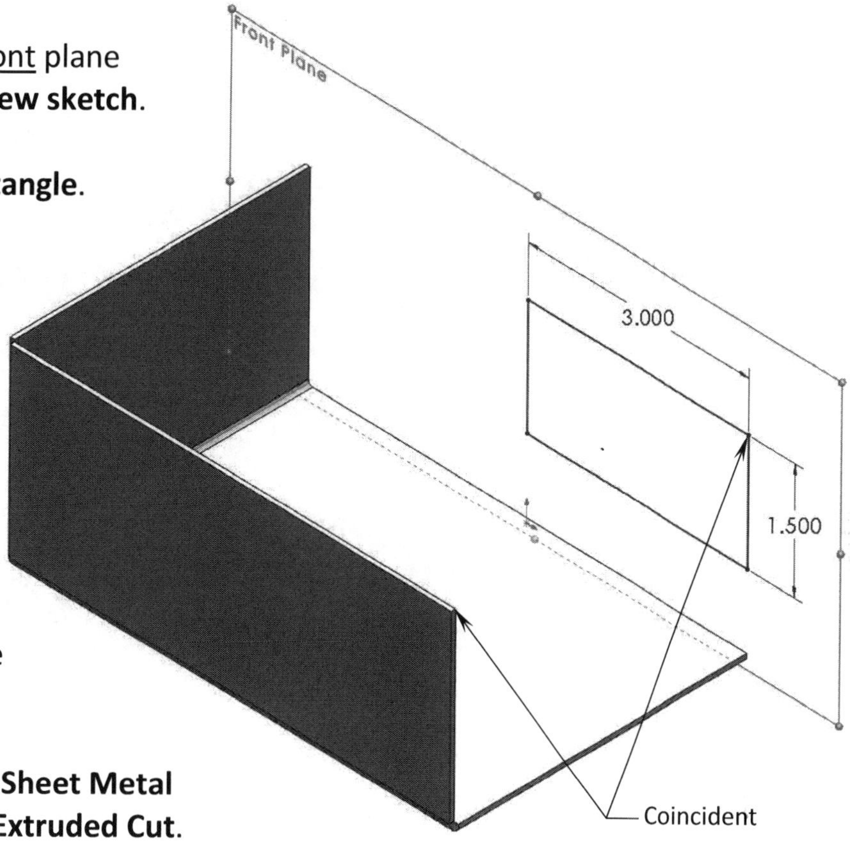

For Direction 1, select: **Through All** and click **Reverse**.

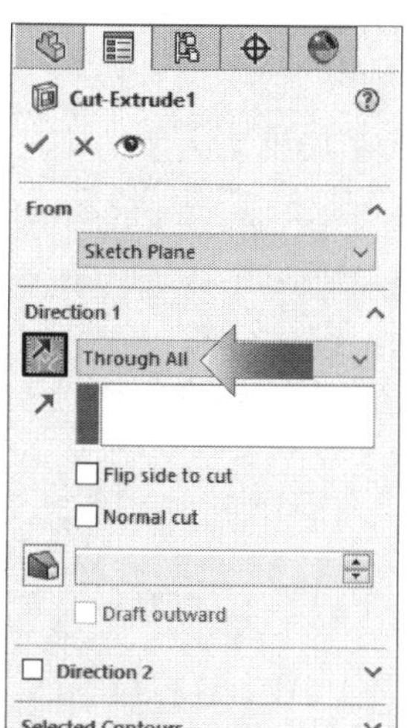

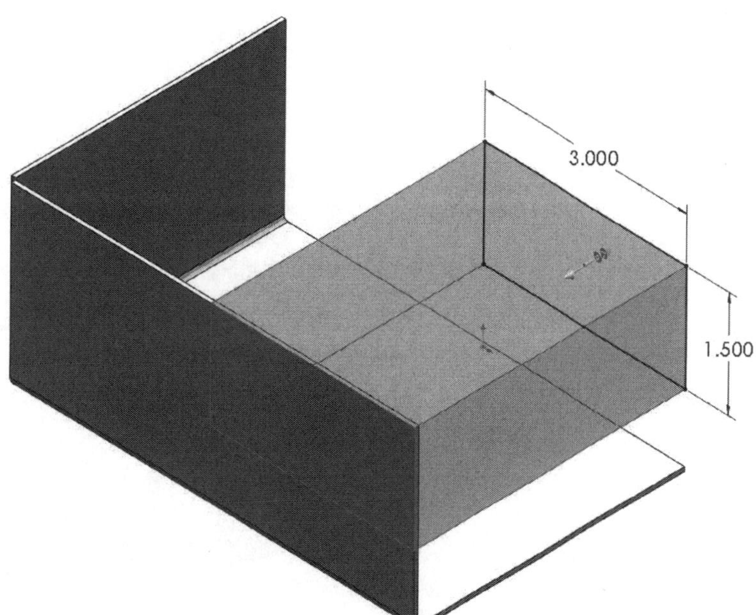

Click **OK**.

5. Creating a miter flange 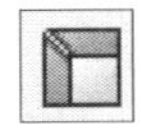 :

Select the top face of the part and open a **new sketch**.

Sketch **2 lines** starting from the outer edge of the flange.

Add the dimensions shown in the image.

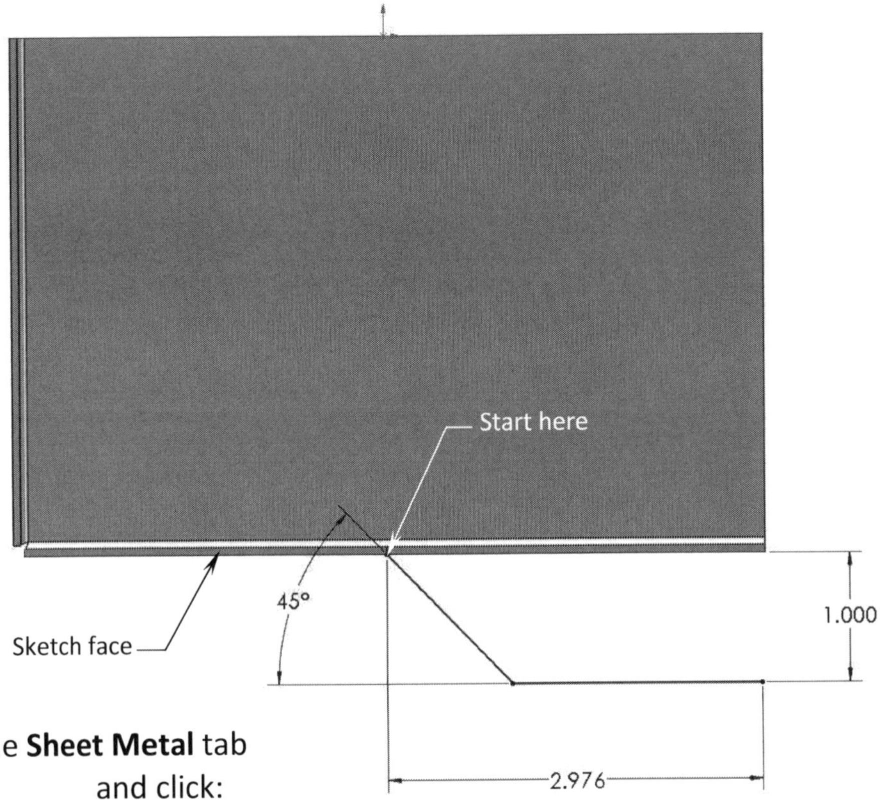

Switch to the **Sheet Metal** tab and click: **Miter Flange**.

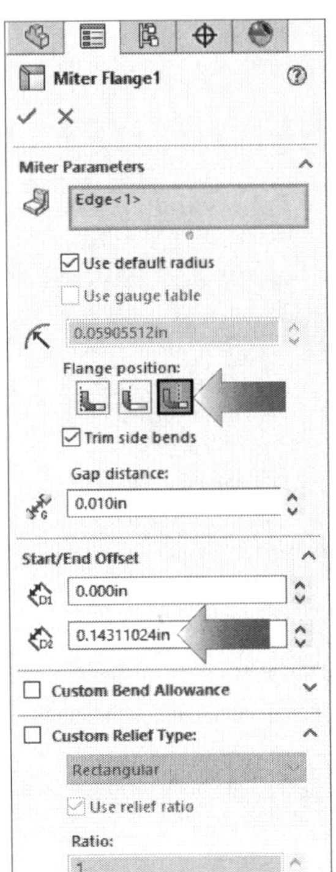

For Flange Position, select **Bend Outside**.

Enable the **Trim Side Bends** box.

Keep the Gap at **.010in**.

For End Offset Distance, enter: **.1431in**.

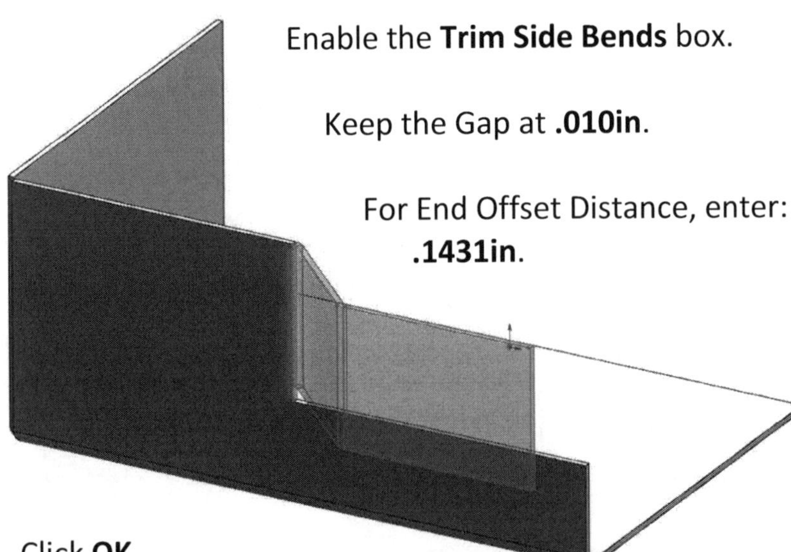

Click **OK**.

6. Adding an edge flange :

Select the bottom edge of the miter flange and click **Edge Flange**.

Move the mouse cursor over to the right and click to lock the direction.

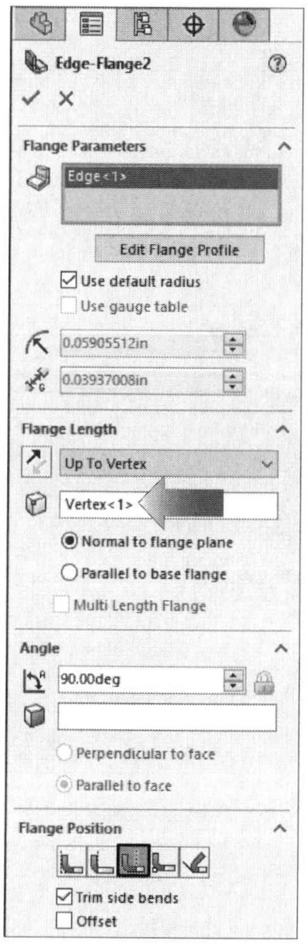

For Flange Length, select **Up to Vertex**.

Select the vertex as noted in the image below.

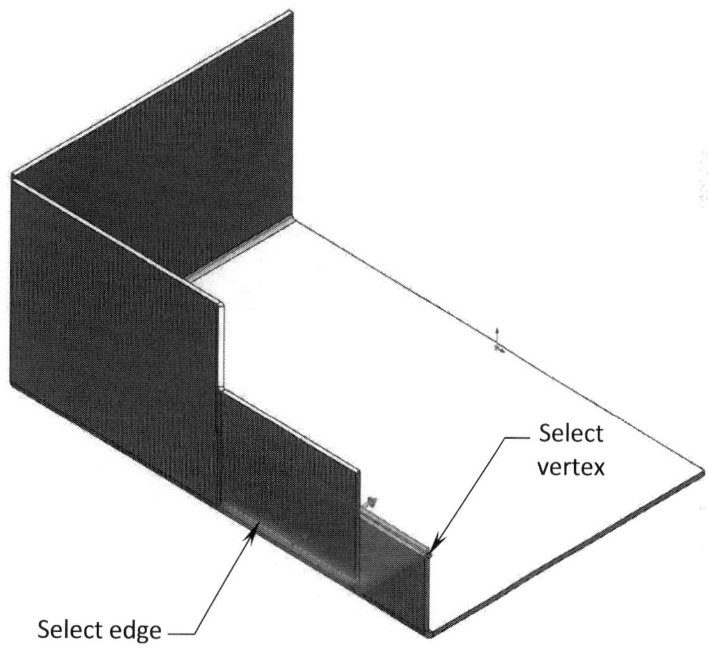

Keep the Bend Angle at **90.00deg**.

For Flange Position, select **Bend Outside**.

Click **OK**.

*Note: The gap between the edge flange and the rectangular cut out is critical; it must stay at **.025in**. at all times.*

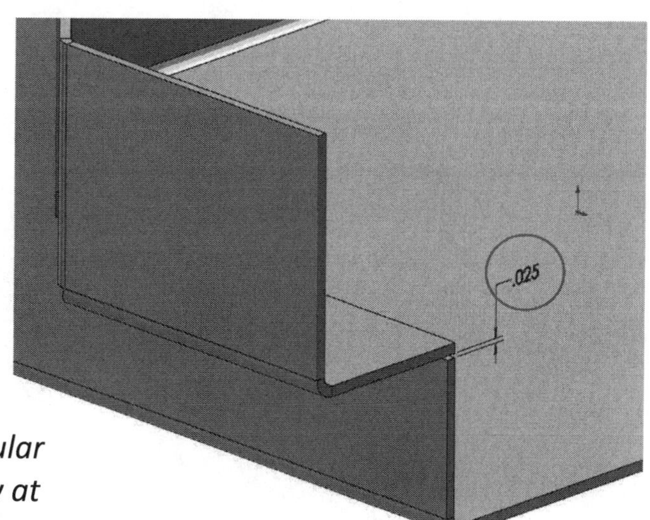

7. Creating a relief cut:

Select the face as indicated and open a **new sketch**.

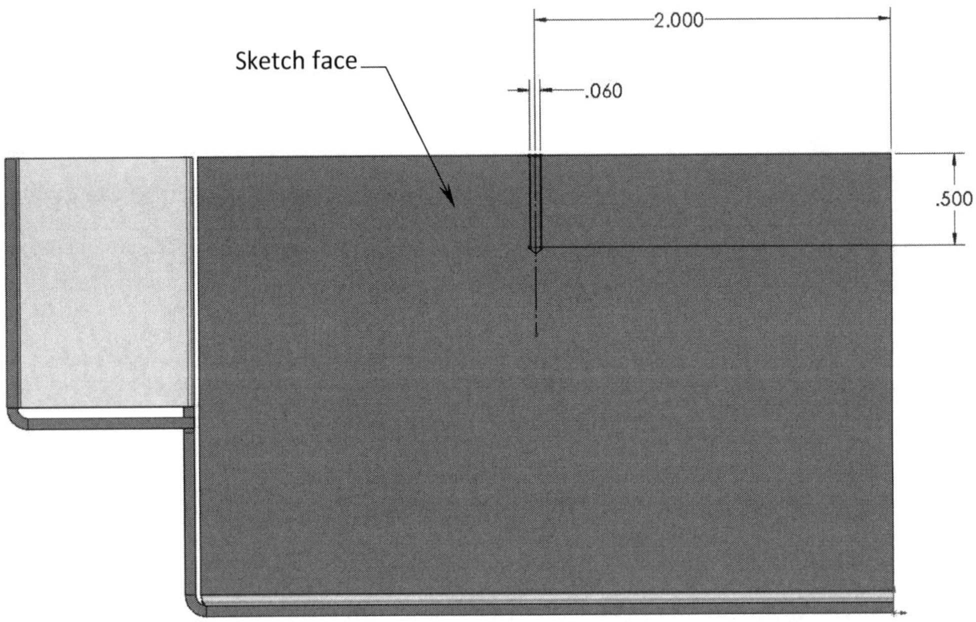

Sketch the profile above and add dimensions to fully define the sketch.

Switch to the **Sheet Metal** tab and click: **Extruded Cut**.

For Direction 1, select **Blind** and enable:
Link to Thickness.

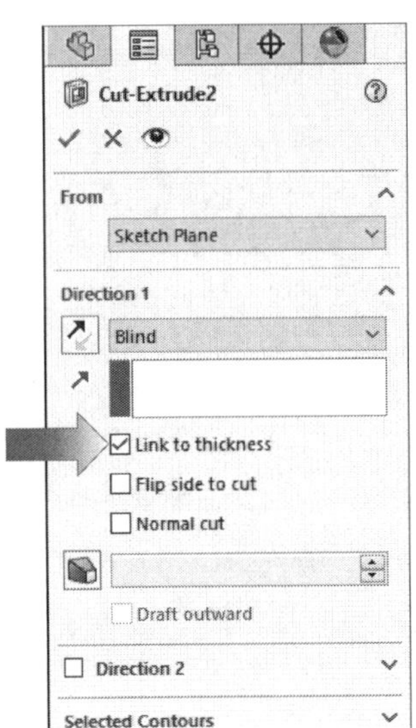

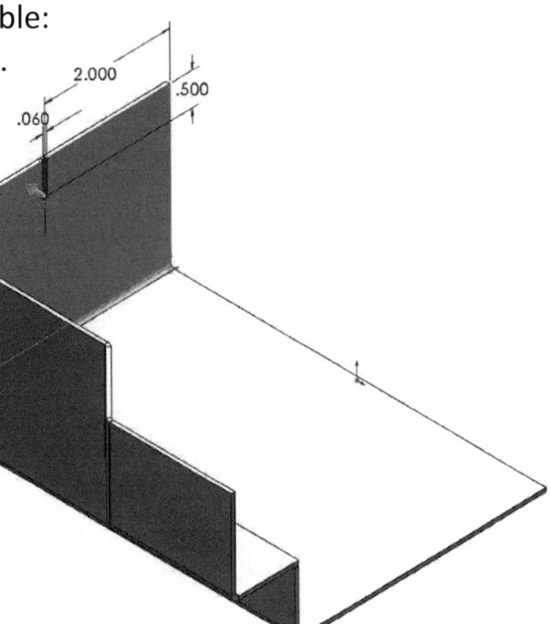

Click **OK**.

8. Adding a hem feature:

Click **Hem**  on the **Sheet Metal** tab.

Select the edge as indicated below.

For Type and Size, select Rolled and enter:
318deg. for Angle and **.1875** for Radius.

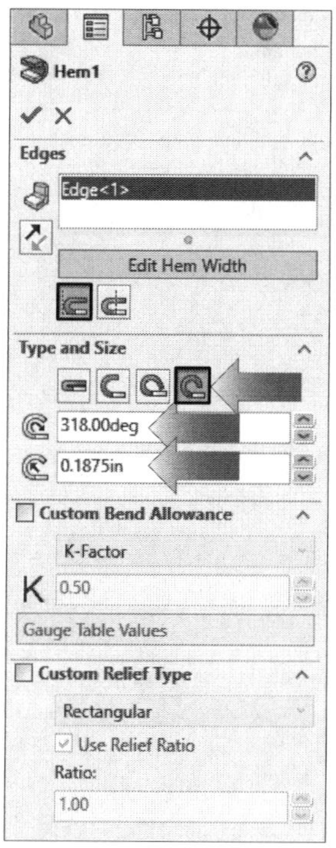

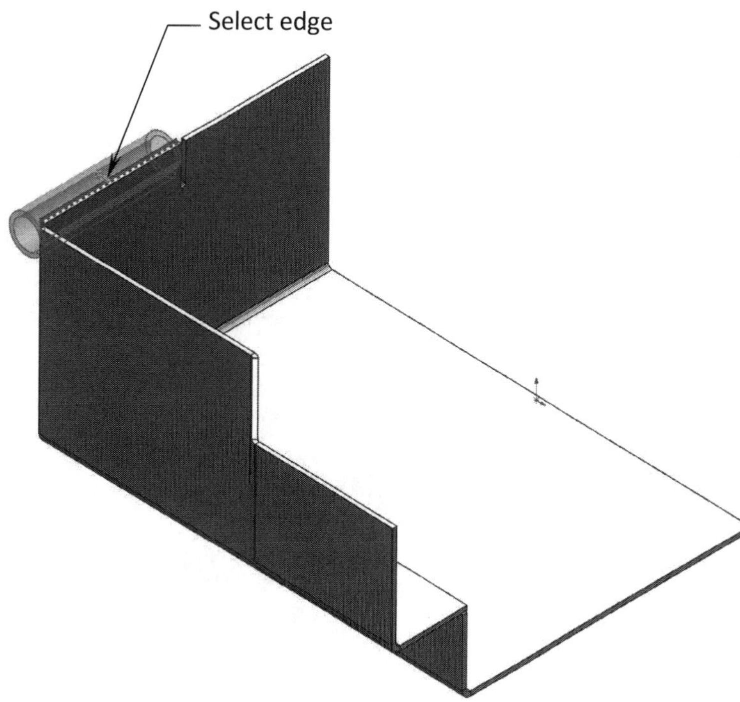

Keep all other parameters at their default values.

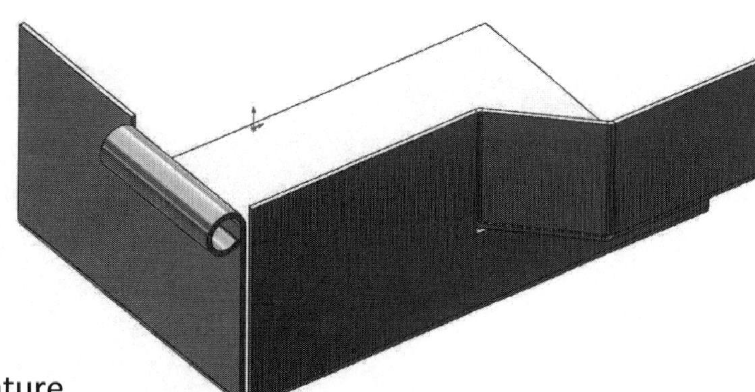

Click **OK**.

Rotate the model and compare your hem feature against the one shown here.

9. Adding a louver:

Expand the **Design Library** on the right side pane.

Expand the **Forming Tools** and the **Louvers** folders.

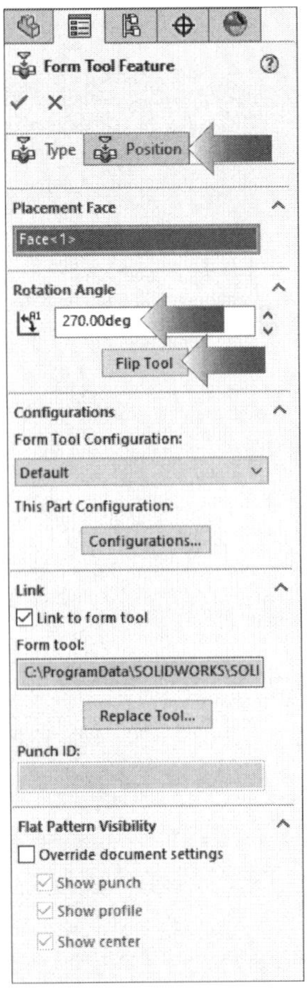

<u>Drag/drop</u> the **Louver** form tool to the <u>inside face</u> of the part.

Change the Rotation Angle to **270deg**.

Click **Flip Tool**.

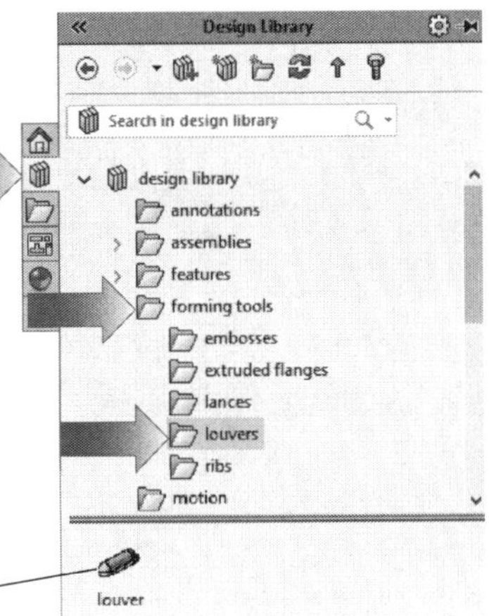

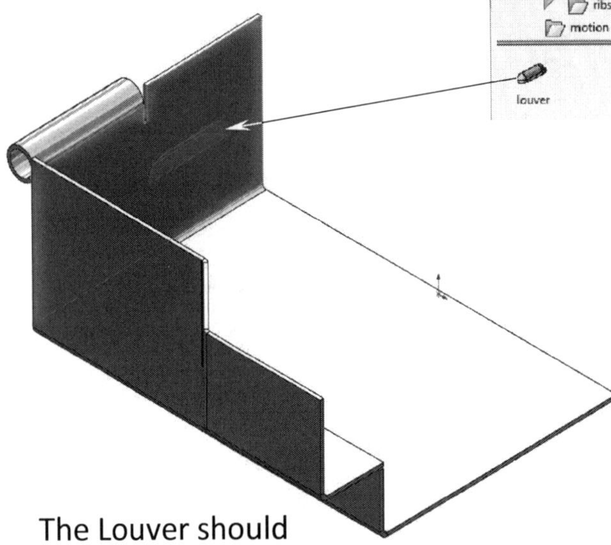

The Louver should protrude outwards.

Click the **Position** tab.

Add the vertical and horizontal dimensions to fully define the sketch.

Click **OK**.

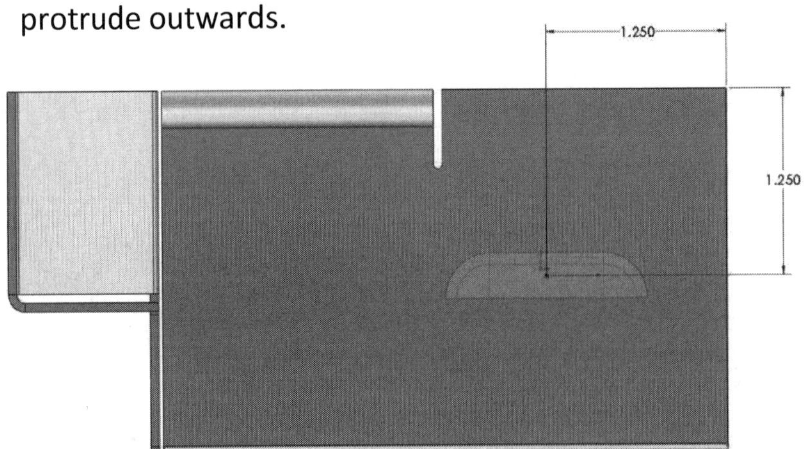

10. Mirroring a body:

Switch to the **Features** tab and click **Mirror**.

For Mirror Face/Plane, select the face on the right side of the part, as noted.

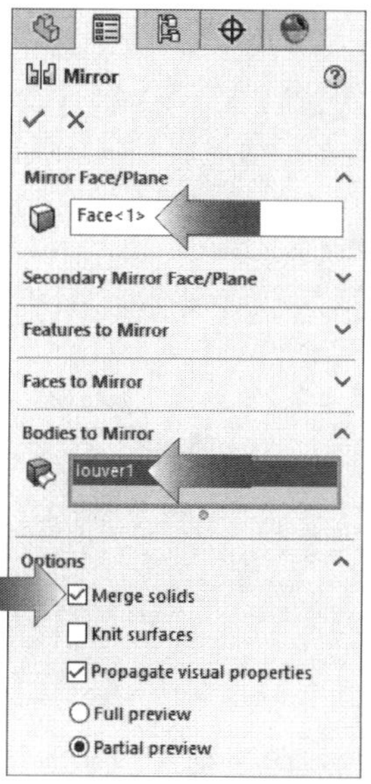

Expand Bodies to Mirror and select the part from the graphics area.

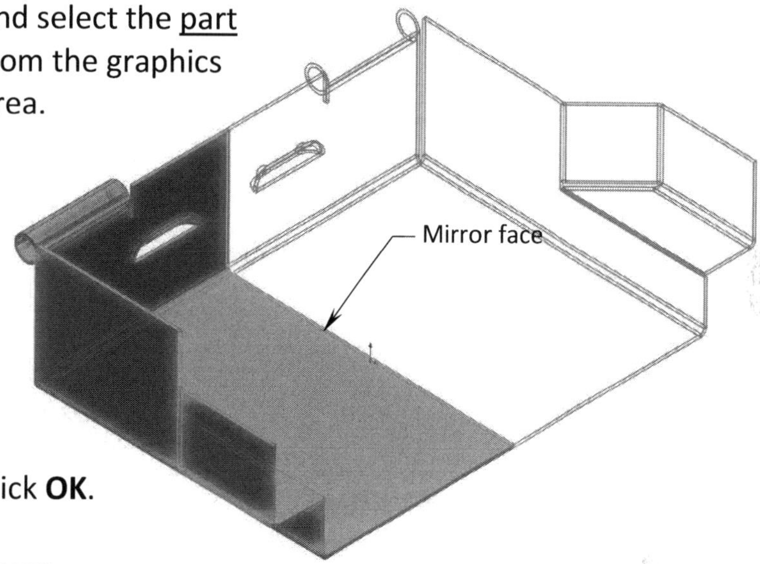

Click **OK**.

11. Calculating the mass:

Switch to the **Evaluate** tab and click **Mass Properties**.

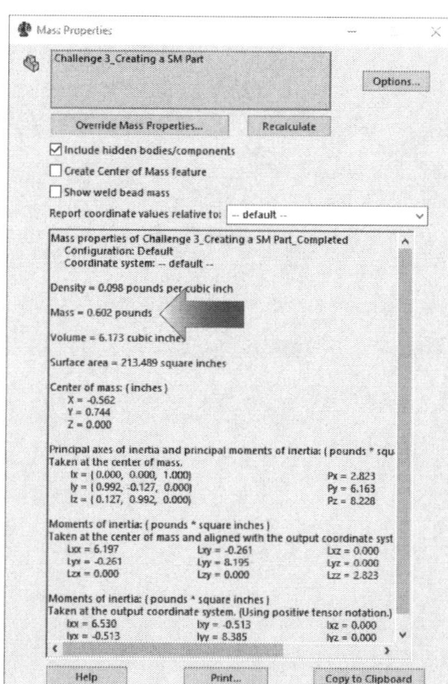

Locate the **Mass** of the part and enter it here: ________________ lbs.

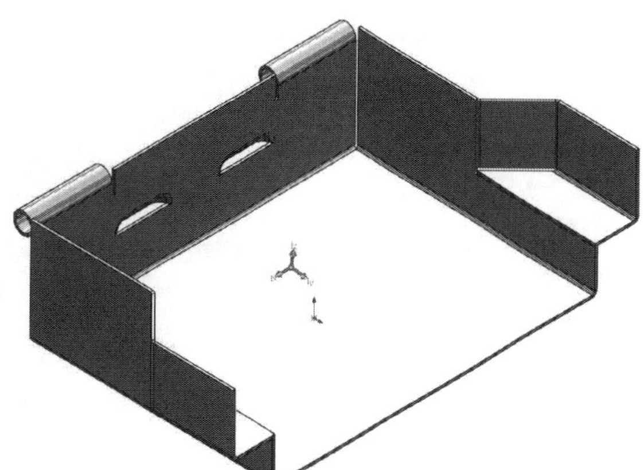

Save your work as **Challenge 3**.

CSWP-SM: Certified SOLIDWORKS Professional Sheet Metal Exam Preparation Materials

Challenge 4 – Using Forming Tools

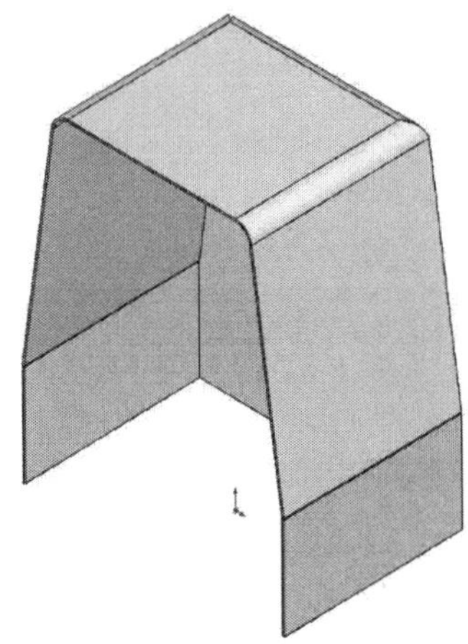

This challenge will test your skills on applying a form tool from the Design Library and then replicating it several times before mirroring the form tools on the opposite side of the part.

1. Opening a part document:

Browse to the Training Folder and open a part document named: **Challenge 4_Modifications**.

2. Adding a Louver formed feature:

Expand the **Design Library**, the **Forming Tools**, and the **Louvers folders**.

Drag/drop the Louver form tool to the face below.

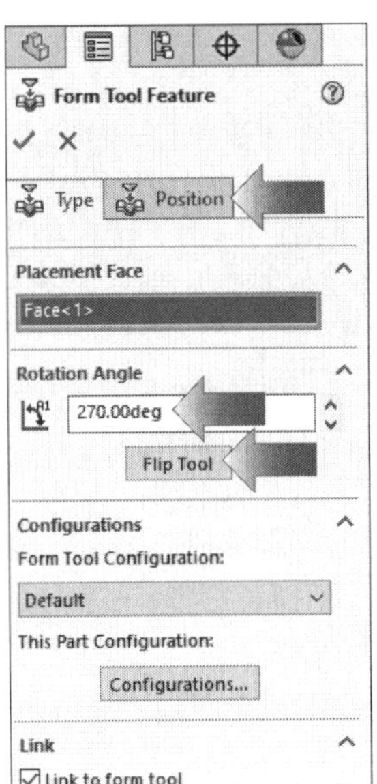

Angle: **270deg**.

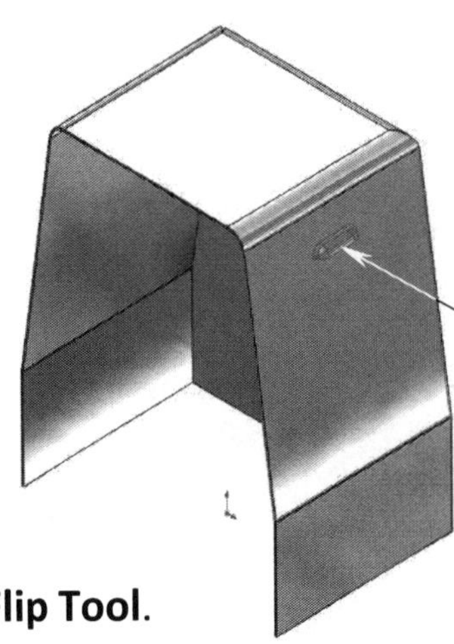

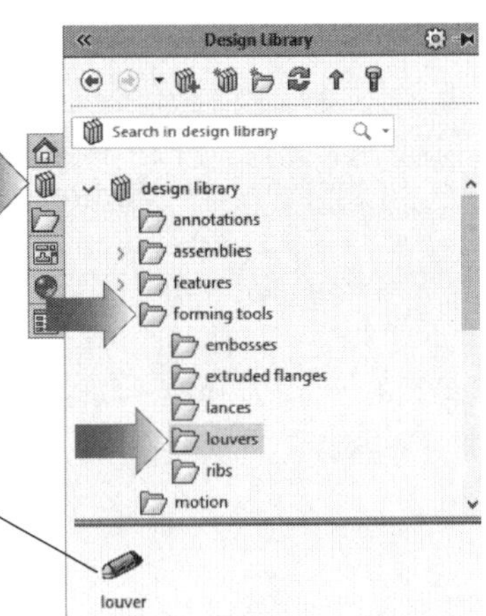

Click **Flip Tool**.

Click the **Position** tab.

Sketch a **vertical centerline** at the mid-point of the top edge.

Add a **Coincident** between the center point of the louver and the centerline.

Add the **1.500** location dimension.

Click **OK**.

Switch to the **Features** tab and click: **Linear Pattern**.

For Pattern Direction, select the vertical edge as indicated below.

Click **Spacing and Instances**.

Enter **.750in**. for Spacing.

Enter **6** for Number of Instances.

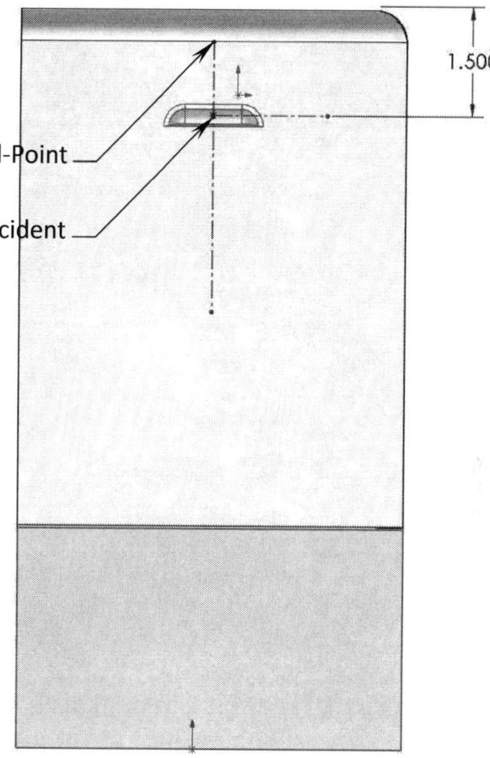

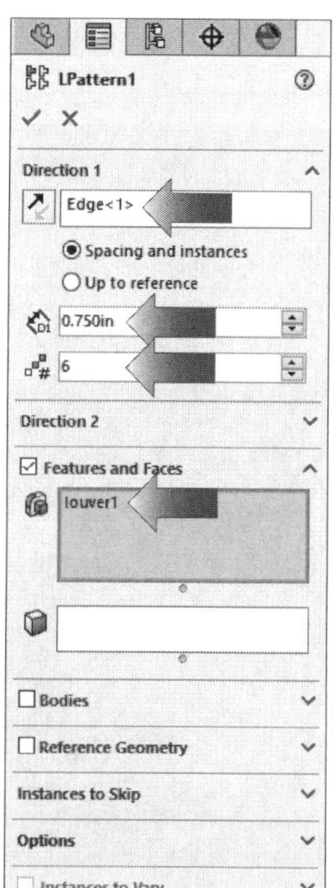

Pattern Direction

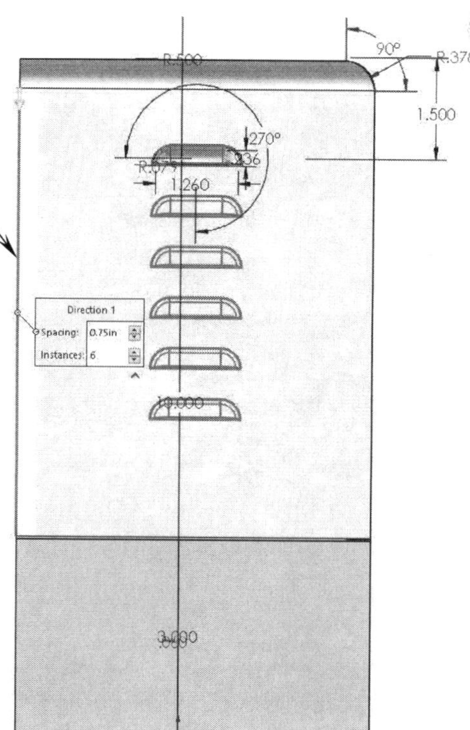

For Features to Pattern, select the **Louver**.

Click **OK**.

3. Mirroring the Louvers:

Click **Mirror** on the **Features** tab.

For Mirror Face/Plane, select the Right plane.

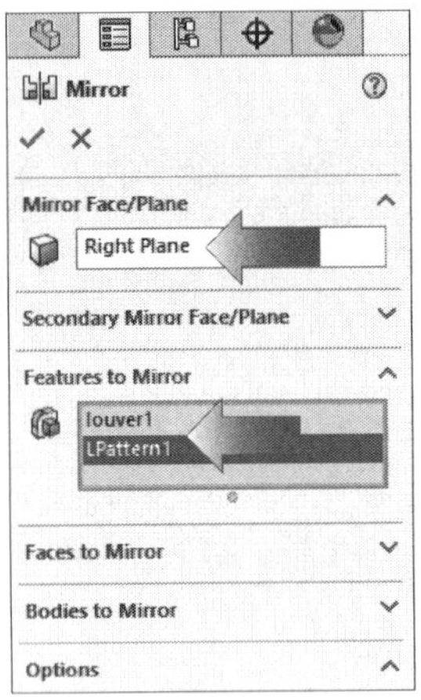

For Features to Mirror, select the **Louver1** and the **LPattern1**.

Click **OK**.

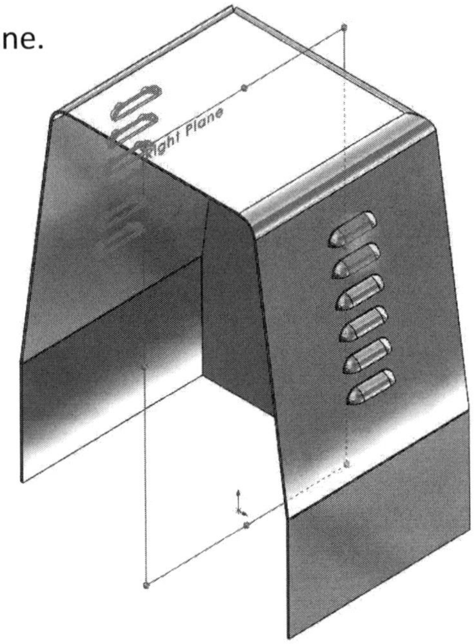

4. Calculating the mass:

Switch to the **Evaluate** tab and click **Mass Properties**.

Locate the mass of the part and enter it here: _______________ lbs.

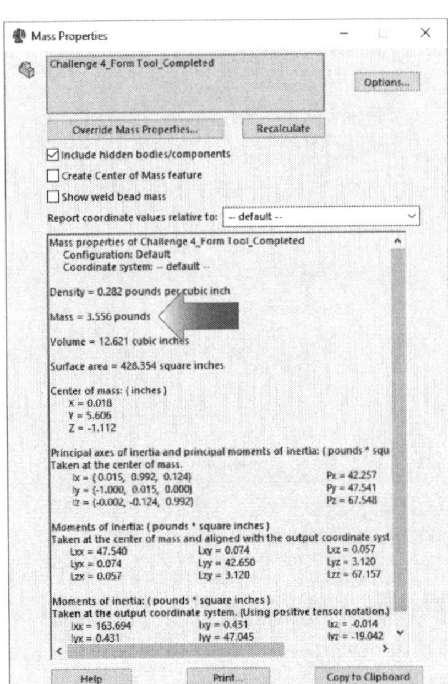

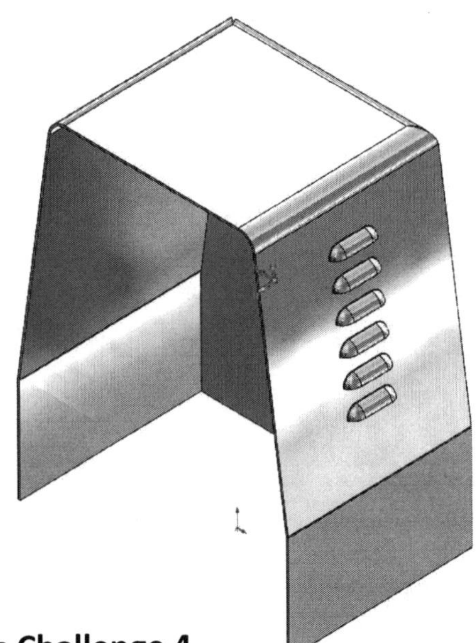

Save your work as **Challenge 4**.

CSWP-SM: Certified SOLIDWORKS Professional Sheet Metal Exam Preparation Materials

Challenge 5 - Creating a Curved Flange

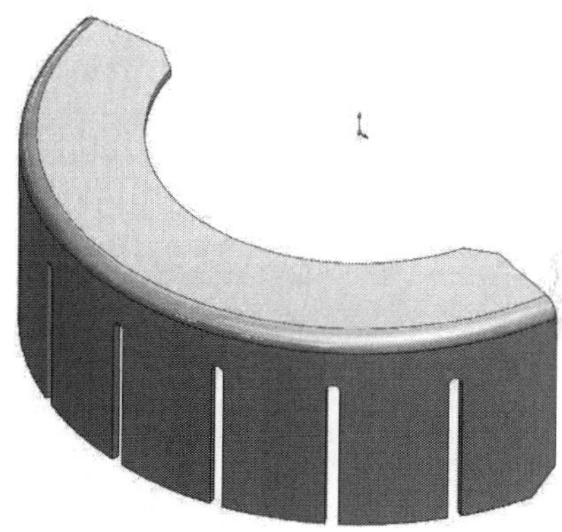

This challenge tests your skills on making a curved flange and orient it as shown in the image.
All sketches must be fully defined with relations and dimensions.

1. Creating a new part:

This model will need to be created from scratch.

Select the Top plane and open a **new sketch**.

2. Creating the 1st sketch:

Sketch **2 Circles** and **3 Centerlines**.

Trim the circles and add the relations to keep the 2 sides symmetrical with each other.

Add the dimensions shown in the image to fully define the sketch.

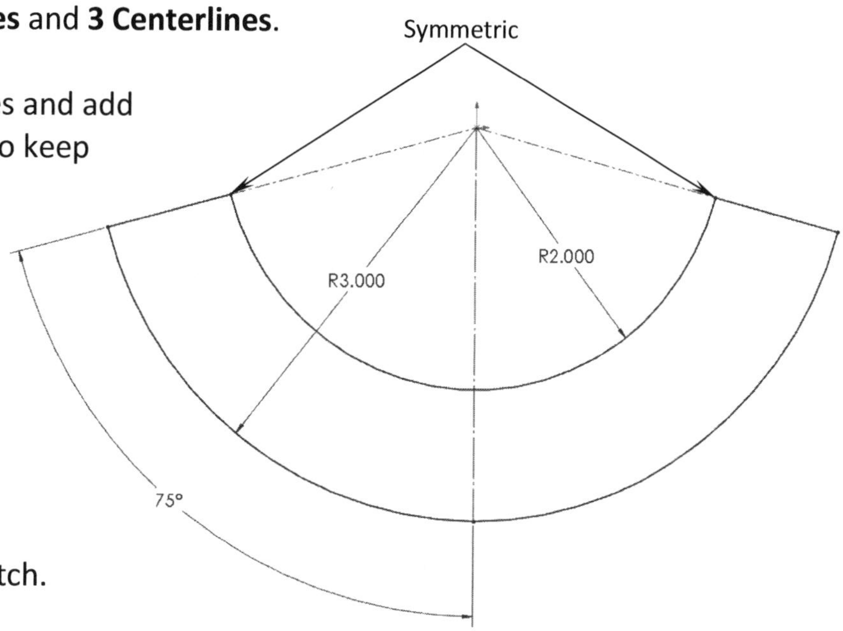

3. Making a base flange:

Switch to the **Sheet Metal** tab.

Select the **Base Flange** tool.

Enable the **Use Gauge Table** checkbox and select:
Sample Table – Aluminum.

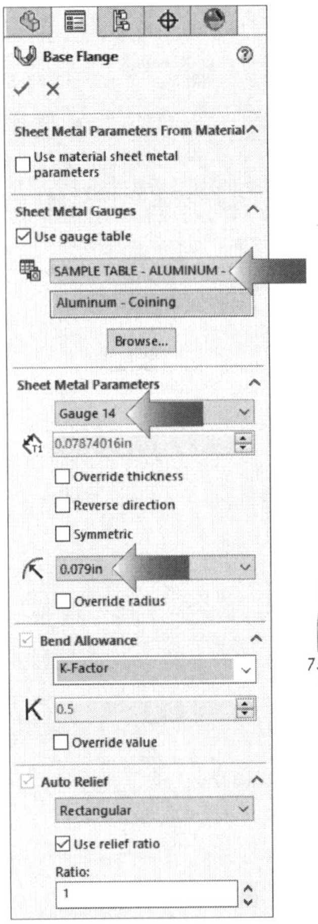

Gauge: **14**

Bend Radius: **.079in**.

K-Factor: **0.5**

Relief: **Rectangular**

Ratio: **1**

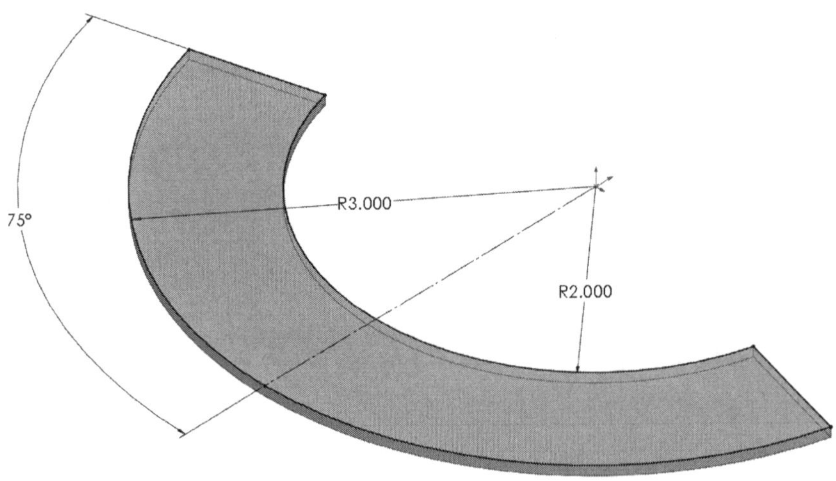

Click **OK**.

4. Making a curved flange:

Click the **Edge Flange** tool on the **Sheet Metal** tab.

Select the **curved edge** as noted and move the mouse cursor downward and click to lock the direction.

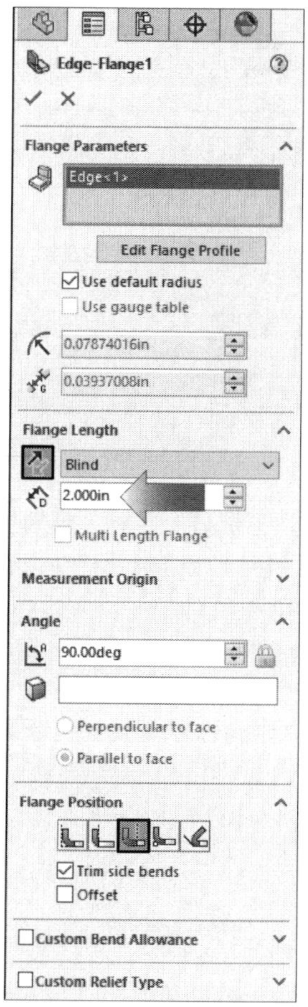

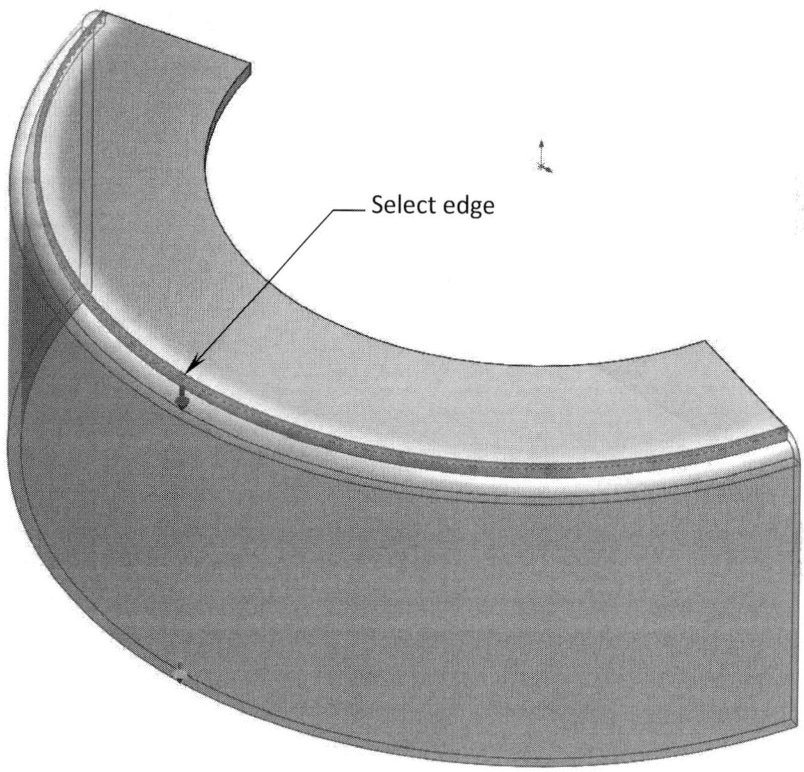

For Flange Length, select **Blind** and enter: **2.00in**.

Keep the Bend Angle at **90.00deg**.

For Flange Position, select **Bend Outside**.

Keep all other parameters at their defaults.

Click **OK**.

5. Adding a slot feature:

Select the Front plane and open a **new sketch**.

Sketch the profile and add the dimensions shown below.

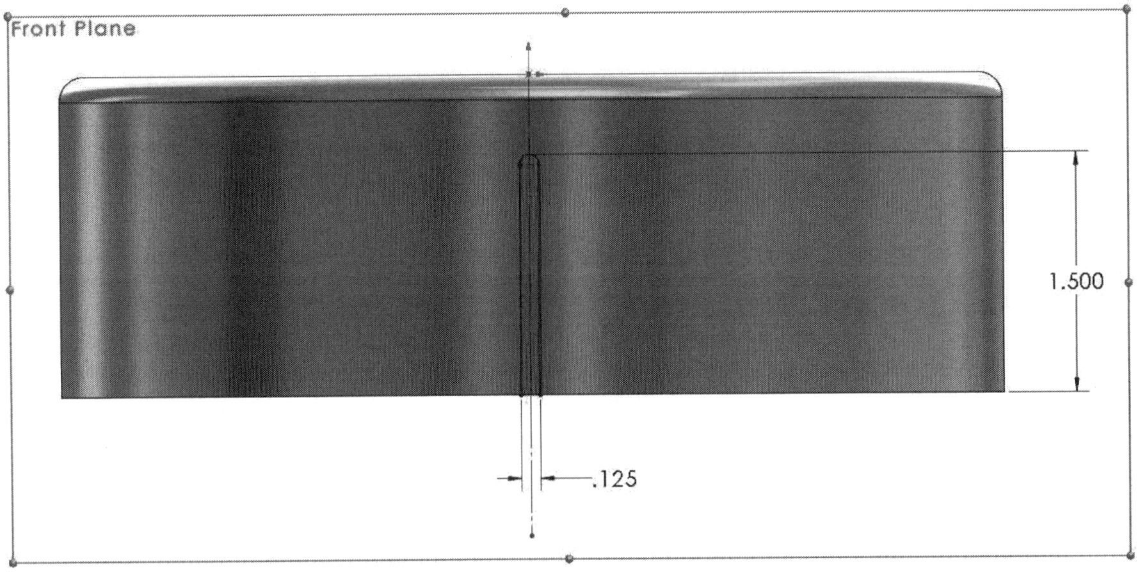

Switch to the **Sheet Metal** tab and click **Extruded Cut**.

For Direction 1, select: **Through All**.

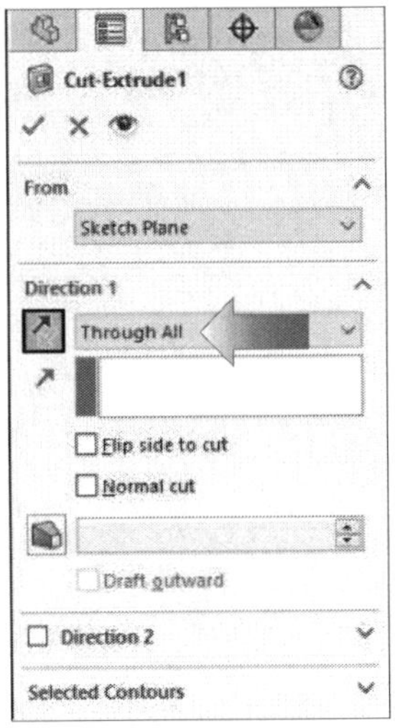

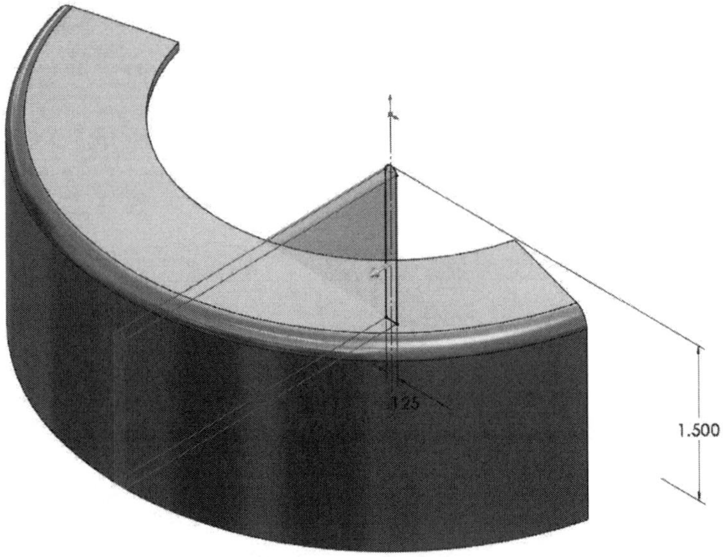

Click **OK**.

6. Pattering the slot:

Switch to the **Features** tab and click **Linear Pattern**.

For Direction 1, select the **circular edge** as indicated below.

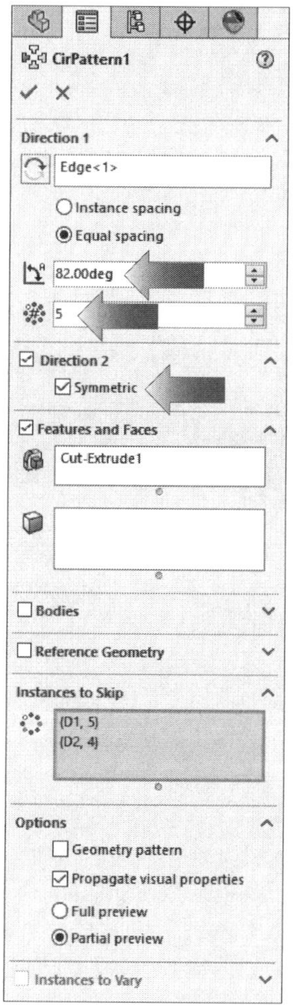

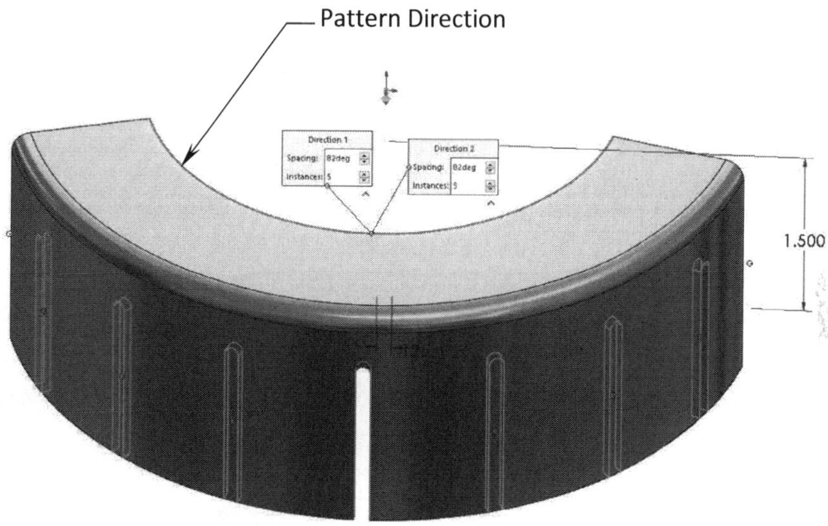

Click **Equal Spacing** and enter **82.00deg**.

Enter **5** for Number of Instances.

Click the Direction 2 checkbox and enable **Symmetric**.

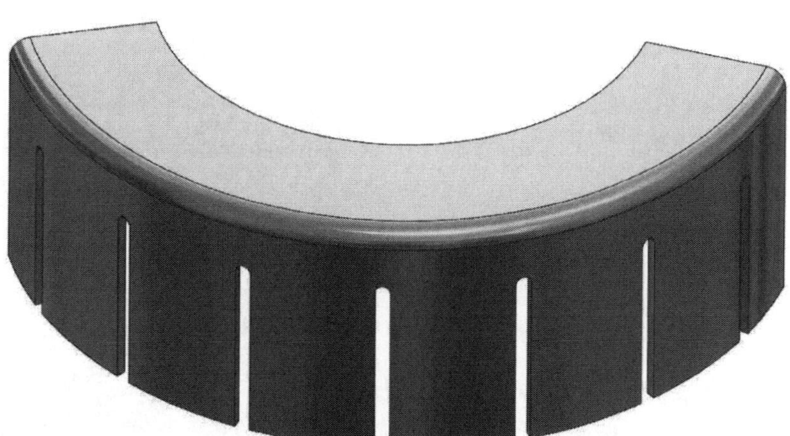

For Features to Pattern, select the **Cut-Etrude1** feature from the Feature-Manager tree.

Click **OK**.

7. Adding chamfer:

Switch back to the **Sheet Metal** tab.

Select: **Corners, Break Corner**.

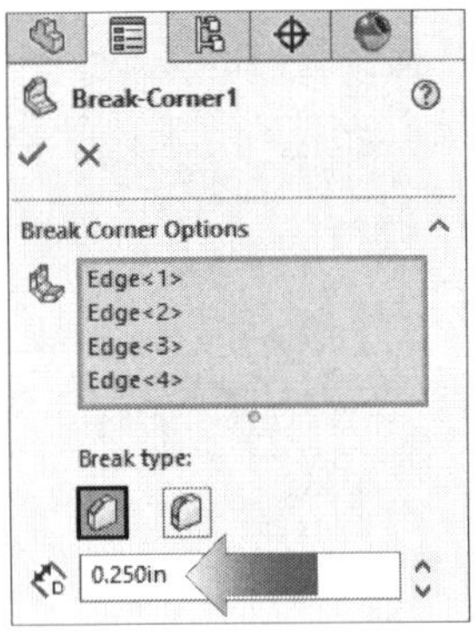

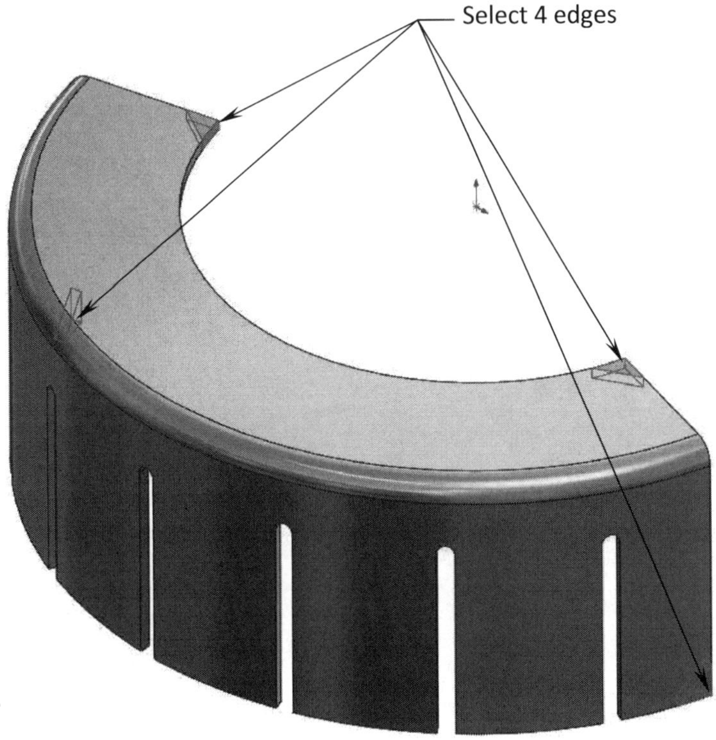

For Edges to chamfer, select **4 edges** as noted.

For Break Type, select **Chamfer**.

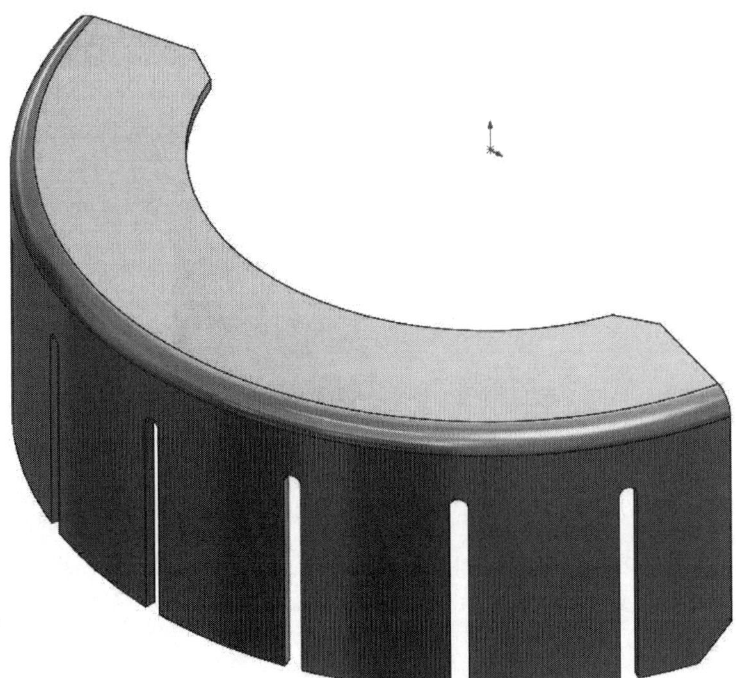

For Distance, enter **.250in**.

Click **OK**.

<u>Note:</u> The chamfer tool in the Features tab is the same as the break corner tool in the sheet metal tab.

8. Calculating the mass:

Assign the material **1060 Alloy** to the model.

Switch to the **Evaluate** tab and click **Mass Properties**.

Locate the mass of the part and enter it here: _________________ lbs.

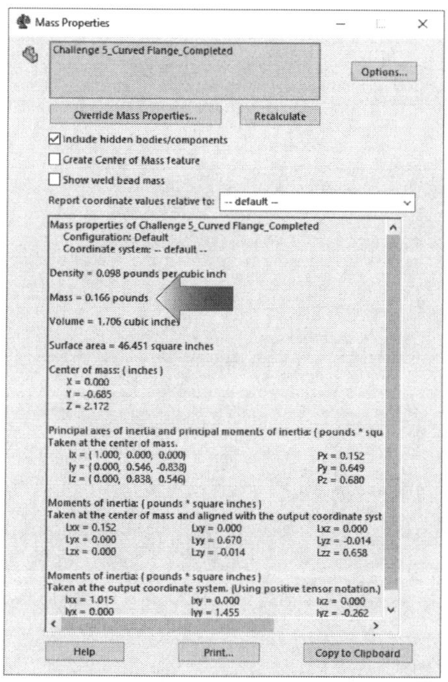

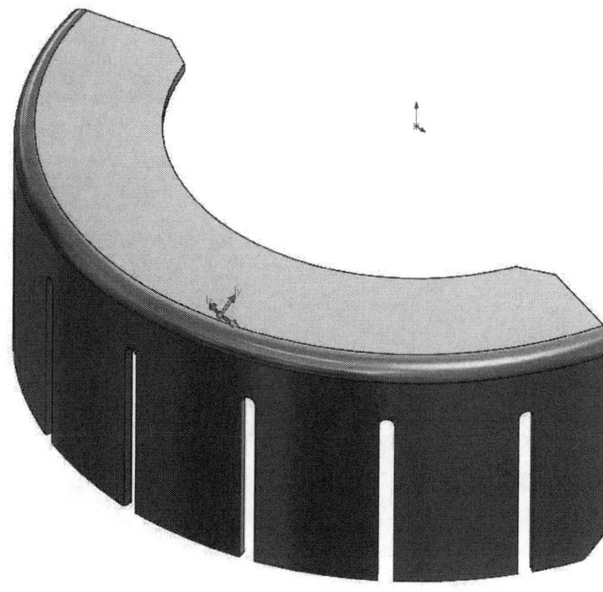

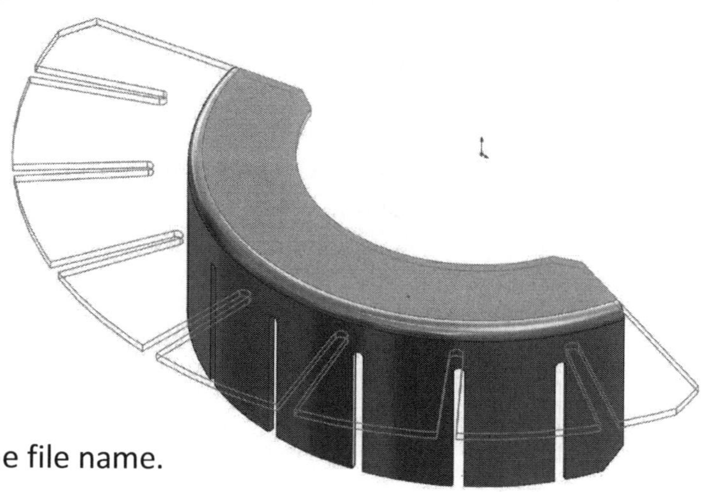

9. Saving your work:

Select **File, Save As**.

Enter: **Challenge 5** for the file name.

Click **Save**.

EXPERT
Mechanical Design
SOLIDWORKS

PROFESSIONAL
Drawing Tools
SOLIDWORKS
PROFESSIONAL
Mold Tools
SOLIDWORKS
PROFESSIONAL
Weldments
SOLIDWORKS
PROFESSIONAL
Sheet Metal
SOLIDWORKS
PROFESSIONAL
Surfacing
SOLIDWORKS

DASSAULT SYSTEMES | The 3DEXPERIENCE Company
CERTIFICATE
CERTIFIED EXPERT
This certifies Your Name
has successfully completed the requirements for
SolidWorks Expert - Mechanical Design
and is entitled to receive the recognition
and benefits so bestowed
AWARDED on MM/DD/Y
C-JXZ123-
Bertrand SICOT
CEO SOLIDWORKS

Glossary

Absorbed
A feature, sketch, or annotation that is contained in another item (usually a feature) in the FeatureManager design tree. Examples are the profile sketch and profile path in a base-sweep, or a cosmetic thread annotation in a hole.

Align
Tools that assist in lining up annotations and dimensions (left, right, top, bottom, and so on). For aligning parts in an assembly.

Alternate position view
A drawing view in which one or more views are superimposed in phantom lines on the original view. Alternate position views are often used to show range of motion of an assembly.

Anchor point
The end of a leader that attaches to the note, block, or other annotation. Sheet formats contain anchor points for a bill of materials, a hole table, a revision table, and a weldment cut list.

Annotation
A text note or a symbol that adds specific design intent to a part, assembly, or drawing. Specific types of annotations include note, hole callout, surface finish symbol, datum feature symbol, datum target, geometric tolerance symbol, weld symbol, balloon, and stacked balloon. Annotations that apply only to drawings include center mark, annotation centerline, area hatch, and block.

Appearance callouts
Callouts that display the colors and textures of the face, feature, body, and part under the entity selected and are a shortcut to editing colors and textures.

Area hatch
A crosshatch pattern or fill applied to a selected face or to a closed sketch in a drawing.

Assembly
A document in which parts, features, and other assemblies (sub-assemblies) are mated together. The parts and sub-assemblies exist in documents separate from the assembly. For example, in an assembly, a piston can be mated to other parts, such as a connecting rod or cylinder. This new assembly can then be used as a sub-assembly in an assembly of an engine. The extension for a SOLIDWORKS assembly file name is .SLDASM.

Attachment point
The end of a leader that attaches to the model (to an edge, vertex, or face, for example) or to a drawing sheet.

Axis
A straight line that can be used to create model geometry, features, or patterns. An axis can be made in several different ways, including using the intersection of two planes.

Balloon
Labels parts in an assembly, typically including item numbers and quantity. In drawings, the item numbers are related to rows in a bill of materials.

Base
The first solid feature of a part.

Baseline dimensions
Sets of dimensions measured from the same edge or vertex in a drawing.

Bend
A feature in a sheet metal part. A bend generated from a filleted corner, cylindrical face, or conical face is a round bend; a bend generated from sketched straight lines is a sharp bend.

Bill of materials
A table inserted into a drawing to keep a record of the parts used in an assembly.

Block
A user-defined annotation that you can use in parts, assemblies, and drawings. A block can contain text, sketch entities (except points), and area hatch, and it can be saved in a file for later use as, for example, a custom callout or a company logo.

Bottom-up assembly
An assembly modeling technique where you create parts and then insert them into an assembly.

Broken-out section
A drawing view that exposes inner details of a drawing view by removing material from a closed profile, usually a spline.

Cavity
The mold half that holds the cavity feature of the design part.

Center mark
A cross that marks the center of a circle or arc.

Centerline
A centerline marks, in phantom font, an axis of symmetry in a sketch or drawing.

Chamfer
Bevels a selected edge or vertex. You can apply chamfers to both sketches and features.

Child
A dependent feature related to a previously built feature. For example, a chamfer on the edge of a hole is a child of the parent hole.

Click-release
As you sketch, if you click and then release the pointer, you are in click-release mode. Move the pointer and click again to define the next point in the sketch sequence.

Click-drag
As you sketch, if you click and drag the pointer, you are in click-drag mode. When you release the pointer, the sketch entity is complete.

Closed profile
Also called a closed contour, it is a sketch or sketch entity with no exposed endpoints, for example, a circle or polygon.

Collapse
The opposite of explode. The collapse action returns an exploded assembly's parts to their normal positions.

Collision Detection
An assembly function that detects collisions between components when components move or rotate. A collision occurs when an entity on one component coincides with any entity on another component.

Component
Any part or sub-assembly within an assembly.

Configuration
A variation of a part or assembly within a single document. Variations can include different dimensions, features, and properties. For example, a single part such as a bolt can contain different configurations that vary the diameter and length.

ConfigurationManager
Located on the left side of the SOLIDWORKS window, it is a means to create, select, and view the configurations of parts and assemblies.

Constraint
The relations between sketch entities, or between sketch entities and planes, axes, edges, or vertices.

Construction geometry
The characteristic of a sketch entity is that the entity is used in creating other geometry but is not itself used in creating features.

Coordinate system
A system of planes used to assign Cartesian coordinates to features, parts, and assemblies. Part and assembly documents contain default coordinate systems; other coordinate systems can be defined with reference geometry. Coordinate systems can be used with measurement tools and for exporting documents to other file formats.

Cosmetic thread
An annotation that represents threads.

Crosshatch
A pattern (or fill) applied to drawing views such as section views and broken-out sections.

Curvature
Curvature is equal to the inverse of the radius of the curve. The curvature can be displayed in different colors according to the local radius (usually of a surface).

Cut
A feature that removes material from a part by such actions as extrude, revolve, loft, sweep, thicken, cavity, and so on.

Dangling
A dimension, relation, or drawing section view that is unresolved. For example, if a piece of geometry is dimensioned, and that geometry is later deleted, the dimension becomes dangling.

Degrees of freedom
Geometry that is not defined by dimensions or relations is free to move. In 2D sketches, there are three degrees of freedom: movement along the X and Y axes, and rotation about the Z axis (the axis normal to the sketch plane). In 3D sketches and in assemblies, there are six degrees of freedom: movement along the X, Y, and Z axes, and rotation about the X, Y, and Z axes.

Derived part
A derived part is a new base, mirror, or component part created directly from an existing

part and linked to the original part such that changes to the original part are reflected in the derived part.

Derived sketch
A copy of a sketch, in either the same part or the same assembly that is connected to the original sketch. Changes in the original sketch are reflected in the derived sketch.

Design Library
Located in the Task Pane, the Design Library provides a central location for reusable elements such as parts, assemblies, and so on.

Design table
An Excel spreadsheet that is used to create multiple configurations in a part or assembly document.

Detached drawing
A drawing format that allows opening and working in a drawing without loading the corresponding models into memory. The models are loaded on an as-needed basis.

Detail view
A portion of a larger view, usually at a larger scale than the original view.

Dimension line
A linear dimension line references the dimension text to extension lines indicating the entity being measured. An angular dimension line references the dimension text directly to the measured object.

DimXpertManager
Located on the left side of the SOLIDWORKS window, it is a means to manage dimensions and tolerances created using DimXpert for parts according to the requirements of the ASME Y.14.41-2003 standard.

DisplayManager
The DisplayManager lists the appearances, decals, lights, scene, and cameras applied to the current model. From the DisplayManager, you can view applied content, and add, edit, or delete items. When PhotoView 360 is added in, the DisplayManager also provides access to PhotoView options.

Document
A file containing a part, assembly, or drawing.

Draft
The degree of taper or angle of a face usually applied to molds or castings.

Drawing
A 2D representation of a 3D part or assembly. The extension for a SOLIDWORKS drawing file name is .SLDDRW.

Drawing sheet
A page in a drawing document.

Driven dimension
Measurements of the model, but they do not drive the model and their values cannot be changed.

Driving dimension
Also referred to as a model dimension, it sets the value for a sketch entity. It can also control distance, thickness, and feature parameters.

Edge
A single outside boundary of a feature.

Edge flange
A sheet metal feature that combines a bend and a tab in a single operation.

Equation
Creates a mathematical relation between sketch dimensions, using dimension names as variables, or between feature parameters, such as the depth of an extruded feature or the instance count in a pattern.

Exploded view
Shows an assembly with its components separated from one another, usually to show how to assemble the mechanism.

Export
Save a SOLIDWORKS document in another format for use in other CAD/CAM, rapid prototyping, web, or graphics software applications.

Extension line
The line extending from the model indicating the point from which a dimension is measured.

Extrude
A feature that linearly projects a sketch to either add material to a part (in a base or boss) or remove material from a part (in a cut or hole).

Face
A selectable area (planar or otherwise) of a model or surface with boundaries that help define the shape of the model or surface. For example, a rectangular solid has six faces.

Fasteners
A SOLIDWORKS Toolbox library that adds fasteners automatically to holes in an assembly.

Feature
An individual shape that, combined with other features, makes up a part or assembly. Some features, such as bosses and cuts, originate as sketches. Other features, such as shells and fillets, modify a feature's geometry. However, not all features have associated geometry. Features are always listed in the FeatureManager design tree.

FeatureManager design tree
Located on the left side of the SOLIDWORKS window, it provides an outline view of the active part, assembly, or drawing.

Fill
A solid area hatch or crosshatch. Fill also applies to patches on surfaces.

Fillet
An internal rounding of a corner or edge in a sketch, or an edge on a surface or solid.

Forming tool
Dies that bend, stretch, or otherwise form sheet metal to create such form features as louvers, lances, flanges, and ribs.

Fully defined
A sketch where all lines and curves in the sketch, and their positions, are described by dimensions or relations, or both, and cannot be moved. Fully defined sketch entities are shown in black.

Geometric tolerance
A set of standard symbols that specify the geometric characteristics and dimensional requirements of a feature.

Graphics area
The area in the SOLIDWORKS window where the part, assembly, or drawing appears.

Guide curve
A 2D or 3D curve is used to guide a sweep or loft.

Handle
An arrow, square, or circle that you can drag to adjust the size or position of an entity (a feature, dimension, or sketch entity, for example).

Helix
A curve defined by pitch, revolutions, and height. A helix can be used, for example, as a path for a swept feature cutting threads in a bolt.

Hem
A sheet metal feature that folds back at the edge of a part. A hem can be open, closed, double, or teardrop.

HLR
(Hidden lines removed) A view mode in which all edges of the model that are not visible from the current view angle are removed from the display.

HLV
(Hidden lines visible) A view mode in which all edges of the model that are not visible from the current view angle are shown gray or dashed.

Import
Open files from other CAD software applications into a SOLIDWORKS document.

In-context feature
A feature with an external reference to the geometry of another component; the in-context feature changes automatically if the geometry of the referenced model or feature changes.

Inference
The system automatically creates (infers) relations between dragged entities (sketched entities, annotations, and components) and other entities and geometry. This is useful when positioning entities relative to one another.

Instance
An item in a pattern or a component in an assembly that occurs more than once. Blocks are inserted into drawings as instances of block definitions.

Interference detection
A tool that displays any interference between selected components in an assembly.

Jog
A sheet metal feature that adds material to a part by creating two bends from a sketched line.

Knit
A tool that combines two or more faces or surfaces into one. The edges of the surfaces must be adjacent and not overlapping, but they cannot ever be planar. There is no difference in the appearance of the face or the surface after knitting.

Layout sketch
A sketch that contains important sketch entities, dimensions, and relations. You reference the entities in the layout sketch when creating new sketches, building new geometry, or positioning components in an assembly. This allows for easier updating of your model because changes you make to the layout sketch propagate to the entire model.

Leader
A solid line from an annotation (note, dimension, and so on) to the referenced feature.

Library feature
A frequently used feature, or combination of features, that is created once and then saved for future use.

Lightweight
A part in an assembly or a drawing has only a subset of its model data loaded into memory. The remaining model data is loaded on an as-needed basis. This improves performance of large and complex assemblies.

Line
A straight sketch entity with two endpoints. A line can be created by projecting an external entity such as an edge, plane, axis, or sketch curve into the sketch.

Loft
A base, boss, cut, or surface feature created by transitions between profiles.

Lofted bend
A sheet metal feature that produces a roll form or a transitional shape from two open profile sketches. Lofted bends often create funnels and chutes.

Mass properties
A tool that evaluates the characteristics of a part or an assembly such as volume, surface area, centroid, and so on.

Mate
A geometric relationship, such as coincident, perpendicular, tangent, and so on, between parts in an assembly.

Mate reference
Specifies one or more entities of a component to use for automatic mating. When you drag a component with a mate reference into an assembly, the software tries to find other combinations of the same mate reference name and mate type.

Mates folder
A collection of mates that are solved together. The order in which the mates appear within the Mates folder does not matter.

Mirror
(a) A mirror feature is a copy of a selected feature, mirrored about a plane or planar face.
(b) A mirror sketch entity is a copy of a selected sketch entity that is mirrored about a centerline.

Miter flange
A sheet metal feature that joins multiple edge flanges together and miters the corner.

Model
3D solid geometry in a part or assembly document. If a part or assembly document contains multiple configurations, each configuration is a separate model.

Model dimension
A dimension specified in a sketch or a feature in a part or assembly document that defines some entity in a 3D model.

Model item
A characteristic or dimension of feature geometry that can be used in detailing drawings.

Model view
A drawing view of a part or assembly.

Mold
A set of manufacturing tooling used to shape molten plastic or other material into a designed part. You design the mold using a sequence of integrated tools that result in cavity and core blocks that are derived parts of the part to be molded.

Motion Study
Motion Studies are graphical simulations of motion and visual properties with assembly models. Analogous to a configuration, they do not actually change the original assembly model or its properties. They display the model as it changes based on simulation elements you add.

Multibody part
A part with separate solid bodies within the same part document. Unlike the components in an assembly, multibody parts are not dynamic.

Native format
DXF and DWG files remain in their original format (are not converted into SOLIDWORKS format) when viewed in SOLIDWORKS drawing sheets (view only).

Open profile
Also called an open contour, it is a sketch or sketch entity with endpoints exposed. For example, a U-shaped profile is open.

Ordinate dimensions
A chain of dimensions measured from a zero ordinate in a drawing or sketch.

Origin
The model origin appears as three gray arrows and represents the (0,0,0) coordinate of the model. When a sketch is active, a sketch origin appears in red and represents the (0,0,0) coordinate of the sketch. Dimensions and relations can be added to the model origin, but not to a sketch origin.

Out-of-context feature
A feature with an external reference to the geometry of another component that is not open.

Over defined
A sketch is over defined when dimensions or relations are either in conflict or redundant.

Parameter
A value used to define a sketch or feature (often a dimension).

Parent
An existing feature upon which other features depend. For example, in a block with a hole, the block is the parent to the child hole feature.

Part
A single 3D object made up of features. A part can become a component in an assembly, and it can be represented in 2D in a drawing. Examples of parts are bolt, pin, plate, and so on. The extension for the SOLIDWORKS part file name is .SLDPRT.

Path
A sketch, edge, or curve used in creating a sweep or loft.

Pattern
A pattern repeats selected sketch entities, features, or components in an array, which can be linear, circular, or sketch driven. If the seed entity is changed, the other instances in the pattern update.

Physical Dynamics
An assembly tool that displays the motion of assembly components in a realistic way. When you drag a component, the component applies a force to other components it touches. Components move only within their degrees of freedom.

Pierce relation
Makes a sketch point coincident to the location at which an axis, edge, line, or spline pierces the sketch plane.

Planar
Entities that can lie on one plane. For example, a circle is planar, but a helix is not.

Plane
Flat construction geometry. Planes can be used for a 2D sketch, section view of a model, a neutral plane in a draft feature, and others.

Point
A singular location in a sketch, or a projection into a sketch at a single location of an external entity (origin, vertex, axis, or point in an external sketch).

Predefined view
A drawing view in which the view position, orientation, and so on can be specified before a model is inserted. You can save drawing documents with predefined views as templates.

Profile
A sketch entity used to create a feature (such as a loft) or a drawing view (such as a detail view). A profile can be open (such as a U shape or open spline) or closed (such as a circle or closed spline).

Projected dimension
If you dimension entities in an isometric view, projected dimensions are the flat dimensions in 2D.

Projected view
A drawing view projected orthogonally from an existing view.

PropertyManager
Located on the left side of the SOLIDWORKS window, it is used for dynamic editing of sketch entities and most features.

RealView graphics
A hardware (graphics card) support of advanced shading in real time; the rendering applies to the model and is retained as you move or rotate a part.

Rebuild
Tool that updates (or regenerates) the document with any changes made since the last time the model was rebuilt. Rebuild is typically used after changing a model dimension.

Reference dimension
A dimension in a drawing that shows the measurement of an item but cannot drive the model and its value cannot be modified. When model dimensions change, reference dimensions update.

Reference geometry
Includes planes, axes, coordinate systems, and 3D curves. Reference geometry is used to assist in creating features such lofts, sweeps, drafts, chamfers, and patterns.

Relation
A geometric constraint between sketch entities or between a sketch entity and a plane, axis, edge, or vertex. Relations can be added automatically or manually.

Relative view
A relative (or relative to model) drawing view is created relative to planar surfaces in a part or assembly.

Reload
Refreshes shared documents. For example, if you open a part file for read-only access while another user makes changes to the same part, you can reload the new version, including the changes.

Reorder
Reordering (changing the order of) items is possible in the FeatureManager design tree. In parts, you can change the order in which features are solved. In assemblies, you can control the order in which components appear in a bill of materials.

Replace
Substitutes one or more open instances of a component in an assembly with a different component.

Resolved
A state of an assembly component (in an assembly or drawing document) in which it is fully loaded in memory. All the component's model data is available, so its entities can be selected, referenced, edited, and used in mates, and so on.

Revolve
A feature that creates a base or boss, a revolved cut, or revolved surface by revolving one or more sketched profiles around a centerline.

Rip
A sheet metal feature that removes material at an edge to allow a bend.

Rollback
Suppresses all items below the rollback bar.

Section
Another term for profile in sweeps.

Section line
A line or centerline sketched in a drawing view to create a section view.

Section scope
Specifies the components to be left uncut when you create an assembly drawing section view.

Section view
A section view (or section cut) is (1) a part or assembly view cut by a plane, or (2) a drawing view created by cutting another drawing view with a section line.

Seed
A sketch or an entity (a feature, face, or body) that is the basis for a pattern. If you edit the seed, the other entities in the pattern are updated.

Shaded
Displays a model as a colored solid.

Shared values
Also called linked values; these are named variables that you assign to set the value of two or more dimensions to be equal.

Sheet format
Includes page size and orientation, standard text, borders, title blocks, and so on. Sheet formats can be customized and saved for future use. Each sheet of a drawing document can have a different format.

Shell
A feature that hollows out a part, leaving open the selected faces and thin walls on the remaining faces. A hollow part is created when no faces are selected to be open.

Sketch
A collection of lines and other 2D objects on a plane or face that forms the basis for a feature such as a base or a boss. A 3D sketch is non-planar and can be used to guide a sweep or loft, for example.

Smart Fasteners
Automatically adds fasteners (bolts and screws) to an assembly using the SOLIDWORKS Toolbox library of fasteners.

SmartMates
An assembly mating relation that is created automatically.

Solid sweep
A cut sweep created by moving a tool body along a path to cut out 3D material from a model.

Spiral
A flat or 2D helix, defined by a circle, pitch, and number of revolutions.

Spline
A sketched 2D or 3D curve defined by a set of control points.

Split line
Projects a sketched curve onto a selected model face, dividing the face into multiple faces so that each can be selected individually. A split line can be used to create draft features, to create face blend fillets, and to radiate surfaces to cut molds.

Stacked balloon
A set of balloons with only one leader. The balloons can be stacked vertically (up or down) or horizontally (left or right).

Standard 3 views
The three orthographic views (front, right, and top) that are often the basis of a drawing.

StereoLithography
The process of creating rapid prototype parts using a faceted mesh representation in STL files.

Sub-assembly
An assembly document that is part of a larger assembly. For example, the steering mechanism of a car is a sub-assembly of the car.

Suppress
Removes an entity from the display and from any calculations in which it is involved. You can suppress features, assembly components, and so on. Suppressing an entity does not delete the entity; you can unsuppressed the entity to restore it.

Surface
A zero-thickness planar or 3D entity with edge boundaries. Surfaces are often used to create solid features. Reference surfaces can be used to modify solid features.

Sweep
Creates a base, boss, cut, or surface feature by moving a profile (section) along a path. For cut sweeps, you can create solid sweeps by moving a tool body along a path.

Tangent arc
An arc that is tangent to another entity, such as a line.

Tangent edge
The transition edge between rounded or filleted faces in hidden lines visible or hidden lines removed modes in drawings.

Task Pane
Located on the right-side of the SOLIDWORKS window, the Task Pane contains SOLIDWORKS Resources, the Design Library, and the File Explorer.

Template
A document (part, assembly, or drawing) that forms the basis of a new document. It can include user-defined parameters, annotations, predefined views, geometry, and so on.

Temporary axis
An axis created implicitly for every conical or cylindrical face in a model.

Thin feature
An extruded or revolved feature with constant wall thickness. Sheet metal parts are typically created from thin features.

TolAnalyst
A tolerance analysis application that determines the effects that dimensions and tolerances have on parts and assemblies.

Top-down design
An assembly modeling technique where you create parts in the context of an assembly by referencing the geometry of other components. Changes to the referenced components propagate to the parts that you create in context.

Triad
Three axes with arrows defining the X, Y, and Z directions. A reference triad appears in part and assembly documents to assist in orienting the viewing of models. Triads also assist when moving or rotating components in assemblies.

Under defined
A sketch is underdefined when there are not enough dimensions and relations to prevent entities from moving or changing size.

Vertex
A point at which two or more lines or edges intersect. Vertices can be selected for sketching, dimensioning, and many other operations.

Viewports
Windows that display views of models. You can specify one, two, or four viewports. Viewports with orthogonal views can be linked, which links orientation and rotation.

Virtual sharp
A sketch point at the intersection of two entities after the intersection itself has been removed by a feature such as a fillet or chamfer. Dimensions and relations to the virtual sharp are retained even though the actual intersection no longer exists.

Weldment
A multibody part with structural members.

Weldment cut list
A table that tabulates the bodies in a weldment along with descriptions and lengths.

Wireframe
A view mode in which all edges of the part or assembly are displayed.

Zebra stripes
Simulate the reflection of long strips of light on a very shiny surface. They allow you to see small changes in a surface that may be hard to see with a standard display.

Zoom
To simulate movement toward or away from a part or an assembly.

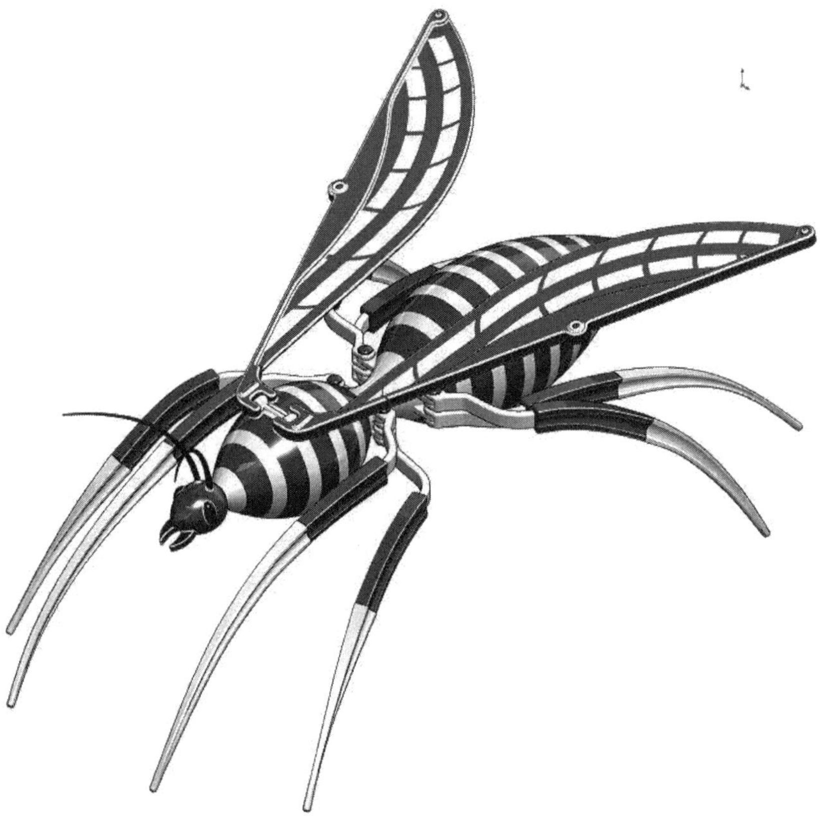

Bug-Bot designed and rendered using SOLIDWORKS

Reference Reading

Materials Science

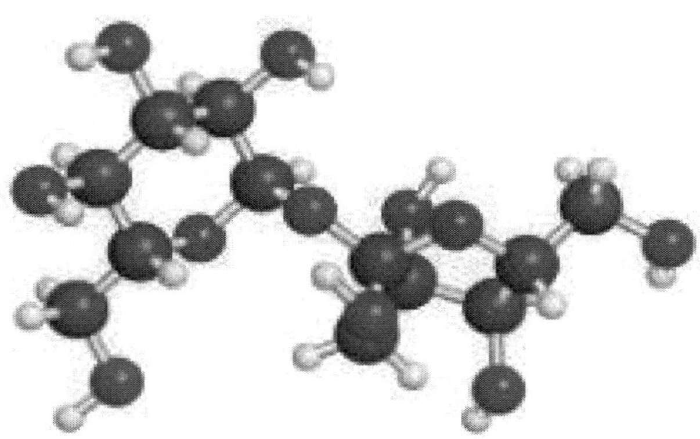

Materials Science

There are roughly 300,000 known materials, encompassing both natural materials like wood and rock, and man-made materials like plastic and glass.
Here is a more detailed breakdown:

- **Natural Materials:**
  These are materials found in nature, such as wood, rock, leather, minerals, and soil.

- **Man-made Materials:**
  These are materials created by humans, including plastics, glass, metals, ceramics, and composites.

- **Materials Science:**
  Materials scientists study how materials work, enabling them to create new materials, combine existing ones, or improve the performance of current materials.

- **Mass of Materials:**
  A study in Nature found that the mass of human-created materials has grown exponentially, reaching 1.1 trillion tons, exceeding the mass of all living things on Earth.

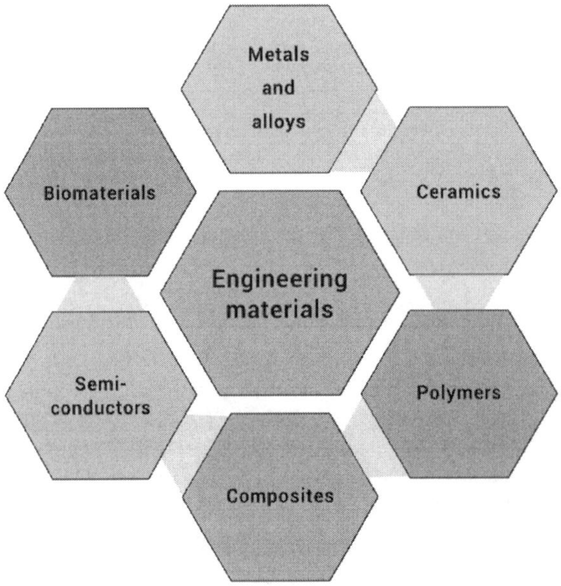

The four main classifications of materials, broadly used in materials science and engineering, are metals, polymers, ceramics, and composites.
Here is a more detailed look at each category:

- **Metals:**
  These are typically characterized by their high strength, ductility, and conductivity. Examples include steel, aluminum, and copper.

- **Polymers:**
  These are organic materials, often synthetic, known for their flexibility, lightweight nature, and resistance to corrosion. Examples include plastics and rubber.

- **Ceramics:**
  These are inorganic, non-metallic materials, often characterized by their high hardness, resistance to high temperatures, and brittleness. Examples include glass, porcelain, and concrete.

- **Composites:**
  These are materials made by combining two or more different materials, often to achieve a combination of properties that are not possible with the individual materials alone. Examples include fiberglass and concrete.

Metals

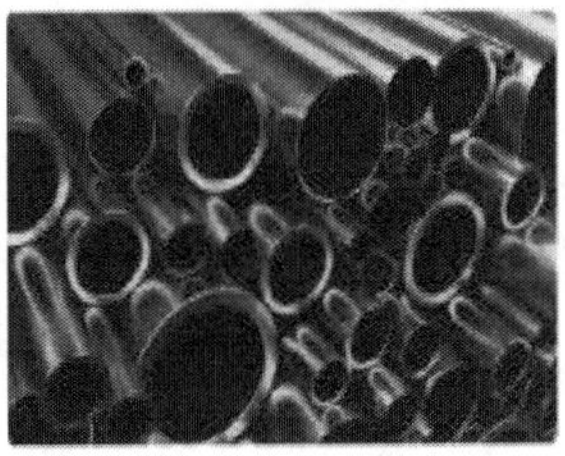

Metals

Some chemical elements are called **metals**. Most elements in the periodic table are metals. These elements usually have the following traits:

1. They can conduct electricity and heat.
2. They can be shaped easily.
3. They have a shiny appearance.
4. They have a high melting point.

Most metals are solid at room temperature, but this does not have to be the case. Mercury is liquid. Alloys are mixtures, where at least one part of the mixture is a metal. Examples of metals are aluminum, copper, iron, tin, gold, lead, silver, titanium, uranium, and zinc. Well-known alloys include bronze and steel.

Many things that are made of metals may, in fact, be made of mixtures of at least one metal with either other metals, or with non-metals. These mixtures are called alloys. Some common alloys are:

- Steel (iron and carbon) (Carbon is a non-metal)
- Brass (copper and zinc)
- Bronze (copper and tin)
- Duralumin (aluminum and copper)
- Gunmetal (copper, tin, and zinc)

People first began making things from metal over 9000 years ago, when they discovered how to get copper from its ore. They then learned how to make a harder alloy, bronze, by adding tin to the copper. About 3000 years ago, they discovered iron. By adding small amounts of carbon to iron, they found that they could make a particularly useful alloy – steel.

Rare metals with high value, like gold, silver and platinum are often used to make jewelry. Metals are also used to make fasteners and screws. Pots used for cooking can be made from copper, aluminum, steel or iron. Lead is very heavy and dense and can be used as ballast in boats to stop them from turning over, or to protect people from ionizing radiation.

Polymers

Polymer

A **polymer** is a substance or material that consists of very large molecules, or macromolecules, that are constituted by many repeating subunits derived from one or more species of monomers. Due to their broad spectrum of properties, both synthetic and natural polymers play essential and ubiquitous roles in everyday life. Polymers range from familiar synthetic plastics such as polystyrene to natural biopolymers such as DNA and proteins that are fundamental to biological structure and function.

Polymers, both natural and synthetic, are created via polymerization of many small molecules, known as monomers. Their consequently large molecular mass, relative to small molecule compounds, produces unique physical properties including toughness, high elasticity, viscoelasticity, and a tendency to form amorphous and semicrystalline structures rather than crystals.

Polymers are studied in the fields of polymer science (which includes polymer chemistry and polymer physics), biophysics and materials science and engineering. Historically, products arising from the linkage of repeating units by covalent chemical bonds have been the primary focus of polymer science. An emerging important area now focuses on supramolecular polymers formed by non-covalent links.

Polyisoprene of latex rubber is an example of a natural polymer, and the polystyrene of Styrofoam is an example of a synthetic polymer. In biological contexts, essentially all biological macromolecules—i.e., proteins (polyamides), nucleic acids (polynucleotides), and polysaccharides—are purely polymeric, or are composed in large part of polymeric components.

Ceramics

Ceramics

Ceramic material is an inorganic, metallic oxide, nitride, or carbide material. Some elements, such as carbon or silicon, may be considered ceramics.

Ceramic materials are brittle, hard, strong in compression, and weak in shearing and tension. They withstand the chemical erosion that occurs in other materials subjected to acidic or caustic environments. Ceramics generally can withstand very high temperatures, ranging from 1,000 °C to 1,600 °C (1,800 °F to 3,000 °F).

A low magnification SEM micrograph of an advanced ceramic material. The properties of ceramics make fracturing an important inspection method.
The crystallinity of ceramic materials varies widely. Most often, fired ceramics are either vitrified or semi-vitrified, as is the case with earthenware, stoneware, and porcelain. Varying crystallinity and electron composition in the ionic and covalent bonds cause most ceramic materials to be good thermal and electrical insulators (researched in ceramic engineering). With such a large range of possible options for the composition/structure of a ceramic (nearly all of the elements, nearly all types of bonding, and all levels of crystallinity), the breadth of the subject is vast, and identifiable attributes (hardness, toughness, electrical conductivity) are difficult to specify for the group as a whole.

General properties such as high melting temperature, high hardness, poor conductivity, high moduli of elasticity, chemical resistance, and low ductility are the norm, with known exceptions to each of these rules (piezoelectric ceramics, low glass transition temperature ceramics, superconductive ceramics). Composites such as fiberglass and carbon fiber, while containing ceramic materials, are not considered to be part of the ceramic family.

Traditional ceramic raw materials include clay minerals such as kaolinite, whereas more recent materials include aluminum oxide, more commonly known as alumina. Modern ceramic materials, which are classified as advanced ceramics, include silicon carbide and tungsten carbide. Both are valued for their abrasion resistance and are therefore used in applications such as the wear plates of crushing equipment in mining operations. Advanced ceramics are also used in the medical, electrical, electronics, and armor industries.

Composites

Composites

A **composite** or **composition material** is a material which is produced from two or more constituent materials.

These constituent materials have notably dissimilar chemical or physical properties and are merged to create a material with properties unlike the individual elements. Within the finished structure, the individual elements remain separate and distinct, distinguishing composites from mixtures and solid solutions. Composite materials with more than one distinct layer are called ***composite laminates***.

Typical engineered composite materials are made up of a binding agent forming the ***matrix*** and a filler material (particulates or fibers) giving ***substance***, e.g.:

- Concrete, reinforced concrete and masonry with cement, lime or mortar (which is itself a composite material) as a binder
- Composite wood such as glulam and plywood with wood glue as a binder
- Reinforced plastics, such as fiberglass and fiber-reinforced polymer with resin or thermoplastics as a binder
- Ceramic matrix composites (composite ceramic and metal matrices)
- Metal matrix composites[2]
- advanced composite materials, often first developed for spacecraft and aircraft applications.

Composite materials can be less expensive, lighter, stronger, or more durable than common materials. Some are inspired by biological structures found in plants and animals. Robotic materials are composites that include sensing, actuation, computation, and communication components.

Composite materials are used for construction and technical structures such as boat hulls, swimming pool panels, racing car bodies, shower stalls, bathtubs, imitation granite, and cultured marble sinks and countertops. They are also being increasingly used in general automotive applications.

Stainless Steel

Stainless Steel

Stainless steel alloys are categorized into austenitic, ferritic, martensitic, duplex, and precipitation-hardening types, each with unique properties and applications, including corrosion resistance, strength, and formability.

Here is a more detailed look at the different types of stainless steel alloys:

1. **Austenitic Stainless Steel:**
   Composition: This is the most common type, characterized by high chromium and nickel content.
   Properties: Non-magnetic, excellent corrosion resistance, good weldability, high strength, and ductility.
   Examples: 304 (18/8 stainless), 316 (with added molybdenum for enhanced corrosion resistance), 303 (machinable).
   Applications:
   Kitchen appliances, food processing equipment, architectural applications.

2. **Ferritic Stainless Steel:**
   Composition: Contains a high percentage of chromium (typically 10.5% to 30%) and little or no nickel.
   Properties: Magnetic, good corrosion resistance, good ductility, and relatively high resistance to stress corrosion cracking.
   Examples: 409, 430.
   Applications: Automotive exhaust systems, kitchenware, and architectural applications.

3. **Martensitic Stainless Steel:**
   Composition: Straight chromium steels without nickel.
   Properties: Magnetic, hardenable (through heat treatment), good strength and hardness, moderate corrosion resistance.
   Examples: 410, 420.
   Applications: Blades, cutlery, and springs.

4. **Duplex Stainless Steel:**
   Composition: A combination of austenitic and ferritic stainless steel, offering a unique blend of properties.

Properties: High strength, excellent corrosion resistance, and enhanced resistance to stress corrosion cracking.
Examples: 2205, 2304.
Applications: Offshore oil and gas, chemical processing, and water treatment.

5. Precipitation Hardening Stainless Steel:
Composition: A type of stainless steel alloy that can be hardened through a heat treatment process.
Properties: High strength, good corrosion resistance, good toughness, and formability.
Examples: 17-4 PH, 630.
Applications: Aerospace, medical implants, and springs.

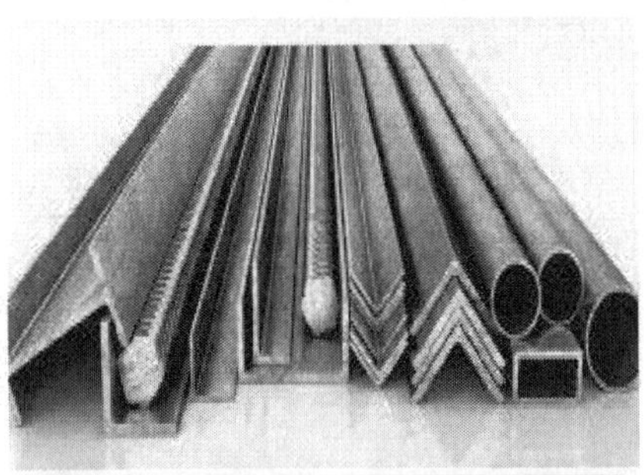

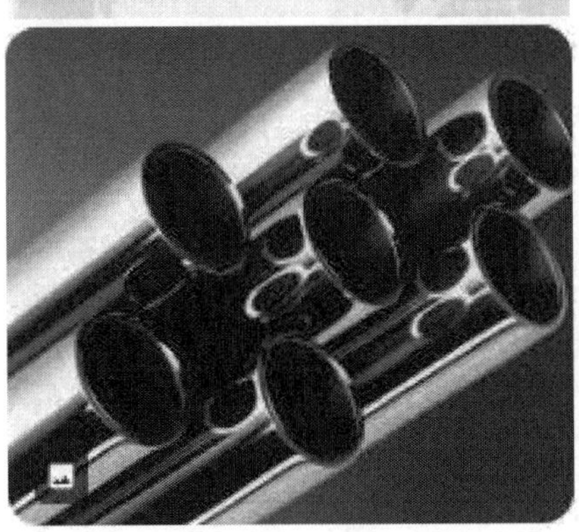

Surgical Steel

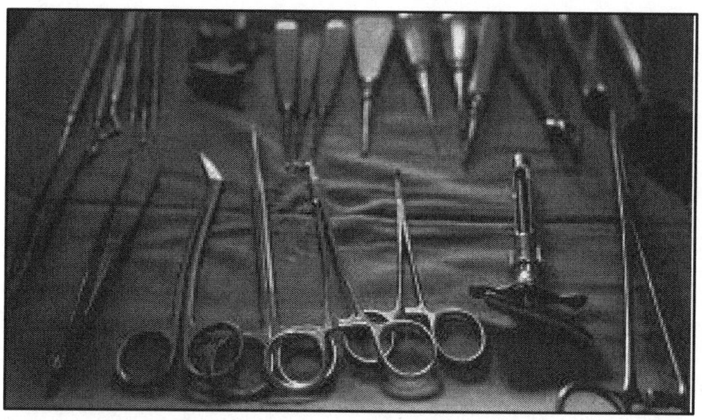

Surgical Steel

Medical grade steel, also known as surgical steel, is a type of stainless steel specifically designed for use in medical and surgical applications. It meets stringent quality and safety standards to ensure compatibility with the human body.

Properties of Medical Grade Steel:

- **Biocompatibility:** Resistant to corrosion and allergic reactions, minimizing the risk of infection or irritation.
- **Strength and Durability:** Provides structural support for medical devices and implants.
- **Heat Resistance:** Can withstand sterilization temperatures without compromising its properties.
- **Corrosion Resistance:** Resists rust and other forms of corrosion, even in bodily fluids.

Common Grades of Medical Grade Steel:

316L: The most widely used grade, known for its excellent corrosion resistance and biocompatibility.

Titanium: A lightweight and hypoallergenic metal with excellent corrosion resistance.

420: A hard and corrosion-resistant steel used for surgical instruments and medical molds.

316LVM: A vacuum-melted version of 316L with even higher purity and biocompatibility.

Applications of Medical Grade Steel:

- Surgical instruments and implants
- Medical devices (e.g., stents, catheters)
- Orthopedic implants
- Dental tools and appliances
- Jewelry and piercings

Aluminum Alloys

Aluminum Alloys

Aluminum alloys are created by combining aluminum with other metals like copper, magnesium, manganese, silicon, tin, nickel, and zinc, each enhancing specific properties like strength, corrosion resistance, and machinability.

Here is a more detailed look:
Common Alloying Elements and Their Effects:

- **Copper (Cu):**
  Increases strength and hardness but can reduce corrosion resistance. Alloys like 2024 are known for their high strength.

- **Magnesium (Mg):**
  Improves strength, corrosion resistance, and weldability. Alloys like 5052 are known for their excellent corrosion resistance.

- **Manganese (Mn):**
  Enhances strength and corrosion resistance, especially in the 3000 series alloys.

- **Silicon (Si):**
  Improves casting properties, strength, and wear resistance. 6000 series alloys often feature silicon and magnesium.

- **Zinc (Zn):**
  Increases strength, particularly in combination with magnesium and copper, as seen in the 7000 series alloys.

- **Tin (Sn):**
  Can be added to certain alloys to improve machinability and corrosion resistance.

- **Nickel (Ni):**
  Used to enhance strength and corrosion resistance in specific applications.

Aluminum Alloys for Medical Applications

6061 aluminum and 6063 aluminum, two medical-grade aluminum alloys, are highly favored in the medical industry due to their combination of strength, machinability, and formability.

Known for its excellent strength and versatility, making it an ideal choice for medical devices that need to withstand wear and stress. It also exhibits good weldability, making it easier to join with other components.

6061 and 7075 aluminum are among the strongest aluminum grades available and are commonly used in high-stress applications. Aluminum grades with lower strength, such as 1100, 3003, and 5052, are often used in applications that do not require high strength.

Aluminum alloys are classified into series based on their primary alloying elements, with common examples including 1000 (pure aluminum), 2000 (copper), 3000 (manganese), 5000 (magnesium), 6000 (magnesium and silicon), and 7000 (zinc) alloys.

Here is a breakdown of some common aluminum alloy series:

- **1xxx Series:**
  These are the purest forms of aluminum, containing at least 99% aluminum, and are known for their excellent corrosion resistance and workability.

- **2xxx Series:**
  Characterized by copper as the primary alloying element, these alloys offer a good combination of strength and toughness but may have lower corrosion resistance compared to other series.

- **3xxx Series:**
  Manganese is the primary alloying element in this series, which offers good formability and corrosion resistance, though they are typically not heat-treatable.

- **5xxx Series:**
  Magnesium is the primary alloying element in this series, resulting in alloys that are known for their moderate to high strength, excellent corrosion resistance, and weldability.

- **6xxx Series:**
  Magnesium and silicon are the primary alloying elements in this series, which offer good strength, corrosion resistance, and weldability, making them suitable for various applications.

- **7xxx Series:**
  Zinc is the primary alloying element in this series, along with smaller amounts of copper, magnesium, and other elements, resulting in high-strength, heat-treatable alloys suitable for aerospace and high-performance applications.

Plastics

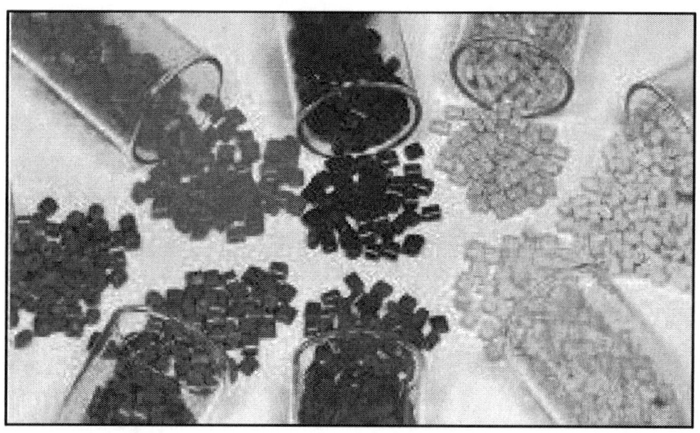

Plastics

Plastics are a vast group of synthetic or semi-synthetic organic compounds, derived from natural materials like crude oil, natural gas, and coal, that are malleable and can be molded into solid objects.

Below are 7 of the most popular and commonly used plastics:

- Acrylic or Polymethyl Methacrylate (PMMA)
- Polycarbonate (PC)
- Polyethylene (PE)
- Polypropylene (PP)
- Polyethylene Terephthalate (PETE or PET)
- Polyvinyl Chloride (PVC)
- Acrylonitrile-Butadiene-Styrene (ABS)

Here is a more detailed look:

- **Definition:**
  Plastics are a diverse class of materials consisting of synthetic or semi-synthetic organic compounds that can be molded into solid objects.

- **Source:**
  They are derived from natural, organic materials like cellulose, coal, natural gas, salt, and crude oil.

- **Production:**
  Plastics are produced through processes like polymerization and polycondensation, where monomers (small molecules) are linked together to form long polymer chains.

- **Malleability:**
  The key characteristic of plastics is their malleability, meaning they can be shaped and molded into various forms.

Common Types of Plastics:

Polyethylene (PE):
A widely used thermoplastic, often used in packaging, bottles, and bags.

- **High-Density Polyethylene (HDPE):** More robust and durable, used in bottles, containers, and pipes.
- **Low-Density Polyethylene (LDPE):** Flexible and milky in color, used in bags and films.

Polypropylene (PP):
A versatile thermoplastic used in a wide variety of applications, including packaging, containers, and fibers.

Polyethylene Terephthalate (PET):
A lightweight, strong, and impact-resistant plastic used for bottles, food containers, and fibers.

Polyvinyl Chloride (PVC):
A strong and versatile plastic used in pipes, flooring, and medical applications.

Polystyrene (PS):
Used in packaging, disposable cups, and containers.

Acrylonitrile-Butadiene-Styrene (ABS):
A tough and durable plastic used in manufacturing, automotive parts, and electronics.

Acrylic (PMMA):
A transparent thermoplastic that can be used as a lightweight, resilient substitute for glass.

Polycarbonate (PC):
A sturdy and resilient material used in engineering and can come in transparent form.

Nylon:
A strong and durable plastic used in textiles, engineering parts, and other applications.

Polyurethane (PU):
A versatile plastic used in foams, coatings, and adhesives.

Polylactic Acid (PLA):
A biodegradable plastic derived from plant starch.

Polytetrafluoroethylene (PTFE):
A plastic material known for its high temperature resistance and non-stick properties.

Index

C

D

E

F

G

H

I

J

K

L

M

N

O

P

Q

R

S

T

U

V

W

Z

Mastering Sheet Metal & Weldments with SOLIDWORKS 2026
Model Library

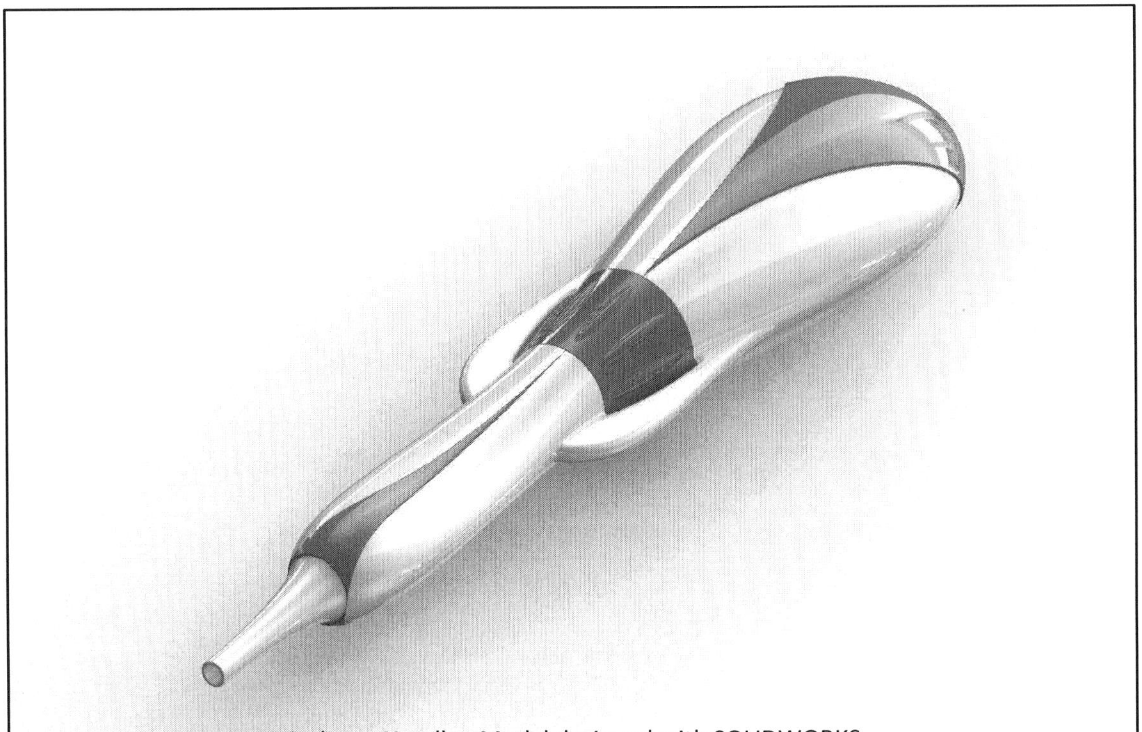

Catheter Handle - Model designed with SOLIDWORKS

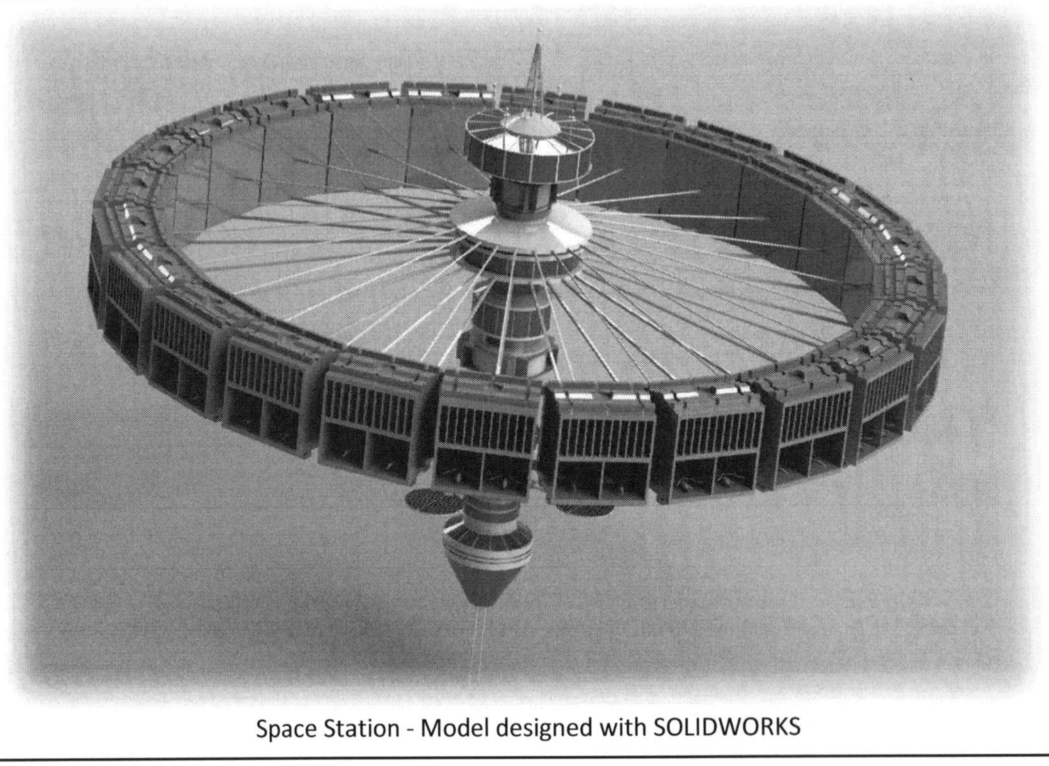

Space Station - Model designed with SOLIDWORKS

Logo Designs - Model designed with SOLIDWORKS

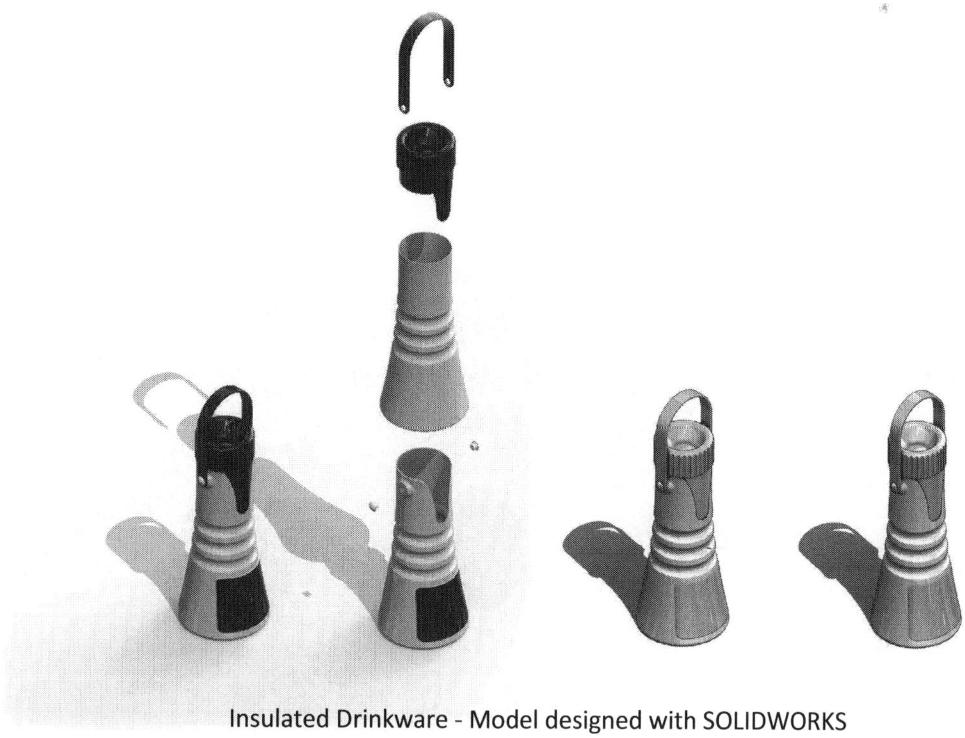

Insulated Drinkware - Model designed with SOLIDWORKS

Bug Bots - Model designed with SOLIDWORKS

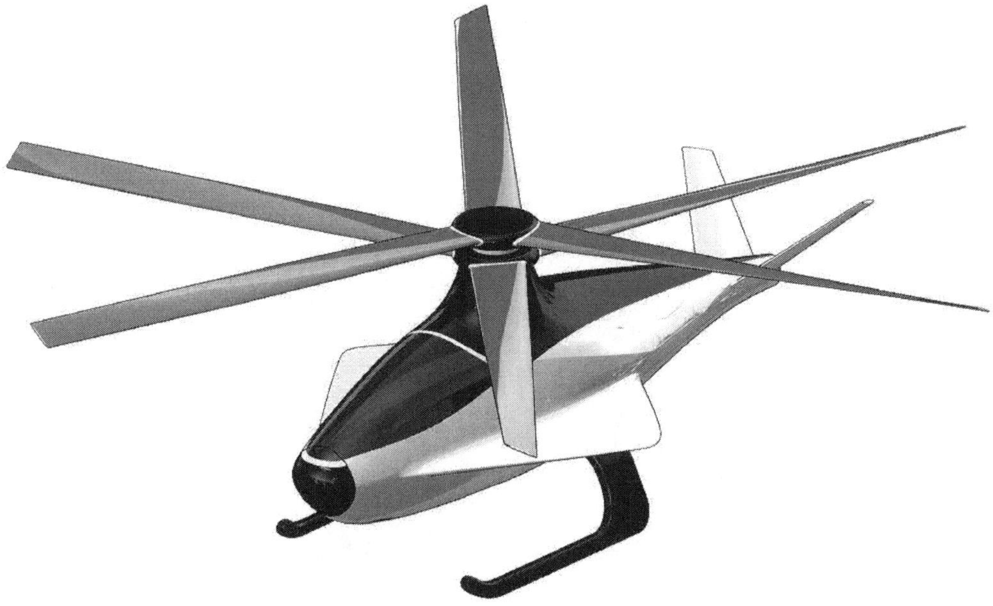

Futuristic Helicopter - Model designed with SOLIDWORKS

Modern Bike - Model designed with SOLIDWORKS

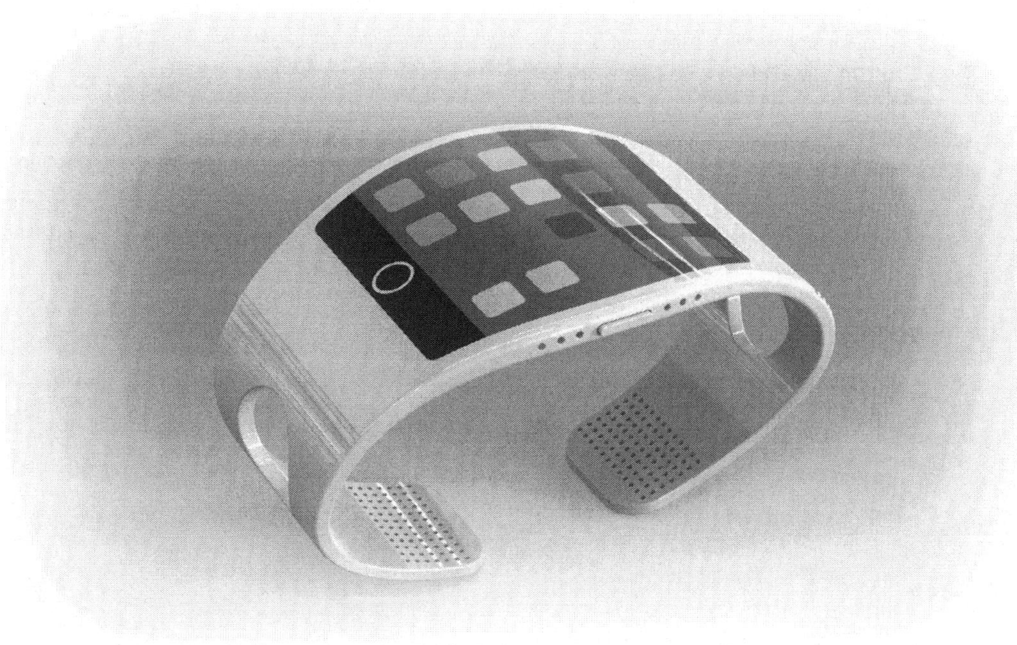

Phone Watch - Model designed with SOLIDWORKS

Modular Robots - Model designed with SOLIDWORKS

Car Mouse - Model designed with SOLIDWORKS

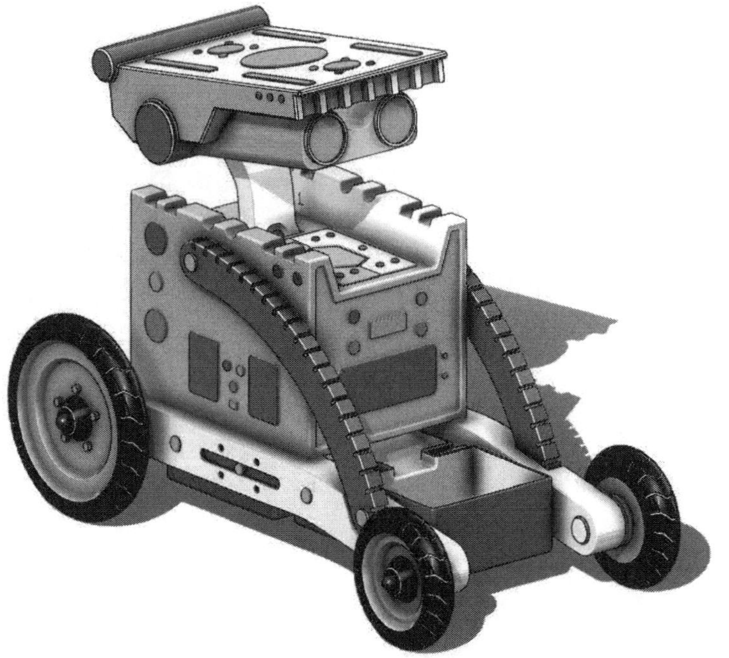

Toy Designs - Model designed with SOLIDWORKS

Helipads - Model designed with SOLIDWORKS

Superyacht - Model designed with SOLIDWORKS

MS Robots - Model designed with SOLIDWORKS

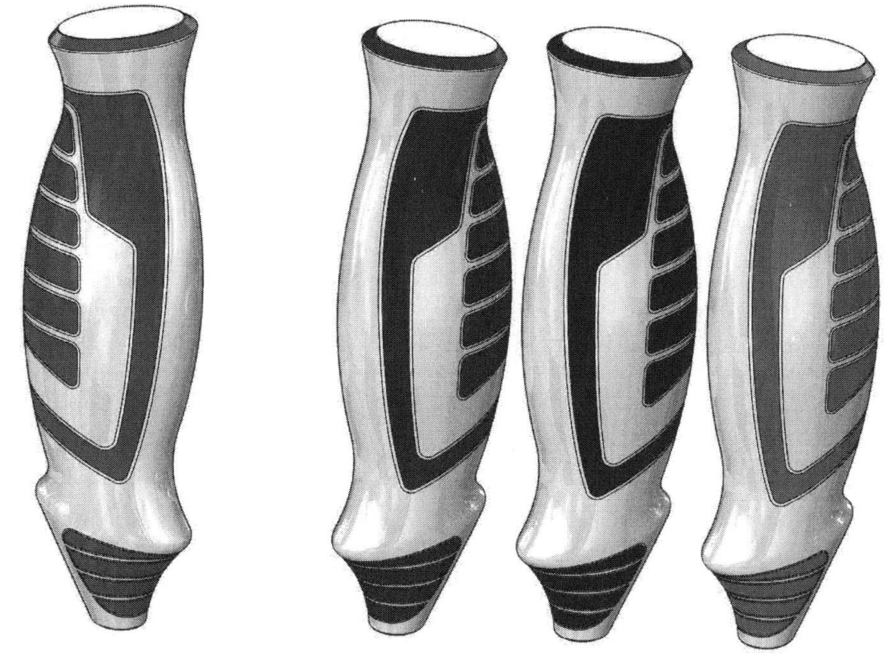

Handle Designs - Model designed with SOLIDWORKS

Helicopter Rotors - Model designed with SOLIDWORKS

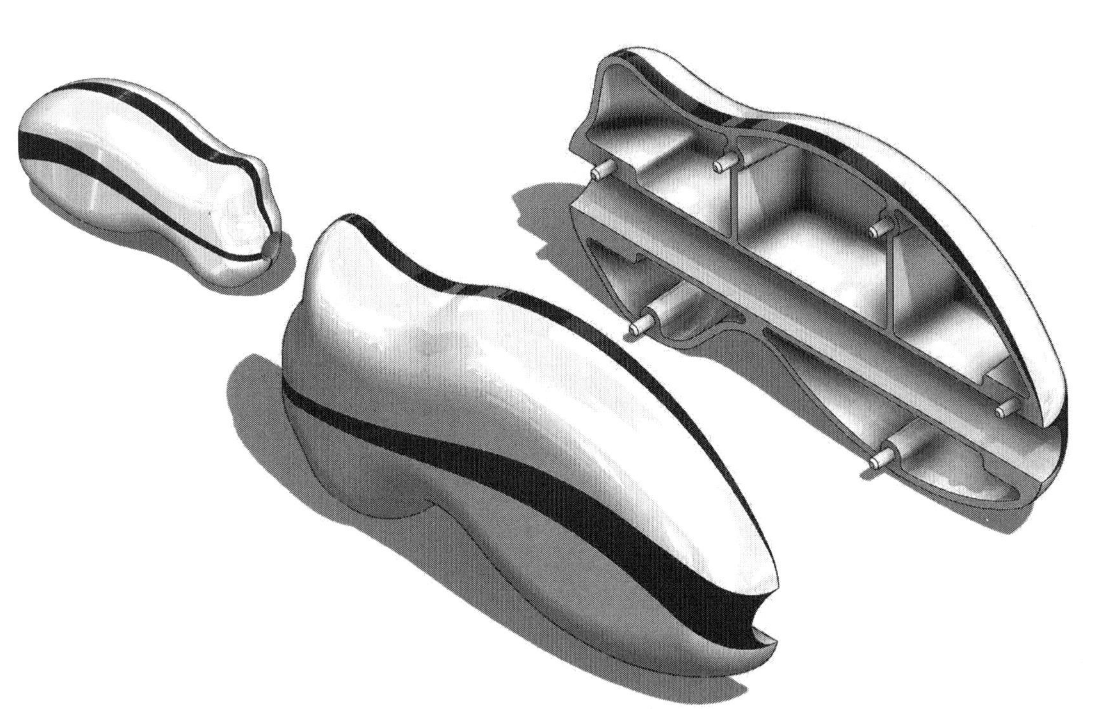

Med-Device Handle - Model designed with SOLIDWORKS

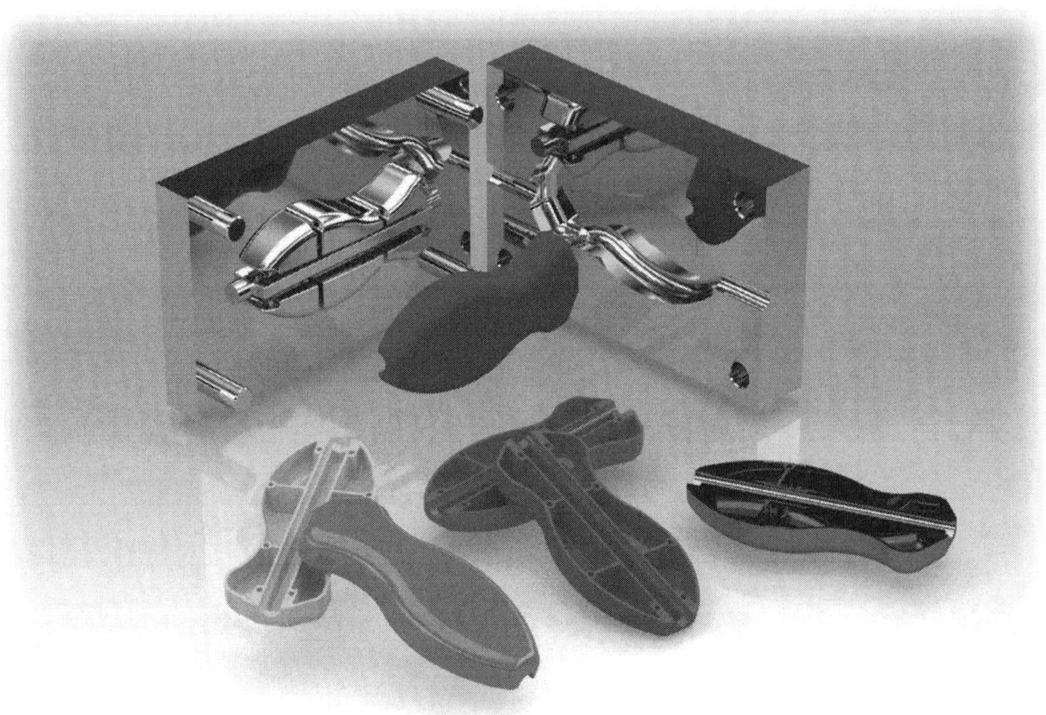

Handle Molds - Model designed with SOLIDWORKS

Ladybug - Model designed with SOLIDWORKS

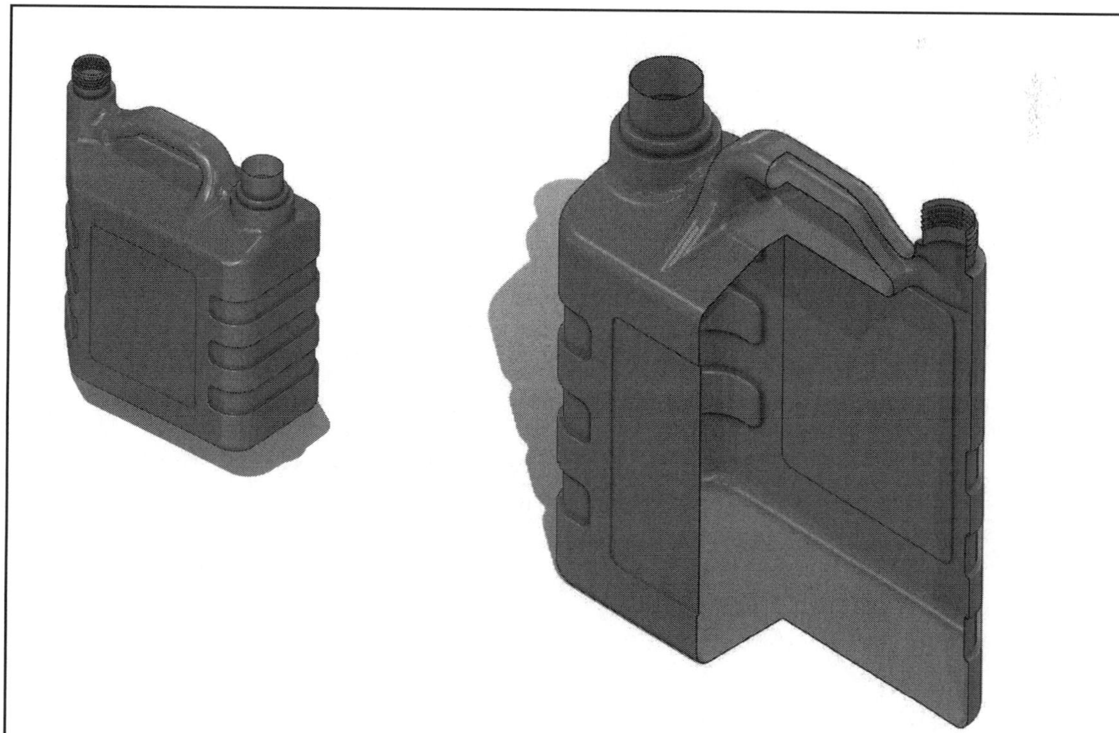

Detergent Container - Model designed with SOLIDWORKS

Blue Angel Aircraft - Model designed with SOLIDWORKS

Helicopter - Model designed with SOLIDWORKS

Concept Car - Model designed with SOLIDWORKS

Concept Car - Model designed with SOLIDWORKS

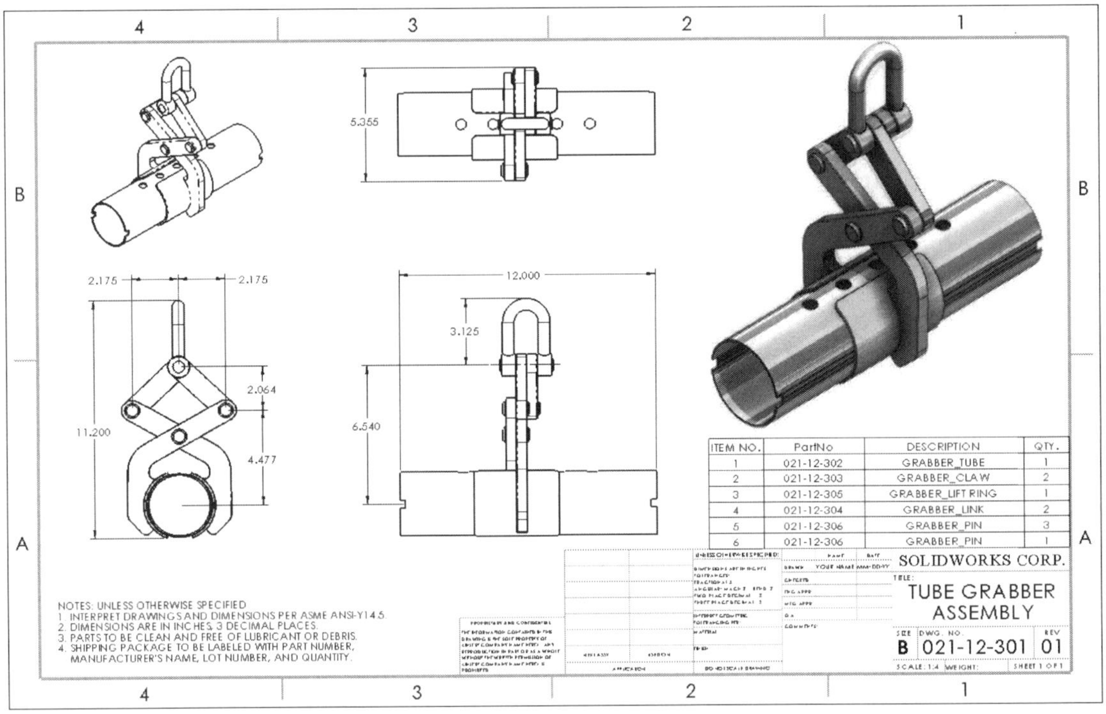

Tube Grabber – Drawing created with SOLIDWORKS

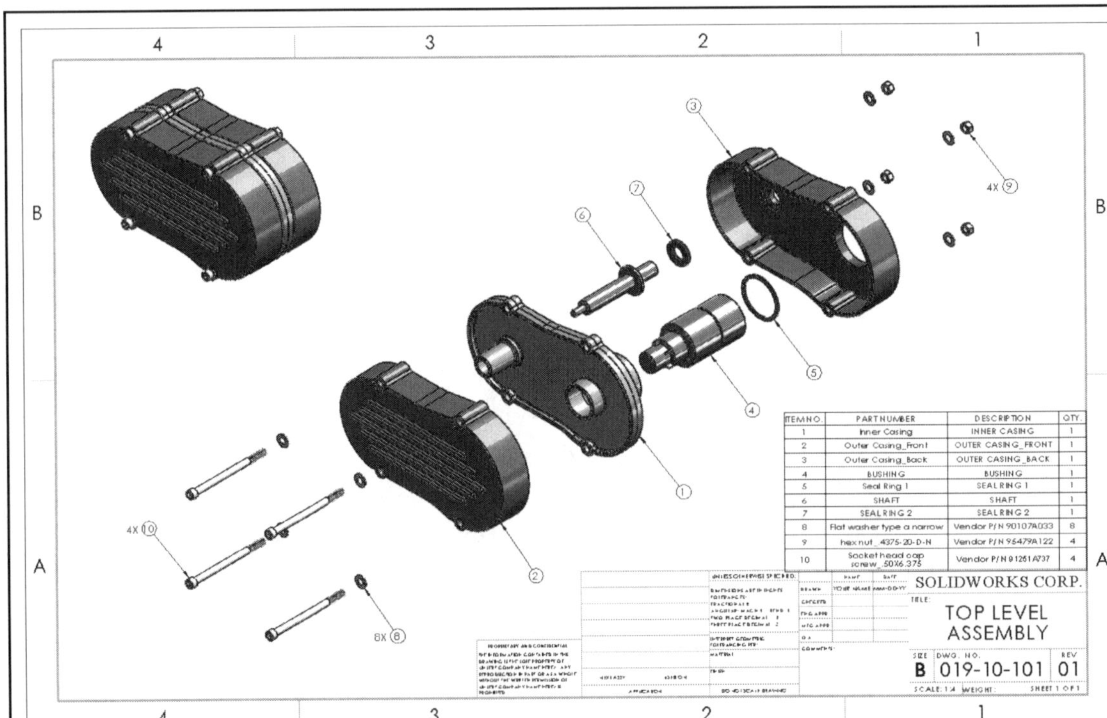

Casted Casing – Drawing created with SOLIDWORKS

Flying Car - Model designed with SOLIDWORKS

Shark Boat - Model designed with SOLIDWORKS

Propeller - Model designed with SOLIDWORKS

3-Way Bracket - Model designed with SOLIDWORKS

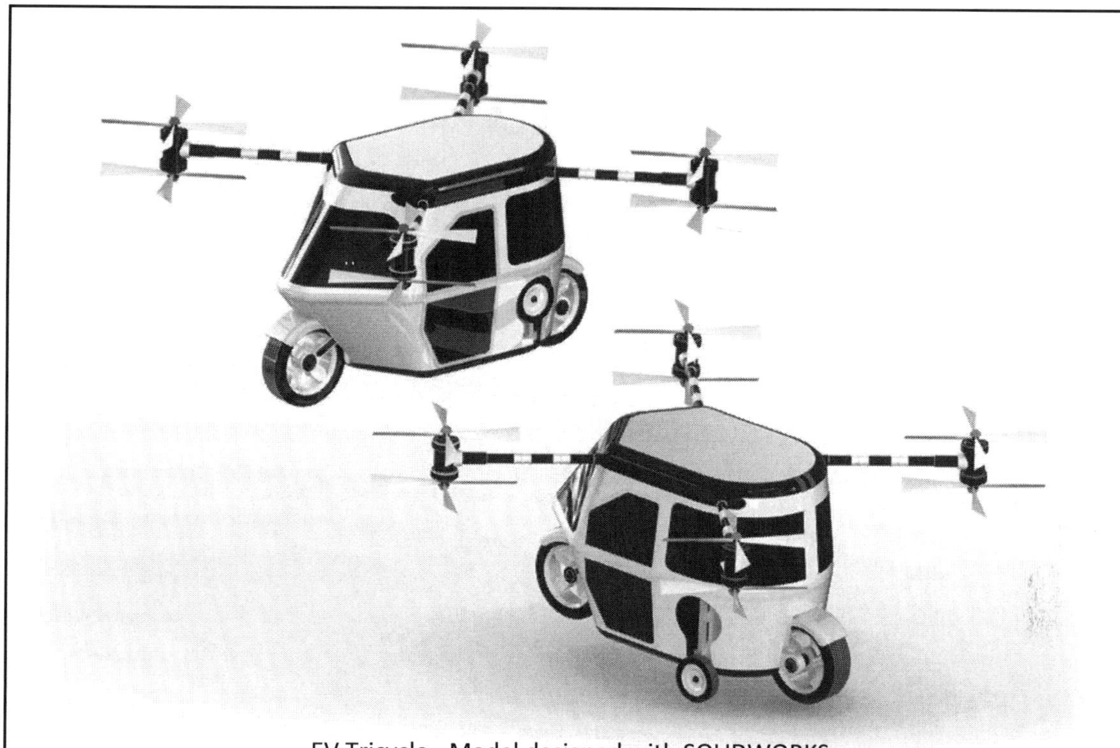

EV Tricycle - Model designed with SOLIDWORKS

Futuristic Car Concepts - Model designed with SOLIDWORKS

Italian Drone - Model designed with SOLIDWORKS

Rolls Royce VTOL Concepts - Model designed with SOLIDWORKS